A Companion to
Gender Studies

BLACKWELL **COMPANIONS IN CULTURAL STUDIES**

Advisory editor: David Theo Goldberg, University of California, Irvine

This series aims to provide theoretically ambitious but accessible volumes devoted to the major fields and subfields within Cultural Studies, whether as single disciplines (Film Studies) inspired and reconfigured by interventionist Cultural Studies approaches, or from broad interdisciplinary and multidisciplinary perspectives (Gender Studies, Race and Ethnic Studies, Postcolonial Studies). Each volume sets out to ground and orientate the student through a broad range of specially commissioned articles and also to provide the more experienced scholar and teacher with a convenient and comprehensive overview of the latest trends and critical directions.

A Companion to
Gender Studies

Edited by

Philomena Essed,
David Theo Goldberg, and
Audrey Kobayashi

Blackwell
Publishing

BLACKWELL PUBLISHING
350 Main Street, Malden, MA 02148-5020, USA
9600 Garsington Road, Oxford OX4 2DQ, UK
550 Swanston Street, Carlton, Victoria 3053, Australia

The right of Philomena Essed, David Theo Goldberg, and Audrey Kobayashi to be identified as the Authors of the Editorial Material in this Work has been asserted in accordance with the UK Copyright, Designs, and Patents Act 1988.

First published 2005 by Blackwell Publishing Ltd

2   2006

Library of Congress Cataloging-in-Publication Data

A companion to gender studies / edited by Philomena Essed, David Theo Goldberg, and Audrey Kobayashi.
    p. cm. — (Blackwell companions in cultural studies ; 8)
    Includes bibliographical references and index.
    ISBN 0-631-22109-3 (alk. paper)
    1. Sex role—Research. 2. Gender identity—Research. 3. Men's studies—Research.
4. Women's studies—Research. I. Essed, Philomena, 1955– II. Goldberg, David Theo.
III. Kobayashi, Audrey Lynn, 1951– IV. Series.

    HQ1075.C656 2005
    305.3′072—dc22

                                                                                2004006865

ISBN-13: 978-0-631-22109-8 (alk. paper)

A catalogue record for this title is available from the British Library.

Set in 11/13pt Ehrhardt
by Graphicraft Ltd, Hong Kong
Printed and bound in the United Kingdom
by TJ International, Padstow, Cornwall

The publisher's policy is to use permanent paper from mills that operate a sustainable forestry policy, and which has been manufactured from pulp processed using acid-free and elementary chlorine-free practices. Furthermore, the publisher ensures that the text paper and cover board used have met acceptable environmental accreditation standards.

For further information on
Blackwell Publishing, visit our website:
www.blackwellpublishing.com

Contents

Contents

Contributors

Madelaine Adelman	School of Justice Studies, Arizona State University, USA
Ifi Amadiume	Department of Religion, African and African American Studies Program, Women and Gender Studies Program, Dartmouth College, USA
Carol Lee Bacchi	Politics, School of History and Politics, University of Adelaide, Australia
Abigail B. Bakan	Political Studies, Queen's University, Canada
Mieke Bal	Amsterdam School for Cultural Analysis, University of Amsterdam, The Netherlands
Vikki Bell	Sociology Department, Goldsmiths College, University of London, UK
Nitza Berkovitch	Department of Behavioral Sciences, Ben Gurion University, Israel
Linda Briskin	Social Science Division/School of Women's Studies, York University, Canada
Irene Dankelman	University Center for Environmental Studies, University of Nijmegen, The Netherlands; Women's Environment and Development Organization, New York, USA
Mona Domosh	Department of Geography, Dartmouth College, USA
Lesley Doyal	School for Policy Studies, University of Bristol, UK
Enakshi Dua	School of Women's Studies, York University, Canada
Philomena Essed	Department of Geography and Planning, University of Amsterdam, The Netherlands; Women's Studies/African-American Studies, University of California, Irvine, USA

Tovi Fenster	Department of Geography and Human Environment, Tel Aviv University, Israel
Ellen Fernandez-Sacco	Office for History of Science & Technology, University of California, Berkeley, USA
Agneta H. Fischer	Department of Psychology, University of Amsterdam, Amsterdam, The Netherlands
Katherine Franke	School of Law, Columbia University, USA
David Theo Goldberg	University of California Humanities Research Institute; African-American Studies/Criminology, Law and Society, University of California, Irvine, USA
Inderpal Grewal	Women's Studies, University of California, Irvine, USA
Ratiba Hadj-Moussa	Sociology, York University, Canada
Judith Halberstam	Department of Literature, University of California, San Diego, USA
Sandra Harding	Department of Education, University of California, Los Angeles, USA
Sara Helman	Department of Behavioral Sciences, Ben Gurion University, Israel
Jennifer Hyndman	Department of Geography, Simon Fraser University, Vancouver, Canada
Tony Jefferson	Department of Criminology, Keele University, UK
Laura Hyun Yi Kang	Women's Studies, University of California, Irvine, USA
Caren Kaplan	Department of Women's Studies, University of California, Berkeley, USA
Kamala Kempadoo	Division of Social Science, York University, Canada
Audrey Kobayashi	Department of Geography, Queen's University, Canada
Nina Laurie	School of Geography, Politics and Sociology, University of Newcastle, UK
Mary Maynard	Department of Social Policy and Social Work, University of York, UK
Amâde M'charek	Department of Political Science, University of Amsterdam, The Netherlands
Cecilia Menjívar	School of Justice Studies, Arizona State University, USA
Toby Miller	Center for Latin American and Caribbean Studies, Department of American Studies/Department of Cinema Studies, New York University, USA

List of Contributors

Lorraine Nencel	Department of Social Research Methodology, Free University, The Netherlands
Joanna Regulska	Department of Women's and Gender Studies and Department of Geography, Rutgers University, USA
Martha Saavedra	Center for African Studies, University of California, Berkeley, USA
Laura Shanner	John Dossetor Health Ethics Center, University of Alberta, Canada
Ella Shohat	Departments of Art and Public Policy, Middle Eastern Studies, and Comparative Literature, New York University, USA
Anita Silvers	Department of Philosophy, San Francisco State University, USA
D. Alissa Trotz	Sociology and Equity Studies/Institute for Women's Studies and Gender Studies, Ontario Institute for Studies in Education, University of Toronto, Canada
Annelies E. M. van Vianen	Department of Psychology, University of Amsterdam, Amsterdam, The Netherlands
Lois A. West	Department of Sociology and Anthropology, Florida International University, USA
Ruth Wodak	Department of Linguistics, University of Vienna, Austria; Collegium Budapest, Hungary
Iris Marion Young	Political Science Department, University of Chicago, USA
Pamela Dickey Young	Department of Religious Studies, Queen's University, Canada

Acknowledgments

We have been concerned in composing *A Companion to Gender Studies* not to opt for exhaustive coverage, an impossible task anyway, but to conjure up and encourage the connections between established and innovative directions in Gender Studies, to consider where the field stands and seems to be forging forward, and to take the tradition seriously while breaking new ground. Thus, we have been particularly interested in indicating emergent thematics into which contemporary Gender Studies has made forays, to draw especially on the expertise of as broad a range of globally located interlocutors as we could muster, in research interests and backgrounds and geographic circulations. The result, we submit, is a rich conversation between themes and contributions long at the heart of Gender Studies and those that new global conditions today are making imperative. We have been insistent throughout to acknowledge the critical ground–clearing, foundational interventions of feminism, without which Gender Studies today would not be conceivable.

For seeing us through the process of editing this volume, we are enormously grateful to the patience and professionalism of the contributors, to the folks at Blackwell, always so supportive, and to colleagues whose guidance and suggestions have enabled us to round off the volume. Andrew McNeillie at Blackwell had the foresight to see the need well ahead of most others for a field-representing volume before the area of Gender Studies could properly be said to be settled. His indomitable editorial partner at Blackwell, Jayne Fargnoli, has patiently prodded us to the point of completion where other editors might understandably have given up on us. Jayne's trust and guidance have been invaluable. The book would have been much longer in the making but for Kim Furumoto at the University of California Humanities Research Institute, whose tireless assistance in editing, suggestions, general good sense, sheer hard labor, and wonderful sense of humor once more enabled a happy outcome.

Philomena Essed
David Theo Goldberg
Audrey Kobayashi

Introduction:
A Curriculum Vitae
for Gender Studies

Philomena Essed, David Theo Goldberg, Audrey Kobayashi

I

"Is it a boy or is it a girl?" Posed at the first moment of life, this question embeds, expresses, and enforces the common normative disposition towards the "path of life." It signals a discursive order in the name and terms of which gender establishes itself at the moment of birth and continues to exert itself, definitive of nearly every human experience. Life is gendered. Gender at birth is at once the rebirth, the generation, of gender. It marks the course of our lives, our curriculum vitae. We hope that this volume, recording highlights in the life of Gender Studies, can serve as one CV among a range of possibilities for the field.

If gender is a constant, however, the ways in which gender is lived are highly fluid, subject to perpetual sociocultural redefinition and to individual interpretation and expression. In the chapters presented here, we attempt to capture that transforming quality of gender as both a constraint upon the ways in which people do things, a barrier to free participation, and a palimpsest of creative expression through which cultural and social practices are worked out, contested, resisted, and often redefined. Gender has a wide range of primary expressions. It (though it is "it" only when it cannot be named) expresses itself through – or as – sexuality, race, class, region, as well as other meaningful designations of human identity. Gender makes a difference not only because it sorts and categorizes humanity, but also because humanity is sorted and categorized by other discursive labels, such as class or race, by experiences in work, play, family, and civic life, which interact with gender to produce a wide variety of outcomes. This *Companion* attempts to reflect, and in multiple ways to represent, that variety.

The essays collected here benefit from the fruits of decades of earlier work by feminist and race critical scholars to understand, analyze, and challenge the distinct ways in which gender serves as a significant marker of social identity. Some of the scholars included here have been on the front lines of gender and race critical work for decades; others are more recent arrivals. All are dedicated to understanding how society is structured as a gendered negotiation of identity, interests, place, and power between what are broadly and traditionally designated as women and men. They necessarily represent a range of disciplines and a variety of theoretical perspectives, as well as a generous set of perspectives on different aspects of gendered life.

To set a context for their contributions, in this introduction we provide an overview of some of the ways in which scholars engage with the slippery terms of gender. Donna Haraway's (1991) history of the contested conceptions of gender reveals the mutually constitutive relationships between the social conditions through which people manifest and elaborate gender in their everyday lives and the practices – always bounded and blinkered – through which academics and other intellectuals have defined gender as an analytical category. This process has always been profoundly political, discursively complex, and ideologically laden. Human history, moreover, is as much about resisting, changing, and denying ascriptions of gender as it is about reinforcing, legitimizing, and normalizing gendered practices. Ironically, these contesting and contrasting practices often occur simultaneously. As a result, even attempts to overcome the effects of gender – rooted in the very historical categories that we wish to challenge – cannot get past gender's overwhelming presence, its "there-ness." To meet the challenges posed by the gender concept today, then, we need to historicize both the social ideas in terms of which gender was established and took hold, and the conditions of lived gender that have defined people's lives.

When feminists of the "first wave" introduced the processes of gender contestation during the latter part of the nineteenth century, their purpose was explicitly political, with little backing from a body of theoretical texts. They were women of the modern era, sufficiently schooled in or confronted by the contradictions of Western thought to see the inequities presented by gendered life, in which men seemed to hold all the power and privilege and women seemed unable to fulfill ambitions beyond the narrow sphere of "womanly" pursuits. They fought to break these bonds. Many analysts have noted the irony of the fact that the first-wave feminists – and in particular the "Blue Stocking" activists for women's suffrage – were drawn almost exclusively from the middle classes, without exception from among white women. On the other hand, a retrospective analysis will show that the fight for freedom did not occur entirely within the self-conscious confines of that suffrage movement. First-year women's studies students in North America, for example, now almost universally learn about Sojourner Truth, whose "Ain't I a Woman?" speech at the 1851 Women's Rights Convention in Akron, Ohio is now hailed as foundational for feminist anti-racism. Born to slavery in 1797, well before it was outlawed in New York state, Sojourner Truth saw herself as playing a role in what was to become a feminist movement, and came to be recognized, through her characteristically courageous and tough-minded public speeches in favor of abolition and against the marginalized status of black women, however begrudgingly, as making a significant contribution to that mission.

If Sojourner Truth represented a distinct and small minority in this regard, second-wave feminism of the second half of the twentieth century, by contrast, is marked by a broadly conscious commitment to link feminist social struggles with theoretical insight. Inspired by writers such as Simone de Beauvoir, and strengthened during a period of social ruptures and challenges to authoritarian structure that occurred during the 1960s led by the likes of Germaine Greer, contemporary feminism is premised on the notion that we need to understand the concept of gender in order to change social relations. For decades, however, second-wave feminism rested on the assumption that "gender" represents a socially constructed category overlaying a more fundamental biological category called "sex." This dualism is both dialectical and ironic. By invoking a distinction between sex and gender, early second-wave feminists were able to challenge *some* gendered practices, especially those surrounding work and careers, on the grounds that if these practices were man-made this also guaranteed their historical contingency. The recognition of women's equality was therefore a matter of choice, not biology. Not so, however, for matters concerning reproduction, which have remained much more firmly embedded in essentialist notions of how childbearing and motherhood limit women's spheres. According to Haraway:

> the political and explanatory power of the 'social' category of gender depends upon historicizing the categories of sex, flesh, body, biology, race, and nature in such a way that the binary, universalizing opposition that spawned the concept of the sex/gender system at a particular time and place in feminist theory implodes into articulated, differentiated, accountable, located, and consequential theories of embodiment, where nature is no longer imagined and enacted as a resource to culture or sex to gender. (1991: 148)

Another dualism well established both in feminist scholarship and women's political movements is that of the relationship between patriarchy and oppositional politics. In 1986 and 1991, Gerda Lerner published a two-volume set entitled *The Creation of Patriarchy* (volume I) and *The Creation of Feminist Consciousness* (volume II). In the first volume, she makes a case for patriarchy as the definitive motif of history, making women central to the production of life and peripheral to the process of defining life's terms. Patriarchal concepts, she claims, are:

> built into all the mental constructs of . . . civilization in such a way as to remain largely invisible. Tracing the historical development by which patriarchy emerged as the dominant form of societal order, I have shown how it gradually institutionalized the rights of men to control and appropriate the sexual and reproductive services of women. Out of this form of dominance developed other forms of dominance, such as slavery. (1991: 3)

In Lerner's binary, patriarchy is opposed by feminist consciousness, which consists of severely constrained, marginalized, and always disadvantaged, but often creative, determined, and heroic, forms of resistance, with the result that:

> More than thirteen hundred years of individual struggles, disappointments and persistence have brought women to the historic moment when we can reclaim the freedom of our minds as we reclaim our past. The millennia of women's pre-history are at an end. We stand at the beginning of a new epoch in the history of humankind's thought, as we recognize that sex is irrelevant to thought, that gender is a social construct and that woman, like man, makes and defines history. (1991: 3)

If one looks at some of the texts used in recent years to introduce students to gender and feminist studies, two things will strike one about the approaches adopted. First, most of these texts assume that studying gender is about studying women. We acknowledge that there has been intense debate concerning the divide between "gender" and "women's" studies, and the respective approaches identified with each. There is an obvious need, now widely noted and acted on, for a corrective to the overwhelming "his-story" that has dominated the academy; we agree that "her-story" both needs to be told and told in relational terms. On the other hand, while there is a vast theoretical literature on the making, meanings, and management of patriarchy, and likewise a rapidly growing literature on the ways in which women experience patriarchy, there is still remarkably little on the ways in which men experience and use patriarchy. In other words, little of "his-story" is written from a feminist perspective, in critical feminist terms. For that reason, we undertake here to present gender as a relationship between the social categories of men and women, with a recognition that we shall not overcome the inequitable and iniquitous effects of gendering without understanding all the various and complex aspects of that relationship, and their interactive, unsettled, sometimes unsettling and shifting connections.

To do so is also to recognize that, as complex as gender can be, human beings are more than gendered, a blend of all the ways in which we have been constituted historically, and of the ways in which we engage the world, individually and in groups. What goes under the concept of gender is a complex and unfixed mix of significant structural and cultural or representational considerations both making and marking social distinctions between those constituted as sexes. Gender accordingly interactively characterizes social structure, individual identities, and signifying practices as well as the normative values embedded in them (Harding 1991; Braidotti 2002). Eisenstein (1996) speaks of the physicality representing the body as a complex set of political meanings that spark hatred through the establishment of otherness. Eisenstein points out that it is the simultaneity of bodily traits in particular combinations – white, male, able-bodied – that at once constitutes and denotes power, by combining in powerful interaction those conditions representing sociocultural elevations and dominance and invoking a set of assertive, complex, and labile fantasies inscribed *upon* the body. For Eisenstein, the discursive properties of race, gender, and the human qualities they engender are written not only on the individual body but also on the body politic, the nation, and on any social structure bearing meaning.

It should be clear that in presenting gender as a set of slippery, simultaneous, and interactive discourses and forces, we do not mean to privilege gender over other forms constituting and inscribing the body. But we do want to give it its historic due and social import, as well as to open up avenues for discussion of how gender has been used historically as a force for the concentration of power upon the male side. Nevertheless, as Judith Butler has made clear, gender is as much a troubled term as a troubling set of conditions and relations, not only because of its historic effects but also because of the new obstacles and contradictions that have resulted from feminist attempts to challenge it. We do not share the view of some radical feminists that other forms of oppression are a result only, or simply, or uniquely of gender. Nor do we wish to present a simplified concept of gender as something that can be deconstructed in order to address most of the world's woes. Like Butler, we do not assume that "there is some existing identity, understood through the category of women, who not only initiate feminist interests and goals within discourse, but constitute the subject for whom political representation is pursued" (1990: 1). Our anti-essentialism, not unlike Butler's, makes no concessions for either gender or sex.

At the same time, the fact that gender – like other forms of bodily and sociocultural identification – makes a difference means that we do not live in an undifferentiated world. In the chapters that follow, the authors have attempted to convey a sense of the range, complexity, relations, and implications of gendered differentiation, and therefore also a sense of the specificity of particular gendered contexts, expressed in particular places, cultural contexts and outcomes, and through particular social formations and imaginations. The gendered sites represented here range across institutions – the family, education, the healthcare system, labor relations – and speak from a variety of global perspectives, incorporating processes of development, location, racial constitution, and elaboration, as well as class specification. In short, the chapters presented in this volume critically reveal old and new ways of establishing, speaking, performing, acting out, and managing difference.

II

We aim in this volume, then, to offer a comprehensive, critical and engaged overview of Gender Studies and to suggest the directions in which the field is headed. The chapters are written by leading and emerging scholars with international reputations who have made important contributions to the topics or areas that they have been commissioned to address. Most of the texts are suitable for quick use as a reference, as well as for classroom usage at the upper division undergraduate level and in graduate courses.

There is heterogeneity in the nature of the contributions, ranging from essay statements, even provocations, to state-of-the-art overviews. Stylistic diversity expresses the impact of different disciplinary backgrounds on the making of Gender Studies. We have tried to be critical but careful not to impose our own paradigmatic dispositions on the contributors, thus leaving space for variety and contradictions, for descriptive, sometimes more disciplinary-bounded approaches, and for theoretical, analytical, transdisciplinary, and transnational distinction in the contributions. At the same time, there is also general coherence and consistency regarding critical disposition, interdisciplinary engagement, and international comparison and multidimensional or intersectional nuance.

Many studies or collections of essays claim to be about gender, but address only women. In our approach to the authors, we asked them not to reduce gender singularly to women as a category. In some cases, of course, the particularities of the area called for explicit emphasis on women, for instance, concerning a particular knowledge gap that needs to be filled. A case in point is Ratiba Hadj-Moussa's chapter about Arab women (chapter 19).

Where relevant, most of the contributions point to the interplay of gender with other markers of social positioning (e.g., dis/privileges associated with class, race, ethnicity, nationality, age, dis/abilities, and sexual orientation). The particular ways in which that could be done are shaped by the location and scope addressed by the essays, and by paradigmatic differences between the approaches. Many contributors are familiar with Race Critical Theory, and therefore engage with race, ethnicity, and racism as critical explanatory and analytical concepts. Mieke Bal's chapter on violence and tradition, for instance (chapter 40), problematizes the racially fashioned gender of the Black Peter ("Zwarte Piet") figure and its function in modern Dutch history. Others have included ethnicity as a more descriptive category. The same holds true for authors' engagements with Queer Studies as a marker of the way sexuality and sexual orientation are included as constitutive categories. Judith Halberstam (chapter 4) provides a state-of-the-art overview of the field – concise, comprehensive, and highly accessible to readers who are less familiar with Queer Studies. Accessibility with regard to contributors' engagement with Disability Studies reveals many gaps. In this respect, the volume is regretfully skewed. Most of the contributions pre-suppose culturally contextualized notions of "ability" as a given. The emerging field of Disability Studies constitutes one of the most interesting (and politically needed) fields of growth in general, most notably in relation to Gender Studies (as it has elsewhere in relation to Postcolonial Studies, for example). This immediately points to some timely themes we would have liked to include: biomedicine, cosmetic surgery, cloning, and the fashion industry are all highly gendered but at the same time remain deeply shaped by (racial, ethnic) norms of bodily and cognitive perfection. Logistics got the better of us, and such interventions will have to wait for other occasions.

This *Companion* is composed so as to serve different academic audiences: students and scholars across the world, and not only in Europe and North America, even though a substantial number of the authors are located (if not initially hailing from) there. In this sense, the volume reflects the rapid globalization of intellectual life, for while most authors are now located professionally in Western academies, many are not necessarily culturally (only) defined by these geographical spaces. In any case, we have welcomed pieces that are not parochial or specific to only one national (social, cultural) context. At the very least, we asked contributors to make some reference to or show the relevance of their analysis to some other contexts. And here, again, it is relevant in some cases to highlight a particular context, otherwise often underrepresented. Take, for instance, Tovi Fenster, writing on "Space and Cultural Meaning" (chapter 34), who focuses on Bedouin women in Israel in order to make the more general point that space is a gendered (and ethnicized, racially fashioned) concept, also explaining how and why.

When all is said and done – everything written, commented upon, revised, and finally wrapped up between covers – there is pleasure in achievement, a sense of accomplishment. But there remains also the definitive din of irrepressible areas that we perhaps might – should – have included but failed to: television and media, information technology, to mention just two not referenced above. A number of classical themes, in any case, notably socialization and psychoanalysis, are subsumed in different contributions.

Regretfully, we must insist on a clichéd but rather unavoidable disclaimer: this volume is not an attempt to be all-inclusive. We have undertaken to produce a companion in the symbolic sense of a friend to engage with, to learn from, to commit to, to take along with one, to argue with, to rely upon, to enjoy. The contributions hold a unified and comprehensive vision of the field and its new directions. The unifying methodological concern has been to identify phenomena that look "neutral" on the surface, but are deeply gendered just beneath, and the text is organized accordingly. Of course, alternatives and cross-cuttings are thinkable – some themes can be categorized under other intersecting headings as well.

III

The volume is structured so as to reflect key characteristics of Gender Studies: *Interdisciplinarity*, *Nonconformity*, and *Reflectivity*. But we seek also to include principal pillars of concern and debate – conceptual *Re-positionings*; *Jurisdictions* or domains of power, governance, and legality; social and geographical *Mobility*; the organization and orderings of *Spatiality*; the virtues and constraints of *Familial* arrangements and relations in different parts of the world, as well as issues having to do with *Physicality*, namely, the possibilities and impossibilities of the body.

Interdisciplinarity

Gender Studies is a broad interdisciplinary project. It focuses critically upon gendered conditions and articulations of social power along with their supporting bodies of knowledge in interaction with additional constitutive markers and expressions of unequal social arrangements. Mary Maynard (chapter 1) lays out the foundation. Emerging from Women Studies, the more extensive and relational domain of Gender Studies ranges across a broad array of disciplines – from arts to medicine, from discourse to geography – while shaping interdisciplinary fields, including Cultural Studies, Race Critical Studies, Queer Studies, Area Studies, and Postcolonial Studies. Part I of this volume emphasizes the generally global – not to be confused with globalizing – scope of Gender Studies. The enormously wide theoretical and analytical range of Gender Studies is encouraging; the geographical scope is dazzling; the ability to assume but then also immediately to reject disciplinary boundaries is beyond the imagination of most other fields. Just for the sake of the argument, read, one after the other, Ella Shohat's article on area studies (chapter 2), Inderpal Grewal and Caren Kaplan's contribution on postcolonial scholarship (chapter 3), Enakshi Dua's piece on global development (chapter 20), and Irene Dankelman's discussion of the environment and sustainable development (chapter 33). That we have placed these articles in different sections exemplifies the overarching thematic ordering we have given to the volume, which we think best represents the most general and generally impressive themes current in Gender Studies. But it is testament also to the broad inter- and transdisciplinary range of the field. Increasing sophistication and broadening of the field – interweaving gender with other dimensions of lived experiences and social structures in a range of geographical locations – is a strength but also a challenge. Is Gender Studies becoming all-inclusive, all-consuming, and, if so, can it continue to be a distinct interdisciplinary field? This volume does not provide unified or even any definitive answers to these questions. Gender Studies is as much an unfinished process as the notion of gender itself is in development, in transition across time. More than anything, we hope that the contributions mapping out this interdisciplinary range will fuel the debate concerning the nature and scope of Gender Studies and related fields.

Re-positionings

Few if any scholars would dispute the fact that feminism is the mother of Gender Studies. *Re-positionings*, the second section of the volume, offers literally what it announces – namely, a discussion of different approaches to fundamental concepts that have been instrumental to shaping the development of Gender Studies: knowledge, power, body, gender. It voices how different streams of thinking and authors relate to these concepts, but without suggesting any completeness. Gender Studies is a field on the move, always in the throes of reconstruction, continuously re-positioning itself in relation to political climates and the politics of knowledge. The developments are not linear. Specific thematic priorities may surface at different times in different countries and locations. There is certainly no universal development implied in the selection of contributions to this section in view of the question "What kinds of shift have taken place between the early 1970s Western perceptions of 'we (homogenously oppressed) women,' on the one hand, and today's questioning of racially produced, arranged, and differentiated masculinities or the culture of flirtation in heterosexual encounters, on the other?"

In an eloquently written essay, Laura Hyun Yi Kang (chapter 5) discusses the profound impact of the second wave of feminist scholars in exposing androcentrism among the gatekeepers of knowledge production, while undertaking to redefine what counts as knowledge, who makes the determination, and on what criteria. More recent elevation of the power of discursive regimes (language as articulating local meanings none of which represent any universal truth) seemed to overshadow any engagement with the materiality of deprivation, of bodies in distress, even as the body assumed abstracted, even idealized, theoretical significance and centrality. And those bodies in distress are overwhelmingly positioned socially by, on the basis, or in terms of gender.

If the disposition of gender, its definition and social positioning, is deeply embedded in epistemological articulations, Amade M'charek (chapter 6) reveals how deep that embeddedness runs. For M'charek shows, by way of a close examination of the laboratory practices of the Human Genome Diversity Project, that far from being the stable affiliate of gender's conceptual variety, biological sex is equally culturally profligate. Genetic sex, as M'charek concludes, shifts in its meanings repeatedly in practice. Sex and gender are not so distinct as they have been assumed to be.

"The body," it turns out then, never really disappeared from the agenda. Iris Marion Young (chapter 7) puts her finger on a related, still controversial, and yet unresolved debate: how does the body relate to gender? She applauds Toril Moi's introduction of the lived body as a rich and flexible concept for theorizing the socially constituted experience of men and women (in all their diversity). At the same time, Young insists, there is no understanding of "the lived" without gender either. Gender relates the particular (uniquely lived bodies) to the structural (gender and other social structures, social expectations, and institutional rules causing deprivations for some while privileging others). Toby Miller (chapter 8) takes us from the "lived body" to the "loved body" – the He Man, as embodied in hegemonic (white) masculinity. Miller contests essentialist notions of masculinity: masculinity is a form of life in transition, revealing complexity and ambiguity. Masculinity is neither a property nor an essence: "Hegemonic Masculinity" serves at once as idealized abstraction and relation of power, oppressing not just women but also, as Miller notes, "the many men excluded from it." Even "subscribers" may realize that the authorizing norms of power it represents are beyond reach, while those subjugated by its imposition (Miller identifies the working class, ethnic or racial minorities, and many immigrants) may be drawn to what the hegemonic model represents or offers.

The division of societies analytically into two discrete camps of men and women representing oppositional gender categories is no longer tenable, if it ever was. Revisiting the power paradigm around sex and sexuality, Lorraine Nencel (chapter 9) seeks to re-position the concept of sexuality as a multilayered, intricate, also playful set of relations where women's and men's behavior cannot be seen as just reinforcing presupposed gender inequities.

Jurisdictions

If the section on re-positioning seeks to intervene in prevailing relations of gendered power, *Jurisdictions* concerns itself with the grounds, range, and styles of expression of gendered authority, whether at the macro or the micro levels. At issue are the underlying fabric and general scope of gendered power, most notably in national configurations and in law. But this section concerns also the modalities of articulation through policy, and its material manifestations in domestic violence locally and in ethnic cleansing and genocide more globally. Thus, at the broader end of the range, Lois A. West (chapter 10) discusses how nations are gendered and gender is enacted through national expression, arguing for an analysis that focuses on the process by which gender differences and conflicts are negotiated and where those processes succeed or break down. Masculinist bias occurs in institutions and practices that fail to cognize women's experience and male social domination, but also in research that often fails to consider the possibilities of such exclusions. But there can be a feminist bias also, West argues, in reducing gender relations to concerns solely about the social roles and positionings of women. West is concerned to analyze the various ways masculinities serve to mold and make nationalism through engendering processes. So she points out that studies of nationalism focus largely on militarized masculinities, on the violence of armed conflict, and in some cases on the rape of women by male perpetrators of conflict and violence. Increasingly drawn into global circuits of movement and circulating populations, states are facing standards of gendered interactivity and the pressure to meet standards of gendered relation not necessarily of their own making.

Where Lois A. West generalizes broadly across national instances, Katherine Franke (chapter 11) offers carefully considered ways focused on particular contexts in which law fashions what we take sexuality to be and how those conceptions are defined, scrutinized, and controlled through a body of law, affecting differentially those whose gender locations differ on socially fashioned criteria. Sexuality, Franke suggests, is especially important because it so deeply serves to mediate relations of gendered power and, accordingly, as an "instrument of gender regulation." The laws surrounding sexuality, she argues, should not so readily reduce to sexual laws just as certain behavior should not so readily be labeled erotic or as sexual offenses, thus covering over other compelling conceptions at work. Franke's broader point is that we should not lose sight of the various ways, in particular contexts, in which sex serves power relations – serves to humiliate, or to eviscerate masculinity, especially in racially charged contexts. Sex regulates. But Franke insists also that we pay close attention to how the various ways practices or behavior not readily characterized as sexual can be erotic within and across gender formations and positionings. In any case, whether and how some act is experienced as sexual – whether as erotic or violent – will depend not on context reductively understood but very often on one's gendered position within broader parameters of relations of power. Sex, Franke concludes, has no a priori normative value but can be put to work legally and culturally for both good and bad.

Carol Lee Bacchi (chapter 12) argues that despite widespread Western claims of gender-neutrality, policy-making, policy application, and policy implication have been shown especially by feminists to be shaped by deeply gendered considerations, most notably to the detriment of women but one could add of gays, lesbians, and transsexuals too. Gender, Bacchi points out, should not simply be treated as indicative of biological sex, as simply a part or characteristic of individuals, but as a structural positioning in social organization and relations. Policy-making thus is a gendering process, often differentially shaping the lives of people occupying distinct social positions, sometimes more deeply defining the social positions that, say, men and women occupy, almost always impacting in contrasting ways on those socially differentiated. Bacchi herself is particularly interested in studying how gendered assumptions in policy-making are understood and applied in particular circumstances and in projects such as affirmative action, cosmetic surgery, and gender mainstreaming. As she points out, where the assumption is that the social problems stem from women being treated like men, the response becomes that women are treated fairly when the conditions they face are like those of men, thus continuing to elevate men's experience as the norm.

Madelaine Adelman (chapter 13) continues the focus on gendered public policy, though directed at the specific set of gendered issues concerning family violence. Domestic violence is traditionally understood in its most common form as men's violence against their women partners. Adelman widens this constrained sense of what counts as family and, accordingly, of the varieties of violence enacted within this expanded set of relationships. She does so in a broader globalized frame, pointing to national differences in conception of domestic violence and in institutionalized responses. She calls attention to research indicating the diminishing of woman battering and violence against women in some national contexts, such as in the US, Britain, and Canada, by institutionalizing it in antiseptic terms as an individualized social or medical problem, often pathologizing women, rather than as one that is socio-structurally prompted. Thus violence against women, Adelman concludes, has largely been "gender neutralized" in these societies rather than "gender accentuated" as a violation of human rights, as it has been under the auspices of UN interventions, holding not just individuals but also states responsible for the vulnerability of women in those societies. Women thus are considered a class facing "gender-specific" violations. This, Adelman shows, can have the unfortunate implication of restricting women's agency and failing to address the structural conditions of women's vulnerability to violence. Gendered social relations, she concludes, shift the meaning, experience, effects, and responses of domestic violence.

Jennifer Hyndman (chapter 14) continues the focus on gender directed violence. She shows, on the basis of well-known case studies, the centrality of gender to various ways of understanding genocide and ethnic violence. Men and women have traditionally been socialized differently to participate in state violence, most notably war, but it is also the case that gender relations, positions, expectations, and behaviors alter as a consequence of institutionalized violence. So the mass disappearance of men as a result of war or ethnic cleansing shifts the social roles and burdens of women as a consequence. But it is also the case that men and women might be differentially targeted in genocidal ethnic cleansing projects. As Hyndman argues, this has a great deal to do with the differential ways men and women are positioned by ethnic nationalisms as well as how those who are taken not to belong to the national body are positioned relative to those who are. But another, more recent factor in such gender differentiation has to do with the fact that the battlefield in wars has now been expanded to include people's bodies, homes, and livelihoods, as well as affective affinities and relations. Hyndman concludes that the application of international conventions and laws offers the best way to prevent instances of genocide or ethnic cleansing in contrast to attempted deterrent punishments of perpetrators, which have no prohibitive effect precisely because they are retrospective.

If Jennifer Hyndman's focus is on crimes against humanity, Tony Jefferson (chapter 15) considers the gendered dimensions, causes, and effects of crime, as well as conceivable responses. Where Madelaine Adelman's attention is directed to domestic violence and especially the impact on women, Jefferson attends to the set of sexual crimes, focusing especially on why the rate of masculine crime is so high, as a way of bringing attention to bear on the particularly gendered dimensions of criminal action and violent crime, their definition, expressions, and implications. Jefferson critically surveys and summarizes the complex nuances of three prevailing accounts of maleness and, by extension, of men's behavior. The first orthodoxy covered by Jefferson reduces male behavior to the "normal masculine personality," to role behavior of the man who has learned what is expected of him in seeking power and domination. The second acknowledges multiple masculinities, recognizing a diversity of male expressions of power as well as the consequential complexity this recognition implies for gender relations. The third account seeks a psychoanalytic explanation for masculine behavior in the desires and investments of contradictory subjects.

Jefferson examines critically what each of these accounts offers by way of explaining high rates of men's sexual violence. In the first account, men's sexual violence seems disturbingly reduced to its masculine nature. In the second account, rape and other violently sexual crimes are group resources for achieving masculinity. And in the third case, men's sexual violence is explained by feminist inspired forms of psychoanalysis by some version of their felt insecurity and inadequacy. Jefferson concludes with the insistence that adequate accounts must necessarily address a careful weaving together of the psychological or inner world with the social in specific circumstances.

Nonconformity

The section on jurisdiction ranges over the nature of normative institutionalizations and authoritative articulations. *Nonconformity*, by contrast, underlies all struggles for justice. It takes courage to question and to reject what is being taken for granted in dominant domains. Sandra Harding (chapter 16) tells the story of the feminist revolution in science: the dismantling of the myth of neutrality in favor of conscious subjectivity, an undertaking deeply controversial from the start. Gender analyses expose the limitations of masculine bias in modern science and technology and the rationality underlying the ideals of modernity, democracy, progress, and so-called civilization. There are few examples where the gendered, classed, and racially inflected perceptions of "civil" and "civilized" are more explicitly hypocritical than in society's responses to prostitution.

Kamala Kempadoo (chapter 17) traces the history of the study of women pathologized and ousted for not conforming to the sexual norms of "proper" womanhood. Today, sex work has become a basis of livelihood for increasing numbers of women and men under new global arrangements. Epistemologically and methodologically, sex work studies are a good example of the nonconventional nature of those directions in gender studies where activism and research intertwine: struggles against the oppression of and discrimination against sex workers have contributed substantially to theory development of the nature of intersections between sexuality and economic life. By definition, activism aims to challenge the status quo. Thus Nitza Berkovitch and Sara Helman (chapter 18) point out that the international women's movement has transformed conventional definitions of human rights by insisting on the recognition of individuals as perpetrators of human rights – think of rape and sexual abuse – rather than the traditional perception that only states can violate human rights. Their account of the history of the gay and lesbian movement lays out the continuing global struggle for the right not to comply with dominant ideologies that take heterosexuality as the only appropriate form of sexuality and desire.

Ratiba Hadj-Moussa (chapter 19) astutely reminds us that women are often a source of resistance. But nonconformity can be much more complex than simply saying "no" to dominant gender expectations. Women's groups in almost every country in the Middle East find themselves in opposition not only to the ruling power but to Islamists as well. Dealing with the latter, some feminists – revolutionaries in disguise – wear the Islamic veil, which renders possible recourse to legitimation for a range of practices on the basis of appeal to the sacred texts. The written sources they seek to master in order to challenge male appropriation of claims to God's authority and legitimation are accordingly made available.

13

Mobility

Mobility is about "moves," "movements," and "mobilization," economically (international development, class, organizational structures), geographically (migration), and in terms of political action (unions). Part V addresses access to means of power and tools for survival; it is about the pursuit of better quality of livelihoods, of the conditions for living. It is no wonder that a number of the chapters in this section emphasize feminist action and women's struggle for social and economic equality. Livelihoods in the South and in the North have been greatly affected by globalization – the gap between rich and poor has increased dramatically, obviously between North and South, but also within both.

On the face of it Enakshi Dua's introduction of the theme "Development under Globalization" (chapter 20) reads as if it is perfectly gender-neutral. Colonization left third world countries with distorted and underdeveloped economic structures. But, as Dua points out, subsequent national economic development projects have not been beneficial to all groups. Development planners have tended to ignore the significance of (poor) women's paid and unpaid labor for national economies. For more than three decades women have been fighting the pervasive ways in which gender operates as an allocation principle, a struggle intensified by the loss of real wages and employment for women under the market manipulations of neoliberal millennial capitalism. As a consequence, globalization has intensified the flight from economic denigrations and from the horrors of war and political oppression, with differential gendered effect.

Cecilia Menjívar (chapter 21) writes about migration movements from South to North and East to West, while at the same time accentuating the gendered nature of migration. Her contribution is exemplary as a gender-balanced approach, exhibiting careful consistency in integrating the lives of men and women in the story of migration. She pictures how immigrants' social positions – shaped by gender, class, race, and ethnicity – mediate the effects that immigration laws and the dynamics of the labor market will have on their lives. Men often lose status with immigration, which can lead to marital conflict and domestic abuse. Highly educated women, too, end up in positions for which they are over-qualified. But in some cases, immigration holds new opportunities for women, in education and employment, and by offering them less restrictive lifestyles. In the process of flight from oppressive circumstances, stereotypical gender perceptions can work to the advantage of women (more assistance compared to men when seen as a helpless woman) but also to their disadvantage (women are more vulnerable to being sexually abused).

Migrants and refugees come from different class positions. For a long time, advocates of Marxist theories played down the obvious variation within class lines. Abigail B. Bakan (chapter 22) shows that class is deeply divided by factors of gender, race, and nationality. Male domination continues to be expressed in terms of significantly lower wages for women, who carry the largest burden of care work, often on top of other income-generating activities. Discrimination

14

against women and resistance against a gender analysis of class interests is also prevalent in unions – traditionally exclusive male bastions.

Linda Briskin (chapter 23) discusses how women workers, not recognizing themselves in union practices, have organized separately, in various parts of the world. In some countries, women have insisted that unions take account of the gender implications in all issues – including restructuring, health and safety, and seniority. Yet, the language of gendering democracy in unions does not sufficiently reflect the intertwining of gender with specific claims for democracy that have emerged from other marginalized groups: ethnic minorities, gay and lesbian workers, as well as disabled workers. Agneta H. Fischer and Annelies E. M. van Vianen (chapter 24) make it clear that unions are just like any other corporate or bureaucratic structure in privileging (white) masculine, heteronormative interests. Gender differences are particularly skewed at the top levels characterized by almost exclusively (white) masculine homogeneity. Senior managers highly value what are viewed as characteristically feminine values, such as positive feedback, loyalty toward colleagues, personal development, and balance between work and care, but when it comes to the actual practice of peer selection the choices are different. Men are considered to be better equipped to perform with charisma, ambition, strong will, self-confidence, assertiveness, and independence. Moreover, leaders are identified on the basis of expressing or being encouraged to express ego-boosting emotions – pride, anger, and irritation – more typically associated with men and less appreciated when expressed by women.

Familiality

Different behaviors associated with men and women betray the ideological underpinning of socialization into culturally specific understandings of femininity and masculinity. These understandings offer a backdrop in terms of how to approach differing conceptions and experiences of family on a global scale. Prevailing family norms in one part of the world may differ from those in other places, and thus may prompt pressures to conform or motivations to rebel specific to that place even if, in a globalizing world, they are prompted by perceptions of differing practices elsewhere. Family, of course, is a contested notion. It supposes familiarity of sorts, emphasizing kin-like relationships. But there are great variations between who are included and the social expectations involved. Should the determination be made on the basis of the household or the bloodline, a combination of both, or is it for the law to determine what and who constitute family? Historically, cross-culturally, as well as within cultures and between generations, the familial, the familiar, and the family merge and overlap. Hence, we have suggested *familiality* as a heading for Part VI of this volume. It is not only the notion of family that is under scrutiny in this section; so too is the universality of gender as a classifying concept in familial relations and expectations. So even as we have opted for an area approach, we hasten to add that we have not tried to be exhaustive. The contributions address the Americas, notably

Latin America and the Caribbean, as well as Europe and Africa. Regretfully, we have not been able to include a contribution on Asia as a region. Almost every collection of this kind faces some crisis of deadline and delivery. This was ours. The ultimate version of the contribution we had commissioned never materialized. We regret the omission.

Local communities in colonized countries, and women and men across the world, have struggled against externally imposed normative definitions of family gender roles. Ifi Amadiume (chapter 25) criticizes the nineteenth-century European-imposed father–son paradigm on the basis of which were applied rights of inheritance and succession depriving African women of land and other property. Yet gender does not sufficiently capture the complexity of African familial relations. This holds true for new developments, such as progressive men who adopt the culture of the "mama husband," a genderless parent. Gender likewise falls short in accounting for traditional arrangements – for instance, of women marrying other women. Such same-sex marriages have often been mistaken for, but have different implications from, (Western) gay and lesbian marriages. The tendency to universalize Western familial concepts is not new. Feminist approaches have rightfully problematized the dominance and privileges of males and elders in a range of African, and in particular Islamic, cultures. But few if any have been successful in bringing back into focus African daughters in relation to their mothers and other women in the lineage, other than only as objects of (male) abuse and exploitation.

D. Alissa Trotz (chapter 26) acknowledges that while we can speak of "the idea" of Caribbean family as such, there is no sense in talking about "*the* Caribbean family.*" Family – that is, kinship relations between men and women of African, Asian, indigenous, and indeed mixed descent – has been a critical site of struggle for Caribbean national autonomy and cultural identity. But studies tend to set against each other the stereotypical "Afro-Caribbean-female-headed-household," on the one hand, and patriarchal Asian arrangements, on the other. These generalizations not only pathologize gender expressions in the Caribbean (as deviant from an idealized Western family image), but also create a false sense of cultural homogeneity across countries and continents. Furthermore, they reduce men in relation to female-headed households to the role of failing fatherhood only. Men also make important contributions to the family as grandfathers, uncles, sons, or in other kin-like roles.

Nina Laurie (chapter 27) makes clear that in Latin America too the culture of poverty paradigm, which was introduced in the late 1970s, has produced an over-emphasis on the homogenized image of family as "female-headed," and as *the* target for development policy strategies. It is true that the poorest households are often headed by women – with or without the presence of male partners/fathers present. But different colonial histories, variants of people of European descent, immigrants and indigenous cultures, rural and urban areas, the differences made by class and ethnicity, and the gender impact of authoritarian regimes on family lives render the idea of "*the* Latin American family" useless. The past decade of accelerated globalization and neoliberal restructuring programs has impacted familial arrangements. Women in the Caribbean, as in Latin America more generally, have increased their involvement in paid labor. Women now participate at greater rates in the informal sector of home-based work, insecure contract and piece-work, and in sex work in the tourism industry. Extended local networks of family form a substantial base for economic activity and support. In addition, transnational remittances – due to migration of male and female family members – contribute to the family household income. Largely neglected in Latin America, but now explicitly coming into focus, are studies of gender and ethnic intersectionality. These studies challenge essentialist notions of gender relations in indigenous communities. Equally problematic, indeed downright insulting, is the hegemonic assumption in mestizo society that no one wants to have any "Indian" ancestry in the family. But tides are changing. Increasingly, the "social capital" of indigenous networks and communities is coming into view.

In Europe, by contrast, gender research on family lacks nuance about the impact of ethnically diverse needs and identities on family formation processes. But by and large, as Joanna Regulska (chapter 28) indicates, families across Europe have become more similar: there is more flexibility in choosing family arrangements. Despite differences between countries, there are similarities in the privileges shared by middle-class and elite families and the challenges faced by single mothers or low-income families. Across the board new generations renegotiate and redefine the conditions under which young women, men, and, more recently, transsexuals make decisions about getting married, forming new unions, or establishing relations. A shift is taking place from kinship relations based on biological ("blood") ties to formation on a social basis. The opposite-sex-legal-marriage-with-two-children model is no longer always normative. Single households are more common, as are single and multiple parents (including grandparents, foster parents, and friends). Gay and lesbian (married) couples are no longer so unusual. Despite more individual choice, the gender distribution and use of power in these diverse arrangements of familiality still depend largely on class, religion, race, ethnicity, sexuality, and culture. Moreover, the idea of family as a safe site has lost credibility. Today, women no longer tolerate physical abuse in silence. Feminist research has put "the" family on the world history map as a site of domestic violence against women and girls.

Physicality

It is probably safe to say that the first public analysis to represent the embodiment of gender, race, and socio-economic intersectionality can be found in Sojourner Truth's famous speech, "Ain't I a Woman?" (1851), referred to earlier. These were her words:

> That man over there says that women need to be helped into carriages, and lifted over ditches, and to have the best place everywhere. Nobody ever helps me into

carriages, or over mud-puddles, or gives me any best place! And ain't I a woman? Look at me! Look at my arm! I have ploughed and planted, and gathered into barns, and no man could head me! And ain't I a woman? I could work as much and eat as much as a man – when I could get it – and bear the lash as well! And ain't I a woman? I have borne thirteen children, and seen most all sold off to slavery, and when I cried out with my mother's grief, none but Jesus heard me! And ain't I a woman?

Then they talk about this thing in the head; what's this they call it? [member of audience whispers, "intellect"] That's it, honey. What's that got to do with women's rights or negroes' rights? If my cup won't hold but a pint, and yours holds a quart, wouldn't you be mean not to let me have my little half measure full?

Then that little man in black there, he says women can't have as much rights as men, 'cause Christ wasn't a woman! Where did your Christ come from? Where did your Christ come from? From God and a woman! Man had nothing to do with Him.

Sojourner Truth here combines a number of key concepts discussed in Part VII of this *Companion*: bodily strength and femininity, reproduction, the deviant body, solidarity, and care. She challenges the equation of femininity with white female physical weakness and helplessness, while firmly claiming as her own womanhood the experience of physical strength, even when under conditions of intense racial exploitation. And she reminds us that, having born many children, as a black woman she has been substantially deprived of the experience of motherhood. Laura Shanner (chapter 29) confirms that, more than 150 years later, women of color all over the world are still being discouraged or even prevented from mothering children. In the name of development aid, international family planning programs are generous in pushing contraceptives but silent on infertility relief. This sharply contradicts the enormous investment in expensive reproductive and genetic technologies in the Western world, primarily tuned to the needs of white and middle-class women. New technologies may offer greater choice on an individual level (for those who can afford them financially), but structurally genetic technology is deeply gendered, racially implicated, and dismissive of physical impairments. Alarming developments point at the fact that high-technology countries exercise increasing medical and state control over the womb, while allowing for technological interventions eventually aimed at materializing desired fetuses "on order." One can imagine a possible scenario whereby women are made legally accountable for preventing prenatal injury, at the cost of their right to decide whether and under which conditions they are willing to offer their wombs as nurturing environments for a fetus to grow. Equally concerning are the social implications of increasing quality control of the fetus in the name of individual choice, cultural tradition, or preventive health. Think of sperm banks offering semen of white, middle-class, highly intelligent donors, alongside the abortion of female fetuses, and socially endorsed interventions to abduct fetuses lacking the promise of bodily perfection.

Historically, the "deviant" body has been the object of disrespect and abuse in subtle and not so subtle ways. Deviance obviously is characterized differently in different periods and places. But there is a longstanding widespread devaluation of the non–male, non–white, non–complete, or differently shaped body. The (still prevalent) projection of dependency on the part of women has a particular gendered form in relation to disabled men. They may feel feminized (or violated in their sense of being a man), for instance when able-bodied men open a door for them. In her revealing discussion of the gender of disabilities (chapter 30), Anita Silvers points out that in cultures that devalue dependency and inflate the importance of self-sufficiency, chronic illnesses and disabilities are perceived as a burden, as lesser forms of life, as deviant rather than as naturally part of the human condition. Silvers's chapter opens with an insightful analogy between race–gender intersectionality and gender disability. She compares black women's vulnerability in being discriminated against as a result of their dislocation from normative female roles to the fragility of discrimination protection for women with disabilities: they are not seen as fitting the normative image of womanhood either. Disabled women (as opposed to disabled men and able-bodied people) face higher unemployment levels and fewer opportunities to find a (male) partner willing to offer the necessary care. The prejudice that assumes that disabled people are by definition overall less competent deprives disabled women from the recognition that, like many able-bodied women, they want to and can provide love and care for family and friends. In other words, impairments are material or physical facts, but disability is a (gendered) social imposition.

Biological characteristics are not the only determinants of health and corporeal well-being. Lesley Doyal (chapter 31) argues that the nature and quality of the daily life of men and women (in racial, economic, and geopolitical contexts) influences their exposure to health risks and their access to resources to live a healthy life. Poverty afflicts the majority of women and men in the (under)developing world, and increases, for example, the risks of childbearing. In the same vein, the cultural devaluation of girls and women manifests itself in a range of health hazards particular to them, including a lack of control over their own fertility, undernourishment, exposure to sex-specific diseases, anxiety, and depression. It is hard to think that the health problems faced by men are a reflection of gender inequality in access to the health resources they need. Men engage more than women in risky behavior, whether to prove their masculinity, to secure even basic resources, or because they are pressed as foot soldiers into political conflict. As a result, men are much more likely than women to get murdered, to die in a car accident or in conflict circumstances, to engage in unsafe sex, or to lose their life in highly dangerous sports activities.

The latter point raises the question of sports, which is undeniably about the body, physicality, and embodied power, but is equally about masculine hegemony. Team sports in particular provide a socializing system for males in the world of political, economic, and social power. Martha Saveedra (chapter 32) contends that modernity has naturalized sport as the masculine code for heterosexual male superiority and domination over the feminine. Sport is by definition a highly competitive, hierarchical, secularized, role-specified, rule-driven, bureaucratically organized, and quantity-oriented field of physical contest. Heterosexual normativity needs constant reassertion and reaffirmation to compensate for the homoerotic effects of male-dominated sports activities: think of the celebration of male muscular physicality and the intimacy of same-sex interactions in team sport. Many sportswomen go a long way to assert their (hyper) heterosexual femininity. Thus the label of "lesbian" continues to be a powerful tool to ridicule and limit women's access to sport. Masculine hegemony in sports has been contested by non-Western examples. The historical exclusion of women from sports, so prevalent in the Western model of sport at least until very recently, is not universal. In China, women athletes excel internationally more than their male counterparts. In Senegal, basketball, one of the sports that provides upward mobility, has turned female players into popular icons. Likewise, African-American sportswomen have been welcomed more generously by their communities than white women in Anglo-Saxon cultures, though (as with their male counterparts) sometimes with mixed relief.

Spatiality

Part VIII, *Spatiality*, includes chapters that are arranged from more general, even global, to more particular or specific locations, which focus on the gendered fashioning and inflecting of each scale. Space serves, on the one hand, as a container and conduit for gender-fashioned events, relations, and activities; on the other hand, space itself is gender-inflected or marked, if not constituted and determined. Development, whether destructive or sustainable, is distributed unequally in and across space, both made and marked by differentiated gendered positioning in prevailing relations of power.

Irene Dankelman (chapter 33) overviews the literature on gender-differentiated relations to nature. Dankelman outlines the history of women's important contributions to a critical environmentalism and illustrates, despite prevailing assumptions to the contrary, that the relation to and effect on people of social space and the environment are far from gender-neutral. She demonstrates in some detail the relation between male-dominated environmental resources and power, on the one hand, and the environmental degradation, resource depletion, and restricted access that have followed as a consequence, on the other. Dankelman stresses, by contrast, the critical role women have played in environmental management and sustainable development.

Tovi Fenster (chapter 34) reflects upon the social arrangement of space as gendered and as gender-experienced. She considers the gendered meanings with which space is infused. Like other chapters in Part VIII, Fenster shows how socio-spatial relations are reflected in and serve to (over-)determine gendered relations of power in the contexts in which they are defined and refined. The codifications of public and private spaces are deeply engendered. Gender marks both how social spaces are categorized and classified and the meanings attached to and associated with them. Space can be both liberating and confining, rendering possible for some what it makes impossible for others. In this light, Fenster also reveals how some of the worst human rights abuses are connected to restrictions and prohibitions within – and to specific and specifically designed – socio-spatial or institutional sites, most notably, but not only, for women.

The gendered marking of space thus is embedded in architectural design and embodiment, a fact little recognized until quite recently. The gendering of architecture is most evidenced in housing and home design, as Mona Domosh (chapter 35) points out in a critically subtle review of the field. Architecture has long been controlled as a discipline – and in its corporate hierarchy – by men and is overwhelmingly practiced by men, and, in societies dominated by Europe and European settlers, by white men. Domosh points out that some cultures explicitly divide living and recreational spaces into female private spaces and male public spaces. And indeed, men and women (and one might add, straight and gay people) tend to inhabit spaces, public and private, differently from each other. She argues that the suburbanization of residential life throughout the West has reflected and reinforced dominant patriarchal relations of social power. Suburbs, for instance, have entailed large, time-consuming distances between home and work, an additional factor that seriously militates against those, almost invariably women, assumed to be primary care-givers seeking employment, especially in higher remunerating sectors of the economy. Accordingly, suburbs have also magnified women's isolation first in the home and then in an automobile culture that is both antisocial and reductive. Men, by contrast, were thrust into factory and office life and assumed to be economic producers, in contrast to the care-giving and consuming roles assumed by women. Indeed, consumptive spaces largely were designed with women in mind, as, for example, in the decorative layout of department stores.

Domosh shows that gendered differentiation equally marks architectural writing, commentary, and criticism. Women are expected to write about interior decoration and furnishing, while building design and urban forms are supposedly the turf and territory of men. But, as she points out critically, space is also largely heteronormative in the uses to which it is put. This heteronormativity is occasionally challenged and disrupted, and almost always in particular parts of cities, by gay and lesbian intervention regarding spatial symbolics and meanings, use, and transversal.

As modern institutions that shape how societies understand their histories and cultural standing, museums both reflect and represent various forms of social relation, most notably those of race, class, and gender. Ellen Fernandez-Sacco reveals the ways in which gender shapes prevailing power relations around museum cultures (chapter 36), but is also embedded in assumptions that underpin institutional conception as well as in the material conditions and culture of the museum. Museums, in their internal organization and positioning in the consumptive economy of the contemporary tourist trade as much as in representation, reflect and express dominant strains in the social order of gender. Fernandez-Sacco expands the realm of the museum to include contemporary cyber-virtual spaces of artistic representation which depend on the invisibly gendered relations of labor for their productive possibility as much as do the spaces of more materially embodied museums. And yet, she argues, these virtualizations make gender determinations for the viewer more ambiguous, more unsure, and sometimes as a consequence more challenging.

As Mona Domosh points out regarding architecture generally, so Fernandez-Sacco demonstrates that museum architecture, in particular, is the province of male architects. Buildings quite literally bear the "brand" of some or other emerging or established architect, who almost invariably is male. More and more, museums are marked or branded in terms of their architectural design and less and less by the content of their art collections. Increasingly, museums partner in circulating "global" traveling exhibitions, realizing art and so beauty as and in global commodities. The buildings, hardly reducible to gendered configurations, nevertheless are deeply informed in their spatial configurations and by extension in their viewer experiences (and often in their collections) by male ideals. Finally, Fernandez-Sacco argues that the shift from manufacturing-based economies to tourist-driven consumptive ones in which museums have come to play such large roles has also entailed significant gender shifts. Manufacturing economies offered reasonably well-paid skilled working-class jobs largely, if not exclusively, to men. Jobs servicing the tourist economy tend to be part-time, temporary, benefit-less, more or less unskilled, and low paying. Needless to say, these positions tend to be inhabited by women and recent non-white immigrants.

Reflectivity

Gender Studies emerges from the tradition of critiquing social injustices. Without reflection on the norms, values, principles, and practices underpinning social structures of gender differentiation and replication, there could be no understanding of issues of justice and injustice, of the many cultural ways in which gender operates. We close the volume, accordingly, with a section on *Reflectivity*, with chapters about the gendering of ethics, religion, discourse, and tradition, and the contribution of these norm-setting domains to engendered social life.

Vikki Bell (chapter 37) argues that ethics, like feminist theory, is intimately concerned with questions of the quality of social life, responsibility, and responsiveness. Feminist theory has been concerned to reveal the contingency of social structures and strictures, to question the values according to which social life is constituted, and to identify harms previously unseen. The prevailing trends in modern ethical theory have understood ethical values to be decontextualized, abstracted, and idealized universals conceived or identified by disembodied reason. As Bell reveals, feminist theory has been at the forefront of demonstrating how such purportedly universal values were representative of masculinist bias and male interests. Feminist ethics, by contrast, has been committed, internal distinctions notwithstanding, to embodied and situated determinations of

22

ethical values and virtues. This commitment to situated and embodied analysis underpins a concern, also, that actual differences, the concrete other, not merely be attended to but that they be taken seriously. Ethics became, in effect, the implemented understanding of the principles and normative practices of intersubjectivity. Bell observes that this shift to the intersubjective carries its own shortcomings as the grounding for ethics and its values, not least its parochial individualism and its own narrow exclusiveness and exclusions, concerns she explores critically in some depth. In short, intersubjective interactions always take place in the context of social relations of power and comprehension. Bell shows how this calls forth less examined ethico-psychological notions of empathy or identification, or of baring and bearing the trace of another within oneself across geographies and temporalities, of love and forgiveness, and ultimately of cultural, linguistic, and normative translation. A gendered ethics, she concludes, concerns both the establishment of norms of social interaction and a constant question of those norms and their grounds of establishment.

Pamela Dickey Young discusses how religious traditions take on gender-based or -bounded considerations (chapter 38). She understands religion to be an organizing structure for comprehending the world and for acting in it. Religious traditions may vary dramatically over time in these interpretive and normative schemes, and official forms might differ, even dramatically, from unofficial ideas and practices taken to inhabit, make up, or inflect the religion. Dickey Young accordingly suggests that while men may occupy official positions of religious authority, women may exert authority or power in less official or formal settings. Religions often identify gender in terms of sex, assigning gendered roles or social positions of relative power on the basis of biological sex and affirmative symbolism to the gender considered more powerful or valuable (almost invariably maleness). Indeed, men may be elevated socially by a prevailing interpretation of a religion because they are considered to be more akin to the deity's imagined gender in the relevant qualities. But in most religions – and this is especially true of what have come to be called fundamentalist interpretations of a tradition – men have also occupied the most powerful positions, hermeneutically and administratively. Dickey Young is right to insist, therefore, that a gendered analysis of religion needs to attend not simply to the gendering of religious symbolism but also to the relation between such symbolism and the forms of social power they engender, reflect, license, or indeed critique. A critical disposition towards these forms of power includes comprehending that just as a particular religion is marked by hierarchical relations of gender power so too are particular religions positioned hierarchically in relation to each other, with Christianity occupying the most powerful position in modernity. In response to these marginalizing positions within traditional religious relations of power, women have often established their own, sometime renegade communities of interpretation and practice, thus stretching the bounds of tradition from the inside out.

If Bell and Dickey Young address prevailing theoretical and institutional reflections on and about the normative, Ruth Wodak considers even broader questions about how people engage each other discursively, the terms of our thinking and judging about ourselves and others, and the framing of our social relations (chapter 39). Wodak shows that women are both invariably overlooked and incorporated in dominant male modes of address, at once including and belittling the status of more than half the people in the world. She is thus particularly concerned about what language implicitly includes and excludes, what it makes possible in terms of gender and what gendered possibilities it cuts off and for whom. She shows that stereotypes, power and hierarchy, and actual behavior are mutually constitutive and interactive, as revealed in the social discourse that dominates. Wodak illustrates that discursive control is exercised by those who exert social power. Gender relationships are ordered through such socio-discursive assertion, providing access for men, other considerations being equal, that women might well be denied.

Where Ruth Wodak is concerned with the way discursive formations and assumptions engender social power and structure gender inequalities, Mieke Bal (chapter 40) closes the volume by reflecting not on how gender (or particular genders) is defined – what gender *is*, as she characterizes it – but on how particular genders are socially positioned – what gender *does*, what effects it enacts. Gender, and sexual behavior, it follows, are socioculturally prompted and promoted, not individually intended or biologically necessitated and so never absolutely necessitated or inevitable. Bal thus reflects (upon) and represents the overriding spirit of the volume, invigorating a robust argument for an anti-essentialist, non-reductive, and complex conception of gender we have aimed at by the choice of topics to promote. But it is also to reveal, as Bal shows, that gender drips with violence, for people are fixed in place not by necessity but by the structural force of social imposition and the sets of assumptions and actions reinforcing socio-structural composition. This is the violence of discipline and repetition, of acting out as expected. Bal argues, and demonstrates through a careful cultural analysis of the tradition of *Zwarte Piet* (Black Peter) – representations that bedevil Dutch society every December – that cultural performance can serve as critical intervention, drawing our attention to the contingent fixings of seemingly natural and so inevitable structural conditions. Bal, in short, helps us to close the volume on a critically encouraging note, vigorously and rigorously revealing that the seemingly inevitable is indeed changeable, that the debilitating socio-structural formations of gender and race are not as fixed as their proponents and supporters might take it for granted.

References

Braidotti, R. (2002) "The Uses and Abuses of the Sex/Gender Distinction in European Feminist Practices," in Gabriele Griffin and Rosi Braidotti (eds.), *Thinking Differently: A Reader in European Women's Studies* (London: Zed Books), pp. 285–310.
Butler, J. (1990) *Gender Trouble: Feminism and the Subversion of Identity* (New York: Routledge).

Eisenstein, Z. (1996) *Hatreds: Racialized and Sexualized Conflicts in the 21st Century* (New York and London: Routledge).

Haraway, D. J. (1991) *Simians, Cyborgs and Women: The Reinvention of Nature* (New York: Routledge).

Harding, S. (1991) *Whose Science? Whose Knowledge?* (Ithaca: Cornell University Press).

Lerner, G. (1986) *The Creation of Patriarchy*, vol. I (Oxford: Oxford University Press).

Lerner, G. (1991) *The Creation of Feminist Consciousness: From the Middle Ages to 1870*, vol. II (New York and Oxford: Oxford University Press).

Truth, S. (1851) "Ain't I a Woman?" available on <http://www.fordham.edu/halsall/mod/sojtruth-woman.html>

PART ONE

Interdisciplinarity

CHAPTER ONE

Women's Studies

Mary Maynard

Introduction

Women's Studies is now established as an important field of study and research across the globe. First appearing in the United States in the second half of the 1960s, courses and degree programs rapidly emerged in other Western countries and in other parts of the world. The emergence of Women's Studies at this time was linked to the political movement and practice of feminism. Women, mainly those who were white and from the West, began more vocally to challenge the discrimination which made them unequal to men in areas such as education, employment, and domestic responsibilities. Women's Studies became linked to the educational wing of feminism in two ways. First, it was pointed out that women tended to be invisible in most academic research and teaching, where the emphasis appeared to be on important men and men's ideas and interests. Second, there was a questioning of the ways in which knowledge was conventionally obtained, with the associated criticism that the methods, concepts, and theories deployed were irrelevant to and, in fact, helped to conceal the lives and experiences of women. Women's Studies activists and scholars aimed to rectify the situation. This was to be done by providing information and analyses about the lives of women, so that they could be used to initiate social changes that would end gender inequality. Linked to this was the need to develop new ways of thinking about doing research and constructing knowledge which would be sensitive to women's circumstances and perspectives.

This chapter offers an overview of some of the major issues in the still growing area of interdisciplinary Women's Studies. It begins by looking at some of the early concerns. This is followed by a discussion of some of the key aspects of debates about "difference." The next section looks at the important, but highly contested, area of postmodernism, before turning to a consideration of masculinity and whiteness. The final section looks at Women's Studies more globally, focusing, in particular, on some interesting and important new arguments in the field of Women and Development. The chapter closes with some brief concluding remarks.

Early Key Concerns

The main issues for Women's Studies during its first 20 or so years of existence may be grouped into three broad themes. These relate to substantive, theoretical, and methodological concerns. Substantive issues refer to those aspects of existence that are important because of the ways in which they structure and frame people's lives and experiences. Initially, Women's Studies teachers and researchers took responsibility for adding women into the existing academic agenda and curricula from which they were largely absent. This meant, for example, including sections on topics such as women and education, women and paid work, women and health, and women and the media in courses, books, and research projects. However, while this early work was important, it was soon recognized that simply adding women's experiences to what was already known about men was, on its own, insufficient. It was argued that there are aspects of women's lives which are specific to them and which are missed by only focusing on a male agenda. Further, it is as necessary to consider the private dimension of life as it is to focus on the public sphere, although the latter was often treated as more significant by men. Thus, new topics, deriving particularly from women's experiences, began to be emphasized. Writers focused on a range of concerns, from domestic responsibilities, to pregnancy and childbirth, to differential use of household resources, to sexuality and heterosexism. One particular focus, which has subsequently developed a considerable body of knowledge, was that of violence towards women, which is often taken to include pornography, sex tourism, and sexual harassment, as well as domestic violence and rape. Analyses of such issues indicate the significance of men's violence in the power they hold over women. Further, the fear of such violence constrains women and limits their freedom of choice and movement. It has been shown that both the reality and the fear of violence act as a form of social control over women worldwide. It is, in part, due to the pioneering nature of Women's Studies research and writing that this matter is now part of a global agenda.

Similarly, early Women's Studies writers were critical of existing theoretical explanations of social inequalities and divisions because of their gender-blindness and failure sufficiently to emphasize women's situation. Commentators tended to identify three major feminist perspectives, each with its own historical tradition and legacy. Liberal feminism was seen as focusing on individual rights, concepts such as equality, justice and equal opportunities, and the legal and policy changes required for women to achieve parity with men. Marxist feminism was portrayed as explaining women's subordination to men in terms of capitalist exploitation. Capitalist economic relations meant not only that women were paid less than men in the workplace but that they were not paid at all for the essential work and services they provided in the household, thereby ensuring their dependence on men. In contrast, radical feminism emphasized a separate system of male domination called patriarchy. Patriarchy was defined as "the system of social structures and practices in which men dominate, oppress and exploit women" (Walby 1990: 20). The concept and theory of patriarchy, it was claimed, allowed the specific nature and circumstances of women's unequal position to be understood.

The third aspect of key early concerns relates to methods of social research. In much of the world, research is only considered to be legitimate and reliable if it is based on ideas about science and objectivity. In terms of understanding the social world and social life, this has meant an emphasis on quantitative research and methods such as questionnaires and surveys. The latter permit the generation of numerical and statistical data which can be generalized across a sample population. Women's Studies researchers have argued, however, that such an approach is not always the most useful when investigating the lives of marginalized groups, including women. This is because they fracture experience and cannot take account of change over time. Further, since the questions to be asked are set and often coded in advance, women's own accounts and understandings tend to be silenced. All such research can do is measure the extent, distribution, and intensity of something that has already been defined as important before the research itself has begun. This may be inappropriate when studying aspects of experience that may not be pre-known. For this reason Women's Studies research has tended to use qualitative methods, particularly semi-structured and unstructured interviews. This enables researchers to see the world through their women participants' eyes, yielding rich, deep, and more holistic information.

As time went on, however, concerns were expressed about aspects of this Women's Studies agenda. Its substantive coverage, for example, tended to be overly Westernized and culturally specific. Initial theoretical formulations began to be regarded as unsatisfactory, since they could never encompass every strand of feminist thinking and were grounded in particular philosophical ideas and ways of thinking that are inimical to other cultural contexts. As a consequence, theories about women and gender relations became much more complex, with a focus on black, lesbian, and various other feminist standpoint positions (Hartsock 1998). In addition, an overemphasis on qualitative research methods is now regarded as underplaying the role of numerical information in demonstrating the extent and severity of women's inequality and subordination. A qualitative approach may also take it for granted that participants are willing to speak, usually in English, to a stranger about most aspects of their lives, which is another ethnocentric assumption. These kinds of concern have been addressed by Women's Studies through acknowledging the importance of "difference."

Difference and Diversity

How to understand the significance of "difference" became one of the most pressing debates within Women's Studies during the 1990s. The fact that there are many forms of gender relations, not only those of white ethnic groups, led to the increasing acknowledgment that women have diverse experiences and that commonalities have to be demonstrated rather than assumed. A significant impetus for this came from women of different ethnicities, cultures, and religions, both in the West and worldwide. It was argued, for example, that, whereas early Women's Studies work on the family had portrayed it as an oppressive institution, this underplayed its role as a bulwark against racism and the positive aspects of extended kinship relations experienced by many ethnic groups. Similarly, writers have pointed out that different groups have differing concepts of equality and justice which are not necessarily the same as those of white feminists in the West. Some Muslim women writers, for instance, have argued for recognition of complementarity rather than equality on the grounds that the latter tends to be articulated in male terms and Western women have failed to gain anything from it except unequal access to the public domain (Afshar 1998). Other issues relate to women's roles in religious, fundamentalist, and nationalist movements, their different experiences of exile, migration, and diaspora, and the gendered nature of genocide and catastrophe. However, crucial to the debate is an increased awareness of the inherent racism of analyses and practices which assume white experiences to be the norm, use these as a basis from which to generate concepts and theories, and fail to acknowledge that women from different cultures and ethnicities are themselves a differentiated group.

The diversity of women's experiences does not relate to ethnicity and cultural context alone. Also important are the ways in which disability influences women's experiences of being female and how a society's responses to disability are, themselves, gendered. Sexual orientation has also become a key focus, with heterosexism – the belief that heterosexuality is better, more normal, natural, and morally right than other forms of sexuality – challenged for the prejudice and discrimination that it enshrines. Differential access to resources, socio-economic status, or social class position are also deeply gendered and have been found to influence life chances and expectations across social groups.

Another aspect of "difference" which has been recognized more recently relates to later life and the process of ageing. In Western cultures this increasingly takes place in a context that celebrates youthfulness and its association with femininity. In contrast, older people, especially older women, tend to be denigrated and treated mainly as social problems, as a drain on scarce resources. Ageism, which may affect the very young as well as those in later life, involves negative stereotypical presumptions about competence, ability, and the need for protection and their supposed correlation with chronological age. For these reasons, age needs to be taken seriously as an aspect of difference.

The emphasis on difference and diversity, however, while an important corrective to previous homogenizing ways of understanding women's lives and positions, is not without its problems. It raises questions about the relationship between the different forms of diversity and how these should be understood and theorized in different geographical locations and cultural contexts. Some commentators have suggested that there is too much emphasis on differences and insufficient concern with the things that women might share and the potential for unified political strategies and action. Such critics argue that by focusing on other forms of diversity, in addition to gender, the feminist project for women is dismantled. Others, though, point out that the differences between women should be celebrated rather than seen as impediments and that women should be able to set their own priorities for analysis and change, rather than having these imposed upon them.

Women's Studies and Postmodernism

In recent years, Women's Studies, along with other subjects and disciplines, has been profoundly influenced by the increasing interest in culture, discourse analysis, and postmodernism. Indeed, the development of cultural studies and Women's Studies has been closely interrelated. While the concept of "postmodernism" is a highly contested one, over which there is little agreement, it is still possible to highlight its main elements and characteristics, particularly in terms of how they have impinged on Women's Studies. The first thing to note is the ways in which culture has been elevated to a major analytic category, arguably replacing ideas about the material world as a key concern. Changes in Western cultural forms, it has been suggested, have led to these becoming increasingly fragmented and highly varied. The plethora of designs, styles, goods for consumption, and ways of living which are now available offer opportunities to break away from previous limited and constricting forms of being. This has implications, in particular, for the construction of identities and subjectivities. For women, this is said to be a positive development because of the potentially wide range of possibilities that are opened up. Postmodern theory questions static portrayals of how the self is socially constructed, emphasizing the role of discourse as well as more organizational structures. The broadening cultural base provides the context for this process. The old certainties about self, rooted in community and class, have been circumvented.

A second, and related, aspect of postmodern thinking concerns ideas about knowledge and its construction. Western theories have generally been formulated in terms of meta-narratives, grandiose frameworks of ideas, such as those of Marx, which attempt to provide generalized and generalizable accounts and explanations. Postmodernism, however, dismisses such a search for truth and all-encompassing knowledge. Instead, knowledge is local, specific, and fragmented. Some Women's Studies writers regard such arguments as important because of the ways in which they accord with ideas about difference. They legitimate and explain the movement of Women's Studies theory away from the initial three perspectives. They are championed for the prominence given to the role of discourse in knowledge construction and to the relative uncertainty of the knowledge that is produced.

Postmodern ideas such as these have had a major influence on some core concerns within Women's Studies. There has been much discussion, for example, about the meaning of gender and whether, and how, it might be distinguished from sex. Conventional arguments used to define sex as the anatomical and physiological differences which distinguish biological females from biological males, with gender referring to the social construction of femininity and masculinity. Others have argued that such a formulation is problematic because it perpetuates the opposition of nature and culture which permeates Western thought. In contrast, postmodern thinkers concentrate on how the categories "woman" and "man" are culturally constructed through discourse. Butler, for instance, argues (1990) that gender is not inherently linked to physiology and anatomical bodies and that there is no reason to believe that there are only two genders. This is a binary opposition based on a heterosexist world-view. For Butler, gender has no pre-given essential existence and femininity only exists to the extent that it continues to be performed. Because performing gender brings gender itself into being, Butler regards the latter as being much less stable than is usually accepted. However, she has been criticized for portraying "women" as a construct with no existence or unity prior to construction through discourse.

By focusing on the ambiguities of gender, Butler is intent on signaling the possibilities of new and non-hierarchical relationships. Gender bending, disrupting conventional sexual and gender binary divisions, is regarded as a way of problematizing both the norm of heterosexuality and the tendency unproblematically to oppose it to homosexuality. These debates are also being informed by queer theory and by forms of gender transgression. This involves playing with gender, especially through the parodying of camp, butch, femme, and drag. It can also involve transsexuality, shifting the boundaries of gender and sexuality with the physical aid of anatomical surgery. However, questions have been raised about how really useful such subversion is as a political strategy and whether transgression is necessarily transformative.

Postmodern work has had a considerable impact on Western Women's Studies in terms both of its content and its forms of thinking, although the nature of this influence has been hotly debated. Some writers are completely dismissive, regarding it as academic pretentiousness or nothing more than a cultural product of late Western patriarchy. Others consider a postmodern position to be the only way forward, with those, such as Brooks (1997), seeing its links with postcolonial thought leading to the dawn of "postfeminism" and the wholesale destabilization of existing theory. Some Women's Studies practitioners, however, have attempted to follow a more tempered stance. They acknowledge that postmodern ideas are useful in thinking about new areas of work, such as that which questions the naturalness of the body, examines the role of autobiographies, or attempts to reconceptualize power. However, they are also wary of "strong" postmodernism, which they see as only fleetingly relating to anything of substance and where meaning seems completely relativistic.

Other Recent Issues

As may be seen so far, the topics and areas covered by Women's Studies have become increasingly varied and are frequently both innovative and at the cutting edge of knowledge. There are two further areas, in particular, which deserve brief consideration.

The first of these is the problematizing of men and of masculinity. It may seem strange to suggest that this is a Women's Studies issue when a major reason for Women's Studies initial development as a subject was the criticism that knowledge and research had previously been almost exclusively male-defined and focused. However, this focus had been on men in a purely genderless sense. There was little direct concern with the social construction of men, being male, or having male characteristics and behavior. For these reasons, the critical study of men and of masculinities is currently a major area of growth, despite some concerns that it detracts from the many projects concerning women that still need to be undertaken. Such work is largely conducted by men who are sympathetic to Women's Studies and who support a feminist approach. However, one recent feminist exception, indicative of the potential benefits to come, is Westwood's research (2000) on masculinity and the diamond trade in India. Focusing on the relationship between masculinity and ethnicity, Westwood displays both the dynamics that led to the trade's success and the processes that may lead to its destruction. She demonstrates how the former has been grounded in both gender relations and in gendered discourses.

The second area of recent debate concerns problematizing the nature of whiteness. Whiteness studies are an expanding area in the US, although their position elsewhere in the world is more precarious. Such work has been made possible by, and largely developed from, black feminists' writing on racism and anti-racism. This has emphasized the difficulties which arise when "race" and gender are still treated as separate categories, leading to black women's continual marginalization in feminist and anti-racist work (Carby 1999; Essed 1996; Twine and Blee 2001). Crenshaw, for instance, develops the concept "intersectionality" to underline how the experiences of women of color are often produced by interlinked patterns of racism and sexism (1995). She argues that these experiences cannot be explained by employing traditional notions of race and gender, but that the ways in which they intersect lead to experiences of a qualitatively different kind from those of white women. By tracing the categories to their intersections, Crenshaw intends "to suggest a methodology that will ultimately disrupt the tendencies to see race and gender as exclusive or separable" (1995: 378).

However, it has increasingly been argued that a similar approach should be extended to whiteness and that there needs to be an analysis of white racialization in relation to gender and anti-racist discussions (Fine et al. 1997). There are a number of reasons why whiteness is seen as an important subject to study. First is the need to counter taken-for-granted assumptions that white people do not have an ethnicity or that such an ethnicity is unproblematically shared. It is argued, for instance, that not to explore what it means ethnically to be white is racist because this "otherizes" those who *are* seen to have an ethnicity, treats them as deviant from some unspecified norm and fails to make visible the privileges associated with being white in racist societies. Second, the meanings and understandings about what is involved in being a white woman and the nature of white femininity have been historically constructed in the context of a colonial and imperialist past. This needs to be analyzed and critiqued if it is properly to be understood and challenged. The third reason for studying whiteness relates to the development of Women's Studies and feminism within racist societies. It is argued that it is only by exploring how whiteness is invisibly embodied within the organization and content of Women's Studies that the tendency to reify Western values and perceptions can be contested. For Women's Studies properly to be inclusive, it is not sufficient simply to compare experiences across cultures. It is also necessary to modify ideas and concepts in relation to understanding cultural difference. Despite concerns that studying whiteness runs the risk of prioritizing white women, as was the case in Women's Studies before issues of ethnic diversity were recognized, protagonists insist that this is an important topic for debate. It is only by understanding how white women (and men) use power that they will be able to recognize their own privilege and take responsibility for the consequences of how it is exercised (McIntosh 1997).

Global Women

Women's Studies has received various forms of support around the world. In the US, for instance, the Ford Foundation has funded women's research centers; the Canadian, Norwegian, and Dutch governments have created professorships in Women's Studies; and the Swedish research council for social sciences and the humanities has instigated Women's Studies fellowships (Walby 2001). Elsewhere, the British Council has helped to support the establishment of Women's Studies programs in India, Jordan, Morocco, and Vietnam. In Japan and Morocco there is increasing concern about levels of violence against women, and in India and Vietnam attention is being paid to the difficulties experienced by older women.

One field of inquiry which broadens understanding of the nature of women's lives in various parts of the world is the "women and development" literature. Although not particularly well integrated with Women's Studies material in the West, this is a major scholarly and practical intervention whose impact is enormous. Attention has been drawn to recent developments in the women and development field and suggestions made for a new paradigm in Development Studies. Chua et al. (2000) argue that the focus on women and development has moved through three broad phases. The original women in development (WID) approach used an equity framework, which pointed to the invisibility of women in the development process and argued that they should be treated on equal terms with men. It was a response to earlier models which treated women and children as welfare recipients and not as agents contributing to economic development. This was followed, in the late 1970s, by women and development (WAD), another way of thinking about the same issues but one that was informed theoretically by Marxist feminism and made the self-organization of women a key aspect of its analysis and practice. It emphasized, in particular, how the first world keeps the third world in a relation of dependency through its development strategies. This was eventually superseded by the "gender and development" (GAD) perspective. GAD is not just about integrating women into development planning. It also aims to use such initiatives as a tool for challenging unequal gender relations and for empowering women.

While sympathetic to these approaches, however, Chua et al. argue that they overemphasize economic and structural factors at the expense of the cultural. They follow the work of Nussbaum in offering what they term a "women, culture, and development" (WCD) paradigm, linking insights from Women's Studies, Cultural Studies and Critical Development Studies (see Nussbaum and Glover 1995). The idea is to create a new interdisciplinary way of understanding gender and the third world "by taking into account the ways in which practices and discourses of gender, culture and the South come together in the everyday lives of women and the Third World" (Chua et al. 2000: 824). They seek to explore the experiences, identities, practices, and representations of third world women, in culturally specific ways, particularly focusing on matters of agency. In this WCD model, they not only carry Women's Studies insights into our under-standing of women and the development process, they also offer an integrated perspective which has potential for Women's Studies more generally.

There are, however, other ways in which women are being encompassed more globally. The first is through the work of scholars such as Chandra Mohanty, whose writings have done much to expose the parochialism of Euro-American feminisms, as well as the male-dominated narratives of the third world (1991a, 1991b, 1997). Mohanty examines the engagement of third world women with feminism in the context of decolonization, national liberation struggles, state regulation, multinational capitalism, and related discursive practices. She con-sistently calls for the rethinking of feminist theories and practices within an increasingly complex transnational and international framework.

A second approach is the focus on women's rights as human rights. Nussbaum (2000) has drawn attention to a United Nations report which indicates that no country treats its women as well as its men. However, because gender inequality is highly correlated with poverty, developing countries have particularly pressing problems, with gender issues related to literacy, income, health, nutrition, male violence, rape, and abuse very much to the fore. Women lack the fundamentals for leading human lives because they are women. Further, traditional human rights frameworks tend to be modeled on male needs and may not be appropriate to meet those of women (Peters and Wolper 1995). Feminists, therefore, argue that it is impossible to separate the struggle for human rights from that for women's rights. Nor is it sufficient simply to extend existing human rights mechanisms to women. Rather, gender-based abuses must be treated as human rights abuses. Such an awareness must also be used to challenge and transform conventional understandings of human rights.

Conclusion

It may be seen that Women's Studies is now a key area of teaching, research, and publishing, with gender acknowledged as being of central analytical and practical concern. In some countries, such as the UK, its integration into other subject areas, such as sociology, history, and literary analysis, has meant that it has become less dependent on specialized centers or courses for its existence. In other parts of the world such centers are crucial to maintaining a high profile and presence for Women's Studies. Since the 1970s, Women's Studies has demonstrated how both policy-making and intellectual work are impoverished if insufficient attention is paid to women. As the contents of this chapter show, the subject is continually being reshaped in terms of both substance and parameters. One crucial aspect of this continues to be the debate about difference, particularly through an engagement with ethnicity, racism, and cultural diversity.

References

Afshar, H. (1998) *Islam and Feminisms. An Iranian Case Study* (London: Macmillan).

Brooks, A. (1997) *Postfeminisms* (London: Routledge).

Butler, J. (1990) *Gender Trouble. Feminism and the Subversion of Identity* (London: Routledge).

Carby, H. V. (1999) *Cultures in Babylon. Black Britain and African America* (London: Verso).

Chua, P., Bhavnani, K.-K., and Foran, J. (2000) "Women, Culture and Development: A New Paradigm for Development Studies?" *Ethnic and Racial Studies* 23/5: 820–41.

Crenshaw, K. W. (1995) "Mapping the Margins: Intersectionality, Identity Politics and Violence Against Women of Color," in K. Crenshaw, N. Gotanda, G. Peller, and K. Thomas (eds.), *Critical Race Theory* (New York: The New Press).

Essed, P. (1996) *Diversity: Gender, Color and Culture* (Amherst, MA: University of Massachusetts Press).

Fine, M., Weis, L., Powell, L., and Wong, L. M. (eds.) (1997) *Off White. Readings on Race, Power and Society* (London: Routledge).

Hartsock, N. C. M. (1998) *The Feminist Standpoint Revisited and Other Essays* (Boulder, CO: Westview Press).

McIntosh, P. (1997) "White Privilege and Male Privilege: A Personal Account of Coming to See Correspondences Through Work in Women's Studies," in R. Delgado and J. Stefancie (eds.), *Critical White Studies: Looking Behind the Mirror* (Philadelphia: Temple University Press).

Mohanty, C. T. (1991) "Cartographies of Struggle: Third World Women and the Politics of Feminism," in C. T. Mohanty, A. Russo, and L. Torres (eds.), *Third World Women and the Politics of Feminism* (Bloomington and Indianapolis: Indiana University Press).

Mohanty, C. T. (1991) 'Under Western Eyes: Feminist Scholarship and Colonial Discourses," in C. T. Mohanty, A. Russo, and L. Torres (eds.), *Third World Women and the Politics of Feminism* (Bloomington and Indianapolis: Indiana University Press).

Mohanty, C. T. (1997) "Women Workers and Capitalist Scripts: Ideologies of Domination, Common Interests and the Politics of Solidarity," in M. J. Alexander and C. T. Mohanty (eds.), *Feminist Genealogies, Colonial Legacies and Democratic Futures* (London: Routledge).

Nussbaum, M. (2000) *Women and Human Development* (Cambridge: Cambridge University Press).

Nussbaum, M. and Glover, J. (1995) (eds.) *Women, Culture and Development* (Oxford: Oxford University Press).

Peters, J. and Wolper, A. (1995) (eds.) *Women's Rights. Human Rights* (London: Routledge).

Twine, F. W. and Blee, K. M. (2001) (eds.) *Feminism and Anti-racism: International Struggles for Justice* (New York: New York University Press).

Walby, S. (1990) *Theorizing Patriarchy* (Oxford: Basil Blackwell).

Walby, S. (2001) "Developments in the Sociology of Gender and Women's Studies," in R. G. Burgess and A. Murcott (eds.), *Developments in Sociology* (London: Prentice Hall).

Westwood, S. (2000) "'A Real Romance': Gender, Ethnicity, Trust and Risk in the Indian Diamond Trade," *Ethnic and Racial Studies* 25/5: 857–70.

Further reading

Afshar, H. (ed.) (1998) *Women and Empowerment: Illustrations from the Third World* (London: Macmillan).

Afshar, H. and Maynard, M. (eds.) (2000) *Ethnic and Racial Studies* 25/5. Special guest-edited volume on Gender and Ethnicity.

Bhavnani, K.-K. (ed.) (2001) *Feminism and "Race"* (Oxford: Oxford University Press).

Bradley, H. (1996) *Fractured Identities. Changing Patterns of Inequality* (Cambridge: Polity).

Brah, A. (1996) *Cartographies of Diaspora* (London: Routledge).

Robinson, V. and Richardson, D. (eds.) (1997) *Introducing Women's Studies* (London: Macmillan).

Walby, S. (1997) *Gender Transformations* (London: Routledge).

CHAPTER TWO

Area Studies

Ella Shohat

When in academic institutions feminism is invoked outside of "Western" spaces, it is often subjected to an (inter)disciplinary order that anxiously and politely sends it "back" to the kingdom of area studies. There the experts of the day, it is assumed, will tell us about the plight of women; each outlandish geographical zone will be matched with an abused bodily part. A doubly exclusionary logic (that which applies to women and to their geography) will quickly allot a discursive space for women as well as for gays/lesbians/bi-/transgenders from the diverse regions of the world. Even within multicultural feminist and queer cartographies of knowledge, the diverse regions are often presumed to be isolated from the "center" and from each other. Such approaches, I am afraid, have become a malady in Women's Studies programs, even those that have made an important step toward multiculturalizing the curriculum.

Here, I want to reflect on a relational understanding of feminism that assumes a non-finalized and conjunctural definition of feminism as a polysemic site of contradictory positionalities. Any dialogue about the fictive unity called "Middle Eastern women" or "Latin American gays/lesbians" – especially one that is taking place within a transnational framework – has to begin from the premise that genders, sexualities, races, classes, nations, and even continents exist not as hermetically sealed entities but rather as part of a permeable interwoven relationality. Interlinking critical maps of knowledge is fundamental in a transnational age, typified by the global "travel" of images, sounds, goods, and populations. A relational multicultural feminist project has to reflect this (partially) new moment that requires rethinking identity designations, intellectual grids, and disciplinary boundaries. We need, I believe, to reflect on the relationships between the diverse interdisciplinary knowledges constituting multicultural/ transnational feminist inquiry: Gender and Sexuality Studies, Ethnic and Race Studies, Area and Postcolonial Studies. Given that there is no single feminism, the question is how we orchestrate these conflictual perspectives in order to rearticulate the feminist terrains of struggle foregrounding the densely woven web of relationality.

In many institutions, multicultural feminists have often faced criticism from feminist colleagues who had perceived multiculturalism as somehow "bad for women" (see Moller Okin 1999). Multiculturalism, in the view of these colleagues, is at best irrelevant and at worst divisive for the feminist cause. And when multicultural and transnational approaches are approved, the solution to the production of knowledge often takes the form of an additive approach. In this sense, I'm not interested in talking about the "Middle East" or "Latin America" as unified categories of analysis. Our challenge, I think, is precisely to avoid a facile additive operation of merely piling up increasingly differentiated groups of women from different regions and ethnicities – all of whom are projected as presumably forming a coherent, yet easily demarcated entity. In contrast, the notion of a relational feminism goes beyond a mere description of the many cultures from which feminisms emerge; it transcends an additive approach which simply has women of the globe neatly neighbored and stocked, paraded in a UN style "Family of Nations" pageant where each ethnically marked feminist speaks in her turn, dressed in national costume. To map histories of women and gays/lesbians we must place them in dialogical relation within, between, and among cultures, ethnicities, and nations.

There is also a tendency in critical discourse to pit the rotating chain of marginalized communities against an unstated "white" or "Western" norm. This discourse assumes a neat binarism of black versus white and Chicana versus Anglo or East versus West and North versus South – a binarism that ironically repositions whiteness and Westerns as a normative interlocutor. This conceptual binarism – as in black versus white or Eastern versus Western – puts on hold all those who do not fit into either category, sitting, as it were, in her couch awaiting her turn to speak. This "on hold" analytical method ends up producing gaps and silences. The relationships among the diverse "others" remain obscure. Therefore our challenge, it seems to me, is to produce knowledge within a kind of a kaleidoscope framework of communities in-relation without ever suggesting that their positionings are identical. It is for this reason that I am not interested in having a clear and neat categorization of spaces allocated to each specific region. I am more concerned with investigating the multichronotopic links in the hopes of creating an intellectual dialogue that bypasses the institutional scenario of Feminist/Queer Studies versus Area Studies. In the first, the logic and discourse of postmodernity applies; in the latter, that of modernization and development.

Even in more critical frameworks within US academia, the production of knowledge tends to reproduce an implicit and even invisible US nationalism. It undergirds certain versions of first world feminism and, at the same time, we can discern the nationalism of certain versions of multiculturalism as articulated by women of color and queer discourses. I think we should especially pay attention to the ways universities erect disciplinary borders and maintain conceptual boundaries that continue to reproduce the discursive overlapping quarantine of interconnected fields of inquiry. For example, the majority of women of the world form the margins of most curricula, fenced off within the Bantustans called "Area Studies" – such as Middle East Studies – as though their lives are not also implicated by US agendas and policies, and as though there are no Middle Eastern women in the US. Although nationalism is often seen as a specifically third world malady, it is no less relevant to the labor, feminist, queer, and multicultural movements within the US. In going through a substantial number of curricula within Ethnic Studies, Women's/Gender Studies, and Queer Studies, it was not difficult to detect a submerged American nationalism that often undergirds such practices and epistemologies, giving us a star-striped nationalism with a tan, a nationalism in drag, and a rainbow nationalism. In my experience on various "diversity committees," I have found that educational institutions often glimpse multiculturalism and feminist/gay/lesbian perspectives through a largely unconscious national-exceptionalist lens. And while I have no quarrel with the idea of a US uniqueness, I do quarrel with the idea that uniqueness is unique to the US. Every nation-state has a palimpsestic uniqueness all its own. And along with that shared uniqueness, we find historical parallels and global links between different national formations. The implicit nationalism of many multicultural, feminist, and gay/lesbian curricula and agendas leads us to miss numerous opportunities for a relational analysis and for a cross-disciplinary and transnational connection.

It is fundamental to deploy a multiperspectival approach to the movement of feminist ideas across borders. We must worry about a globalist feminism that spreads its programs around the world as the universal gospel, just as we have to be concerned about a localist feminism that surrenders all dialogue to the dead-end of an overpowering relativism. One of the challenges facing multicultural/transnational feminism has to do with the translations of theories and actions from one context to another. In an Arab/Muslim context, where feminism is often denounced as a Western import and where Arab/Muslim women articulate their version of what constitutes gender struggle, what would it mean to deploy a post-structuralist perspective that would critique the notions of experience, authenticity, and essentialism? What kind of relational maps of knowledge would help illuminate the negotiation of gender and sexuality as understood in diverse contexts, but with an emphasis on the linked historical experiences and discursive networks across borders? While one does not have to subscribe to any grand Theory with a capital "T," it would be foolish to deny that theorizing forms a forceful element in the envisioning of (any) social and political change. The multicultural feminist project as seen in *Talking Visions* for example (Shohat 1998) attempted to synthesize the contribution of post-structuralism for multicultural feminism with that of historical materialism. Such a project gave an expression to the dilemmas resulting from, on the one hand, the difficulty with fully embracing an empiricist approach to experience – a method that implies the possibility of a direct access to a prediscursive reality; and, on the other, the difficulty with fully subscribing to a post-structuralism in which experience never seems to exist outside the discourses that mediate them. I was hoping, in other words, to transcend a referential verism (for example, that writing about experiences directly reflects the real) without falling into a hermeneutic nihilism whereby all texts become nothing more than a meaningless play of signification. Experience and knowledge within a multicultural/transnational feminist project, in this sense, have to be defined as dialogical concepts that can be understood as a set of discursive practices based on personal and communitarian interlocution, an interlocution situated in historical time and geographical space.

Some third world women and US women of color have at times denounced theory itself as inherently Western, and as an impediment to activism. They have critiqued white, Western, or – to be more precise – Eurocentric theories for eliding the experiences of women of color. This indispensable critique, however, should not allow us to forget (a) the importance of looking critically at activist practices and of theorizing them as part of feminist agendas; (b) the awareness that every practice is undergirded by some kind of theory, philosophy, worldview, or discursive grid – even when the practitioners claim not to have a theory; (c) the fact that theorizing and theories are not a Western monopoly, a view that would inscribe in reverse a colonialist vision of the "West" as theoretical mind and the "non-West" as unreflecting body; (d) that third world women and women of color have themselves contributed to theorizing not only by writing theory per se, but also by their own multi-axis thinking and activism which has challenged multiple hegemonic discourses. In this sense, activism itself can be seen as a form of theorizing, a practical testing of ideas. Ironically, I think that many activists have underestimated their own historical contribution to the West's questioning of totalizing narratives.

In contrast, some feminist writers (such as Nelly Richards, Wahneema Lubiano, Inderpal Grewal, Caren Kaplan, and others) have insightfully suggested that postmodernism, for example, is relevant for women of color and third world women. The various post-theories (post-structuralism, postmodernism, postcolonialism) are indeed useful tools, albeit problematic ones for a multicultural feminist project. Here, one may address this question from a different angle as well. The critique offered by anti-colonial third-worldist discourses was a crucial element in generating the critique of totalizing master narratives in the first place. Both structuralist semiotics and third-worldism had their long-term historical origins in a series of events that undermined the confidence in European modernity: the Holocaust (and in France the Vichy collaboration with the Nazis), the postwar disintegration of the last European empires, and the third world anti-colonial revolution. Although the exalted term "theory" was rarely linked to anti-colonial theorizing, third-worldist thinking had an undeniable impact on first world "theory" (see Shohat and Stam 1994; Stam 2000). The structuralists codified, on some levels, arguments made by anti-colonial thinkers. The critical work of "denaturalization" performed by what one might call the left wing of semiotics – for example Roland Barthes's dissection of the colonialist implications of a *Paris Match* cover showing a black soldier saluting the French flag – cannot be detached from the third-worldist critique of European master narratives performed by such francophone anti-colonial writers as Aime Cesaire ([1955] 1972) and Franz Fanon (1961). Levi-Strauss's crucial turn from biological to linguistic models for a new anthropology was, to some extent, motivated by his visceral aversion to a biological anthropology deeply tainted by anti-Semitic and colonialist racism. Indeed, it was in the context of decolonization that UNESCO asked Levi-Strauss to do the research that culminated in his "Race and History" (1952), where the French anthropologist rejected any essentialist hierarchy of civilizations (see Stam 2000).

The crisis of modernity is inseparable from Europe's loss of its privileged position as the model for the world. The discursive withdrawal from projecting Europe as a spokesperson on behalf of the Universal came into existence through and in relation to the critique of European Humanism, explicitly addressed by Fanon in *The Wretched of the Earth*. The shared concern of the feminist and the anti-colonial movements over the transformation of the "Other" from object to subject of history has to be understood in this historical conjuncture. It is hardly a coincidence that Simone de Beauvoir ([1949] 1969) charts "The Birth of the Free Woman" in images that are reminiscent of and allude to the black struggle in the US and the anti-colonial struggle in the third world. Indeed, blacks and women in the US, as numerous black feminists have suggested, began an uneasy dialogue over their parallel and intersected battles for political representation more than a century ago. What is at stake, however, is the non-dialogical and unilateral historiography that narrates the emergence of feminism as a linear march from pre-modernity to modernity and postmodernity. As with Eurocentrism, which sees Europe as the unique source of meaning, as the world's center of gravity, as an ontological "reality" to the rests of the world's shadow, so monocultural feminism simply traces its formation back to a Western modernity pictured as devoid of all dialogue with ambient anti-racist and anti-colonial struggles. This narrative also simplistically suggests that postmodernism – seen alone and unaided by any critical thought "outside" of the imaginary space of the West – has opened up a space for diverse "Others." The implied openness of this narrative, paradoxically, reveals its own closedness. While, it is a common wisdom in Feminist Studies to euphorically link modernity to the rise of feminism, it can be argued that the crisis of modernity in the wake of anti-colonial and anti-racist interrogation has also helped shape a different conception of feminism itself, one that has begun to free itself from the white man's and the white woman's burden of Enlightenment and its concomitant narrative of progress.

Feminist thought is also often caught up in a tension between essentialist and anti-essentialist discourses. While post-structuralist gender, queer, and postcolonial theories entail the rejection of essentialist articulations of identity as well as bio-logistic and transhistorical determinations of gender, race, and sexual identity, a desire for political agency leads to support for "affirmative action," implicitly premised on the very categories elsewhere rejected as essentialist, leading to a paradoxical situation in which theory deconstructs totalizing myths, while activism has to nourish them. (Women from the Middle East face multiple exclusions in the US, yet they do not qualify for "affirmative action" – but this topic requires another debate.) One of the challenges for multicultural/transnational feminism, then, is to articulate its project in relation to the issue of gender essentialism, on the one hand, and cultural essentialism, on the other. Looking into popular debates about women both in the US and in the Middle East, we can see that it isn't easy to puncture the essentialism balloon about what "America" is and what "Arab," "Jew," or "Iranian" is and what "women" and "men" are all about. And, as we know, that kind of essentialist discourse tends to take precedent over analysis of power relations.

I want to insist that the concept of *relationality* should not be confused with cultural *relativism*. Although the concept of relationality goes back to structural linguistics, I am using it here in a translinguistic dialogic and historicized sense. The project of multicultural feminism has to be situated historically as a set of contested practices, mediated by conflictual discourses, which themselves have repercussions and reverberations in the world. A cultural relativist approach would oblige us to accept veiling or cliterodectomy, for example, as simply representing a different cultural norm, and therefore a legitimate practice of another culture. (In fact, this argument has found an echo within the US legal system, known as a "cultural defense" to justify a variety of gender-based abuses such as wife-battering within an immigrant community.) At the same time, it is important to avoid a universalist formulation of feminism, one premised on Eurocentric discourse of modernity versus pre-modernity or developed versus underdeveloped – concepts grounded in the feminist version of a Promethean civilizing mission.

Therefore, to articulate a complex critique of such practices as cliterodectomy, we would have to try to achieve the following: dissect the global media's tendency to fetishistically focus on rituals that involve sexual organs and expose them as ambivalent sites of voyeuristic pleasure; avoid a Eurocentric framing narrative that would transform a conjunctural praxis into the essence of a culture, nation, or region, where cliterodectomy, for example, would be represented as being at the very kernel of Egyptian, African, or Muslim culture; examine such oppressive practices in relation to other forms of oppressive practices of body mutilation and gendered pathologies in the "West," thereby avoiding the ascription of the cultural superiority to the "West," implicit in the double whammy of downplaying Western abuses and amplifying everyone else's abuses; dispute the idea that traditions are coherent, static, and uninterrupted in any culture; compare the discourses about such practices associated with "tradition" with the technologically based practices – such as cosmetic surgery – associated with postmodernity; examine the active complicity of women themselves in performing such oppressive practices, rather than suggest that they are merely passive victims of patriarchy; look into the ways the practice is contested within the community rather than produce a misleading image of a homogenous community; interrogate Eurocentric versions of feminism which envision the elimination of such practices as entailing (even if only subliminally) a total cultural assimilation to the West; study the history of the practice in relation to the voices of dissent, rather than manufacture narcissistic rescue narratives towards otherized cultures; examine such practices in the context of worsening social conditions due to destructive globalization policies and IMF-generated poverty, whereby women's bodies become the symbolic site of "preserving" tradition, an issue often addressed by fundamentalist religious organizations but overlooked by the state apparatus and transnational institutions; analyze critically the transnational asymmetries inherent in legislation around gender, immigration, and human rights, in which support for gender-based asylum often recycles old colonial tropes of dark women trapped in hopelessly retrograde and brutal societies.

Thus, to truly have a relational analysis, we would have to address the operative terms and axes of stratifications typical of specific contexts, along with the ways these terms and stratifications are translated and reinvoiced as they "travel" from one context to another. For example, historically, questions of race are less central in the Middle East and North Africa where the operative terms have more to do with religion. In this sense, I do not define multicultural/transnational feminism either as an universalist project or as a cultural relativist project. The universalizing Enlightenment discourse, which has been the subject of much postmodern critique, is a form of philosophical dogmatism; it excludes dialogue by making it impossible. Relativism, meanwhile, also excludes dialogue by making it pointless, since within "I'm OK, you're OK" logic everything is legitimate and therefore not debatable. At times, however, hegemonic feminism has challenged gender-based essentialism, while simultaneously inscribing notions of cultural essentialism. "Difference" became central for writings by women of color and third world women writers, and, in some quarters, it became associated with the idea of "Eastern" or African superiority over "Western" culture, virtually inverting Eurocentric hierarchical discourses. While gender essentialism challenged patriarchal ideologies, it did not necessarily challenge the essentialist discourses about gender and sexuality altogether. Similarly, arguments for cultural differences among women (hetero-, bi-, or lesbian) interrogate the colonialist ideologies about difference as implying the superiority of Western culture, but again do not necessarily interrogate the notion of cultural essence altogether. By bringing together multiculturalism and feminism within a transnational framework, we can try to avoid replicating the idea of essentialist cultural differences among women. Therefore, to raise the question of difference among women (hetero-, bi-, or lesbian) for me is not about delineating some essentialist ideas about the cultural differences between Western and third world women, but rather about looking at different positioning vis-à-vis the histories of power, especially since the advent of colonialism. Having said that, I have not been interested in difference for the sake of difference, but rather in dialogical encounters of differences. My argument is not that "We are all different," a truism which forms the basis for cultural relativist arguments. My point is rather that multicultural feminism is a situated practice in which histories and communities are mutually co-implicated and constitutively related, open to mutual illumination.

Take the question of feminist historiography as an example. Third world women's involvement in anti-colonialist struggles was often not seen as relevant for feminism in feminist writings. I have proposed to reread the history of third world women, especially within anti-colonial struggles, as a kind of subterranean, unrecognized form of feminism and as a legitimate part of feminist historiography, even if the activists themselves do not label it as feminism. Multicultural feminists have to disinter stories of survival from the rubble of the master narrative of progress. Historically, colonized women had been deeply involved in anti-colonialist and anti-racist movements, long before their dialogue with the Women's Movement. It is often their activism within anti-colonialist and anti-racist movements that led to their political engagement in feminism. This type of anti-patriarchal and even, at times, anti-heterosexist work within anti-colonial struggles will remain marginal to the feminist canon as long as only one feminism retains the power of naming and narrativizing. The debate about what constitutes a legitimate feminist epistemology for a long time has had to do with the privileging of single-issue feminism over a multi-axis analysis. Recognizing invisible feminist histories is crucial for rearticulating what constitutes legitimate spaces, moments, and subjects of feminist studies.

We need to make connections in conceptual terms linking issues of gender and sexuality in the context of colonialism, imperialism, and third world nationalism on the one hand, and race and ethnicity and multiculturalism on the other. Many literary studies of culture and empire privilege the nineteenth and twentieth centuries, but one could trace colonial discourses back to 1492, linking representations of "tradition" and globalization with contemporary discourses about, for example, modernity and postmodernity. The Columbus story for me was a way to trace Orientalism far back and to show the links between the Reconquista in Spain – the expulsion of Jews and Muslims in 1492 – and the Conquista of America in the same year, in terms of the travelling discourses and practices (Shohat 1999). I tried to show the historical discursive links between the Americas and the Orient prior to the formation of contemporary geopolitics. Perhaps the first modern orientalist was none other than Columbus. After his arrival in the Caribbean island of Hispaniola, he wrote to the Spanish throne praising the war against both Muslims and Jews, and thanking the queen for having sent him to the regions of India to convert its people to the holy faith. Here, discourses about Muslims, Jews, and (Asian) Indians crossed the Atlantic during Spain's continental reconquista, arming the conquistadors with a ready-made us-versus-them ideology aimed at the regions of India, but applied instead toward the indigenous peoples of the accidentally discovered continent. European campaigns against Muslims and Jews, as well as against other so-called heretics and agents of Satan, such as witches, made a mammoth apparatus of racism and sexism available for recycling in the new continents. The colonial misrecognition inherent in the name "Indian" underlines the linked imaginaries of East and West Indies. Indeed, Columbus took to "India" (i.e. to the Americas) conversos, fluent in Semitic languages, who were expected to speak to the Indians in their own language. (Was it with the help of such translators that Columbus wrote with great confidence and knowledge about the Carib and Arawak cultures?) My point is that the American colonial discourse did not simply take in orientalist discourse, but was constituted by it. And later on, colonial discourse, which was itself shaped within the Americas, Sub-Saharan Africa, and East and South Asia, impacted on the formation of specific orientalist discourse directed at North Africa and West Asia – territories colonized quite late in the imperial game.

My point in making such links is to reimagine the study of regions in a way that transcends the traditional dogmatism of area studies. I have tried to show the links that preceded the contemporary "global village." As Robert Stam and I tried to argue (1994), globalization is not a completely new development; it must be seen as part of the much longer history of colonialism in which Europe attempted to submit the world to a single "universal" regime of truth and global institution of power. The 500-year colonial domination of indigenous peoples, the capitalist appropriation of resources and the imperialist ordering of the world formed part of a massive world-historical globalizing movement that reached its apogee at the turn of the century. Globalization theory, in this sense, has its roots in a diffusionist view of Europe's spreading its people, ideas, goods, and economic and political systems around the world. Thus, patriarchal colonial diffusionism has undergone a series of metamorphoses: it transmuted into modernization theory in the late 1940s and 1950s, embracing the idea that third world nations would achieve economic take-off by emulating the historical progress of the West; and it transmuted in the 1980s into globalization theory. Women of the "underdeveloped" world, it was assumed, would have to be further modernized to "catch up."

Terms such as "underdeveloped" and "developing" project an infantilization trope on a global scale. These terms have implied the political and economic immaturity of diverse Calibans suffering from a putative inbred dependency on the leadership of the diverse modernizing forces. The *in loco parentis* discourse of paternalistic gradualism assumed the necessity of rescue narratives and the integration of peoples in the "far" corners of the "global village" into the vision of the "advanced" and "mature" nation-states. Liberal academic curricula and well-meaning human rights programs thrive on a binarist demarcation of opposing twin concepts of modernity: tradition and science versus religion. In this sense, modernization functions as the bridge between two opposite poles within a narrative that paradoxically assumes the essential superiority of Euro-hegemonies, while simultaneously generating programs to transform the underdeveloped community "into" modernity. Within this discourse, the "developing" world always seems to lag behind, somehow, not simply economically, but also culturally, condemned to a perpetual game of catch-up in which it can only repeat on another register the history of the "advanced" world. When the first world reaches the stage of capitalism and postmodernism, the developing world hobbles along toward modernism and the beginnings of capitalism.

Like the discourse of the sociology of modernization, the economics of development, and the aesthetics of postmodernism, Eurocentric versions of transnationalism covertly assume a telos toward which "traditional" cultural practices are presumed to be evolving. Performed within the discursive framework of development and modernization, the study of third world aesthetics tends to produce a Eurocentric narrative of "cultural development." Such a narrative also produces segregated notions of temporality and spatiality. A more adequate formulation of these transnational relationships would not see any world as either "ahead" or "behind." Instead, it would see all the worlds as coeval, living the same historical moment but under diverse modalities of subordination and hybridization. The spatiality and temporality of cultures as lived is scrambled, palimpsestic in all the worlds, with the pre-modern, the modern, and the postmodern coexisting and interlinked globally.

To place gender studies and area studies in critical dialogue would require a multichronotopic form of analysis, particularly in terms of the ways in which geographies are imagined and knowledge is mapped within academic institutional practices. It would ask us to place the often-ghettoized histories, geographies, and discourses in hopefully politically and epistemologically synergetic relations. It would require critical voices to look for ways in which variegated pasts and presents parallel and intersect, overlap and contradict, analogize and allegorize one another.

Notes

This text was written as a lecture given in conjunction with book-signing events for *Talking Visions: Multicultural Feminism in a Transnational Age* (Cambridge, MA: MIT Press, 1998; pbk 2001). The arguments here are based on my introduction to the book. I would like to thank Robert Stam for generously allowing me to use some shared material from our co-authored work (Shohat and Stam 1994). A shorter version of this piece appeared as "Area Studies, Transnationalism, and the Feminist Production of Knowledge," *Signs* 26/4 (summer 2001), a special issue on Globalization and Gender, coedited by A. Basu, I. Grewal, C. Kaplan, and L. Malkki.

References

Cesaire, A. ([1955] 1972) *Discourse on Colonialism*, trans. Joan Pinkham (New York and London: Monthly Review Press).

de Beauvoir, S. ([1949] 1969) *The Second Sex*, trans. H. M. Parshley (London: New English Library).

Fanon, F. (1961) *The Wretched of the Earth*, trans. Constantine Farrington (New York: Grove Weidenfeld).

Moller Okin, S. (1999) "Is Multiculturalism Bad for Women?" in Joshua Cohen, Matthew Howard, and Martha C. Nussbaum (eds.), *Is Multiculturalism Bad for Women?* (Princeton: Princeton University Press).

Shohat, E. (1998) *Talking Visions: Multicultural Feminism in a Transnational Age* (Cambridge, MA: MIT Press; pbk 2001).

Shohat, E. (1999) "Taboo Memories, Diasporic Visions: Columbus, Palestine, and Arab-Jews," in May Joseph and Jennifer Natalya Fink (eds.), *Performing Hybridity* (Minneapolis: University of Minnesota Press).

Shohat, E. and Stam, R. (1994) *Unthinking Eurocentrism* (London: Routledge).

Stam, R. (2000) *Film Theory* (Oxford: Blackwell).

CHAPTER THREE

Postcolonial Scholarship

Inderpal Grewal and Caren Kaplan

The history of modern imperialism bears directly upon the condition of women and relations of gendered power in the modern period. The politics of anti-colonial and anti-imperial feminisms have emerged over the last two decades as a central question in feminist scholarship, linking the issue of gender to key terms such as modernity, transnationalism, and globalization. In examining the gender relations produced by colonial and anti-colonial projects from the eighteenth to the twentieth century, there is increasing evidence to suggest that these relations are not to be understood simply as historical evidence of past occurrences. Rather, as new forms of colonialism pervade the contemporary world, it remains crucial to understand the continuities between colonial and postcolonial projects and to articulate the new forms of feminist theory that are required to address these changing conditions.

In the 1980s, Postcolonial Studies emerged as an academic field within which discourse analysis of the texts produced by the colonial governments, scholars, explorers, merchants, and travelers became an important method. Influenced by post-structuralist approaches to archives, material culture, and literature, discourse analysis encouraged interdisciplinary examinations of subjects and topics that had previously been solely the realm of nationalist or Orientalist historiography. Overtly political and thus accused of bias, Postcolonial Studies brought in new scholarly approaches to present a perspective that had received little recognition in the academy. Relying on post-structuralist interventions into the formation of knowledge in modernity, colonial discourse approaches high-lighted the ways in which the cultures of colonialisms informed the construction of identities, geopolitics, and the social.

However, almost from its inception, debates about the meaning and the scope of Postcolonial Studies characterized the field. In particular, scholars argued over whether the word "post" suggests that colonialism is over or whether it means that new forms have supplanted the earlier ones. While it cannot be said that colonialism has ended, it can certainly be argued that new forms of colonialism have been emerging throughout the modern period. For example, one way to

51

come to grips with the terrifyingly unequal power relations of the contemporary world is to examine what Achille Mbembe (1992) calls the "postcolony" – that is, the way that formerly colonized nation-states produce new relations of power that are linked to the structures of the colonial past but are also differentiated through new kinds of local and national elite formations. However, scholars such as Ella Shohat argue (1992) that this emphasis on a kind of "post"-ness ignores the many places around the world where direct settler colonialism continues. In addition, Anne McClintock points out (1992) that Postcolonial Studies often ignores the colonies at "home" in the US. Questions have also been raised about the temporal overlapping of Colonial and Postcolonial Studies; in particular, as Ella Shohat asks (1992), when does the postcolonial begin, since anti-colonial struggles have occurred throughout modernity? Or, as Frankenberg and Mani argue (1993), the postcolonial should not be seen as one formation, since the experience of persons from colonizing countries may be quite different from that of persons from countries that are colonized. Such critiques indicate the ways in which Postcolonial Studies became widely divergent, producing new analytic strategies within many different disciplines and fields.

Thus Postcolonial Studies cannot be seen as a clearly defined, bounded area of study, but as a set of changing practices in academic sites that connect questions of modernity to colonialism, and which insist that current forms of power in financial, cultural, aesthetics, and media arenas are linked to imperial and colonial practices.[1] But how did this shifting, multifaceted field come about? How can we understand, historically, the emergence of Postcolonial Studies in the Western academy in the early 1980s? There are several key reasons that can be given here.

First, many formerly colonized countries gained independence during the post-war period, while there emerged new movements for resistance to neocolonial interventions in other regions. As countries gained independence, these fledgling nation-states were faced with many challenges. How, for instance, was the nation to be imagined now that it was an independent state? What kind of education, civil society, industry, etc. was best for this new nation-state? How to deal with the continued presence of the former colonial powers everywhere – in education, in economic policy, in trade, in social transformation, and in cultural struggles? These kinds of question were raised and addressed by intellectuals and writers, forming a body of work that can be termed "postcolonial" in that it followed the formal end of colonization and struggled with the cultural, political, and economic effects of decolonization.

Secondly, in the 1960s political upheavals occurred around the world that were characterized by concerns about the impact of global finance, militarization, growing nuclear threats, Cold War alliances and tensions, and labor struggles. The non-aligned movement of the formerly colonized nations created new alliances between some states in Africa, the Middle East, and Asia. Pan-Africanism, pan-Arabism, and other transnational solidarity movements grew during this time period. Within the US, similar upheavals led to civil rights struggles as many non-white groups came to assert their rights before the nation-state. Second-wave feminist movements also occurred at this time in the US and Europe, as women demanded rights from and struggled against the nation-state. Feminists in the newly decolonized countries fought to articulate the new gendered subjects of the modern nation-states (Jayawardena 1986). Looking at feminist movements through the lens of such upheavals reveals that in the last few decades feminist politics have been integral to social change and transformation on a global scale (Enloe 1993).

Thirdly, the migrations of people from the formerly colonized countries to the US and Europe (and Australia as well) formed twentieth-century diasporas, bringing the third world into the first world. There was a dramatic increase in the visibility and impact of numbers of non-white people who had earlier been figured as distant "Others" within the heart of the colonial metropolis. These changes in population created a crisis in national identity and citizenship as well as new subcultures of resistance within Europe and North America. The cultural productions of these diasporic communities have been marked by critiques of civil society along with new versions of interdisciplinary studies that destabilize the conventions of Area Studies. For example, the notion of a "Black Atlantic" or the "Silk Route" or the new field of Pre-colonial Studies produce new objects of study of regions previously assumed to be demarcated by nation-state boundaries (see, for example, Gilroy 1993).

Fourthly, race- and gender-based movements in North America and much of Europe became focused around claiming an identity. For example, seeing themselves as "ethnic" groups, US race-based movements practiced cultural nationalism – that is, seeing minority, non-white cultures as nations (Gilroy 1993; James 1969; Rodney 1981; Steady 1981[2]). Connecting themselves to third world decolonization movements, US anti-race movements claimed that they too were the "third world" within the "first world," with similar characteristics of underdevelopment such as substandard education, healthcare, and housing (Mohanty et al. 1991). The emergence of multiculturalism in the US, Canada, and the UK, first as a vanguard movement of racialized identity and then as a form of national pluralism somewhat endorsed by multinational corporations and the nation-state, has transformed national and, increasingly, global politics. Linking gender to analyses of race and class, multiculturalism produced models of subjectivity that became focused on multiple and simultaneous oppressions (Anzaldua 1990; hooks 1981; Moraga and Anzaldua 1981; Shohat and Stam 1995).

Fifthly, massive economic changes also occurred during this period. New technologies of communication, transportation, media, finance, and militarization produced more wealth and more inequality than ever before (Appadurai 1996; Harvey 1990; Soja 1989). Modern international entities such as the United Nations and its financial bodies such as the International Monetary Fund and the World Bank realigned corporate and governmental power by inextricably linking the domestic to the international (Leyshon and Thrift 1997). For instance, the funding of development projects in the third world by the World Bank led to an emphasis on Western-style modernization through industrialization and away from more localized forms of agriculture and economic activity (Escobar 1995). Many of the critiques of this form of development point to the impact on women's activities in the home and outside, their altered power relations within the family and community, and their continued exploitation on an international scale (Beneria 1982; Gallin et al. 1989; Mohanty 1991; Sen and Grown 1987).

These five points suggest that Postcolonial Studies emerged as a field within a historical context in which questions of colonization and decolonization were debated by new groups of scholars in diverse locations. In the US academic context, postcolonial scholars, using the critiques of knowledge made possible by civil rights and feminist movements, linked the humanities and social sciences to the ongoing reconsolidation of power in the "West." The central terms of the debates in Postcolonial Studies were the relations between culture, imperialism, and nationalism (Balibar and Wallerstein 1991; Bhabha 1990; Hobsbawm 1990; Kandiyoti 1991; Parker et al. 1992; Said 1993; Sangari and Vaid 1990). Looking at culture as a site of competing and shifting representations rather than as a set of primordial or authentic traditions, scholars began to examine how nations and empires created powerful images and information about other places and people. For example, in his landmark work *Orientalism* (1978), Edward Said revealed that such modes of producing knowledge created the "Orient" as a zone of "Otherness," that is, as a space whose cultural practices were believed to be barbaric, uncivilized, and different from those of the so-called "West." Said argued that culture must be studied as a key site within which colonial power was exercised.

While Said's work provided feminists with the tools to understand the colonized subject as "Other," Gayatri Spivak's theoretical interventions into poststructuralism, literary criticism, and postcoloniality opened up an entirely new field of feminist scholarship (Spivak 1993, 1987, 1999; Spivak and Harasyn 1990). Starting in the early 1980s, Spivak challenged colonialism's missionary projects, especially those that attempted to "civilize" or "rescue" women in non-Western countries. Questioning the obsession of the West with the body of the non-white, non-Western woman, Spivak critiqued representational practices in the work of first world feminists who reproduced Orientalist and colonialist discourses. For example, Spivak argued (1988b) that Julia Kristeva's writings on China proposed new forms of universality and difference through which the "classical" East was revered but contemporary China was treated with contempt. Examining colonial cultural formations, Spivak focused on the "subaltern" woman who did not have the power to represent herself in these modern discourses of power. Her concern with the gendered subject who is the least powerful in hierarchies of power formed the basis of her critique of Western feminism as a globalizing, missionary project in which older forms of inequality were continued in new ways. Since feminists constantly "negotiate" with the "structures of violence" that enable them to come to "voice," Spivak argued (1988a) that there is no pure space from which to speak. Spivak's groundbreaking work revealed the centrality of imperialism and capitalism in the formation of gender identity within the history of modern Europe and the US.

Following these interventions by Spivak and Said, the relationship between imperialism and cultural representation emerged as an important area of work in feminist Postcolonial Studies. Here feminists examined the ways in which colonial patriarchies depicted women through political discourses that produced ideas about race, gender, sexuality, religion, and class that remain influential to this day. The "civilizing" practices of modern European imperialism generated specifically gendered forms of colonial discourse within which the figure of woman played a key role in ideas about nation. Postcolonial feminist scholarship critiqued the ways in which what were called "cultural practices," such as sati, seclusion, footbinding, veiling, arranged marriages, and female circumcision, came to symbolize the "barbarism" of non-Western cultures (McClintock 1995; Shohat 1991). More recently, gendered colonial symbols are visible in the media as debates over the "hijab" (headcovering), in attacks on Muslim fundamentalism, sensational accounts of sex tourism, and efforts to legislate against what is being called FGM ("Female Genital Mutilation") (see, for example, Gunning 1992; Grewal and Kaplan 1996; Kirby 1987; Lionnet 1992). These representational practices produce images of third world women as objects or victims who require first world assistance or direction. Within "Western feminism," representations of a victimized third world woman were created from a combination of popular and elite information cultures.

Increasingly, feminist scholars have taken up the study of the circulation of these colonial discourses in popular culture. For example, colonial photographs and journals such as *National Geographic* are discussed in terms of representational politics of gender, race, class, and nation (Lutz and Collins 1993). Museums of ethnography and natural history have been analyzed in relation to the history of collecting, and the rise of Western sciences of medicine, anthropology, and other social sciences. Studies of sports such as cricket and golf and "international" tournaments such as the Olympics draw upon postcolonial modes of critique. Film Studies has intersected Postcolonial Studies in numerous ways to examine Hollywood as well as documentary and ethnographic cinema (Trinh 1989; Shohat 1991; Tobing Rony 1996). For instance, Ella Shohat has focused on the depiction of "Eastern" women in twentieth-century Hollywood cinema as a *terra incognita*, that is, as "virgin" territory that must be conquered by a masculine imperial power. Gayatri Spivak refers (1985) to this imperialist project as one in which "brown women are saved by white men from brown men." As the work of scholars such as Reina Lewis (1995) and Sarah Graham-Brown (1988) reveals, both popular and elite culture generate gendered colonial discourses.

Many of these Orientalist and colonialist images were produced by people who traveled to the regions in question sometimes for pleasure but very often in the service of government or corporate interests. While Said had based his analysis of nineteenth-century Orientalist discourse on the narratives of travelers from Britain to what had been termed the "Middle East," feminist scholars studied the accounts of female as well as male travelers. In considering this new archive, travel narratives by ordinary European women became texts that could be studied to examine how colonial discourses pervaded women's culture. In Western women's studies, which for many years did not include postcolonial approaches, many of these women travelers had been seen as heroines for leaving domesticity to venture into unknown lands (Barr 1989). Postcolonial feminist scholars argued against this kind of romanticization, showing that this so-called practice of resistance was instead based on imperial tropes and reliance upon colonial power structures (Grewal 1996; Kaplan 1995, 1996; Mills 1991; Pratt 1992; Ware 1992).

These critiques generated by Postcolonial Studies intervene in the notion, produced by Anglo-American cultural feminism, that women can form a "global sisterhood," as Robin Morgan (1984) has called it, in which women have common interests, common agendas, and common oppressions. This presumption also suggested that all patriarchies were the same and were linked. The feminist scholarship on travel and postcolonialism contradicts this belief, arguing that there is no single global patriarchy. Rather, patriarchies are divergent, often collaborating as well as conflicting. Thus women do not have "natural" common interests since their gendered formation within different nationalisms produces various feminist subjects. Instead of seeing nationalism and feminism as existing in opposition to one another, such scholarship has argued that these were often collaborative and linked.

The emergence of a "third world women" coalition project suggested that the colonial divide existed between women as well, with "third world women" on one side and "first world women" on the other (Mohanty et al. 1991; Parmar and Amos 1984). Such a politics emerged from feminists in Europe and North America who critiqued the erasure of issues of race within feminist movements and who argued that they too were colonized peoples undergoing a process of decolonization. Feminists who worked in the third world researched the ways in which race, nationalism, and class became fault lines within feminism, dividing women of the "global north" from those in the "global south." Increasingly linked to Postcolonial Studies, European and US feminists began to focus on the divisions and conflicts between women rather than their similarities, and thus to think about different feminisms rather than one global feminist project. The emphasis on difference rather than similarities illuminates the gendered production of imperial cultures in particular ways that reveal the imbrication of feminisms with nationalism.

The contemporary study of nationalism has relied heavily upon Benedict Anderson's theorization (1983) of the nation as an "imagined" community that is formed through material practices such as print and other media within modern culture. Yet Anderson's analysis does not address the ways in which these material practices consolidated new patriarchies. While anti-colonial movements used nationalism in order to gain independence from European domination, the current history of nationalism has raised many important concerns about its

progressive as well as its reactionary dimensions (including masculinist recupera-
tions of "tradition"). Feminist postcolonial scholarship came to see nationalism
as a process in which new patriarchal elites gain the power to produce the generic
"we" of the nation (Kaplan et al. 1999). More and more, feminists argued that
the homogenizing project of nationalism draws upon female bodies as the symbol
of the nation to generate discourses of rape, motherhood, sexual purity, and
heteronormativity.

The critique of nationalism has emerged to analyze both sides of the colonial
divide – that is, to examine the ways in which anti-colonial nationalisms within
colonized countries and the imperial nationalism of the colonizers were both
productive of new forms of gender. In fact, feminist postcolonial scholarship came
to emphasize the hegemonic forms of power and complicity between colonizers
and colonized that "recast" new patriarchies. Sangari and Vaid (1990) made the
important point that feminist analysis was necessary to examine all kinds of
nationalisms that emerged in relation to colonialism, and that such nationalisms
relied on the figure of the woman to articulate both power and difference. Such
a project involves the work of feminist historians, anthropologists, and literary
scholars to articulate the new forms of gender that arose with colonial modernity
in particular sites and periods. As a result, the study of modernity in specific
places around the world has now become integrally connected to the examination
of colonialism and imperialism; how women became "modern" in different places
has become a key issue in feminist scholarship.[3] Such scholarship has enabled
new connections and conversations between scholars working in what has been
called "Area Studies" and those working in the so-called West.

These conversations have led feminists to the conclusion that nationalisms are
not just patriarchal. If the study of European women travelers revealed the ways
in which Eurocentric discourses about the colonized woman as victim of her
culture became widespread, they also suggest that these women travelers were
expressing nationalist ideas about the superiority of their country and their
capabilities and the inferiority of colonized Others. This explains why, for instance,
British women in the late nineteenth century continued to believe that their own
countries were havens of freedom when they themselves did not have the vote,
and were struggling for their rights. It can also explain why many working-class
women in Britain, locked in labor struggles, could still support the project of
British colonialism. It also explains the ways in which anti-colonial and cultural
nationalisms produced their own gendered forms of power. Nationalism creates
these misrecognitions – that is, a deliberate and ideological forgetting – and such
practices continue to this day as postcolonial elites divided by gender and sexuality come to participate in new cosmopolitanisms within transnationality (see
Grewal 2005).

By paying attention to the interactions between women from different nations,
it was possible to understand the nature of what are being called "transnational"
relations – i.e. relations across national boundaries. By such a transnational
analysis, one can get a quite different picture of the relation of feminism to

nationalism. This kind of analysis contradicts the popular belief that feminism exists in an antagonistic relation to nationalism. The complexity of nationalism is that although nationalism and feminism are often opposed, such opposition cannot be seen simply as resistance to nationalism because often one cannot exist without the other and often one is constructed only through the other.

Given this very heterogeneous and multifaceted world, relations between women become just as complicated as those between societies or between nations. Rather than simply use the model of information retrieval about a plurality of women around the world, a postcolonial approach enables us to think about gender as a constellation of practices and identities in a world whose boundaries have changed. Since recent scholarship has shown us that gender, class, religion, and sexuality produce different kinds of women in relation to different kinds of patriarchies, postcolonial feminist scholarship provides a more complex view of how modern gender binaries are produced around the world under colonial and postcolonial conditions. In addition, the impact of global forces such as colonialism, modernization, and development, and the ways in which these rely upon colonial legacies for specific and historicized gendering practices have created new negotiations, inequalities, and asymmetries.

Postcolonial Studies has thus been a crucial site for examining the complexity of the relationship between nationalism and feminism. Consequently, it can also enable an understanding of the ways in which contemporary racisms, nationalisms, and gendered subordinations are produced in relation to each other. Postcolonial Studies has enabled us to understand this increasingly interconnected world. For instance, scholars examine, on the one hand, the ways in which feminist communities are being produced in cyberspace (Cherny and Weise 1996; Haraway 1991), and on the other hand, the new female industrial worker in multinational assembly lines (Ong 1987; Freeman 2000), or the increasingly female population in prisons in metropolitan locations (Davis and Dent 2001). Postcolonial Feminist Studies is a useful place to do this work since academic pursuits are not merely abstractions within an ivory tower but are the political and ideological struggles in a workplace whose product is knowledge. The production of such knowledge is integral to public policy and to social struggles, as well as to cultural and political identities. The academy is not just a reflection of a distanced society, but is an integral part of the way the nation-state reproduces its concerns. Thus, Postcolonial Studies addresses many of the tensions arising out of the historical context of Western imperialism including the vexed gender politics of neocolonial formations.

Notes

1 For instance, Dirlik (1997) fails to recognize this aspect of the field.
2 These works reveal the influence of anti-colonial movements within black struggles for civil rights in the US and Europe.

3   See several essays in the journal *Positions: East Asia Cultures Critique* (various issues) for work on modernity and gender in Japan, China, and Korea.

References

Anderson, B. (1983) *Imagined Communities: Reflections on the Origin and Spread of Nationalisms* (London: Verso).

Anzaldua, G. (ed.) (1990) *Making Face, Making Soul: Haciendo Caras* (San Francisco: Aunt Lute Foundation Books).

Appadurai, A. (1996) *Modernity at Large* (Minneapolis: University of Minnesota Press).

Balibar, E. and Wallerstein, I. (eds.) (1991) *Race, Nation, Class* (London: Verso Press).

Barr, P. (1989) *The Memsahibs: In Praise of the Women of Victorian India* (London: Century).

Beneria, L. (1982) *Women and Development: The Sexual Division of Labor in Rural Societies* (New York: Praeger/ILO).

Bhabha, H. (ed.) (1990) *Nation and Narration* (New York: Routledge).

Cherny, L. and Weise, E. R. (1996) *Wired Women: Gender and New Realities in Cyberspace* (Seattle, WA: Seal Press).

Steady, F. C. (1981) *The Black Woman Cross-Culturally* (Cambridge, MA: Schenkman Publishing Co.).

Davis, A. and Dent, G. (2001) "Prison as a Border: A Conversation on Gender, Globalization and Punishment," *Signs* 26/4: 1235–41.

Dirlik, A. (1997) "The Postcolonial Aura: Third World Criticism in the Age of Global Capitalism," in Anne McClintock, Ella Shohat, Aamir Mufti (eds.), *Dangerous Liaisons: Gender, Nation, and Postcolonial Perspectives* (Minneapolis: University of Minnesota Press), pp. 492–500.

Enloe, C. (1993) *Bananas, Beaches, and Bases: Making Feminist Sense of International Politics* (Berkeley: University of California Press).

Escobar, A. (1995) *Encountering Development: The Making and Unmaking of the Third World* (Princeton, NJ: Princeton University Press).

Frankenberg, R. and Mani, L. (1993) "Crosscurrents, Crosstalk: Race, 'Postcoloniality,' and the Politics of Location," *Cultural Studies* 7 (May): 292–310.

Freeman, C. (2000) *High Tech and High Heels in the Global Economy: Women, Work, and Pink-Collar Identities in the Caribbean* (Durham: Duke University Press).

Gallin, R., Aronoff, M., and Ferguson, A. (eds.) (1989) *The Women and International Development Manual*, vol. 1 (Boulder, CO: Westview).

Gilroy, P. (1993) *The Black Atlantic: Double Consciousness and Modernity* (Cambridge, MA: Harvard University Press).

Graham-Brown, S. (1988) *Images of Women: The Portrayal of Women in the Photography of the Middle East, 1860–1950* (London: Quartet Books).

Grewal, I. (1996) *Home and Harem: Nation, Gender, Empire and the Cultures of Travel* (Durham, NC: Duke University Press).

Grewal, I. (2005) *Transnational America* (Durham, NC: Duke University Press).

Grewal, I. and Kaplan, C. (1996) "*Warrior Marks*: Global Womanism's Neo-Colonial Discourse in a Multicultural Context," *Camera Obscura* 39 (September): 5–33.

Gunning, I. (1992) "Arrogant Perception, World-Travelling and Multicultural Feminism: The Case of Female Genital Surgeries," *Columbia Human Rights Law Review* 23: 189–248.

Haraway, D. (1991) "A Cyborg Manifesto: Science, Technology, and Socialist-Feminism in the Late Twentieth Century," in *Simians, Cyborgs and Women: The Reinvention of Nature* (New York: Routledge).

Harvey, D. (1990) *The Condition of Postmodernity* (Cambridge, MA: Basil Blackwell).

Hobsbawm, E. (1990) *Nations and Nationalisms Since 1798* (Cambridge: Cambridge University Press).

hooks, b. (1981) *"Ain't I a Woman?" Black Women and Feminism* (Boston: South End Press).

James, C. L. R. (1969) *A History of Pan-African Revolt* (Washington, DC: Drum & Spear Press).

Jayawardena, K. (1986) *Feminism and Nationalism in the Third World* (London: Zed Books).

Kandiyoti, D. (1991) *Women, Islam, and the State* (Philadelphia: Temple University Press).

Kaplan, C. (1995) "'Getting to Know You': Travel, Gender, and the Politics of Representation in Anna and the King of Siam and The King and I," in Roman de la Campa, E. Ann Kaplan, and Michael Sprinker (eds.), *Late Imperial Culture* (London: Verso), pp. 33–52.

Kaplan, C. (1996) *Questions of Travel: Postmodern Discourses of Displacement* (Durham: Duke University Press).

Kaplan, C., Alarcon, N., and Moallem, M. (eds.) (1999) *Between Woman and Nation: Nationalisms, Transnational Feminisms, and the State* (Durham, NC: Duke University Press).

Kirby, V. (1987) "On the Cutting Edge: Feminism and Clitorodectomy," *Australian Feminist Studies* 5 (Summer): 35–55.

Lewis, R. (1995) *Gendering Orientalism: Race, Femininity and Representation* (London: Routledge).

Leyshon, A. and Thrift, N. (eds.) (1997) *Money Space: Geographies of Monetary Transformation* (London: Routledge).

Lionnet, F. (1992) "Feminisms and Universalisms: 'Universal Rights' and the Legal Debate Around the Practice of Female Excision in France," *Inscriptions* 6: 98–115.

Lutz, C. and Collins, J. L. (1993) *Reading National Geographic* (Chicago: University of Chicago Press).

Mbembe, A. (1992) "Prosaics of Servitude and Authoritarian Civilities," *Public Culture* 5/1: 123–48.

McClintock, A. (1992) "The Angel of Progress: Pitfalls of the Term 'Postcolonial'," *Social Text* 31/32: 84–98.

McClintock, A. (1995) *Imperial Leather: Race, Gender and Sexuality in the Colonial Contest* (New York: Routledge).

Mills, S. (1991) *Discourses of Difference: An Analysis of Women's Writing and Colonialism* (New York: Routledge).

Mohanty, C. (1991) "Under Western Eyes: Feminist Scholarship and Colonial Discourses," in Chandra Mohanty, Ann Russo, and Lourdes Torres (eds.), *Third World Women and the Politics of Feminism* (Bloomington and Indianapolis: Indiana University Press).

Mohanty, C., Russo, A., and Torres, L. (eds.) (1991) *Third World Women and the Politics of Feminism* (Bloomington and Indianapolis: Indiana University Press).

Moraga, C. and Anzaldua, G. (1981) *This Bridge Called My Back* (Watertown, MA: Persephone Press).

Morgan, R. (1984) *Sisterhood is Global: The International Women's Movement* (New York: Anchor).

Ong, A. (1987) *Spirits of Resistance and Capitalist Discipline: Factory Women in Malaysia* (Albany: State University of New York Press).

Parker, A., Russo, M., Sommer, D., and Yaeger, P. (eds.) (1992) *Nationalisms and Sexualities* (New York: Routledge).

Parmar, P. and Amos, V. (1984) "Challenging Imperial Feminism," *Feminist Review* 17: 3–20.

Pratt, M. L. (1992) *Imperial Eyes: Travel Writing and Transculturation* (New York: Routledge).

Rodney, Walter (1981) *How Europe Underdeveloped Africa* (Washington DC: Howard University Press).

Said, E. (1978) *Orientalism* (New York: Vintage Press).

Said, E. (1993) *Culture and Imperialism* (New York: Knopf).

Sangari, K.-K. and Vaid, S. (eds.) (1990) *Recasting Women: Essays in Indian Colonial History* (New Brunswick, NJ: Rutgers University Press).

Sen, G. and Grown, C. (eds.), *Development, Crises, and Alternative Visions: Third World Women's Perspectives* (New York: Monthly Review).

Shohat, E. (1991) "Gender and the Culture of Empire: Toward a Feminist Ethnography of the Cinema," *Quarterly Review of Film and Video* 13: 45–84.

Shohat, E. (1992) "Notes on the Post-Colonial," *Social Text* 31/32: 99–113.

Shohat, E. and Stam, R. (1995) *Unthinking Eurocentrism* (New York: Routledge).

Soja, E. (1989) *Postmodern Geographies: The Reassertion of Space in Critical Social Theory* (London: Verso).

Spivak, G. C. (1985) "Three Women's Texts and a Critique of Imperialism," in Henry Louis Gates Jr., *"Race," Writing and Difference* (Chicago: University of Chicago Press), pp. 262–80.

Spivak, G. C. (1987) *In Other Worlds* (New York: Routledge).

Spivak, G. C. (1988a) "Can the Subaltern Speak?" in Cary Nelson and Lawrence Grossberg (eds.), *Marxism and the Interpretation of Culture* (New York: Routledge), pp. 271–313.

Spivak, G. C. (1988b) "French Feminism in an International Frame," in *In Other Worlds: Essays in Cultral Politics* (New York: Methuen), pp. 134–53.

Spivak, G. C. (1993) *Outside in the Teaching Machine* (New York: Routledge).

Spivak, G. C. (1999) *A Critique of Postcolonial Reason: Towards a History of the Vanishing Present* (Cambridge, MA: Harvard University Press).

Spivak, G. C. and Harasyn, S. (eds.) (1990) *The Postcolonial Critic: Interviews, Strategies, Dialogues* (New York: Routledge).

Tobing Rony, F. (1996) *The Third Eye: Race, Cinema, and Ethnographic Spectacle* (Durham, NC: Duke University Press).

Trinh, M. T. (1989) *Woman, Native, Other* (Bloomington: University of Indiana Press).

Ware, V. (1992) *Beyond the Pale: White Women, Racism and History* (London: Verso).

CHAPTER FOUR

Queer Studies

Judith Halberstam

Recently, I have heard colleagues and students alike bemoan the decline of queer theory. Some say that queer theory is no longer in vogue; others characterize it as fatigued or exhausted and lacking in keen debates. Still others wax nostalgic for an earlier moment in the history of Queer Studies in the academy and queer life outside the academy and accuse a new generation of queer theorists and activists of having dropped the ball on the politics of the queer project. These vague rumblings of queer theory and its discontents are accompanied by rumors of certain powerful university presses no longer having faith in queer publications. Is Queer Studies in some kind of decline? In this short chapter I want to take stock quickly of the field by situating Queer Studies within the larger terrain of interdisciplinary studies, locating it in relation to pedagogy and digital media and describing some of the areas of debate within Queer Studies as they have emerged in recent conferences.

Gay Shame/Gay Pride

> If queer is a politically potent term, which it is, that's because, far from being capable of being detached from the childhood scene of shame, it cleaves to that scene as a near-inexhaustible source of transformational energy.
> Eve Sedgwick 1995

At a recent conference on "Gay Shame" organized by David Halperin and Valerie Traub, the possibility that Queer Studies might be merely one part of a corporatization of gay culture was raised. Many scholars opposed gay shame to gay pride and characterized gay shame as the structure of feeling appropriate to an earlier paradigm of sexual variance and sexual politics. Gay pride, however, was associated with contemporary mobilizations of consumption and gentrification and was excoriated as the assimilationist wave of a gay neoliberalism. The "gay shame rubric" allowed for some interesting exchanges about the contemporary foci of Queer Studies, and I want to begin here by tracing these exchanges in order to highlight some areas of conflict and dialogue in Queer Studies now.

Sedgwick and others, who have written so eloquently about gay shame, posit an early childhood experience of sexual shame that has to be reclaimed, reinterpreted, and resituated by a queer adult who, armed with a theoretical language about his or her sexuality, can transform past experiences with abjection, isolation, and rejection into legibility, community, and love. Gay shame, in this scenario, becomes the deep emotional reservoir upon which an adult queer sexuality draws, for better or for worse. And the sexual and emotional scripts which queer life draws upon, and which oppose the scripts of normativity, are indebted oddly to this early experience with shame, denial, and misrecognition. When we seek to reclaim gay shame and we oppose the normativity of a "gay pride" agenda, we embrace these awkward, undignified, and graceless childhoods and we choose to make them part of our political future.

The annexing of shame to queer within the temporal space of "anteriority" has been a huge part of several influential projects in Queer Studies: Warner's critiques of "normal" (2000), Sedgwick's theory of "shame" (1993), and Bersani's work on "homos" (1996) all find rich archives of sexual variance in the temporal lag between homo and gay. And in Crimp's forthcoming work, "Queer before Gay," queer is very explicitly the pre-history of gay, a history that must not be left behind in the rush to gay pride but which must be excavated in all its contradiction, disorder and eros. While these projects make some useful disconnections between queer life and the seeming inevitability of homonormativity, there are also some problems that attend to characterizing shame as normal's "other" and then positioning it as a past that must be reclaimed. The three most obvious problems have to do with, first, glorifying the pre-Stonewall past; second, idealizing youth itself, the territory of gay shame after all; and, finally, as Berlant suggests (2000: 74), the interest in shame tends to force us to focus upon "a too psychically invested subject."

Why are these things problematic? First, the focus on the past fails to recognize or credit in any way the contemporary anti-homonormative queer politics which often emerge in transgender arenas or in relation specifically to race and immigrant communities (we notice that the homo-norms like their critics are often white gay men). And so, when we make "gay pride" into the sum total of contemporary queer politics, we simply are not looking closely enough at the alternatives. Second, "gay shame" has a tendency to universalize the self who emerges out of a "shame formation" (often a white and male self whose shame in part emerges from the experience of being denied access to privilege). And third, discussions about gay shame betray a kind of casualness about the effects of shame upon others. Warner warns about this (2000) when he writes: "What will we do with our shame? And the usual response is to pin it on someone else." Warner is exactly right, but let's remember that the projection of shame elsewhere is neither random nor unpredictable. In the Warhol film that Crimp writes about (2000), the body that is made to bear the marks of shame, that is forced to squirm under the camera's gaze, and that is forced to be painfully vulnerable is a Puerto Rican drag queen. As Larry LaFontaine recently wrote to Douglas Crimp in an open letter, this racial dynamic reveals the symbiotic relationship between white shame and brown bodies.

Obviously, shame is multifaceted and can be brought on by psychic traumas as brutal as physical bullying and as seemingly benign as mute indifference. But shame records a failure to be powerful, legitimate, proper – it records the exposure, in psychoanalytic terms, of the subject's castration; indeed, in a psychoanalytic framework, one would be tempted to say that castration is central to shame and that shame is central to femininity. And so, the shame experienced by white gay men in childhood has to do with the exposure of their femininity and the dramatization of their failure to access the privilege that has been symbolically reserved for them. The sissy boy is the incarnation of shame and so we should not be surprised to find that the centerpiece of today's gay pride movements has to do with the reclamation of gay masculinity.

It needs to be pointed out that, for the butch lesbian, her masculinity is not in and of itself shameful when she is a child (we do tolerate tomboys in a way that is unthinkable for the sissy boy). It is the butch's failure to become properly feminine at adolescence that prompts the shame and so we should say that some lesbian subjectivities have much less to do with shame than most gay white male subjectivities. Indeed, butch embodiment has been theorized by Butler in relation to "melancholy" and is situated in the two most famous novels of lesbian masculinity, *The Well of Loneliness* and *Stone Butch Blues*, as defiant singularity in one and heroic isolation in the other. Butchness gives rise to the blues, to rage, and finally to a political sensibility that is shared by other female subjects who experience themselves as disenfranchised – namely feminism. Shame is a gendered form of sexual abjection, it belongs to the feminine, and while we are not in the habit of naming the particularity of male forms of emotional being, in this case, in the case of white gay manhood, I suggest we start.

Finally, while I see why people may want to hold on to shame, nourish and nurture a close relation to shame, build upon the negative but deeply erotic nature of shame, I want to offer here a caution against gay shame by way of a quick consideration of Pedro Almodovar's latest film, *Talk To Her*. This film, which should have been called "Talk To Her . . . because she is in a coma and cannot talk back to you and she won't know or mind what you do to her even if you rape her while all the while seeming to be basically a good guy if a little closeted . . . ," breaks its audiences down into those who hate it and those who love it: lesbians hate it and gay men love it. Falling into the category of those who hate this film, who despise its pathetic dependence upon aesthetic mastery to represent the most trite and insulting narratives about women and men, I nonetheless understand that *Talk To Her* has much to say about gay shame and its consequences. Indeed, Almodovar's film offers us two solutions to the discomfort of gay shame.

First, "Work it out or normalize it": the film, and contemporary gay pride politics, suggest that gay white men can work through gay shame by producing normative masculinities and presenting themselves as uncastrated, muscular, whole. This occurs by cleaving to the ordinary and the quiet. In the film this role is fulfilled by Marco the seemingly straight man who pursues the masculine woman, the bullfighter, and whose desire is triangulated through her onto her ex and Benigno.

Second, "Project it elsewhere or aestheticize it": the white gay male experience of shame is often managed through the act of projection, which Douglas Crimp describes so well in his essay on Mario Montez. There, Andy Warhol, the original "thin white duke," projects shame, castration, and vulnerability onto the feminized and racialized body of a Puerto Rican drag queen and in the process creates an illusion of mastery. In *Talk To Her*, it is Benigno who projects his shame elsewhere – onto the body of a mute woman, a dancer who lies in a coma after a car accident. He and Marco bond over their care for their comatose women and the two women represent two different sides of gay male projection. While the former female bull fighter is essentially the fag hag, the castrated and unlucky woman whose castration stands in for the fag's own shame and who often becomes a source of humor, the former dancer occupies the role of the diva – Koestenbaum's Jackie Onassis or opera singer, Warhol's Marilyn Monroe – the idealized and phallic woman who often becomes an excuse for exquisite but dangerous investments in beauty and art. While the fag hag is used and abused, the diva is cared for and talked to; the fag hag is an emblem, the diva a trophy, the fag hag is openly despised and secretly worshipped, the diva is openly worshipped and secretly despised. Both are summarily massaged, admired, and utterly destroyed.

Feminist gay shame

An option that neither Almodovar nor Warhol entertains is that gay shame can be used, in all its glorious negativity, in ways that are feminist and anti-racist. The glory of the drag queen is that she takes pride in her shame; just the names alone – Vaginal Crème Davis for example – step in where others fear to tread. The form of subject formation that Munoz (1999), in reference to the work of Vaginal Crème Davis, has called "disidentification" also leads us to a place where shame can be transformed into something that is not pride, but not simply damage either. And finally, we could look to a gay white text like Michael Cunningham's *The Hours*, and see how the sensibility of gay male shame can be routed through women without destroying them in the process. *The Hours* produces compelling schemas of queer temporalities, shows us vividly the meaning of queer before and after gay, and it depicts in unflinching detail the deaths of at least two of its main characters. But at its conclusion both shame and the woman have survived – a small triumph and a signpost to the next queer moment.

Queer Studies Now

It is my distinct impression that Queer Studies has recently experienced a paradigm shift, one not completely described by the "gay shame/gay pride" binary, and that, far from being over, Queer Studies in the academy is flourishing in the work of a new generation of scholars who have had the benefit of a training in queer theory at the graduate level. Much of the most exciting work in this new moment of Queer Studies refuses to see sexuality as a singular mode of inquiry and instead makes it a central category of analysis in the study of racialization, transnationalism, and globalization. Some of this work can be considered to define new fields such as Queer Ethnic Studies, Queer Postcolonial Studies, and Transgender Studies. Examples include: Manalansan's ethnographic work (2003) on diasporic Filipino gay men; Ferguson's work (2004) on the history of sociology and its projection of deviance onto the black family; Gopinath's work on South Asian queer cultural production (1995); Keeling's work (2002) on black spectatorship and queer black cinema; and Valentine's ethnography of transgender sex workers in New York City (2003).

It is true that there are still not many jobs in Queer Studies specifically and indeed a focus on queer thematics can often take excellent candidates out of the running for traditionally conceived jobs. But sexuality makes its way regularly onto laundry lists of areas of interests. And perhaps that is just the way we like it – Queer Studies does not seem to be on the verge of institutionalization, and so work on sexuality continues in a variety of disciplinary venues but belongs to none of them. While Feminist Studies finds its place in Women and Gender Studies programs in the university and studies of race and racialization tend to be associated with Ethnic Studies, the study of sexuality goes on in sociology, literature, history, and anthropology departments among others, but sexuality is also part of the curriculum in Gender Studies and Ethnic Studies programs. The problem with not having a clear institutional home is, of course, that the study of sexuality is central to no single discipline or program and in fact may be taught everywhere and nowhere simultaneously. However, the advantage of the stealth approach to the study of sexuality is that it remains multidisciplinary, a promiscuous rogue in a field of focused monogamists.

Queer Studies, because it is without a disciplinary home, offers a potent critique of disciplinarity itself. In a chapter entitled "The Means of Correct Training" in his *Discipline and Punish*, Foucault tells us that "discipline 'makes' individuals" and he goes on to describe the institutional structures that train "moving, confused, useless multitudes of bodies and forces into a multiplicity of individual elements" (1979: 170). The disciplines themselves obviously emerge out of the reorganization of power and knowledge that molded the modern university in the late nineteenth and early twentieth century. Given what we know about disciplinary power and the way it works on behalf of liberal regimes, and given the enormous shifts in both knowledge base and cultural forms in the last hundred years, I think we are justified in asking today: Why hold onto the disciplines in the forms that they now exist? Currently, the most exciting places in most universities to do work are peripheral sectors often called "programs" and distinguished in some way from "departments" and "disciplines." Programs often invite interdisciplinary work and they offer a place from which to reconceptualize the organization of knowledge. At present, such sectors tend to be home to many of our sexuality programs if only because the disciplines are constructed around canonical bodies of knowledge which almost deliberately repress the study of difference by selecting areas of study under the misleading rubric of "excellence."

Situating Queer Studies within programs rather than departments encourages the field to be multidisciplinary. Because of this inevitable multidisciplinary focus, then, new work in Queer Studies seems to have overcome what was experienced in earlier moments as a stand-off between the social sciences and humanities. Social scientists often accused humanities scholars in Queer Studies of only reading texts and of producing impossibly abstract theories of embodiment and difference, while Queer Cultural Studies scholars accused the social scientists of being anti-theoretical and too invested in the "real" and the "community." A consciously cultivated multidisciplinarity offers a much-needed detour around such debates and encourages queer scholars to use the methodologies that best match their projects rather than finding projects that allow them to use the discipline-appropriate methods.

In my own work, I have had to deploy participant observation as well as textual analysis and I think of what I do as Queer Cultural Studies. My current project offers a sense of interdisciplinary Queer Studies. My book suggests what queer life loses when it is wholly accommodated within mainstream ideologies of family. *In a Queer Time and Space: Transgendered Bodies, Subcultural Lives* (Haberstam 2005) contains an analysis of the explosion of queer urban subcultures in the last decade. My larger purpose is to examine the ways in which many queer communities experience and spend time in ways that are very different from their heterosexual counterparts. Queer uses of time and space develop in opposition to the institutions of family, heterosexuality, and reproduction. By making queerness an outcome of temporality, life scheduling, and eccentric economic practices, we detach queerness from sexual identity and we come closer to understanding Foucault's comment that "homosexuality threatens people as a way of life" rather than as a way of having sex. At a moment when so many middle-class gays and lesbians are choosing to raise children in conventional family settings, it is important to study queer life modes that offer alternatives to family time and family life. So this book includes a critique of the rise of the gay family. Since family structures are everywhere considered to be "right" and respectable, and since so many GLQT (gay, lesbian, queer, transgender) civil rights groups are calling for the recognition of the gay family, there is something counterintuitive about offering such a critique. But, in this book, I hope to show that the boom in gay families is not simply a testament to increased levels of tolerance for gays and lesbians; it may also be evidence of a subtle enforcement of compulsory reproduction. As 30-something bourgeois gay men and lesbians use new reproductive technologies to generate their own families, we must ask whether these families challenge dominant notions of kinship and community or whether they consolidate traditional, conservative, and even reactionary notions of kinship and community in a new site.

My work has participated in some interesting conversations about queer pedagogy and the need to take Queer Studies beyond the university and into public arenas that often get called reductively "the community" or "the real world." Among the many important new developments in Queer Studies in recent years is the emergence of a cadre of queer public intellectuals. Queer public intellectuals are those people who refuse the boundaries between community and campus, activism and theory, classroom and club. And queer public intellectuals are committed to multiplying the sites within which Queer Cultural Studies happens and to recognizing cultural producers as theorists and theorists as contributors to the circulation of ideas beyond the university. Stuart Hall has described Cultural Studies in general as a place where intellectual and political commitments may often clash productively. He has commented that Cultural Studies draws attention "not just because of its sometimes dazzling internal theoretical development but because it holds theoretical and political questions in an ever irresolvable but permanent tension" (1992: 284). As Cultural Studies and Queer Studies become institutionalized and professionalized, Hall implies, a "theoretical fluency" emerges among practitioners that may well be at odds with the original political goals of the field. Sustaining the public intellectual is one way for Cultural Studies to uphold what Hall describes as "the responsibility of transmitting . . . ideas . . . knowledge, through the intellectual function, to those who do not belong, professionally, in the intellectual class" (ibid.: 281). At the same time, we need a division of labor: not all Queer or Cultural Studies scholars need to be public intellectuals; not all public intellectuals need to be professors; and not all queer scholarship needs to be accessible. And so, while some people want to serve as translators between the academy and the nightclub, others might want to defamiliarize language, experience, and the realm of "common sense."

Gibson and McHoul point out that Cultural Studies was created in the university when a new class of student (the scholarship boy or gifted working-class pupil) entered the arena. In the 1950s these new students brought fresh questions and experiences to the classroom and they forced university teachers to respond to them by refusing to respect the boundaries of disciplinary knowledge. Gibson and McHoul write: "Cultural studies, then, is not interdisciplinary for the sake of being so; interdisciplinarity is not its willed departure, the volunteered flag of its curricular radicality – at least not at this moment. Interdisciplinarity, on the contrary, arises out of structural institutional necessity" (2001: 25). We are at one of those historical moments in the humanities when new forms of study, mostly interdisciplinary, will surely emerge, not because humanities scholars are "playing with categories" or trying to be radical, but because new questions from new students studying new forms of culture force us all, of necessity, to move far beyond the disciplinary boundaries that have encased our own graduate training. The challenge for a new generation of scholars will be to pursue the projects that feel urgent to them while still remaining eligible for jobs in the fields that dominate the marketplace. The challenge for my generation is to change the marketplace so that original, daring, and ambitious work can be recognized, funded, rewarded, and, above all, encouraged.

The mixing of methods and the eccentric selection of objects of inquiry has also allowed queer scholars to disrupt the logic of coherence that creates a term like "LGBT" (lesbian, gay, bisexual, transsexual). As Sedgwick writes: "there can't be an a priori decision about how far it will make sense to conceptualize lesbian and gay male identities together. Or separately" (1990: 36). And we might add that it may or may not make sense to study Ls and Gs with Ts: I would argue that in many cases, for example, it does *not* make sense to study gay men and lesbians together, as we saw in the example of "gay shame," and we should be very willing to break up the moniker of "gay" and "lesbian" – particularly in relation to queer history. It has also become very clear recently that transgender histories and lesbian histories may overlap, but they are not identical. Indeed, the sense that transsexuality and transgenderism have been both cannibalized and overlooked by LGB Studies has created some intense conversations in recent years in community forums.

A queer pedagogy must also try to break with the oedipal deadlock that creates and sustains intergenerational conflict. To first-wave queer theorists, I would say: let's not become a generation of whiners complaining about what the youth of today doesn't know, how poorly trained they are, how apolitical they have become, etc. To generation Q'ers I would say avoid the "kill daddy/mommy" syndrome of critical labor within which you are right because those who came before you are wrong. I know from my own work that what I do is utterly dependent upon the work of people who did queer work long before the *Journal of Homosexuality* or GLQ (gay, lesbian, queer) even existed. I think the future of queer pedagogy is fully dependent upon the recognition of Queer Studies' varied and complex past and that is a history that we need to teach, pass on, and learn from.

Finally, while Queer Studies offers a potent critique of disciplinarity and pedagogy, it also offers an interesting interface with new digital technologies and the development of smart classrooms and web-based learning. I recently taught a class in Critical Gender Studies at the University of California at San Diego on "Gender, Sexuality, and Subcultures." Using web technology, I was able to create a website for the class which links students to sites like Mr. Lady records and other independent dyke labels; I was also able to put music on digital reserve for the students to listen to, thereby creating an archive of subcultural materials that will remain part of the library and enable students to find out about, write about, and connect with small queer bands and queer zines and all manner of ephemera which otherwise could not be studied. These databases create a new future for queer history by making a place for materials that otherwise would be lost in the ebb and flow of a paper history. With flexible and innovative notions of archiving, canonicity, disciplinarity, and intellectual labor in hand, we can catch a glimpse of a queer future within which Hothead Paisan or Vaginal Crème Davis becomes as important to Queer Studies as Freud or Lacan. Rumors of the demise of Queer Studies have been greatly exaggerated.

References

Berlant, L. (2000) "Two Girls Fat and Thin," in Stephen M. Barber and David Clark (eds.), *Regarding Sedgwick* (New York: Routledge).

Bersani, L. (1996) *Homos* (Cambridge, MA: Harvard University Press).

Crimp, D. (2000) "Mario Montez: For Shame," in Stephen M. Barber and David Clark (eds.), *Regarding Sedgwick* (New York: Routledge).

Ferguson, R. (2004) *Aberrations in Black: Toward a Queer of Color Critique* (Minneapolis, MN: University of Minnesota Press).

Foucault, M. (1979) *Discipline and Punish: The Birth of the Prison* (New York: Vintage Books).

Gibson, M. and McHoul, A. (2001) "Interdisciplinarity," in Toby Miller (ed.), *A Companion to Cultural Studies* (Oxford: Blackwell Publishing).

Gopinath, G. (1995) "'Bombay, UK, Yuba City': Bhangra Music and the Engendering of Diaspora," *Diaspora* 4/3 (Winter): 303–22.

Halberstam, J. (2005) *In a Queer Time and Space: Transgendered Bodies, Subcultural Lives* (New York: New York University Press).

Hall, S. (1992) "Cultural Studies and Its Theoretical Legacies," in L. Grossberg, C. Nelson, and P. Treichler (eds.), *Cultural Studies* (New York: Routledge).

Keeling, K. (2002) "In the Interval: Franz Fanon and the 'problems' of Visual Representation." Ph.D. dissertation, University of Pittsburgh.

Manalansan, M. (2003) *Global Divas: Filipino Gay Men in the Diaspora* (Durham, NC: Duke University Press).

Munoz, J. E. (1999) *Disidentifications: Queers of Color and The Performance of Politics* (Minneapolis, MN: University of Minnesota Press).

Sedgwick, E. K. (1990) *Epistemology of the Closet* (Berkeley and Los Angeles: University of California Press).

Sedgwick, E. K. (1993) *Tendencies* (Durham, NC: Duke University Press).

Sedgwick, E. K. (1995) *Shame and Its Sisters: A Silvan Tompkins Reader* (Durham, NC: Duke University Press).

Valentine, D. (2003) "I Know What I Am: The Category of 'Transgender' in the Construction of Contemporary US Conceptions of Gender and Sexuality." Ph.D. dissertation, New York University.

Warner, M. (2000) *The Trouble With Normal* (Cambridge, MA: Harvard University Press).

PART TWO

Re-positionings

CHAPTER FIVE

Epistemologies

Laura Hyun Yi Kang

Introduction

Gender Studies benefits substantially from the way feminism has changed the very nature of perceiving knowledge. The term "feminist epistemology" has been widely invoked, but there is no consensus on what it exactly constitutes. In addition to the contestation around the meaning of "feminist," there is a wide array of meanings for the second term, "epistemology," which ranges from a specific discipline to a distinct subdiscipline of philosophy to a broader, multidisciplinary usage of the word to substitute for "thought" or "knowledge." Feminist epistemology sometimes signals a distinctively feminist branch of epistemology and at other times signals a particular branch of feminist theory, which explores the politics of gender in knowledge production and validation. This chapter will first outline these various definitions of "feminist epistemology." Then it will move on to a discussion of the feminist critiques of the assumptions of traditional "epistemology proper" defined as "a theory of knowledge in general."

Because of these masculinist biases and blind spots of traditional epistemology, some feminists have concluded that epistemology and feminism are incompatible, which is also the argument of those who seek to defend epistemology from the improper politicization of knowledge by feminists. Others acknowledge these problems but conclude that feminists need to remain critically engaged with the field of epistemology because of its influence in shaping criteria for truth and justification in other disciplines, which in turn have material consequences in the world and in women's lives. However, such discussions about the limits and possibilities of "feminist epistemology" have mostly confined its purview to a disciplinarily narrow "epistemology proper" and to certain fields of study seen as more rigorous in their exploration of what matters about knowledge, namely the natural and biological sciences, the history of philosophy, and certain social sciences. The arts and humanities and interdisciplinary fields of study, where there has been important and innovative work in both feminist critiques of dominant knowledge and new methods of feminist knowledge production, are consequently left out of much existing discussion of feminist epistemology and are thus epistemologically devalued.

In addition to these kinds of knowledge and discipline, specific constituencies of women are also marginalized and reduced as significant contributors to the ongoing conversation of what counts as "feminist epistemology." I discuss the very particular invocations of "women of color" as distinctly embodied and experientially burdened subjects and the more recent efforts to add a "multicultural," "global," and "postcolonial" dimension to the discussions on feminist epistemology, which tend to figure "women of color" and women in other places largely as corporeal bodies or bodies of identity and not as bodies of knowledge that can substantively alter and advance the existing discussions of epistemology. The conclusion thus argues for a broader framing of a pluralized "feminist epistemologies," which includes a critique of disciplinarity and begins to consider the possibilities of interdisciplinarity for a feminist politics of knowledge production.

Definitions of Feminist Epistemology

"Feminist epistemology" has been defined in terms that vary from "women's ways of knowing" or "women's knowledge" to a more gender-inclusive "feminist knowledge" to a more disciplinarily specific "feminist work in epistemology" (Alcoff and Potter 1993: 2). Early attempts to posit a unique "women's knowledge" as distinct from "men's knowledge" were problematically predicated upon a universally shared "women's experience," which came under criticism as essentialist and homogenizing from many feminists across the disciplines (Collins 1986; Haraway 1991; Scott 1992). There was a move, then, to focus upon the significance of *gender*, whereby the designation of "feminist" would encompass more than knowledge about, by, and for women. Pointing to "influential arguments avowing that women, per se, do not exist," Alcoff and Potter add that "to refer to a liberatory project as 'feminist' cannot mean that it is only for or about women" (1993: 4). As early as 1987, Harding went so far as to assert that men conducting research from "a feminist perspective" can contribute to "the emancipation of women which inquiries *by women* cannot achieve" (1987c: 12; italics in original). This broader designation of "feminist epistemology" thus encompasses matters of everyday knowledge drawn from women's lives to a range of methods and methodologies for studying gender across the disciplines.

The body of writings that comprise "feminist work in epistemology," which is often confused with or supported by the invocation of a professionally disciplined group of subjects called "feminist epistemologists," can be divided further into four different yet linked projects. First, there has been a significant body of work devoted to identifying and critiquing the biases against "women's ways of knowing" in the field of epistemology proper and philosophy more broadly. Defining "women's knowledges" as a "knowing how" or "a skilled activity," Alcoff and Potter argue that these knowledges have been delegitimated by the normative privileging of the propositional "knowing that" in traditional epistemology (1993: 11). Second, there is a body of work devoted to identifying "gender-specific ways of knowing" by highlighting the significance of gender both to the construction of knowledge and to the definition and enforcement of the criteria for what counts as true knowledge. This privileging of gender as a central axis in the production and classification of knowledge has come under criticism, leading to concerted efforts to acknowledge, if not explicate, multiple axes of race, ethnicity, class, sexuality, and nationality. Third, a more recent usage of "feminist work in epistemology" describes efforts to identify and analyze a more general "politics of knowledge," which is attentive to the play of power and knowledge framed more broadly. Alcoff and Potter point to "a new research program . . . moving beyond critique to reframe the problematic of knowledge," which encompasses diverse feminisms "often having in common only their commitment to unearth the politics of epistemology" (ibid.: 3). Fourth, there is a more historically and institutionally narrow designation that refers to a specific set of texts that mark an earlier moment of academic feminist studies, but one that is no longer relevant to describing a more diverse range of works that have since emerged. For example, Alcoff and Potter explain their retention of the "feminist" designation as a way to identify a particular historical trajectory of work that "did in fact begin (among those who are identified with mainstream academic feminism) as work on gender issues in the theory of knowledge" (ibid.: 4). In this narration, "gender" continues to enjoy a historical primacy if no longer a singular analytic privilege in the expanding reconfigurations of what counts as "feminist epistemology."

Feminist Critiques of Epistemology Proper

Feminist critiques of the field of epistemology proper have had two main aims: first, to show how its traditional theories of knowledge and scientific method are androcentric, and, second, to explicate, defend, and refine what are considered distinctively feminist scientific practices and knowledges. Feminist critics have focused upon five common features of traditional epistemology, which have led to the marginalization of women as both objects and subjects of knowledge:

- the assumption of the isolated individual as the exemplary agent of knowing;
- a commitment to a notion of objectivity that separates subjects from objects of knowledge;
- the ideal of abstract universal knowledge;
- a privileging of the context of justification over the context of discovery; and
- the upholding of the natural sciences and their allied scientific method as paradigmatic.

I will briefly summarize each of these five points of feminist critique as well as some alternatives offered by feminists.

In characterizing the process of how we gain knowledge, traditional epistemology privileges independent perception and memory (as belonging to a lone, isolated thinker) over testimony from other people (Code 1991: 111). Instead, Nelson (1993) has proposed the importance of what she calls "epistemological communities," since key to the definition and justification of knowledge is what counts as "evidence," which is socially determined and collectively agreed upon. Nelson is careful to clarify that she does not mean that these communities are comprised of "individuals who, as individuals, know in some logically or empirically 'prior' sense" (ibid.: 124) but that we can only know *as* members of communities. Potter (1993) makes a similar point about the primacy of the community of knowers over the individual knower, but focuses on the social nature of language as key to this communal formulation of knowledge.

There have been extensive criticisms of the masculinist definition of objectivity, which has secured traditional epistemology as an androcentric discourse that conceives of knowledge as domination over an object. An assumption of a clear separation of the knower from the object of knowledge enables and ensures this mastery. As Code writes, "the subject's demonstrated ability to manipulate, predict, and control the behavior of his own objects of knowledge is commonly regarded as evidence par excellence that he knows them" (1991: 140). Harding argues against this tendency by emphasizing that objects of knowledge are socially constructed. Even the trees, rocks, and electrons studied in the natural sciences, are "social objects" due to "the contemporary general cultural meanings that these objects have for everyone, including scientists" and also "through the shapes and meanings these objects gain for scientists because of earlier generations of scientific discussions about them" (1993: 64–5). Therefore, objects of knowledge are always already discursively constituted by (other) subjects of knowledge, and there cannot be a clear separation of subject from object. This point is linked to the feminist contention against the individualized conception of the knower in traditional epistemology.

Feminists have also interrogated the privileging of abstract universal knowledge over practical, localized knowledges. Code describes this as "the method of abstracting simplified (and hence clarified) exemplary knowledge to demonstrate the possibility, verifiability, and appropriate strategies for justifying knowledge claims" (1991: 111). Since there is an emphasis upon the knower as an isolated individual, the specific, social identity of different knowers, or what Code describes as the "privileges of class, race, ethnicity, and gender," are considered as "irrelevant" to the research process and more importantly to the final abstracted product or knowledge (ibid.: 27).

Closely related to this privileging of abstraction, several feminist scholars have also pointed to the epistemological priority attributed to the context of justification over the context of discovery. In other words, it matters more whether and how the final end product can be justified as knowledge than how that knowledge was produced and by whom. Longino points to the philosophical distinction and privileging of the justification of knowledge claims against the process and context of discovery, which involve certain methods of investigation whose very selection over other methods and whose specific application "limit what we get to know about" (1993: 101). Furthermore, she presses for considering the importance of "both the context of assumptions that supports reasoning and the social and cultural context that supports scientific inquiry" (1990: 219).

Finally, feminist critiques have focused upon how traditional epistemology upholds natural sciences and the scientific method as paradigmatic for other branches and methods of knowledge production. Instead, some feminists have insisted upon crucial differences between knowing things and knowing people. Code would insist on how, in trying to know other human beings, "knowers are kept on their cognitive toes" (1991: 38). She therefore argues that the social sciences offer a better paradigm of responsible and rigorous knowledge production than the natural sciences. From a different angle, Haraway has argued for a feminist way of knowing which grants agency not only to other persons but also to non-human objects of knowledge such as animals and machines. She adds: "The point is paradigmatically clear in critical approaches to the social and human sciences where the agency of people studied itself transforms the entire project of producing social theory" (1991: 198).

The Incompatibility of Feminism and Epistemology

There are two very different arguments for the untenability of a "feminist epistemology" insofar as feminism and epistemology are seen as constitutively incompatible. On the one hand, there is the resistance from traditional or mainstream epistemologists who find that feminism politicizes and particularizes epistemology, which is supposed to be devoted to the project of a *general* theory of knowledge and standards for justification. Rather than a general theory of knowledge, feminist work in epistemology foregrounds "the impact of the social status as well as the sexed body of the knower upon the production of knowledge" (Alcoff and Potter 1993: 2). This incompatibility results in a "contradictory pull between the concrete and the universal" (ibid.: 1). On the other hand, Code argues that the field of epistemology proper is so thoroughly androcentric that feminists should abandon it in favor of producing knowledges that are practically useful for women. In other words, there can be no "feminist epistemology" within the inherited terms of producing and justifying knowledge in traditional epistemology, which Code (1991) refers to alternatively with philosophy as a discipline.

There have been several attempts to situate feminist epistemology as part of a branch of what is referred to as social epistemology, which considers the significance of social forces, including the social identity of the knower and the context of discovery, to the production of knowledge (Longino 1990). Nelson has argued for feminists to *not* give up on the field of epistemology proper and the philosophy of science because "the theories developed within these enterprises play a significant role in shaping and legitimating methodologies, self-understandings, and knowledge claims of various institutions granted cognitive authority (the sciences, academic disciplines, and other institutions that define the grounds for and shape social policy)." She adds that these institutions "have had deleterious consequences for women and others denied cognitive authority" and that an abandonment of epistemology "threatens to minimize the force of feminist critiques aimed at revealing those consequences and identifying their sources and implications" (1995: 43).

Kinds of Feminist Epistemology

Despite both traditional rejections of feminist arguments and feminist skepticism toward the field of epistemology proper, there have been various attempts to formulate what are considered distinctively feminist epistemologies. Notably articulated by Sandra Harding (1987b), most taxonomies of feminist epistemologies delineate three in particular: feminist empiricism, feminist standpoint theory, and feminist postmodernism. I will review these three in further detail.

Feminist empiricism identifies the sexism and androcentrism in traditionally empiricist accounts of women and gender. Empiricism upholds direct observation, and logical analysis can serve as a reliable foundation of knowledge. However, prevailing accounts of biological male superiority or universal male dominance are biased insofar as they ignore or fail to consider empirical data to the contrary. Unlike traditional empiricism, then, feminist empiricism holds that the social identity of the researcher as well as the "context of discovery" are important in shaping the conclusions and additional hypothesis drawn from the research. However, feminist empiricism diagnoses the problem with existing scientific accounts as one of sexist bias on the part of particular researchers rather than the general methods and methodological norms of scientific inquiry. Consequently, the solution is to remove these biases and the very methods of science can aid in the purging of these biases. Feminist empiricism also holds that the added presence of women researchers will lead to less biased research findings since women are more likely to detect and correct androcentric biases of traditional empirical research. It matters *who* is conducting the research but not necessarily *how* they are doing so as long as they follow legitimate methods.

Rather than a wholesale endorsement, "feminist empiricism" better describes various feminist critiques and modifications of traditional empiricism. In endorsing "a modest, pared down empiricism, one that shuns metaphysical meaning postulates and restricts itself to epistemology," Longino proposes what she calls a "contextual empiricism," which is attentive to the "background assumptions" that guide the definition of evidence and how they express the shared and embedded values of a specific scientific community (1990: 215–16). Longino further adds that these assumptions and values are the products of social activity and interaction. Following from Longino, Cudd also upholds a "contextual empiricism" that is accompanied by "a policy of multiculturalism within science and a policy of race and gender equality in the society as a whole" (1998: 51).

Feminist standpoint theory places even greater epistemological significance upon the social position of the researcher in the knowledge produced. Articulated by Dorothy Smith, Nancy Hartsock, Hilary Rose, and Patricia Hill Collins, feminist standpoint theory combines elements of Marxism and object-relations theory to argue that knowledge is not abstract or neutral, but differentially available to different social actors and scholars. Because knowledge is grounded materially in lived experiences, those in the position of the oppressed have access to a clearer, less biased understanding of social realities since they are less likely to benefit materially from the continued existence of the relations of oppression. Smith (1987) argued that the local and everyday lived realities of women produce a unique "women's standpoint" that cannot be captured by sociology's abstract masculinity. Collins (1986, 1990) extended this critique of a specifically disciplinary epistemology in proposing a unique black women's standpoint. Drawing attention to the multiplicity of social differences and inequalities, Collins argued, "It is more likely for Black women as members of an oppressed group to have critical insights into the condition of our own oppression. . . . [W]e are the only group that has experienced race, gender, and class oppression as Black women experience them" (1990: 33–4). These experiences enable the formulation of what she calls a distinctive "Black feminist thought." However, as Collins is careful to clarify, black feminist thought is itself partial and "situated" and so the knowledges of groups that occupy other standpoints are necessary for a fuller critical account of social structures and social relations. Feminist standpoint theorists have repeatedly stressed that this is not an epistemological relativism since such a feminist standpoint is gained not only from the mere *experience of* oppression but in a conscious and active *struggle against* oppression. Hartsock (1983) thus clarified that a feminist standpoint is a "practical achievement," which is "scientifically preferable" to the knowledges produced from the standpoint of the privileged or the oppressor.

Since its formulation in the 1980s, there have been several feminist critiques and revisions of feminist standpoint theory. Haraway has critiqued the neat correspondence of being and knowing, of identity and knowledge in feminist standpoint theory. Rather than an enabling starting point for critical thinking, Haraway points to the dangers of assuming the coherence and unmediated knowability of one's identity if it entails forgetting the contingency of "being" whereby "self-knowledge requires a semiotic-material technology linking meanings and bodies" (1991: 192). Upholding instead the picture of a "split and contradictory self," she clarifies, "Splitting, not being, is the privileged image for feminist epistemologies of scientific knowledge" (ibid.: 193). The presumed correspondence and possible stability, even if a practical achievement, of being, seeing, and knowing in one unified subject militates against the possibilities for multiple and flexible solidarities that require an ability "to see together without claiming to be another" (ibid.).

Harding has attempted to avoid the possible relativism and essentialism of feminist standpoint theory by suggesting the efficacy of multiple standpoints rather than a singular standpoint. Since the privileged lives of those in the ruling groups prevent their members from critically seeing the hierarchical relations of ruling, Harding (1991) proposes that rather than seeing standpoint as an end point or final achievement of the oppressed, all of us must "start off from" the experiences of oppressed groups or "marginal lives" on the way to a more broadened social analysis that is able to take many different standpoints into consideration. Clarifying that the goal of standpoint theory is not confined to revealing the truth of the lives of the oppressed group, Harding reframes the work of Smith as "enabl(ing) us to understand women's lives, men's lives, and the relations between the two" (1995: 342). She also emphasizes that feminist standpoint theory does not argue that feminist knowledges proceed naturally and directly from women's experiences, and that only women can produce a feminist standpoint and feminist knowledges, since "Men, too, can learn to start their thought from women's lives" (ibid.: 343). Here we see a broadening of feminist knowledge beyond "women's ways of knowing" and "women's experiences" to something that encompasses male knowers who seek critical awareness about gender.

A major criticism of feminist standpoint theory has focused upon the lack of consideration about differences and hierarchies among women or, for that matter, any collectivity delineated by a single axis of identification and inequality such as race, class, or nationality. Hekman (1997) attributes the debates around differences among women as a significant force in the decline of feminist standpoint theory in the 1980s along with the decline of Marxism and the emergence of postmodernism and post-structuralism. As Longino narrates: "Feminists from racial and ethnic minorities compelled the advocates of standpoint theory to recognize that the material conditions and experiences of women differed significantly to undermine any notion of a unified standpoint" (1999: 338). Several feminists have since formulated and refined this picture of several different, overlapping, and contradictory social and cultural positions and consequently epistemological positions. More recently, Mohanty elaborates upon feminist standpoint theory to posit that "the particular standpoint of poor indigenous and Third World/South women provide the most inclusive viewing of systemic power" (2003: 511).

Longino has identified two specific problems with feminist standpoint theory, which others have also pointed to. First, she asks how one could adjudicate among various feminist standpoints when "Women occupy many social locations in a racially and socially stratified society" (1993: 107). Longino further critiques the move to pluralize the concept of a singularly shared and privileged feminist standpoint when she points out: "Standpoints as multiple and assumable become more like perspectives and the materiality of the original standpoint theory is lost" (1999: 334). Second, there was the matter of its disciplinary leanings. Given that feminist standpoint theory was "developed by and for social scientists," Longino adds, "it has been difficult to see what its implications for the natural sciences might be," especially given their "distorted epistemic ideal – objectivity as radical detachment" (ibid.: 334). Arguing that the alternative to this masculinist bias in the natural sciences need not necessarily invoke feminine differences or a specific standpoint available to women and unavailable to men, Longino supports Fox-Keller's object-relations theory-inflected proposal for a "dynamic objectivity," which "does not seek power over phenomena but acknowledges instead the ways in which phenomena are complexly interdependent." Longino underscores how "Dynamic objectivity is not presented as a typically feminine epistemological orientation but as an alternative to an epistemological orientation associated with both masculine psychological development and masculinist gender ideology" (ibid.: 108).

Harding (1987b) characterizes both feminist empiricism and feminist standpoint theory as "transitional epistemologies," since each is invested in retaining certain elements of traditional epistemologies – namely empiricism and Marxism – even as they critique and seek to remedy certain androcentric biases and blind spots. Harding argues furthermore that one need not choose between feminist empiricism and feminist standpoint theory, especially since they are critical and radical departures from empiricism and Marxism. Choosing one or the other may entail an unnecessary and unproductive alliance with one or the other of these two androcentric frameworks. Unlike the claims of both feminist empiricism and feminist standpoint theory to be advancing the cause of objectivity in science, feminist postmodernism is skeptical of the reach for scientific objectivity itself. Feminist postmodernism further resists any universalizing narratives of reason or authenticity. Harding identifies two strands of feminist postmodernism, one influenced by continental theories of semiotics, deconstruction, and psychoanalysis, and another manifesting itself in "writings of women of color." I will explore these two forces separately.

Hekman (1990) was an early proponent of the usefulness of postmodernism for a rethinking of feminist epistemology. Focusing specifically on feminist work in the social sciences, Hekman has argued that they have made a limited intervention because they still subscribe to the modernist presupposition of an autonomous, knowing subject and the possibilities for objectivity that animates its masculinist epistemology. Instead, she argues that postmodernism, represented for her largely by the work of Michel Foucault, can produce two important insights for feminism: (1) that the replacement of the masculinist biases of social science epistemologies with a feminist perspective will *not* produce greater objectivity; (2) that the pursuit and defense of this masculinist version of objectivity in the social sciences bespeaks a "fear" of admitting that the social sciences are "feminine" discourses especially in contrast to the "harder" natural and physical sciences. Feminists then contribute to this unequal epistemological gendering by subscribing to the possibilities for a scientific objectivity modeled on the natural sciences. Relying on the Foucauldian argument that what distinguished the modern episteme from classical episteme is that humans are now both the subjects and objects of knowledge, thus making knowledge a field of power and contestation over the human, Hekman argues that the androcentric social sciences have compromised further their special epistemological claim to know the "social" by only being able to examine a part, a gendered part of it.

Other feminists have been more hesitant about adopting postmodernism wholesale. In "Epistemologies of postmodernism," Benhabib (1990) outlines the postmodernist rejection of the modern episteme as "an episteme of domination," but disagrees with Lyotard in that she advocates "formulating minimal criteria of validity for our discursive and political practices" (ibid.: 125). Bordo identifies a "feminist gender skepticism" or "a new skepticism about and the use of gender as an analytical category" as the result of "a recent academic marriage which has brought indigenous feminist concerns over the ethnocentrisms and unconscious racial biases of gender theory into a theoretical alliance (a highly programmatic appropriation of) the more historicist, politically oriented wing of poststructuralist thought (e.g., Foucault, Lyotard)" (1990: 135). In a similar alignment of "writings by women of color" with feminist postmodernism, Harding characterizes the interventionary critiques of "women of color" too generically as arguing that there are "many stories that different women tell about the different knowledge they have" (1987a: 188). While this body of work is sometimes included as part of feminist standpoint theory and sometimes as part of feminist postmodernism, I would categorize their sustained critiques of the racism and ethnocentrism of feminism as another strand of feminist epistemologies, which is sometimes referred to as "difference feminism."

Bodies and Knowledges

Arguing that "[t]he attribution of epistemic privilege to socially marginalized subjects is not a feminist innovation," Bar On (1993: 85) makes an important distinction between the Marxist attribution of epistemic privilege to the proletariat and feminist standpoint theory's privileging of women. Unlike the lower-middle class, which has some investments in capitalism and the "dangerous class" of the "chronically unemployed," the proletariat is distinguished by how "its social marginality is a function of [its] economic centrality" (ibid.: 86). Bar On argues that feminists like Hartsock who have attempted to apply this Marxist model to the situation of women have not argued similarly that "women's social marginality is a function of women's centrality in a systematically organized relation with men," thus leading to a different calculus in which the degree of one's social marginalization determines the degree of one's epistemic privilege. This, however, leads straight to the problem of accounting for a multiplicity of marginalizations among women. Either one could assert the epistemic privilege of one kind of subject over another, of one kind of marginalization over another, or one could argue that all subjects are equally marginalized, which begs the question that Bar On asks: "Does epistemic privilege matter?" (ibid.: 89). One recurrent tactic exercised by feminists has been to authorize the knowledge or standpoint of those groups of women who are deemed as most marginalized from some implicit center so that "epistemic privilege then becomes a function of the distance from the center" (ibid.). Bar On cites the claiming of just such a privileged consciousness in the work of Marilyn Frye (for lesbians) and Gayle Rubin (for women who practice non-normative forms of sexual relations). This perceived distance from a center can be quantified and compounded when one takes into account multiple oppressions, since "the multiple ways in which a person can be socially marginalized can be seen as cumulative." In this problematic assumption of a single center and a grounding of epistemic privilege in "identity and practices," Bar On cautions against the epistemic privileging of any one body or group based solely upon their greater marginalization. Even as it might authorize some women to speak about and for themselves, "an authority they do not have if everyone is equally capable to know them and their situation" (ibid.: 95), this logic of epistemic privilege could also delimit the range of knowledges that can be claimed by the multiply marginalized, such as "women of color" who can speak with authority only when they speak for themselves and about their experiences, but not necessarily about any broader matters of knowledge. For instance, Collins's 1986 essay, "Learning from the Outsider Within," is most widely invoked and often aligned with feminist standpoint theory in its insistence upon the uniqueness of a black woman's standpoint. However, often overlooked in more recent reviews of the field of feminist epistemology is the essay's critique of the disciplinary protocols of sociology.

There have been some efforts to point to the epistemological significance and innovations of the interventions of "women of color" and the intersectional analysis they have formulated and revised. Harding characterizes this contribution of "women of color" as a "matrix theory" that "enables us to think how each of us has a determinate social location in the matrix of social relations that is constituted by gender, class, race, sexuality and whatever other macro forces shape our particular part of the social order" (1995: 344). However, this reformulated theory is still attributed to "women of color and others who *started off their thought from women of color's lives*" (ibid.; original italics). More recently, casting "multiculturalism" as a "cognitive virtue of scientific practice" that can lead to "better science," indeed to a more objective science, Cudd attempts to challenge the prevalent dismissal of such interventions by "feminists and marginalized others" as "merely a practical point about doing science, not an epistemic point" (1998: 59). Instead, she argues that the social identity of the people who do science matters epistemologically to the kind of knowledges that are produced. However, she still emphasizes the determining significance of who the scientists are, since "the minority and women scientists themselves will be more likely to recognize the false, prejudiced assumptions about race and gender that have lurked in the background, guiding scientists as they interpret evidence and build theories" (ibid.). Noting the disciplinary resistance to acknowledging the philosophical and epistemological significance of the writings of Minh-ha Trinh, Patricia Hill Collins, and Gloria Anzaldúa, Nye (1998) makes a similar proposal to include these writings, especially as they have inspired feminist philosophers on questions of knowledge. If "feminist epistemology" has moved on from a focus on "women" to "gender" and onto "feminist" interrogations of knowledge in general, it appears that the figure of embodied women lingers in reference to "women of color."

A similar embodiment can be seen in another recent effort to expand the boundaries of feminist knowledges through global, international, postcolonial, and transnational framings. As with earlier framings of the "writings of women of color," there is a tendency to include this geographically "other" constituency of women and feminists in terms that clearly outline their outsidedness to epistemology and philosophy, thus preserving their disciplinary borders as the sites of a general investigation and theorization of knowledge while defending against charges of racist exclusion and ethnocentrism. In their editorial introduction to a volume titled, *Decentering the Center: Philosophy for a Multicultural, Postcolonial, and Feminist World*, Narayan and Harding acknowledge "the extent to which feminist philosophy must and does draw on the texts, data, and concerns of work in other disciplines, responding to the challenges they pose and the illuminations they provide" (2000: viii). These other disciplines include political science, social geography, economics, and psychology. Later on, they write: "Multicultural and postcolonial feminist writings often do not look much like contemporary philosophic work in either their styles or their concerns. Nevertheless, many of these writings have contributed important insights and analyses to feminist philosophy" (ibid.: xi). Code (1998) discerns an "implicit" epistemological argument for how to "think globally" in the work of Mohanty's 1997 essay. Thus, a disciplinary boundary, which is also a racialized and national boundary, is maintained around philosophy and its feminist disciples.

While feminist interventions in the fields of traditional epistemology and philosophy are important and necessary, I propose a broader framing of feminist epistemologies along several registers. First, there needs to be a more critical examination of how different feminist knowledges are bound by particular disciplinary protocols, which are historically shifting and institutionally constrained. Even though the field of epistemology proper lays claim to a study of knowledge in general, there is no single, properly disciplined space for such interrogations of the power/knowledge nexus of disciplinarity itself. Second, such a critical understanding of disciplinarity would also enable attention to be given to a greater range of feminist knowledges and methodologies in the arts and humanities. It may further assist in conceiving of innovative multimedia understandings of "feminist epistemologies" beyond the social and natural sciences. For instance, the visual arts and musicology offer provocative alternative modes of knowing and experiencing gender. Foster (1998) has proposed choreography as a useful prism for conceptualizing gender as performance. Third, rather than figuring epistemological diversity in terms of the bodies and identities of different women and men, I propose that feminists study the interdisciplinary fields of Queer Studies, Ethnic Studies, Critical Race Studies, and the various area studies as specific epistemological formations that have shaped and will shape the future of what counts as feminist knowledges. These interdisciplinary studies offer a rich archive of methodologies and epistemologies for thinking about a range of women, genders, and feminisms beyond the traditional disciplines. Their simultaneous and conjoined investigations of history, culture, and political economy can critically re-member the partiality of disciplinary divisions and their knowledge-making practices. This critical engagement in a broader project of interrogating what counts as knowledge within and across particular disciplines and interdisciplinary fields is one way in which a critical Gender Studies could distinguish itself from the older Women's Studies.

References

Alcoff, L. and Potter, E. (1993) "Introduction: When Feminism Meets Epistemology," in L. Alcoff and E. Potter (eds.), *Feminist Epistemologies* (New York: Routledge).

Bar On, B.-A. (1993) "Marginality and Epistemic Privilege," in L. Alcoff and E. Potter (eds.), *Feminist Epistemologies* (New York: Routledge).

Benhabib, S. (1990) "Epistemologies of Postmodernism: A Rejoinder to Jean-Francois Lyotard," in L. J. Nicholson (ed.), *Feminism/Postmodernism* (New York: Routledge).

Bordo, S. (1990) "Feminism, Postmodernism, and Gender-Skepticism," in L. J. Nicholson (ed.), *Feminism/Postmodernism* (New York: Routledge).

Code, L. (1991) *What Can She Know? Feminist Theory and the Construction of Knowledge* (Ithaca, NY: Cornell University Press).

Code, L. (1998) "How to Think Globally: Stretching the Limits of Imagination," *Hypatia* 13/2: 73–86.

Collins, P. H. (1986) "Learning from the Outsider Within: The Sociological Significance of Black Feminist Thought," *Social Problems* 33: S14–S30.

Collins, P. H. (1990) *Black Feminist Thought: Knowledge, Consciousness, and the Politics of Empowerment* (Boston: Unwin, Hyman).

Cudd, A. (1998) "Multiculturalism as a Cognitive Virtue of Scientific Practice," *Hypatia* 13/3: 43–61.

Foster, S. L. (1998) "Choreographies of Gender," *Signs* 24/1: 1–33.

Haraway, D. (1991) *Simians, Cyborgs, and Women: The Reinvention of Nature* (New York: Routledge).

Harding, S. (1987a) "Conclusion: Epistemological Questions," in S. Harding (ed.), *Feminism and Methodology* (Bloomington, IN: Indiana University Press).

Harding, S. (ed.) (1987b) *Feminism and Methodology* (Bloomington, IN: Indiana University Press).

Harding, S. (1987c) "Introduction: Is There a Feminist Method?" in S. Harding (ed.), *Feminism and Methodology* (Bloomington, IN: Indiana University Press).

Harding, S. (1991) *Whose Science? Whose Knowledge? Thinking from Women's Lives* (Ithaca: Cornell University Press).

Harding, S. (1993) "Rethinking Standpoint Epistemology: 'What is Strong Objectivity'?" in L. Alcoff and E. Potter (eds.), *Feminist Epistemologies* (New York: Routledge).

Harding, S. (1995) "'Strong Objectivity': A Response to the New Objectivity Question," *Synthese* 104: 331–49.

Hartsock, N. C. M. (1983) "The Feminist Standpoint: Developing the Ground for a Specifically Feminist Historical Materialism," in S. Harding and M. B. Hintikka (eds.), *Discovering Reality: Feminist Perspectives on Epistemology, Metaphysics, Methodology, and Philosophy of Science* (Boston: D. Reidel Publishing Company).

Hekman, S. J. (1990) *Gender and Knowledge: Elements of a Postmodern Feminism* (Cambridge: Polity).

Hekman, S. J. (1997) "Truth and Method: Feminist Standpoint Theory Revisited," *Signs* 22/2: 341–66.

Longino, H. (1990) *Science as Social Knowledge: Values and Objectivity in Scientific Inquiry* (Princeton: Princeton University Press).

Longino, H. (1993) "Subjects, Power and Knowledge: Description and Prescription in Feminist Philosophies of Science," in L. Alcoff and E. Potter (eds.), *Feminist Epistemologies* (New York: Routledge).

Longino, H. (1999) "Feminist Epistemology," in J. Greco and E. Sosa (eds.), *The Blackwell Guide to Epistemology* (Malden, MA: Blackwell Publishers).

Mohanty, C. (1997) "Women Workers and Capitalist Scripts: Ideologies of Domination, Common Interests, and the Politics of Solidarity," in M. J. Alexander and C. P. Mohanty (eds.), *Feminist Genealogies, Colonial Legacies, Democratic Futures* (New York: Routledge).

Mohanty, C. (2003) "'Under Western Eyes' Revisited: Feminist Solidarity Through Anticapitalist Struggles," *Signs* 28/12: 499–535.

Narayan, U. and Harding, S. (2000) "Introduction," in U. Narayan and S. Harding (eds.), *Decentering the Center: Philosophy for a Multicultural, Postcolonial, and Feminist World* (Bloomington, IN: Indiana University Press).

Nelson, L. H. (1993) "Epistemological Communities," in L. Alcoff and E. Potter (eds.), *Feminist Epistemologies* (New York: Routledge).

Nelson, L. H. (1995) "The Very Idea of Feminist Epistemology," *Hypatia* 10/3: 31–50.

Nye, A. (1998) "It's not Philosophy!" *Hypatia* 13/3: 107–16.

Potter, E. (1993) "Gender and Epistemic Negotiation," in L. Alcoff and E. Potter (eds.), *Feminist Epistemologies* (New York: Routledge).

Rose, H. (1987) "Hand, Brain, Heart: A Feminist Epistemology of the Natural Sciences," in S. Harding and J. F. O'Barr *Sex and Scientific Inquiry* (Chicago: University of Chicago Press).

Scott, J. W. (1992) "Experience," in J. Butler and J. W. Scott (eds.), *Feminists Theorize the Political* (New York: Routledge).

Smith, D. (1987) "Women's Perspective as a Radical Critique of Sociology," in S. Harding (ed.), *Feminism and Methodology* (Bloomington, IN: Indiana University Press).

CHAPTER SIX

Genetic Sex

Amâde M'charek

Introduction

Biological sex has long been considered a stable, universal factor, the biological counterpart of gender. While this distinction is easily taken for granted, I learned otherwise when I entered the laboratories of the Human Genome Diversity Project. By way of introduction, let me first say something general about this project. During my study of the Human Genome Diversity Project (Diversity Project), I was struck by its mutual absence and presence (M'charek 2000). The Diversity Project was initiated in 1991 by population geneticists who aimed to map human genetic variation on a global level. Their aim was an internationally coordinated scientific endeavor to sample and map genetic variation between populations all over the world, and to reconstruct the migration history of humans. The Project soon became controversial because of an emphasis placed on "isolated populations" and "indigenous people." It was associated with bad science and scientific racism. In debates about the Diversity Project, it seemed to me that the Project contributed to organized criticism not only of this particular initiative, but also of other practices such as the patenting of genes derived from the cell material of indigenous people (see Lock 2001; Haraway 1997; Hayden 1998). Thus not only was the aim of the Project a globalized approach to genetic diversity; its effect was also a globally organized criticism.

However, when I began studying the Diversity Project, focusing less on these debates and more on how scientists studied genetic diversity in laboratories, I started to ask myself some questions. Where is the project? And how is it practiced as such? The geneticists I talked to were indeed conducting diversity studies, but none of them seemed to be involved in the project, even though their names would appear on lists of the organization and I would find them attending conferences of the Diversity Project. They preferred not to view their work as part of this project but treated it in isolation.[1] It seemed to me that the "global" as an endeavor of the Diversity Project had become a contaminated category.

There is a second category that is contaminated in particular contexts: biological sex. Especially within the field of Gender Studies, since the nature/culture debates in the 1970s and the sex/gender distinction in the 1980s, little attention has been paid to "biological" sex. Differences between men and women were best understood as cultural. Gender became the field of study, debates, and interventions. Biological sex remained the universal but not so relevant reference. Some scholars, however, suggested that the issue of biological sex is much too important to be left in the realm of scientific discourse, and much too complex to be treated as a stable reference (Butler 1990; Haraway 1991a, 1991b; Mol 1985). Whereas gender was treated as the contextual, constructed, and mediated category, biological sex became its universal and unified other.

My aim is to locate these contaminated versions of the global (genetic sex and the Diversity Project) in scientific practice.[2] I will for this purpose enter a laboratory where genetic diversity is being studied. I focus on practices where studies of genetic lineage are at issue and where a two-sexed model is applied: the mitochondrial DNA and the Y-chromosome. The main topic is genetic sex, but the analyses will shed light on how the Diversity Project is practiced in laboratories.

What is Genetic Sex?

Human geneticists know the sexes as XX and XY. Critics of this binary scheme have argued that the XX and XY scheme fails to pay any attention to culture. My aim in this chapter is to show that neither of these approaches takes into account the practices of genetics. Difference between the sexes is neither a natural quality embodied in individuals nor a cultural additive. Rather, it is an effect of interfering practices where the sexes are deemed relevant. Thus, instead of taking culture as the fact after biology, I view culture as part and parcel of biology, and examine sex differences in the practices of genetics.

Feminist scholars have delivered a large corpus of literature showing that science – and especially biology – is, just like any other practice, gendered. They have shown that it is gendered in terms of who does the research, revealing a male bias and bringing to the surface the contributions of women in science. Others have examined the language of science, providing insight into hierarchies in the designation of agency, and about biases between objects categorized as masculine and others as feminine. Still others have considered scientific methods, arguing that these could be seen as masculine. This research showed that methods establish a distinction and a hierarchy between a (masculine) subject of research, namely the scientist, and a (feminine) object of research, namely nature.[3] These approaches have led to one basic feminist claim concerning sexual differences: "gender" can be found everywhere.[4] "You just have to put on gender glasses to see it," as one scholar once put it to me. Once I had been in the laboratories, however, the sexual distinction I found seemed banal, the kind of distinction that I could have learned about in any other environment. And I saw nothing specific to *genetic sex* in laboratory practices. Population geneticists' accounts of human history talk about men and women and their different migration histories. But how does it *materialize* in laboratories and where can it be traced?

The strategy I propose and will follow here is not one of putting on "gender glasses," as that approach does not necessarily set the focus appropriately and could render what is looked at oblique. Moreover, putting such glasses on metaphorically exposes the wearer to the danger not only of predefining – if not essentializing – the sexes and what counts as sex differences, but also of developing a blind spot for the irrelevance of the sexes in particular practices.

Instead, I follow a strategy proposed by Annemarie Mol, Donna Haraway, and others, a strategy of locating objects in practices. From this perspective, a universal claim, such as the claim that sex differences are universal and thus also part of genetics, gives rise to these questions: where is genetic sex and how is it performed (Haraway 1991c; Mol 1985, 1990, 2002)? The strategy of locating enables us to map the specific contours of a universal claim in particular contexts and to make practices visible in which such a claim does not hold. For this purpose I will consider two practices: the practice of genealogy and the specific ways in which it is tied to studies of genetic lineage; and the practice of DNA and how this is involved in studies of genetic diversity. However, it is important to emphasize that differences between these sites are analytical rather than ontological. The differences do not correspond to the classic division between "mental labor" and "manual labor." They rather point to a gradient of technologies, spaces, and problem-solving procedures that are important in either practice.

Archaeology of the Human Genome: Facts and Artifacts of Genealogy

"Archaeology of the Human Genome" is part of the title of a paper by population geneticists Arndt von Haeseler, Antti Sajantila, and Svante Pääbo (1996). This paper – let us call it the Archaeology paper – provides a literature review and argues for the potential of genetic data in reconstructing human history, especially when the two-sexed model of mitochondrial DNA and Y-chromosomal DNA are considered. The paper opens as follows:

> Many of us, especially in our youth, are interested in the lives of our parents and immediate family; then again, as members of a particular group or population, we like to know about the life of our ancestors; finally, as members of the human race, we are fascinated with the question of human origins. [. . .] However, early humans left traces of their activities not only in the form of their bones and artefacts. They also passed on to us their genomes. Every genome is made up of about three billion base-pairs, several of which experience mutations in each

generation, and, as the way in which these mutations accumulate in populations are influenced by how populations expand, contract, split and merge, the study of genetic variation has the potential to yield a great deal of information regarding our history.

Under the heading "A bit of theory," it goes on:

All individuals have parents, and some individuals have the same parent(s). The consequence of these trivial facts is that as genealogical lineages in a population trace back over generations, they will occasionally coalesce to common ancestors. There will be fewer and fewer ancestors as one goes back. Eventually, all female lineages will trace back through a series of consecutive mothers to one single mother and all male lineages will similarly trace back to a single father, that is, the most recent common ancestors (MRCAs) on the maternal and paternal side. . . . If the demographic history of a population is unknown, it can be reconstructed from the patterns of nucleotide substitution in the genome. DNA sequences from mitochondrial (mt) genome and those from the majority of the Y-chromosome are particularly useful as they are passed on without recombination from mother to daughter and from father to son. Consequently these sequences can be traced back directly to the genealogical maternal or paternal MRCAs. Autosomal DNA sequences, which are inherited through both males and females and occur in two copies per individual, trace back to "biparental" MRCAs that are on the average four times as old as maternal and paternal MRCAs. (Haeseler et al. 1996: 135)

Genealogy, Genetic Lineages, and Technologies of the Sexes

The choice of the term "archaeology" in the title of the paper quoted indicates that genetic similarities and differences come with a story about the past.[5] A story about populations. Much as archaeological artifacts are viewed as records of human history, mutations in DNA and the way these are distributed among populations are treated as records of population histories. On the assumption that all populations have one origin, genetic differences in particular can be read as events in the past, contributing to stories about when and how populations diverged or merged, reduced in size or grew. As the quote indicates, mtDNA and the Y-chromosome are considered very useful for studying these events. Especially because neither recombines (i.e., they are inherited unchanged from mother or father), these DNA systems represent the maternal and the paternal line of inheritance, which can be traced back to one ancestral mother and one ancestral father. Before addressing these two systems, let us take a closer look at how genealogy is practiced in studies of genetic lineage and at the relevance of sex in these studies.

The trivial fact of genealogy mentioned in the Archaeology paper, namely the fact that all individuals have parents, demarcates an involved relation between genealogy and genetic lineage. From a genealogical perspective, going back in time means to unfold a greater complexity in biological kinship. It makes more and more individuals appear as part of "the family," as ancestors of a specific individual (see, e.g., Strathern 1992: esp. 83–4). From the perspective of an individual, this amelioration of ancestors can be represented by the form of a V. While the intersection between the two arms of this letter indicates a contemporary moment in time where there is one individual, their divergence points deeper and deeper into history, making progressively more ancestors appear, represented by the space between the two arms. By contrast, however, the Archaeology paper contends that there "will be fewer and fewer ancestors as one goes back." This suggests that from the perspective of genetic lineage, the genealogical V should rather be turned upside down, to become a Λ instead. At issue here is not an ever-growing family but an ever-shrinking "family" the farther one goes back in time. But how should we understand this type of genealogy, how should we understand the occurrence of a Λ?[6]

Although the opening sentence of the Archaeology paper evokes the idea that population genetics is interested in individuals and where they come from, groups of individuals are the field's main objects of study. Populations. Population genetics studies how groups of individuals relate to each other and reconstructs the development of these relations through history. Thus the object of study, many individuals and not one, explains the Λ. The space at the bottom (the largest divergence between the two arms) stands for a group of individuals, a population in a contemporary moment in time. But what is the relevance of Λ and *why* does not each of these individuals have his or her own V-shaped genealogy? The answer lies in *how* geneticists study individuals and for what purpose.

Geneticists do not study all genetic material, but focus on very limited fragments of DNA. Their aim is a study of lineage for particular parts of the DNA. Tracing the lineage of a DNA fragment, geneticists take into account only those "parents" who contributed by passing it on. Others are left out. Doing so, the farther geneticists go back in time, the fewer ancestors and the more lineage they can presuppose. Ultimately, so the quote indicates, this genetic information coalesces in two ancestors: a mother and a father. While V stands for the genealogy of an individual and in the context of DNA would require studying large amounts of genetic information, Λ stands for a specific type of genealogy, one that has one DNA fragment as its topic and so helps establish genetic lineage. Whereas V is about how the individual is connected *to* predecessors, Λ is about how individuals are connected to each other *via* predecessors. This indicates the importance of the fact that all individuals have parents in studies of lineage, and attributes a specific meaning to that fact. Although "parenthood" is pivotal for studies of genetic lineages, parents become necessary passage points of a DNA fragment. They are relevant not so much as individual males and females but as the means of producing lineage. Thus, in studies of genetic lineage the sexes are not relevant as male and female parents but as sources of reproduction and as passage points through which genetic lineage can be established.

The Archaeology paper states that mtDNA and the greater part of the Y-chromosomal DNA are especially appreciated for studying genetic lineage, because they escape recombination. Let us briefly ponder these two systems. Unlike the Y-chromosome, mtDNA is to be found in the cytoplasm (the medium surrounding the nucleus) and not in the nucleus. It is passed on via the mother only. Males and females receive their cytoplasm and thus inherit their mtDNAs from their mothers. Males cannot pass it on to their offspring. This system of inheritance accounts for a maternal lineage. The Y-chromosome shows a different pattern of inheritance that accounts for a paternal lineage. Only males carry Y-chromosomes and pass them on to their sons. From the perspective of the individual, however, there are other differences between the two systems. In the mtDNA approach there is no difference between males and females. They both have mtDNA. But from the perspective of the Y-chromosome, male and female individuals differ. Only males carry this chromosome. What does this difference between the two DNA systems tell us about the relevance of sex in studies of genetic lineage?

The story of mtDNA in particular indicates that geneticists are not interested in the sex of the individual. Even though males do have them, their mtDNAs are considered to be part of the female system of inheritance. Interestingly enough, the Archaeology paper even excludes males from that system. It is stated there that mtDNA is passed on "from mother to daughter." This suggests that fathers are analogously acknowledged not for the fact that they *carry* a Y-chromosome, but for the fact that they *pass it on* to their sons. Thus, in practices of genetic lineage sex is performed not so much as a quality of an individual but rather as a pattern of inheritance. Sex differences are not located in individuals but in genetic kinship.

This specific relevance of sex can be viewed further if we take the most recent common ancestors (MRCAs) into account. The paper mentions three categories of MRCA: one single mtDNA mother, one single Y-chromosomal father, and a third type of MRCA consisting of many single autosomal "biparents" ("autosomal" refers to the 44 chromosomes located in the nucleus and inherited from both parents). Both maternal (mtDNA) MRCA and paternal (Y-chromosome) MRCA are estimated to have occurred about 200,000 years ago; the "biparental" MRCAs, however, may be four times older, so the Archaeology paper suggests. This implies that from a genetic perspective, our MRCAs do not necessarily have to coincide with individuals or with actual parents. From this perspective, MRCAs can best be seen as partial products of genetic lineage. In line with this, DNA is handled as a variety of technologies which, together with a Λ-type genealogy, contributes to those lineages. Moreover, as I have argued in the case of genetic lineage, genetic sex is performed not as a quality of individuals but rather as a pattern of inheritance or – better – a technology of lineage. Similarly, DNA is treated not so much as an essential feature of individuals but as a technology "embodying" different systems for producing lineage leading to different MRCAs.[7] Taking the mtDNA and Y-chromosomal systems into account, this treatment of

DNA can therefore be seen as a technology for producing sexualized genetic lineages.

Next to the sexualized model of XX-XY, in genetics there exists the model of mtDNA and Y-chromosome. I have focused on the latter not only because it plays a central role in studies of genetic lineage, but also to *denaturalize* the former as the category par excellence to know the sexes. Moreover, in the practice of genealogy and for the purpose of studying genetic lineage, sex difference is not so much a quality of individuals, but rather that of genetic lineage. Lineage, as was shown, is invested with theory, interests, and points of departure. While genealogy (as we know it outside the lab) is about *origin* and identity, lineage is about *connections* and the partiality of these. Given this partiality of lineage and parenthood, "origin" can never be natural. It is always situated, dependent on technologies and practices. Lineage in this sense is a form of what Marilyn Strathern (1991) has called "partial connections." It is enabled by technologies, and produces compatibility (among groups of individuals or a population) without comparability. In the next part of this chapter I will turn my attention to the practice of DNA, or the practice of producing data at the bench. We will see what happens to genetic sex in that particular setting.

The Ir/relevance of Sex in Laboratory Practice

In my study of the Diversity Project I conducted a participant observation in two laboratories. The Laboratory for Molecular Evolution and Human Genetics (let's call it Lab P) was one of these laboratories. In the course of my research in Lab P, I was working on a project aimed at comparing two "bottlenecks" (a reduction in genetic diversity due to factors such as a reduction in population size), one in the Sinai Desert and one in Finland, by studying the Y-chromosome. For this purpose, the Finnish population was compared to that of Sweden and the Sinai populations to those living along the Nile. Mitochondrial DNA studies have shown a reduced diversity in Finns when compared to the Swedish, and the same has also been found for three Y-chromosomal markers tested (see Sajantila et al. 1996). The case of the Sinai Desert looked slightly different. MtDNA there showed a high diversity as in the rest of Egypt, whereas the three Y-chromosomal markers showed a reduced diversity. Lab P was interested in testing more loci on the Y-chromosome to explain this difference and to see whether that difference still holds when more markers are applied. Abdel-Halim Salem, who was working on both the Finnish and Sinai populations, familiarized me with the project and we continued working on it together.

Before we started testing the markers, Salem drew a map of Egypt to show me where the populations along the Nile and in the Sinai live. Discussing the populations of the Sinai, he explained to me that most of the samples we had in the lab, except for the samples he (a medical doctor) had collected himself, were assembled in the 1960s by an Israeli population geneticist. These were serum samples[8] and since they were so old, their quality was not always that good. The set of Y-chromosomal markers we were about to use for the Finland–Sinai project were sent to Lab P by a Dutch laboratory in Leiden. Salem showed me the set of primers, some control samples (tested in Leiden) and the protocol. We went through it, talked about how to establish the PCR condition, and started testing the markers for a number of samples from a population called Sawarka (Sinai).[9] Once the markers appeared to work, we extended our work of typing them to more individuals. The strategy Salem proposed was to do one population at a time for all markers and then move on to the next.

After I had finished typing one marker (DYS 390) for all the Sawarka samples, I found only two alleles, i.e. two variable fragments of DNA. Instead of going on to the next marker, I decided first to compare these results with those of another population, Jabalya. Jabalya was an exception in the Sinai. Previous studies had shown that unlike other populations in this region, it showed no reduction in diversity on the Y-chromosome.[10] I was of course curious as to whether that would hold for this marker as well. I was unable to discuss the change in method with Salem since he was abroad, so I took the samples from the refrigerator and started running the PCRs. From the 36 samples that I tested none of them showed a band on the agarose gel.[11] I then thought that perhaps the bands were not very strong and that they could nevertheless be detected by the ALF™, which is a more precise visualizing technology. So I booked one ALF™ for the next day. But the end result was not positive either. When Salem came back, I told him about the "Jabalya problem." Although he was at first a little annoyed that I had changed the schedule, when I showed him the collection of samples that I was typing he laughed and said, "Now we can be sure that the samples are females." It appeared that I had been trying to type the Y-chromosomes of females.

We walked over to another part of the lab where he showed me a file in which I could find information about Lab P's samples. It contained different kinds of information, about when and where the samples had been collected and by whom they had been supplied to the lab, and in some cases information about their sex could be found. He told me that if this file did not contain information about the sex of the samples I could have a look at his personal file on the Sun computer, where he had stored his raw data, including data about the three Y-chromosomal markers that he had typed earlier. He explained that with some of the samples it was unclear whether they were male or female, and stated, "I don't even know if all non-males are females." This is especially a problem of serum samples, because if they fail to work for nuclear DNA, you cannot determine whether this is due to deterioration of the DNA or because they are females and do not have a Y-chromosome.

Following this episode we started reorganizing the samples according to sex. We first took a second collection of the Jabalya samples and separated the two sexes in the boxes and then did the same for the other populations. Then I made a list of all the Sinai samples that are known to be males and recorded this information in my lab journal.

Ordering and Enacting the Sexes

In practices of genealogy, sex mattered as a pattern of inheritance. It mattered in the way it helped to establish genetic lineage. However, in a DNA practice, as a procedure of producing data at the bench, the sex of the samples had become a significant part of studying DNA.

Compared to mtDNA, studies of the Y-chromosome are rather new in the field of population genetics. MtDNA has been used extensively ever since the 1970s. The first population studies on the Y-chromosome, however, appeared in the early 1990s, and it was only in 1995 that a number of Y-chromosomal markers were discussed as being informative for the purpose of population studies. In Lab P the first Y-chromosomal markers were introduced in late 1995 and the lab's first paper reporting work carried out using these markers appeared in 1996 (Sajantila et al. 1996; Salem et al. 1996). This information reflects the organization of daily work in Lab P and the relevance of sex in doing DNA.

Working on the Y-chromosome, it is relevant that some individuals (namely males) have a Y-chromosome and others do not. Are these then females? Just as in the Jabalya case, the absence of Y-chromosomal alleles was read as extra information about the female sex of those samples. This allelic information contributes to a "practice of chromosomes," i.e. a practice of XX-XY. In this practice the sexes are performed as presence or absence of the Y-chromosome. However, working with rather old samples showed that this distinction is not "natural." Absence of a Y-chromosomal allele did not necessarily mean that the individual from whom the sample was taken was a female. In such cases, the sex of the samples is an effect of good or deteriorating DNA. Presence of a Y-chromosomal allele makes a sample into a male sample. Its absence, however, does not make a sex difference. Sex difference could therefore be seen as a local and contextual laboratory product, invested by the quality of individual samples and their relevance for a particular experiment. Thus, in a practice of deteriorating DNA, sex is performed not as a quality of a *sampled individual* but as that of an *individual sample*.

Laboratories reflect the activities carried out in such space, and the organization of the space is often centered around such activities (Garfinkel 1996: esp. chs. 1 and 7; Lynch 1997: esp. ch. 1). For example, in the lab there are cupboards above each bench containing most of the chemical solutions needed for the specific work conducted at that bench, and there is always a set of pipettes, pipette tips, and latex gloves within easy reach. The samples are also subject to this type of organization. There is a spatial division between different populations, which are preferably stored in separate boxes. But old and new samples, i.e. serum and blood samples, also tend to be stored in separate boxes. Sex, however, did not bring about such a spatial division. Males and females were mingled and placed in the same boxes. So how should we understand a mutual relevance and irrelevance of sex differences? How should we understand the pivotal role of sex in Y-chromosomal DNA, and the virtual absence of sex in the organization of work?

Whereas I had problems seeing any system in the numbers assigned to the samples (some series had unsystematic numbers, such as "101," "7125," or "77&78"; others had a number and a letter referring to the name of the population, such as "B9," "B31," or "B91"; still others had a number and two letters such as "FB25" or "MB29," indicating males or females of that same population[12]), Salem seemed to have the relevant information at hand. Simply by looking at the containers of DNA he would indicate to me when the samples were gathered, which of the samples were male or female – and, so he told me, he even knew personally some of the people represented by the samples he had collected himself. This information was neither absent nor irrelevant, even though it was not visible to a newcomer. This also applied to information about the sexes. Having worked much longer with the samples, Salem could be said to have embodied that information. My knowledge of the samples was limited, so I had to mobilize other practices of knowing the sexes by consulting the written records, the "Sample file," and raw data in the "Sun computer." For Salem, these practices had already become part of the letters and numbers that were written on the cups. Moreover, since he had been engaged in collecting some of the samples, other repertoires of enacting the sexes were at his disposal. These repertoires consisted not only of written records and previous experience in the lab but also of an anatomical way of determining the sexes, such as the presence or absence of breasts. Salem's knowledge regarding the samples in the lab was thus based on an interference between different repertoires and different practices where the sexes were performed (Haraway 1991a; Strathern 1991).[13] On the other hand, I had to introduce another way of establishing the sexes, namely that of creating a visual distance between male and female samples. By making a spatial division in the boxes and drawing up a list of all the male samples in my lab journal, I created a means of transforming these different ways of knowing the sexes which became pivotal parts of doing DNA.

As indicated above, work conducted on the Y-chromosome is rather new in population studies as well as in Lab P. The populations we were typing for the Y-chromosome were first studied using mtDNA. From the perspective of mtDNA, the sex of the individual is not relevant. Any human sample will do, even those whose sex can no longer be determined.[14] Thus the storage of samples according to population, or even according to the DNA quality of the samples, can be seen as reflecting a former practice, a practice of doing mtDNA. Although the lab was moving away from mtDNA,[15] and although it had already conducted Y-chromosomal research for which sex did matter, the samples occupied "the same place" as before. The changed practice was not reflected in *how* the samples were organized spatially. Rather, it was operative as a management of different repertoires of performing the sexes.

Doing Lineage: Making Sexes

In this chapter we have encountered two practices in studies of genetic lineage and viewed how sex difference is enacted in these. First, we have considered the practice of genealogy, where the sex could be located not so much in the individual as in genetic lineage. MtDNA was treated as a technology to trace a maternal lineage and Y-chromosomal DNA helped to produce a paternal lineage. By contrast, in the second practice, at the bench where samples were being studied the sex of the individual became relevant. This has not always been the case. With the introduction of Y-chromosomal research in studies of genetic lineage, the samples were treated as derived from women or men. Thus, in this particular laboratory it is a change in technology that has introduced a sexual division between samples. However, this division is not self-evidently a matter of DNA. Among other things, the sex of the samples may be enacted as information in the written records, as good or deteriorating DNA, as knowledge about how and from whom the samples were taken in the field, or as a spatial division between the collection of samples in the laboratory. To be sure, genetic sex is not a list of references, such as these, to an individual. Rather, it is a management of different repertoires of making sex differences. And information in the DNA is just one of these. This management of repertoires does not stop with the collection of data, or at the bench, but goes on in the analyses of data and the writing down of the results for publication. In that process, the various ways in which sex difference is enacted tend to be subsumed. For example, although the two systems of inheritance (mtDNA and Y-chromosome) point back to *partial ancestors* that do not have to coincide with individuals or parents (MRCA's), the presupposition of individuals is crucial for geneticists. To interpret genetic lineage and to produce accounts about the history of populations, information in the Y-chromosome is read as data about men and information in the mtDNA as data about women. Both particles thus help to produce complementary accounts about the history of populations, revealing men and women, whenever you look back in time.

Even though the sex/gender distinction has been productive for feminist politics, it has too long been read as nature versus culture. If we take biological sex to be a metaphorical onion, many studies aimed to take away the various layers of that onion and to identify these as gender (see, e.g., Bleier 1988; Keller 1986; Harding 1986; Jacobus et al. 1990). The core of such an onion would then represent the biological, the universal but not so relevant other of gender: that which is stable and which escapes normativity. However, as we know, an onion does not have a core. My treatment of genetic sex here was aimed at destabilizing this distinction. In her study on primatology, Donna Haraway states the following: "The boundary between sex and gender is the boundary between animal and human, a very potent optical illusion and *technical achievement*" (1988: 95; italic added). Even if this distinction may be relevant at times or even if it may perform itself, it has taken away the opportunity to investigate and question the biological. With the recent interest in the body, the biological has entered center stage. An ever-growing corpus of literature is showing how the body is enabled by technologies, making oblique the very distinction between nature and technology.[16] In this chapter I have taken genetic sex – one could say, the ultimate identifier of sex difference – as my object of investigation. My treatment of it departs from the fact that biological categories do not exist by themselves but are enabled by technologies. Even though geneticists may present us with stable objects, if we take their practices into account it becomes clear that genetic sex shifts and changes all the time. There is no stable reference. And this in itself questions the very distinction between sex and gender. We find ourselves confronted with two unknown variables; variables that take specific forms if we situate them somewhere.

Notes

My gratitude goes to many colleagues, especially the members of the Laboratory for Evolution and Human Genetics (Munich), who made the lab a place I kept returning to. I also thank the Deutscher Akademischer Austauschdienst (DAAD) and the Netherlands Organization for Scientific Research (NWO) for kindly supporting my research in Munich.

1   I have studied two "European" laboratories over a period of one year: the Forensic Laboratory for DNA Research in Leiden, The Netherlands, and the Laboratory for Molecular Evolution and Human Genetics in Munich, Germany. I met various other European and non-European geneticists at meetings and conferences on human genetic diversity.

2   Within the field of Science and Technology Studies there exists a large corpus of literature in which scientific knowledge is investigated as culture and practice. See, for example, Pickering (1992). For an overview of laboratory studies, see Knorr-Cetina (1995).

3   Both feminism and feminist studies of science constitute a large and contested terrain. I can hardly do justice to the diversity within these domains nor acknowledge the many inspiring works of different kinds, such as that of Evelyn Fox Keller or that of Sally Hacker, Donna Haraway, Annemarie Mol, and Judith Butler, by talking simply, as if it were that, about "feminist scholars." Nor can I do justice to the elaborate studies contributed to the field of science studies by feminist scholars and feminists in general. For early contributions to the latter see, for example, two edited issues; Bleier (1988) and Harding (1986). My interest in genetics is very much indebted to, and inspired by, the work of Evelyn Fox Keller. Sally Hacker taught me that one should engage in science and technology to make a political difference; Donna Haraway's work gave me the promise of combining socialist, feminist, and anti-racist politics with academic work and doing science studies; Annemarie Mol's and Judith Butler's works showed that there were other ways of theorizing sex or gender, making it possible for me to relate to it. Moreover, from Annemarie Mol's work I learned to focus on processes of doing science and their normative involvement in scientific objects. (See Keller 1986, 1992a, 1992b, 1995; Hacker 1989; Haraway 1989, 1991a; Hirschauer and Mol 1990; Mol 1985, 1991.)

4   My use of "sex" and not "gender" is deliberate, even though the English language puts some constraints on its use. I apply it not only to destabilize the seemingly neat distinction between sex (as being biology) and gender (as being culture), but also in accord with my claim that culture is part and parcel of genetic practices. For an elaboration on sex and gender and especially on its use in Dutch feminist studies, see Mol 1998. On the traffic of the concept of gender between languages, and on distinctions between sex and gender, see Haraway 1991b.

5 The reference to archaeology points to a heated debate between disciplines, namely between genetics and palaeontology. The battle is about human origin, and about which discipline has the best access to it. An example of such a debate is that between the paleontologists Alan Thorne and Milford Wolpoff on the one hand, and Alan Wilson and Rebecca Cann on the other. The issue is not only which sources provide the best evidence of human history and origin, but also how the spread of humans around the world came about, and the multiregional theory versus the African origin theory. See Thorne and Wolpoff 1992; Wilson and Cann 1992. In an interview, population geneticist Mark Stoneking talked about this ongoing debate and made clear the privileged view of genetics as follows: "We geneticists know that our genes must have had ancestors, but palaeontologists can only hope that their fossils had descendants" (interview with author at The Laboratory for Evolution and Human Genetics in Munich, March 11, 1997).

6 For an elaborate examination of different types of genealogical trees, see Bouquet 1995; see also Claudia Castañeda's treatment of genealogical trees in medicines as technologies (paper presented at the EASST Annual Meeting, Lisbon, Portugal, 1998).

7 For an analysis of how both DNA and the cell are treated as technologies, see Rheinberger 1997.

8 Blood serum is the fluid which precipitates when blood clots.

9 PCR, Polymerase Chain Reaction, is a DNA fragment copying technology using a thermostable enzyme. This procedure not only produces more DNA, making it easier to study, but a chemical group (such as a fluorescent group) is also attached to the copies in order to visualize them using ultra violet or laser beams.

10 The origin story of Jabalya states that it was founded in the seventeenth century as a monastery by Christian monks. Its population became intermixed both as a result of pilgrimages and because of the fact that Jabalya was traditionally a passage point for those wishing to cross the desert.

11 Agarose is a gel-like substance which sets (polymerizes) at room temperature. By placing small fragments of DNA (in the prepared slots) in the gel, and placing the whole gel under an electronic currency, the DNA fragments start to migrate. The relation between the distance of the migrated DNA fragments on the gel and the time they were given to move is an indicator of the length of such a fragment.

12 Lab P does not assign new numbers to samples that come into the lab. Whatever number the samples have, this is how they are stored. It is a practical method because most of the samples are collected by other laboratories or scientific groups. Keeping records of who supplied the samples and when, and adopting their nomenclature offers a way of communicating what is and is not already in the lab when new deliveries arrive.

13 For an elaboration on interfering practices, see Law 2000. On the relevance of breasts in medical practices of trans-sexuality, see Hirschauer 1998.

14 Old samples work better for mtDNA than for nuclear DNA. The reason for this is that each human cell contains a large number of copies of mtDNA.

15 Professor Svante Pääbo, interview with author at The Laboratory for Evolution and Human Genetics in Munich, February 4, 1997.

16 Most notably so in the work of Haraway 1991b, but also in that of among many others, e.g., Butler 1990, 1993.

.References

Bleier, R. (ed.) (1988) *Feminist Approaches to Science* (New York and Oxford: Pergamon Press).

Bouquet, M. (1995) "Exhibiting Knowledge: The Tree of Dubois, Haeckel, Jesse and Rivers at the Pithecanthropus Centennial Exhibition," in M. Strathern (ed.), *Shifting Contexts: Transformations in Anthropological Knowledge* (London and New York: Routledge).

Butler, J. (1990) *Gender Trouble: Feminism and the Subversion of Identity* (London: Routledge).

Butler, J. (1993) *Bodies that Matter: On the Discursive Limits of "Sex"* (London: Routledge).

Casteñeda, C. (1998) "Heredity in Science and Medicine" (paper presented at the EASST Annual Meeting, Lisbon, Portugal).

Garfinkel, H. (1996 [1967]) *Studies in Ethnomethodology* (Cambridge, MA and Oxford: Blackwell Publishers).

Hacker, Sally (1989) *Pleasure, Power, and Technology: Some Tales of Gender, Engineering and the Cooperative Workplace* (London and Sydney: Unwin Hyman).

Haraway, D. J. (1988) "Primatology Is Politics by Other Means," in R. Bleier (ed.), *Feminist Approaches to Science* (New York, Oxford: Pergamon Press).

Haraway, D. J. (1989) *Primate Visions: Gender, Race, and Nature in the World of Modern Science* (London and New York: Verso).

Haraway, D. J. (1991a) "A Cyborg Manifesto: Science, Technology, and Socialist-Feminism in the Late Twentieth Century," in *Simians, Cyborgs, and Women: The Reinvention of Nature* (London: Free Association Books).

Haraway, D. J. (1991b) "Gender for a Marxist Dictionary: The Sexual Politics of a Word," in *Simians, Cyborgs, and Women: The Reinvention of Nature* (London: Free Association Books).

Haraway, D. J. (1991c) "Situated Knowledges: The Science Question in Feminism and the Privilege of Partial Perspective," in *Simians, Cyborgs, and Women: The Reinvention of Nature* (London: Free Association Books).

Haraway, D. J. (1997) *Modest Witness@Second Millennium.FemaleMan Meets OncoMouse: Feminism and Technoscience* (New York and London: Routledge).

Harding, J. (ed.) (1986) *Perspectives on Gender and Science* (London and New York: The Falmer Press).

Hayden, C. (1998) "A Biodiversity Sampler for the Millennium," in S. Franklin and H. Ragoné (eds.), *Reproducing Reproduction: Kinship, Power, and Technological Innovation* (Philadelphia: University of Pennsylvania Press).

Hirschauer, S. (1998) "Performing Sexes and Genders in Medical Practices," in M. Berg and A. Mol (eds.), *Differences in Medicine: Unraveling Practices, Techniques, and Bodies* (Durham, NC and London: Duke University Press).

Hirschauer, S. and Mol, A. (1995) "Shifting Sexes, Moving Stories," *Science, Technology & Human Value* 20: 368–85.

Jacobus, M., Keller, E. F., and Shuttleworth, S. (eds.) (1990) *Body/Politics: Women and the Discourses of Science* (New York: Routledge).

Keller, E. F. (1986) *Reflections on Gender and Science* (New Haven: Yale University Press).

Keller, E. F. (1992a) "Nature, Nurture, and the Human Genome Project," in Daniel J. Kevles and Leroy Hood (eds.), *The Code of Codes: Scientific and Social Issues in the Human Genome Project* (Cambridge: Harvard University Press).

Keller, E. F. (1992b) *Secrets of Life, Secrets of Death: Essays on Language, Gender and Science* (New York: Routledge).

Keller, E. F. (1995) *Refiguring Life: Metaphors of Twentieth Century Biology* (New York: Columbia University Press).

Knorr-Cetina, K. (1995) "Laboratory Studies: The Cultural Approach to the Study of Science," in S. Jasanoff, G. E. Markle, J. C. Petersen, and T. Pinch (eds.), *Handbook of Science and Technology Studies* (Thousand Oaks, London, New Delhi: Sage).

Law, J. (2000) "On the Subject of the Object: Narrative, Technology, and Interpellation," *Configurations* 8: 1–29.

Lock, M. (2001) "The Alienation of Body Tissue and the Biopolitics of Immortalized Cell Lines," *Body & Society* 7: 63–91.

Lynch, M. (1997) *Scientific Practice and Ordinary Action: Ethnomethodology and Social Studies of Science* (Cambridge: Cambridge University Press).

M'charek, Amâde (2000) *Technologies of Similarities and Differences: On the Interdependence of Nature and Technology in the Human Genome Diversity Project* (Amsterdam: Thesis).

Mol, A. (1985) "Wie Weet Wat een Vrouw Is? Over de Verschillen en de Verhoudingen Tussen de Disciplines," *Tijdschrift voor Vrouwenstudies* 21: 10–22.

Mol, A. (1990) "Sekse, Rijkdom en Bloedarmoede: Over Lokaliseren als Strategie," *Tijdschrift voor Vrouwenstudies* 42: 142–57.

Mol, A. (1991) "Wombs, Pygmentation and Pyramids: Should anti-Racists and Feminists Try to Confine 'Biology' to its Proper Place?" in A. van Lenning and J. Hermsen (eds.), *Sharing the Difference* (London and New York: Routledge).

Mol, A. (1998) "Dit Geslacht Dat Zoveel Is: Een Conversatie Tussen een Onbekend Aantal Onbekenden van Wie Slechts ÉÉn zich Bekend Zal Maken," *Tijdschrift voor Genderstudies* 1: 13–15.

Mol, A. (2002) *The Body Multiple: Ontology in Medical Practices* (Durham, NC and London: Duke University Press).

Pickering, A. (ed.) (1992) *Science as Practice and Culture* (Chicago and London: The University of Chicago Press).

Rheinberger, H.-J. (1997) "Von der Zelle zum Gen: Repräsentationen der Molekularbiologie," in H.-J. Rheinberger, M. Hagner, and B. Wahring-Schmidt (eds.), *Räume des Wissens: Representation, Codierung, Spur* (Berlin: Akademie Verlag).

Sajantila, A. et al. (1996) "Paternal and Maternal DNA Lineages Reveal a Bottleneck in the Founding of the Finnish Population," *Proc. Natl. Acad. Sci.* 93 (October): 12035–9.

Salem, A. et al. (1996) "The Genetics of Traditional Living: Y-chromosomal and Mitochondrial Lineages in the Sinai Peninsula," *American Journal of Human Genetics* 59 (September): 741–3.

Strathern, M. (1991) *Partial Connections* (Savage, MD: Rowman and Littlefield).

Strathern, M. (1992) *After Nature: English Kinship in the Late Twentieth Century* (Cambridge: Cambridge University Press).

Thorne, A. G. and Wolpoff, M. H. (1992) "The Multiregional Evolution of Humans," *Scientific American* (April): 28–33.

von Haeseler, A., Sajantila, A., and Pääbo, S. (1996) "The Genetic Archaeology of the Human Genome," *Nature Genetics* 14: 135–40.

Wilson, A. C. and Cann, R. (1992) "The Recent African Genesis of Humans," *Scientific American* (April): 22–7.

CHAPTER SEVEN

Lived Body versus Gender

Iris Marion Young

In her thorough and provocative essay "What Is a Woman?" Toril Moi argues that recent feminist and queer theorizing has brought us to the end of a constructivist gender rope. While feminist theory of the 1970s found a distinction between sex and gender liberating both for theory and practice, subsequent feminist and queer critiques have rightly questioned the distinction. By destabilizing categories both of biological sex and gender identity, recent deconstructive approaches to feminist and queer theorizing have opened greater possibilities for thinking a plurality of intersecting identities and practices. Deconstructive challenges to the sex/gender distinction have increasingly abstracted from embodiment, however, at the same time that it has rendered a concept of gender virtually useless for theorizing subjectivity and identity. At this theoretical pass, Moi proposes (2001) that we throw over the concept of gender altogether and renew a concept of the lived body derived from existential phenomenology, as a means of theorizing sexual subjectivity without danger either of biological reductionism or of gender essentialism.

I am persuaded by Moi's argument, but I am not ready to accept her conclusion. In this chapter I will sort out why, on both counts. I will examine the logic of the evolution of gender theory on which Moi reflects, review her arguments for why gender is not a useful category of theorizing, and explain my reasons for applauding her turn to a concept of lived body. I will argue that Moi's argument is, however, incomplete. While she is correct that gender is a problematic concept for theorizing subjectivity, there are or ought to be other aspects of feminist and queer theorizing that cannot do without a concept of gender. By reflecting on Moi's account of recent feminist and queer theorizing, we discover that these aspects, which concern social structure more than subjectivity and identity, have been relatively neglected. The oppression of women and queers occurs through systemic processes and social structures which need description that uses different concepts from those appropriate for describing subjects and their experience. Moi's proposal to reconstitute a concept of the lived body helps for the latter, but for the former we need a reconstituted concept of gender.

The Sex/Gender Distinction

Early feminist appropriations of what until then had been an obscure psychological distinction between gender, as referring to self-conception and behavior, and sex, as referring to anatomy and physiology, were very theoretically and politically productive. At this theoretical moment, challenging the conviction that "biology is destiny" was an important feminist project. In order to argue for opening wider opportunities for women, we needed ways to conceptualize capacities and disposition of members of both sexes that distanced behavior, temperament, and achievement from biological or natural explanations. A distinction between sex and gender served this purpose. Feminists could affirm that of course men and women are "different" in physique and reproductive function, while denying that these differences have any relevance for the opportunities members of the sexes should have or the activities they should engage in. Such gender rules and expectations are socially constituted and socially changeable. Much of this early second-wave feminist theorizing invoked an ideal of equality for women that envisioned an end to gender. "Androgyny" named the ideal that many feminists theorized, a social condition in which biological sex would have no implications for a person's life prospects, or the way people treated one another (including, importantly, in the most consistent of these theories, one's choice of sex partners). These androgynous persons in the transformed liberated society would have no categorically distinct forms of dress, comportment, occupations, or propensities toward aggression or passivity, associated with their embodiment. We would all be just people with various bodies (see Ferguson 1991 for one statement of the androgynous ideal).

This appeal to an ideal of androgyny did not last long. Some of the turning-point texts of feminist theory in the late 1970s and early 1980s turned instead to accounts of the social and psychological specificities of femininely gendered identity and social perspective derived from gender roles. While not at all explained by biological distinctions between men and women, nevertheless there are deep social divisions of masculine- and feminine-gendered dispositions and experience which have implications for the psychic lives of men and women, their interactions with one another, and their dispositions to care for children or exercise authority. Nancy Chodorow (1978), Carol Gilligan (1982), Nancy Hartsock (1983), and others developed theories of feminine gender identities as expressing a general structure of subjectivity and social standpoint in significant ways defining the lives and possibilities of most women.

No sooner had such a general account of feminine gender identity emerged than it came under attack as "essentialist." These accounts assume mothering as defining the experience of most women. They fail to inquire about the differences that race or class positioning make to caring practices, and they assume that women are or wish to be in relationships with men. They extrapolate from the historical specificity of twentieth-century affluent urban nuclear families and occupations structures, ignoring historical and cross-cultural specifications in the organization of family and work. Although the criticisms were not always voiced in the fairest way, most feminist theorists took these points to heart.

Queer theory broke into this dissolution of gender theory in the person of writers such as Diana Fuss and Judith Butler. Because Moi focuses on Butler's subversion of the sex/gender distinction, and I will support Moi's conclusion in specific respects, I will follow Moi in this focus.

In *Gender Trouble* (1990), Butler questioned the motive of feminist theory to seek a theory of gender identity. Feminists believe they need such a general theory of gender, she argued, in order to know what is the subject of feminist politics. Feminism has no meaning as a specific transformative social movement, it is thought, without an account of the "agent" of change, the subject to be liberated; that subject is "woman," and "gender" is the concept that displays what a woman is. As gendered, "women" are distinct from the biological sex: female. Butler argued, however, that the feminist distinction between sex and gender nevertheless retains a binarism of stable categorical complementarity between male and female, which reproduces a logic of heterosexual normativity. The very distinction between sex and gender ought to be put in question in order to challenge any reliance on a distinction between nature and culture, or any conception that subjects have inner lives to which an idea of stable gender identity corresponds. Gender is nothing other than a social performative. The discursive rules of normative heterosexuality produce gendered performances that subjects reiterate and cite; the sexing of bodies themselves derives from such performatives. In this process of reiterated gender performance, some persons become constituted as abject, outside the heterosexual binary. Radical politics, then, consists in troubling the gender binaries and playing with gender citation.

In response to the critical reaction of some commentators that her theory of gender as performance makes bodies and sexual identity simply a product of discourse, in *Bodies That Matter* (1993) Butler argues that the materiality of sexed bodies is itself socially constituted. She insists that such production of bodies is not "idealist," and that a valuation of "materialism" over "idealism" itself relies on a questionable binary logic.

Moi does not refute Butler's arguments, which she takes to be cogent, given their terms and methods. She argues nevertheless that ideals of subjectivity and sexuality have become increasingly abstract in this train of theorizing that begins with the sex/gender distinction and ends by deconstructing a material/ideal dichotomy. It is not clear at this point what lived problems the theory addresses or how the concepts help people understand and describe their experience. Butler successfully calls into question the logic of the sex/gender distinction, yet her theorizing never goes beyond these terms and remains tied to them. This line of critique, Moi argues, calls for throwing off the idea of gender altogether as useful for understanding subjectivity and identity. Queer theory and practice bend gender meanings, aiming to loosen them from the normative polarities of hegemonic masculinity and femininity. Moi suggests that queer and feminist theorists should make a break with gender altogether.

Moi's Alternative: The Lived Body

For an alternative to the categories of sex and gender, Moi proposes to return to the framework of existential phenomenology on which Simone de Beauvoir relies. The central category for this theoretical approach is that of the *lived body*. A reconstituted concept of the lived body, Moi argues, would offer feminists an idea that can serve the function we have wanted from the sex/gender categorization, without bringing its problems.

The lived body is a unified idea of a physical body acting and experiencing in a specific sociocultural context; it is body-in-situation. For existentialist theory, *situation* denotes the produce of *facticity* and *freedom*. The person always faces the material facts of her body and its relation to a given environment. Her bodily organs have certain feeling capacities, and function in determinate ways; her size, age, health, and training make her capable of strength and movement in relation to her environment in specific ways. Her skin has a particular color, her face determinate features, her hair particular color and texture, each with their own aesthetic properties. Her specific body lives in a specific context – crowded by other people, anchored to the earth by gravity, surrounded by buildings and streets with a unique history, hearing particular languages, having food and shelter available, or not, as a result of culturally specific social processes that make specific requirements on her to access them. All these concrete material relations of a person's bodily existence and her physical and social environment constitute her *facticity*.

The person, however, is an actor; she has an ontological freedom to construct herself in relation to this facticity. The human actor has specific projects, things she aims to accomplish, ways she aims to express herself, make her mark on the world, transform her surroundings and relationships. Often these are projects she engages in jointly with others. *Situation*, then, is the way that the facts of embodiment and social and physical environment appear in light of the projects a person has. She finds that her movements are awkward in relation to her desire to dance. She sees the huge city with its thousand year history as an opportunity for learning about her ancestors. "To claim that the body is a situation is to acknowledge that the meaning of a woman's body is bound up with the way she uses her freedom" (Moi 2001: 65).

How does Moi propose that the idea of the lived body might replace that of gender, and the distinction between sex and gender? Like the category of sex, that of the lived body can refer to the specific physical facts of bodies, including sexual and reproductive differentiation. "Woman" and "man" name the physical facticity of certain bodies, some with penises, others with clitorises and breasts, each with differing experiences of desire and sexual feeling. A category of lived body, moreover, need not make sexual difference dimorphous; some bodies have physical traits like those of men in certain respects or those of women in others. People experience their desires and feeling in diverse ways that do not neatly correlate with sexual dimorphism or heterosexual norms. As a lived body, moreover, perceptual capacities and motility are not distinct from association with sexual specificity; nor is size, bone structure, or skin color. Most important for the proposal Moi makes, the concept of the lived body, unlike the concept of sex, is not biologistic. It does not refer to an objectivist scientific account that generalizes laws of physiology and function. A scientific approach to bodies proceeds at a significantly higher level of abstraction than does a description of bodies as lived. The idea of the lived body thus can bring the physical facts of different bodies into theory without the reductionist and dichotomous implications of the category of "sex."

The idea of the lived body, moreover, refuses the distinction between nature and culture that grounds a distinction between sex and gender. The body as lived is always enculturated: by the phonemes a body learns to pronounce at a very early age; by the clothes the person wears that mark her nation, her age, her occupational status; and in what is culturally expected or required of women. The body is enculturated by habits of comportment distinctive to interactional settings of business or pleasure; often they are specific to locale or group. Contexts of discourse and interaction position persons in systems of evaluation and expectations which often implicate their embodied being; the person experiences herself as looked at in certain ways, described in her physical being in certain ways; she experiences the bodily reactions of others to her, and she reacts to them. The diverse phenomena that have come under the rubric of "gender" in feminist theory can be redescribed in the idea of lived body as some among many forms of bodily habitus and interactions with others that we enact and experience. In such redescription we find that Butler is right in at least this respect: it is a mystification to attribute the ways of being associated with the category "gender" to some inner core of identity of a subject, whether understood as "natural" or acquired.

The idea of the lived body thus does the work the category "gender" has done, but better and more. It does this work better because the category of the lived body allows description of the habits and interactions of men with women, women with women, and men with men in ways that can attend to the plural possibilities of comportment, without a necessary reduction to the normative heterosexual binary of "masculine" and "feminine." It does more because it helps avoid a problem generated by use of ascriptive general categories such as "gender," "race," "nationality," and "sexual orientation" to describe the constructed identities of individuals, namely the additive character that identities appear to have under this description. If we conceptualize individual identities as constituted by the diverse group identities – gender, race, class, sexual orientation, and so on – there seems to be a mystery both about how persons are individualized, and how these different group identities combine in the person.

Return to a category of lived body brings us back to each person with such diversities. Each person is a distinctive body, with specific features, capacities, and desires, which are similar to and different from those of others in a determinate respect. She is born in a particular place and time, is raised in a particular family setting, and all these have specific sociocultural histories that stand in relation to the history of others in particular ways. What we call categories of gender, race, ethnicity, etc. are shorthand for a set of structures that position persons, a point to which I will return. They are not properly theorized as general group identities that add together to constitute individual identities. The individual person lives out her unique body in a socio-historical context of the behavior and expectations of others, but she does not have to worry about constituting her identity from a set of generalized "pop-beads" strung together (Spelman 1988).

By means of a category of the lived body, then, "One can arrive at a highly historicized and concrete understanding of bodies and subjectivity without relying on the sex-gender distinction that Butler takes as axiomatic" (Moi 2001: 46). The idea of the lived body recognizes that a person's subjectivity is conditioned by sociocultural facts and the behavior and expectations of others in ways that she has not chosen. At the same time, the theory of the lived body says that each person takes up and acts in relation to these unchosen facts in her own way.

To consider the body as a situation is to consider both the fact of being a specific kind of body and the meaning that concrete body has for the situated individual. This is not the equivalent of either sex or gender. The same is true for "lived experience," which encompasses our experience of all kinds of situations (race, class, nationality, etc.) and is a far more wide-ranging concept than the highly psychologizing concept of gender identity (Moi 2001: 81).

Is the Lived Body Enough?

Toril Moi argues that a concept of the lived body serves feminist theoretical purposes better than a concept of gender. She defines those purposes as providing a theory of subjectivity and the body, and providing an understanding of what it means to be a woman or man in a particular society (2001: 4, 36, 14). Feminist theory, she says, ought to become a project of dispelling confusions concerning bodies, sex, sexuality, sexual difference, and the power relations among women and men, heterosexuals and homosexuals (ibid.: 120). This last phrase about power relations is extremely vague. Depending on how it is specified, the scope of theorizing power relations might fall beyond what I take as Moi's major emphasis in defining the tasks of feminist theory. She defines this theory as focusing on subjectivity, who one is as an agent, the attributes and capacities one has for experience, the relations with others that contribute to one's sense of self.

I find Moi's discussion of the logic of gender theorizing, the dilemmas that have developed for it, and the increasing abstraction it seems to have been forced to in order to respond to these dilemmas. These problems with a concept of gender have surfaced at least partly because gender aims to be a general category, but subjectivity is always particular. Moi's appropriation of the concept of the lived body offers more refined tools for theorizing sexed subjectivity, and the experience of differently situated men and women, than does the more blunt category of gender. Agreeing with this means dispensing with gender altogether, but only if the projects of feminist and queer theories consist just in theorizing subjectivity. But I think they do not. The debates about gender and essentialism that Moi aims to bring to a close with her arguments have, I think, tended to narrow the interests of feminists and queer theorists to issues of experience, identity, and subjectivity. Her discussion clears the way for asking whether other aspects of a project for feminist and queer theory have been obscured by these debates, for which a resituated concept of gender might still be needed. In the remaining pages of this chapter I want to suggest that a concept of gender is important for theorizing social structures and their implications for the freedom and well-being of persons.

As I understand them, feminist and queer theory consist not only in giving an account of the meaning of the lives of women and men in all their relational and sexual diversity. Nor is it only about analyzing how discourses construct subjects and the stereotypical or defamatory aspects of some of these discourses that contribute to the suffering of some men and women who fall on the wrong side of normalizing processes. Feminist and queer theories are also projects of social criticism. These are theoretical efforts to identify certain wrongful harms or injustices, locate and explain their sources in institutions and social relations, and propose directions for institutionally oriented action to change them. This latter set of tasks requires the theorist to have an account not only of individual experience, subjectivity, and identity, but also of social structures.

In other writings I have begun to articulate a concept of social structure specifically directed at the project of giving institutional account of sources of injustice and in response to the dilemmas of ascribing group identities. There remains a great deal of work to be done to theorize social structures in a way adequate to the practical demands of feminist and queer politics. Briefly, here, by the term social structure I mean a way of looking at societies that is at a more "macro" level than the way of looking at them that focuses on individual experience. Structure denotes the confluence of institutional rules and inter-active routines, mobilization of resources, and physical structures which con-stitute the historical givens in relation to which individuals act, and which are relatively stable over time. Structures also connote the wider social outcomes that result from the confluence of many individual actions within given institu-tional relations, whose collective consequences often do not bear the mark of any person's or group's intentions, but nevertheless serve differentially to enable and constrain further possibilities for action. Social structures are that about their social environment that individuals experience as the way things are which offer opportunities or limit their options to set and enact goals for themselves.

Structures are the larger-scale social processes that come before and follow upon individual actions, into which individuals, their actions, and interaction are inserted (Young 2000: esp. ch. 3; 2001).

To describe and explain some of the structures and processes that effect differential opportunities and privileges in contemporary society, I suggest, we cannot do without a concept of gender. Feminist and queer theories need conceptual tools to describe the rules and practices of institutions that presume differing roles for men and women, and/or which presume that men and women are coupled with each other in intimate relations. We need tools for understanding how and why certain patterns in the allocation of tasks or status recognition remain persistent in ways that limit the options of many women and of most people whose sexual and intimate choices deviate from heterosexual norms. Notice that something important happens to the concept of gender, however, when we understand it as a tool for theorizing structures more than subjects. We no longer need to ascribe a single or shared gender identity to persons we describe as men and women.

My own effort to respond to critiques of early feminist theories of gender turned in this direction of theorizing gender as an attribute of social structures more than of persons. In "Gender as Seriality: Thinking About Women as a Social Collective" (1997) I draw on a concept from Sartre's later philosophy, his idea of a series. Gender, I suggest there, is best understood as a particular form of the social positioning of lived bodies in relation to one another within historically and socially specific institutions and processes that have material effects on the environment in which people act and reproduce relations of power and privilege among them. On this account, what it means to say that individual persons are "gendered" is that we all *find ourselves* passively grouped according to these structural relations, in ways too impersonal to ground identity. There I proposed that there are two basic axes of gender structure: a sexual division of labor and normative heterosexuality. Here, I will take a lead from Bob Connell (1987) and add to these a third axis: gendered hierarchies of power.

The structuring of work and occupations by gender is a basic aspect of all modern societies (and many pre-modern societies), with far-reaching consequences for the lives of individuals, the constraints and opportunities they face. The core of a gendered division of labor in modern societies is the division between "private" and "public" work. An aspect of the basic structure of these societies is that the work of caring – for persons, their bodily needs, their emotional well-being, and the maintenance of their dwellings – takes place primarily in unpaid labor in private homes. While recent decades have seen some changes in the allocation of this work between men and women, it is still the case that this unpaid caring and household work falls primarily to women. The operations of the entire society depend on the regular performance of this work, yet it goes relatively unnoticed and little valued. The persons to whom this work is assigned have less time and energy to devote to other tasks and activities than do those who do less of it. This gendered division of labor persists apparently because people collectively do not wish to organize broadly funded public services that take more collective responsibility for care work. Despite many significant changes in gender ideas and ideology in contemporary societies, there has been little change in this basic division of labor. Indeed, neoliberal economic policies across the globe have had the effect of retrenching this division where it may have loosened.

Feminist social and political theory in the last 20 years has documented dozens of ways that this gendered structure constrains the opportunities of those persons doing unpaid care work, mostly women. They work longer hours than others and are rendered dependent on other people for provision of their needs, which makes them vulnerable to poverty or abuse. Feminist researchers have also documented how this basic structure underlies occupational divisions in public paid work according to gender. When occupations involve caring, they tend to become female-gendered. Because many women arrange their public work lives in relation to caring responsibilities, only a relatively small number of occupations welcome them, which helps keep wages low in those occupations. The structuring of both private and public work along these lines exhibits gendered hierarchies of status and power, not to mention financial reward.

It might be thought that these structural consequences of a sexual division of labor describe Western industrial societies primarily. Theorized at the right level of categorical generality, however, similar structures describe much about many less developed countries, especially in urban life. As some feminist scholars of development have argued, for example, both government policy and the policies of international organizations such as the International Monetary Fund implicitly rely on the assumption that unpaid domestic labor is infinitely expandable, and that household caretakers are available to take up the slack in meeting the needs of their family members when food subsidies are slashed, school fees go up, or health clinics are closed.

A structural account of the sexual division of labor, that is, does not assume that this division of labor has the same content across societies. It is a theoretical framework that asks whether there are tasks and occupations usually performed by members of one sex or the other, and/or whether the social norms and cultural products of the society tend to represent certain tasks or occupations as more appropriately performed by members of one sex or the other. For any society, both today and in the past, the answer is usually yes, but there is nevertheless considerable variation among them in *which* occupations are sex associated, the ideologies often legitimating these associations, how many tasks are sex typed, and what implications this sexual division of labor has for the distribution of resources among persons, their relative status, and the constraints and opportunities that condition their lives.

A second axis of gender structuring in our society is normative heterosexuality. This structuring consists in the diverse institutional and ideological facts that privilege heterosexual coupling. These include the form and implications of many legal institutions, many rules and policies of private organizations in allocating positions and benefits, the structuring of schooling and mainstream media to accord with these institutions, as well as the assumptions many people make in their everyday interactions with others. Together, such social facts make structures with differential consequences on the lives of different men and women, and which sometimes produce serious suffering or wrongful limitations on freedom. The system of normative heterosexuality significantly constrains the lives of men and women, with all their varying sexual and desiring inclinations, motivating some to adjust their lives in ways they believe will bring them material reward and acceptance, and others to care about lives in the interstices of social relations where their desires and projects do not fit, or openly to rebel.

Cheshire Calhoun argues (2000) that lesbian and gay subordination is different in form from the structural constraints on the lives of women or people of color, for example. Whereas structures of female subordination or institutionalized racism confine people perceived as belonging to certain categories as having certain places or positions, Calhoun argues that persons who transgress heterosexual norms have no legitimized place at all in political citizenship, civil society, or private spheres. Structures of normative heterosexuality constrain lesbians and gay men by enforcing their invisibility.

An institutionalized valuation of particular associations of maleness or masculinity conditions hierarchies of power in ways that constrain the possible actions of many people and seem quite resistant to change. Positions and practices of institutionalized and organized violence are most important here – military and police forces, prison systems, etc. In general, the structuring of state institutions, corporations, and other bureaucracies according to hierarchies of decision-making authority and status afford some people significant privileges and freedom, and these are usually men, at the same time that they limit, constrain, and subordinate others, including most women and many men. Gendered hierarchies of power intersect with a sexual division of labor and normative heterosexuality in many ways to reproduce a sense of entitlement of men to women's service and an association of heterosexual masculinity with force and command.

When describing social structures as gendered, it is necessary neither to make generalizations about men and women nor to reduce varying gender structures to a common principle. A gendered occupational division of labor may strongly code certain occupations as female and others as male, and these codings may have far-reaching implications for the power, prestige, and material reward that incumbents of each enjoy. Nothing follows from this, however, about what most men or most women do for a living. Recognizing the structures of normative heterosexuality may well result in theorizing plural understandings of gender, varying rules and practices that make expectations on men and women regarding sexual interaction, relation of adults and children, social aesthetics, relationship of persons to workplace roles, and so on, that do not share a common logic and in some respects may be in tension with one another. The most important thing about the analysis is to understand how the rules, relations and their material consequences produce privileges for some people that underlie an interest in their maintenance, at the same time that they limit options of others, cause relative deprivations in their lives, or render them vulnerable to domination and exploitation.

In this chapter I have agreed with Toril Moi's proposal that the existential phenomenological category of the lived body is a richer and more flexible concept than gender for theorizing the socially constituted experience of women and men than either concepts of sex or gender. The lived body is particular in its morphology, material similarities, and differences from other bodies. I have argued, moreover, that this proposal should not mean dispensing with a category of gender, but rather confining its use to analysis of social structures for the purposes of understanding certain specific relations of power, opportunity, and resource distribution. An obvious question arises at this point, as to the relation of lived bodies to these structures.

The existentialist concept of being in situation enables a theory of address this question, which I do not have the space here to develop with the detail it requires. Bodies as lived find gender structures as an aspect of the facticity of their lives. Much about that gendered facticity – the expectations of others, the way they treat one another, the rules the institutions enforce, and so on – conditions the way the individual subject sees herself and her possibilities for action. Each person nevertheless deals with gendered facticities in her own way, constituting her own idiosyncracies and trying to realize goals she sets for herself within parameters sometimes very constrained by social structures. Thus theorizing subjectivity as lived body and social structure through gender are not alternatives, but complementary aspects of projects of feminist and queer theory.

Note

This is a shortened version of an essay, "Lived Body vs Gender: Reflections on Social Structure and Subjectivity," published in *Ratio: An International Journal of Analytic Philosophy* 15/4 (December 2002): 410–28.

References

Butler, J. (1990) *Gender Trouble* (New York: Routledge).

Butler, J. (1993) *Bodies that Matter* (New York: Routledge).

Calhoun, C. (2000) *Feminism, The Family, and the Politics of the Closet: Lesbian and Gay Displacement* (Oxford: Oxford University Press).

Chodorow, N. (1978) *The Reproduction of Mothering* (Berkeley: University of California Press).

Connell, R. W. (1987) *Gender and Power* (Stanford: Stanford University Press).

Ferguson, A. (1991) "Androgyny as an Ideal for Human Development," in *Sexual Democracy: Women, Oppression and Revolution* (Westview: Allen and Unwin).

Gilligan, C. (1982) *In a Different Voice* (Cambridge, MA: Harvard University Press).

Hartsock, N. C. M. (1983) *Money, Sex and Power: Toward a Feminist Historical Materialism* (Boston: Northeastern University Press).

Moi, T. (2001) "What is a Woman?" in *What is a Woman and Other Essays* (Oxford: Oxford University Press).

Spelman, E. (1988) *Inessential Woman: Problems of Exclusion in Feminist Thought* (Boston: Beacon Press).

Young, I. M. (1997) "Gender as Seriality: Thinking about Women as a Social Collective," in *Intersecting Voices: Dilemmas of Gender, Political Philosophy and Policy* (Princeton: Princeton University Press).

Young, I. M. (2000) *Inclusion and Democracy* (Oxford: Oxford University Press).

Young, I. M. (2001) "Equality of Whom? Social Groups and Judgments of Injustice," *Journal of Political Philosophy* 9/1 (March): 1–18.

Young, I. M. (2002) "Lived Body vs Gender: Reflections on Social Structure and Subjectivity," *Ratio: An International Journal of Analytic Philosophy* 15/4 (December): 410–28.

CHAPTER EIGHT

Masculinity

Toby Miller

Introduction

Men were once the implicit center of most political discourse, social organization, and intellectual inquiry – universal subjects of truth whose achievements, failures, milestones, foibles, and bodies were historical and biological markers of human endeavor and nature. Now, they are subject to specific attention and problematization by researchers, governments, and corporations. Feminist political, personal, and scholarly work, in particular, has been crucial in both asserting the centrality of women to social, scientific, and intellectual life, and calling on men to become objects of study as gendered subjects rather than universal models, in ways that address sexual violence, political power, conversational domination, and media attention – in short, the way of life that characterizes contemporary society and its continued privileging of male images, interests, and experiences.

There was a burst of writing and thinking about men in the 1980s and '90s across the human sciences and social movements. The last 20 years have witnessed, for example, an emergent men's movement and men's studies. Largely a first world discourse about men's rights, nurturance, feelings, and confusion, it draws on the misogyny and anti-Semitism of the psychoanalyst C. G. Jung as much as any other source ("poor, poor, pitiful me – I'm the bad guy? I think I'll go hug a tree" – see Bly 1991 for exemplification). On the other hand, this period has also been marked by queer theory, a largely first world discourse about the logocentric interdependency of gay and straight and the centrality of queerness to "normalcy" ("we're inside you, we are you, mere 'tolerance' of us is no escape from that reality") (see Messner 1997; Warner 1993). The result crosses the gamut from a regressive, self-justifying literature on self-help to excoriating social critiques (Connell 1992: 735; Kimmel 1992).

In this chapter, I survey some literature on masculinity from the perspective of the most influential critical analysis of masculinity in the social sciences – R. W. Connell's thesis of hegemonic masculinity – then test its utility through two case studies of what are often thought of as key sites of symbolic male domination: first, the world of sports; and second, the figure of James Bond. It will be my contention that first world masculinity has been profoundly destabilized by a combination of socio-economic and cultural change, such that even these super-symbols of conventional maleness evidence major ongoing shifts in what counts as masculinity. These are signs of hope in a world that continues to be dominated by men, all the way from the sphere of governmental politics to the repertoire of sexual desire available to women.

But first it is necessary to outline conventional, reactionary accounts of masculinity. Away from overtly politically committed analyses, four discourses articulate the knowledge system of science with gender. They are essentialist approaches that endow particular forms of conduct by men as biological or customary practices that are intrinsic to maleness as both an evolutionary and a behavioral description. These four approaches are gender science, categorization analysis, sex roles, and psychoanalysis.

Revisiting 1970s debates about how to establish the femininity of sportswomen, Butler (1998: 109–11) has pointed out the multiple irony of positivistically applied gender science: that the oscillation in sex testing between chromosomal and hormonal signs registered both an anxiety to fix identity once and for all, and the unattainability of acultural, ahistorical absolutes. This anecdote references the restless search both for the essence of masculinity (by science and the political-cultural right) and for the means of transforming masculinity (by feminists and the political-cultural left). Categorization labels certain physical and behavioral norms as male or female in terms of either nature or society. So, masculinity is thought to involve qualities such as practicality, violence, desire, competitiveness, a bluff approach to feelings, and a teleological orientation to attaining goals. Activities coded as male are evaluated to see whether they "contaminate" women who participate in them. Sex-role analysis accounts for differences in the uptake of social practices by girls and boys through socialization. These stereotypes of masculinity can be reinforced or undermined by family upbringing, social change, ideological training, and media contradictions. And androgyny studies "permit" intermingled behavior across gender (Dewar 1993: 151–7).

There have also been some important psychoanalytic contributions to understanding masculinity. Badinter (1995: x, 32–3) identifies a "requirement" that masculinity differentiate itself from femininity. Men's lives come from the bodies of women, from whom they must disentangle their identities. This struggle produces numerous effects: for instance, that women are less emotionally disturbed during adolescence and live longer, and men resent women whilst also questioning the role of their fathers. Badinter draws on the Oedipus myth, which concerns a man whose feet are brutally bound and disfigured as a child by his father, and who unwittingly carries out a prediction that he will kill his father and marry his mother. On discovering the fact, Oedipus tears his eyes out. This story helps to explain the transfer of boys' affection from mothers to other women, and accounts for succession and rivalry in male life. It takes violence as the narrative touchstone of masculinity (Barratt and Strauss 1994: 43–5). The literary-theological anthropologist René Girard (1992: 145–9) also focuses on violence. He suggests there is a tripartite and mimetic character to male desire, "not only a subject and an object but a third presence as well: the rival." Both the subject and the rival want the object. This is not due to its innate properties. Rather, the rival's desire "alerts the subject to the desirability of the object." Girard identifies sacrificial violence as the key to holding together social formations that lack a fully achieved juridical apparatus. A subject is selected, onto whom the tensions of a group can be projected: sometimes an enemy and sometimes a friend. This sacrificial figure is a surrogate.

Against these mystical, socio-biological, and social-psychological approaches, distributive critics emphasize inequalities of opportunity and power. A sociological model displaces a psychological one, but it remains a liberal position: as long as the preconditions are in place for equilibrium, whatever happens from that point is meant to be, with society in need of equalization, not transformation. By contrast, the left problematizes the overall historical, social, economic, and cultural mythology of masculinity (M. Hall 1993; Hargreaves 1986: 48, 30–1; Mitchell and Dyer 1985: 96–7; Park 1994: 70).

Hegemonic Masculinity

Most of this latter, more critical research into men draws its inspiration from the idea that we live in an era of "hegemonic masculinity" (HM). The concept's lineage is to be traced to the writings of Antonio Gramsci, as picked up and redisposed by R. W. Connell. For Gramsci, an Italian Marxist writing from jail in the mid-1930s, hegemony is a contest of meanings in which a ruling class gains consent to the social order by making its power appear normal and natural. Ordinary people give "spontaneous" consent to the "general direction imposed on social life by the dominant fundamental group" as a consequence of the education and entertainment provided by intellectuals. The society contains old cultural meanings and practices, no longer dominant but still influential, and emergent ones, either propagated by an upcoming class or incorporated by the ruling elite. These discourses are expressed by intellectuals, who work at "superstructural 'levels'" to forge the "hegemony which the dominant group exercises throughout society" (1978: 12).

Connell, an Australian Marxist writing from Australian and US research universities in the 1980s and '90s, applies this notion of consent-through-incorporation to gender relations, especially masculinity. Combining theories of imperialism with feminism, he articulates the history of North Atlantic commercial republics expanding into the rest of the world with contemporary anthropological study. The result makes Western European and North American white male sexuality isomorphic with power (men seek global dominion and desire, orchestrated to oppress women) albeit countered/modified by the liberal promises of modernity. Those promises displaced highly formalized, ritualistic performances of femininity and masculinity that had endured and progressed within different formations around the world – a freedom that also facilitates the rationalization of imperialism and neocolonialism. HM encompasses obvious sexism – rape, domestic violence, and obstacles to female occupational advancement – and more subtle "tactics" of domination, such as the exclusion of women from social environments and sports teams, and lopsided media interest in the lives and bodies of men. Connell calls for critical investigations of masculinity across the state, work, the family, sexual practice, and organizational life (1987; 1993: 602; 1995: 185–99; 1996; 1998).

Of course, HM (straight, strong, domineering) oppresses not only women, but also the many men excluded from it, while even "subscribers" may find its norms of ultimate power and authority to be unattainable. And it does not appeal to everybody. HM's articulation against women and homosexuals makes it unpopular with vast numbers of people. At the same time, many men who feel socially weak (the working class, minorities, and many immigrants) may find the hegemonic model appealing, even though the sources of their powerlessness lie in the monetary and racial economy, not in some need to struggle against women and gays (Messner 1997: 7–8, 12; Rowe 1997: 124). Connell himself argues (1990; 1995) that male identity is complex and polyvalent, with no singular set of qualities consistently marked as masculine. Masculinity and men's bodies (symbolically conceived as unitary) are contested sites, fraught with contradictions.

Connell's social theory is impressive, notably in its attention to history. But critics point to the fact that the histories he sketches tend to be brief and conveniently selected, such that the work sometimes reads like neat ideal types overlaying messy evidence. Counter-examples to a narrative of Western domination abound in the third world, and there are also significant aspects of everyday male conduct that are about selflessness and the desire to build and share, not destroy or dominate – so Mexican men may carry babies around, and macho may be much more complicated than stereotypes allow (Badinter 1995: 25–6; Davis 1997: 555, 563; Gutmann 1996; Kimmel 1992: 167).

The thing about hegemony as a concept is that it explains everything and nothing in a circular motion. Tending to lack a dynamic of history made at specific sites, it accounts for seemingly resistive moves to domination as a function of repressive tolerance, or as co-opted by ruling logics. Such moves are rarely investigated for themselves, but as symptoms of politics from elsewhere, and this "elsewhere" is the given of whoever currently rules. Aspects of everyday conduct that are inconsistent with standard political moves are understood in the same way. But perhaps they have nothing to do with consent to domination elsewhere and are actually site-specific, or articulated with dynamics other than HM. Does HM allow for a time when men are not *being* men, when their activities might be understood as discontinuous, conflicted, and ordinary, rather than interconnected, functional, and dominant – when nothing they do relates to the overall subordination of women or their own self-formation as a gendered group? Put another way, can HM allow for a time when a man is not *being* a man? when his activities might be understood in utterly different ways, rather than being reduced to logics of sexual urge and agent? Coleman (1990: 193, 195) has identified two discourses that interrogate masculinity. The first presents a dramaturgical view: men act their gender in public performances through practices that together amount to a role. By contrast, the second discourse treats its object as a hidden truth to be understood through symptomatic readings. In each case, various practices catalogued as "masculine" could be ascribed to other performances: teaching, voting, policing, or cooking. Masculinity is an occasioned activity, not a system.

When men are judged as such, and present themselves in anticipation of such processes, masculinity "takes place." Rather than looking behind masculine representations of the body as a phallic stand-in, we can follow ethnomethodology's lead and view gender as an occasioned, multiperspectival matter that emerges from social situations. In McHoul's (1997) hands, ethnomethodology demonstrates that the apparently normal is in fact a contingently achieved series of actions. So New York performance artist Diane Torr's "Drag King" workshop for women who are keen to adopt male forms of bodily comportment as a means of controlling space urges participants to come with a "fake penis (the most convincing is a piece of tubular bandage, stuffed with cotton wool and sewn at either end – don't make it too large!!)." Masculinity is present; men are not.

The man simply "is" most of the time; masculinity emerges when it is called up (Coleman instances an occasion when a man is asked to carry a bag conventionally coded as feminine and becomes aware of sexual difference). Such moments are not secretions of what is otherwise denied: there are often no things to deny and nothing beneath the surface. If there are, they may not be part of a broader, coherent problematic, because too many other possible contexts must be accounted for (bell-ringing, color, age, newsprint readership, gardening-appliance purchase, or criminal activity) to encompass the diverse practices of all men all the time under this handily tidy sobriquet. For its very tidiness leads down one of two paths: either men constantly monitor their performance of masculinity, ensuring a seamless weave with no grammatical mistakes and specific semantic and syntactical shifts that underscore their gender; or they are constituted unconsciously and collectively by a mass ideology that can only be uncovered through the heroics of theorists. Rather than these remorseless antinomies, we would do better to aim the study of gender in the direction of explicit, knowable – and hence realistically contestable – occasions of maleness (Coleman 1990: 197–8).

However we differ, most analysts agree that the crucial issue for discussing men is power: that everywhere one *turns*, men seem to be *in* power, but everywhere one *listens*, they seem to feel power*less*. I want to suggest, contra Badinter and Girard, that this feeling is historically contingent and political, rather than timelessly universal and psychological; and, contra Connell, that it is a partially positive by-product of the commodification of male beauty.

All Change When Capital Changes

The brutal deindustrialization that has cut the economic underpinnings of first world working-class masculinity since the 1970s has also seen a dramatic shift of capital into the services sector, the entertainment complex that is a cradle of Northern, especially US, wealth. Beauty is as much a part of male discourse today as toughness, while grace is the avowed compatriot of violence. These antinomies have always enjoyed *frottage*, but their relationship has become crucial to marketing both individuals and cultural practices in ways that were occasional and casual in earlier times. Governmentality, the refinement of human bodies through rationalization and utilitarianism, connects to capital accumulation, but in a dispersed network of power that cannot be explained in terms of a unilinear connection between laboring and consuming forces. It is equally driven by the search for individual health and happiness, via the conditioned and consuming body, sex appeal, and self-discipline. Just as the bourgeoisie has managed to be the most revolutionary class in history, so its means of reification, in all their sophistication, have had both beneficial and baleful consequences. The requirement for capitalism to generate new forms of consumption has driven masculinity and heteronormativity into a condition of unparalleled flux, as capital targets queers and straight women by sexualizing the male body. As a result, the progressive displacement of speech by sight as a critical hermeneutic method, which began in early-modern Europe, at last moves onto men in the sexual way that colonized women much earlier.

We can see this in the context of emergent advertising trends. The 1980s saw two crucial conferences that helped shift the direction of global advertising: "Reclassifying People" and "Classifying People." Traditional ways of understanding consumers – race and class – were supplanted by categories of self-display, with market researchers dubbing the 1990s the decade of the "new man." Lifestyle and psychographic research became central issues in targeting consumers, who were divided between "moralists," "trendies," "the indifferent," "working-class puritans," "sociable spenders," and "pleasure seekers," with men further subdivided into "pontificators," "self-admirers," "self-exploiters," "token triers," "chameleons," "avant-gardicians," "sleepwalkers," and "passive endurers" (Fox 1989; Nixon 1996: 99). These innovative classifications were harbingers of new male targets for capitalist consumption.

Gay magazines circulate information to businesses about the spending-power of their putatively childless, middle-class readership – *Campaign*'s slogan in advertising circles is "Gay Money Big Market Gay Market Big Money." And there has been a corollary surge in interest from the heartland of capitalism. The 1990s brought US TV commercials showing two men furnishing their apartment together at Ikea, and Toyota's male car-buying couple. Meanwhile, Hyundai began appointing gay-friendly staff to dealerships, IBM targeted gay-run small businesses, Subaru advertisements on buses and billboards had gay-advocacy bumper stickers and registration plates coded to appeal to queers, and Volkswagen commercials featured two men driving around in search of home furnishings. (These campaigns are known as "encrypted ads." They are designed to make queers feel special for being "in the know" whilst not offending straights who are unable to read the codes.) Polygram's classical music division has a special gay promotional budget, Miller beer was a major supporter of Gay Games '94, Bud Light sponsored the 1999 San Francisco Folsom Street Fair ("the world's largest leather event"), and Coors introduced domestic partner employee benefits to counteract its anti-gay image of the past (this was echoed by the major auto manufacturers in 2000). In the late 1990s, Sony, Smirnoff, and Telstra sponsored Sydney's Gay and Lesbian Mardi Gras Festival. The spring 1997 US network TV season saw 22 queer characters across the prime-time network schedule, and by 2001 there were 30 – clear signs of niche targeting. The first successful gay initial public offering, an Australian newspaper and real-estate firm, emerged in 1999, while gay and lesbian websites were drawing significant private investment. Bruce Hayes, an "out" gay man who won a swimming relay gold medal for the US at the 1984 Los Angeles Olympics, was a key figure in Levi Strauss's 1998–9 Dockers campaign. The next year, Procter & Gamble, the nation's second-largest advertiser, dropped plans to advertise on a projected TV talk show by anti-queer advice-giver Laura Schlessinger following lobbying efforts (Alsop 1999a, 1999b; Bank 1999: B1; Cahill 1997: 34; Elliott 1998; O'Connor 1997; Rawlings 1993; Rutenberg and Elliott 2000). Such commercial decisions were simply not made until the mid-1990s.

Thanks to this commodification of the male subject, he is brought out into the bright light of narcissism and purchase. In related developments, male striptease shows performed for female audiences (extremely rare up to the 1970s) reference not only changes in the direction of power and money, but also a public site where women paid to see male genitalia, treating men as sex-objects. During the 1998 men's World Cup Soccer tournament, the French Sexy Boys Band offered special strip shows for "*les filles sans foot*" ("girls without soccer/girls who couldn't care less"). The Band has been performing in Paris since 1993 to sell-outs – its all-female audiences must book two weeks in advance. And the US Chippendales (est. 1978) toured Northern Europe across the spring and summer of 1999 to crowds of women – *The Full Monty* (1997) writ large, even though some female spectators found the reversal of subject positions far from easy. The group now markets its own merchandise and also licenses its name (Burke 1999; Dyer 1992: 104; Harari 1993; Jenkins 1998: 92).

The North American middle-class labor market sees wage discrimination by beauty amongst men as much as women, and major corporations frequently require executives to tailor their body shapes to the company ethos, or at least encourage employees to cut their weight in order to reduce healthcare costs to the employer. In 1998, 93 percent of US companies featured related programs for workers, compared to 76 percent in 1992. American Academy of Cosmetic

Surgery figures indicate that more than 6,500 men had face-lifts in 1996, and 680,000 had other cosmetic procedures. In 1997, they accounted for a quarter of all such procedures, and the following year straight couples were frequently scheduling surgery together (up 15 percent in a year). Between 1996 and 1998, male cosmetic surgery increased 34 percent, mostly through liposuction (which has quadrupled since 1990). Gay men reportedly often use steroids for cosmetic purposes, and a third of all "greying" male US workers in 1999 colored their hair to counter the effect of aging on their careers. Mid-town Manhattan now offers specialists in ear-, hand-, and foot-waxing, with men comprising 40 percent of the clientele. As of 1997, the annual US market for men's toiletries was US$3.5 billion.

On the health front, young males are beginning to experience the kind of somato-mimetic problems of young women – and no wonder. Consider *Playgirl* magazine. Its male centerfolds have undergone comprehensive transformations over the past quarter century: the average model has lost 12 pounds of fat and gained 25 pounds of muscle. GI Joe dolls of the 1960s had biceps to a scale of 11.5 inches, an average dimension. In 1999, their biceps were at a scale of 26 inches, beyond any recorded bodybuilder. Similar changes have happened to other dolls, such as *Star Wars* figures. There are probable correlatives: in 1997, 43 percent of US men up to their late fifties disclosed dissatisfaction with their appearance, compared to 34 percent in 1985 and 15 percent in 1972. Subscriptions to the bodybuilding magazine *Men's Health* went from 250,000 in 1990 to 1.5 million in 1997. The new century brought reports of a million men diagnosed with body dysmorphic disorder and the invention of the "Adonis Complex" by psychiatrists to account for the vastly increased numbers of eating and exercise disorders among men (60 percent of such disorders are now reported by women and 40 percent by men). This suggests that dissatisfaction with one's body has crossed genders. What Tien calls "the rising tide of male vanity" has real costs to conventional maleness ("Marketplace" 1999; Bordo 1999: 217; Burstyn 1999: 217; Freudenheim 1999; S. S. Hall 1999: 33; Hamermesh and Biddle 1994; Lemon 1997: 30; Pope et al. 2000: 12, 18, 27, 31, 43, 47, 54; Stein 1999; Tien 1999; Wheeler 1999). To interrogate these changes on a site-specific basis, here are two investigations that illustrate how complex and contradictory masculinity can be, even at its acme – sports and spying.

Boys and Balls: Sports

The HM model seems to fit sport's ideological apparatus, where aggression, bodily force, competition, and physical skill are primarily associated with straight maleness (Cahn 1993: 344). Sport has been a crucial site for training and expressing male violence, both on and off the field. This is evident from the record of domestic assault and public attacks on bystanders by athletes. It includes 56 pro US footballers charged with domestic violence between 1989 and 1994 and high-profile murder charges arising from the 1999–2000 pro football season ("Out of Bounds" 1996: 1050; Rowe 1997: 123). Messner argues that:

> Football, based as it is on the most extreme possibilities of the male body . . . is clearly a world apart from women, who are relegated to the role of cheerleaders/ sex objects on the sidelines. . . . In contrast to the bare and vulnerable bodies of the cheerleaders, the armored bodies of the football players are elevated to mythical status, and as such, give testimony to the undeniable "fact" that here is at least one place where men are clearly superior to women. (1990: 213)

In an in-depth interview with an Australian sporting professional who seemingly embodies HM, Connell's subject is asked about the meaning of being a man. He replies in negative terms: to be a man is to "Not be a gay." The exclusion of male desire for other men from the definition of masculinity occurs in the context of all-male competition and single-sex affinity on and off the sporting field. Connell (1990) observes a profound contradiction in this "articulation of self and body." The body is invested with narcissistic social currency as an object for professional improvement and success, but this narcissism is unstable and can never be satisfied. The commodified body requires constant self-surveillance and renewal if it is to remain competitive and hence marketable to sponsors.

McKay says: "any male Australian athlete will verify . . . [that] the most insulting accusation a coach can make about a player's performance is to say that he 'played like a sheila' or a 'poofter'" (1991: 55). In Schwartz's words, "being or appearing homosexual will bring shame to the team and the sport" (1997: 56). No surprise, then, that British heavyweight boxer Lennox Lewis reacts to queries about dating with "I'm fully 110 per cent a ladies' man. You don't have to worry about me" (quoted in Smith 1999). HM's homophobia and misogyny are personified by infamous ex-Indiana University basketball coach Bobby Knight. Consider this hysterical 1985 assault on one player:

> You never push yourself. You know what you are Daryl? You are the worst fucking pussy I've ever seen play basketball at this school. The absolute worst pussy ever. You have more goddamn ability than 95 percent of the players we've had here but you are a pussy from the top of your head to the bottom of your feet. An absolute fucking pussy. (Quoted in Eitzen 1999: 84)

But masculinity, understood as a set of dominant practices of gendered power, is no longer the exclusive province of men, either as spectators, consumers, or agents. "Female masculinity" can now be rearticulated as a prize rather than a curse (Halberstam 1998). The capacity of sport to ideologize masculine superiority has been destabilized as women have struggled to gain greater access. Increasing numbers of women are competing in traditionally male sports like powerlifting, body-building, the martial arts, football, rugby, and ice hockey, and women often outperform men in stamina-based events. The year 2000 saw the formation of a Women's Professional Football League and Tonya Butler winning a football scholarship to junior college and successfully kicking extra points, while Laila Ali followed in her father's career footsteps with several boxing knockouts and a 2001 defeat of Joe Frazier's daughter ("Catching Up with Tonya Butler" 1999–2000; Billings 1999–2000). Women's entry into customarily male preserves illustrates the "double movement of containment and resistance" that characterizes cultural struggles among dominant and sub-ordinate groups (S. Hall 1981). On the one hand, the presence of vigorous and robust women athletes demonstrates that sporting prowess is not "naturally" masculine. On the other, the presence of physically powerful females precipitates attempts by men to limit women's aspiration and resistance (Disch and Kane 1996; McKay 1992; Ndalianis 1995; White and Gillett 1994).

In addition to "infiltrating" the field, women have become desirable consumers of masculinity in and as spectator sports. In the mid-1990s, National Football League (NFL) administrators discerned a threat to the game's man appeal from other media forms and faced mothers who objected to their sons playing so mindlessly violent a sport. The League responded by hiring Sara Levinson to run marketing – the first woman to be employed in its central office executive group other than as a secretary. The NFL wanted her to push merchandising spin-offs and attract female audiences via what became known as the "Women's Initiative," named because "[o]ur research indicates that women like the tight pants on the players." High-school co-educational football was introduced, along with Levinson's new *argot*, which talked of the NFL as a brand, not something quasi-holy (Seabrook 1997). Meanwhile, male players were complaining about the ritual objectification of standing near-naked as hundreds of administrators, owners, coaches, medics, scouts, and other men calibrated their bodies at meat-market conventions (Burstyn 1999: 137). Clearly, changes are afoot that under-cut HM as an analysis and as a problem even in male sports, supposedly the heartland of brutal male domination.

Spying on Men: James Bond

Another key site for testing the HM model is the cinema, where it seems plausible to construct a genealogy of brutal white masculinity appearing on the Hollywood screen via the genre of action adventure. Such a history would examine James Bond in his various incarnations since 1962 and connect him to such Reagan-era icons as Sylvester Stallone, Arnold Schwarzenegger, and Bruce Willis. But it is my argument that Bond's gender politics are far from a function-alist world of total domination by straight, orthodox masculinity. As I have noted, excoriating evaluations of women's bodies have long been a pivotal node of consumer capitalism. Now, slowly in many cases but rapidly in others, the process of bodily commodification through niche targeting has identified men's bodies as objects of desire, and gay men and straight women as consumers. Masculinity is no longer the exclusive province of men, either as spectators, consumers, or agents of power. And Bond was an unlikely harbinger of this trend.

Because Bond is such a complex series of social texts, his film persona needs to be understood across sites, starting with the originary novels. Their trace was significant to film reviewers of the day, and it provides an abstraction from contemporary viewing positions in order to get at "the affective structure" of Bond (Bergonzi 1958: 221). This structure spoke to 8-year-old Jay McInerney (later a prominent New York night-time novelist) when the film *Doctor No* (1962) was released. Bond had come "to save America, and not incidentally to liberate me from my crew cut and help me to meet girls." McInerney's parents forbade him to see the film because it was said to be "racy" and because his father's domestic mastery was attested by Jay's hairstyle (McInerney 1996: 13).

Many British critics of the mid-1960s interpreted Bond as a symptom of imperial decline, evidenced in his lack of moral fiber, and an open sexuality that assumed the legitimacy of strong women desiring heterosexual sex outside marriage (Cannadine 1979: 49–50; Denning 1992: 223). This aspect made Bergonzi deride Bond as not "an ideal example for the young," because women are "only too eager to make love to *him*" (1958: 222, 225). The Salvation Army's *War Cry* journal objected to the same tendency (Woolf 1990: 86). Bond represented the casual pleasures that derived from a perverse intermingling of US consumer culture with European social welfare – what the *New Statesman*, in a celebrated essay on Bond, referred to as "our curious post-war society" (Johnson 1958). Connery stood for the right and the space – for men *and* women, albeit in unequally gendered ways – to be sexual without being "committed," and he also symbolized polymorphous sexuality (Bold 1993: 320). In *Doctor No*, Fleming describes Honeychile Rider's buttocks as "almost as firm and rounded as a boy's." This drew a rebuke from Noël Coward: "Really, old chap, what could you have been thinking of?" (quoted in Richler 1971: 343). Any scan of the popular sociology and literary criticism of the time indicates how threatening this was to the right, which drew analogies between the decline of Empire and the rise of personal libertarianism (Booker 1969: 42–3; Cannadine 1979: 46, 49–50; Houston 1964–5).

For all his supposed association with fast-living, high-octane sex, and a dazzling life, Bond basically eschews sex in the novels, leaving the desiring women who surround him in a state of great anxiety. Attempts to match Bond with other literary-historical figures, notably via claims that the novels are based on either *Beowulf* or *Sir Gawain and the Green Knight*, explain this rejection of women as Fleming's "medieval blueprint" of chaste valor (Harris 1990: 30–1; Webb 1968). But it's more than that:

God, it was turning towards his groin! Bond set his teeth. Supposing it liked the warmth there! Supposing it tried to crawl into the crevices! Could he stand it? Supposing it chose that place to bite? Bond could feel it questing amongst the first hairs. (Fleming 1990: 65)

Of course, "it" is Dr. No's centipede heading for "that place." Everyone recalls the spider doing the same in the film – after which, Connery runs to the bathroom and is violently ill. But the steadfast way with which Bond eschews sex in the original stories might as well have made it a human being that "liked the warmth there," for all the horror of intimacy.

Bond's terror about "that place" is also evident in the book *Casino Royale*. Le Chiffre tortures him with "a three-foot-long carpet-beater in twisted cane." The details are fetishistically enumerated in three pages of purple Fleming prose that describes the evil mastermind making his way across what he calls Bond's "sensitive part," while the latter awaits "a wonderful period of warmth and langour leading into a sort of sexual twilight where pain turned to pleasure and where hatred and fear of the torturers turned to a masochistic infatuation" (Fleming 1966: 119–22).

In *Doctor No*, Bond is confronted with his desire for Honeychile Rider, her "left breast . . . hard with passion. Her stomach pressed against his." In response he "must stay cold as ice . . . Later! Later! Don't be weak" (Fleming 1990: 142). Bond risks being taken down by desire, the threat of woman exhausting man's capacity to control his environs and be transcendent. This refusal draws a mocking retort when Honey addresses him in the third person: "His arms and his chest look strong enough. I haven't seen the rest yet. Perhaps it's weak. Yes, that must be it. That's why he doesn't dare take his clothes off in front of me" (ibid.: 144). Conservative novelist-pop philosopher Ayn Rand, who adored the 007 books for what she saw as their unabashed romanticism and heroic transcendence, was appalled by the films because they were laced with "the sort of humor intended to undercut Bond's stature, to make him ridiculous" (1971: 138).

These qualities of self-parody are key aspects to the unstable masculinity on display. Connery's Bondian sex is fairly progressive for its day, with the sado-masochistic aspects, predictably, too much for US critics: *Newsweek* condemned Connery in *Doctor No* as of interest solely to "cultivated sado-masochists" (quoted in Anez 1992: 314). Identical critiques came from the Communist Party youth paper, *Junge Welt*, in the German Democratic Republic, and from the Vatican City's *L'Osservatore Romano* (Sann 1967: 34). Britain's *Daily Worker* found an "appeal to the filmgoer's basest instincts" and "perversion," while on the other side of politics, the *Spectator* deemed the film "pernicious." *Films and Filming* called the "sex and sadism" a "brutally potent intoxicant" and identified Bond on-screen as a "monstrously overblown sex fantasy of nightmarish proportions." He was "morally . . . indefensible" and liable to produce "kinky families" (quoted in Barnes and Hearn 1998: 16–17, 26–7). But for feminist cultural historian Susan Douglas, then, like McInerney, growing up in the US, *Doctor No*, for example, was a sign that "sex for single women [could be] glamorous and satisfying" (1994: 72).

The producers cast Connery knowing full well that he was not the ruling-class figure of the novels, in the hope that he would appeal to women sexually and encourage cross-class identification by men (Broccoli with Zec 1998: 171). Co-producer Albert Broccoli called this "sadism for the family" (quoted in Barnes and Hearn 1998: 20). Connery was frequently criticized as a "wuss" during the 1960s, in keeping with the notion that his s/m style embodied the weak-kneed and decadent cosseting that was losing an Empire. *Time* labeled him a "used-up gigolo" after *Doctor No* (ibid.: 16) while many US magazines objectified him mercilessly by listing his bodily measurements (Dore 1996: 11).

In *Doctor No*, Connery hands his card to a woman he meets in a club and invites her to "come up and see him some time." This is an invitation for the woman (Eunice Gayson as Sylvia Trench) to exercise her desire – which she does, astonishing him by breaking into his apartment within the hour. He encounters her practicing golf in his rooms, attired in just a business shirt. *Thunderball* (1965) finds Connery chided by Fiona Volpe (Luciana Paluzzi):

> I forgot your ego, Mister Bond. James Bond, who only has to make love to a woman and she starts to hear heavenly choirs singing. She repents, then immediately returns to the side of right and virtue. But not this one. What a blow it must have been – you, having a failure.

The equal legitimacy of male and female extra-marital desire lives contradictorily within Bond's violent patriarchal attitudes. So it should be no surprise to find that the first *Sunday Times* magazine color supplement (1962) features Mary Quant clothing, worn by Jean Shrimpton and photographed by David Bailey; a state-of-the-nation essay on Britain; and a James Bond short story – or that the inaugural *Observer* equivalent includes fashions from France and stills from the forthcoming Bond movie (Booker 1969: 49, 238). This is the all-powerful brute at work, with women cowering defensively?

Connery's prior careers as Scottish Mr. Universe, Carnaby Street model, and Royal Court Shakespearian background the intersection of body, style, action, and performance perfectly. In gesturing against McInerney Senior's crewcut, Connery showed that the look of a man could transcend his class background and *politesse*. This was a postmodern figure of beautiful male commodification *avant la lettre*, exquisitely attractive to many women and men who either shared or read through his sexism and racism to enjoy goodness, excitement, and parody (Bold 1993; Manning 1990: 13; Synnott 1990). From the first, Connery was the object of the gaze, posing in 1966 besuited for *GQ* and bare-cleavaged for *Life*, making it clear that sexiness did not have to be associated with a choice between ruggedness and style (McInerney 1996: 26, 32) – the harbinger of a new male body on display. Something similar is happening in feminist "slash lit" fanzines that recode male bonding from TV action series as explicitly sexual, depicting hyper-stylized, hugely tumescent cocks at play in sado-masochistically inflected pleasure (Penley 1992, 1997). Such texts trope Cyril Connolly's 1963 spoof "Bond Strikes Camp," which finds M coming out as gay and 007 a transvestite. So the articulation of Bond with hypermasculinity does not quite withstand close inspection. It suggests that his massive appeal across time, space, and viewer is referencing something deeper than the reinforcement of HM.

Conclusion

Masculinity is a form of life in transition, a mode of social domination of quite terrifying force and completeness that is coming unstuck and having to renew itself, with unintended consequences. It is difficult indeed to know which direction masculinity will take. Clearly, the study of masculinity will continue to be influenced by both the conservative assumptions outlined earlier and, on the left, by Connell's HM formulations. Whatever path is taken from here on, however, will need to take into account the transformations in relations of looking that have been engendered by capitalism and exemplified here. I do not, however, suggest that we are close to putting an end to the immense social inequalities that, in era after era and place after place, characterize male–female relations. The violence and domination of patriarchy may in fact undergo renewal with men's responses to this new commodification. In no sense, then, do I regard the changes I have outlined as a wholesale revolution that should cause men any real grief – we/they still get to "run" most aspects of life. But the traditional overcoding, the rampant overvaluation, of male desire for women, and the corollary undercoding, undervaluation, of male desire and female desire for men, are in transition. Our analyses of these trends need to change as well, if we are to understand them and engage in a cultural politics that brings gender relations closer to equality and open to negotiation.

Paul Smith says: "Masculinity isn't always a pleasant thing to behold, and it's always difficult, sometimes unpleasant to write about – it's certainly a difficult thing in just about every respect." Smith points out that when masculinity is "understood simply as a given," there is little room for transforming it. But once it is identified as partial and contingent, its "state of silent and indefinite normality over and against which difference was both established and measured" is made audible, definite, and itself subject to difference (1996: ix). In my view, masculinity is best viewed not as a property or an essence, but as a series of contingent signs and practices that exercise power over both men and women – and to "know" it is to shift it, not just to love it.

Note

Thanks to David Goldberg for comments.

References

"Catching Up with Tonya Butler" (1999–2000) *Sports Illustrated for Women* (winter–spring): 17.

"Marketplace" (1999) National Public Radio, June 3.

"Out of Bounds: Pro-Sports Leagues and Domestic Violence" (1996) *Harvard Law Review* 109/5: 1048–65.

Alsop, R. (1999a) "Are Gay People More Affluent Than Others?" *Wall Street Journal* (December 30): B1, B3.

Alsop, R. (1999b) "But Brewers Employ In-Your-Mug Approach," *Wall Street Journal* (June 29): B1.

Anez, N. (1992) "James Bond," *Films in Review* 43/9–10: 310–19.

Badinter, E. (1995) *XY: On Masculine Identity*, trans. L. Davis (New York: Columbia University Press).

Bank, D. (1999) "On the Web, Gay Sites Start to Click," *Wall Street Journal* (September 28): B1, B6.

Barnes, A. and Hearn, M. (1998) *Kiss Kiss Bang! Bang! The Unofficial James Bond Film Companion* (Woodstock: Overlook Press).

Barratt, B. B. and Straus, B. R. (1994) "Toward Postmodern Masculinities," *American Imago* 51/1: 37–67.

Bergonzi, B. (1958) "The Case of Mr Fleming," *Twentieth Century* (March): 220–8.

Billings, L. (1999–2000) "Minnesota Vixens," *Sports Illustrated for Women* (winter–spring): 46–7.

Bly, R. (1991) *Iron John: A Book About Men* (Reading: Addison-Wesley).

Bold, C. (1993) "'Under the Very Skirts of Britannia': Re-Reading Women in the James Bond Novels," *Queen's Quarterly* 100/2: 310–27.

Booker, C. (1969) *The Neophiliacs: A Study of the Revolution in English Life in the Fifties and Sixties* (London: Collins).

Bordo, S. (1999) *The Male Body: A New Look at Men in Public and in Private* (New York: Farrar, Strauss and Giroux).

Broccoli, A. with Zec, D. (1998) *When the Snow Melts: The Autobiography of Cubby Broccoli* (London: Boxtree).

Burke, R. M. (1999) "Chippendales Let It All Hang Out in Europe," *Wall Street Journal* (April 8): A16.

Burstyn, V. (1999) *The Rites of Men: Manhood, Politics, and the Culture of Sport* (Toronto: University of Toronto Press).

Butler, J. (1998) "Athletic Genders: Hyperbolic Instance and/or the Overcoming of Sexual Binarism," *Stanford Humanities Review* 6/2: 103–11.

Cahill, P. (1997) "Pink Power's Diversity Carries Cash Clout," *Variety* (September 15–21): 34, 44.

Cahn, S. K. (1993) "From the 'Muscle Moll' to the 'Butch' Ballplayer: Mannishness, Lesbianism, and Homophobia in US Women's Sport," *Feminist Studies* 19/2: 343–68.

Cannadine, D. (1979) "James Bond & the Decline of England," *Encounter* 53/3: 46–55.

Coleman, W. (1990) "Doing Masculinity/Doing Theory," in Jeff Hearn and David Morgan (eds.), *Men, Masculinities and Social Theory* (London: Unwin Hyman).

Connell, R. W. (1987) *Gender and Power: Society, the Person, and Sexual Politics* (Cambridge: Polity).

Connell, R. W. (1990) "An Iron Man: The Body and Some Contradictions of Hegemonic Masculinity," in Michael A. Messner and Don Sabo (eds.), *Sport, Men, and the Gender Order: Critical Feminist Perspectives* (Champaign: Human Kinetics Press).

Connell, R. W. (1992) "A Very Straight Gay: Masculinity, Homosexual Experience, and the Dynamics of Gender," *American Sociological Review* 57/6: 735–51.

Connell, R. W. (1993) "The Big Picture: Masculinities in Recent World History," *Theory and Society* 22/5: 597–623.

Connell, R. W. (1995) *Masculinities* (Berkeley: University of California Press).

Connell, R. W. (1996) "New Directions in Gender Theory, Masculinity Research, and Gender Politics," *Ethnos* 61/3–4: 157–76.

Connell, R. W. (1998) "Masculinities and Globalization," *Men and Masculinities* 1/1: 3–23.

Connolly, C. (1963) *Previous Convictions* (New York: Harper & Row).

Davis, K. (1997) "Was will der Mann?: Some Reflections on Theorizing Masculinity," *Theory and Psychology* 7/4: 555–64.

Denning, M. (1992) "Licensed to Look: James Bond and the Heroism of Consumption," in Francis, M. (ed.), *Contemporary Marxist Literary Criticism* (London: Longman).

Dewar, A. (1993) "Sexual Orientation in Sport: Past, Present, and Future Alternatives," in Alan G. Ingham and John W. Loy (eds.), *Sport in Social Development: Traditions, Transitions, and Transformations* (Champaign: Human Kinetics).

Disch, L. and Kane, M. J. (1996) "When a Looker is Really a Bitch: Lisa Olson, Sport, and the Heterosexual Matrix," *Signs: Journal of Women in Culture and Society* 21/2: 278–308.

Dore, K. (1996) "Public School Playboy: The Image of James Bond in America in the Sixties," Unpublished ms.

Douglas, S. J. (1994) *Where the Girls Are: Growing Up Female with the Mass Media* (New York: Times Books).

Dyer, R. (1992) *Only Entertainment* (London: Routledge).

Eitzen, D. S. (1999) *Fair and Foul: Beyond the Myths and Paradoxes of Sport* (Lanham: Rowman & Littlefield).

Elliott, S. (1998) "Levi Strauss Begins a Far-Reaching Marketing Campaign to Reach Gay Men and Lesbians," *New York Times* (October 19): C11.

Fleming, I. (1966) *Casino Royale* (London: Pan).

Fleming, I. (1990) *Doctor No* (New York: Berkeley).

Fox, C. (1989) "Decade of the 'New Man' is Here," *Australian Financial Review* (January 21): 46.

Freudenheim, M. (1999) "Employers Focus on Weight as Workplace Health Issue," *New York Times* (September 6): A15.

Girard, R. (1992) *Violence and the Sacred*, trans. P. Gregory (Baltimore: Johns Hopkins University Press).

Gramsci, A. (1978) *Selections From the Prison Notebooks of Antonio Gramsci*, trans. and ed. Quentin Hoare and Geoffrey Nowell-Smith (New York: International Publishers).

Gutmann, M. C. (1996) *The Meanings of Macho: Being a Man in Mexico City* (Berkeley: University of California Press).

Halberstam, J. (1998) *Female Masculinity* (Durham: Duke University Press).

Hall, M. A. (1993) "Gender and Sport in the 1990s: Feminism, Culture, and Politics," *Sport Science Review* 2/1: 48–68.

Hall, S. (1981) "Notes on Deconstructing 'The Popular'," in Raphael Samuel (ed.), *People's History and Socialist Theory* (London: Routledge & Kegan Paul).

Hall, S. S. (1999) "The Bully in the Mirror," *New York Times Magazine* (August 22): 30–5, 58–65.

Hamermesh, D. S. and Biddle, J. E. (1994) "Beauty and the Labor Market," *American Economic Review* 84/5: 1174–94.

Harari, F. (1993) "The New Face of Beauty," *Australian* (June 18): 15.

Hargreaves, J. (1986) *Sport, Power and Culture* (Cambridge: Polity).

Harris, H. R. (1990) "New Light on James Bond," *Contemporary Review* 256/1488: 30–4.

Houston, P. (1964–5) "007," *Sight and Sound* 34/1: 14–16.

Jenkins, E. (1998) *Tongue First: Adventures in Physical Culture* (New York: Henry Holt).

Johnson, P. (1958) "Sex, Snobbery, and Sadism," *New Statesman* (April 5): 430–2.

Kimmel, M. S. (1992) "Reading Men: Men, Masculinity, and Publishing," *Contemporary Sociology* 21/2: 162–71.

Lemon, B. (1997) "Male Beauty," *Advocate* 738 (July 22): 30–2.

McHoul, A. (1997) "On Doing 'We's': Where Sport Leaks into Everyday Life," *Journal of Sport & Social Issues* 21/3: 315–20.

McInerney, J. (1996) "How Bond Saved America – And Me," in Jay McInerney, Nick Foulkes, Neil Norman, and Nick Sullivan, *Dressed to Kill: James Bond the Suited Hero* (Paris: Flammarion).

McKay, J. (1991) *No Pain, No Gain? Sport and Australian Culture* (Sydney: Prentice Hall).

McKay, J. (1992) "Sport and the Social Construction of Gender," in Gillian Lupton, Patricia M. Short, and Rosemary Whip (eds.), *Society and Gender: An Introduction to Sociology* (Sydney: Macmillan).

Manning, M. (1990) "Futile Attraction," *New Statesman and Society* 3/122: 12–13.

Messner, M. A. (1990) "When Bodies are Weapons: Masculinity and Violence in Sport," *International Review for the Sociology of Sport* 25: 203–19.

Messner, M. A. (1997) *Politics of Masculinities: Men in Movements* (Thousand Oaks: Sage).

Mitchell, S. and Dyer, K. (1985) *Winning Women: Challenging the Norms in Australian Sport* (Ringwood: Penguin).

Ndalianis, A. (1995) "Muscle, Excess and Rupture: Female Bodybuilding and Gender Construction," *Media Information Australia* 75 (February): 13–23.

Nixon, S. (1996) *Hard Looks: Masculinities, Spectatorship and Contemporary Consumption* (New York: St. Martin's Press).

O'Connor, J. J. (1997) "Coming Out Party: The Closet Opens, Finally," *New York Times* (April 30): C18.

Park, R. J. (1994) "A Decade of the Body: Researching and Writing About the History of Health, Fitness, Exercise, and Sport, 1983–1993," *Journal of Sport History* 21/1: 59–82.

Penley, C. (1992) "Feminism, Psychoanalysis, and the Study of Popular Culture," in Lawrence Grossberg, Cary Nelson, and Paula A. Treichler (eds.), *Cultural Studies* (New York: Routledge).

Penley, C. (1997) *NASA/TREK: Popular Science and Sex in America* (London: Verso).

Pope, H. G. Jr., Phillips, K. A., and Olivardia, R. (2000) *The Adonis Complex: The Secret Crisis of Male Body Obsession* (New York: Free Press).

Rand, A. (1971) *The Romantic Manifesto: A Philosophy of Literature*, rev. edn. (New York: Signet).

Rawlings, S. (1993) "Luring the Big Boys," *B and T* 43/1923 (February 12): 18–19.

Richler, M. (1971) "James Bond Unmasked," in Bernard Rosenberg and David Manning White (eds.), *Mass Culture Revisited* (New York: Van Nostrand Reinhold).

Rowe, D. (1997) "Big Defence: Sport and Hegemonic Masculinity," in Alan Tomlinson (ed.), *Gender, Sport and Leisure: Continuities and Challenges* (Meyer and Meyer Verlag).

Rutenberg, J. and Elliott, S. (2000) "Advertiser Shuns Talk Show as Gay Protest Gains Power," *New York Times* (May 19): A21.

Sann, P. (1967) *Fads, Follies and Delusions of the American People* (New York: Crown).

Schwartz, H. L. (1997) "Out of Bounds," *Advocate* 729 (March 18): 56–9.

Seabrook, J. (1997) "Tackling the Competition," *New Yorker* (August 18): 42–51.

Smith, P. (1996) "Introduction," in Paul Smith (ed.), *Boys: Masculinities in Contemporary Culture* (New York: Westview Press).

Smith, T. W. (1999) "When (Heavyweight) Words Collide," *New York Times* (March 11): D2.

Stein, J. (1999) "Only His Hairdresser Knows for Sure," *Time* (July 19): 78.

Synnott, A. (1990) "The Beauty Mystique: Ethics and Aesthetics in the Bond Genre," *International Journal of Politics, Culture, and Society* 3/3: 407–26.

Tien, E. (1999) "The More Hairless Ape," *New York Times* (June 20): 3.

Warner, M. (ed.) (1993) *Fear of a Queer Planet* (Minneapolis: University of Minnesota Press).

Webb, B. L. (1968) "James Bond as Literary Descendent of Beowulf," *South Atlantic Quarterly* 67/1: 1–12.

Wheeler, D. L. (1999) "Could Boys Get 'Barbie Syndrome'?" *Chronicle of Higher Education* (June 11): A22.

White, P. and Gillett, J. (1994) "Reading the Muscular Body: A Critical Decoding of Advertisements in 'Flex' Magazine," *Sociology of Sport Journal* 11/1: 18–39.

Woolf, M. (1990) "Ian Fleming's Enigmas and Variations," in Clive Bloom (ed.), *Spy Thrillers: From Buchan to le Carré* (New York: St. Martin's Press).

CHAPTER NINE

Heterosexuality

Lorraine Nencel

Introduction

Almost 20 years have passed since the relationship between gender and sexuality – a relationship that in its extreme equated the two – was brought into question. Several publications (Caplan 1987; Ortner and Whitehead 1981; Snitow et al. 1983; Vance 1984; Weeks 1986), now classics, provided space to analyze and theorize sexuality in its own right. Snitow et al., one of the earlier studies in the field, describes sexuality as follows: "As we create masculinity and femininity, so we also make love. Sexuality is a construct" (1983: 10). In her introduction to *Pleasure and Danger* Vance states: "Despite the many interrelationships of sexuality and gender, sexuality is not a residual category, a subcategory of gender; nor are theories of gender fully adequate to account for sexuality" (1984: 10). Vance and Snitow et al. were driven by developments particularly relevant to the North American context in reply to the feminist conceptualizations of sexuality as dangerous and oppressive. Their volumes offered a theoretical alternative that supported another feminist political agenda. Valverde describes this controversy as the time "in which feminists who emphasize sexual danger, and thus seek to control male abuse and protect and/or empower women, are opposed to those who emphasize the need for taking risks in the pursuit of both the theory and practice of women's sexual pleasure" (1989: 237).

Caplan (1987), working from a cross-cultural anthropological perspective, also emphasizes the cultural specificity of the construct of sexuality and the need to study it independently and in its articulation with gender. The contributions of Gay Studies, Third Gender Studies (Kulick 1998; Prieur 1998), as well as studies that originated out of concern for AIDS prevention (Parker et al. 1991, 2000) have firmly anchored the premise in the social sciences that sexual and gender identities need not coincide, reflect, or conform to each other: one's gender identity is not naturally one's sexual identity or vice versa; both are socially and culturally constructed within specific dynamics in historical contexts. Additionally, just like gender, sexuality is constituted by and an expression of relations of power. In sum, these theoretical perspectives have strengthened the intricate relationship between sexuality and gender and at the same time have legitimated their analytical independence.

Nonetheless, heterosexual sexuality is underrepresented in the literature. This does not mean that it has not been researched. In anthropology, for example, it has been studied vis-à-vis kinship and reproduction. Despite the cultural diversity found in kinship systems and reproductive relations, heterosexual sexuality was not studied as a cultural construct, but taken as a societal given. In part, it was this recognition and its far-reaching consequences of silencing other sexualities that inspired the growth and institutionalization of Queer Studies (Rubin 1985). The cultural dynamics of (hetero-)sexuality has gained more importance in reproductive health and AIDS prevention studies, but, as Obermeyer states, "focusing almost exclusively on the practical consequences of behaviour. Frequently consisting of inventories – does one engage in such and such practice, how frequently, how many partners one has, how often one achieves satisfaction, etc. – such studies tend to reify behaviours and fail to provide explanations for their existence or understand their meaning for actors" (2000: 239). Comparatively speaking, since the 1980s the study of heterosexual sexuality has been less dynamic and innovating than the studies on non-hegemonic expressions of sexuality.

In the study of heterosexual sexuality the concept power is given a prominent place. It is debatable whether its positioning as such has always contributed favorably to developing sexuality theories of heterosexuality. The primary concern, whether made explicit or not, is with the way gender power relations affect heterosexual women's experience of their sexuality. Depending on which position the researcher leans towards in the debate on sexuality – roughly speaking, is it dangerous or pleasurable? oppressive or empowering? – the research will be directed to proving their standpoint. The simplification of this complex relation between gender, power, and (hetero-)sexuality has produced research that allocates script-like roles to women and men with programmatic outcomes. In its two extremes, women are made into victims by sexual practices which objectify them and entirely benefit men, or women's actions are interpreted as challenging hegemonic structures of sexuality, when perhaps all they are actually doing is "having fun." Far too little work is being done on the pleasurable side of these relations. Women's experiences are still too often being analyzed in a framework that (implicitly) defines concepts such as agency as synonymous with "resistance." Studies that focus on empowerment as the objective often end up presenting a checks and balance version of empowerment, or representing reality as an accumulative process – have women become empowered through their experiences? how can their empowerment increase? Neither of these two approaches does justice to the intricacies of men's and women's sexual experiences.

This approach to heterosexual sexuality has determined the directions of research for far too long. It is too entangled in feminist political agendas that have commendable objectives but are founded on feminist mores that do not create the space necessary to explore the intricacies of (hetero-)sexuality. This way of seeing the relationship between power and sexuality has taken on paradigmatic proportions. The need to unsettle this paradigm has become increasingly apparent. Hence, the objective of this chapter is twofold. First, it aims to examine three different areas – work, masculinity, and female sexuality – in which sexuality is studied in relation to gender and how it is constituted by power. The reason these areas were chosen is simple. Studies on gender, labor, and workplace relations have often been concerned with sexuality in work: several of the studies discussed below attempt to analyze the interaction among gender, sexuality and power without becoming too entangled in the snares of this paradigm. They offer surprising insight into the subject. The choice to concentrate on studies concerning masculinity and female sexuality is logical in a chapter concerning heterosexual sexuality where the players are men and women. In addition, since the mid-1990s studies on masculinity have increased substantially. It is interesting to take an analytical glimpse into what is being done on (hetero-)sexuality within this new and exciting area.

The exploration of (hetero-)sexuality and power will be undertaken with a review of recently published articles. This methodological choice gives insight into what I have called the "praxis of academia." Instead of basing the analysis on contemporary theory and the "classics," it is a challenge to analyze the subject by reviewing how it is developing in everyday academia. Is the power paradigm beginning to show signs of fatigue or is it still firmly anchored?

The second objective of this chapter intends to go beyond the point of unsettling the power paradigm and scramble up even further the relation among gender, sexuality, and power, creating more space to explore concepts such as sexual subjectivity, pleasure, sexual objectification, and their relation. Based on the review that follows, the final section will deal with what is needed to develop an alternative perspective on gender, power, and (hetero-)sexuality.

Workplace Sexuality: Sexual Harassment versus Flirting

In 1988, Rosemary Pringle published a pioneering study on Australian secretaries and described the place of sexuality in the workplaces as being everywhere performed self-presentations, dress, jokes, and gossips in affairs, fantasies, and sexual harassment. Pringle was one of the first academics to study office relations in terms of power, gender, and sexuality. Her study showed that, as absurd as it is to imagine the workplace as gender neutral, it is unthinkable to consider the workplace as sex neutral. "Gender and sexuality are central not only in the boss–secretary relation but in all workplace power relations" (1988: 84).

Since the mid-1990s there have been some interesting studies conducted in regard to power, femininity, and sexuality on the work floor. Theses studies can be divided along geographical as well as disciplinary boundaries. The first group has been dominated by studies conducted in the West and concern sexual harassment: its definition, causes, consequences, and organizational responses (Bowes-Sperry and Tata 1999). Research has been primarily conducted in the disciplines of sociology, psychology, and law. Although these studies have made sexual harassment visible and have presented ideas to modify this type of behavior in the workplace, they leave little room for exploring the other areas of sexual work-floor dynamics. Other studies included here address this bias and criticize its one-sided approach (Powell and Foley 1999; Rogers and Henson 1997; Williams et al. 1999). These studies illustrate that consensual relations are as equally telling of sexual work-floor dynamics as coercive ones. Problematic in both these perspectives is the conceptualization of the workplace as a controlled organizational entity separated from a broader social context.

The second group of research is represented in the majority by anthropological or ethnographic studies carried out in Latin America or the Caribbean. It is not a coincidence that Latin America and the Caribbean are amply represented in this perspective. In part, this can be attributed to the high integration of sexuality in gender relations in society at large (Nencel 1996, 2001; Melhuus and Stølen 1996). Additionally, unlike Western ethnographic studies of organizations, the research agendas of the anthropologist go beyond studying the organization as an isolated locus. These ethnographies search for answers to questions that give insight into how these workplace experiences are related to, express, or reflect broader social issues and/or relations (Farnsworth-Alvear 1997; Freeman 2000; Nencel unpublished; Salzinger 2000; Yelvington 1995, 1996). They do not predefine the significance of sexual relations beforehand; rather, they attempt to explore its significance in the work-floor context. Flirting is one relation that has received considerable attention. In a study on workers' sociability in Medellín Colombia (1935–50) Farnsworth-Alvear (1997) calls flirting a "sociable relationship," which, along with arguing and fighting, "challenge public codes of femininity as much as they challenge work rules." Yelvington's study (1995, 1996) of a factory in Trinidad shows different dimensions of the significance of flirting, not only as an instrument of domination, but also as a tactic for women to resist. In this workplace situation, flirting not only sexually objectifies women, but also women's active participation in flirting relations objectifies men. Salzinger sees flirtation in a Mexican maquiladora as a "social relation that defines and frames the interactions of supervisors and workers overall" (2000: 86). Sexual objectification and desire are essential relations in the production system of the factory she studied: "Productivity at Panoptimex is born out of the routinized sexual objectification of women workers by their male superiors" (ibid.: 82).

In their ethnographic detail, these studies show how notions of sexuality fuse into the construction of femininity, how work practice and work-floor relations reflect and reproduce gender hierarchies and inequalities, as well as how these sexual relations work and rework class and ethnic relations within the workplace and beyond. Within this field, power relations are constituted in interaction between men and women, bosses and workers, customers and workers. The outcome of the process of sexual objectification – which in one mainstream current of feminist research is indicated as the causal factor of women's victimization or oppression – is not assumed but, rather, challenged, resulting in less predictable outcomes. Loe's study on female waitresses working in an American chain restaurant Bazooms, in which women's breasts contribute to the restaurant's success, shows how "power, gender roles, sexual identities, and harassment are in constant flux with each interaction among the players" (1995: 399). Loe analyzes the constraints as well as how women negotiate and alter their situation through their agency. Wood's (2000) study on female strippers – considered by most to be the ultimate example of the sexually objectified woman – analyzes the interaction between the strippers and the customers and reveals that power is a contested, negotiated social resource that is constantly being enacted by men and women. Power relations reinforce traditional notions of masculinity, simultaneously giving the dancer ultimate control over the customer. In my ongoing research project on secretaries in Lima Peru, the state's (unsuccessful) attempt to forbid women to wear a miniskirt at work is an excellent illustration of how the values and norms embedded in the process of sexual objectification are interwoven into gender relations as well as work-floor dynamics. However, it is only one of the layers constituting the construction of sexuality: how these norms and values are subjectively experienced can give an alternative reading to this story.

Finally – and extremely significant – these studies make a serious attempt to conceptualize women as sexual subjects. Their subjective experiences are essential for understanding how power relations, whether constraining or pleasurable, are constructed. This becomes even more significant when we take account of the fact that in several of the cultures where these studies have taken place, women's sexuality is perceived of as passive or not talked about for fear of tainting their reputations. By positioning women as sexual subjects, these studies provide alternative readings of women's sexuality which, in turn, challenge cultural hegemonic imagery. Contrastingly, men's sexuality has always been considered active and voracious. It is since the 1990s that the study of masculinity has been completely incorporated in gender studies. This has contributed to undoing the universal oppositional social category men.

Sexuality, Power, and Masculinity

In the 1990s the growing interest in the study of masculinity led to various publications that deconstructed this concept, disclosing the dynamics that reinforce hegemonic imageries of masculinity as well as other images that contradict or offer alternative notions. Anthropological studies have revealed – as we no longer can talk of "the universal woman" – that it is absurd to talk about a singular masculinity or analyze men's action solely as a causal factor of women's oppression. Accompanying this is a critical analysis of the conventional representation of power conceived of as "if it were both an abstraction located in concepts, beliefs and ideologies 'out there' and also a substantive property which can be won, exchanged or lost. Such a concept of power focuses attention on institutions, on formal relations between the powerful and the weak, and on men" (Cornwall and Lindisfarne 1994: 23) – and, it can be added, ignores the daily practices of individuals and groups of men in how they construct their sexual selves (e.g. Gutmann 1996). The study of masculinity and power is not confined to anthropology. New journals such as *Men and Masculinities*, founded in 1999, illustrate that the study of masculinity is multidisciplinary.

Gough (2001) describes how male British university students negotiate their masculinity in different social arenas (the pub vs. the university) strategically "biting their tongues" to produce different desired outcomes; the development agency Oxfam dedicated an issue of its journal *Focus on Gender* to men and masculinity (Sweetman 1997). In reproductive health studies men's subjective experiences are presently given a prominent position in research. However, Obermeyer's observation (cited earlier) is also relevant to this sub-area of study.

As in feminist studies on femininity, in this genre of masculinity studies gender is conceptualized as a multilayered, plural construct. And, like feminist studies, gender is analyzed in all its multidimensional richness, while heterosexual sexuality is not always treated with equal intensity. The relationship between gender and sexuality in the construction of masculinity needs further exploration. Exceptions such as Connell's (1995) and Seidler's (1997) work on masculinity are serious in-depth studies that show how sexuality informs gender processes. My own work (1996) concerning the construction of men's sexual selves in Lima Peru illustrates how men's projections of sexual desire construct labels of female gender identity and, as such, reinforce existing power relations. The analysis of men's subjective sexual experiences in different moments of their lives whittled away at the all-encompassing concept of the macho to reveal different masculinities which are partially constructed by the sexual choices men make in their lives. Although the study of heterosexual masculinity gives contents and insight into hegemonic notions of power and debunks them when necessary, they leave the power paradigm basically intact, studying men from the position of control, whether they have it, want it, or not. Despite this shortcoming, the study of men as "engendered and engendering subjects" (Gutmann 1997) has provided several vital pieces in the gender jigsaw puzzle of relations supporting analysis of male and female sexuality as a relational concept (see Holland et al. 1998). This in turn creates new questions that encourage female sexualities to be studied from a broader perspective.

Studying Female Sexuality

Present-day studies of female sexuality have produced two developments. First, there is a growing number of studies particularly, but not exclusively, in the North which conceptualize women as sexual subjects who are sexually active individuals, inquire into their sexual practices and subjective experiences, and analyze how they position themselves in relation to male heterosexual power (Giffin 1998; Holland et al. 1998; McCallum 1999; Meadows 1997; Roberts 1995; Stewart 1999). Thus, the sexual dynamics of different groups of women is becoming more visible. Hand in hand with the first development is the second. This increasing interest in women's sexual experience is turning out rich empirical material, nonetheless; the queries are generally limited to issues related to the power paradigm. Stewart's (1999) study on young Australian women, predominantly from Anglo-Australian origins, illustrates how they are reworking the "givens" of heterosexual practice, accordingly producing positive changes. It is interesting to note that many studies being done on female heterosexual sexuality concern young women. This is far from coincidental, but is most likely based on the assumption that change is more likely to be seen in young women's and men's relationships. It goes without saying that change is easier to detect within the younger generations; however, this assumption potentially silences the experiences of other groups in which change in sexual norms and practices are less perceptible. Meadows's (1997) choice to study the experiences of sexuality for a group of mid-life women is not arbitrary. Her decision to concentrate on this group is a methodological attempt to counteract this tendency. Meadows describes the experience of the sexuality of these women as being, unlike that of young women, positive; they enjoy more self-esteem and openly talking about pleasure and sexual desire. Through the years they have experienced personal empowerment.

A noteworthy study that is an outcome of a 10-year research project – the Women, Risk, and AIDS Project (Holland et al. 1998) – not only analyzes sexuality as a relational concept and, therefore, consistently approaches it from both a masculine and feminine perspective; it also illustrates how young British women and men create their (sexual) identities from their opposing sides of the power paradigm – men want sex and women want love and relationships. Hence, we learn how women consent or resist male power, to what extent these women have been able to empower themselves or feel disempowered, and how men uphold their power.

What all these studies have in common is that they depart from a predefined definition of gender inequality in which the power constituted in institutionalized heterosexual sexuality is a masculine possession. Consequently, they show the dynamics of its workings, or test their research material against this relation to draw conclusions about women's empowerment and the (potential) changes this induces in gender relations of power. Hoskins's critique of the WRAP study is also valid for the other studies discussed here. She asserts that the study reinforces "heteronormative and gender values. This raises questions about the purpose of feminist academic research, in particular, whether it should concentrate on empowerment or highlighting where there still is patriarchal control" (2000: 144). Giffin goes further and gives an excellent critique of the concept of empowerment in relation to heterosexuality and AIDS prevention. She asserts: "When the demand for empowerment in sexuality is put in abstract, ahistorical terms on . . . it reduces the terms of heterosexuality to power relations and control, making no contribution to redefining these relationships in substantive terms. Beyond empowerment, the same limitation might be said to apply to abstract calls for 'autonomy' and 'liberty' in sexuality. As Jeffrey Weeks has put it, we must address the question of 'Freedom from what?'" (1998: 155). Thus, more calls are being made to break with this feminist academic tradition and discover new ways to analyze (hetero-)sexuality.

Unsettling the Power Paradigm

The study of sexuality relies too heavily on the dynamics of gender power relations for its own analysis. Research is all too often orchestrated by underlying principles that seek to demonstrate the mechanisms of gender inequity or search for ways to empower women or show their empowerment. Reinforcing this is the positioning of men and women as oppositional gender categories. Many studies on heterosexual sexuality are primarily concerned with how oppositional gender relations are expressed and affect women in their sexual experience and practices. Moreover, women's subjectivity is enframed by the power paradigm. Although there is a growing tendency to emphasize agency instead of victimization, and this can be considered a positive turn, it is the flipside in the power paradigm, engineered through the same theoretical construction. There is still a need to develop even further theoretical frames that support research and analysis of heterosexual sexuality in its own right.

Finally, in heterosexual sexuality studies, gender is approached as a multilayered concept and often sexuality is not. Consequently, it is easy to trace how gender informs sexuality, but questions remain concerning other possible configurations such as the influence sexuality has on gender, where they conflate, when they diverge, etc.

This overview not only indicates the elements that theoretically obstruct the development of the relation between gender and sexuality; it also suggests directions to unsettle the power paradigm on which it is so firmly anchored. These thoughts can be synthesized in a theoretical frame that includes a multilayered concept of sexuality and focuses on understanding the diverse processes of interactions taking place. A multilayered concept of sexuality provides space for the analysis of sexual ideologies, discourses, and imageries. It includes the analysis of sexual meanings produced by different actors such as religious or state institutions. It provides the possibility to research the process of objectification – a powerful process that often has negative consequences for women: reinforcing the control of and power over women and their sexuality. Furthermore it analyzes interactions between individuals in different positions of power and in different locations: men and women in the workplace, at home, in recreation. It analyzes the sexual meanings these interactions produce, a diversity of relationships such as flirting, sexual harassment, abuse or violence, and the

139

dynamics of sexual practices, attitudes within consensual relations. Finally, there is a subjective layer in which men and women are conceptualized as sexual subjects. In contrast to women being analyzed as objects, they are approached as subjects with sexual likes and dislikes, who may enact and embody the process of objectification and even consider this empowering, as well as reject and create other scenarios which include, for example, pleasurable sexual experiences, experiences of empowerment or victimization. This multilayered concept dissolves the tensions that previously existed between the various dyads that were discussed above, simply by placing them side by side and approaching them as feasible options informing men's and women's constructions of their sexual selves.

Finally, it is necessary to study the different types of interaction taking place. There are interactions between people that constitute power, gender, and sexual relations. There are processes of interaction between the different layers of the concept of sexuality. For instance, how do the sexual ideologies developed by the state inform employment policies which, in turn, condition work-floor dynamics? Lastly, there are processes of interaction between identity markers such as gender and sexuality and axes of difference such as race (Stoler 1991), ethnicity, and class. Of course it is unrealistic to expect a study of (hetero-)sexuality to include all the elements discussed here; nevertheless, departing from a multilayered definition of sexuality that tunes in to processes of interaction may be the first step to an approach to heterosexuality that leaves the conventional power paradigm behind without disregarding the power relations that inform women's sexual experiences in all their varieties and delights.

References

Bowes-Sperry, L. and Tata, J. (1999) "A Multiperspective Framework of Sexual Harassment," in G. N. Powell (ed.), *Handbook of Gender and Work* (London: Sage).

Caplan, P. (ed.) (1987) *The Cultural Construction of Sexuality* (London: Tavistock Publications).

Connell, R. W. (1995) *Masculinities* (Cambridge: Polity).

Cornwall, A. and Lindisfarne, N. (1994) "Dislocating Masculinity: Gender, Power and Anthropology," in A. Cornwall and N. Lindisfarne (eds.), *Dislocating Masculinity* (London: Routledge).

Farnsworth-Alvear, A. (1997) "Talking, Fighting, Flirting. Workers' Sociability in Medellín Textile Mills, 1935–1950," in J. D. French and D. James (eds.), *The Gendered Worlds of Latin American Women Workers* (Durham, NC: Duke University Press).

Freeman, C. (2000) *High Tech and High Heels in the Global Economy* (Durham, NC: Duke University Press).

Giffin, K. (1998) "Beyond Empowerment: Heterosexualities and the Prevention of AIDS," *Social Science and Medicine* 46/2: 151–6.

Gough, B. (2001) "'Biting Your Tongue': Negotiating Masculinities in Contemporary Britain," *Journal of Gender Studies* 10/2: 169–85.

Gutmann, M. C. (1996) *The Meanings of Macho. Being a Man in Mexico City* (Berkeley: University of California Press).

Gutmann, M. C. (1997) "Trafficking in Men: The Anthropology of Masculinity," *Annual Review of Anthropology* 26: 385–409.

Holland, J., Ramazanoglu, C., Sharpe, S., and Thomson, R. (1998) *The Male in the Head. Young people, Heterosexuality and Power* (London: Tufnell Press).

Hoskins, B. (2000) "Young Women's Sexuality: All Bad New?" *Feminist Review* 66: 142–6; also in *American Anthropologist* 99/3: 574–85.

Kulick, D. (1998) *The Gender of Brazilian Transgendered Prostitutes* (Chicago: Chicago University Press).

Loe, M. (1995) "Working for Men at the Intersection of Power, Gender, and Sexuality," *Sociological Inquiry* 66/4: 399–421.

McCallum, C. (1999) "Restraining Women: Gender, Sexuality and Modernity in Salvador da Bahia," *Bulletin of Latin American Research* 18/3: 275–93.

Meadows, M. (1997) "Exploring the Invisible: Listening to Mid-Life Women about Heterosexual Sex," *Women's Studies International Forum* 20/1: 145–52.

Melhuus, M. and Stølen, K. (1996) *Machos, Mistresses, Madonnas. Contesting the Power of Latin American Gender Imagery* (London: Verso).

Nencel, L. (1996) "Pacharacas, Putas and Chicas de su casa: Labelling, Femininity and Men's Sexual Selves in Lima, Peru," in M. Melhuus and K. Stølen (eds.), *Machos, Mistresses, Madonnas. Contesting the Power of Latin American Gender Imagery* (London: Verso).

Nencel, L. (2001) *Ethnography and Prostitution in Peru* (London: Pluto Press).

Nencel, L. (unpublished) "Que Viva La Minifalda. The State, Sexual Objectification and the Workplace. Secretaries in Lima, Peru." Paper presented at Gender and Latin American Studies Day, CEDLA/Belle van Zuylen Institute, May 2001, Amsterdam.

Obermeyer, C. M. (2000) "Sexuality in Morocco: Changing Context and Contested Domain," *Culture, Health & Sexuality* 2/3: 239–54.

Ortner, S. B. and Whitehead, H. (1981) *Sexual Meanings: The Cultural Construction of Gender and Sexuality* (Cambridge: Cambridge University Press).

Parker, R., Barbosa, R. M., and Aggleton, P. (eds.) (2000) *Framing the Sexual Subject* (Berkeley: University of California Press).

Parker, R. G., Herdt, G., and Carballo, M. (1991) "Sexual Culture, HIV Transmission, and AIDS Research," *The Journal of Sex Research* (special issue) 28: 77–98.

Powell, G. N. and Foley, S. (1999) "Romantic Relationships in Organizational Settings. Something to Talk About," in G. N. Powell (ed.), *Handbook of Gender and Work* (London: Sage).

Prieur, A. (1998) *Mema's House. On Transvestites, Queens, and Machos* (Chicago: University of Chicago Press).

Pringle, R. (1988) *Secretaries Talk. Sexuality, Power and Work* (Australia: Allen & Unwin; London: Verso, 1989).

Rogers, J. K. and Henson, D. (1997) " 'Hey, Why Don't you wear a Shorter Skirt?' Structural Vulnerability and the Organization of Sexual Harassment in Temporary Clerical Employment," *Gender and Society* 11/2: 215–37.

Rubin, G. (1985) "Thinking Sex: Notes for a Radical Theory of the Politics of Sexuality," in C. Vance (ed.), *Pleasure and Danger. Exploring Female Sexuality* (Boston: Routledge & Kegan Paul).

Salzinger, L. (2000) "Manufacturing Sexual Subjects. 'Harassment', Desire and Discipline on a Maquiladora Shopfloor," *Ethnography* 1/1: 67–92.

Seidler, V. J. (1997) *Man Enough. Embodying Masculinities* (London: Sage).

Snitow, A., Stansell, C., and Thompson, S. (1983) "Introduction," in A. Snitow, C. Stansell, and S. Thompson (eds.), *Powers of Desire* (NewYork: Monthly Review Press).

Stewart, F. J. (1999) "Femininities in Flux? Heterosexuality and (Safe) Sex," *Sexualities* 2/3: 275–90.

Stoler, A. L. (1991) "Carnal Knowledge and Imperial Power: Gender, Race and Morality in Colonial Asia," in M. Di Leonardo (ed.), *Gender at the Crossroads of Knowledge: Feminist Anthropology in the Post-Modern Era* (Berkeley: University of California Press).

Sweetman, C. (ed.) (1997) "Men and Masculinity," in *Oxfam Focus on Gender* (Oxford: Oxfam).

Valverde, M. (1989) "Beyond Gender Dangers and Private Pleasures: Theory and Ethics in the Sex Debates," *Feminist Studies* 15/2: 237–54.

Vance, C. (1984) "Pleasure and Danger: Towards a Politics of Sexuality," in C. Vance (ed.), *Pleasure and Danger. Exploring Female Sexuality* (Boston: Routledge and Kegan Paul).

Weeks, J. (1986) *Sexuality* (London: Tavistock Publications).

Wood, E. A. (2000) "Working in the Fantasy Factory," *Journal of Contemporary Ethnography* 29/1: 5–31.

Williams, C. L., Guiffre, P. A., and Dellinger, K. (1999) "Sexuality in the Workplace: Organizational Control, Sexual Harassment, and the Pursuit of Pleasure," *Annual Review of Sociology* 25: 73–93.

Yelvington, K. A. (1995) *Producing Power. Ethnicity, Gender and Class in a Caribbean Workplace* (Philadelphia: Temple University Press).

Yelvington, K. A. (1996) "Flirting in the Factory," *Journal of the Royal Anthropological Institute* 2: 313–33.

PART THREE

Jurisdictions

CHAPTER TEN

Nation

Lois A. West

This chapter argues for a need to engender the study of nations and nationalism by using a sociological perspective of gender process. Nation-states are not constructed in thoroughly gender-segregated environments, but as interactions between females and males, majorities and minorities, the local and global. This notion of interaction, of process, needs to be better incorporated into Nation Studies through the incorporation of multiple perspectives of interaction.

Gender analyses have lacked a sense of process in Nation/alism Studies partly because of bias – both masculinist and feminist. Bias hindered process analysis when there was an underlying assumption that females and males live in segregated worlds where one group would get analyzed, while another would get ignored. This has been further complicated by the underlying assumption of feminist theory that the sexes are continuously embroiled in processes of conflict and struggle.

Another point has to do with lack of consensus on the meanings of "gender," "nation/state," "transnationalism," and "globalization," which has hindered understandings and praxis. As Wilford observes: "Contesting theories of nation-alism, debates about the relationship between ethnicity and 'race,' ambivalence about the celebration of 'difference,' together with the problematization of 'women' as an organizing construct, all combine to lay a conceptual and political mine-field" (1998: 1).

What is increasingly needed are the process perspectives – the places and theories of the negotiations between males and females over reproduction, par-enthood, payment for work, ideologies, and state policies, as these construct nation-states and beliefs about "the nation." What is also needed is a more careful consideration of consensus and common ground, rather than the assump-tion of struggle. This is particularly evident where differences get negotiated and worked out to the good of all involved parties. First, an examination of how bias limits conceptualizations.

Masculinist Bias

Early feminist theory has criticized male scholars for ignoring the experiences and understandings of females, which they took to be identical to their own (masculinist bias). They thought they were speaking for everyone (universalism bias). As a report by the United Nations Population Fund (2000: 1) put it: "The reality of women's lives has been invisible to men. This invisibility persists at all levels, from the family to the nation." Restrictions placed on women's opportunities and choices, "have been considered either unimportant or non-existent, either accepted or ignored." What Grant (1991) calls a "gender bias" in international relations theory is really a masculinist bias in that women continue to be overwhelmingly left out of state-building except as behind-the-scenes actors (see Sluga 2000 for a discussion of where women were in the post-World War I peace process).

In a 1999 call for papers from a Dakar-based gender research group, researchers critically pointed out that, "few African men have undertaken gender sensitive research, or seriously considered working on any aspect of gender or gender relations" (CODESRIA 1999). Kaplan and Grewal criticize "masculinist marxism," and they take to task: "This refusal to engage scholarship on gender reproduces institutional patriarchies through academic 'gatekeeping' rather than encouraging affiliation and exchange. The denial or rejection of gender as a crucial category of analysis refuses attention to the subject positions of people who fall under the category of 'subaltern'; the proletariat as a universal category ignore the uneven divisions between men and women, as well as between first and third world constructions of class as inflected by race" (1999: 352–3).

Masculinist bias continues to affect scholarship in all disciplines, albeit no less in the subfield of gender and nationalism. Frye argues that when males take themselves and other males in their cultures as paradigm cases, they create a "paradigm-case category." Based on their experiences, they create prototypes and cognitive frames (understandings) where "people's judgments of similarities and differences among things in such categories are asymmetrical" (2000: 50). This creates "problematic generalization," overgeneralization, and ethnocentrism because we do not see other paradigms or experiences than our own when we are not engaged with them. Masculinist bias overgeneralizes from man to generic men.

Some scholars remain proud of their bias: Fukuyama argues that while it looks like women are "feminizing" the international relations world, masculinism is "natural" because male violence is rooted in evolutionary male aggression. Male-dominated states are necessary because of "male tendencies to band together for competitive purposes, [men] seek to dominate status hierarchies, and act out aggressive fantasies toward one another [which] can be rechanneled but never eliminated" (1998: 36). Once we understand this viewpoint, he asserts, we see how women must adopt the masculine paradigm: men set the state and nation-building standard so the standard must be male – a masculinist bias. This bias also reveals continuing disagreement over the role of biology or social construction in human behavior. Pryke (1998) argues that this is especially an issue in studying nationalism and sexuality because it becomes impossible to separate biology from sexuality and nation-building where nationalism focuses on population and natalism or racist eugenics and genocide. Untangling the linkages gets complex and coming down on the side of biology is handy for reinforcing masculinist bias, as Fukuyama demonstrates.

Feminist Bias

Where there is masculinist bias there is also feminist bias. Since the development of men's studies in the 1980s, feminists continue to disagree about the role of men in relation to the study of women and gender. Feminist bias occurs when the category of "gender" comes to really mean "women-only." One author exclaimed – in his book title – *Gender is Not a Synonym for Women* (Carver 1996). In the practice of Women's Studies, scholars sometimes use "gender" but mean women. In an Australian university course on gender, public policy, and the state, the syllabus reads: "While we use the language of 'gender,' we will mainly focus on women, as putting gender on the agenda is, in the first instance, about recognizing and addressing women's absence" (Victoria University, Gender on the Agenda 2000).

Feminists Peterson and Runyan use "gender" to refer to men in their definition of "gendered nationalism," which they define as reference "to the construction of a national identity and solidarity based on masculinist notions of self-determination and autonomy, which is at the expense of women's self-definitions and solidarity. Historically, gendered symbols, identities, and divisions of power, labor, and resources have been central features of nationalism" (1993: 190). Here gender and nationalism are male-dominated by power relations. Bracewell argues that putting men as dominant and women as other in "the discursive construction of nations. . . . seems to have made men as such invisible . . . too often treated . . . as stable, undifferentiated categories, and have posited a straightforward equation between male interests, masculinity and nationalism" (2000: 566). What this bias neglects are the diversities among men and the complexities of social interactions.

Feminist bias overgeneralizes to men and women: feminist analyses of states and nations are replete with references to patriarchal domination and power struggles between men and women without reference to cases that do not fit this paradigm. Baden and Goetz (1997) argue that the use of "gender" in the discourses at the 1995 United Nations Conference on Women in Beijing in becoming a synonym for women did not include the "relational aspects of gender, of power and ideology, and of how patterns of subordination are reproduced." In examining gender and nationalism, Mayer argues that nationalism, gender, and sexuality set up an "Us" versus "Them" distinction, where "The empowerment of one gender, one nation or one sexuality *virtually always* occurs at the expense and disempowerment of another" (2000a: 1; my emphasis).

Walby (2000) argues for theorizing gender in nations as "gender regimes," a concept put forth by Connell (1990) as integral to social "struggles." These regimes are comprised of six structures and two forms. One entire structure is male violence. Of the two forms, one is domestic, where women are "confined to the household," and is compared to the other, the public, where the patriarchal strategy is to "segregate and subordinate" women. In this framework, nations and states are comprised of conspiring males and subordinated females in social relations dominated by conflict. Feminist bias overgeneralizes to entire societies, not individual actors. Social relations are rooted in power relations that are worked out conflictually and we do not see where we might find consensuality, commonality, and peaceful coexistence. Assuming that *all* men participate in male privilege or that *all* females are victimized by differential citizenship in systems of social control is a gross overgeneralization and undermines agency, one of the intents of feminist theory.

Female Agency

One outcome of feminist bias has been a focus on female agency – where women's social movement organizing has led to substantive influences on states and nations and improvement in the status of women at the local, national, and global levels. Some of the best current research has been on the intersections between understandings of female identities, ethnicity, and nationalism. Much of this work focuses on cultural constructions, representations, and ideologies.

In twentieth-century examples, women who worked for women's rights (not always comfortable with the feminist label) worked within the parameters of nationalist movements to change policies towards women on both a national (West 1997a) and international level (Goodman 1998; Wichterich 2000, ch. 6). In my own ethnographic work, I focused on cases where women's efforts to improve the status of women in their nation coincided with efforts at state-building. I termed this social movement intersection "feminist nationalism," and included social movement women's organizations such as the umbrella organization GABRIELA, which has been noteworthy for its cross-class alliances, and the Kilusan ng Manggagawang Kababaihan in the Philippines, which worked in alliance with the male-dominated Kilusang Mayo Uno (West 1997b). Feminist leaders in Quebec have been very instrumental in pushing women's agendas at the local and state levels as they assert Québécois nationalism (LeClerc and West 1997). Yet my academic enterprise led to contestation and misrepresentation where I did not expect them. After mislabeling my book's title, Cockburn (2000: 624) alleges that I argue that feminism is integral to all nationalisms. But I include and consider examples of cases where feminist nationalism was missing (in most of Europe: see Kaplan 1997). This academic argumentative framework places me in a social hierarchy. The movement organizations analyzed by Cockburn reflect the "anti-essentialism" of current female agency social movements where feminism and nationalism coincide – similar to movements described in my collection.

What neither Cockburn nor I do, however, is generate broader theory. Where and during what historical conditions do feminism and nationalism coincide? How do they coincide if nationalism is masculinized? Analysts can take the elements of feminism and nationalism and push coincidence or lack of it further, which could lead to broader theory. Perhaps the ways in which feminism resides within masculinized nationalisms makes untangling gender more difficult. Research seeks to understand the variabilities of masculinities in the construction of nationalism to clarify engendering processes.

Male Diversity

Much of the literature on nationalism focuses on armed conflict because so many twentieth-century national groups were and are still embroiled with states that perpetuate differing kinds of militarized masculinisms. At the turn of the twenty-first century, there were more than three dozen major armed conflicts in the world, with many of them rooted in or linked to nationalist struggles – from Indonesia/Timor, Israel/Palestine, Chechnya/Russia, Serbia/Albania onwards (Smith 2001).

North American nationalism, in the latter part of the twentieth century, came to the forefront in the wake of the September 11, 2001 terrorist attacks in New York City and Washington, DC. These actions seemed motivated by peculiar notions of a masculinized religious nationalism most oppressive to women. That war is a male-dominated activity is no longer taken-for-granted as only a fact of biological aggression, but is explored in relationship to the social formations of masculine identities, male homosocial groupings, and male sexualities. War affects men as well as women, but not *all* men are responsible for all wars. Recent research focuses on the critical ways in which the ideologies of masculinities may affect the social constructions of nations and states. There is a particular interest in the nature of militarized nationalisms, warring states, and masculine diversities – of the ways imagined communities are imagined and then acted out by certain groups of men. Nagel (1998) argues that in many cases, manhood is "patriotic" and womanhood "exalted." A "sexualized militarism" constructs enemy men as wimps and hypersexualized enemy women as sluts. Certain kinds of cultural masculinities sexualize gender when a man's sexual potency gets links to the defense of one's nation (see Aretxaga 1998; Korac 1998; Mayer 2000a, 2000b; Pryke 1998). Ehrenreich argues the importance of a sociology of emotion which is difficult to dissociate from the body: masculinized nationalism gets tied up with war because of "the human capacity for intense feelings of group identification . . . rituals of collective defense – who derived a pleasurable thrill from it . . . the experience of confronting danger as a group . . . that can arouse a kind of exhilaration" (1997: 197). "The nation, as a kind of 'organism,' exists only through the emotional unity of its citizens, and nothing cements this unity more decisively than war" (ibid.: 202).

Yuval-Davis examines the kinds of war-making activities in relationship to the sexual division of labor. She considers that perhaps where war had a "front" and "rear" with a "home front" there may be a greater division than when there is no front and women fight alongside men (she gives the example of the Incas fighting the Spanish: 1997: 95). She suggests the role of social structures, but adds "Constructing the position of women in the military around the dichotomies of combat/non-combat and front/rear are, therefore more a result of ideological constructions on womanhood and manhood in society than a reflection of considered decisions based on objective difficulties of incorporating women into combat roles" (ibid.: 103).

Underlying the social construction of understandings of nations and states are the cultural ideologies of masculine and feminine. One theme in the differentiation between nation and state is that nations are symbolized by women and states by men. One's national group is associated with mother, kin, blood, land (mother earth), whereas a government/state is associated with the male citizen who must protect the nation from invasion (rape) and occupation under threat of losing the nation (see Pettman 1996a, 1996b), a "feminized motherland, a masculinized sovereign state" (Elshtain 1992). Overgeneralizing to states and nations without specifying them misses the important historical comparative viewpoint of *which* nations and states and under what conditions?

A popular idea in Men's Studies is that "hegemonic masculinities" get socially constructed in relation to "subordinate masculinities." That some men construct social hierarchies, which they perpetuate to advantage a few at the expense of many others, has been analyzed in different cross-cultural frameworks. Divergent masculinities underlie the social construction of differing nationalisms. Nelson (1998) argues that the idea of American national identity developed from the 1780s to the 1850s as a kind of white "civic fraternity" of American manhood. White manhood became the marker for civic unity under developing capitalism, although how much this ideology translated nationally can be debated given the North/South split. Hoganson (1998) argues that understanding the cultural construction of what it meant to be an "American man" is critical to understanding the US role in the Spanish/Philippine–American Wars. An economic crisis in the early 1890s threatened men's new-found roles as economic providers to the family, but men could create new roles by joining the fight to "save" Cuba and the Philippines from Spanish aggression. This "manly" (as opposed to "effete") job motivated "politically powerful men [who] drew on their understandings of appropriate male conduct when deciding how the nation should act" (1998: 204) which meant to call up a war. (See an exploration of dominant US cultural masculinity at the turn of the twentieth century in Kimmel

1996.) Male elites asserted their cultural understandings/ideologies of the need to be aggressive to excite other men and propel and justify two wars under the guise of a certain kind of masculinized American nationalism.

Much of the literature on debates over the role of women and homosexuals in the US military considers "the dilemma of how to protect, uninterrupted, the existing connection between nationalism and masculinity" (Allen 2000; Mayer 2000b: 16; Yuval-Davis 1997). American militarized masculinism incorporates heterosexism as well as sexism, homophobia as well as a certain kind of American hegemonic masculinity that gets taken for granted by many military men in their love of the homosocial military male subculture which affirms their American nationalism and their masculinity.

The effects of colonialism get examined in relation to other twentieth-century masculinized nationalisms. American colonialism imported West Point military academy militarism, with its hazing rituals and codes of honor (as well as its hardware), to the Philippines in the 1930s with the establishment of a Philippine national army and the Philippine Military Academy (PMA). McCoy argues the importance of examining the nature of male homosocial groupings in gender identity, cultural adaptation, and standards of honor: "Although the PMA adopted the West Point program almost intact, Filipino cadets mediated between the state's new model of maleness and society's existing standards creating their own vision of military masculinity" (1995: 698). Pre-colonial Philippine males already had initiation rituals, codes of honor and friendship, violence and aggressiveness, which melded with imported traditions into a unique militarized masculine nationalism and which carried on throughout the Philippines' twentieth-century political history.

Other cases link militarized masculinity to nationalism in the former Yugoslavia (Korac 1996), Dominican Republic (Krohn-Hansen 1997), Germany (Linke 1997), and Israel (Mayer 2000b). Religion gets linked up in India with a critique of "masculine Hinduism" (Banerjee 1999). Militarized masculinism affects women in Indonesia, where a masculinized nationalism constructs a "national feminine" (Sunindyo 1998). In Thailand, the scripting of Thai women in the Miss Thailand beauty pageant fits with a militarized masculinist nationalism (Callahan 1998).

Some of the best work has been done on rape in the wars in the former Yugoslavia, where women's sexuality and reproduction became linked to militarized masculinism: "[I]t is in part this link between nationhood and reproduction that made the use of rape in the Yugoslav war such a powerful weapon" (Gal and Kligman 2000: 26). One good example of a gender process perspective is Bracewell's analysis of the issue of rape in Kosovo. She argues: "Serb-Albanian relations in Kosovo were presented as a matter of competing masculinities, with the bodies of women serving as the markers of success or failure" (2000: 572). A crisis of communism in Eastern Europe in the late 1980s; continuing economic crises; low Serb birth rates; women's continuing agency either in support of Serb traditionalism and nationalism or as anti-war feminists joined by anti-war

Serbian men refusing their call-up or deserting (ibid.: 579): all paint a picture of diversity within complexity – a process of competing gender ideologies, regimes, and media constructions. Strong Serb masculine, militarized nationalism (as opposed to bestial Albanians) depended on vulnerable Serb domestic femininity against any peace activists.

Bracewell further links these ideologies to practical consequences: war and national conflict saw a rise in family violence, "not just in mixed marriages" (between Serbs and non-Serbs), and also in legislation that limited abortion, taxed childless couples, controlled women's access to certain kinds of work, criminalized homosexuality, and seized property of draft evaders and deserters (ibid.: 584). Bracewell concludes that the nationalism of Serbia in the latter twentieth century "can be seen as making it clear who the real men were. . . . [T]he calls for a reassertion of national dignity were structured by a shared understanding of masculinity." Thus, she argues for "a more differentiated and dynamic perspective on the interactions of gender and nation. Both gender and national are best seen as relational identities . . . created through a process of highlighting difference" (ibid.: 585). Where her analysis rested on struggles over identities and counter-identities and power relations, she shows these as processes of negotiations between men and women as diverse subjects of complex action which provides a good example of the gender process perspective.

Not all analyses of masculinity and nationalism focus on militarism. Some look at other important cultural symbols – as with same-sex soccer and cross-sex tango in the nationalism of Argentina (Archetti 1999) or where Japanese nationalist identity gets configured with masculinity, transnationalism/globalization, race, gender and sex, class, and cultural and economic imperialism in the Japanese suit campaign (Kondo 1999). Other important work examined the relationship between colonialism, nationalism, masculinity, and labor in the Caribbean (Lewis 2000). The notion of a "national identity" as socially constructed and engendered through cultural forms develops the "imagined community" tradition (Anderson 1991).

Global Materialism and the End of Nationalism?

Engendering nationalism as the shared community of nations with similar national aspirations but differing gender traditions means going beyond imagination to examining materialism and history where gender narratives are viewed as linked to economic and political realities (Hasso 1998). During the twentieth century, the number of sovereign states grew from 50 in 1900 to 190 by the end of the century. Fewer than 20 were ethnically homogenous, and many ethnic groups found themselves in states as "minorities" in majority-dominated relationships (Schaeffer 1997: 298). Colonization created arbitrary states, splitting nations such as the Kurds, and post-World War II decolonization processes redrew state lines, spawning social movements bent on separatism. Under these social conditions, ethnicity, religion, and social movements become as important as gender in understanding contemporary nationalism, and this is evidenced in the intersections in the current literature. While there is still much on the construction of ethnic and national identities, increasingly there is a goal to move "beyond national identities," as a 1999 issue of *Social Justice* proclaimed.

One move beyond imagining identities means a welcome reaffirmation of the importance of historical materialism. Nationalism, state-building, and gender and ethnic/race relations are seen as created or influenced by processes of economies, globalization of capital, information, population, and transnationalism ("the cultural specificities of global processes": Ong 1999: 4), as well as the activities of actors in national and global social movements. Margolis (2000: 5) argues that gender relations can only be understood within the cultural materialism of "productive and reproductive imperatives." For her, the social construction of gender roles and cultural ideologies most often follows changes in the organization of domestic and capitalist production and in the increasing control that women are getting over human reproduction.

Global capitalist development creates social changes in agriculture, industrialization, urbanization, and technological development, all of which draw women from the home into the marketplace. Women working in paid employment have moved from traditional family economies to dual-earning family wage economies. Sophisticated reproductive technologies increasingly free women to pursue waged work, which creates a challenge to change the notion of women-only domestic labor. As these changes affect gender relations on a global scale, domestic and work worlds remain gender segregated and economically stratified due as much to cultural ideologies as to structural organization. Margolis believes that while feminism "indeed made women question the low pay and segregation of female labor . . . women's consciousness was raised . . . by the material conditions of their lives, by the disjunctions between ideology and reality" (2000: 156). In this scenario, ideologies do not create women's and men's definitions or status in nation-states; material realities and the development of capitalism do. Ong asserts: "Our challenge is to consider the reciprocal construction of practice, gender, ethnicity, race, class, and nation in processes of capital accumulation" (1999: 5).

Analysts reason that global capitalism (the processes of globalization) will end the nation-state (transnationalism trumps nationalism). Japanese corporate leader Ohmae (1995) argues that as information, industry, investment, and individuals flow more freely across national borders, the nation-state becomes irrelevant. Where wars created national boundaries, increasingly regions ("region-states") will do so, as private capital is used to build infrastructure rather than sovereign states. Brodkin believes that "capitalism now has a power perhaps greater than ever in its history to cross, even dissolve national boundaries" (2000: 237). With corporations constituting half of the world's largest economies and with Wal-Mart bigger than Greece, a global capitalist economy will erode both states and nationalism: the way in which states construct national subjects reflects the way capital organizes production and labor through gender, race, and ethnic delineations (ibid.: 238). A state's "race-making" (who gets defined as having color) or "racial formation" (Omi and Winant 1994: the economic and political practices which shape racial meanings) help to create national meanings as importantly as defining who is male or female.

Ostry and Nelson argue that "cross-border economic integration and national political sovereignty have increasingly come into conflict, leading to a growing mismatch between the economic and political structures of the world" (1995: xvii). A nation's domestic policies conflict with international standards, as an Afghani representative of the Taliban discovered on his 2001 US tour: at every stop he met American women protesting the treatment of Afghani women. The radical decline in Afghani women's status under the Taliban became an international rallying cry for activists, who organized with Afghani women's protests cross-nationally online and then in national demonstrations before the September 11 attacks. NGOs used the international press and computer networks to make their cause into a media phenomenon. Capitalist development (computer technologies, the internet, consumer culture – now all globalized) made organizing easier in confronting a national group's gender relations with an international audience, and demonstrated the role of the media in reinforcing or challenging gender relations and nationalism (for other cases, see Tartakovskaya 2000; Zarkov 1997). This organizing helped to lay the groundwork for the call for and seating of Afghan women in the post-Taliban government.

With increasing transmigration (people moving across borders for better or different jobs), transnationalism (migrants moving across national boundaries) adds "nationality" to jobs and "diaspora capitalisms" (Layoun 1998; Ong and Nonini 1996). Current research examines the meaning of ethnicity and nationalism in transnational environments: where people are migrating and taking on dual citizenship, living in multiple localities, and taking on "collective identities." Alarcon et al. query whether, "in an era of globalization, it is appropriate to ask how post-modernity produces feminist practices that can be seen as part of the transnational circulation of cultures and politics as well as material goods" (1999: 15). Capitalism spurs transnational migration, challenging categories of national/foreigner, male/female (Kim 1998).

Currently, the development of information and communication technologies has created a globalized mass media which reveals how a single nation or state's gender standards compare with other cases. Cross-national economic and political analyses demonstrate to policy-makers how policies and laws affect gender status and set up international standards for progress. This standard can challenge nationalist projects and cultural histories, such as that seen with the Taliban, with organizing efforts providing the potential to improve women's status. For example, a group of Nordic countries established a gender equity plan to encourage their governments to achieve greater representation of women. As a result, the European Union routinely publishes gender equity statistics, which show France to be a laggard: while 45 percent of Sweden's legislators are women, only 8.7 percent of France's are (Daley 2001b). Arguing for "parity" (not a quota), French feminists were able to pass legislation to oblige political parties to field an equal number of female and male candidates in elections. Belgium has a quota which states that a third of their lists must consist of women, while political parties in Spain, Austria, and Germany put quotas on themselves. French women candidates have generated laws to dispense morning-after pills in schools and created a civil pact for gay partners (Daley 2001a; see also United Nations 2000).

Social movement actors use advanced internet technologies to wage campaigns that ranged from improving women's status to ending child labor and slavery, from simply getting the information out to letter-writing, fund-raising, and event-organizing. Organizing women's movements against rape during the war in the former Yugoslavia led to an international war crimes tribunal that convicted Bosnian Serbs for rape and sexual enslavement (Benderly 1997). While rape has been viewed as a war crime since the mid-nineteenth century, convictions were difficult to obtain until the 1990s. The United Nations is paying attention to rape and sexual enslavement in East Timor by militias and to the abuse of women in refugee camps (Crossette 2001: 5).

Women's political participation in nations and states remains a mixed bag. South African women were able to pass a historic "women's budget." Latin American women worked to see that women's interests would be taken into account in state policies, but "For all the variability of Latin American state forms and the diversity of gender-state relations, no state, even the most apparently radical, achieved anything approaching gender equality in the political sphere." Feminist attempts "to reconcile rights, social justice, and motherhood with national interests may have ceded too much ground to defenders of masculine privilege" (Molyneux 2000: 70). Afghan women were seated in the post-Taliban government, albeit in very small numbers. Women's political gains throughout the latter part of the twentieth century were slow and uneven, yet gains were made nonetheless and inequality gaps continue to close.

Toward a Gender Process Perspective

What this newer work demonstrates is that engendering nations must include a sense of process and complexity. A gender process perspective would not begin with the assumption of struggle, but of process – that females and males are involved in complex daily interactions which may privilege some at the disadvantage of others, or in which interests can be negotiated through to common ground. A dynamic perspective takes all the social actors into account: a perspective can privilege the female or male without ignoring any group. The social construction of gender does not occur in a vacuum, but in complex interactions with race, ethnicity, class, biology, culture, and economies – local, national, and globalized. Research on engendering nation is moving in that direction, but as long as Gender Studies remains in "special issues" on nationalism rather than as an integrated study, bias remains and complexity may be lost.

Incorporating divergent masculinities and female agencies within a global environment of international capitalism, transnational mass media, developing technologies, migratory populations, and "flexible citizenship" moves us beyond masculinist or feminist bias into gender process. The ways in which globalization may be improving some women's status (see, for example, Traub 2001), while making it difficult for others (see special *World Development* gender issues for 1995 and 2000), can be considered as well as the ways certain kinds of masculinities provide the justification and ideologies underlying militaristic nationalism which pacifist masculinities challenge. While the former broadens nationalism to incorporate women and feminism, the latter differentiates between men who are causing the problems of nationalism and those seeking solutions. Certainly one solution is the development of a concept of a global citizen who respects the uniqueness that ethnic and gender identities provide to nations and shares in the belief that we are all citizens of the same planet. One possible example would be the recognition of Jerusalem as a "global" city to be governed by an international coalition. Many of us wish to maintain the ideals and possibilities of prosperity and peace for all, not just for some. And this idealism can play out in real-life daily social interactions, which a gender process perspective can reveal.

References

Alarcon, N., Kaplan, C., and Moallem, M. (1999) "Introduction: Between Woman and Nation," in Caren Kaplan, Norma Alarcon, and Minoo Moallem (eds.), *Between Woman and Nation: Nationalisms, Transnational Feminisms, and the State* (Durham: Duke University Press).

Allen, H. (2000) "Gender, Sexuality and the Military Model of U.S. National Community," in Tamar Mayer (ed.), *Gender Ironies of Nationalism: Sexing the Nation* (London: Routledge).

Anderson, B. (1991) *Imagined Communities: Reflections on the Origins and Spread of Nationalism* (London: Verso).

Archetti, E. (1999) *Masculinities: Football, Polo and the Tango in Argentina* (Oxford: Berg).

Aretxaga, B. (1998) "What the Border Hides: Partition and the Gender Politics of Irish Nationalism," *Social Analysis* 42/1: 16–32.

Baden, S. and Goetz, A. M. (1997) "Who Needs [Sex] When You Can Have [Gender]?" *Feminist Review* 56: 3–25.

Banerjee, S. (1999) "Warriors in Politics: Religious Nationalism, Masculine Hinduism and the Shiv Sena in Bombay," *Women and Politics* 20/3: 1–26.

Benderly, J. (1997) "Rape, Feminism, and Nationalism in the War in Yugoslav Successor States" in Lois West (ed.), *Feminist Nationalism* (New York: Routledge).

"Beyond National Identities: Social Problems and Movements" (1999) *Social Justice* 26/3.

Bracewell, W. (2000) "Rape in Kosovo: Masculinity and Serbian Nationalism," *Nations and Nationalism* 6/4: 563–90.

Brodkin, K. (2000) "Global Capitalism: What's Race Got to Do With It?" *American Ethnologist* 27/2: 237–65.

Callahan, W. (1998) "The Ideology of Miss Thailand in National, Consumerist, and Transnational Space," *Alternatives* 23/1: 29–61.

Carver, T. (1996) *Gender is Not a Synonym for Women* (Boulder, CO: Lynne Rienner).

Cockburn, C. (2000) "The Anti-Essentialist Choice: Nationalism and Feminism in the Interaction Between Two Women's Projects," *Nations and Nationalism* 6/4: 611–29.

CODESRIA (Council for the Development of Social Science Research in Africa), Multinational Working Group on Gender and National Politics in Africa (1999) "Call for Research Proposals" <http://www.sas.upenn.edu/African_Studies/codesria/gender.htm>.

Connell, R. W. (1990) "The State, Gender, and Sexual Politics: Theory and Appraisal," *Theory and Society* 19.

Crossette, B. (2001) "A New Legal Weapon to Deter Rape," *New York Times*, Outlook (March 4): 5.

Daley, S. (2001a) "French Parties Scramble for Women to Join Ticket," *New York Times* (February 4): 1.

Daley, S. (2001b) "French Twist: Parity, Thy Name is Woman," *New York Times*, Opinion (February 11): 4.

Ehrenreich, B. (1997) *Blood Rites: Origins and History of the Passions of War* (New York: Metropolitan Books, Henry Holt & Co).

Elshtain, J. B. (1992) "Sovereignty, Identity, Sacrifice," in Spike Peterson (ed.), *Gendered States: Feminist (Re)Visions of International Relations Theory* (Boulder, CO: Lynne Rienner).

Frye, M. (2000) "Ethnocentrism/Essentialism: The Failure of the Ontological Cure," in The Social Justice Group at The Center for Advanced Feminist Studies, University of Minnesota (ed.), *Is Academic Feminism Dead? Theory in Practice* (New York: New York University Press).

Fukuyama, F. (1998) "Women and the Evolution of World Politics," *Foreign Affairs* 77/5: 24–40.

Gal, S. and Kligman, G. (2000) *The Politics of Gender After Socialism: A Comparative Historical Essay* (Princeton: Princeton University Press).

Goodman, J. (1998) "Transnational Contestations: Social Movements Beyond the State," Association paper of the International Sociological Association.

Grant, R. (1991) "The Sources of Gender Bias in International Relations Theory," in Rebecca Grant and Kathleen Newland (eds.), *Gender and International Relations* (Bloomington: Indiana University Press).

Hasso, F. S. (1998) "The 'Women's Front:' Nationalism, Feminism and Modernity in Palestine," *Gender & Society* 12/4: 441–65.

Hoganson, K. L. (1998) *Fighting for American Manhood: How Gender Politics Provoked the Spanish-American and Philippine-American Wars* (New Haven: Yale University Press).

Kaplan, C. and Grewal, I. (1999) "Transnational Feminist Cultural Studies: Beyond the Marxism/Poststructuralism/Feminism Divides," in Caren Kaplan, Norma Alarcon, and Minoo Moallem (eds.), *Between Woman and Nation: Nationalisms, Transnational Feminisms, and the State* (Durham, NC: Duke University Press).

Kaplan, G. (1997) "Feminism and Nationalism: The European Case," in Lois West, *Feminist Nationalism* (New York: Routledge).

Kim, H. S. (1998) "Sexualized and Ethnicized Body Politics in the Transnational Era," Association Paper of the International Sociological Association.

Kimmel, M. (1996) *Manhood in America: A Cultural History* (New York: The Free Press).

Kondo, D. (1999) "Fabricating Masculinity: Gender, Race, and Nation in a Transnational Frame," in Caren Kaplan, Norma Alarcon, and Minoo Moallem (eds.), *Between Woman and Nation: Nationalisms, Transnational Feminisms, and the State* (Durham, NC: Duke University Press).

Korac, M. (1996) "Understanding Ethnic-National Identity and Its Meaning: Questions from Women's Experience," *Women's Studies International Forum* 19/1&2: 133–43.

Korac, M. (1998) "Ethnic-Nationalism, Wars and the Patterns of Social, Political and Sexual Violence against Women: The Case of Post-Yugoslav Countries," *Identities: Global Studies in Culture and Power* 5/2: 153–81.

Krohn-Hansen, C. (1997) "The Construction of Dominican State Power and Symbolisms of Violence," *Ethnos* 62/3&4: 49–78.

Layoun, M. N. (1998) "The Nation in Transculturation and the Gendered Spaces of the Diaspora: Woman/Man and Citizenship," *Revista Crítica de Ciencias Sociais* 50: 27–46.

LeClerc, P. and West, L. A. (1997) "Feminist Nationalist Movements in Quebec: Resolving Contradictions?" in Lois A. West (ed.), *Feminist Nationalism* (New York: Routledge).

Lewis, L. (2000) "Nationalism and Caribbean Masculinity," in Tamar Meyer (ed.), *Gender Ironies of Nationalism: Sexing the Nation* (London: Routledge).

Linke, U. (1997) "Gendered Difference, Violent Imagination: Blood, Race, Nation," *American Anthropologist* 99/3: 559–73.

Margolis, M. L. (2000) *True to Her Nature: Changing Advice to American Women* (Prospect Heights, IL: Waveland Press).

Mayer, T. (2000a) "Gender Ironies of Nationalism: Setting the Stage," in Tamar Meyer (ed.), *Gender Ironies of Nationalism: Sexing the Nation* (London: Routledge).

Mayer, T. (2000b) "From Zero to Hero: Masculinity in Jewish Nationalism," in Tamar Meyer (ed.), *Gender Ironies of Nationalism: Sexing the Nation* (London: Routledge).

McCoy, A. (1995) "'Same Banana': Hazing and Honor at the Philippine Military Academy," *The Journal of Asian Studies* 54/3: 689–726.

Molyneux, M. (2000) "Twentieth-Century State Formations in Latin America," in Elizabeth Dore and Maxine Molyneux (eds.), *Hidden Histories of Gender and the State in Latin America* (Durham, NC: Duke University Press).

Nagel, J. (1998) "Masculinity and Nationalism: Gender and Sexuality in the Making of Nations," *Ethnic and Racial Studies* 21/2: 242–69.

Nelson, D. D. (1998) *National Manhood: Capitalist Citizenship and the Imagined Fraternity of White Men* (Durham, NC: Duke University Press).

Ohmae, K. (1995) *The End of the Nation State: The Rise of Regional Economies* (New York: Free Press).

Omi, M. and Winant, H. (1994) *Racial Formation in the United States from the 1960s to the 1990s* (New York: Routledge).

Ong, A. (1999) *Flexible Citizenship: The Cultural Logics of Transnationality* (Durham, NC: Duke University Press).

Ong, A. and Nonni, D. (eds.) (1996) *Ungrounded Empires: The Cultural Politics of Chinese Trans-nationalism* (New York: Routledge).

Ostry, S. and Nelson, R. R. (1995) *Techno-Nationalism and Techno-Globalism: Conflict and Cooperation* (Washington, DC: The Brookings Institution).

Peterson, S. and Runyan, A. S. (1993) *Global Gender Issues* (Boulder, CO: Westview Press).

Pettman, J. J. (1996a) "Boundary Politics: Women, Nationalism and Danger," in Mary Maynard and June Purvis (eds.), *New Frontiers in Women's Studies: Knowledge, Identity and Nationalism* (London: Taylor & Francis).

Pettman, J. J. (1996b) *Worlding Women: A Feminist International Politics* (Sydney: Allen & Unwin).

Pryke, S. (1998) "Nationalism and Sexuality: What Are the Issues?" *Nations and Nationalism* 4/4: 529–46.

Schaefer, R. K. (1997) *Understanding Globalization: the Social Consequences of Political, Economic, and Environmental Change* (Lanham: Rowman & Littlefield Publishers).

Sluga, G. (2000) "Female and National Self-Determination: a Gender Re-Reading of 'The Apogee of Nationalism'" *Nations and Nationalism* 6/4: 495–521.

Smith, Colonel D. (2001) "The World at War January 1, 2001," *The Defense Monitor* 30/1: 1–8.

Sunindyo, S. (1998) "When the Earth is Female and the Nation is Mother: Gender, the Armed Forces and Nationalism in Indonesia," *Feminist Review* 58: 1–21.

Tartakovskaya, I. (2000) "The Changing Representation of Gender Roles in the Soviet and Post-Soviet Press," in Sarah Ashwin (ed.), *Gender, State and Society in Soviet and Post-Soviet Russia* (London: Routledge).

Traub, J. (2001) "Keeping Up with the Shidhayes," *The New York Times* (April 15), pp. 32–7.

United Nations (2000) *The World's Women 2000: Trends and Statistics* (New York: United Nations).

United Nations Population Fund (2000) *The State of the World Population 2000: Lives Together, Worlds Apart: Men and Women in Time of Change* (New York: UNPF).

Walby, S. (2000) "Gender, Nations and States in a Global Era," *Nations and Nationalism* 64: 523–40.

West, L. A. (1997a) "Introduction: Feminism Constructs Nationalism," in Lois A. West (ed.), *Feminist Nationalism* (New York: Routledge).

West, L. A. (1997b) *Militant Labor in the Philippines* (Philadelphia, PA: Temple University Press).

Wichterich, C. (2000) *The Globalized Woman: Reports from a Future of Inequality*, trans. Patrick Camiller (Australia: Spinifex Press).

Wilford, R. (1998) "Women, Ethnicity and Nationalism: Surveying the Ground," in Rick Wilford and Robert L. Miller (eds.), *Women, Ethnicity and Nationalism: The Politics of Transition* (London: Routledge).

World Development (1995) 23/11.

World Development (2000) 28/7.

Yuval-Davis, N. (1997) *Gender and Nation* (London: Sage).

Zarkov, D. (1997) "Pictures of the Wall of Love: Motherhood, Womanhood and Nationhood in Croatian Media," *European Journal of Women's Studies* 4/3: 305–39.

CHAPTER ELEVEN

Law

Katherine Franke

When I was living in New Haven a number of years ago, a miracle happened that drew people by the thousands to witness evidence of the Divine. A crucifix had been found to appear in the body of an oak tree in the middle of Worchester Square. I went to have a look: after all, how often do you get to see that kind of thing? Not surprisingly, at first I couldn't see anything but the usual trunk and limbs of a tree. Yet a believer took the time to show me what was really there, something that my untrained eye could not at first see: the cross on which Jesus Christ had been crucified. Well, maybe there was something there.[1]

To the believers, the shape of the oak tree was evidence of something that was really there: a corporeal manifestation of an omnipresent Divine Being. For them, once you've seen the crucifix, you really can't not see it: you can't un-see it. For most people, sex is like the Divine Being: it is an obscure and powerful domain that reveals itself in expected and unexpected places, and is immediately visible to the trained eye. Indeed, once you see it, it's hard to look away. Like the tree in Worchester Square, the human body is an "inscribed surface" that is discursively marked in such a way that renders certain body parts and particular behaviors essentially sexual (Foucault 1977: 148).

What are we seeing when we recognize something as sexual? How do we know what makes a practice sexual in nature? How do we distinguish a practice that is fundamentally sexual from one that is not? I ask these questions in order to beg two more normative questions: why do we do so? and what happens to what we "know" once we have done so? My curiosity derives from a concern that to call something sexual is to say at once too much and not enough about the meaning of a practice or body part so named.

When men in a workplace make life intolerable for their female co-workers by calling them sexual names, putting up pictures of naked women, and touching their breasts and behinds, their conduct – unwelcome conduct of a sexual nature – is legally described as sexual harassment. When a group of male police officers viciously assault a man in their custody by shoving a toilet plunger in his anus, those cops are charged with aggravated sexual abuse. When an adult male forces a 10-year-old boy to fellate him, this man is arrested for having sexually molested a minor. These offenses receive special legal regulation by our civil and criminal laws as sexual misconduct. But the use of excessive violence by a police officer when placing handcuffs on a suspect, the aggressive use of choke holds, or chaining a stranger to a pipe in the basement – whatever crimes these are, they are not sex crimes, or so the law tells us.

By focusing, often exclusively, on what we regard to be the sexual aspect of certain types of conduct, we tend to ignore or eclipse the ways in which sex operates "as an especially dense transfer point for relations of power" (Foucault 1990: 103) – often gender, race, or sexual orientation-based power. For a complex set of reasons, we almost intuitively label some behavior as sexual; take workplace sexual harassment, for instance. Yet, if pressed, most people would not be able to either identify or defend a set of criteria they apply in such nominalist moments. To uncover a satisfactory and stable definition of sex is, to borrow an expression from Abraham Lincoln, like undertaking to shovel fleas: "You take up a shovelful, but before you can dump them anywhere they are gone" (see Donald 1995: 389). It is the initial regulatory move, the marking of behavior as fundamentally sexual, that I want to interrogate. If it is in fact true that "there is not some ahistorical *Stoff* of sexuality, some sexual charge that can be simply added to a social relationship to 'sexualize' it in a constant and predictable direction, or that splits off from it unchanged" (Sedgwick 1985: 6), then it is worth asking what we are doing and what we are missing when we assume that such *Stoff* exists.

The questions I ask directly here are ones I first considered in my earlier work on sexual harassment (1997). There, I explored how workplace sexual harassment could be a species of sex discrimination. I criticized both courts and commentators who identified the wrong of sexual harassment to lie in the sexual nature of the conduct. Rather, I argued, sexual harassment must be understood as a technology of sexism; that is, as a tool or instrument of gender regulation which feminizes women as sexual objects and masculinizes men as sexual subjects (Franke 1997: 691, 730–47, 762–72).

In this chapter, I push these insights about the use of sex as a technology of sexism one step further by probing two more fundamental questions: first, why do certain practices get labeled as sexual? And, second, what flows from their being so designated? I explore the ostensibly denotative practice of naming particular behavior as primarily sexual in nature by examining two contexts in which the label "sexual," understood as erotic, occludes the way sex mediates other social relations of power. In each setting, I argue that we make a grave mistake when we interpret certain behavior as primarily erotic in nature. This mistake, I argue, is amplified in the legal treatment of these practices as sex crimes, or sexual offenses. First, I look to ritualized practices in the Highlands of Papua New Guinea, where boys as young as 7 are forced to fellate older men for a period of up to eight years as part of the process of becoming a man. At first impression, most nonnative interpreters of ritualized man–boy fellatio conclude, without hesitation, that this conduct is fundamentally erotic in nature – how can it not be so? In fact, Western anthropological readings of these practices first described them as sodomy, and today the behavior is most commonly referred to as ritualized or institutionalized homosexuality (see, e.g., Creed 1984: 157, 158; Herdt 1981, 1984; Williams 1936: 158).[2] I provide an alternative reading of the ritualized semen practices of the Sambia that illustrates the way ingestion of semen is undertaken primarily in the service of teaching and reinforcing the cultural power and supremacy of both men and masculinity, while at the same time teaching and reinforcing the cultural subordination and inferiority of women and femininity. In this regard, semen practices play a role in Sambia culture similar to that played by workplace sexual harassment in ours.

Next I examine the assault of Abner Louima, a black man who was attacked by white New York City police officers in August 1997. Louima sustained serious injuries after several police officers severely beat him, then forced the wooden handle of a toilet plunger into his rectum, and then removed it and forced the soiled handle into Louima's mouth. The sexual nature of the police conduct animated much of the outrage expressed by the public, the press, and legal authorities in the weeks following the assault. Prosecutors initially charged the white police officers arrested in connection with the assault of Louima with sex crimes.[3] Two aspects of this case are worthy of examination. First, why should we consider this assault a sex crime? Second, by reading the assault as primarily sexual, important insights about the way sex is used as an instrument of gender- and race-based humiliation and injury are elided or at least minimized.

Do these examples instruct that we best desexualize crimes like rape and forced sex with children? There are compelling arguments in favor of such a reformation of the laws regulating behavior traditionally treated as sex crimes. Indeed, Foucault made such an argument in the mid-1970s. Surely, the problems that inhere in the project of differentiating sexual assault from a punch in the face suggest that one should give serious consideration to the position that "there is no difference, in principle, between sticking one's fist into someone's face or one's penis into their sex" (Foucault 1988: 200). Ultimately, however, I reject such a wholesale move given that the material experience of sexual assault by its victims instructs that "they cannot afford to jump into the realm of the ideal and pretend that . . . sex (the genitals) is the same as other parts of the body" (Bell 1991: 83, 89). Rather, I suggest that law-enforcement officials, the media, and the public more generally should analyze cases of this nature on a case-by-case basis, so as to fashion arguments in a way that highlights the multivalent nature of these crimes, where appropriate, without perpetuating the essentialization of certain body parts and human behaviors as fundamentally sexual.

Through these examples, I hope to illustrate the productivity of sex – that is, how sex gets put to work in the service of myriad power relations. Sometimes sex is used to satisfy erotic desire; sometimes it accomplishes reproduction; sometimes it does both. Sometimes sex pays the rent; sometimes it sells cars, cigarettes, alcohol, or vacations in Mexico. Sometimes sex is used to subordinate, or has the effect of subordinating, another person on the basis of gender or race, or both.

To understand sex as a fundamentally erotic drive, and as a "natural given which power tries to hold in check [e.g., the prosecution of sex crimes], or as an obscure domain which knowledge tries gradually to uncover [e.g., anthropological discoveries of primitive homosexuality]" (Foucault 1990: 105), is to risk two grave errors. First, once something is classified as sexual we understand its meaning primarily in erotic terms and lose sight of the ways sex is easily deployed as an instrumentality of multiple relations of power. Second, we are likely to understand the erotic to be present in too few human behaviors insofar as we deny or ignore the role of the erotic in behavior less susceptible to being read as "sexual."

Seminal/Sexual Practices

In *Guardians of the Flutes*, anthropologist Gilbert Herdt provided an initial monograph of what he terms "ritualized homosexuality" among the Sambia, a tribe in the Eastern Highlands of Papua New Guinea. For the Sambia, the process of becoming a man is not one that may be left to nature, as is the case with girls, but must be accomplished by the ritualized intervention of culture. Thus, beginning at around the age of 7, boys commence a process of ritualized masculinization that is completed only when a young man fathers a child. This process starts with a series of ritualized practices designed to purge the polluting and feminizing effects of contact with women from the male body. Herdt terms these "egestive rites" designed to "remove internal, essentially 'foreign' material believed acquired through intimate, prolonged contact with one's mother (and other females)" (1981: 204–5, 223).[4]

Boys are first required to undergo cane-swallowing: canes are forced down their throats so as to induce vomiting and defecation, thereby purging food belonging to the mother from the male body – a necessary prerequisite for masculinization. Second, nose-bleeding is undertaken to remove the pollution of menstrual blood remaining in the male body. Stiff, sharp grasses are thrust into the boy's nose until blood flows, thereby removing the "bad blood" from his body. It is a matter of "urgent concern that the mother's contaminated blood be removed from boys; otherwise male biological development is impeded." Men alone conduct these rituals, keeping them hidden from women in the community; to effectuate this, the boys are sworn to secrecy (ibid.: 224–6, 262–5).[5]

Next follow the "ingestive rites"; this is where all the attention is paid by those intrigued by the practices of this culture. "The most important early ingestive rite of all," according to Herdt, is that of fellatio. Sambia men believe that without the daily ingestion of semen, a boy's body will not mature into that of a man, and he may likely wither and die. Thus, "repeated inseminations create a pool of maleness: the boy, it is believed, gradually acquires a reservoir of sperm inside his semen organ. . . . The semen organ changes from being dry and hard to fleshy, moist, and then firm. . . . Semen gradually transforms the initiate's body too. It internally strengthens his bones and builds muscles." According to these beliefs, boys must avoid all interaction with women, including their mothers, and must fellate older men on a daily basis until they reach adolescence, about the age of 15, at which time they switch roles and are fellated by younger boys. These bachelors, as Herdt calls them, are fellated by initiates until the woman they marry begins menstruation. At that point, Sambia culture dictates that they cease same-sex seminal practices and engage only in heterosexual coitus. Again, males closely hold these ingestive rites secret; indeed, the men threaten the boys with death should they reveal any of this information to women (ibid.: 227, 232–4, 236, 252).[6]

Thus, you have what Herdt describes as "ritualized homosexuality." Herdt is careful not to describe the Sambia as homosexual.[7] In fact, it is the distinction between homosexual practices and homosexual identity that constitutes the central conundrum of Sambia culture for Herdt. How is it that "seven-to-ten-year-old Sambia boys are taken from their mothers when first initiated into the male cult, and thereafter experience the most powerful and seductive homosexual fellatio activities," yet "they emerge as competent, exclusively heterosexual adults, not homosexuals"? The boys "experience [ritualized fellatio] as pleasurable and erotically exciting. Yet, in spite of this formidable background, the final outcome is exclusive heterosexuality." It is precisely because "homosexual behavior" among the Sambia men can be explained neither by genetic determinism nor social learning theory that Herdt finds the Sambia so fascinating (ibid.: 2–3, 8). According to what theory of sexual identity acquisition can "normal" adult heterosexuality evolve out of ritualized childhood same-sex sex?

Initial accounts of Sambia culture by Western anthropologists simply failed to mention the same-sex seminal practices described above.[8] Herdt, among other anthropologists, attributed this omission to a larger refusal in anthropology to regard sexuality as a legitimate subject of ethnographic inquiry.[9] In Papua New Guinea, this oversight quickly yielded to revulsion and condemnation by Western anthropologists, accompanied by aggressive efforts by missionaries to dissuade the locals from such perversion.[10] Indeed, many of the practices observed by Herdt in his early fieldwork no longer persist in Sambia culture (ibid.: 607–8).[11] Herdt, however, was one of the first Western observers to encounter the Sambia practices and declare: Look, homosexuality. Hallelujah, we are everywhere! Thus, with *Guardians of the Flutes*, his edited collections, and subsequent writings on the Sambia,[12] Herdt has "established a framework for the study of homosexualities cross-culturally" (Elliston 1995: 848). Through the scientific lens of anthropology, Herdt has, therefore, undertaken the task of shedding light on the "obscure domain" of the homo-sex drive in New Guinea.

From virtually all vantage points, commentators have interpreted Sambia semen practices as both erotic and homosexual – homoerotic (e.g. Herdt 1991:

606–7). How can one deny the sexual nature of fellatio? or the homoerotic nature of fellatio between men? It is this way of knowing these practices that I want to contest. From the perspective of the fellated, fellatio involves arousal, penile erection, ejaculation – surely this practice is about the bachelors "getting off." Herdt's fieldwork documents the fact that the bachelors truly enjoy and seek out sex with boys. Similarly, the boys seem to enjoy, to varying degrees, their "erotic relationships" with the bachelors. For this reason, Herdt is willing to characterize some of these unions as "lover relationships."[13]

Herdt finds Sambia culture an interesting subject of ethnographic study because of its exotic manifestation of the erotic; others would, no doubt, be aghast at the way adult men sexually exploit young boys. The ritualized nature of the practice merely compounds the sexual violation. Just as I have cautioned against understanding workplace sexual harassment as a fundamentally sexual activity, so too there is danger in interpreting Sambia semen practices as fundamentally erotic (Franke 1997: 729–47). Deborah Elliston has argued: "to identify the man–boy 'homosexual' practices as 'ritualized homosexuality' imputes a Western model of sexuality to these Melanesian practices, one that relies on Western ideas about gender, erotics, and personhood, and that ultimately obscures the meanings that hold for these practices in Melanesia" (1995: 849).

Among the interesting questions to be posed in analyzing semen practices among the Sambia are those regarding the purpose of these practices. Is the fellatio undertaken in the service of satisfying individual erotic desire, or in the service of advancing broader cultural norms that have, no doubt, a sexual component? Herdt poses this question, and ultimately determines to maintain the centrality of the erotic in his interpretation of Sambia initiation rituals. He expresses concern about ethnographies that tend to "ignore, dismiss, trivialize, or even invalidate the actor's homoerotic meanings and desires" (1991: 606–7). He is determined not to "deodorize the erotic and peripheralize the homoerotic ontology" (ibid.: 607).[14] Herdt is not alone in this concern. Gerald Creed, while expressing some criticisms with respect to Herdt's interpretations of Sambia culture, echoes a commitment to keep a focus on the erotic: "The actual physical and erotic aspects of homosexuality . . . are often overlooked when it is treated as institutionalized behavior. Institutionalized homosexuality is still sex and it may still serve a pleasurable function. Analyses that neglect this fact are incomplete" (1984: 160).

It is exactly this "homoerotic ontology" that concerns me. Why should we assume that the central meaning of Sambia initiation practices is sexual, that is, erotic? To ask this question thoughtfully requires the category "sexual" to be broken down into constitutive parts. To describe the semen practices as homoerotic, as Herdt and Creed insist, is to collapse several important concepts that deserve disaggregation. For Herdt, one must understand the male erection as the product of arousal, and arousal must be defined in erotic terms.[15] Yet men can become aroused such that they achieve penile erections for a range of reasons independent of an erotic response to another person or situation.[16] It has been well documented that men can have erections associated with non-sexual fear, sleep, full bladders, violence, and power (Dekker and Everaerd 1989: 353, 361; Langevin 1983: 8). Alfred Kinsey has observed that, for boys, erection and ejaculation are easily induced by "non-sexual" sources such as carnival rides, fast bicycle rides, sitting in warm sand, setting a field afire, war motion pictures, being chased by police, and, my two personal favorites, seeing one's name in print and hearing the national anthem. Kinsey concluded, however, that by their late teens males have been conditioned to respond primarily to "direct physical stimulation of the genitalia, or to psychic situations that are specifically sexual" (Kinsey et al. 1948: 164–5). Notwithstanding this general conditioning, "a romantic context is not a necessary condition for sexual arousal, in either men or women" (Dekker and Everaerd 1989: 361).

Therefore, there is reason to question interpretive strategies that tend to essentialize certain bodily responses, such as the male erection, as fundamentally erotic or romantic in nature. To the extent that "Herdt posits a tautologous ordering of eroticism that makes penile erection contingent on a kind of arousal that is by definition erotic" (Elliston 1995: 854), he is making just this mistake in interpreting Sambia culture.

Similarly, I want to resist the inclination to essentialize certain practices as undertaken principally to satisfy erotic desire. Of course, this issue arises in what I have described elsewhere as "the ongoing intramural debate within feminism about whether rape should be understood as a crime of violence or sex" (Franke 1997: 740). Rather than consider the question of sex and power in relation to rape in antinomous terms, consider the following examples. In ancient Rome, when a husband caught another man in bed with his wife, it was acceptable punishment for the husband and/or his male slaves to orally or anally rape the male offender (Richlin 1992: 215, 256). So too, oral and anal rape were used as a punishment in medieval Persia for various crimes.[17] Although it is possible that the person administering the punishment in these circumstances derived some erotic satisfaction from these practices, to characterize them as fundamentally erotic in nature is to radically pervert their meaning. Of course, I don't mean to imply that practices of this kind are subject to "correct" interpretations, because they do not possess meaning independent of interpretation. However, I do think some interpretations better reflect the ways the practices are understood by the participants, the significance they hold in the cultures in which they take place, and the unique ways in which sex can be a powerful tool to inflict myriad forms of harm.[18]

Thus, I want to challenge the inclination to declare man–boy fellatio in Melanesia a principally homoerotic practice. Rather, I prefer that we understand these activities not as homoerotic or homosexual, but as homosocial. Like Eve Kosofsky Sedgwick, I believe that the descriptor "homosocial" provides better purchase on the relation between and among men in Sambia society. Rather than reduce that relation to the erotic, to describe it as homosocial leaves room for the role of the erotic while recognizing the "range of ways in which sexuality functions as a signifier" (Sedgwick 1985: 7)[19] for and instrument in the enforcement of power relations. The work that sex does can be and often is at once symbolic and material, productive and reproductive, pleasurable and dangerous. Close examination of the Sambia male initiation rituals reveals that semen practices function symbolically, metonymically, and literally in the transmission of an ideology of gendered power.

Rather than evidencing the expression of man–boy love or desire, ritualized semen practices among the Sambia must be understood relative to their location in larger gender norms in their society. Sambia culture is fundamentally sexually polarized and sexually segregated.[20] Strict divisions of labor and ritual taboos regulating physical contact between the sexes are in evidence throughout the culture. From the time when boys are first isolated from all women at about the age of 7, they are taught to disparage women as dangerous creatures whose body fluids can pollute men and deplete their masculine substance. Women are frequently referred to as "dirty polluters," and men engage in purification rites after coitus, such as nose-bleeding, to rid their bodies of female contamination. So dangerous is the threat of pollution from women that public and private spaces are strictly sex-segregated. During the initiation process, men teach boys the reality of the threat that women pose to both maleness and masculinity (Herdt 1981: 28–9, 162, 244–5; 1997: 113).[21]

Accompanying the notions of female danger for Sambia are concomitant beliefs about the tremendous material and symbolic power and value of semen. According to Herdt and Stoller, "semen is the most precious human fluid . . . more precious than even mother's milk." Semen is related to human reproduction and growth in several ways. First, men orally inseminate their wives prior to conception, believing that the semen prepares the wife's body for making babies, as well as for lactation when the semen is converted into milk. After oral insemination, the couple engages in repeated vaginal insemination, depositing semen into the woman's womb, where it is transformed into a fetus. Multiple inseminations are necessary for this evolution to come off because the creation of a baby requires a critical mass of semen (Herdt and Stoller 1990: 60, 62, 63; interestingly, more semen is necessary to make a girl than a boy).

Semen is also necessary for human growth. Thus, "initial growth for every fetus occurs through semen accumulation." Babies grow from the ingestion of breast milk; the Sambia believe women's breasts transform semen into milk. After weaning, young girls continue to grow on their own due to the presence of female blood in their systems. Growth in boys, however, requires daily ingestion of semen in order to develop their skin, bones, and male features (ibid.: 65, 62).

Thus, the Sambia is a highly sex-stratified culture in which men are superior to and vilify women and in which men exclusively possess the elixir necessary for human reproduction and growth. In light of the central role that semen plays in the Sambia gender-based belief system, it would be careless to understand the transmission of semen, either between males or between males and females, solely or even primarily as an erotic practice. Given that fellatio between men and boys is explicitly undertaken to effect the transformation of boys from a feminized to a masculinized state, and is part of a larger indoctrination process whereby the boys learn of and internalize gender norms premised on male superiority, the integrity of an interpretation of these practices that understands them as primarily erotic in nature is quite questionable.

To be fair, Herdt does acknowledge the role that "ritualized homosexuality" plays in the masculinization of boys as they become initiated into "the whole male sexual culture" (1997: 121). But he fails to see the indispensable relation that masculinity bears to misogyny and gender hierarchy within Sambia culture. Herdt's insistent focus on Sambia homoeroticism denies him the opportunity to appreciate the degree to which notions of the superiority of men and the inferiority of women are mutually constitutive within the Sambia culture. Deborah Elliston describes these practices as "traumatic lessons in social hierarchy for the initiates. . . . Ritual teachings about men's and women's differences inculcate among men a generalized suspicion and fear of women while simultaneously exalting men's abilities and supremacy; together these teachings instantiate a gender hierarchy" (1995: 855). To represent their man–boy semen practices as being only about male sexuality or only about men elides the systemic nature of sex and gender norms as regulatory ideals among Sambia men and women.

Herdt observes the Sambia and represents the same-sex semen practices as fundamentally homoerotic, thereby neglecting the role these practices play in both the creation and maintenance of male supremacy in Sambia culture. If it is true across cultures that "the body requires incessant ritual work to be maintained in its sociocultural form" (Beidelman 1997: 244), then we must acknowledge the ways sexual practices produce not only sexual identity, but corporal and social identity as well; "the sutures of [social identity] become most visible under the disassembling eye of an alternative narrative, ideological as that narrative may itself be" (Sedgwick 1985: 15). Thus, the man–boy semen practices of the Sambia, while astonishing at first, provide an instructive opportunity to challenge the inclination to essentialize certain practices as erotic. I turn next to a less exotic, although no less astonishing, incident that further illustrates the danger in essentializing certain behavior as sexual/erotic. The Sambia and the assault of Abner Louima both illustrate how the classification of practices as sexual holds the danger of obfuscating how sex "both epitomizes and itself influences broader social relations of power" (ibid.: 13).

Anal/Sexual Practices

On the night of August 9, 1997, Abner Louima was leaving the Rendez-Vous, a nightclub in Brooklyn, New York popular among Haitian immigrants in the city, when the police arrived to break up a fight that had broken out between club patrons. "The white cops started with some racial stuff," Louima later reported. "They said, 'Why do you people come to this country if you can't speak English?'

They called us niggers." One police officer believed Louima had knocked him down during the altercation. The officer later declared, "No one jumps me and gets away with it." Officers pushed Louima to the ground, handcuffed him, and delivered him to the 70th Precinct – beating him severely on the way. Louima was charged with disorderly conduct, obstructing governmental administration, and resisting arrest.[22]

Once at the police station, officers strip-searched Louima in a public area, and, with his pants down, took him into the men's room, where they brutally assaulted him:

> My pants were down at my ankles, in full view of the other cops. They walked me over to the bathroom and closed the door. There were two cops. One said, "You niggers have to learn to respect police officers." The other one said, "If you yell or make any noise, I will kill you." Then one held me and the other one stuck the [wooden handle of a toilet] plunger up my behind. He pulled it out and shoved it in my mouth, broke my teeth and said, "That's your s—t, nigger." Later, when they called the ambulance, the cop told me, "If you ever tell anyone . . . I will kill you and your family."[23]

Louima was then taken to a jail cell, and only after other prisoners complained that he was bleeding did the police call for an ambulance. Louima required surgery to repair a pierced lower intestine and a torn bladder. He remained in the hospital for two months recovering from the injuries he sustained from the police officers at the 70th Precinct.[24]

It took a short while for the media to learn of this vicious assault, but once they did the headlines screamed: "Police Sodomize Suspect," "Suspect Claims Police Raped Him with Plunger," "Officer Accused of Sexually Brutalizing Suspect Arrested."[25] Members of the Haitian community marched in protest against this outrageous form of police brutality, waving toilet plungers and carrying signs declaring the cops to be "Criminals," "Perverts," "Rapists."[26] A retired transit police officer who attended the march exclaimed: "That's a foul and sordid act they performed on that man."[27] New York City Mayor Rudolph Giuliani exclaimed that the attack was "personally repulsive to him" and that the cops charged with the assault were "perverted."[28] Immediately after the event, several police officers who were associated with Justin Volpe, one of the officers charged with assaulting Louima, claimed that the Rendez-Vous was a gay club and that Louima's injuries stemmed from violent anal sex he had engaged in while at the club.[29] When the two police officers arrested in connection with the assault appeared for their arraignment, courthouse protesters taunted the cops by calling them "faggots."[30] The district attorney charged the officers with aggravated sexual abuse and first-degree assault, both crimes for which they could receive a maximum sentence of 24 years.[31] Only later were the charges against the police amended to include a racial bias crime for which the maximum sentence is, interestingly enough, only four years.[32]

It was precisely the sexual aspect of this assault that provoked journalists to grant Louima the moniker, "America's most famous victim of police brutality since Rodney King."[33] Sure, the police get carried away from time to time, shoot at fleeing suspects when deadly force isn't called for, choke a suspect to death with a choke hold, or even rape female prostitutes in a brothel they had raided.[34] But, as *Village Voice* journalist Richard Goldstein observed: "None of these documented cases arouse the outrage of this 'barbaric' act, which . . . is only supposed to happen in the Third World. *Here in the land of the free, when it comes to police brutality, we draw the line at raping a man.*"[35]

That this crime was heinous cannot be denied, but is it best characterized as a sex crime? What exactly was sexual about this assault? As Goldstein asked: "What's sex got to do with it?" Virtually every report of the case mentions early in the article that Louima is married and has children, and nightly news broadcasts regularly showed pictures of Louima and his family in the days following the assault.[36] What is more, the assailants were portrayed by the media as healthy heterosexuals.

So why call it a sex crime? The easy answer is tautological: the allegations fit the description of a sex crime as set out in New York criminal law. But what is a sex crime? There are several ways to differentiate a sexual assault from a non-sexual assault: (1) it is motivated by the erotic desire of the perpetrator; (2) it involves contact with the perpetrator's or the victim's sexual body parts (e.g., vagina, breasts, or penis) or involves acts that are typically regarded as sexual (e.g., kissing, fellatio, sexual intercourse); or (3) it is experienced as sexual by the victim.

New York criminal law defines criminal sexual offenses to be rape, sodomy, sexual misconduct, sexual abuse, aggravated sexual abuse, and course of sexual conduct against a child.[37] Two of these crimes explicitly anchor the crime's sexual nature, in whole or in part, in the satisfaction of sexual desire: criminal sexual abuse and course of sexual conduct against a child. The Penal Law defines criminal sexual abuse as sexual contact with another person by force or when the person is incapable of granting consent. Course of conduct against a child is committed when, among other things, a person engages in aggravated sexual contact with a child younger than 11 years of age. As a foundation for these two violations, the Penal Law defines "sexual contact" as "any touching of the sexual or other intimate parts of a person not married to the actor *for the purpose of gratifying sexual desire of either party.*"[38]

Because the satisfaction of sexual desire must be accomplished by touching sexual or intimate parts, it must be those parts that make this conduct a sex crime. But what are sexual or other intimate parts? Courts have found the chest, the upper leg, the leg, the mouth, and the navel to be "sexual or intimate parts" for purposes of the criminal sexual abuse statute.[39] Further, it has been established that "'intimate parts' is much broader than the term 'sexual parts'" and that "intimacy . . . must be viewed within the context in which the contact takes place. . . . A body part which might be intimate in one context, might not be intimate in another."[40] So really, any body part could be considered as sexual or intimate depending on the context. It appears that it is the perpetrator's erotic desire that sexualizes the body part, thus making contact with that body part a sex crime.

But it cannot be the perpetrator's desire that sets some crimes apart as sex crimes. Sexual misconduct, rape, sodomy, and aggravated sexual abuse are all premised on penetration of the vagina, rectum, or mouth.[41] The satisfaction of sexual desire is irrelevant to these crimes. So, at least for purposes of the criminal law, these body parts are essentially sexual.

This brief tour through New York criminal law illustrates that those behaviors labeled sex crimes bear, at best, a family resemblance to one another. The answer to the question "What makes something a sex crime?" is not revealed in the positive law itself. Instead, a complex set of interpretive moves is required to ascribe a sexual nature to the behavior. Some of the symbolic work is done endogenously by one or both of the parties involved, and some of it is done exogenously by those who act as public interpreters of the behavior: prosecutors, judges, and juries. But in all cases, that which makes the crime sexual "is a discursive formation . . . not a fact or property of the body" (Bell 1991: 86; Bell attributes this argument to Foucault).

So what rendered the assault of Abner Louima a sex crime? Of course, it was the penetration of his rectum. But why? Surely we would not want to ground the sexual nature of the crime in the erotic pleasure, latent or otherwise, that the officers received from performing this act. Louima certainly did not experience this assault as erotic. Nor would we want to say that the violent insertion of a wooden handle in a person's rectum is intrinsically a sexual act, or that all acts involving a rectum are to be so construed.

Nevertheless, most people would want to say that there was something particularly wrong with this assault that distinguishes it from an equally violent punch in the face or a kick in the ribs. Justin Volpe, the police officer charged with principal responsibility for Louima's injuries, was quoted as having said to other cops on the night of the assault: "I had to break a man."[42] In this comment lies the key for understanding the power and the wrong of the assault on Louima. I suggest that the power of the assault principally lies not in its sexual nature, *simpliciter*, but in the unique way that it humiliated Louima as a black man. For white men, particularly white police officers, to assault a black man anally is one of the most powerful ways to assault black masculinity. Tragically, Louima is not the first man to experience this kind of assault. At least six black men, all immigrants, have complained that a white police officer abducted them, took them to an isolated place in Queens, and anally raped them at gunpoint. The victims and witnesses report that the cop threatened them with death if they spoke to the authorities about these assaults.[43] What distinguished Louima's assault from other incidents of police violence was not that it was sexual, but that the police officers were caught.

A preoccupation with the supposedly sexual nature of these assaults deflects attention away from the gender- and race-based nature of this crime. Here we have an example of what is commonly thought to be a sexual act being used as an instrument of gender- and race-based terror.[44] One cannot understand the meaning of this conduct without taking into account its gender- and race-based significance. To view it as primarily sexual is to make the same mistake as that made by Herdt in Melanesia: it is to essentialize certain conduct and body parts as sexual, and to occlude the ways in which "the sexual" can be deployed as the instrumentality by which other forms of power and supremacy are cultivated. After all, the Louima incident began with a police officer telling him: "You niggers have to learn to respect police officers."[45]

What is more, hypersexualizing the Louima assault carries the additional danger of normalizing other violent police practices because they aren't sexually barbaric. Recall Richard Goldstein's observation: "When it comes to police brutality, we draw the line at raping a man." Other non-sexual forms of police violence may be regrettable, but many may view this behavior as a kind of police-based *droit du seigneur*. In fact, it may well be the case, as Goldstein argues, that there is a kind of sadist satisfaction that accompanies the use of handcuffs, choke holds, or other excessive methods of police restraint, such as hog-tying suspects. To regard the Louima assault as the exception, where perverted cops acted completely beyond the pale, "prevents us from imagining that cops who specialize in [violent] tactics might find them exciting."[46] To over-eroticize the treatment of Louima carries the danger of under-eroticizing police tactics that do not involve penetration of a "sexual or intimate body part." After all, if, as Kinsey suggested, young men can get aroused by being chased by police, why shouldn't police get aroused when running after suspects? Misconduct charges filed against a police officer in Seattle lay bare the erotic potential of routine police practices.[47]

Which, of course, prompts the most fundamental of questions: is it the sexual/erotic nature of any of these practices that makes them wrong? For the most part, I think not. It seems to me that these incidents should be analyzed to uncover the way the sexual/erotic operates as a particularly efficient and dangerous conduit with which to exercise power. Thus, to say that the Louima assault was sexual is at once to say too much and not enough about it. This simple construction of the injury of Louima's assault occludes the particularly gendered and raced salience of anal penetration for a Caribbean black man. "They have always taken us for this frail and vulnerable community," said Tatiana Wah, a Haitian activist who was one of the organizers of the march protesting the police assault of Louima.[48] The anal assault of Louima, performed not in private, but in front of an audience of white cops on their turf, effectively enacted the perceived frailness and vulnerability of Haitian men.

How best to avoid the erasure of racial- or gender-based subordination by and through the invocation of the sexual? In the section that follows, I consider the desexualization of sodomy, rape, and other assaults labeled sex crimes.

The Desexualization of Violence

Beginning with *The History of Sexuality*, Michel Foucault developed a theory of the discursive truth of sex and, for present purposes, a critical analysis of the means by which certain forms of knowledge-based power are deployed such that sexuality gets anchored in certain parts of the body (1990: 57–63).[49] The examples I provide above from New York criminal law illustrate quite well Foucault's point: criminal law does not merely pick out the set of practices that are truly sexual in nature, but, rather, certain body parts or practices become sexual by virtue of their regulation by law. As a result, different parts of the body become attached to different fields of knowledge: when we interrogate practices involving the genitals, we are, by definition, learning something sexual.

Shortly after the publication of *The History of Sexuality*, Foucault entered into a set of discussions with feminists about rape (1988: 200–4; Bell 1991: 84–7). Given his concerns about the dangers of punishing sexuality, Foucault poses the question: "What should be said about rape?" In these conversations, he urges the position that "when one punishes rape one should be punishing physical violence and nothing but that. . . . It may be regarded as an act of violence, possibly more serious, but of the same type, as that of punching someone in the face" (1988: 200–1).[50] Well, Foucault is unequivocally weighing in on the violence side of the sex versus violence debate among feminists about the meaning of rape.[51]

In response to the women who objected to his insistence on desexualizing rape, Foucault reveals his true concern. By making rape a "sex" crime, we are once again anchoring sexuality in certain parts of the body, and in so doing, "the body is discursively marked [thereby] construct[ing] certain parts of the body as more important than others" (Bell 1991: 92). By bestowing this "special" status on parts of the body marked sexual, "sexuality as such, in the body, has a preponderant place, the sexual organ isn't like a hand, hair, or a nose. It therefore has to be protected, surrounded, invested in any case with legislation that isn't that pertaining to the rest of the body" (Foucault 1988: 201–2).

Many feminists would respond: so what's wrong with that? Sexual assaults *are* different. Foucault's concern derives from the way the deployment of sex in this fashion occludes the way power operates on the body, "ordering it as it studies, organizing its movements as it observes, categorizing as it probes. In this way, power, or power/knowledge, produces our understanding of the body" (Bell 1991: 87). Thus, for Foucault, sex is not a thing we have or do, but is instead a regulatory ideal. Judith Butler expresses a similar interest in the ways "sex" "produces the bodies it governs" and in so doing, produces bodies that matter, and bodies that don't (1993: 1).[52] Wendy Brown pushes these Foucauldian insights in yet another direction, illuminating the danger of a rights-based politics that is built on the naturalization of identity which is, in fact, the result of a regulatory ideal: "disciplinary productions of identity may become the site of rights struggles that naturalize and thus entrench the powers of which those identities are the effects" (1995: 120).

It is the regulatory power of sex that Foucault seeks to interrupt by questioning the need to treat rape differently from a punch in the face. To his mind, we stand to gain much and lose little by punishing the physical violence of rape "without bringing in the fact that sexuality was involved" (1988: 202).

For the most part, I find myself in agreement with Foucault's theoretical point, yet I think Monique Plaza is right when she argues that women, in particular, cannot afford the jump into the "realm of the ideal" (1980: 28, 35). Although in principle, there is much to Foucault's suggestion that we treat rape and "non-sexual" assault as crimes of violence, to recommend such a change in the positive laws at this moment means that rape victims will bear the transition costs of this representational reform. That is, rape victims will continue to experience rape as an assault to their sexual body during the period in which the withdrawal of regulation by sex crime laws transforms the way we know the body.

To reconcile the tension between the damage done by laws that perpetuate "the sexual" as a regulatory ideal, and the cost to rape victims of demanding that the law not recognize a sexual aspect to their injury, we need to think rather more synthetically about sexual violence specifically and sexuality more generally. These two cases illustrate how inclined we usually are to view sex as something that is either entirely present or entirely absent from a particular practice. The frames we apply to practices like that of the Sambia or the violence perpetrated against Abner Louima lack the nuance that can at once recognize the sexual as constitutive of the activity's meaning, while not exhausting that meaning. Rather, the law and our critical gaze must see how sex works synthetically with a range of other productive and destructive vectors of power in these moments.

Of course, all cultures sexualize different body parts and behaviors in myriad ways. In a sense, I am urging a reverse sociology of the erotic. Rather than studying the ways fingers, toes, lips, ears, penises, vaginas, or anuses become eroticized across cultures, I am concerned with the way body parts and practices, once sexualized, cannot escape a signification process by which contact with those body parts and the enactment of those practices are always already and exclusively understood to be sexual. This reverse sociology will better enable us to appreciate legally and culturally how sex is put to work for bad, as well as for good.

Notes

1 The Blessed Virgin Mary seems to appear all the time in Queens, New York. In fact, there are ads in the subway announcing a phone number you can call, for only $1.50 a minute, to receive information about the most recent sightings of the BVM.

2   Herdt asks, for instance, "Why should a society of manly warriors believe that a boy must be orally inseminated to become masculine? What happens when this conviction is implemented through prolonged ritualized homosexuality?" (1981: 1).

3   Merrill Goozner, "NYC Cut in Crime Has a Brutish Side," *Chicago Tribune*, August 16, 1997.

4   Herdt provides the name Sambia as a pseudonym for the tribe's true name to "protect the identities of those who trusted [him] and to guard the community's ritual cult, which still remains a secretive way of life in the strict sense of the term. Sambia men explicitly stipulated that no part of [his] original material be allowed to circulate within Papua New Guinea" (1981: xvi). Herdt summarized the Sambia beliefs as follows: "Femininity is thought to be an inherent development in a girl's continuous association with her mother. Masculinity, on the other hand, is not an intrinsic result of maleness; it is an achievement distinct from the mere endowment of male genitals. Masculine reproductive maturity must be artificially induced, by means of strict adherence to ritual techniques" (ibid.: 160).

5   Herdt observes that cane-swallowing was abandoned sometime around 1964 because it was too painful (1981: 223 n.29).

6   See also 1981: 281–2, noting an interim stage when boys approaching puberty take an active role in motivating younger boys to join them as fellators.

7   "It is crucial that we distinguish from the start between homosexual identity and behavior" (1981: 3 n.2).

8   Herdt cites a number of early Melanesian studies that ignored same-sex seminal practices (1984: 2).

9   See ibid.: 3, recognizing that, as of 1984, "sex remains one of the 'taboo' subjects in anthropology." See also Weston 1993: 339: "Throughout the first half of the century, most allusions by anthropologists to homosexual behavior remained as veiled in ambiguity and as couched in judgment as were references to homosexuality in the dominant discourse of the surrounding society." Herdt attributed three additional factors to this failure: (1) a lack of data; (2) the tendency for writers still to view homosexual behavior as universally deviant, unnatural, or perverse; and (3) the use of authorities viewing only heterosexuality as "normal" (1984: 3).

10   See Herdt 1991: 603, 607, which addresses the negative response of white missionaries, government officers, and Western agents to the "boy-inseminating man."

11   One must wonder how Herdt's published work may have contributed to the extinction of the very practices he set out to document.

12   Herdt 1984 (a collection of articles addressing same-sex sexual practices in different societies in the South Pacific region); 1982 (analyzing male maturation rites in Papua New Guinea); 1997: 81–8, 112–23.

13   Herdt observes: "Men are not simply biding time by fooling around with initiates. Boys were their first erotic partners. For this reason, and other personality factors, bachelors are sometimes passionately fond of particular boys" (1981: 288). See also ibid.: 282, 319 and 1991: 611, discussing the protections and bonds that may develop between bachelors and boys.

14   "Do boy-inseminating relationships, one must wonder, express erotic desire?" (Herdt 1991: 603). Herdt recognizes and rejects two interpretative trends that largely dismiss the erotic nature of Melanesian homosexuality. The first trend treats such practices as "purely customary ritual practice" (ibid.: 607).

15   "It is a necessary redundancy to say that without sexual excitement – as signified by erections in the inspirer and bawdy enthusiasm in the inspired boy – these social practices would not only lie beyond the erotic but, more elementarily, would not exist" (Herdt 1991: 613).

16   As noted by Vanggaard: "It appears, then, that emotions and impulses other than erotic ones may cause erection and genital activity in men; just as, in the baboon, mounting and penetrating to show superiority, or sitting on guard with legs apart and penis threateningly exposed show erection of an asexual origin. . . . The same will probably have been the case with the Bronze Age people of Scandinavia – or of northern Italy for that matter – since they equated

phallic power with the power of the spear, the sword and the axe, as we can see from their perroglyphs" (1972: 102).

17 "'A favourite Persian punishment for strangers caught in the Harem or Gynæceum is to strip and throw them and expose them to the embraces of the grooms and Negro slaves'" (Vanggaard 1972: 101, quoting Richard Burton, "Thousand Nights and a Night," *Terminal Essay X* (1885): 235).

18 As Foucault noted, "Sexuality is not the most intractable element in power relations, but rather one of those endowed with the greatest instrumentality: useful for the greatest number of maneuvers and capable of serving as a point of support, as a linchpin, for the most varied strategies" (1990: 103).

19 Sedgwick recognizes that aspects of the Sambia culture fit within her "homosocial continuum." (See also 1985: 5.)

20 One clear example of this polarization is found in the many spatial segregations evidenced by the Sambia culture. The male "clubhouse," sire of many of the masculinization rites, is off-limits to women (see Herdt 1981: 74–5). Similarly, female "menstrual huts" are strictly avoided by men (ibid.: 75). This spatial segregation operates in many other areas, including domiciles and footpaths (ibid.: 75–6).

21 Herdt observed that, in the Sambia culture, "Men hold that women may pollute them by simply 'stepping over' . . . above, or beside them, or by touching persons, food, or possessions. During their menstrual periods women leave their houses and retire to the menstrual hut, which is situated slightly below the hamlet. Men and initiates completely avoid the area of the hut. Likewise, women must not walk near the men's clubhouse or look inside" (1981: 75). Domestic arrangements are also organized around the danger of male pollution by women. On entering a house, women immediately must squat near the doorway, thereby reducing the possibility of transferring their polluting fluids to men in the house (ibid.: 75–6).

22 See Richard Goldstein, "What's Sex Got to Do with It? The Assault of Abner Louima May Have Been Attempted Murder. But It Was Also Rape," *Village Voice*, September 2, 1997: 57; Hayes, "Haitian's Beating May Have Been Case of Mistaken Identity, Punch," *Arizona Republic*, August 22, 1997: A11 (reporting that witnesses claimed that another individual, not Louima, threw the punch against Officer Volpe); Mike McAlary, "The Frightful Whisperings from a Coney Island Hospital Bed," *New York Daily News*, August 13, 1997: 2 (quoting Louima as he lay in his hospital bed four days after the attack); UPI File, "Report: Officer Boasted after Attack," August 19, 1997, available in Lexis, Nexis Library (reporting the alleged statement of Justin Volpe, New York City police officer; one report stated: "the officers became furious when he protested his arrest, twice stopping the patrol car to beat him with their fists"). See also David Kocieniewski, "Injured Man Says Brooklyn Officers Tortured Him in Custody," *New York Times*, August 13, 1997: B1.

23 McAlary, "The Frightful Whisperings from a Coney Island Hospital Bed," 2. Louima recounted the incident to a newspaper: "'The cops pulled down my pants in front of the desk sergeant.' . . . 'They marched you naked across the precinct?' 'Yes.' 'There were other cops around?' 'Yes. There was the sergeant and other cops. They saw.' 'And they said nothing?' 'I kept screaming, "Why? Why?" All the cops heard me, but said nothing.' 'What they said to me I'll never forget. In public, one says, "You niggers have to learn how to respect police officers"'" (Mike McAlary, "Victim and City Deeply Scarred," *New York Daily News*, August 14, 1997: 4).

24 Kocieniewski, "Injured Man," B1. Tom Hayes, "Officer Accused of Sexually Brutalizing Suspect Arrested," *Arizona Republic*, August 13, 1997: 1 (as reproduced by a number of newspapers). *Newsday*, "Louima Starts on a Long Road Back," October 12, 1997: A39.

25 J. Zamgba Browne, "Police Sodomize Suspect: The Tale of Torture at 70th Precinct," *New York Amsterdam News*, August 20, 1997: 1; *Salt Lake Tribune*, "Suspect Claims Police Raped Him with Plunger," August 14, 1997: A13; Hayes, "Officer Accused," 1. See also "New York

Officer Surrenders in Sexual Assault on Immigrant," *Los Angeles Times*, August 14, 1997: A18; "Cop Surrenders on Sexual Brutality Charges," *San Diego Union & Tribune*, August 14, 1997: A12.

26 See Vinette K. Pryce, "A Week of Outrage, Pain and Celebration," *New York Amsterdam News*, September 10, 1997: 1, which contains a photograph of a protester at a march holding a sign saying "Criminals, Perverts, Rapists."

27 Charles Baillou, "Marchers Blast Police Barbarism at City Hall," *New York Amsterdam News*, September 10, 1997: 8.

28 David Firestone, "Giuliani's Quandary: Mayor Who Linked Name to Police Success Is Now Facing a Very Ugly Police Failure," *New York Times*, August 15, 1997: A1. The press reported that, during the assault of Louima at the 70th Precinct, one of the officers said: "This is Giuliani time, not Dinkins time" (Eleanor Randolph, "In Police Abuse Case, Giuliani's Balance Tested," *Los Angeles Times*, August 16, 1997: A1). But see Carolina Gonzalez and Bill Hutchinson, "Sharpton Promises He'll Defend Louima," *New York Daily News*, January 19, 1998: 8, reporting that Louima was then unsure of whether the officer actually made this statement. Mayor Giuliani provided a quite interesting response to reports of the officer's alleged comment: "The remark is as perverted as the alleged act" (in Randolph, A1).

29 John Sullivan, "New Charges Filed in Police Brutality Case," *New York Times*, August 22, 1997: B3.

30 Goldstein, "What's Sex Got to Do with It?" 57.

31 See Goozner, "New York Cut in Crime," 1; see also New York Penal Law §120.10 (McKinney 1998) (first degree assault); New York Penal Law §130.70 (first degree aggravated sexual abuse).

32 See "2 NYC Officers Get New Charge in Haitian's Beating," *Boston Globe*, September, 1997, A8; see also New York Penal Law §240.31 (first degree aggravated harassment).

33 Mike McAlary, "Home Sweet Heartache: Love Alone Won't Aid Louima in Brooklyn," *New York Daily News*, October 10, 1997: 3.

34 A New York City commission report provides two examples of police overzealousness: "One officer from a Brooklyn North precinct told us how he and his colleagues once threw a bucket of ammonia in the face of an individual detained in a precinct holding pen. Another cooperating officer told us how he and his colleagues threw garbage and then boiling water on a person hiding from them in a dumbwaiter shaft" (City of New York, Commission to Investigate Allegations of Police Corruption and the Anti-Corruption Procedures of the Police Department, Commission Report (1997): 47; hereafter Mollen Report). Also see Amnesty International, United States of America, Police Brutality and Excessive Force in the New York City Police Department (1996): 26, 37–54.

35 Goldstein, "What's Sex Got to Do with It?" 57; emphasis added.

36 See, e.g., Charles Baillou, "Angry Haitians March at the 70th Precinct in Brooklyn," *New York Amsterdam News*, August 27, 1997: 1; "The Blue Wall, Police Brutality and Police Silence," *Nightline*, ABC, August 22, 1997.

37 See New York Penal Law §§55 130.00C.85 (McKinney 1998 and Supp. 1998; listing New York's sex offenses). The New York Penal Law defines sexual misconduct as:

1 Being a male, he engages in sexual intercourse with a female without her consent; or
2 He engages in deviate sexual intercourse with another person without the latter's consent; or
3 He engages in sexual conduct with an animal or a dead human body. (§330.20)

"Deviate sexual intercourse" is defined as "sexual conduct between persons not married to each other consisting of contact between the penis and the anus, the mouth and penis, or the mouth and the vulva" (§130.00(2)). First degree sexual abuse occurs when: a person subjects another person to sexual contact:

1 By forcible compulsion; or
2 When the other person is incapable of consent by reason of being physically helpless; or
3 When the other person is less than eleven years old. (§130.65)

First degree aggravated sexual abuse occurs when: a person inserts a foreign object in the vagina, urethra, penis or rectum of another person causing physical injury to such person:

1 By forcible compulsion; or
2 When the other person is incapable of consent by reason of being physically helpless; or
3 When the other person is less than eleven years old. (§130.70(1))

First degree course of sexual conduct against a child occurs when, "over a period of time not less than three months in duration, [a person] engages in two or more acts of sexual conduct, which includes at least one act of sexual intercourse, deviate sexual intercourse or aggravated sexual contact, with a child less than eleven years old" (§130.75; see also §130.80, second degree course of sexual conduct against a child).

38 New York Penal Law §130.00(3); emphasis added. In its entirety, "sexual contact" means: "Any touching of the sexual or other intimate parts of a person not married to the actor for the purpose of gratifying sexual desire of either party. It includes the touching of the actor by the victim, as well as the touching of the victim by the actor, whether directly or through clothing."

39 See *People v. Cammarere*, 611 N.Y.S.2d 682, 684 (App. Div. 1984); *People v. Gray*, 607 N.Y.S.2d 828, 829 (App. Div. 1994); *People v. Graydon*, 492 N.Y.S.2d 903, 904 (Crim. Ct. 1985); *People v. Rondon*, 579 N.Y.S.2d 319, 320–1 (Crim. Ct. 1992); *People v. Rivera*, 525 N.Y.S.2d 118, 119 (Sup. Ct. 1988); *People v. Belfrom*, 475 N.Y.S.2d 978, 980 (Sup. Ct. 1984).

40 *People v. Rivera*, 119.

41 The New York Penal Law provides as follows. Sexual intercourse, defined as "its ordinary meaning and occur[ing] upon any penetration, however slight," New York Penal Law §130.00(1) (McKinney 1998), is a necessary element of sexual misconduct (§130.20), rape (§130.35), and sodomy (§130.50). Aggravated sexual assault requires "insert[ion] of a foreign object in the vagina, urethra, penis, or rectum of another person" (§130.70).

42 See Goldstein, "What's Sex Got to Do with It?" 57.

43 Earl Caldwell, "Police Sodomy in Queens: The Column the Daily News Killed," *New York Amsterdam News*, August 27, 1997: 12. The "black" newspapers in New York reported these incidents at great length, but none of the "white" papers has mentioned them. See Earl Caldwell, "Earl Caldwell to the *Daily News* . . . 'I warned you. You fired me,'" *New York Amsterdam News*, August 27, 1997: I: "The major papers seemed to have a blackout of the story. The *Daily News* had published nothing. The *New York Times* had published no story either."

44 In a characteristically laconic passage in *Beloved*, Toni Morrison depicts the acrid humiliation suffered by African American men on a chain gang who are forced each morning by white male guards to put on their own chains, kneel down in a row, and fellate the guards on demand (1987: 107–8). I read this passage not to be principally about the expropriation of sex from African American men, but rather about the routine ways sexual practices were used to degrade these prisoners.

45 See McAlary, "Frightful Whisperings," 2, quoting Louima's recollection of an officer's statement just prior to the insertion of a plunger into Louima's anus.

46 Goldstein, "What's Sex Got to Do with It?" 57.

47 After flirting with a female bartender while on his break, a male police officer followed her when she drove home from work, pulled her over, and teasingly said, "Now you know what it's gonna be like to be arrested. . . . He then took her out of the car, handcuffed her, grabbed her hair and pulled her head back and began to fondle her sexually" (Ronald K. Firten, "County Officer Faces Charges of Misconduct," *Seattle Times*, October 24, 1998: A7).

48 Richard Goldstein and Jean Jean Pierre, "Day of Outrage," *Village Voice*, September 9, 1997: 44, quoting Tatiana Wah.

49 Foucault writes: "Is 'sex' really the anchorage point that supports the manifestations of sexuality, or is it not rather a complex idea that was formed inside the deployment of sexuality?" (1990: 152).

50 Foucault sets up the discussion with the provocative declaration that "in any case, sexuality can in no circumstances be the object of punishment."

51 See, e.g., Franke 1997: 740–4, discussing the debate among feminists concerning the proper meaning of rape: as a crime of violence or sex.

52 In addressing Foucault's "regulatory ideal," Butler notes: "sex not only functions as a norm, but is part of a regulatory practice . . . whose regulatory force is made clear as a kind of productive power, the power to produce – demarcate, circulate, differentiate – the bodies it controls."

References

Beidelman, T. O. (1997) *The Cool Knife: Imagery of Gender, Sexuality, and Moral Education in Kaguru Initiation Ritual* (Washington, DC: Smithsonian Institution Press).

Bell, V. (1991) "Beyond the 'Thorny Question': Feminism, Foucault and the Desexualisation of Rape," *International Journal of the Sociology of Law* 19: 83.

Brown, W. (1995) *States of Injury: Power and Freedom in Late Modernity* (Princeton University Press).

Butler, J. (1993) *Bodies That Matter: On the Discursive Limits of "Sex"* (New York: Routledge).

Creed, G. W. (1984) "Sexual Subordination: Institutionalized Homosexuality and Social Control in Melanesia," *Ethnology* 23: 157.

Dekker, J. and Everaerd, W. (1989) "Psychological Determinants of Sexual Arousal: A Review," *Behavior RES and Therapy* 27: 353

Donald, D. H. (1995) *Lincoln* (New York: Touchstone).

Elliston, D. A. (1995) "Erotic Anthropology: 'Ritualized Homosexuality' in Melanessa and Beyond," *American Ethnologist* 22: 848.

Foucault, M. (1977) *Language, Counter-Memory, Practice: Selected Essays and Interviews*, ed. Donald F. Bouchard, trans. Donald F. Bouchard and Sherry Simon (Ithaca, NY: Cornell University Press).

Foucault, M. (1988) *Politics, Philosophy, Culture: Interviews and Other Writings 1977–1984*, ed. Lawrence D. Kritzman, trans. Alan Sheridan et al. (New York: Routledge).

Foucault, M. (1990) *The History of Sexuality*, trans. Robert Hurley (New York: Vintage Books).

Franke, K. M. (1997) "What's Wrong with Sexual Harassment?" *Stanford Law Review* 49: 691.

Herdt, G. H. (1977) *Same Sex, Different Cultures: Gays and Lesbians across Cultures* (Boulder: Westview Press).

Herdt, G. H. (1981) *Guardians of the Flutes* (New York: McGraw-Hill).

Herdt, G. H. (ed.) (1982) *Rituals of Manhood: Male Initiation in Papua New Guinea* (Berkeley: University of California Press).

Herdt, G. H. (1984) "Ritualized Homosexual Behavior in the Male Cults of Melanesia, 1862–1983: An Introduction," in Gilbert H. Herdt (ed.), *Ritualized Homosexuality in Melanesia* (Berkeley: University of California Press).

Herdt, G. H. (1991) "Representations of Homosexuality: An Essay on Cultural Ontology and Historical Comparison, Part II," *Journal of the History of Sexuality* 1: 603.

Herdt, G. H. and Stoller, R. J. (1990) *Intimate Communications: Erotics and the Study of Culture* (New York: Columbia University Press).

Kinsey, A. C. et al. (1948) *Sexual Behavior in the Human Male* (Philadelphia: W. B. Saunders Co.).

Langevin, R. (1983) *Sexual Strands: Understanding and Treating Sexual Anomalies in Men* (Hillsdale, NJ: L. Erlbaum Associates).

Morrison, T. (1987) *Beloved* (New York: Knopf).

Plaza, M. (1980) "Our Costs and Their Benefits," *M/F: A Feminist Journal*: 28.

Richlin, A. (1992) *The Garden of Priapus: Sexuality and Aggression in Roman Humor*, rev. edn. (Oxford: Oxford University Press).

Sedgwick, E. K. (1985) *Between Men: English Literature and Male Homosocial Desire* (New York: Columbia University Press).

Vanggaard, T. (1972) *Phallós: A Symbol and Its History in the Male World*, trans. Thorkil Vanggaard (New York: International Universities Press).

Weston, K. (1993) "Lesbian/Gay Studies in the House of Anthropology," *Annual Review of Anthropology* 22: 339.

Williams, F. E. (1936) *Papuans of the Trans-Fly* (Oxford: The Clarendon Press).

CHAPTER TWELVE

Policy

Carol Lee Bacchi

Policy and gender have a contested relationship in Western democracies. The declared goal is a gender-blind polity and gender neutrality is embraced as a means to that end. On the other hand, feminists insist that a wide range of policies play a significant role in entrenching women's subordination. Some point out that gender neutrality as a formal arrangement fails to touch the lives of most women. Others declare gender neutrality an impossible and undesirable goal. The purpose of this chapter is to work through the implications of these various positions and in the process to put forward a slightly different perspective which I believe moves the discussion in fruitful directions.

Policy Studies and Policy Practice: Feminist Interventions

A conventional understanding of the policy process is that it involves well-considered legislative and legal responses to social problems and social needs (Bacchi 1999: Part I). In this understanding, rational and detached policy-makers make well-intentioned attempts to improve the lives of citizens. The domain is public decision-making to regulate public activities. Citizens' private lives are considered to be their own.

More recent studies have challenged this understanding in a number of ways. First, by drawing attention to the fact that governments may refuse to act in some situations, the judgment involved in pursuing certain policy directions is revealed. In addition, a close analysis of policies suggests the non-innocent way in which problems are understood (Bacchi 1999). "Non-innocent" is not meant to imply deliberate malfeasance, but the necessary involvement of values and presuppositions in the policy-making process. In addition, the focus has shifted from state-generated decisions to the interrelationship between the state and other institutions, including the professions and the family. We have here a much broader social canvas than is traditionally assumed.

Feminists have played a significant role in reshaping policy studies. They have shown, for example, how the separation of public from private activities, with the former deemed to be the domain of government scrutiny, places women at risk of abuse. The demarcation between so-called public and private activities also ignores the role of government in shaping relations between women and men through the privatizing of caring responsibilities (Olsen 1985; Pateman 1983). In addition, assumptions about the appropriate roles of women and men have been shown to lodge deep within welfare policies which often assume a wife at home (Orloff 1993). Gender is often used as a shorthand to refer to these processes.

But the relationship between policy and gender has been complicated by the explicit commitment of Western democracies to gender neutrality. Since the 1960s there have been moves toward eradicating the "different treatment" of women. The goal has been declared to be equal treatment and a gender-blind polity. To this end, legislation was introduced which banned discrimination on the basis of sex (Lacey 1995). With a similar goal of equal treatment, welfare regimes in some countries have moved toward a sameness model for benefits (Shaver 1993).

A large number of feminist studies expose the hidden gender subtext in formal "gender-neutral" programs. A few examples will illustrate the varied nature of these challenges. Uma Narayan (1997) points to the inadequacies of formally gender-neutral immigration laws which ignore women's dependent immigrant status if they face abuse and violence. Lorna Weir calls the discourse of population planning "neosexist in its gender neutrality and incorporation of status of women concerns with minimal programme linkage" (1994: 15–16). She points out that anti-natalist programs have overwhelmingly intervened in women's bodies, "constructing having children as a phenomenon of the female body." Baker and Tippin (1999) point out how recent employability policies in Australia, New Zealand, and Canada have falsely treated beneficiaries as gender-neutral beings without family responsibilities, with particularly dire outcomes for mothers on low incomes.

Gender neutrality remains a problem for feminists, however. The question has become whether the goal ought to be *genuine* gender neutrality or something else. And if something else, what would this look like? As DiQuinzio and Young point out, while some feminists believe that treating women in the same way as men would be an improvement over current policy, others "challenge the efficacy of gender neutrality in promoting women's interests" (1997: ix).

Meanings of Gender in Policy Analysis

With this background, it becomes important to reflect upon the meanings of gender employed in these debates. In government policy around sex discrimination, for example, there is often slippage between the terms "gender-neutral" and "sex-neutral," and between "gender-blind" and "sex-blind." This slippage indicates that "gender" is being used as a synonym for "sex," as simply another way of referring to categories of people, to men and women. In this usage, gender (like sex) is seen to be a part of a person rather than a way of shaping social relations. It follows that, in this understanding, on the grounds that all individuals should be treated alike, gender becomes something to be bracketed off in designing policy.

Recent gender theory challenges this static, individualistic characterizing of gender. The series editors of *Revisioning Gender* (Ferree et al. 1999: xi, xiii) note the key shift from conceptualizing gender as an individual trait to focusing on gender as a principle of social organization. The goal, they tell us, is to "no longer take dichotomous gender for granted but to begin to explain the meaning of gender itself." Fiona Wilson (1996; cited in Benschop and Doorewaard 1998: 789) makes a similar point in her plea: "Instead of looking at gender as a difference perhaps we need to look . . . at how this is 'done'." To bring this insight to Policy Studies, we need a more dynamic understanding of gender as a process and of policy as a gendering process, drawing attention to the role of law and policy in shaping the lives of women and men. On this understanding, gender cannot be bracketed off; rather, its implications need to be confronted.

Identifying the workings of gender as a process is not a straightforward task, however. While many policies incorporate gendered assumptions based on stereotypical characterizations of masculinity and femininity, it is not always possible to "read off" how these assumptions will be applied to men and women. Moreover, gendered assumptions can be and are used at times to structure other hierarchical relations, between heterosexual and homosexual, for example. The challenge then is to interrogate the ways in which gender plays a part in the creation of hierarchies among social groups. To meet this challenge, we need policy analyses which bring together the study of concepts *and* their uses (see Bacchi 1996).

Many feminists have been involved in identifying the presence of gendered assumptions in foundational concepts in much Western law and policy. These analyses are often produced by feminist political philosophers (e.g., Lloyd 1984; Pateman 1983) and feminist legal theorists (Naffine 1990; Smart 1989). They have made the case that the Western concept of equal opportunity and the notions of justice and rights associated with this concept privilege a political subject who is constituted as rational, individuated, and abstracted from body. This characterization is shown to map onto a masculine stereotype, with the clear characterization of women and femininity in Western philosophy as emotional, attached to particular others (Benhabib 1992), and embodied. Using this kind of analysis, it is possible to say that the constructed separation between public and private in the understanding of governmental roles is itself a gendered understanding. So too it could be argued that the description of policy studies as rational and detached mimics the masculine stereotype. But what are we to do with these insights? What is achieved by drawing attention to the deeply gendered character of foundational concepts in approaches to policy?

Feminist policy analysts have detailed the differential impact of a range of policies on women and men, highlighting how women do less well under these policies. This kind of analysis often pays heed to the gendered character of basic concepts, but has as a primary target drawing attention to the ways in which these concepts have gendered effects. Sometimes, "gendered" in these studies is meant to capture the ways in which policies reinforce traditional roles for men and women, with men as breadwinners and women as providers of support services in the home (Sainsbury 1994). Sometimes, "gendered" refers only to a differential impact on women and men, with women earning less pay than men or with women being less well represented in public institutions (European Commission 1998). Most recently, feminists have called for "gender" to become an aspect of mainstream policy studies (Mazey 2000: 334). As often as not, what is meant here is that mainstream Policy Studies needs to incorporate an assessment of how policies affect women.

While all these studies have their uses, I recommend focusing upon the specific ways in which gendered assumptions in policies are interpreted in specific contexts, how these concepts are used in relation to particular projects. The task is to examine how gendered concepts are *applied* in the lives of diverse groups of men and women. A starting premise here is that gendered terms and concepts are not a seamless web, that there are contradictions within their very framing, and that they can be and are deployed in a variety of ways to accomplish diverse political purposes (Bacchi 1996; Lacey 1995). This approach puts the focus on the activity involved both in shaping the lives of women and men, and in using gendered concepts for other purposes. This makes it equally important to map the operation of gendered assumptions onto other marginalized groups.

This approach moves us past the dilemma around gender neutrality. As we saw above, mainstream commitments to "gender neutrality" work with an understanding of gender as the ontological categories of men and women. With this understanding, "neutrality" means simply equal treatment of these two groups. There is no recognition here of the active role of law/policy in constituting these groups. By contrast, a focus on concepts *and* their uses suggests the need to emphasize the role of policies in creating gendered effects in the lives of women and men such that men are placed hierarchically above women. "Neutrality" would then mean addressing these effects, not ignoring them. This could and would involve active intervention on behalf of women. It also means keeping an eye on the uses of gendered concepts in the creation and reinforcement of other hierarchies along racial lines and along other markers of "difference." The following cases illustrate what it means to study gendered concepts *and* their uses.

Affirmative Action: When is Gender Neutrality Not Neutral?

In Western democracies, the focus of this discussion, there has been concern about the relationship between affirmative action and anti-discrimination policies. Because the goal is held to be a "gender"- (and race-)blind polity, affirmative action for designated groups is denigrated for freezing the very categories we should be intent on eliminating. As a result, affirmative action is located as an *exemption* to anti-discrimination legislation, "allowable" for a period of time to assist targeted groups to improve their situation. In Sweden, which has created a separate directive for "positive action," the term generally used in Europe, the goal of a "gender"-blind polity has meant that positive action for women has to be matched by positive action for men (Bacchi 1996: ch. 6).

Because "gender" is taken to inhere in people, equal treatment is deemed to be an appropriate goal. So, for example, Australia's Affirmative Action (Equal Employment Opportunity for Women) Act (1986) stipulated that nothing in the legislation would contravene appointment by merit (Bacchi 1996: 82). Both men and women, we are told, will be judged by the same criteria. These criteria are placed outside gendering processes, whereas in many contexts merit has a gendered character and gendered effects. For example, if it is held to be meritorious to leave one's family for extended periods of time and to spend long hours at work, fewer women than men are likely to get hired or promoted given the current division of domestic duties. Moreover, this conception of merit will make it difficult to shift the current privileging of career over family in employment policy.

The insistence in Sweden that you cannot have positive action for women without having positive action for men demonstrates even more pointedly the problems with a defense of "gender-neutral" equal treatment. Positive action has been used to move men into teaching positions usually held by women on the grounds that it will help reduce gender segregation in the workforce and will alter children's stereotypes about the roles men and women can fill. However, with the shift from heavy industry to service occupations, a large number of men are seeking employment in jobs traditionally dominated by women. By encouraging this to take place, the policy entrenches groups of women in low-paying jobs or out of work altogether (ibid.: 113).

In another Swedish case, a regional development policy offered government subsidies to firms that hired 40 percent of the "underrepresented sex," who were invariably women. Although framed in gender-neutral language, policy-makers had no doubt about the outcome: more women would be hired. Nor was the motivation a gender-neutral one. The concern was to "create the prerequisites for a balanced population in the different parts of the country" (ibid.). The goal then was to enlist women in a civilizing of the frontier in a way similar to that described by Eveline (1995) in a study of the Western Australian Argyle mines where women were targeted for affirmative action because it was assumed that they would improve men's lives.

In the hiring of teachers, a supposedly gender-neutral hiring policy put women out of jobs. In the regional development program, an apparently gender-neutral hiring policy had as its goal firming up traditional gender relations. The cases are very different in some ways. In the first, women lose jobs; in the second, they gain them. The similarity is that in both cases gender neutrality reinforces the subordination of women, in the labor force and in their relationships with men. Gender-neutral policies which treat gender as a characteristic of people instead of recognizing the ways in which policy is a gendering process thus play a role in enshrining the hierarchical positioning of some men over some women.

Thinking about gender as a part of a person locates "difference" within people instead of seeing difference as something produced in the relationships between people (Bacchi 2001). In affirmative action, this has the effect of setting targeted groups in competition with each other. That is, women are seen as a separate category, separate from ethnic minorities or blacks, for example. As a result, in the United States, women are made to compete *against* minority-groups for a 10 percent "set-aside" quota of highway contracts (Bacchi 1990: 170). To challenge a notion of neutrality which demands only equal treatment, and a vision of equity which places marginalized groups in competition with each other, we need to emphasize the activity involved in shaping social relations between diverse groups of women and men. A gender analysis scrutinizes the role of gender in these processes.

Gender-neutrality and Somatophobia (fear of the body)

Above, I noted that feminist political philosophers and feminist legal theorists have identified deeply gendered assumptions in the foundational concepts of Western laws, assumptions which link masculinity with rationality and detachment from others, and femininity with embodiment and emotion. Nicola Lacey (1995: 16) has pointed out that feminists are in danger of misreading a number of political situations if they insist that these assumptions map onto the bodies of men and women in some straightforward way. Recent research by myself and my colleague, Chris Beasley, reinforces this conclusion. We have located a mind/body dichotomy operating within Australian social policy. In an examination of recent legislation around ART ("Artificial" Reproductive Technology) and cosmetic surgery, we find two kinds of citizens being produced: those who are deemed to be in control of their bodies and hence autonomous citizens in the liberal cast, meaning less oversight by government; and those who are deemed to be controlled by their bodies and hence open for forms of regulation and control. This dichotomy is one which many feminist authors have identified as gendered; that is, mind is classically associated with masculinity and body with femininity.

We find, however, that women are located on both sides of the dualism – that women are not always constituted as the opposite to mind-men-masculinity. Around ART, women are constituted as controlled by body and on these grounds their political "autonomy" is compromised. Specifically, in relation to "Artificial" Insemination by Donor, the husband's consent is deemed to be necessary, although it is recognized that this compromises women's "autonomy." The grounding principle which allowed the New South Wales Law Reform Commission to reach this conclusion was clearly articulated: "Promotion and support of the heterosexual and married family is a justifiable policy for the legislature to adopt" (Bacchi and Beasley 2002). By contrast, in the recent New South Wales Select Committee Report on Cosmetic Surgery (NSW 1999), both men and women are constituted as gender-neutral consumers of medical services who in general ought to be left "free" to make decisions about their bodies. Here, the model of mind controlling body operates to justify limited regulation of the cosmetic surgery industry.

In both cases mind is privileged over body. In ART women are deemed to lose control of their assumed right to "autonomous" decision-making because their sexed bodies are involved in the reproduction of heterosexual and married families. In cosmetic surgery, both men and women are generally constituted as rational consumers of bodily modification. These examples show that privileging mind over body, which clearly maps onto the privileging of masculinity over femininity in Western philosophy, may not necessarily always map onto men and women in anticipated ways. Therefore, the task becomes, not simply challenging this mind/body dichotomy at an abstract level, but drawing attention to the ways it figures in other political agendas, in one case to bolster conventional marital arrangements and in another to set up the cosmetic surgery industry as virtually self-regulating.

Attention to the political projects accomplished through the uses or application of gendered assumptions, such as the mind/body dualism, means keeping a sharp eye on the ways in which they foster distinctions between other groups of citizens, between whites and blacks, between the abled and disabled, for example, in ways that privilege some over others (see Hill Collins 1997; Seymour 1998). Shifting the focus from gender as a part of people to gendering as a political process creates the opportunity to examine the impact of gendered assumptions on the creation of hierarchical social relations beyond those between "men" and "women," a project of pressing concern for contemporary feminisms. Hill Collins (1999: 263) calls this a "logic of intersectionality," which redefines gender as "a constellation of ideas and social practices that are historically situated within and that mutually construct multiple systems of oppression."

Gender Mainstreaming or Gender Sidelining?

Mainstreaming has become a buzz-word for a shift in approach to institutional change. In essence, it refers to devolution of responsibility and accountability for addressing gender issues to the sub-units of an organization. The argument is that directives from the top are unlikely to be taken up. Hence, in many cases a move to mainstreaming has meant the removal of separate units dedicated to equal opportunity on the grounds that these were having little impact. The approach has been the focus of development organizations from the 1990s (Baden and Goetz 1997: 4). Mazey (2000: 342) traces its origins to the Nordic countries and to the Netherlands. In 1995 the concept was endorsed at the fourth World Conference on Women in Beijing and the following year the European Commission adopted a formal commitment to gender mainstreaming. The latter defined mainstreaming as "not restricting efforts to promote equality to the implementation of specific measures, but mobilizing all general policies and measures specifically for the purpose of achieving equality" (European Commission 1998: 5–6).

Putting aside for the moment questions of resources and monitoring, it is important to interrogate the presuppositions behind the mainstreaming agenda and where these lead. One way to do this, I suggest, is to examine models for implementation, and in these to interrogate meanings of gender. The questions become: just what are you mainstreaming when you mainstream "gender"? What does it mean to mainstream "gender"? To produce answers to these questions, I take a close look at the European Union's 1998 *Guide To Gender Impact Assessment* (European Commission 1998).

The *Guide* uses gender in two quite different ways. In a section elaborating "basic concepts," it offers separate definitions of "sex" and "gender," marking a distinction between biological and social differences, a distinction popular in early second-wave feminism (European Commission 1998: 5). In this usage, "gender" becomes a cultural cloak which can be removed, revealing "true" men and women. With this baseline, the role of policy in shaping the lives of women and men may well become difficult to discern. This conception of gender as a part of people which needs ideally to be removed results, for example, in an endorsement of a "gender-neutral" approach to positive action, placing men in women's teaching jobs, an approach criticized above (ibid.: 11–12). In addition, the *Guide* suggests that this teaching requires people who are "unskilled or semi-skilled," thereby accepting a conventional and gendered characterization of caring work as unskilled.

Paradoxically, even as the *Guide* insists that "gender" is separate from the biological categories of men and women, so gender is used as a shorthand for "men and women." We can see this in the way in which a gender-based assessment begins with an analysis of sex-disaggregated statistics to see if women and men appear as significantly different in relation to a range of policies. In this usage, the goal becomes preventing policy proposals "from further reinforcing *existing* differences – in participation, distribution of resources, discriminatory norms and values and structural direct or indirect discrimination" (ibid.: 11; emphasis added).

This descriptive use of gender does not address the "relational aspects of gender, of power and ideology, and of how patterns of subordination are reproduced"

(Baden and Goetz 1997: 3). A focus on "existing differences" does not tell us how these differences come to be. In effect, the goal becomes evening out the impact of a range of policies rather than interrogating their premises. For example, in the *Guide*, the legitimacy of the goal of "eliminating labour market rigidities" is taken to be axiomatic (European Commission 1998: 11). As Lacey (1995: 6) explains, when the focus is simply a disparity in the treatment of men and women, "equalisation was almost invariably in one direction – towards a male norm." As I have argued elsewhere (Bacchi 1999: 69), this kind of analysis encourages us to think that women will be liberated when they have work conditions like men, or pay comparable to similar groups of men. It is difficult in this framing to challenge the appropriateness of those work conditions or those male pay rates. Rather, we need to examine the impact of gendered assumptions in creating/reinforcing social hierarchies and in framing lives we may not wish to lead.

Conclusion

As we can see from these examples, there is a great deal at stake in the meaning of gender that we use. If we restrict our analysis to the impact of law/policy on "existing" men and women, we fail to interrogate the role of law and policy in shaping hierarchical relations among diverse groups of men and women. To capture the dynamic role of law/policy, it may be more useful to produce a "*gendering* impact assessment" than a "gender impact assessment." This could involve the examination of statistical differences among men and women around a variety of indicators but this would mark the beginning rather than the end of the exercise. The task is not simply to "even out" these effects on women and men, but to probe the assumptions which result in these effects and the role they play in sustaining hierarchical relations among diverse groups of women and men.

References

Bacchi, C. (1990) *Same Difference: Feminism and Sexual Difference* (Sydney: Allen & Unwin).
Bacchi, C. (1996) *The Politics of Affirmative Action: "Women," Equality and Category Politics* (London: Sage).
Bacchi, C. (1999) *Women, Policy and Politics: The Construction of Policy Problems* (London: Sage).
Bacchi, C. (2001) "Dealing with 'Difference': Beyond 'Multiple subjectivities'," in P. Nursey-Bray and C. Bacchi (eds.), *Left Directions: Is There a Third Way?* (Perth: University of Western Australia Press).
Bacchi, C. and Beasley, C. (2002) "Citizen Bodies: Is Embodied Citizenship a Contradiction in Terms?" *Critical Social Policy* 22/2: 324–52.
Baden, S. and Goetz, A. M. (1997) "Who Needs [Sex] When You Can Have [Gender]? Conflicting Discourses on Gender at Beijing," *Feminist Review* 56 (summer): 3–25.
Baker, M. and Tippin, D. (1999) *Poverty, Social Assistance and the Employability of Mothers: Restructuring Welfare States* (Toronto: University of Toronto Press).

Benhabib, S. (1992) *Situating the Self: Gender, Community and Postmodernism in Contemporary Ethics* (Cambridge: Polity).

Benschop, Y. and Doorewaard, H. (1998) "Covered by Equality: The Gender Subtext of Organizations," *Organization Studies* 19/5: 787–805.

DiQuinzio, P. and Young, I. M. (1997) "Introduction," in P. DiQuinzio and I. M. Young (eds.), *Feminist Ethics and Social Policy* (Bloomington: Indiana University Press).

European Commission (1998) *A Guide to Gender Impact Assessment: Employment & Social Affairs, Equality Between Women and Men* (Luxembourg: Office for Official Publications of the European Communities).

Eveline, J. (1995) "Surviving the Belt Shop Blues: Women Miners and Critical Acts," *Australian Journal of Political Science* 30/1: 91–107.

Ferree, M., Lorber, J., and Hess, B. B. (eds.) (1999) *Revisioning Gender* (London: Sage).

Hill Collins, P. (1997) "Towards an Afrocentric Feminist Epistemology," in S. Kemp and J. Squires (eds.), *Feminisms* (Oxford: Oxford University Press; article first published in 1990).

Hill Collins, P. (1999) "Moving Beyond Gender: Intersectionality and Scientific Knowledge," in M. M. Ferree, J. Lorber, and B. B. Hess (eds.), *Revisioning Gender* (London: Sage).

Lacey, N. (1995) "Feminist Legal Theory Beyond Neutrality," *Current Legal Problems* 48/2: 1–38.

Lloyd, G. (1984) *The Man of Reason* (London: Methuen).

Mazey, S. (2000) "Introduction: Integrating Gender – Intellectual and 'Real World' Mainstreaming," *Journal of European Public Policy* 7/3: 333–45.

Naffine, N. (1990) *Law and the Sexes* (Sydney: Allen & Unwin).

Narayan, U. (1997) "Male-order Brides: Immigrant Women, Domestic Violence, and Immigration Law," in P. DiQuinzio and I. M. Young (eds.), *Feminist Ethics and Social Policy* (Bloomington: Indiana University Press).

NSW (New South Wales) Select Committee (1999) *The Cosmetic Surgery Report.* Report to the NSW Minister for Health, October. Chair, Merrilyn Walton. <http://www.asnsw.health.nsw.gov.au/heal . . . rs/mediareleases/1999.oct/21-10-99/htr> (accessed October 10, 2000).

Olsen, F. (1985) "The Myth of State Intervention in the Family," *University of Michigan Journal of Law Reform* 18/4: 835–64.

Orloff, A. S. (1993) "Gender and the Social Rights of Citizenship: The Comparative Analysis of Gender Relations and Welfare States," *American Sociological Review* 58 (June): 303–28.

Pateman, C. (1983) "Feminist Critiques of the Public/Private Distinction," in Stanley Benn and Gerald Gaus (eds.), *Private and Public in Social Life* (London: Croom Helm).

Sainsbury, D. (ed.) (1994) *Gendering Welfare States* (London: Sage).

Seymour, W. (1998) *Remaking the Body: Rehabilitation and Change* (London: Routledge).

Shaver, S. (1993) *Women and the Australian Social Security System: From Difference Towards Equality*, Social Policy Research Centre, Discussion Paper No. 41 (New South Wales: University of New South Wales).

Smart, C. (1989) *Feminism and the Power of Law* (New York: Routledge).

Weir, L. (1994) "The Regulation of Gender, Reproduction and Sexualities," in M. Valverde (ed.), *Radically Rethinking Regulation: Workshop Report* (Centre of Criminology: University of Toronto).

Wilson, F. (1996) "Research Note: Organizational Theory: Blind and Deaf to Gender?" *Organization Studies* 17/5: 825–42.

Further reading

Beasley, C. and Bacchi, C. (2000) "Citizen Bodies: Embodying Citizens – A Feminist Analysis," *International Feminist Journal of Politics* 2/3: 337–58.

Butler, J. (1993) *Bodies that Matter: On the Discursive Limits of "Sex"* (New York: Routledge).

Gatens, M. (1996) *Imaginary Bodies: Ethics, Power and Corporeality* (New York: Routledge).

O'Connor, J., Orloff, A. S., and Shaver, S. (1999) *States, Markets, Families: Gender Liberalism and Social Policy in Australia, Canada, Great Britain and the United States* (Cambridge: Cambridge University Press).

Randall, V. and Waylen, G. (eds.) (1998) *Gender, Politics and the State* (London: Routledge).

Sainsbury, D. (1999) *Gender and Welfare State Regimes* (Oxford: Oxford University Press).

Thornton, M. (1995) "The Seductive allure of EEO," in Norma Grieve and Ailsa Burns (eds.), *Australian Women: Contemporary Feminist Thought* (Melbourne: Oxford University Press).

CHAPTER THIRTEEN

Domestic Violence

Madelaine Adelman

Public concern with what many now refer to as domestic violence is not new. What is always new is the place of gender and the idealization of gendered social relations in explanations of and responses to domestic violence. In this chapter I will highlight the shifting relationships between gender (and gendered social relations in the form of heterosexuality) and domestic violence by discussing theories about and action aimed at ending domestic violence. I am particularly concerned with how current theorizing and action takes place during a time period and in places where domestic violence discourse is produced through sometimes overlapping processes of institutionalization and globalization. In doing so, I also will point to emerging issues surrounding the relationship between gender and domestic violence, including the convergence of gender and other identities of difference, women's violence, same-gender domestic violence, and the multiplicity of masculinities.

Regulating Domestic Violence and Maintaining Male Dominance

According to historians and feminist scholars (Ferraro 1996; Gordon 1988; Pleck 1987), individuals, communities, organizations, and states have challenged (as well as instituted or perpetuated) in a variety of ways the type and level of violence used within families. Historically, these challenges have been gendered in the sense that community members, religious leaders, social reformers, and state authorities aimed their critiques at husbands who used what was considered to be excessive violence against their wives (and sometimes their children). Over time, domestic violence theorizing and action were based on understandings of violent men either as sinful, deviant, or out-of control, or as hypermasculine. Mainstream solutions to the gendered nature of domestic violence were (and continue to be in some quarters) a vision of idealized gender relations based on domesticated but dominating men and vulnerable but virtuous women living together in nuclear families. Accompanying this vision are racialized and nation-alized distinctions between good and bad families as well as deserving and undeserving victims (Bynum 1992; Merry 2000; Razack 1998).

Over the last 150 years, feminist theorizing about domestic violence at times has paralleled mainstream or conservative solutions to domestic violence, par-ticularly those advocating the criminalization of domestic violence (Ferraro 1996; Pleck 1987). Although some domestic violence reformers also focused on the lack of women's rights and problems inherent to the patriarchal family, nineteenth- and twentieth-century work mostly centered on state regulation of family life, the criminalization of certain physical forms of wife-beating, and the punishment of wife-beaters. Beginning in the 1970s, however, a radical revisioning of gender relations guided feminist action around wife-beating and other, related forms of violence against women (Schechter 1982). Along with demands for equal protection and state intervention, the US battered women's movement called for a transformation of the American family from an institution based on gender hierarchy to one based on gender equality. Accordingly, woman-battering could not be eliminated without structural transformations of gender roles, identities, and relations. Rather than see batterers as deviant men, radical feminists under-stood men's use of violence as a means to reinforce their already existing social dominance. Other feminists identified patriarchal gender relations along with white supremacy and capitalism as major causes of domestic violence.

Gendered Symmetry or Asymmetry?

During the past 30 years, scholars and activists have debated whether domestic violence is truly a gendered phenomenon. Methodologically and theoretically, this debate focuses on measures of gender symmetry or asymmetry of violence used by intimate partners (Kurz 1993). As a result of differences in research design and data analysis as well as political commitments, there are deep fissures between those advocating gender symmetry through a family violence (FV) approach and those who understand domestic violence as another asymmetrical form of violence against women (VAW) (Dobash and Dobash 1992).

Family violence advocates recognize that women are more likely to be assaulted in their own homes and/or murdered by male (ex)-intimates; they have also demonstrated the seriousness and pervasiveness of domestic violence. However, they do not hold gender as central to explaining and solving the problem of domestic violence. Instead, FV researchers define domestic violence as one means among many for negotiating interpersonal conflict. Methodologically, family violence researchers de-link gender and domestic violence by studying it along-side other forms of family violence such as child abuse and neglect, sibling violence, and elder abuse and neglect (see, for example, Barnett et al. 1997). The de-linking of gender and domestic violence also occurs when family violence researchers concentrate on measuring rates of violence and, in doing so, isolate violence from its social and cultural context, failing, for example, to distinguish between gendered offensive and defensive violence (for a detailed critique of the Conflict Tactics Scales instrument used in FV research, see Johnson 1998: 26–8). Some versions of the family violence approach include gender inequality in marriage as one factor among many (e.g. stress, anger, poor communication, perceptions of powerlessness) that may cause domestic violence.

In contrast, researchers in the violence against women tradition maintain that gender is central to understanding the dynamics, regulation, and prevention of domestic violence (Dobash and Dobash 1979; Stanko 1985; Websdale 1998; Yllo and Bograd 1988). VAW researchers understand domestic violence as a complex process by which mostly men attain and maintain power and control over female intimate partners. Feminist domestic violence discourse in the United States (and more recently across the globe) draws on several key concepts, including the power and control wheel. This model, based on battered women's reports, was created by members of the Domestic Abuse Intervention Project (DAIP) in the mid-1980s to describe and explain what represents to many a near universal dynamic of battering. Battering is a patterned process consisting of coercive and controlling behaviors including but not limited to those related to the body (such as isolation, sexual violence, physical violence) and the mind (such as emotional abuse, intimidation, and threats). Other fundamental components of the power and control wheel include male privilege, use of children, and minimizing, blaming, or denying the abuse (Domestic Abuse Intervention Project 2001). Employing the key concept of power and control, VAW researchers study domestic violence in conjunction with other gendered forms of violence such as sexual harassment and rape.

Unlike some academic theorizing, the debate between family violence and violence against women is not limited to the pages of social science and humanities journals. Domestic violence research, often sponsored by state agencies such as the National Institute of Justice, also shapes the possibility of public policy interventions (and their funding), legislation reform, media representations, and the ways ordinary citizens think about and respond to domestic violence.

Institutionalization and Gender Neutralization

The way in which a social problem is framed determines in large part its solution. The transformation of a social condition to a social problem constitutes a process whereby (often competing) frames are used to define, explain, and fix "it." Social movements, not necessarily unified to begin with, struggle to have their frame(s) adopted by stakeholders with requisite status, power, and resources. In case studies of the United States, Canadian, and British battered women's movements, scholars have observed a pattern of institutionalization that involves translation, appropriation, and, for the most part, gender neutralization of woman battering (Dobash and Dobash 1992; Ferraro 1996; Walker 1990). This is seen through the naming of the problem as family or domestic violence and the criminalization and medicalization of domestic violence as a social problem.

Gillian Walker conducted an institutional ethnography of the Canadian battered women's movement's "struggle that increasingly t[ook] place on the terrain of the state" (1990: 72). She was particularly interested in tracing how members of the movement and their allies were involved in "translating the local concerns of the women's movement activists to the national level" (Walker 1990: 56). This translation process resulted in the subsequent appropriation and absorption of wife-battering into two distinct but related and competing discourses on family violence and wife assault. Each discourse triggered a different set of meanings and solutions. The wife assault discourse triggered a criminalization of wife-battering aimed at state-based punishment of individual batterers and protection of individual battered women, while the family violence discourse triggered social services aimed at treating problems within the family unit. Walker concludes:

> What is important in the process studied here is not the specifics of the recommendations to a particular provincial government, which may or may not have been acted on, but the framework for action that has been set up. . . . Feminist concerns about the coercion and abuse of women and children in the context of oppression and inequality are subsumed under theories of a sick society in which individuals can be prosecuted but basically need treatment and cure. (ibid.: 214–15)

Similar patterns may be observed in the United States, where the institutionalization of domestic violence is developing in a time period in which politicians and other stakeholders value "family values" and criminalization over women's safety. The translation and appropriation of woman-battering to family or domestic violence results directly in the gender neutralization of the social problem. This is evident not only in the adoption of gender-neutral terminology, but also in the legal codes that result in the arrest and conviction of battered women for their use of resistant violence (Johnson and Ferraro 2000) and treatment plans that pathologize battered women.

By the turn of the twenty-first century, at least in the United States, the gender-neutral family violence approach had apparently won the day. Indeed, Ferraro refers to the current state of domestic violence discourse as a "genderless code" (1996: 78). However, gender is accentuated in the transformation and globalization of domestic violence from a social condition to a violation of women's human rights.

Globalization and Gender Accentuation

Domestic violence discourse has been gender neutralized or degendered over the last two decades in the United States through the "achievement" of state institutionalization and bureaucratization. In stark contrast, at the global level, gender accentuation is observed in the institutionalization and globalization of gender violence. Specifically, domestic violence has been newly defined as a form of gender violence and, as such, a violation of women's human rights (Bunch and Carillo 1991; O'Toole and Schiffman 1997). This major transformation from social condition to social problem framed as a human rights violation is a result, in large part, of women activists, members of recognized non-governmental organizations, and state representatives across the globe meeting together, sharing stories of inequality, discrimination, and violence, and, eventually, creating regional and global networks organized against gender violence. This process was supported, in part, by United Nations World Conferences on Women, held first in Mexico City in 1975 and subsequently in Copenhagen (1980), Nairobi (1985), and Beijing (1995).

It was during the 1993 Vienna Conference on Human Rights that the United Nations formally embraced the notion that women's rights were human rights; at the same conference, violence against women was affirmed as a violation of women's human rights. During the last decade, gender violence activists have organized and demanded the promulgation of UN recommendations and declarations regarding gender violence as well as the development of global and state-level bureaucracies to implement and regulate this new "women's rights as human rights" regime. Non-governmental organizations such as Amnesty International and Human Rights Watch have quickly endorsed the idea that the specific experiences of women should be taken into account by those monitoring human rights abuses.

One of the more innovative components of the women's rights as human rights concept is the revitalization of state responsibility and accountability for human rights violations. Women's human rights activists have interpreted international law to center on state responsibility for the enactment and application of gender equality in law and society. In addition to debates over the meaning of gender equality and whether a particular state-level law provides it, the gendering of human rights has introduced new ideas about state accountability for human rights violations. Whereas human rights violations were previously construed as those acts perpetrated by the governing on the governed (i.e. relations between individuals and the state), the gendering of human rights principles demands that member states regulate relations between individuals within the state. This means, for example, that states are instructed to consider and regulate relations between family members. In other words, women's rights as human rights transforms domestic violence from an individual, privatized trouble to a violation of women's fundamental human rights to equality, security, liberty, integrity, and dignity.

The United Nations General Assembly approved the Declaration on the Elimination of Violence Against Women in December 1993. This declaration calls on states to condemn violence against women, in all its forms; to refrain from engaging in violence against women; and to "punish acts of violence against women, whether those acts are perpetrated by the state or by private persons."[1]

State governments are now specifically charged with preventing the occurrence of and protecting women from gender violence as well as building "new ways for women to win justice and redress when they are targeted for violence" (Human Rights Watch 2000).

Converging Identities and Domestic Violence

The globalization of domestic violence as a violation of women's human rights sets women apart as vulnerable to gender-specific abuses. This women-as-class approach provides much-needed language and tools to organize against such harms. It also allows for the global recognition of a wide variety of locally defined harms under the rubric of gender violence. Yet, the globalization of domestic violence, with its strong reliance on gender, and the always, already potential for gendered victimization, may produce unintended consequences.

The globalization of domestic violence and the resultant association and identification of women with victimization may delimit the agency of women (Heberle 1996) and/or may funnel funds toward anti-violence initiatives without providing support for eradicating the conditions that make women vulnerable to violence and men entitled to maintain authority through violence in the first place. It may also distract attention away from any cultural variations in the use of violence, particularly women's (Burbank 1996). In addition, the primacy of gender may freeze idealized commonalities among (battered) women, positing norms that are actually based on a dominant group's understanding of gender, gender relations, kinship, and domestic violence. It also may obscure differences among women (e.g. race, class, nation, sexuality) and the contexts in which they live (e.g. rurality, militarism, migration, colonialism) that combine to shape experiences of and responses to domestic violence (Abraham 2000; Adelman 2000; Lancaster 1992; McGillivray and Comasky 1999; Websdale 1998). Finally, the presumption of the centrality of gender often insures that "state protection of battered women is enabled only through the production of racialized difference along with the erasure of its very production" (Adelman 2004). Sherene Razack, for example, demonstrates how, when a woman refugee seeks asylum in the West from gender-based persecution such as domestic violence, she must "cast herself as a cultural Other, that is, as someone fleeing from a more primitive culture" (1998: 92). Future studies of globalization may contribute to complex understandings of the place of gender and other converging identities within domestic violence discourse.

Gender, Sexuality, and Domestic Violence

The overwhelming majority of domestic violence discourse unreflectively focuses on violence among heterosexual couples, whether dating, cohabitating, or married.

This is interesting given that lesbians made up a substantial portion of the battered women's movement, establishing shelters for battered women, pushing for legislative changes, and running state-wide coalitions against domestic violence. Even more puzzling is that, in spite of the fact that numbers of formerly battered women embrace asexuality and/or same-sex desire as a political act, personal preference, or as a means of avoiding the gender associated with violence and dominance, separatism – or the rejection of heterosexuality per se – was never a fundamental part of feminist theorizing about domestic violence. The closest feminist research on domestic violence gets to interrogating heterosexuality or contributing to critical heterosexuality studies is when it situates the study of woman-battering within marriage as a way of pointing out the patriarchal nature of the institution, the widespread social and cultural support for the maintenance of such a family form, and the difficulties faced by wives when they leave their husbands (Dobash and Dobash 1979; Websdale 1998).

Current writing on domestic violence, be it popular or academic, continues to assume that battering occurs within opposite-gender intimate dyads. In spite of this, few domestic violence researchers consider the intersection of (hetero)sexual and gender identities. Is compulsory heterosexuality rather than gender respons-ible for the pervasiveness of domestic violence? Can gender be isolated from theories and experiences of heterosexuality? Is there something specific about heterosexual intimacy that creates conditions for domestic violence? To what extent do heterosexuality and heterosexism form the context in which gendered power is maintained through domestic violence? Drawing on his research with men who batter, Jeff Hearn argues that men's heterosexuality informs and is informed by men's violence against known women; in other words, "men's violence to women is structured *through men's* heterosexuality and vice versa" (1998: 218; emphasis in original). While I find this position theoretically com-pelling, recent research on same-sex or same-gender domestic violence begins to challenge presumptions regarding any exclusive connection between gender, heterosexuality, and domestic violence.

Activists and researchers alike draw significant parallels between opposite-gender and same-gender domestic violence, while adjusting the definition of domestic violence to match the absence of putative gender differences within same-gender domestic violence (Leventhal and Lundy 1999; Renzetti 1992). For example, to explain the dynamic of same-gender domestic violence, the Wingspan Domestic Violence Project uses an adapted version of the DAIP power and control wheel in which "male privilege" has been replaced with "entitlement." Entitlement refers to a batterer "treating partner as inferior; using differences against partner . . . ; demanding that your needs always come first; and interfering with partner's job, personal needs, family obligations, and sleep" (Wingspan Domestic Violence Project 2000: 16). Does this adjustment or gender neutralization, intended to reflect the lived realities of lesbians and gay men, imply that gender may not be central to the meaning and manifestation of domestic violence? If this is true, it begins to collapse the foundation of feminist theorizing on and actions against domestic violence. Instead, perhaps the degendering of same-gender domestic violence suggests that interest in and access to power and control often associated with masculinity and men are not limited to those considered to be biological males or heterosexual in the societies in which they live. In this scenario, gender remains central to explanations and response to domestic violence in that the desire for power and control and the meaning and performance of gender is de-linked from biological sex. What remains unexamined is the cultural context in which the desire for and access to masculine power and control is structured and enforced to the exclusion of women (heterosexual and lesbian) and some men.

Multiple Masculinities

Domestic violence discourse focuses primarily on battered women. Why do women stay? What happens when they leave? What services and resources do they need in order to live in safety and free from violence? The narrow exceptions to this pattern are the initiatives aimed at men who batter, often referred to as "batterer intervention programs," and the studies and commentaries thereof. Program frameworks and curricula vary nationally and internationally. Some are interested in decreasing men's use of violence without losing their authority in the home (often found in Christian-based interventions); others focus on men learning to limit their use of violence by managing their anger. In these, men are taught to anticipate and interrupt their violence by engaging in a number of individual reflective exercises, although depending upon the program and instructor(s), little may be said about the root reasons that cause men to become angry. There are also programs that attempt to educate men on the costs of a violence-based masculinity (e.g. partner may leave) and offer an alternative form of peaceful masculinity based on egalitarian gender relations.

Women's Studies, Feminist Studies, and now Gender Studies scholars each have contributed to the idea that men possess or perform gendered identities. While early domestic violence research relied on a unified, universal, and homogenous notion of patriarchy and male dominance, those who study the construction of masculinity have begun to address the production of multiple masculinities, including its dominant and/or hegemonic forms. Scholars demonstrate how, as a result of inequalities and differences based on class, race, sexuality, and gender, some individuals and groups of men neither desire nor are able to embody hegemonic masculinity. This interest in differentiation among men is echoed in the work of psychologists who produce personality profiles of distinct types of men who batter. The work most allied with Gender Studies, however, is that which would explore the multiple meanings of masculinity and violence produced through a convergence of race, class, and sexuality.

Readers of this volume may have assumed a deep and perhaps obvious connection between gender and domestic violence. What I have tried to demonstrate above is the constantly shifting place that gender and gendered social relations occupies in domestic violence discourse. When observed vertically, over time, through the institutionalization of domestic violence in the United States, gender shifts from a central to a marginal place in domestic violence discourse, resulting in gender neutralization. When considered from a horizontal perspective, via the globalization of domestic violence as a form of gender violence and as a violation of women's human rights, gender holds a central place, resulting in gender accentuation. Future theorizing about same-gender domestic violence, differences among women, as well as masculinities may contribute to the continuation of tensions surrounding the place of gender as well as inter- and intra-gender social relations in domestic violence discourse.

Note

1 United Nations General Assembly Resolution 48/104 of December 20, 1993, Declaration on the Elimination of Violence against Women, http://www.unhchr.ch/huridocda/hur . . . mbol)/ A.RES.48.104.En?Opendocument> (last accessed October 5, 2000).

References

Abraham, M. (2000) *Speaking the Unspeakable: Marital Violence Among South Asian Immigrants in the United States* (New Brunswick, NJ: Rutgers University Press).

Adelman, M. (2000) "No Way Out: Divorce-related Domestic Violence in Israel," *Violence Against Women* 6/11: 1223–54.

Adelman, M. (2004) "Domestic Violence and Difference," *American Ethnologist* 31/1: 131–41.

Barnett, O., Miller-Perrin, C., and Perrin, R. (1997) *Family Violence Across the Lifespan; An Introduction* (Thousand Oaks, CA: Sage).

Bunch, C. and Carillo, R. (1991) *Gender Violence: A Development and Human Rights Issue* (Rutgers, NJ: Center for Women's Global Leadership).

Burbank, V. (1996) *Fighting Women: Anger and Aggression in Aboriginal Australia* (Berkeley: University of California Press).

Bynum, V. (1992) *Unruly Women: The Politics of Social and Sexual Control in the Old South* (Chapel Hill: University of North Carolina Press).

Dobash, R. E. and Dobash, R. (1979) *Violence Against Wives* (New York: Free Press).

Dobash, R. E. and Dobash, R. (1992) *Women, Violence and Social Change* (New York: Routledge).

Domestic Abuse Intervention Project (2001) "Power and Control and Equality Wheel" <http://www.duluth-model.org/daippce.htm> (last accessed May 16, 2001).

Ferraro, K. (1996) "The Dance of Dependency: A Genealogy of Domestic Violence Discourse," *Hypatia* 11/4: 77–91.

Gordon, L. (1988) *Heroes of Their Own Lives: The Politics and History of Family Violence* (New York: Penguin).

Hearn, J. (1998) *The Violences of Men* (London: Sage).

Heberle, R. (1996) "Deconstructive Strategies and the Movement Against Sexual Violence," *Hypatia* 11/4: 63–76.

Human Rights Watch (2000) "What Will It Take? Stopping Violence Against Women: A Challenge to Governments" <http://www.hrw.org/backgrounder/wrd/fiveplus.htm> (last accessed May 16, 2001).

Johnson, H. (1998) "Rethinking Survey Research," in R. Emerson Dobash and Russell Dobash (eds.), *Rethinking Violence Against Women* (Thousand Oaks, CA: Sage).

Johnson, M. and Ferraro, K. (2000) "Research on Domestic Violence in the 1990s: Making Distinctions," *Journal of Marriage and the Family* 62: 948–63.

Kurz, D. (1993) "Physical Assaults by Husbands: A Major Social Problem," in Richard Gelles and Donileen Loseke (eds.), *Current Controversies on Family Violence* (Newbury Park, CA: Sage).

Lancaster, R. (1992) *Life is Hard: Machismo, Danger, and the Intimacy of Power in Nicaragua* (Berkeley: University of California Press).

Leventhal, B. and Lundy, S. E. (eds.) (1999) *Same-sex Domestic Violence* (Thousand Oaks, CA: Sage).

McGillivray, A. and Comaskey, B. (1999) *Black Eyes All of the Time* (Toronto: University of Toronto Press).

Merry, S. (2000) *Colonizing Hawai'i: The Cultural Power of Law* (Princeton: Princeton University Press).

O'Toole, L. L. and Schiffman, J. (eds.) (1997) *Gender Violence: Interdisciplinary Perspectives* (New York: New York University Press).

Pleck, E. (1987) *Domestic Tyranny: The Making of American Social Policy against Family Violence from Colonial Times to the Present* (Oxford: Oxford University Press).

Razack, S. (1998) *Looking White People in the Eye: Gender, Race, and Culture in Courtrooms and Classrooms* (Toronto: University of Toronto Press).

Renzetti, C. (1992) *Violent Betrayal: Partner Abuse in Lesbian Relationships* (Newbury Park, CA: Sage).

Schechter, S. (1982) *Women and Male Violence: The Visions and Struggles of the Battered Women's Movement* (Boston: South End Press).

Stanko, E. (1985) *Intimate Intrusions: Women's Experiences of Male Violence* (London: Routledge and Kegan Paul).

Walker, G. (1990) *Family Violence and the Women's Movement: The Conceptual Politics of Struggle* (Toronto: University of Toronto Press).

Websdale, N. (1998) *Rural Woman Battering* (Thousand Oaks, CA: Sage).

Wingspan Domestic Violence Project (2000) *Abuse and Violence in Same-gender Relationships: A Resource for the Lesbian, Gay, Bisexual, and Transgender Communities* (Tucson: Wingspan Domestic Violence Project).

Yllo, K. and Bograd, M. (eds.) (1988) *Feminist Perspectives on Wife Abuse* (Newbury Park, CA: Sage).

CHAPTER FOURTEEN

Genocide and Ethnic Cleansing

Jennifer Hyndman

The politics and processes of genocide and ethnic cleansing are highly gendered. Men and women are targeted differently during systematic campaigns to eliminate a particular cultural or ethnic group, and yet discernible patterns of violence can be traced. This chapter outlines definitions of genocide and ethnic cleansing, sketching the importance of gender to each. A brief discussion of nationalism, militarization, and economic stakes follows in order to provide an analytical framework in which to think about the connections among all three terms. Contemporary examples of these phenomena are discussed in this context. Finally, responses to addressing genocide and ethnic cleansing are surveyed from a feminist perspective.

A Word on Gender

This short chapter takes gender broadly to mean the masculine and feminine identities associated with men and women that vary across space, time, cultural, and socio-political contexts. Gender is also a relational concept that allows one to compare the meanings, expectations, and material practices of men with those of women. The ways in which men and women are militarized (socialized to participate in a war), for example, are quite distinct. Likewise, the positions of men and women within a nationalist discourse tend to be distinct, especially along gender lines. Women are often constructed as reproducers of the nation, while men are its warriors and protectors. Perhaps most importantly, gender relations and identities are dynamic. They are not fixed and are subject to change. The work and responsibilities of women from Srebrenica (Bosnia-Herzegovina), for example, have changed dramatically since the disappearance and murder of most men in that town in July 1995. This chapter aims to demonstrate the ways in which gender relations shape particular practices of genocide and ethnic cleansing.

Genocide

The term "genocide" was coined by Polish jurist Raphael Lemkin during the execution of Hitler's final solution. "Lemkin was deeply aware of the atrocities being committed across Europe, which were being carried out largely on racial grounds and which were affecting one ethnic group in particular, the European Jewish community" (Stoett 2000: 34). The word is derived from the Greek word for race or people, *genos*, and the Latin *caedere* (cide), meaning to kill. The intersection of gender and race thus becomes an important analytical consideration.

While rooted in the experience of the Holocaust, the concept has widened with the passage of time and the crimes committed to destroy specific national, ethnic, racial, or religious groups. Many groups, from Ukrainians to Roma peoples to East Timorese to Biafrans, have been subject to such systematic violence. Some commentators suggest that genocide appropriately describes the colonial treatment of indigenous peoples of North America, Australia, New Zealand, Southern Africa, Northern Europe, and Guatemala. The struggles of these peoples are ongoing and in no way should genocide be considered a plight of the past.

A legal definition of genocide can be found in article 2 of the 1948 Convention on the Prevention and Punishment of the Crime of Genocide, which defines the term as:

> any of the following acts committed with the intent to destroy, in whole or in part, a national, ethnical, racial or religious group: killing members of the groups; causing serious harm, bodily or mental, to members of the group; deliberately inflicting conditions calculated to bring about the group's destruction; imposing measures to prevent births within the group; forcibly transferring children of the group to another group.

The Convention makes it possible to charge individuals and non-state actors with the "crime of genocide," but the complicity or active participation of the state is normally part of genocide.

There are all kinds of debates around what constitutes genocide. For example, the murderous Khmer Rouge campaign in Cambodia between 1975 and 1979 involved the killing of its own people. Thus some commentators have suggested that Pol Pot could not be charged with genocide because no specific group was racially "othered." Similarly, some analysts contend that Idi Amin's rampage against Ugandans of South Asian ancestry in the 1970s was not genocide because the group constituted political enemies, not racial ones. The line is fine in drawing such distinctions, and the strong emotive power of invoking the term will ensure that such debates continue.

The recent recognition of rape and sexual assault as weapons of war and acts of genocide in international law points to the gender dimensions of genocide. These will be discussed in the final section.

Ethnic Cleansing

Ethnic cleansing refers to the elimination of an unwanted ethnic or cultural group from a society, achieved through genocide, forced migration, rape, torture, and/or forced assimilation. Generally, ethnic cleansing occurs in a delineated territory from which unwanted others are purged. This may involve forced removal of a people from specific territory, the destruction of the group through targeted killing, rape, and pillaging of homes. In the process, those affected are dispossessed of home, land, and livelihood, in addition to loss of life.

Such systematic policies and processes of elimination occur quite differently for women than for men. For example, rape and sexual assault were major measures by which Serbian forces attempted to "cleanse" Bosnian Muslim women and Catholic Croat women from areas of Bosnia-Herzegovina. Several *patterns* of rape have been documented in Bosnia, and these required considerable logistical coordination, pointing to a policy of ethnic cleansing, rather than an incident. One of the five patterns outlined by Salzman (1998) identified sexual violence as an occurrence in conjunction with looting and intimidation before the fighting broke out in a given region. The second pattern is correlated with the fighting itself, during attacks on villages. In the third pattern, detention facilities and "collection centers" were the sites of rape. The fourth pattern of sexual violence took place in rape camps that were established in buildings such as hotels, schools, hospitals, factories, auditoriums, and barns. Frequently, women in these centers were told that their captors wanted to impregnate them, thus demonstrating that rape and forced impregnation constitute a form of ethnic cleansing. Finally, the last pattern of sexual violence identified occurred in camps established as centers of prostitution to service soldiers returning from the front line. In contrast to the fourth pattern, where punishment was the aim, the goal in this case was to provide sex for men returning from fighting. These women were mostly killed.

Men who were subject to "cleansing" could be found in other camps. Prison camps were established in Bosnia-Herzegovina for all captured enemy men of fighting age. While women have often fought in wars, both as soldiers (US women in the Persian Gulf in 1990) and as guerillas (Nicaraguan women as part of the Sandinista movement in the 1970s), in this war they were not considered the principal combatants or potential fighters. The men who found themselves in these camps were starved and malnourished during their imprisonment (see *Welcome to Sarajevo*, a film shot in conjunction with the BBC, using original footage from the 1992–5 war in Bosnia-Herzegovina).

These examples illustrate the multiple ways in which ethnic cleansing was enacted and the multiple venues employed to conduct these patterned processes in highly gendered ways. It is critical to remember that many marriages – and thus families – comprised people from different ethnic/racial groups. Before the 1990s, when nationalisms were fueled by particular political leaders, ethnic/

national identity was not an issue. Most people identified as "Yugoslavian" rather than "Serbian," "Croatian," or "Bosnian Muslim."

In Kosovo, a province of the Republic of Serbia and part of the Federal Republic of Yugoslavia, ethnic cleansing was perpetrated through the widespread burning of homes, summary executions, and the forced migration of ethnic Albanian Kosovars to neighboring states during the spring of 1999. In a controversial effort to stop ethnic cleansing, NATO forces began air attacks, ostensibly on military installations and strategic infrastructure. Civilians were also killed. The rationale of using state-sanctioned violence (by NATO countries) to stop state-sponsored violence by the government of Slobodan Milosevic has been hotly debated, especially by feminists (Cockburn 2000).

Drawing on more historical examples, we find that Joseph Stalin's regime perfected the crime of ethnic cleansing between 1937 and 1949, when more than two million people of 13 nationalities were deported from their homelands to remote areas of the USSR (Stoett 2000). The first wholesale deportation involved the Soviet Koreans, relocated to Kazakhstan and Uzbekistan to prevent them from assisting Japanese spies and saboteurs. The effectiveness of this operation led the state to adopt, as standard procedure, the deportation of whole ethnic groups suspected of disloyalty. In 1941, the policy affected Soviet Finns and Germans; in 1943, the Karachays and Kalmyks were forcibly relocated; in 1944, the massive deportation affected the Chechens, Ingush, Balkars, Crimean Tatars, Crimean Greeks, Meskhetian Turks, Kurds, and Khemshils; and, finally, the Black Sea Greeks were moved in 1949 and 1950. The nationalist battles for sovereignty and autonomy from Russia in the 1990s have clear antecedents in these earlier projects of ethnic cleansing.

One final example from Southeast Asia illustrates ethnic cleansing in a contemporary context. The military government of Burma has used forced relocation based on ethnic identity since the late 1980s. The country is composed of at least seven major nations/ethnic groups, but those who are not ethnic Burmans (Burmans are perceived by the government to be allies) and who live in key cities of political importance have been forcibly relocated to more rural destinations, generating a steady stream of internally displaced persons and refugees. This example illustrates one set of outcomes that have direct implications for other states, thus rendering ethnic cleansing a political issue for governments across the world.

The Politics of Nationalism and Militarization

It is not possible to address the meanings and importance of ethnic nationalism and militarization in a comprehensive manner in this brief chapter. But neither can one understand the motivation and rationale given for these systematic efforts to wipe out entire groups of people without some reference to them. Gender politics and power relations are at the center of both nationalist and ethnic-nationalist projects. A distinction can be made between "ethnic nationalism" and "civic nationalism" whereby the former refers to an appeal based on blood loyalty linked to authoritarianism, and the latter speaks to a multiethnic society bound together by shared democratic traditions and the rule of law rather than divisive ascribed loyalties (Ignatieff, cited in Stasiulus 1999).

A great deal of feminist research on nationalism focuses on the role of gender in the construction and reproduction of ethnic-national ideologies (Giles and Hyndman 2004). Nationalism may seek to homogenize differences under the unifying discourse of the nation; it nonetheless generates contradictory positions for women, as symbols of cultural purity, agents of resistance against western domination, and subjects of the nationalist patriarchal family. Nationalism is not a fixed notion, nor can it claim a unitary subject that bears nationality separate from gender, race, caste, class, and religious identity. It thus intersects with gender relations and racism in particular permutations and combinations. Nationalist projects demand attention because of the ways in which they construct and claim women as part of the nation, and because of the ways in which belonging is used as a basis for eliminating women and men of other nations.

Men too are cast in specific roles in relation to the nation. It is men who are generally expected to defend the integrity of the nation and its territory, which generally includes the bodies of "their" women. Being male connotes certain social roles in a context where nationalism and militarization intersect: men tend to be seen as the principal combatants and can therefore be the first targets in campaigns to eliminate or force out a particular ethnic/national group. When the patriarchal, exclusionary nation is militarized, most often by men though not solely, processes of ethnic cleansing and genocide can proceed. The process of militarization affects women and men quite differently across gender lines, and across geographical and historical context. Two brief examples from different parts of the world illustrate this point.

The case of Rwanda

Between April and July of 1994, a set of unimaginable events transpired in the Great Lakes region of Africa, specifically in Rwanda, with the genocide of Tutsis and moderate Hutus. An estimated 500,000 to 1 million people were killed, often with machetes and other blunt instruments. The short period and systematic nature of the killing point to a well-coordinated, state-sponsored strategy to eliminate Tutsis and those Hutus married to Tutsis or sympathetic to a multiethnic society. The international community, including the UN and its major donor countries, did virtually nothing until the Tutsi rebels living in Uganda at the time took control of Rwanda and forced much of the civilian population and the perpetrators of the genocide into refugee camps in (then) Zaire and nearby Tanzania.

It is estimated that 250,000 women were raped during the Rwanda genocide. "Tutsi women were targeted for sexual objectification and dehumanization by the genocidal propaganda disseminated by the Hutu regime; Hutu men were exhorted to rape and torture Tutsi women" (Drumbl 2000: 23). What is perhaps more disturbing is that this behavior was not seen as deviant; rather, the murder, torture, rape, and mutilation of members of one ethnic group by those of another is normalized during a genocide.

The case of Bosnia-Herzegovina

Between 1992 and 1995, brutal and systematic campaigns of ethnic cleansing in Bosnia displaced more than half the population. As noted earlier, rape camps and prison camps where subjects were literally starved, often to death, were tools of this campaign to dispossess enemy nations. Subsequently, hundreds of thousands of people became dependent on humanitarian aid, especially in the designated safe havens where violence precipitated terror and generated rapid urbanization to the "safe" cities and towns, leaving large parts of the countryside abandoned.

This international humanitarian intervention was a highly political project. At first, the UN Security Council designated the six safe cities and posted peacekeepers at each location. When several of the safe havens came under fire, insufficient numbers of UN troops were in place to defend the people who were seeking refuge there. This raised a horrible dilemma for UN humanitarian organizations: should they authorize a humanitarian corridor to get civilians at risk out of the region, and by doing so facilitate the very ethnic cleansing that the perpetrators of the attack aimed to achieve? Or should they let people stay and pay the consequences? The latter scenario was not really an option, though if peacekeeping forces had been stronger and had had more comprehensive rules of engagement, they may have been able to fend off attackers. This example illustrates the conundrums faced by UN bodies when they attempt to protect those made vulnerable by campaigns of ethnic cleansing. They can sometimes become inadvertently complicit in the campaign.

With the signing of the Dayton Accord in 1995, Bosnia-Herzegovina was divided into two ethnically/nationally-based republics: the Muslim-Croat Federation that comprises 51 percent of the land area, and the Republic of Srbska which is more homogeneously Serbian. Some feminist commentators contend that the Dayton Accord signaled the end of multi-ethnic society in Bosnia-Herzegovina, despite guarantees that all displaced people could return to their original homes from before the war. The Accord is viewed by many as a compromise that does not do enough to mitigate and overcome the ethnic nationalism that started the war. Many people, especially women, remain displaced from their homes in the "other" parts of the country (i.e. Bosnian Muslim women from Srebrenica in Sarajevo).

Responses to Genocide and Ethnic Cleansing

International conventions and laws are the major instruments to address and ideally prevent acts of genocide and ethnic cleansing. As noted earlier, the 1948 Convention on the Prevention and Punishment of the Crime of Genocide was born of the atrocities committed during World War II, particularly the Holocaust. In a more recent context, international criminal tribunals have been established to hear cases from the wars in Yugoslavia and Rwanda, as well as in other countries (i.e. Cambodia). In 1998, the Treaty of Rome established, in principle, the International Criminal Court. The court was ratified by the requisite number of countries and signed, even by the US in the last days of the Clinton Administration, late in 2000. The administration of George W. Bush has since "unsigned" the treaty, removing US support for the Court because, says the government, it may implicate US soldiers and/or political leaders who perform and/or authorize acts interpreted as genocide and other war crimes. Nonetheless, arrangements for the Court have gone ahead, promising an international legal mechanism to try war crimes.

The intransigence of the US in ratifying UN conventions is also well known and worth noting, given its purported role as champion of democracy and human rights. International treaties undergo extensive examination and scrutiny before they are ratified in the United States; it can take several years for a treaty to be ratified after it is signed. For example, it took the US more than 30 years to ratify the Convention on the Prevention and Punishment of the Crime of Genocide, and the Convention on the Elimination of All Forms of Discrimination Against Women, which was signed by the US 17 years ago, has still not been ratified. Adopted by the General Assembly of the UN in 1989, the Convention on the Rights of the Child has also not been ratified by the US, a state that has increasingly acted beyond the purview of international norms and treaties.

On the UN front, the Security Council issued its first resolution on Women, Peace, and Security on October 31, 2000, calling on member states and all parties to conflict to pay attention to the gender dimensions of rights, protection, and participation in conflict reduction. The appointment of women to decision-making positions and as special representatives was also promulgated in the document, the first ever by the Security Council to link women, peace, and (in)security.

From a feminist perspective, new developments in the realm of international tribunals prove to be Janus-faced: on the one hand, private/public divides are being challenged through the international legal system, specifically by the two War Crimes Tribunals for the Former Yugoslavia and Rwanda.[1] Gendered crimes are no longer private acts to be endured in silence. On the other hand, the idea of a tribunal that hands out sentences in an international court – seen as an "enemy court" by the US – is punitive and does not necessarily constitute a feminist strategy for attaining justice. In June 1996, for the first time in history, the tribunal for Yugoslavia prosecuted rape as a weapon of war and a "crime against humanity." It issued indictments for the arrest of eight men, charged with sexual assault for the purposes of torture and enslavement. Ample evidence that men used rape to terrorize, humiliate, and contaminate the women of opposing ethnic groups in Bosnia–Herzegovina led to the indictments. "To rape women with impunity and to mark their bodies with the symbols of the other side is to assert domination and to symbolically assault ethnic identity in its most protected space" (Coomaraswamy 1999: 10).

Men were also raped and sexually mutilated; in some cases they were forced to rape or sexually mutilate other men. People's bodies are construed as territory and become the sites of public violence on which symbolic constructions of the nation and its boundaries take place.

The ruling that rape is a weapon of war, however, is significant because it publicizes sexual violence as a weapon of war. Sexual violence and rape are as old as war itself, but until now these issues have been rendered invisible or incidental because they were dismissed as private acts, the "aberrational practices of errant soldiers" (Coomaraswamy 1999: 3). The tacit theater of war was the battlefield, the public space around which the rules of war – the Geneva Conventions – have been written. But the public/private divide between the battlefield and civilian bodies has dissolved. People's bodies, homes, communities, and livelihoods have become the battlefields of contemporary conflict. By identifying rape as a strategic weapon of war, its violence is recorded as a public act, and punishment for such crimes is legitimized. Rape is not simply an addition to international humanitarian and human rights law. It represents a new category of crime that reorganizes the scale and scope of punishment, and recasts what counts (that which is public) and what does not (that which is considered private). The safety of a person and her body, as the finest scale of geopolitical space, is politicized.

In one sense, these changes may be celebrated as feminist victories, but, as Dianne Martin has noted, these legislative outcomes of feminist law reform may, in fact, run counter to the goals motivating reform. The increased criminalization of gendered crimes and hate crimes, including ethnic cleansing and genocide, reinforces the retributive model of criminal justice. As Martin says:

> Feminist activism was engaged originally with criminal law reform because so much about the criminal justice system was at worst abusive and at best inattentive to human needs, particularly the needs of women and victims of violence. Little about the criminal justice system merited feminist support and much required amendment, particularly the essentially nineteenth-century patriarchal values that (still) dominate criminal law doctrine. However, the reform agenda moved beyond challenging the criminal justice system as a whole, and acquired some new allies, with their own agendas. One of the most troubling, and most ubiquitous of the new initiatives is the attempt to use the criminal trial, and the punishment that it justifies, as an occasion of healing and closure for crime victims. (Cited in Drumbl 2000: 22)

The international criminal tribunals demonstrate a similar pattern of punitive and retributive criminal justice (ibid.).

One must consider the context of such crimes and the goals of any response: is the aim reconciliation among segments of a shattered society? Is it punishment, so that by prosecuting perpetrators a local sense of justice is achieved, and civil society can be reconstructed? Is the aim political, i.e. to bring major war criminals to "justice" for the satisfaction of certain allied governments on a more international scale? Alternative models of seeking justice for the survivors of ethnic cleansing campaigns and genocide demand more attention. The viability of truth commissions, held in the countries where crimes are alleged to have taken place, offer an attractive if not always a viable possibility.

Linking gender, genocide, and ethnic cleansing is a fraught and challenging project. Militarization and ethnic nationalism shape racial, national, and gender identities in specific ways. What is perhaps clearest from this short chapter is that the person, and not the state, is the most crucial scale of geopolitical space and security. The bodies of both men and women are the sites at which militarized violence is perpetrated during systematic campaigns to eliminate or force out particular ethnic, national, and/or religious groups.

Note

1   One criticism of this talk revolved around the very "humanist" notions of justice and politics described. While I understand the limitations of what I have called "UN humanism," I am not simply endorsing the ways in which justice is meted out by the international war crimes tribunals. As Dianne Martin and Mark Drumbl have written, "the increased criminalization of gendered crimes and hate crimes represents a reinforcement of retributive criminal justice model," one that may well be counter-intuitive to feminist politics (in Drumbl 2000: 22). One must consider the context of such crimes and the goals of any response: is the aim reconciliation among segments of a shattered society? Is it punishment, so that by prosecuting perpetrators a local sense of justice is achieved, and civil society can resume? Is the aim political, i.e. to bring major war criminals to "justice" for the satisfaction of certain allied governments on a more international scale? I thank Adrienne Burk for her insights on these geographies of justice and collective memory. Thanks also to Dan Hiebert for making me think much more about these issues.

References

Cockburn, C. (2000) "Women in Black: Being Able to Say Neither/Nor," *Canadian Woman Studies* 19/4 (special issue "Women in Conflict Zones"): 5–10.

Coomaraswamy, R. (1999) "A Question of Honour: Women, Ethnicity, and Armed Conflict," Third Minority Rights Lecture, May 25, Hotel Intercontinental, Geneva, Switzerland.

Drumbl, M. (2000) "Punishment Goes Global: International Criminal Law, Conflict Zones, and Gender (In)equality," *Canadian Woman Studies* 19/4 (special issue "Women in Conflict Zones"): 22–7.

Giles, W. and Hyndman, J. (2004) *Sites of Violence: Gender Politics in Conflict Zones* (Berkeley: University of California Press).

Salzman, T. (1998) "Rape Camps as a Means of Ethnic Cleansing: Religious, Cultural, and Ethical Responses to Rape Victims in the Former Yugoslavia," *Human Rights Quarterly* 20/2: 348–78.

Stasiulis, D. (1999) "Relational Positionalities of Nationalisms, Racisms, and Feminisms," in C. Kaplan, N. Alarcón, and M. Moallem (eds.), *Between Woman and Nation: Nationalisms, Transnational Feminisms, and the State* (Durham, NC and London: Duke University Press).

Stoett, P. (2000) *Human and Global Security: An Exploration of Terms* (Toronto: University of Toronto Press).

Further reading

Brownmiller, S. (1994) "Making Female Bodies the Battlefield," in A. Stiglmayar (ed.), *Mass Rape: The War Against Women in Bosnia-Herzegovina* (Lincoln and London: University of Nebraska Press).

Cockburn, C. (1998) *The Space Between Us* (London: Zed Books).

Enloe, C. (1993) *The Morning After: Sexual Politics at the End of the Cold War* (Berkeley: University of California Press).

Enloe, C. (2000) *Maneuvers* (Berkeley: University of California Press).

Gourevitch, P. (1998) *We Wish to Inform You that Tomorrow We Will be Killed with our Families: Stories from Rwanda* (New York : Farrar, Straus, and Giroux).

Jayawardena, K. (1986) *Feminism and Nationalism in the Third World* (London: Zed Books).

Sharp, J. P. (1996) "Gendering Nationhood: A Feminist Engagement with National Identity," in N. Duncan (ed.), *Bodyspace: Destabilising Geographies of Gender and Sexuality* (New York and London: Routledge).

CHAPTER FIFTEEN

Crime

Tony Jefferson

Introduction

Until comparatively recently, criminology, along with other social sciences, was largely gender-blind; that is, it tended to talk about its subject matter of crime, criminalization, and control as if it made no difference that its dramatis personae of offenders, law-makers, police officers, prison guards, judges, and the like are overwhelmingly male. The introduction of "the question of woman" by contemporary feminists inaugurated a period of much greater gender awareness. Now, every first-year student knows that, in thinking about crime, gender "makes a difference." Beyond that, however, given theoretical differences in thinking about gender, and the fact that gender is never the sole relevant factor where crime is concerned, matters become less clear. This brings me to the main object of this overview, namely, to offer a broad route map to the terrain of gender and crime, focused through key theoretical shifts in conceptualizing gender, and exemplified using one broad category of crime: namely, sexual violence. Given the variety of very different behaviors covered by the term "crime," from fiddling tax returns to genocide, only some of which, some of the time, attract the "criminal" label, as well as limitations of space, a selective approach to the examples of crime used is unavoidable.

My choice of sexual violence is governed by the simple fact that gender considerations have had most impact here. Like Daly (1998), my primary focus will be on lawbreaking, or crime, and not issues to do with either criminalization or criminal justice. However, unlike Daly and most other reviewers whose primary interest has been women and crime, my main focus will be on men and crime. This is for two reasons. The first, pragmatic one is that much of this overview is a revised and updated version of my earlier article on "masculinities and crimes" (Jefferson 1997a). The second, principled one is that such a focus enables me to address what Heidensohn concludes are the "crucial" questions, "intellectually and politically." These are: "Not what makes women's crime rates so low, but why are men's so high" (2002: 523). Moreover, it is in relation to thinking about issues to do with male offenders and masculinity that some of the most significant shifts in gender theorizing have taken place.

The (Re)Discovery of the Female Offender

However, it is appropriate to start briefly with women and crime since this was the topic where gender-based analyses first surfaced in criminology (Heidensohn 1968, 1985; Leonard 1982; Smart 1976). "Gender and second-wave feminism," Segal reminds us, "were born together, at the close of the 1960s" (1999: 38). Traditionally, sexual difference was presumed to determine social destiny and the subordinate position of women was, in consequence, inevitable. The idea of gender changed all that. Gender refers to the socially learned patterns of activity and the cultural norms associated with being a man (masculinity) or a woman (femininity) in a given society (Oakley 1972). By making a distinction between biological "sex" and acquired "gender," it made women's subordination a function of gender, not sex. Since male domination was a function of the power of masculinity, it was, potentially, changeable. From this broad, feminist starting point, gendered critiques of the discipline ensued. These emphasized the general neglect of female offenders, and, when they were not overlooked, their distorted depiction. This work also noted that explanations of men's crimes benefited from a variety of critical, sociological approaches, but work on female offenders remained stuck in a theoretical time warp, little changed from the nineteenth-century work of Lombroso and Ferrero (1895), riddled with unreconstructed individualistic, deterministic assumptions rooted in biology and psychology, and sexist stereotypes (Heidensohn 1985; Leonard 1982; Smart 1976).

The marginalization and distortion of women within both mainstream and critical criminology prompted attention to two key issues, which Daly and Chesney-Lind identified as the "gender ratio problem"[1] (why do men commit more crimes than do women) and the "generalizability problem" (are theories of criminality developed on the basis of male offenders applicable also to female offenders?) (Daly and Chesney-Lind 1988). Despite increases in women's share of offending in both Britain and the US, crime's male-dominated gender ratio is criminology's most robust and enduring finding, both historically and cross-culturally (Heidensohn 2002: 496).[2] But attempts to explain women's greater conformity have not been terribly successful, as Heidensohn unflinchingly notes:

> In reviewing theories of female criminality in recent times, Pollock Byrne [*sic*] makes a succinct if gloomy point: "Unfortunately feminist criminology has not offered any comprehensive theory to supplement those it has criticized" (1990:

25). It is hard to disagree with this. Despite a considerable body of work in the field, theoretical crocks of gold have failed to appear. (Ibid.: 522)

One reason has to do with the inadequacies of seeking simply to insert women into existing criminological theories in pursuit of "gender-neutral" theories, an approach associated with non-feminist or liberal feminist analyses (Daly 1998: 94). Another has to do with the problems of trying to produce a *general* theory of crime, however gender-aware. Heidensohn, for example, after discussing the efforts of various authors to produce gender specific versions of control theory,[3] is forced to conclude that the results have been inconclusive, while remaining "a widely cited component of most efforts to discuss women and crime" (2002: 522). Some might want to argue that gender awareness alone cannot compensate for a theory's inadequacies, and those of control theory have been well documented (cf. Taylor 2001). More hopeful, to my mind, are those approaches, based on detailed looks at women in connection with particular categories of crime, which are alert to what Daly (1998: 94–9) summarizes as "gendered crime" (broadly, the gender-differentiated social organization of specific crimes), "gendered pathways to law breaking" (broadly, the gendered particularities of biographical routes into specific crimes), and "gendered lives" (broadly, the gender-specific social conditions of offenders' lives). Taking any or some of these themes, one might "provide a partial window of understanding on gender and crime" (ibid.: 100). I could not agree more. However, for all the sociological sophistication, sensitivity to gender, and awareness of other relevant factors such as class, race, and age, approaches of this kind remain purely social, hence equivalent to the studies of masculinity and crime that I characterize below as stage 2 approaches.

Framing a survey of this kind is never easy and probably always contentious. However, it is arguable that the issue of "*equity*," with men the comparator, animated much of the early work cited above. Heidensohn certainly thought so, and called it "the first and most widely-debated theme in this field" (2002: 497). Gelsthorpe (2002: 118) is more agnostic when she suggests that early critiques drew generally from different feminist positions. But she does acknowledge that, "in criminal justice practice there were strivings for 'equality'" (ibid.: 119). The academic equivalent of such strivings was a raft of studies into women's treatment within the criminal justice system, concerned to see whether women were treated the same as men and, if not, how and to what extent did gender discrimination operate (cf. Allen 1987; Eaton 1986). This constituted the second area of interest opened up by feminist attention to the female offender. The debates these studies ignited have been important and inevitably contentious, hinging on whether women were the beneficiaries of a chivalrous "leniency" or, conversely, the victims of a harsher (in)justice, the latter a consequence of being judged "doubly deviant" (transgressors of both the law and gender norms) or of being subject to greater, especially medicalized, interventions in their lives. However, because they are about criminal justice and not about crime matters, they are beyond the scope of this review.

This brings us to the third broad field of inquiry that the new gender-awareness made possible: namely, women as victims of crime. For my purposes, several things are important about this new arena. First, this focus on female victimization originates outside academic criminology, being the product of the US feminist movement. These highly political connections, with their activist orientations, still mark much of the work in this area. Second, the focus shifts decisively from equality to sexuality, with radical feminism playing a vanguard role. This marked a crucial and highly contentious shift. As Segal (1999: 38–9) unerringly put it, "the most extravagant trouble for gender theory would emerge from its ties to that third term to which 'sex' and 'gender' have long been wedded: 'sexuality'." Third, as this work deals with women as victims and not as offenders, it, too, is beyond the reaches of this review. However, since this work had much to say about men as offenders, it constituted, I would argue, the starting point for thinking about masculinity and crime. Consequently, it represents an appropriate point to shift our attention from female to male offenders, but without losing the gendered nature of our gaze.

Engendering Male Crime

In introducing the topic of masculinity, Connell discusses the three strands – the psychoanalytic, the social psychological, and "recent developments in anthropology, history and sociology" (1995: 7) – that have, in their different ways, produced knowledge about masculinity in the twentieth century. Adapting this to facilitate my discussion of the relationship of this theorizing to the crime question, my framework will be structured to emphasize the significant theoretical shifts. Thus, I start with what I call "orthodox accounts and the 'normal' masculine personality." Whether of the psychoanalytic or the social psychological kind, their central theoretical product has been that of a relatively fixed and unitary "normal" masculine personality, the result of a successful oedipal resolution in its psychoanalytic variant, and of successful "sex-role" learning in its social psychological one. The two subsequent shifts both postdate contemporary feminism. The first of these (Connell's "recent developments"), I call "the social break with orthodoxy: power and multiple masculinities." This is characterized theoretically by the concepts of multiple masculinities, power (since these masculinities are always structured in relations of domination/subordination), and an insistence on the social (or institutional) dimension to masculinities. The second shift is the moment of feminist and poststructuralist engagements with more recent and radical developments in psychoanalytic theorizing. I call this "the psychoanalytic break with orthodoxy: contradictory subjectivities and the social." The principal feature of this development is the (re)discovery and reworking of the fragile, contingent, and contradictory character of masculinity (and femininity), without losing sight of the social.

Tony Jefferson

Orthodox Accounts and the "Normal" Masculine Personality

It was Freud who, as a turn-of-the-century Viennese physician struggling to make sense of his patients' troubled lives, first "noticed" what we would now call gender.[4] Their difficulties in living a gendered existence were central to his clinical case-studies. These laid the basis for a new understanding very different from the taken-for-granted one where maleness was a "natural" product of biological sex. Utilizing his revolutionary ideas about repression and the unconscious, and novel methods (dream analysis and free association) for symptomatically "reading" what had been repressed, he came to see the importance of early parent–child relations, especially the tangled mixture of love and jealousy he found there, to the formation of sexuality and gender in adulthood. The crucial stage in this development he called the oedipal complex, the moment when, for boy children,[5] fear of the potentially castrating father wins out over desire for the mother. This leads, through internalization of his father's prohibitions (the formation of the super-ego), to identification with the masculine. This is also the moment when the cultural prohibitions of civilization win out over individual desire.

For Freud, this masculinity was built upon a constitutional bisexuality, and a complex mix of pre-oedipal desires and identifications. Hence, it was always multilayered, consisting of masculine and feminine elements, conflict-ridden and fragile. Moreover, this "impure" basis makes neurotics of us all. Freud saw no discontinuity between "normal" and pathological mental processes. But the history of mainstream psychoanalysis, in its pursuit of acceptance and respectability, was to be one of increasing conservatism, and a concomitant sanitization and simplification of its theory. Thus, by the mid-twentieth century, psychoanalytic orthodoxy effectively held that a successful resolution of the oedipal complex paved the way to mental health and the gender "normality" of adult heterosexuality and marriage; by contrast, an unsuccessful resolution underlay various pathological conditions and assorted gender "perversions," including homosexuality.

The social psychological equivalent of the "normal," post-oedipal masculine personality of mainstream psychoanalysis is the "normal" man of sex role theory. He is someone who has successfully learned his social script – the cultural norms and expectations of "being a man" in our society: the male sex role. This idea emerged in the 1950s when "sex difference" research – the myriad attempts from the 1890s on to measure "scientifically" how men and women differ psychologically – met up with role theory, the efforts by social scientists from the 1930s to think how positions in social structures get reproduced. This conjunction produced the (now conventional) idea that the psychological differences between men and women (their "sex differences") result from the learning of the cultural norms and behavior appropriate to their sex – their "sex role" (thus reproducing the social categories, men and women). Masculinity is thus the male sex role internalized.

216

Talcott Parsons identified the origins of the male and female sex roles to be in the functional requirements of small groups like the family for role differentiation. He produced his influential distinction between "instrumental" and "expressive" roles, a distinction which remained within the realm of social explanations (Parsons and Bales 1956). "Most often," however, as Connell reminds, "sex roles are seen as the cultural elaboration of biological sex differences" (1995: 22). In other words, there is at the heart of most sex role theory a depressing circularity: sex roles are derived from cultural norms which, in turn, are based in innate differences.

Ironically, the early sex difference research, conducted by the first generation of women admitted into North American research universities, found that psychological differences between the sexes are small or non-existent (a finding which echoes Freud's radical findings about the mixture of masculinity and femininity in all of us). But somewhere along the way, this radical challenge to the doctrine of innate sex differences gets lost, despite the continuing failure of the welter of subsequent research to find many differences. Moreover, although the social nature of the theory allows for change, for new cultural norms to be transmitted, and for the possibility of role-conflict, in practice, and especially before the advent of contemporary feminism, the theory rests largely on highly static, conservative assumptions: that role-expectations are clearly defined, unproblematically internalized, and normative. Consequently, the personalities so produced contribute to the mental health and social stability of society. Mainstream sex role theory thus produces a social parallel to mainstream psychoanalysis: in both, conflict and contradiction are effectively erased, the continuity between normality and pathology is severed, and masculinity and femininity become polarized terms.

The Social Break with Orthodoxy: Power and Multiple Masculinities

Once male social scientists followed the lead of feminist historians, anthropologists, and sociologists in their gendered recasting of women's lives with complementary reexaminations of the lives of men *as men*, a number of important shifts occurred. Historical and anthropological evidence showed something of the empirical *diversity* in masculinities, cross-culturally and in different historical time periods, although much of the work remains wedded theoretically to the idea of male sex roles. There has, however, also been a stronger focus on the *institutional sites* – labor market, the law, the state, colonialism, etc. – wherein cultural norms pointed up by role theory are embedded. This attention to the dynamic, changing nature of masculinities and to the institutional sites of such transformations has led to a recognition, by some, that masculinity is not simply an external role to be passively internalized, a mere product of socialization, but something constructed in the interactional and institutional struggles of everyday life, an achievement of *practice*. The idea of competing masculinities struggling within institutional settings, and within the broader class, race, and other social relations that constrain these, has rendered this work sensitive to power differences *between men*, as well as the more usual feminist focus on inequalities between men and women.

Of course, not all this new work manages to be properly sensitive to all four issues of diversity, institutions, practice, and power. Linking them up coherently in a single theoretical frame is hard enough, let alone putting them to work on concrete cases. Connell's own efforts in this regard are seminal (1987, 1995). First, the centrality of practice and hence the idea that gender relations are historically constructed; second, the idea that the constraints on gender relations are multiple, composed specifically of three interrelated but irreducible structures of labor, power, and cathexis (roughly, sexuality);[6] third, the notion that the historical play of gender relations operates at the various levels – personality, gender regime (institutional), gender order (societal) – which jointly comprise society; finally and most famously, his adaptation of Gramsci in coining the idea of hegemonic and subordinate masculinities to make sense of the relation between competing masculinities (later extended to include "complicit" and "marginalized" masculinities, see Connell 1995: 79–81).

What remains unclear in Connell's work, especially given his obvious interest in psychoanalysis (Connell 1994), is why he puts an unspecified "practice" in command. His short definition of masculinity regards it as "simultaneously a place in gender relations, the practices through which men and women engage that place in gender, and the *effects* of those practices in bodily experience, personality and culture" (1995: 71; my emphasis). To my mind, this Sartrean commitment to practice (Sartre was hostile to the psychoanalytic idea of unconscious motivations) and to personality as constituted by the practices that collectively define a life ignores another possibility: one that makes subjectivity and the role of the unconscious central, but without losing a grip on the social. *That* is the contribution of recent developments in psychoanalytic theorizing, to which I now turn.

The Psychoanalytic Break with Orthodoxy: Contradictory Subjectivities and the Social

"Ultimately, the worth of psychoanalysis in understanding masculinity will depend on our ability to grasp the structuring of personality and the complexities of desire at the same time as the structuring of social relations, with their contradictions and dynamisms" (Connell 1995: 20–1).

In my view, Connell has not himself properly realized this aspect of his project. The reason has to do with his commitment to what some would now regard as a very modernist notion of structure, when much of the new, radical psychoanalytic theorizing is post-structuralist, and approaches the task heavily influenced by Foucault, discourse, and what has come to be known as the "turn to language." Now is not the time to enter the fray on the vexed question of the relation between discourse and the "real" (see Jefferson 1994), but the idea of social discourses offering up a range of subject positions (a development of Foucault's deterministic idea that discourses position subjects) seems to put the question of motivation/investment/identification/desire (call it what you will for the moment) back at the heart of the matter. How, for example, do subjects come to take up (desire/identify with) one (heterosexual) rather than another (homosexual) subject position within the competing discourses of masculinity? This route makes unavoidable a re-engagement with the split, contradictory subject of psychoanalysis, if Connell's "practice" is to be fully understood. Where else are the complex and contradictory origins of desire taken seriously, as Connell (1994) himself has so persuasively argued?

The authors who have been most influential in rendering this subject of psychoanalysis socially literate are Jaques Lacan, Melanie Klein, and other more recent Object Relations theorists (see Minsky 1996, 1998). Lacan's linguistically influenced revisions of traditional Freudian theory, principally his notion that it is the child's entry into the social world of language (and hence into Foucault's discursive realm) that founds the unconscious and self-identity, provide a significant opening towards a (non-reductive) social understanding of the psyche. The revisionist work of Melanie Klein and Object Relations theorists, especially their emphases on the importance of relational defense mechanisms (such as "splitting" off unwanted "bad" parts of the self and "projecting" them into others, where they can be disowned) and on early "object relating," laid a further basis for an understanding of the psyche which is simultaneously social (cf. Rustin 1991, 1995). Chodorow's object relations-influenced account probably has been the most influential to date in theorizing about masculinity. She argued that the emotional dynamics underpinning the process of separation from the mother are different for girls and boys, leaving boys with *the* problem of masculinity, namely, how to relate, and girls with *the* problem of femininity, namely, how to separate (Chodorow 1978). Its widespread appeal probably had more to do with its recognizable sociology than its psychoanalytic argument, a point she now recognizes, since she has gone on to criticize this work for giving "determinist primacy to social relations" (1989: 7; see also Chodorow 1994). This also goes to show how difficult it is to work seriously with both personality and social relations "simultaneously."[7] Nonetheless, in this area we have no other option.[8] Let us see now how my three models can help us understand shifts in approaches to the question of men, masculinities, and particular crimes.

Sexual Violence: Rape, Sexual Abuse, Murder

This cluster of crimes in which sex is somewhere implicated is undoubtedly the area on which thinking about masculinity has impacted most, not surprisingly perhaps, given the importance of sexuality to constructions of masculinity. Indeed, it was the path-breaking writings of American radical feminists on rape in the 1970s (Brownmiller 1976; Griffin 1971) which, being the first to notice and theorize the gendered nature of rape, effectively kick-started the whole current interest in theorizing the relationship between forms of masculinity and certain crimes.

Amir's sociological findings based on convicted rapists in Philadelphia (1967, 1971) had already begun to challenge the image of the rapist as psychopathic stranger, the "monster" lurking in the bushes that has traditionally dominated the commonsense discourse on rape. But its relationship to masculinity escaped him. Moreover, in characterizing 19 percent of the rapes as "victim-precipitated" (victim retracting consent after first agreeing, or not reacting strongly enough), he seemed to be blaming the female victim, thus provoking feminist ire. The feminist interventions finally scotched any notion that rape was an activity undertaken only by abnormal or pathological males, most impressively in Brownmiller's monumental historical and cross-cultural cataloguing of the ubiquity of rape. Further, these writings moved beyond the psychological and sociological characteristics of convicted rapists to connect rape to the (patriarchal) organization of society as a whole. In Brownmiller's case, rape was actually the *foundation* of "the patriarchy" (1976: 17). Finally, and most controversially, *all* men were implicated. As Brownmiller provocatively put it, rape "is nothing more or less than a conscious process of intimidation by which *all men* keep *all women* in a state of fear" (ibid.: 15; emphases in original), an idea that produced the feminist slogan: "all men are potential rapists." From being a *criminal* act committed by a minority of *deviant* men, rape had become a key tactic in the social control of women and the reproduction of male dominance.

In terms of my three-stage model of theorizing masculinity, these early feminist writings straddle the first two stages. In linking masculinity to patriarchal social relations and thus emphasizing the centrality of power, these move beyond the narrow oedipal and sex-role frames characteristic of orthodox accounts of masculinity. In other ways, though, they fail to surmount orthodox thinking. Masculinity is conceptualized in the singular, effectively *the* ideology underpinning the range of practices and institutions that collectively constitute *the* all-embracing system of male domination that is patriarchal society. Second, the notion of how individual men come to acquire patriarchal, masculine values, whether these were seen as rooted in biology (as they were for Brownmiller) or culture (as became more common), is, like sex-role theory, implicitly deterministic: Weber's "iron cage."

One interesting attempt to move beyond these limitations is contained in Box (1983). First, he categorized rape into a number of types, ranging from the brutally "sadistic" to the manipulative "exploitation" rape, which, he argued, were differently motivated. Then he analyzed these in relation to a multifactorial model of causation involving economic inequality, the law, "techniques of neutralization," as well as what he calls the "masculine mystique." In doing this, he takes an important step toward multiplicity without actually breaking with the notion of a singular "culture of masculinity." What he does suggest is that men's differential access to socio-economic resources, and different relationships to cultural stereotypes of masculinity, will affect both the motivation to rape and the kind of rape that is likely to result. Crucially, he attempts to explain the profile of imprisoned rapists, who tend to be lower class and to be largely convicted of "anger" or "domination" rapes. He suggests that masculine sex-role socialization in the lower class contexts of socio-economic powerlessness and a "subculture of violence" could begin to account for this profile (on homicide, see also Polk 1994). Box also makes the important point that, for the sadistic rapist (the rarest category), the "masculine mystique" factor is all-important. (This, as we shall see below, provides a point of connection with later work on serial killing.) Whereas radical feminism had all men down as "potential" rapists, thus effectively answering the question of what function rape plays in a patriarchal society, Box was attempting to answer a more traditional criminological question: namely, which men actually become so.

James Messerschmidt's book, *Masculinities and Crime* (1993), offers probably the most sustained attempt by a criminologist to rethink this relationship away from the deterministic reductionism of early radical feminist theorizing, and thus breaks decisively with orthodox accounts. In so doing, he does for criminology what Connell has done for the study of masculinity more generally. From Giddens (1976, 1981) he takes the idea of a practice-based approach to social structure, and from Acker (1989) the notion that gender, race, and class relations are implicated simultaneously in any given practice. He combines these insights with Connell's (1987) concepts of a multiply structured field of gender relations and hegemonic and subordinated masculinities. Finally, he borrows from phenomenology the idea of the "situational accomplishment" of gender (Fenstermaker et al. 1991; Goffman 1979; West and Zimmerman 1987). The result of this creative synthesis sees crime as a resource for the situational accomplishment of gender (Messerschmidt 1993: 79). It is a form of "structured action," a way of "doing gender," which simultaneously accomplishes (or "does") class and race. Men's resources for accomplishing masculinity, as with those of Box's rapists, will vary, dependent on their positions within class, race, and gender relations. These differences will be reflected in the salience of particular crimes as masculinity-accomplishing resources. For those at the bottom of racial and class hierarchies, with consequently reduced opportunities for the accomplishment of hegemonic masculinity, crime can be particularly salient.[9]

Messerschmidt then proceeds to put his theory to work to explain a whole range of crimes, including those of the powerful. His examples included an analysis of the infamous Central Park rape case in which a white woman jogger was repeatedly raped and left near to death. At the time of the analysis, four teenage Afro-American youths had been convicted of the crime, accompanied by reports that they had been jubilantly celebrating ("wilding") throughout. Messerschmidt argued that this exemplified his thesis: the rape and the "wilding" behavior were a group resource for accomplishing masculinity in a context of class and race disadvantage where other such resources are pitifully few. Subsequently, a lone male confessed to the crime and the youths' convictions were quashed. Although this meant that this particular case was obviously not an example of group "wilding," Messerschmidt (personal communication) still feels that the general point about group rape being a resource for accomplishing masculinity in particular contexts is borne out by numerous examples, including group rapes by school and college athletes (cf. Benedict 1997; Lefkowitz 1997), and those reported to Bourgois (1995, 1996) by young Puerto Rican crack dealers in New York City.

Although this approach constitutes an advance on the early radical feminist explanations, what it singularly fails to do is problematize why some young men "choose" this particular form of behavior to accomplish their masculinity when other similarly located men, thankfully, do not. In other words, it is a purely sociological theory about which *groups* of men are more or less likely to get involved in particular sorts of crime; it has nothing to say about which *particular man or men* from any given group (usually only a fraction of the group) are likely to do so. Take the fact of the differential involvement of men in a group rape: some are initiators of the assault, some are active participants, some are onlookers, and some simply leave the scene. This was certainly true of one of the most detailed case studies on record, the Glen Ridge case, which involved the sadistic and degrading sexual assault on a retarded young woman by a group of advantaged high school athletes (Lefkowitz 1997). Although the sexist culture of masculinity of the athletes, supported by a collusive community, provided the *necessary* context which made the case possible, what was also needed for a *sufficient* explanation was an understanding of what set it off, what enabled the transition from possibility to enactment. In this case, the initiators were two particular boys. Lefkowitz's detailed attention to their biographical details revealed that both had exhibited serious behavioral problems and certain indications of dangerousness well beforehand. Without these particular young men with their particular biographies, I contend that this particular group rape would not have taken place (Jefferson 1998; see also Jefferson 1999).

In short, to understand why particular men rape entails taking the psychic dimension of subjectivity seriously, especially its contradictoriness; not seeing the self, as Messerschmidt implicitly does, simply as unitary and rational, reflexively monitoring behavior in the light of the responses of others (1993: 77). This oversocialized, essentially Meadian version of the self (Mead 1934) helps explain the fact that the examples given of "doing gender" all end up explaining the reproduction of gender (and race and class).[10] This is despite the stated theoretical importance of practice (doing). It is this emphasis on constraints, on structure rather than action, which explains the ultimately deterministic feel to the analyses. It also reveals the limits of a purely social break with the prevailing theoretical orthodoxy.

Another study operating within a broadly similar theoretical framework, but linked to an idea from cultural anthropology that the core properties of hegemonic masculinity in patriarchal societies are "procreation," "provision," and "protection," is that of Kersten (1996). In this, he attempts to explain contemporary (and puzzling) differences in rape rates between Australia, where rates are high, Japan, where they are low, and Germany, which has rates somewhere between the two. The high (and rising) rates in Australia are explained broadly in terms of the effects of the continent's "deep social, cultural and economic crisis" on the traditional "national masculinity" built on "physical prowess and independence." This, Kersten argues, affects both the newly marginalized, for whom crime, including rape, becomes a resource for accomplishing masculinity (following Messerschmidt), and those attempting to live up to "hegemonic masculinity." In the latter case, the difficulties of rearing and providing for families heighten the salience of the purely protective dimension of "good" masculinity, and, in consequence, "the image of the rapist as stranger." Thus, rising rape rates are connected to increases in rape behavior *and* to heightened sensitivities, to underlying structural changes, and to their (differential) impact on competing masculinities. In Japan, by contrast, masculinity and assaultive behavior are not mutually implicated, for a whole host of reasons – cultural, organizational, even architectural – that Kersten attempts to spell out. It is a valiant attempt to think masculinity onto the notoriously difficult terrain of comparative criminology; though, as with Messerschmidt, it remains locked into an exclusively social frame.

Both Messerschmidt and Kersten demonstrate something of the enormous influence that the notion of hegemonic masculinity has had within criminology. However, it has also become clear that the term has been seen increasingly as problematic (Collier 1998; Donaldson 1993; Hood-Williams 2001; Jefferson 2002a; MacInnes 1998; Wetherell and Edley 1999; Whitehead 1999, 2002). I suggest that this has something to do with its structuralist logic. However, it is also my view that not all post-structuralist alternatives to conceptualizing masculinity are adequate. By looking at two specific and very sophisticated examples of post-structuralist attempts to go beyond Connell, I hope to show the nub of theoretical problems that they, too, present.

Richard Collier's book, *Masculinities, Crime and Criminology* (1998) is probably the most sustained challenge from within criminology to the idea of hegemonic masculinity. His argument, in brief, is that the term is of "limited use" in trying to understand the complexities of an actual male subject. This is mainly because:

What is actually being discussed in accounts of (hegemonic) masculinity and crime is, in effect, a range of popular ideologies of what constitute ideal or actual characteristics of "being a man" (Hearn 1996). Hegemonic masculinity appears to open up an analysis of the diversity of masculinities (subordinate, effeminate, non-capitalist?) whilst simultaneously holding in place a normative masculine "gender" to which is then assigned the range of (usually undesirable/negative) characteristics. (ibid.: 21)

The resulting picture, he suggests, is highly reductive:

> [T]he argument that "real men" (that which is ascribed the status of "hegemonic" masculinity) are inherently oppressive continues to override any investigation of the complexity of behaviour of men in their everyday relations with women and other men. (ibid.: 22)

It is not difficult to see how Messerschmidt's (1993, 1997) catalogue of criminals might fit this criticism. They may all be doing masculinity differently, depending on their location in gender, race, and class relations, but they are all indubitably doing bad not good.

Thus far, I can agree with the argument. However, the trouble begins when we come to Collier's own approach to the problem. He first describes what his task is *not* about: "To 'deconstruct' the heterosexual man of criminology is not, in itself, sufficient to understand the contours of the formation of individual subjective commitments in any particular instance" (1998: 31–2). In other words, explaining "*why* fragmented positionings may be held together by individuals in such a way as to produce the subjective experience of 'identity'" (ibid.: 32; emphasis in original), the question of "choosing," investing in, or identifying with different subject positions, is not his concern. Rather, his is the more "modest" task of exploring "subjectivity as embodiment, subjectivity as the lived experience of a (specifically masculine) body as it is socially and culturally inscribed" (ibid.). Subsequent chapters offer various concrete examples of this approach, including a consideration of the "spree" killer Thomas Hamilton, who gunned down a classroom of children in Dunblane, Scotland, in 1996, killing 16 children and their teacher, and injuring 17 more children. His conclusion to the chapter talks of having "presented an interpretative genealogy of how the 'silencing' of masculinity is achieved in one particular context and instance" (ibid.: 121). Yet two pages earlier, in a recap of his argument, he has this to say: "Thomas Hamilton, in trying to masculinise himself within the ideals of traditional heterosexual masculinity, can be read as attempting to forge a more commanding and potent sense of himself as a man (Jackson 1995: 28)" (ibid.: 119).

Collier then spells out how Hamilton did this, concretely: by "his involvement in (at least) three major activities [namely] . . . his participation in youth clubs . . . his involvement with firearms and gun clubs . . . and, finally . . . in his ultimate invasion, reframing and destruction of the largely feminised space of the primary school at Dunblane" (ibid.). Now I may be misunderstanding this, but it seems to me that, despite disavowals, Collier *is* offering an explanation of Hamilton's subjectivity. To what else can the phrase "in trying to masculinise himself . . ." be referring? Or, take the argument: "In seeking to carve out an identity for himself 'in a different framework that seemed to offer . . . some status and self-respect' (Jackson 1995: 16)" (Collier 1998: 118). Doesn't this address directly the disavowed "why" question? Certainly Jackson (whose 1995 pamphlet Collier invokes in aid) was concerned to explain masculine subjectivity.

Whether or not I am right in my interpretation of Collier's analysis of Hamilton, there is a problem. If it is an (unknowing) attempt to explain Hamilton's subjectivity as well as a genealogy, it is confusing theoretically since it offers no resources for thinking through the former question. If it is, as claimed, only a genealogy, a deconstruction of the "textual" Hamilton in press discourses interpreted through the absent "sexed" body of Hamilton, it is fine as far as it goes, but inadequate precisely because it doesn't explain how the particular discursive interpretations argued to inscribe Hamilton "*as a man*" come to be lived, subjectively, something that is surely necessary if we are properly to envision the complex subjects that Collier's critique of hegemonic masculinity rightly presumes. This is an example of the weakness of a purely discursive turn.

Wetherell and Edley, on the other hand, do claim to engage the psychological dimension of masculinity. They are critical of Connell for "a lack of specification on how hegemonic masculinity might become effective in men's psyches" (1999: 337). However, their own Lacanian-inspired "psycho-discursive" solution fails to produce an inner world and therefore fails to deliver on its promise. Based on tape-recorded interviews with 61 men, they described the patterns of identification they found in parts of their interviews as examples of "imaginary positioning" (ibid.: 342). By that they mean, in an argument that draws on Lacan and Barthes, "[A]n external voice from without is . . . mispresented [hence "imaginary"] as a voice from within" (ibid.: 343). Since their interviewees took up diverse and sometimes mixed positions, they proposed that Connell's hegemonic "norms are in fact discursive practices" (ibid.: 353) and that:

> identification is a matter of the procedures in action through which men live/talk/ do masculinity . . . these procedures are intensely local (situationally realized) and global (dependent on broader conditions of intelligibility). They represent the social within the psychological. . . . What we mean by character or identity is partly the differential, persistent and idiosyncratic inflection of these procedures over time in the course of a life. . . . These procedures are a particular class of discursive practice which we call psycho-discursive. (ibid.)

In other words, their efforts to understand "[w]hat happens psychologically" (ibid.: 337) in the negotiations between actual men and hegemonic masculinity, to combine "insights from the ethnomethodological/conversation tradition . . . with those stemming from poststructuralist and Foucauldian notions of discourse" (ibid.: 338), remain resolutely social ("the social within the psychological"). Interviewees might resist, but there is no escaping the iron hand of discourse. Men's masculinities, it seems, are the (discursive) accounts through which they communicate them. Effectively, men are no more than the sum of their talk. Since there is a refusal to contemplate a pre-discursive or non-discursive realm, all psychological processes (such as motives, emotions and desires) and biographical elements that underpin the crucial question of identification are reduced to forms of "discursive accomplishment" (ibid.: 335). For all its sophistication, this remains a social psychology without an irreducible inner world.

Despite their dissatisfactions with hegemonic masculinity, Wetherell and Edley, like Collier, failed to transcend what I call the "purely social break" characteristic of stage 2 thinking on masculinities and crime. The complexities of men's experiences evaded them. One could argue that the return to (a socially literate) psychoanalysis within feminism, my third stage in thinking about masculinities, was prompted, ultimately, by some of the felt disjunctions between personal experience (which had always been a serious object of attention in feminism) and available feminist theory: for many women, for example, their love of and desire for particular men contradicted their theoretical understandings of men-in-general as oppressors, aggressors, potential rapists. Progress in turning a similar spotlight on men's experiences has been slight, but instructive.

Books recounting men's experiences of rape, as rapists, are rare. I know of two: Beneke (1982) and Levine and Koenig (1983).[11] Reading these, what is striking is the disjunction between feminism's traditional depiction of the rapist as the personification of power and how these men experienced themselves ("I had a kind of phobia about women, I just felt I wasn't good enough for them, like really inside"; "women often made me feel inferior," Levine and Koenig 1983: 78, 84). Here, Frosh's psychoanalytic notion "of the *incoherence* of the masculine state, of the way its ideological claims to effectiveness and power are built on a continuing denial of weakness and dependence" (1994: 99; emphasis in original) has telling, concrete purchase. Perhaps, though, what is needed to shift the terms of the debate is the authority of a sociologist like Giddens (1992: 122): "a large amount of male sexual violence now stems from insecurity and inadequacy rather than from a seamless confirmation of patriarchal dominance."

These ideas have been developed most in two case-studies, both by feminists, one a professor of English, the other a journalist, of the serial, sexual murderer Peter Sutcliffe, the so-called "Yorkshire Ripper" (Ward Jouve 1988; Smith 1989). The question of serial killing has generated a small publishing industry of its own. It may be useful, therefore, to outline the main strands, so as to distinguish clearly my own focus. First, there is the work on sadistic sexual murder of feminist writers like Cameron and Frazer (1987) and Caputi (1987), and, more generally on the killing of women, of Radford and Russell (1992). In this work, the masculinity of the violence is certainly central, most thought-provokingly in Cameron and Frazer's idea that the "common denominator" of sex-murderers is not misogyny, since not all their victims are women, but "a shared construction of . . . masculinity" in which the "quest for transcendence" is central (1987: 166–7). However, because masculinity and patriarchy are conceptualized in the singular, theoretically speaking, this work is a continuation (along with a whole range of other work on violence against women) of the tradition inaugurated by the work of Brownmiller and Griffin on rape.

Second, there is the emergent positivistic criminological literature responding to an apparently novel crime phenomenon (Holmes and De Burger 1988; Lester 1995; Levin and Fox 1985). Definitions, profiles, and typologies are central, based upon the careful assembling of what is known about killers' backgrounds, personalities, motives, methods, victims, and killing locations. The resulting portraits, I concluded elsewhere, "traverse the spectrum from insanity and psychopathy, through instability, trauma, anti-social personality and sexual sadism to various versions of 'normality'" (Jefferson 2002b: 156). Where the fact of the predominance of male perpetrators is noticed, it is merely one of a number of factors. The explanation offered is highly orthodox: for example, the pressure on men who feel weak to live up to the powerful sex-role norms expected of them (Levin and Fox 1985: 53). The understanding of Freud and the unconscious is risible (Holmes and De Burger 1988: 98). The third strand is the biographical accounts of particularly heinous killers written by journalists. These now constitute a whole sub-genre of biographical writing. The final strand is certain feminist appropriations of these journalistic accounts. It is these that interest us here.

Once Peter Sutcliffe acquired his "Yorkshire Ripper" tag, and thus became linked in the popular imagination to "Jack the Ripper,"[12] the interest of journalists and academic feminists[13] was assured – with the usual division of labor. The former have done the leg-work, attended the trial, conducted the interviews, and produced detailed but essentially descriptive accounts of the case; the latter have offered their feminist-inspired theoretical re-readings. Only Smith, a feminist and a journalist who reported on the trial, manages both. Of the re-readings, it is the brilliant discussions of Sutcliffe's fragile and conflicted masculinity, in both Smith and Ward Jouve, that begins to develop the contours of an understanding of masculinity that is both socially literate and psychoanalytically complex.

Connell's assertion that it is in the "detail of cases" that the deployment of psychoanalytic ideas will greatly assist our understanding of masculinity (1995: 34), is superbly exemplified in these two accounts. They reach similar conclusions. Both tell the story of a boy who is painfully torn between the tough, masculine values of father, brother, and working-class neighborhood, the mantle of masculinity required of him, and the quiet, gentle femininity of his beloved, long-suffering mother, with whom he strongly identified. They show something of the multiple ambivalences that this contradiction produced: the cruel cross-pressures of the socially required versus the psychically desired (but socially punished). And they outline many of the contingencies that, in repeatedly demonstrating his failure to live up to the social expectations of manliness, led him first to blame the feminine in himself, to hate part of himself, and then externalize that hatred and destroy women.

It was a grisly resolution. It was not inevitable. It was in some sense chosen. But it is a resolution and a choice that displays a logic only when understood within the detail of a life observed through a lens of masculinity which is simultaneously social and psychic, alert to the multiple contradictions within and between these dimensions, the anxieties and ambivalences these set up, and the compounding influence of contingencies. It is the strength of both the accounts of Smith and Ward Jouve that they do render Sutcliffe's life comprehensible, at least after a fashion. They both draw on journalistic accounts, but transform

227

them by noticing and accounting for a host of apparently inconsequential, over-looked details, thus rendering them theoretically meaningful.

This work has had little impact on the rape debate, which is still heavily influenced by radical feminism. Three decades on, discussions of the various violences against women are still effectively centered on unmasking the many visages of "male power" (in the singular). This is evident in studies of the (patriarchal) assumptions and practices in the conduct of rape investigations and trials that produce high "attrition rates" and low rates of conviction (Adler 1987; Chambers and Millar 1983, 1986; Grace et al. 1992; Lees 1996; Lees and Gregory 1995). It is also evident in the work on rape in war, as Gelsthorpe's summary of the literature reveals: "war crimes such as rape or mass rape are an expression of the gender order or of a militarised masculinity (Enloe 1983; MacKinnon 1994; Nikolic-Ristanovic 1996a, 1996b)" (2002: 127). Some US feminists, however, have changed tack completely and rejected this orthodoxy as a form of "victim-feminism" (Paglia 1992; Roiphe 1993). They regard its picture of woman-as-victim, passively powerless, as one that simply reinforces the conventional stereotype of the weak, helpless woman. These new "power" (or "post-") feminist voices have emerged out of the complex sexual and racial politics on US campuses which engendered the debate about "political correct-ness" (Dunant 1994; Hollway and Jefferson 1996).[14] In particular, Paglia and Roiphe blame the growth of concern about campus "date-rape" (Boumil et al. 1993) on feminist extensions of the definition of rape (to include verbal as well as physical coercion, or any sex felt by the victim to be violating; see Roiphe 1993: 68–70), and generally bemoan the denial of an active female sexuality in the dating scenario (Paglia 1992: 49–74). Since both Paglia and Roiphe hail from the humanities and not the social sciences, and their purposes were primarily polit-ical, it is not surprising that they end up postulating a responsible, "choosing" female subject, a simple inversion of radical feminism's passive victim of male power (see also Grant 1994).

However, in putting women's sexuality back into the picture, by suggesting that she too is a sexual agent, these new feminist voices reconnected with a dimension that had become obscured by radical feminism's preoccupation with (male) sexuality as power. Still absent was more adequate theorizing of gendered subjectivity. It is this dimension that more recent work on particular date-rape cases is trying to develop (Hollway and Jefferson 1998; Jefferson 1997b), using a theory of subjectivity derived from combining Foucault's notion of (social) discourses with various (psychoanalytically-derived) concepts, such as anxiety and the defenses of splitting and projection, in order to explain the discursive positions adopted (Hollway 1989; Jefferson 1994). Testing this approach on particular cases has involved deconstructions of existing journalistic accounts, highlighting those facts left unexplained, and reconstructions showing how sense can be made of ignored facts, once unconscious motivations and ambivalent feelings, and the anxieties and defensive splittings/projections these give rise to (for both parties) are recognized. The subjectivities that emerge from such analytical reconstructions turn out to be complexly and contradictorily gendered, a conclusion in line with Ward Jouve and Smith on the "masculinity" of Sutcliffe. Further support for the idea of ambivalence in this area can be found in Phillips's fascinating interview-based study with young female students in the US exploring their experiences of intimate relations, including their experiences of coercive sex: "throughout their interviews, women spoke of confusion, of contradictory emotions, of not knowing what to think" (2000: 8). Bravely, she adds, "for many of the young women in this study, rape *is* about sex, *as well as* about violence. . . . Many women report saying yes when they want to say no, and saying no when they want to say yes or maybe" (ibid.: 14).

A further instance of the fruitful rereading of journalistic accounts, one that is alert to the question of masculinity and the importance of addressing social and psychic dimensions, is Jackson's pamphlet on the James Bulger case (1995; see also Jefferson 1996c). Its relevance here is that James's murder by two boys (James was a 2-year-old, his killers were both aged 10) was preceded by a symbolic rape. It was a shocking and gruesome case, provoking widespread public revulsion and incomprehension and, perhaps inevitably, much recourse to demonizing discourses. What the journalist David Smith does in his excellent book on the case is first remind us that killing by children is not new, then meticulously assemble the available evidence, and finally offer an explanation based on the unhappiness, mistreatment, and powerlessness that was characteristic of both boys' lives. He offers this explanation reluctantly, trusting initially that an explanation would emerge from the detail, thus nicely demonstrating the difference between the journalistic and the academic approach. What Jackson does is to take up the neglected issue of masculinity and show how the boys' lives could be understood as attempts to build up a more powerful sense of masculine identity, in the twin contexts of a powerlessness imposed by the frameworks that regulated them (family and school), and the "idealised fantasy images of hypermasculine toughness, dominance and invulnerability" (1994: 22) provided by the media and the male peer group, which exerted both a pull and a pressure. The resulting truancy, "rape," and the killing of the toddler James are all read in this light, with the killing seen as an attempt to master their own anxieties and fears about their own babyishness by violently projecting them onto James, and destroying them there. Once again, there are obvious parallels with the Ward Jouve and Smith accounts of Sutcliffe.

One of the things the Bulger killing did was to re-ignite interest in the case of Mary Bell, the girl who was convicted of strangling two small children in 1968 when she was 11. Gitta Sereny's *The Case of Mary Bell*, first published in 1972, was republished in a new edition in 1995 with a new preface and an appendix about the death of James Bulger. Although Mary Bell was labeled a psychopath by two psychiatrists, thereby securing a conviction for manslaughter on the grounds of diminished responsibility, the similarity between her emotionally impoverished and rejecting background and her troublesome responses and those of the two boy killers of James is striking. For Sereny, the emotional damage that all three children shared is the crucial feature, not their gender (which is never raised). Whether she is right or not, these cases suggest two things at least to bear in mind when thinking about masculinity. One is a reminder of the complex fluidity of gender formation, a point being developed most interestingly in the theoretical work of Jessica Benjamin (1995a, 1995b, 1998). How else explain Mary Bell's extremely "masculine" fearlessness and inability to feel? This would seem to warn against pinning everything on gender difference and ignoring what the sexes share by virtue of being human. Secondly, if masculinity is used over-inclusively as an explanatory concept, the role of other significant factors may be obscured.

It might be in this spirit that we could usefully return to traditional crimino-logical texts like West (1987) on sexual violence. There, the various portraits of rapists, paedophiles, etc., where weakness and inadequacy seem more in evidence than their social power as men, could surely benefit by more attention to the question of masculinity. On the other hand, his detailing of a variety of factors may alert us to the dangers of a too-inclusive use of the concept of masculinity (cf. Walklate 2001: 73).

Lest this focus on individual cases serves to obscure the ultimate object of attention, let me end this section by refocusing on the broadest possible meaning of the social, on what Bob Connell (1993) calls "the big picture." Take some-thing like the rise of fascism in inter-war Germany, which, with its genocidal outcome, ought to be of some interest to criminologists. So far as I know, no serious commentator has ever tried to deny fascism's complex social roots. But, in the wake of the Frankfurt School's efforts to understand the psychic under-pinnings of its mass appeal, who would now deny the need also to understand the complexities of fascism's psychological roots? As Ehrenreich tellingly puts it, in her Foreword to the first volume of Theweleit's extraordinarily rich account of the fantasies of fascist Freikorpsmen, "the problem [with sociological or Marxist theories of fascism] . . . is that these theories have very little to tell us about what we ultimately need most to understand, and that is murder" (Theweleit 1987: xi).

Understanding the roots of fascist violence is at the heart of Theweleit's work. Authority and the construction of the authoritarian personality were central to the Frankfurt school's understanding of fascism. For Theweleit (1987, 1989) it is the attraction of violence, and its origins in the construction of the particular masculinities of the men of the Freikorps, specifically their fear and hatred of the feminine, which is paramount. His work can thus be seen as a (very rich) case-study in masculinity. In attending to the connections between fantasy life and politics, it is sensitive to both psychic and social levels. The question Theweleit leaves open is how different was the psychic constellation of these men from that of other men. But, in the light of the present "big picture," in which neither war, genocide, nor torture can be consigned safely to the historical past, it would seem madness to leave the question of masculine subjectivities out of account. As Benjamin and Rabinbach say in their Foreword to Theweleit's second volume:

"no other work dives so deeply into the fantasies of violence, or into warfare itself as a symbolic system of desire . . . in this world of war the repudiation of one's own body, of femininity, becomes a psychic compulsion which associates masculinity with hardness, destruction, and self-denial" (Theweleit 1989: xiii).

Conclusion

It is common to end a review of this kind by stressing both how far the debate has progressed and what remains to be done. Heidensohn, for example, emphasizes the advances in knowledge about women and crime, the increased recognition of the field in academic and public policy circles, the challenges in store from new research on masculinity and crime, and the distance still to travel: "this has been a long journey which has not yet taken us very far" (2002: 523–4). Gelsthorpe, in her review, highlights the new theoretical "openness" within feminism, especially to questions of epistemology, and the "advances" within criminology attributable to "new ways of thinking" (about reflexivity, personal experience, intertextuality, the blurring of boundaries, and identity), but points out that these developments do not mirror each other and that the criminological "heartlands" remain untouched by any of this. Nevertheless, she is cautiously optimistic about the "scope for positive dialogue" between feminism and criminology (2002: 135). For Carrington, feminist criminology is now characterized by turbulence and diversity, a broadening of interest to include masculinity and the "power effects" of social differences other than gender, and the solid achievements of revitalizing radical criminology and creating the sub-discipline of victimology (2002: 134–7). Future challenges include, still, how to deal with a largely unreconstructed criminology, the ethnocentrism of both criminology and some versions of feminism, and, more generally, the pull of universalizing categories (like woman). What is needed are specific political interventions: "The more specific the challenge to masculinist expressions of power and phallocentric constructions of knowledge . . . the more dangerous and compelling the feminist intervention" (ibid.: 136).

Despite different emphases and levels of specificity, I would contend that these three different attempts at a conclusion (at least my summaries of them) do not offer necessarily incompatible statements. I find myself in broad agreement with all of them. It is tempting, therefore, simply to leave it at that. Job done. However, I feel the need to add something more specific about the nature of the intellectual challenge ahead, given that the field is now so "open," "turbulent," and diverse. Another way of thinking about this new intellectual pluralism ushered in by post-structuralist and postmodern approaches to knowledge is to focus on the theoretical eclecticism they would appear to warrant. The benefits of this have been enormous, liberating us all from theoretical rigidities and false certainties of the old heritage of the many varieties of structuralism. Welcome though this is in all kinds of ways, the price of the new uncertainty can be a lack of clarity or confusion about important intellectual distinctions; a sense that the new intellectual freedom means that "anything goes." Or, more accurately, that, since all approaches have something to offer, each should be encouraged. I want to end by saying something, briefly, about the future of research into masculinity and crime that involves being more prescriptive than that.

As we saw, the turn to post-structuralism has no single meaning. Probably for many it is synonymous with the turn to discourse, a term that usually signifies Foucault. Within criminology, Foucault is now one of the subject's most cited authors. For those interested in matters of criminalization or criminal justice, this is hardly surprising, given Foucault's excitingly novel approaches to such matters. Even if he is approached somewhat warily, usually as part of "a continual contest" (Bell 1993: 14) in the case of feminism, his presence is too massive to ignore. Much of the best work in criminology is indebted to Foucault's analytical concepts. But, as we saw in the work of Collier (1998) and Wetherell and Edley (1999), the Foucauldian-influenced ideas of "interpretative genealogy" and the "psycho-discursive" have not proved adequate in thinking about the inner world of masculine subjectivity. Nor will any notions derived from the idea of discourse, unless they can be deployed, in combination with other concepts, in a way that respects the irreducibility of an inner world. My concern is that much of the renewed interest in questions of identity, welcome though it is, is not respectful of this irreducibility: it knows its Foucault but forgets its Freud.

This brings us to the other meaning of the turn to post-structuralism that I explored, the one that does respect the importance of the inner world without forgetting the social: namely, that associated with contemporary psychoanalytic feminism – my third stage. My contention is that without taking these feminist-inspired, psychoanalytically informed approaches seriously, there will be little progress in thinking about masculinity and crime. I have tried to show what specific contributions such properly psychosocial approaches to masculinity have made in the area of one particular crime category: namely, sexual violence. I have also indicated that such contributions are marginal rather than central. This is partly because of criminology's reluctance to take seriously either psychoanalysis or crime causation (as opposed to criminalization and criminal justice matters), since both are associated (erroneously as I hope to have demonstrated in various ways above) with "individualism," a much discredited notion, as we saw in early feminist approaches to women and crime. But it is also because of the stranglehold that an activist-oriented radical feminism, now somewhat diluted with doses of Foucauldian discourse no doubt, still exerts on the topic of sexual violence. As a man, it has always been hard to "speak truth to power" on such matters. But, if we are serious about Heidensohn's "crucial" questions, about why men's crime rates are so high, and concerned, as she is, that "this has been a long journey which has not yet taken us very far" (2002: 524), the truth is that we can no longer ignore contemporary, feminist psychoanalytic contributions, nor remain ignorant of the distance these have traveled from traditional, bowdlerized versions of Freudianism.

Notes

1 I would prefer the term "sex-ratio" when the reference, as it is here, is to men and women. However, just as gender has become (erroneously and confusingly in my view, but almost invariably) a synonym for sex, it is more common to talk, as Daly and Chesney-Lind (1988) do, of the "gender ratio."

2 Crime's male-dominated gender ratio varies between 5 and 7 to 1 using official figures and drops to about 3 to 1 using self-report studies (which tend to focus on less serious offenses).

3 One of the few attempts to produce a general theory of crime, control theory stresses the importance of various social bonds in protecting people from delinquency (Hirschi 1969).

4 For Freud, the issue was the relationship between sexual difference and sexuality and not, as it was to become for feminists, the question of male power. However, as Segal (1999: 41) points out, "It is the psychoanalyst Robert Stoller who is usually credited with introducing 'gender' as an explanatory concept into the social sciences in 1968" (although Harrison and Hood-Williams (2002: 9) bestow the honor on Oakley (1972)).

5 Space does not permit the complementary sketching of the girl child's path; suffice to say that this, especially the notion of "penis envy," alienated many feminists from the Freudian tradition.

6 In a later book, Connell (2000: 26) introduced a fourth structure and called it "symbolism."

7 A useful starting point, which I explore more fully elsewhere (Jefferson 2002a), is the distinction, made by MacInnes, between "sexual *genesis*" ("being born *of* a man *and* a woman") and "sexual *difference*" ("being born *as* a man *or* a woman") (1998: 17; emphases in original).

8 See Chodorow 1999; Elliott 1992, 1996, 1998; Elliott and Frosh 1995; Froggett 2002; Frosh 1991, 1994; Frosh et al. 2002; Gadd 2000, 2003; Henriques et al. 1984/1998; Hollway and Jefferson 1996, 1998, 2000; Hood-Williams 2001; Jackson 1990, 1995; Jackson and Pratt 2001; Jefferson 1994, 1996a, 1996b, 1996c, 1997a, 1997b, 2002a, 2002b; Layton 1998; Richards 1994; Rustin 1995.

9 Messerschmidt makes the same argument about girls and femininity, in explaining girls' involvement in gangs (1997: 67–87).

10 See, for example, Messerschmidt's analysis of male violence using individual case-studies (2000).

11 I discount books like Scully's (1990). Though this purports to be a study of convicted rapists, the men's experiences are so heavily interpreted through a conventional sociological feminism that, whatever the men have to say is returned to them effectively (and unperceptively) reduced to "justifications" and "excuses" (ibid.: 134). Similarly, descriptive studies of imprisoned rapists based partly on interview material (which are rare in this country) assist little (see Grubin and Gunn 1990).

12 Caputi (1987: 7) called "Jack the Ripper," the "father" to the "age of sex crime." Between 1975 and 1981, the "Yorkshire Ripper" murdered 13 women and seriously wounded 7 others.

13 For journalistic accounts, see Beattie 1981; Burn 1984; Cross 1981; Smith 1989; Yallop 1981. Academic feminist writings on the case include Bland 1984; Hollway 1981; Ward Jouve 1988.

14 David Mamet's play and subsequent film, *Oleanna*, about a college professor accused of sexual harassment and rape, and Michael Crichton's best-selling book, *Disclosure* (also made into a film) about a male victim of sexual harassment, are two popular manifestations of the debate.

References

Acker, J. (1989) "The Problem with Patriarchy," *Sociology* 23/2: 235–40.
Adler, A. (1987) *Rape on Trial* (London: Routledge & Kegan Paul).

Allen, H. (1987) *Justice Unbalanced: Gender, Psychiatry and Judicial Decisions* (Milton Keynes: Open University Press).

Amir, M. (1967) "Victim Precipitated Forcible Rape," *Journal of Criminal Law, Criminology and Police Science* 58: 493–502.

Amir, M. (1971) *Patterns in Forcible Rape* (Chicago: University of Chicago Press).

Beattie, J. (1981) *The Yorkshire Ripper Story* (London: Quartet/Daily Star).

Bell, V. (1993) *Interrogating Incest: Feminism, Foucault and the Law* (London: Routledge).

Beneke, T. (1982) *Men on Rape* (New York: St Martin's Press).

Benedict, J. (1997) *Public Heroes, Private Felons: Athletes and Crimes Against Women* (Boston: North Eastern University Press).

Benjamin, J. (1995a) "Sameness and Difference: Toward an 'Over-inclusive' Theory of Gender Development," in A. Elliott and S. Frosh (eds.), *Psychoanalysis in Contexts* (London: Routledge).

Benjamin, J. (1995b) *Like Subjects, Love Objects: Essays on Recognition and Sexual Difference* (New Haven: Yale University Press).

Benjamin, J. (1998) *Shadow of the Other: Intersubjectivity and Gender in Psychoanalysis* (New York: Routledge).

Bland, L. (1984) "The Case of the Yorkshire Ripper: Mad, Bad, Beast or Male?" in P. Scraton and P. Gordon (eds.), *Causes for Concern* (Harmondsworth: Penguin).

Boumil, M. M., Friedman, J., and Taylor, B. E. (1993) *Date Rape: The Secret Epidemic* (Deerfield Beach, FL: Health Communications Inc.).

Bourgois, P. (1995) *In Search of Respect: Selling Crack in El Barrio* (Cambridge: Cambridge University Press).

Bourgois, P. (1996) "In Search of Masculinity: Violence, Respect and Sexuality among Puerto Rican Crack Dealers in East Harlem," in T. Jefferson and P. Carlen (eds.), *Masculinities, Social Relations and Crime*, Special Issue of *British Journal of Criminology* 36/3: 412–27.

Box, S. (1983) *Power, Crime and Mystification* (London: Tavistock).

Brownmiller, S. (1976) *Against Our Will: Men, Women and Rape* (Harmondsworth: Penguin).

Burn, G. (1984) *Somebody's Husband, Somebody's Son: The Story of Peter Sutcliffe* (London: Heinemann).

Cameron, D. and Frazer, E. (1987) *The Lust to Kill: A Feminist Investigation of Sexual Murder* (Cambridge: Polity).

Caputi, J. (1987) *The Age of Sex Crime* (London: The Women's Press).

Carrington, K. (2002) "Feminism and Critical Criminology: Confronting Genealogies," in K. Carrington and R. Hogg (eds.), *Critical Criminology: Issues, Debates, Challenges* (Cullompton, Devon: Willan).

Chambers, G. and Millar, A. (1983) *Investigating Sexual Assault* (Edinburgh: HMSO).

Chambers, G. and Millar, A. (1986) *Prosecuting Sexual Assault* (Edinburgh: HMSO).

Chodorow, N. J. (1978) *The Reproduction of Mothering: Psychoanalysis and the Sociology of Gender* (Berkeley: University of California Press).

Chodorow, N. J. (1989) *Feminism and Psychoanalytic Theory* (London: Yale University Press).

Chodorow, N. J. (1994) *Femininities, Masculinities, Sexualities: Freud and Beyond* (Lexington, KT: The University Press of Kentucky).

Chodorow, N. J. (1999) *The Power of Feelings: Personal Meaning in Psychoanalysis, Gender, and Culture* (New Haven: Yale University Press).

Collier, R. (1998) *Masculinities, Crime and Criminology* (London: Sage).

Connell, R. W. (1987) *Gender and Power: Society, the Person and Sexual Politics* (Cambridge: Polity).

Connell, R. W. (1993) "The Big Picture: Masculinities in Recent World History," *Theory and Society* 22/5: 599–623.

Connell, R. W. (1994) "Psychoanalysis on Masculinity," in H. Brod and M. Kaufman (eds.), *Theorizing Masculinities* (London: Sage).

Connell, R. W. (1995) *Masculinities* (Cambridge: Polity).

Connell, R. W. (2000) *The Men and the Boys* (Cambridge: Polity).

Cross, R. (1981) *The Yorkshire Ripper: The In-depth Study of a Mass Killer and His Methods* (London: Granada).

Daly, K. (1998) "Gender, crime and criminology," in M. Tonry (ed.), *The Handbook of Crime and Punishment* (New York: Oxford University Press).

Daly, K. and Chesney-Lind, M. (1988) "Feminism and criminology," *Justice Quarterly* 5: 497–538.

Dobash, R. E. and Dobash, R. (1979) *Violence Against Wives: A Case Against Patriarchy* (New York: Free Press).

Donaldson, M. (1993) "What is Hegemonic Masculinity?" *Theory and Society* 22: 643–57.

Dunant, S. (ed.) (1994) *The War of the Words: The Political Correctness Debate* (London: Virago).

Eaton, M. (1986) *Justice for Women?* (Milton Keynes: Open University Press).

Elliott, A. (1992) *Social Theory and Psychoanalysis in Transition: Self and Society from Freud to Kristeva* (London: Routledge).

Elliott, A. (1996) *Subject to Ourselves: Social Theory, Psychoanalysis and Postmodernity* (Cambridge: Polity).

Elliott, A. (ed.) (1998) *Freud 2000* (Cambridge: Polity).

Elliott, A. and Frosh, S. (eds.) (1995) *Psychoanalysis in Contexts: Paths between Theory and Modern Culture* (London: Routledge).

Enloe, C. (1983) *Does Khaki Become You? The Militarization of Women's Lives* (London: Pluto).

Fenstermaker, S., West, C., and Zimmerman, D. H. (1991) "Gender Inequality: New Conceptual Terrain," in R. L. Blumberg (ed.), *Gender, Family and Economy* (Newbury Park, CA: Sage).

Froggett, L. (2002) *Love, Hate and Welfare: Psychosocial Approaches to Policy and Practice* (Bristol: The Policy Press).

Frosh, S. (1991) *Identity Crisis: Modernity, Psychoanalysis and the Self* (London: Macmillan).

Frosh, S. (1994) *Sexual Difference: Masculinity and Psychoanalysis* (London: Routledge).

Frosh, S., Phoenix, A., and Pattman, R. (2002) *Young Masculinities: Understanding Boys in Contemporary Society* (Basingstoke: Palgrave).

Gadd, D. (2000) "Masculinities, Violence and Defended Psycho-social Subjects," *Theoretical Criminology* 4/4: 429–49.

Gadd, D. (2003) "Reading Between the Lines: Subjectivity and Men's Violence," *Men and Masculinities* 5/4: 333–54.

Gelsthorpe, L. (2002) "Feminism and Criminology," in M. Maguire, R. Morgan, and R. Reiner (eds.), *The Oxford Handbook of Criminology*, 3rd edn. (Oxford: Oxford University Press).

Giddens, A. (1976) *New Rules of Sociological Method* (London: Hutchinson).

Giddens, A. (1981) "Agency, Institution and Time-Space Analysis," in K. Knorr-Cetina and A. V. Cicourel (eds.), *Advances in Social Theory and Methodology: Toward an Integration of Micro- and Macro-Sociologies* (Boston: Routledge and Kegan Paul).

Giddens, A. (1992) *The Transformation of Intimacy* (Cambridge: Polity).

Goffman, E. (1979) *Gender Advertisements* (New York: Harper and Row).

Grace, S., Lloyd, C., and Smith, L. J. F. (1992) *Rape: From Recording to Conviction*. Research and Planning Unit Paper 71 (London: Home Office).

Grant, L. (1994) "Sex and the Single Student: The Story of Date Rape," in S. Dunant (ed.), *The War of the Words* (London: Virago).

Griffin, S. (1971) "Rape: The All American Crime," *Ramparts* (September): 26–35.

Grubin, D. and Gunn, J. (1990) *The Imprisoned Rapist and Rape* (London: Dept of Forensic Psychiatry, Institute of Psychiatry).

Harrison, W. C. and Hood-Williams, J. (2002) *Beyond Sex and Gender* (London: Sage).

Hearn, J. (1996) "Is Masculinity Dead? A Critique of the Concept of Masculinity/Masculinities," in M. Mac an Ghaill (ed.), *Understanding Masculinities* (Buckingham: Open University Press).

Heidensohn, F. (1968) "The Deviance of Women: A Critique and an Enquiry," *British Journal of Sociology* 19/2.

Heidensohn, F. (1985) *Women and Crime* (London: Macmillan).

Heidensohn, F. (2002) "Gender and Crime," in M. Maguire, R. Morgan, and R. Reiner (eds.), *The Oxford Handbook of Criminology*, 3rd edn. (Oxford: Oxford University Press).

Henriques, J., Hollway, W., Urwin, C., Venn, C., and Walkerdine, V. (1984/1998) *Changing the Subject: Psychology, Social Regulation and Subjectivity* (London: Methuen/Routledge).

Hirschi, T. (1969) *Causes Of Delinquency* (Berkeley: University of California Press).

Hollway, W. (1981) "'I Just Wanted to Kill a Woman.' Why?: The Ripper and Male Sexuality," *Feminist Review* 9: 33–40.

Hollway, W. (1989) *Subjectivity and Method in Psychology: Gender, Meaning and Science* (London: Sage).

Hollway, W. and Jefferson, T. (1996) "PC or not PC: Sexual Harassment and the Question of Ambivalence," *Human Relations* 49/3: 373–93.

Hollway, W. and Jefferson, T. (1998) "'A Kiss is just a Kiss': Date Rape, Gender and Subjectivity," *Sexualities* 1/4: 405–23.

Hollway, W. and Jefferson, T. (2000) *Doing Qualitative Research Differently: Free Association, Narrative and the Interview Method* (London: Sage).

Holmes, R. M. and De Burger, J. (1988) *Serial Murder* (London: Sage).

Hood-Williams, J. (2001) "Gender, Masculinities and Crime: From Structures to Psyches," *Theoretical Criminology* 5/1: 37–60.

Jackson, D. (1990) *Unmasking Masculinity: A Critical Autobiography* (London: Unwin Hyman).

Jackson, D. (1995) *Destroying the Baby in Themselves: Why Did the Two Boys Kill James Bulger?* (Nottingham: Mushroom Publications).

Jackson, D. and Pratt, S. (2001) "The Fear of Being Seen as White Losers," *Education and Social Justice* 3/2: 25–9.

Jefferson, T. (1994) "Theorising Masculine Subjectivity," in T. Newburn and E. A. Stanko (eds.), *Just Boys Doing Business? Men, Masculinities and Crime* (London: Routledge).

Jefferson, T. (1996a) "From 'Little Fairy Boy' to 'the Compleat Destroyer': Subjectivity and Transformation in the Biography of Mike Tyson," in M. Mac an Ghaill (ed.), *Understanding Masculinities: Social Relations and Cultural Arenas* (Buckingham: Open University Press).

Jefferson, T. (1996b) "'Tougher than the Rest': Mike Tyson and the Destructive Desires of Masculinity," *Arena Journal* 6: 89–105.

Jefferson, T. (1996c) "The James Bulger Case: A Review Essay," *British Journal of Criminology* 36/2: 319–23.

Jefferson, T. (1997a) "Masculinities and Crimes," in M. Maguire, R. Morgan, and R. Reiner (eds.), *The Oxford Handbook of Criminology*, 2nd edn. (Oxford: Clarendon Press).

Jefferson, T. (1997b) "The Tyson Rape Trial: The Law, Feminism and Emotional Truth," *Social and Legal Studies* 6/2: 281–301.

Jefferson, T. (1998) "Review of *Our Guys: The Glen Ridge Rape Case and the Secret Life of the Perfect Suburb* (1997) by B. Lefkowitz," *British Journal of Criminology* 38/2: 329–30.

Jefferson, T. (1999) "Review of *Public Heroes, Private Felons* and *Athletes and Acquaintance rape* (1998) both by J. Benedict," *British Journal of Criminology* 39/2: 329–31.

Jefferson, T. (2002a) "Subordinating Hegemonic Masculinity," *Theoretical Criminology* 6/1: 63–88.

Jefferson, T. (2002b) "For a Psychosocial Criminology," in K. Carrington and R. Hogg (eds.), *Critical Criminology: Issues, Debates, Challenges* (Cullompton, Devon: Willan).

Kersten, J. (1996) "Culture, masculinities and violence against women," in T. Jefferson and P. Carlen (eds.), *Masculinities, Social Relations and Crime*, Special Issue of *British Journal of Criminology* 36/3: 381–95.

Layton, L. (1998) *Who's That Girl? Who's That Boy? Clinical Practice Meets Postmodern Gender Theory* (Northvale, NJ: Jason Aronson).

Lees, S. (1996) *Carnal Knowledge: Rape on Trial* (London: Hamish Hamilton).

Lees, S. and Gregory, J. (1995) *Rape and Sexual Assault: A Study of Attrition* (London: Islington Council).

Lefkowitz, B. (1997) *Our Guys: The Glen Ridge Rape Case and the Secret Life of the Perfect Suburb* (Berkeley: University of California Press).

Leonard, E. B. (1982) *Women, Crime and Society: A Critique of Criminology Theory* (New York: Longman).

Lester, D. (1995) *Serial Killers: The Insatiable Passion* (Philadelphia, PA: The Charles Press).

Levin, J. and Fox, J. A. (1985) *Mass Murder: America's Growing Menace* (New York: Plenum).

Levine, S. and Koenig, J. (eds.) (1983) *Why Men Rape* (London: Stag).

Lombroso, C. and Ferrero, W. (1895) *The Female Offender* (London: T. Fisher Unwin).

MacInnes, J. (1998) *The End of Masculinity: The Confusion of Sexual Genesis and Sexual Difference in Modern Society* (Buckingham: Open University Press).

MacKinnon, C. (1994) "Rape, Genocide, and Women's Human Rights," in A. Stiglmayer (ed.), *Mass Rape: The War Against Women in Bosnia-Herzegovina* (Lincoln: University of Nebraska Press).

Mead, G. H. (1934) *Mind, Self and Society* (Chicago: University of Chicago Press).

Messerschmidt, J. (1993) *Masculinities and Crime* (Maryland: Rowman and Littlefield).

Messerschmidt, J. (1997) *Crime as Structured Action: Gender, Race, Class and Crime in the Making* (Thousand Oaks, CA: Sage).

Messerschmidt, J. (2000) *Nine Lives: Adolescent Masculinities, the Body and Violence* (Boulder, CO: Westview).

Minsky, R. (1996) *Psychoanalysis and Gender: An Introductory Reader* (London: Routledge).

Minsky, R. (1998) *Psychoanalysis and Culture: Contemporary States of Mind* (Cambridge: Polity).

Nikolic-Ristanovic, V. (1996a) "Domestic Violence Against Women in the Conditions of War," in C. Sumner, M. Israel, M. O'Connell, and R. Sarre (eds.), *International Victimology* (Canberra: Australian Institute of Criminology).

Nikolic-Ristanovic, V. (1996b) "War and Violence against Women," in J. Turpin and L. Lorsentzen (eds.), *The Gendered New World Order: Militarism, Development and the Environment* (New York: Routledge).

Oakley, A. (1972) *Sex, Gender and Society* (London: Temple Smith).

Paglia, C. (1992) *Sex, Art, and American Culture* (New York: Vintage).

Parsons, T. and Bales, R. F. (1956) *Family Socialization and Interaction Process* (London: Routledge and Kegan Paul).

Phillips, L. M. (2000) *Flirting with Danger: Young Women's Reflections on Sexuality and Domination* (New York: New York University Press).

Polk, K. (1994) *When Men Kill: Scenarios of Masculine Violence* (Cambridge: Cambridge University Press).

Pollock-Byrne, J. (1990) *Women, Prison and Crime* (Belmont, CA: Wadsworth).

Radford, J. and Russell, D. E. H. (eds.) (1992) *Femicide: The Politics of Women Killing* (Buckingham: Open University Press).

Richards, B. (1994) *Disciplines of Delight: The Psychoanalysis of Popular Culture* (London: Free Association Books).

Roiphe, K. (1994) *The Morning After: Sex, Fear and Feminism on Campus* (New York: Little Brown & Co.).

Rustin, M. (1991) *The Good Society and the Inner World: Psychoanalysis, Politics and Culture* (London: Verso).

Rustin, M. (1995) "Lacan, Klein and Politics: The Positive and Negative in Psychoanalytic Thought," in A. Elliott and S. Frosh (eds.), *Psychoanalysis in Contexts: Paths Between Theory and Modern Cultures* (London: Routledge).

Scully, D. (1990) *Understanding Sexual Violence: A Study of Convicted Rapists* (Boston: Unwin Hyman).

Segal, L. (1999) *Why Feminism? Gender, Psychology, Politics* (Cambridge: Polity).

Sereny, G. (1972) *The Case of Mary Bell* (London: Arrow; republished 1995, London: Pimlico).

Smart, C. (1976) *Women, Crime and Criminology* (London: Routledge and Kegan Paul).

Smith, D. J. (1994) *The Sleep of Reason: The James Bulger Case* (London: Century).

Smith, J. (1989) "There's only one Yorkshire Ripper," in J. Smith, *Misogynies* (London: Faber).

Taylor, C. (2001) "The Relationship Between Social and Self-control: Tracing Hirschi's Criminological Career," *Theoretical Criminology* 5/3: 369–88.

Theweleit, K. (1987) *Male Fantasies*. Vol. 1: *Women, Floods, Bodies, History* (Cambridge: Polity).

Theweleit, K. (1989) *Male Fantasies*. Vol. 2: *Male Bodies: Psychoanalysing the White Terror* (Cambridge: Polity).

Walklate, S. (2001) *Gender, Crime and Criminal Justice* (Cullompton, Devon: Willan).

Ward Jouve, N. (1988) *"The Street-Cleaner": The Yorkshire Ripper Case on Trial* (London: Marion Boyars).

West, D. (1987) *Sexual Crimes and Confrontations* (Aldershot: Gower).

West, C. and Zimmerman, D. H. (1987) "Doing Gender," *Gender and Society* 1/2: 125–51.

Wetherell, M. and Edley, N. (1999) "Negotiating Hegemonic Masculinity: Imaginary Positions and Psycho-discursive Practices," *Feminism and Psychology* 9/3: 335–56.

Whitehead, S. (1999) "Review Article: Hegemonic Masculinity Revisited," *Gender, Work and Organization* 6/1: 58–62.

Whitehead, S. (2002) *Men and Masculinities: Key Themes and New Directions* (Cambridge: Polity).

Yallop, D. A. (1981) *Deliver us From Evil* (London: Macdonald Futura).

PART FOUR

Nonconformity

CHAPTER SIXTEEN

Science and Technology

Sandra Harding

Introduction

The method of Western modern sciences was supposed to generate value-neutral, objective, disinterested facts about nature's order. Yet feminist analyses have shown how these methods and facts have been permeated by gendered values and interests. To be sure, this is so to different degrees and in different ways for different sciences.[1] Nevertheless, standard ways of conceptualizing and practicing scientific method appear to leave research incapable of achieving cultural neutrality in principle, not just in practice. Moreover, gender analyses have shown how in at least some research contexts cultural neutrality is undesirable; culture is also productive of knowledge, not just an obstacle to it. Who does science can influence what we will know about the world.

This work has been immensely controversial from the very beginning. One reason is that Western modern sciences and technologies (WMST) and their logics are central to ideals of modernity, democracy, progress, and "civilization." These ideals help to constitute individuals' and social institutions' identities and conceptions of what are legitimate and important missions. Challenges to these ideals on behalf of women can appear impertinent, arrogant, and wrongheaded, and even deeply disturbing. Yet these gender perspectives on science have become increasingly influential, shaping even national and international policy agendas in such areas as health, the environment, science education, and third world development policies. In this way they have become a significant force in current renegotiations of ideals of modernity, democracy, progress, and "civilization."

Scientific and technological change is always a site for political struggle. Which groups will receive the benefits and which will bear the costs of such changes? Moreover, when gender relations are renegotiated, other significant kinds of social relation are always also at issue – such as class, race, sexuality, and empire. Thus gender perspectives on scientific and technological change always have implications for such other social struggles.

In this chapter, I will identify central themes from the European and North American accounts and from accounts that start off from women's lives in the so-called developing world (from the North and the South[2]). The concluding section proposes clues to several directions that future work in these fields may well pursue.

One note of caution before turning to these projects. There is no single, monolithic feminism or, thus, preferred way to do gender analyses. The terms "feminism" and "gender" both have diverse meanings and uses, and the choices of when to use which term and what to mean by it are always controversial. As a start, we can note that "gender" can be used in two ways. It can refer to the objects of empirical study that are "out there" prior to inquirers' observation of them, that is to men and women and to gendered structural and symbolic social relations, or to the analytic framework that researchers bring to their inquiries – to the study of how gendered individuals, social structures, and systems of meaning are socially produced. Both foci have been important to Feminist Science and Technology Studies. As indicated, in both cases gender should be understood as being always in a mutually constituting relationship with class, race, ethnicity, sexuality, and other structural and symbolic social systems.

Northern Feminist Science and Technology Studies (STS)

In Europe and the United States these analyses have been produced under the influence of more than three decades of the women's movement and, during the same period, of post-positivist social studies of science and technology. The latter have sought to display the integrity of moments in modern science's past with their social eras instead of only with their intellectual histories, as historian Thomas Kuhn (1970) put the point. Thus feminist analyses show how modern sciences have been integrated with the gender relations of their historic eras. The focus here will be on identifying a few main themes within five topics that have proved especially fruitful, if disheartening: sexist and androcentric discrimination through the processes and results of scientific research, sciences' social structures, science education, technology design, and in epistemologies and philosophies of science.

Scientific Sexism

Our Bodies, Ourselves: The Boston Women's Health Guide was published in 1970. This pioneering start to the women's health movement revealed the ignorance that had directed physicians' interactions with patients as well as policies of the medical-industrial complex. Contrary to conventional warnings about the bad effects of politics on the growth of knowledge, it took a coalition of feminist scientists and political activists to launch this new focus of research. Evidently, some kinds of politics can advance the growth of knowledge.[3] At the same time, feminist biologists began to criticize sociobiology's claims about the naturalness of women's subordination to male domination. One group organized "genes and gender" programs at annual meetings of the American Association for the Advancement of Science, and produced some of the first readers on gender and science (Tobach and Rosoff 1978, 1979, 1981, 1984). Feminist biologists and the women's health movement have remained powerful forces in feminist Science Studies (Fausto-Sterling 1994).

Meanwhile, criticisms of sexist and androcentric methods and results of research in history and the social sciences had also begun to appear (Harding 1987). These provided resources for public policy struggles. For example, the US legal system was slowly forced to recognize the necessity of taking a feminist position on rape, domestic abuse, sexual harassment, women's "equal worth" at work, and the "rational woman" standard in liability cases. Social science research figured in struggles over lesbian mothers, "deadbeat dads," and wages or recompense for women's housework. Equally significant were the ways this work revealed the empirical and theoretical inadequacies of social theories in every discipline. Since the natural sciences have social histories, this work has also influenced gender-focused histories, sociologies, and philosophies of science and technology. It has even shaped studies of sciences one might presume to be most immune to cultural influences, such as physics and astronomy at the origins of modern science (Merchant 1980; Schiebinger 1989, 1993), Boyle's chemistry (Potter 2000), early twentieth-century physics and biology (Keller 1984), contemporary high-energy physics (Traweek 1988), and molecular biology (Spanier 1995).

Discriminatory Social Structures

Beginning in the nineteenth century, critics had decried discrimination against girls and women in the social structure of science, mathematics, medicine, and engineering (Rossiter 1982, 1995; Schiebinger 1989, 1993). These struggles were far from over in the 1970s. The formation of women's caucuses in natural and social science disciplines and of women's organizations in universities and in industry carried on these campaigns.

Today, when the formal barriers against women's access to science and engineering education, degrees, publication, lab appointments, and membership in scientific societies finally are illegal in Europe, the US, and many other parts of the world, it remains challenging to identify and then eliminate powerful continuing sources of discrimination.[4] The MIT Women and Science Report (Massachusetts Institute of Technology 1999) created shock waves in many elite science and engineering departments as it revealed the ways in which society's gender norms, including expectations of women's obligations to family, continue to discriminate in different ways against both senior and junior MIT women faculty. In the developing world, the lack of economic resources and social welfare services for families insures that girls' domestic obligations will cause them to drop out of school long before they could gain any science education or, for many, even achieve basic literacy. On the other hand, many countries outside the North have far higher proportions of women on science faculties and national science policy agencies than does the US or Western European nations. This isn't always the result of feminist activism. Instead, to understand the causes of such variation requires close attention to diverse factors, including national science and techno-logy policy, and different opportunities available to nations' science projects in the global political economy (Harding and McGregor 1996; Koblitz 1996).[5]

Science Education

Early equity approaches to remedying girls' and women's underrepresentation in the sciences and engineering assumed that girls and women were deficient in the abilities and talents necessary to compete for careers in these fields. They had "math anxiety," didn't like dissecting frogs, and were lacking in analytic skills. More recent work shifted the focus to deficiencies in pedagogy, curriculum, and the goals of both science and science education (Brickhouse 1994; Kelly 1981, 1987; Rosser 1986, 1993). Perhaps most illuminating has been the emergence of a critical focus on the masculinized culture of science and science education, and on how "doing science" is a way of constituting certain kinds of social identity. While the identities formed through doing science have conventionally been masculine ones, girls have also used their love of doing science to constitute distinctive feminine identities, and in different ways for girls of different racial and ethnic identities (Brickhouse 2001). This work on education offers resources to historians and sociologists of science more generally.

Meanwhile, there is reason to rejoice that equity efforts have paid off, at least in many science classrooms,[6] though little such success is yet visible in most fields of professional science education. Moreover, equity is just one of the goals of feminist work in science education.[7] For example, in a more comprehensive sense of the term, feminists have drawn attention to the "scientific illiteracy" of elites about the gender projects of scientific research and its various institutions, from science and technology museums to *National Geographic* and "Discovery" TV programs.

Gender and Technology

From the beginning of the women's movement in the 1970s, there were projects intended to gain access for women to technological skills and practices from which they had been excluded. For example, courses on car maintenance and on repairing household technologies were offered through the new women's centers. Women were encouraged to enter male territories in the construction trades and the emerging information technologies, as well as agriculture and engineering schools. Accounts of women inventors appeared.

But it took the arrival of social constructivist analyses in Technology Studies to open the way for deeper understandings of how technologies themselves were gendered. First, the object of study shifted from the nature of the "hardware" itself to the nature and processes of technological change, processes that are usually sites of interlocked class, race, empire, culture, and – yes – gender struggles, and thus participate in the emergence of new social formations. Second, such change was understood to have three components: changes in "hardware" (the conventional meaning of technology); changes in the skills required to design, use, and repair the hardware; and changes in the organization of labor with such skills. Who did and who didn't get to design, use, and repair cars, washing machines, and computers? Thus, third, explanations of technological change require attention to how class, race, culture, and gender projects of the larger social formations instigate technological change (Cockburn 1985; Noble 1995; Wajcman 1991). Moreover, scientific methods are themselves technologies of knowledge production. In this way, social aspects of technological change permeate sciences' cognitive, technical cores.[8]

Epistemological Androcentrism

Epistemologies of scientific knowledge have been presumed to be as culturally neutral as the physics and chemistry achievements that they try to explain. Yet it was normal scientific assumptions and practices through which sexist and androcentric accounts were legitimated as objective ones – as "good biology," sociology, or psychology. The very standards of science appear to be sexist and androcentric. Certainly, it is annoying to encounter overt and covert sexism in the behaviors of individual scientists. But these individual and intended behaviors are not the cause of the sexist and androcentric beliefs and practices identified above. Instead, it is institutional assumptions, practices, and cultures, larger social assumptions, and "civilizational" or philosophic standards that create and maintain the legitimacy of sexist and androcentric scientific accounts.[9] Feminists have had to revise and strengthen standards for the objectivity, rationality, and good methods of the sciences. Here I point to two such projects focused on objectivity and good methods.

How can a science maximize objectivity when the adequacy of its assumptions and practices is measured in terms of the latter's distance from "the feminine," from characteristics associated with women or femininity? Familiar exemplary logics of scientific research consistently prescribe the masculine side (first below) of a series of gendered dualisms: objectivity versus subjectivity, rationality versus irrationality and emotionality, mind versus matter or body, "hard" natural sciences versus "soft" social sciences.[10] Feminist scholars have produced critical accounts of such standards, and proposals for both overtly feminine and more effectively gender-neutral standards.[11]

Another focus has been to improve the exemplary methods, in the sense of epistemologies, of research. Feminist standpoint epistemologies are perhaps the most influential of these, emerging independently from sociologists of knowledge, political philosophers, and philosophers of science, and providing a comprehensive political/epistemological framework for thinking about what and how knowledge gets produced and legitimated (Collins 1999; Haraway 1991; Harding 1986, 1991, 1998; Hartsock 1983; Rose 1984; Smith 1987, 1990a, 1990b).[12] As a "rational reconstruction" it proposes that feminist research has succeeded in producing such empirically sound and theoretically more comprehensive analyses in natural and social sciences by starting off thinking about its projects "from women's lives" instead of from the dominant conceptual frameworks of the disciplines that are themselves grounded in the lives of those men who design and manage social institutions and their practices. It has insisted that all knowledge is "situated knowledge," in Haraway's phrase (1991). The disciplines are part of the apparatus of "ruling" in modern, Western kinds of societies, as sociologist Dorothy Smith (1987) puts the point. They work up the complex and confusing phenomena of daily life into categories and causal maps such that administrators can manage legal, economic, welfare, educational, medical, and other agencies and institutions. Women as well as men from exploited groups have been excluded from designing and managing both those institutions and the disciplinary projects that service them.

Thus the lives of women and of other exploited groups can continue to provide a valuable starting point or subject position from which research can be designed to reveal "the conceptual practices of power" in Smith's phrase (1990a). Note that though standpoint approaches start off from the lives of women and other exploited groups, their point is to "study up." What is distinctive about them is not that they study women, but that they provide "institutional ethnographies" of, for example, the legal mind (MacKinnon 1982), or disciplinary frameworks in sociology (Collins 1999; Smith 1987, 1990a, 1990b), political philosophy (Hartsock 1983), or medical/health research (Martin 1987).

In three decades, feminist critical perspectives on WMST have become significant players in more general projects of rethinking modernity, democracy, and social progress. Yet they remain Eurocentric and "part of the problem" for the majority of the world's citizens to the extent that they fail to engage with critical perspectives provided by multicultural and postcolonial science and technology studies, to which we now turn.

Southern Feminist Science and Technology Studies

Women in the South want from science much of what women in the North value, from improved access to appropriate science and technology education and work to better access to effective healthcare and workplace technologies, and to safe and flourishing natural environments (Braidotti et al. 1994; Gender Working Group 1995; Kettel 1995; Harding and McGregor 1996; Shiva 1989; Smith 1999). Moreover, WMST are tightly linked to ideals in the South, too, of modernity, democracy, and social progress. For many citizens of the South, as in the North, to get to think in the terms of modern, international sciences and engineering is to enter high status global conversations, to become citizens of the world. WMS methods and the facts they produce are often experienced as a welcome alternative to traditional discriminatory and just plain ineffectual beliefs and practices in the developing world.

Yet much Southern science and technology thinking, including feminist work, occurs in the context of three science and technology movements that emerged after World War II. These expand the horizons of everyone's understandings of sciences around the globe, and of the ideological and material conditions for the successes of WMST themselves. These are the comparative ethnoscience movement, the "science and empires" movement, and the postcolonial criticisms of Northern development policies, practices, and philosophies.[13]

The comparative ethnoscience movement has had two goals. One is to show the local, cultural features of European sciences and technologies by analyzing them with the methods anthropologists had developed to study the production of knowledge in non-Western societies. Undermining the "exceptionalist" assumption that only ignorance and false beliefs, not WMST's production of truths, were suitable objects for social explanation, these accounts insisted on methodological symmetry in the study of WMST and other local knowledge systems, as they put the point. In effect, they pursued on a postcolonial global map historian Thomas Kuhn's project of showing the integrity of moments in WMST with their historic eras.[14]

This project had the effect of beginning to level the playing field for evaluating achievements of Southern science and technology, which could no longer be devalued on the grounds that they alone contained cultural elements (Selin 1997). This project has sparked the creation of indigenous knowledge national ministries, conferences, and journals.[15] It has brought global attention to intellectual property rights for indigenous knowledge, and to the need to expand "real science" to include much more than Northern science studies have been willing to countenance.

This project also has drawn attention to ways that women have a distinctive standpoint on nature wherever women and men are assigned different interactions with their bodies and the world around them. Women, like men, become repositories of systematic, effective knowledge about nature developed through such interactions. This knowledge must constantly be revised as women's natural and social environments change – deserts expand, farmland is eroded, toxics permeate water and food supplies, new diseases spread, new ideas arrive on television or from culturally new neighbors or international agencies.

247

A second context for Southern feminist work is the "science and empires" movement among historians. A central focus here is the question of causal relations between the two great marks of modernity – the "Voyages of Discovery" and the emergence of modern sciences in Europe. These scholars demonstrated how each had required the success of the other for their own success. European expansion (the "Voyages") required the development of what we could call oceanography, climatology, and astronomy of the Southern Hemisphere in order for ships to reach the Americas and return to Europe. The Europeans also needed better cartography, and knowledge of the unfamiliar flora, fauna, and geology of the lands on which they wanted to settle and establish economically profitable enterprises. They needed knowledge of the threats to life and health and remedies to diseases that they encountered in the new lands. In turn, modern sciences needed the funding, support, and transportation that expansionist projects could provide. The systematic knowledge they developed responded to the needs of the advancing European empire. The systematic ignorance they produced alongside it was marked by disinterest in the needs of the indigenes they encountered, and in all but economic "development." Which leads us to the third movement, and the implications for women of all three science and technology studies movements.

By the 1990s it became clear that four decades of Northern development policies had produced only systematic mal- and de-development for precisely those peoples whose standard of living development was supposed to rise – the 70 percent or so of the world's most economically and politically vulnerable peoples living in the South. It was the "investing classes" in the North and their economically advantaged allies in the South who had benefited from these policies. From its origins, development was conceptualized as the transfer of Northern science and technology and their rationality to the South. So the failures of development began to reflect directly on limitations of Northern science and technology that had previously been virtually invisible to the North (Sachs 1992). Coalitions of Southern and Northern feminists worked through governmental and non-governmental organizations to draw attention to the fact that since women and their children are disproportionately represented in the politically and economically most vulnerable groups, development has increased the vulnerability of the vast majority of the world's women (Braidotti et al. 1994). European expansion had always been experienced as brutal conquest by the societies encountered by the Europeans in the Americas, Asia, Australia and the Pacific Islands, and Africa. However, feminist understandings of the effects of late twentieth-century "development" policies illuminated heretofore unforeseen effects on women of the "Voyages of Discovery." Today even the International Monetary Fund and the World Bank have come to recognize these effects. Must more WMST in a world of political and economic inequality continue to increase the gap between the "haves" and the "have-nots"?

Southern feminist approaches to science and technology have helped to create a new map for Northerners and their feminist concerns. However, the work of getting pro-democratic national and international responses to such concerns still lies ahead of us all.

What are other possible future directions for feminist work?

More Future Directions

One ongoing, difficult project has been to expand fruitful relations between these diverse feminist projects and the work of women scientists. Many of the researchers, scholars, and activists who have created feminist science and technology projects have brought their science expertise and concerns to this feminist work.

Nevertheless, for most scientists, women and men, the use of unfamiliar and suspect philosophy, social science, and humanities languages and conceptual frameworks, as well as of the intellectual and political assumptions of Southern feminists' projects, have seemed daunting and alienating. Yet National Science Foundation (NSF) and other national, regional, and now even international funders have been sponsoring projects that assist scientists in understanding and using the resources of the feminist STS literatures in teaching and in designing research projects. Two recent collections provide especially useful resources for such projects: Mayberry et al. 2001; Wyer et al. 2000. Especially interesting here is Weasel's analysis of how scientists could use the European "Science Shop" model, a kind of "pro bono" commitment, to organize scientific research responding to women's needs in local communities (Weasel 2001).

Another promising project is to follow the direction of Brickhouse's work to expand issues in science education beyond those of access. How do people learn science? What can be considered science for kindergarten through undergraduate college? How could learning to do science help to create citizens invested in both democratic sciences and democratic societies (Brickhouse 2001)?

Finally, the emergence of information technologies at the base of the global economy has only begun to come into focus in feminist science and technology analyses. The most obvious concern here is how to counter their being used to further disempower women at work (Balka and Smith 2000; Mitter, forthcoming). Another topic is the exploration of how problematic masculinity projects are developed through virtual reality activities. A third, barely conceptualized project is to understand the role that the emergence of the information society is playing in the "end of patriarchalism," the constitution of women's movements, and of new forms of family, reproduction, and sexuality (Castells 1997).

To conclude, feminist science and technology concerns have been gathering steam around the globe over more than three decades. As usual, when feminist frameworks are used to try to add women's and gender issues to the purportedly value-neutral conceptual frameworks and agendas of existing disciplines, institutions, and policy-making, the gendered dimensions and limitations of the latter become visible. Feminist science and technology projects, with all their diversity, uncertainties, and conflicts, will continue to provide valuable resources for pro-democratic social transformations.[16]

Notes

1 In the US, "science" unmodified refers to the natural sciences. Europeans use the term to cover both natural and social sciences, and even the insights of literature and the arts – it means knowledge. I shall focus here primarily on the natural sciences, with only occasional sidetrips into the social sciences.

2 The 1992 United Nations' Conference on Environment and Development in Rio de Janeiro produced in the media the language of "North" and "South" to replace the earlier "developed" versus "underdeveloped" and "first world" versus "third world" terminologies. The latter originated in US and European 1950s foreign relations policies, and the far older orientalist language of the "West" versus the rest. Of course, "North/South" is literally inaccurate (Japan is economically in the "North"; much of Eastern Europe, as well as "Northern" inner cities, are in the "South"). Moreover, any such dualism is inherently problematic, naturalizing a homogeneity within each category and an essential opposition between them in ways that are empirically unjustified, theoretically questionable, and politically problematic. However, I use this contrast strategically here to sketch out global patterns documented in the literature cited.

3 Environmental and AIDS research had a similar start-up pattern.

4 An internet search for "women in science and technology" will probably turn up half-a-dozen or more sites where such issues are discussed. These sites come and go: eight were running in January 1995; none of these was still operating in May 2001.

5 The Third World Organization for Women in Science (TWOWS) provides an important international network "supporting the advancement of girls and women in science and technology." It sponsors national chapters, conveys news of jobs, fellowships, workshops, conferences, on-line dialogues, etc. Electronic versions of its newsletter may be found at <http://www.ictp.trieste.it/~twas/twows.html>

6 Brickhouse reports: "Girls are as likely to be enrolled in some advanced high school science courses as boys (AAUW 1998) and are as numerous in some scientific college majors as boys (e.g. biology). Furthermore, sex differences in achievement are small or non-existent (Third International Mathematics and Science Study 1997)" (2001: 282).

7 Brickhouse (1998) provides a good review of an array of such issues.

8 In different ways, this was an insight of both Foucault and Kuhn. It is developed in Hacking (1983) and Rouse (1987).

9 Note that it is masculinity, not just femininity, that is the issue in these accounts. See Noble (1992, 1995) for two influential historical studies of the masculinity of modern sciences and technology.

10 Moreover, as we shall see the Southern STS point out, these standards were similarly measured in terms of their distance from whatever was thought of as "the primitive" – for example, magic, superstition, and ethnosciences, not to mention products of the "savage mind," in the memorable words of French anthropologist Levy-Bruhl (1910).

11 On these objectivity projects, see Harding (1991, 1998); Keller (1984); E. Lloyd (1996). On constitutive versus contextual scientific values, see Longino (1990). On rationality, see G. Lloyd (1984); Rooney (1994).

12 For interesting recent accounts see Garcia Selgas (forthcoming), and Rouse's evaluation (1996) of feminist philosophy of science more generally.

13 For an overview of these movements and their implications for philosophies of WMST, see Harding (1998). See also Braidotti et al. (1994); Haraway (1989); Harding (1993); Harding and McGregor (1996); Shiva (1989); Smith (1999); and UNCSTD (1996) for a diverse set of

feminist accounts that start off from the lives of women in the South. For influential writings from the three Southern STS movements that have shaped much of this feminist work, see Brockway (1979); Crosby (1987); Goonatilake (1984, 1992); Headrick (1981); Hess (1995); Joseph (1991); Kaptchuk (1983); Kumar (1991); Lach (1977); McClellan (1992); Nandy (1990); Needham (1954ff, 1969); Petitjean (1992); Sabra (1976); Sachs (1992); Selin (1997); Watson-Verran and Turnbull (1995); Weatherford (1988).

14   Three influential such accounts were Latour and Woolgar's (1979) study of the production of truth in a biochemical laboratory; Donna Haraway's (1989) study of the merging of functionalism in biology and sociology in primatology studies at the Yerkes Labs in Atlanta in the context of prison, military, and industrial concerns for controling the behaviors of captive populations; and Sharon Traweek's (1988) comparative study of the practices of Japanese and US/European high-energy physics.

15   See especially the Indigenous Knowledge and Development Monitor: <http://www.nufficcs.nl/ciran/ikdm/>

16   My thanks to Katherine Ann Muir for her assistance in the preparation of this essay.

References

American Association of University Women (1998) *Gender Gap: Where Schools Still Fail Our Children* (New York: Marlowe & Company).

Balka, E. and Smith, R. (2000) *Women, Work and Computerization* (Boston: Kluwer).

Boston Women's Health Book Collective (1970) *Our Bodies, Ourselves*.

Braidotti, R., Charkiewicz, E., Hausler, S., and Wieringa, S. (1994) *Women, the Environment, and Sustainable Development* (Atlantic Highlands, NJ: Zed Books).

Brickhouse, N. (1994) "Bringing in the Outsiders: Reshaping the Sciences of the Future," *Journal of Curriculum Studies* 26/4: 401–16.

Brickhouse, N. (2001) "Embodying Science: A Feminist Perspective on Learning," *Journal of Research in Science Teaching* 38/3: 282–95.

Brickhouse, N. (1998) "Feminism and Science Education," in B. J. Fraser and K. G. Tobin (eds.), *International Handbook of Science Education* (Boston: Kluwer).

Brockway, L. H. (1979) *Science and Colonial Expansion: The Role of the British Royal Botanical Gardens* (New York: Academic Press).

Castells, M. (1997) "The End of Patriarchalism: Social Movements, Family, and Sexuality in the Information Age," in *The Information Age: Economy, Society and Culture*, vol. 2: *The Power of Identity* (Oxford: Blackwell Publishers).

Cockburn, C. (1985) *Machinery of Dominance: Women, Men, and Technical Know-How* (London: Pluto Press).

Collins, P. H. (1999) *Black Feminist Thought: Knowledge, Consciousness, and the Politics of Empowerment* (New York: Routledge).

Crosby, A. (1987) *Ecological Imperialism: The Biological Expansion of Europe* (Cambridge: Cambridge University Press).

Fausto-Sterling, A. (1994) *Myths of Gender: Biological Theories about Women and Men* (New York: Basic).

Garcia Selgas, F. (forthcoming) "From Standpoint Theory to Situated Knowledge: Feminist Epistemology for Critical Social Theory in Postmodernity."

Gender Working Group, UN Commission on Science and Technology for Development (1995) *Missing Links: Gender Equity in Science and Technology for Development* (Ottawa: International Development Research Centre).

Goonatilake, S. (1984) *Aborted Discovery: Science and Creativity in the Third World* (London: Zed Books).

Goonatilake, S. (1992) "The Voyages of Discovery and the Loss and Rediscovery of the 'Other's' Knowledge," *Impact of Science on Society* 167: 241–64.

Hacking, I. (1983) *Representing and Intervening* (Cambridge: Cambridge University Press).

Haraway, D. (1989) *Primate Visions: Gender, Race, and Nature in the World of Modern Science* (New York: Routledge).

Haraway, D. (1991) "Situated Knowledges: The Science Question in Feminism and the Privilege of Partial Perspectives," in *Simians, Cyborgs, and Women* (New York: Routledge).

Harding, S. (2001) "After Absolute Neutrality: Expanding 'Science'," in Maralee Mayberry, Banu Subramaniam, and Lisa Weasel (eds.), *A New Generation of Feminist Science Studies* (New York: Routledge).

Harding, S. (ed.) (1987) *Feminism and Methodology: Social Science Issues* (Bloomington: Indiana University Press).

Harding, S. (1998) *Is Science Multicultural? Postcolonialisms, Feminisms, and Epistemologies* (Bloomington: Indiana University Press).

Harding, S. (1986) *The Science Question in Feminism* (Ithaca: Cornell University Press).

Harding, S. (ed.) (1993) *The "Racial" Economy of Science: Toward a Democratic Future* (Bloomington: Indiana University Press).

Harding, S. (1991) *Whose Science? Whose Knowledge? Thinking From Women's Lives* (Bloomington: Indiana University Press).

Harding, S. and McGregor, E. (1996) "The Gender Dimension of Science and Technology," in Howard J. Moore (ed.), *UNESCO World Science Report* (Paris: UNESCO).

Hartsock, N. (1983) "The Feminist Standpoint: Developing the Ground for a Specifically Feminist Historical Materialism," in Sandra Harding and Merrill Hintikka (eds.), *Discovering Reality: Feminist Perspectives on Epistemology, Metaphysics, Methodology, and Philosophy of Science* (Dordrecht: Reidel/Kluwer).

Headrick, D. R. (ed.) (1981) *The Tools of Empire: Technology and European Imperialism in the Nineteenth Century* (New York: Oxford University Press).

Hess, D. J. (1995) *Science and Technology in a Multicultural World: The Cultural Politics of Facts and Artifacts* (New York: Columbia University Press).

Joseph, G. G. (1991) *The Crest of the Peacock: Non-European Roots of Mathematics* (New York: I. B. Tauris).

Kaptchuk, T. J. (1983) *The Web That Has No Weaver: Understanding Chinese Medicine* (New York: Congdon and Weed).

Keller, E. F. (1984) *Reflections on Gender and Science* (New Haven: Yale University Press).

Kelly, A. (ed.) (1981) *The Missing Half: Girls and Science Education* (Manchester: Manchester University Press).

Kelly, A. (ed.) (1987) *Science for Girls?* (Philadelphia: Open University Press).

Kettel, B. (1995) "Key Paths for Science and Technology: On the Road to Environmentally Sustainable and Equitable Development," in Gender Working Group, UN Commission on Science and Technology for Development, *Missing Links: Gender Equity in Science and Technology for Development* (Ottawa: International Development Research Centre), pp. 27–54.

Kirkup, G., Janes, L., Woodward, K., and Hovenden, F. (eds.) (2000) *The Gendered Cyborg: A Reader* (London: Routledge).

Koblitz, A. H. (1996) "Challenges in Interpreting Data," in Sandra Harding and Elizabeth McGregor, "The Gender Dimension of Science and Technology," in Howard J. Moore (ed.), *UNESCO World Science Report* (Paris: UNESCO), pp. 27–8.

Kuhn, T. S. (1970) *The Structure of Scientific Revolutions*, 2nd edn. (Chicago: University of Chicago Press).

Kumar, D. (1991) *Science and Empire: Essays in Indian Context (1700–1947)* (Delhi, India: Anamika Prakashan and National Institute of Science, Technology, and Development).

Lach, D. F. (1977) *Asia in the Making of Europe*, vol. 2 (Chicago: University of Chicago Press).

Latour, B. and Woolgar, S. (1979) *Laboratory Life: The Social Construction of Scientific Facts* (Beverly Hills, CA: Sage).

Levy-Bruhl, E. G. L. (1910) *Les Fonctions mentales dans les sociétés inférieures* (Paris: Presses Universitaires de France), trans. as *How Natives Think* (London: Allen and Unwin, 1926).

Lloyd, E. (1996) "Science and Anti-Science: Objectivity and its Real Enemies," in Lynn Hankinson Nelson and Jack Nelson (eds.), *Feminism, Science, and the Philosophy of Science* (Dordrecht: Kluwer).

Lloyd, G. (1984) *The Man of Reason: "Male" and "Female" in Western Philosophy* (Minneapolis: University of Minnesota Press).

Longino, H. (1990) *Science as Social Knowledge* (Princeton: Princeton University Press).

MacKinnon, C. (1982) "Feminism, Marxism, Method, and the State: An Agenda for Theory," *Signs* 7: 3.

Martin, E. (1987) *The Woman in the Body A Cultural Analysis of Reproduction* (Boston: Beacon Press).

Massachusetts Institute of Technology (1999) *A Study on the Status of Women Faculty in Science at MIT*. Available online at <http://web.mit.edu/fnl/women/women.html>

Mayberry, M., Subramaniam, B., and Weasel, L. (eds.) (2001) *A New Generation of Feminist Science Studies* (New York: Routledge).

McClellan, J. E. (1992) *Colonialism and Science: Saint Domingue in the Old Regime* (Baltimore: Johns Hopkins University Press).

Merchant, C. (1980) *The Death of Nature: Women, Ecology and the Scientific Revolution* (New York: Harper & Row).

Mitter, S. (forthcoming) "Europe and the Developing World in the Globalized Information Economy: Employment and Distance Education."

Nandy, A. (ed.) (1990) *Science, Hegemony and Violence* (Delhi: Oxford University Press).

Needham, J. (1954ff) *Science and Civilization in China*, 7 vols. (Cambridge: Cambridge University Press).

Needham, J. (1969) *The Grand Titration: Science and Society in East and West* (Toronto: University of Toronto Press).

Noble, D. (1992) *A World Without Women: The Christian Clerical Culture of Western Science* (New York: Knopf).

Noble, D. (1995) *The Religion of Technology* (New York: Knopf).

Petitjean, P., et al. (eds.) (1992) *Science and Empires: Historical Studies about Scientific Development and European Expansion* (Dordrecht: Kluwer).

Potter, E. (2001) *Gender and Boyle's Law of Gases* (Bloomington: Indiana University Press).

Rooney, P. (1994) "Recent Work in Feminist Discussions of Reason," *American Philosophical Quarterly* 31/1: 1–21.

Rose, H. (1984) *Love, Power, and Knowledge* (Bloomington: Indiana University Press).

Rosser, S. (1993) "Female Friendly Science: Including Women in Curricular Content and Pedagogy in Science," *The Journal of General Education* 42/3: 191–220.

Rosser, S. (1986) *Teaching Science and Health from a Feminist Perspective: A Practical Guide* (Elmsford: Pergamon Press).

Rossiter, M. (1982) *Women Scientists in America: Struggles and Strategies to 1940* (Baltimore: Johns Hopkins University Press).

Rossiter, M. (1995) *Women Scientists in America: Before Affirmative Action* (Baltimore: Johns Hopkins University Press).

Rouse, J. (1987) *Knowledge and Power: Toward a Political Philosophy of Science* (Ithaca, NY: Cornell University Press).

Rouse, J. (1996) "Feminism and the Social Construction of Scientific Knowledge," in Lynn Hankinson Nelson and Jack Nelson (eds.), *Feminism, Science, and the Philosophy of Science* (Dordrecht: Kluwer).

Sabra, I. A. (1976) "The Scientific Enterprise," in B. Lews (ed.), *The World of Islam* (London: Thames and Hudson).

Sachs, W. (ed.) (1992) *The Development Dictionary: A Guide to Knowledge as Power* (Atlantic Highlands, NJ: Zed Books).

Schiebinger, L. (1989) *The Mind Has No Sex? Women in the Origins of Modern Science* (Cambridge, MA: Harvard University Press).

Schiebinger, L. (1993) *Nature's Body: Gender in the Making of Modern Science* (Boston: Beacon).

Schiebinger, L. (1999) *Has Feminism Changed Science?* (Cambridge, MA: Harvard University Press).

Selin, H. (ed.) (1997) *Encyclopedia of the History of Science, Technology, and Medicine in Non-Western Cultures* (Dordrecht: Kluwer).

Shiva, V. (1989) *Staying Alive: Women, Ecology, and Development* (London: Zed Books).

Smith, D. E. (1987) *The Everyday World as Problematic: A Sociology for Women* (Boston: Northeastern University Press).

Smith, D. E. (1990a) *The Conceptual Practices of Power: A Feminist Sociology of Knowledge* (Boston: Northeastern University Press).

Smith, D. E. (1990b) *Texts, Facts, and Femininity: Exploring the Relations of Ruling* (New York: Routledge).

Smith, L. T. (1999) *Decolonizing Methodologies: Research and Indigenous Peoples* (London: University of Otago Press).

Spanier, B. (1995) *Im/partial Science: Gender Ideology in Molecular Biology* (Bloomington: Indiana University Press).

Third International Mathematics and Science Study Center (1997) *Science Achievement in the Primary School Years: IA's Third International Mathematics and Science Study*, ed. A. Beaton, et al.

Tobach, E. and Rosoff, B. (eds.) (1978, 1979, 1981, 1984) *Genes and Gender*, vols. 1–4 (New York: Gordian).

Traweek, S. (1988) *Beamtimes and Lifetimes* (Cambridge, MA: MIT Press).

UNCSTD (1995) (United Nations Commission on Science and Technology for Development Gender Working Group) *Missing Links: Gender Equity in Science and Technology for Development* (Ottawa: International Development Research Center).

Wajcman, J. (1991) *Feminism Confronts Technology* (University Park: Pennsylvania State University).

Watson-Verran, H. and Turnbull, D. (1995) "Science and Other Indigenous Knowledge Systems," in S. Jasanoff, G. Markle, T. Pinch, and J. Petersen (eds.), *Handbook of Science and Technology Studies* (Thousand Oaks, CA: Sage).

Weatherford, J. M. (1988) *Indian Givers: What the Native Americans Gave to the World* (New York: Crown).

Weasel, L. (2001) "Laboratories Without Walls: The 'Science Shop' as a Model for Feminist Community Science in Action," in Maralee Mayberry, Banu Subramaniam, and Lisa Weasel (eds.), *A New Generation of Feminist Science Studies* (New York: Routledge).

Wyer, M., et al. (eds.) (2000) *Women, Science, and Technology: A Feminist Reader* (New York: Routledge).

CHAPTER SEVENTEEN

Prostitution and Sex Work Studies

Kamala Kempadoo

Prostitution has been a persistent theme in the study of society since the nineteenth century, although it was only in the second half of the twentieth century that it fully entered social studies as a subject worthy of full academic consideration. In this chapter I identify four main approaches in social studies and research, according to assumptions and explanations about sexual and gender relations. I define the most recent approach as "Sex Work Studies." It is important to keep in mind that while each trend is presented as distinct, there are many overlaps, borrowings, and blendings that have occurred between them and with other ideas that are not described here. The approaches therefore should not be treated as discrete or autonomous, but rather can be read as trends in which a specific account of gender and sex dominate political, theoretical, and social work on prostitution at different periods in history.

Regulationism and Female Pathology: The Public Health Approach

The most evident social studies on prostitution date to the first part of the nineteenth century in Western Europe and the United States, where political, social, and economic conditions gave rise to studies of society directed by positivistic methods as used in the natural sciences, distinct from religion and philosophy. These studies rested heavily upon longer-standing patriarchal and Christian discourses of sex and gender, and the work by Parent-Duchalet (1836), Paul Lacroix (1851) and William Acton (1968; first published in 1858) became the cornerstones for social scientific understandings of prostitution. Of concern to the early nineteenth-century scientists was the spread of venereal disease, particularly syphilis, and of prostitution as a health threat to the social body. Prostitution was assumed to be a universal social phenomenon derived from an inherently promiscuous male nature, an inalienable masculine right to regular heterosexual intercourse, and women's innate disposition towards licentiousness.

These gendered "natures" were thought to be exacerbated by social and economic conditions of Western European and American urban life at the time. Prostitution, it was claimed, would never completely disappear, "since the vicious instincts to which it corresponds are, unfortunately, inborn in the human species" (Lacroix 1851: 2). Notions of sex as primal, irrational, uncontrollable, uncivilized, and sinful were foundational building blocks.

Extensive research was carried out to delineate "the problem," and tens of thousands of prostitutes were surveyed in urban centers. However, even though researchers argued that social conditions were of overriding importance in the constitution of the prostitute, and that prostitution was a vice that ruined women, threatened "purity and peace of community," destroyed female honor, and corrupted society "to the core," the studies unequivocally located women as the source of the problem. A stereotype of woman as the inevitable "whore" became firmly anchored in the approach.

While producing a scientific explanation for the social phenomenon of prostitution, this approach legitimized a double standard. On the one hand, prostitution was accorded a natural place in human societies and deemed a necessary and inevitable part of the social whole, within which a male demand for sex was taken for granted. On the other, women involved in prostitution were identified as social deviants who were to be carefully monitored and regulated in order that they did not disrupt public morality and health. "Promiscuous" sexual activity was deemed a male right, whereas women were condemned for similar behavior. Informed by such scientific approaches, state regulations of prostitutes were designed, specifying mandatory medical examinations of women in prostitution, seclusion or imprisonment of infected women, police supervision, and the creation of specific zones or sites where prostitution could be practiced. The social disease, or "pestilence," was to be contained by the state within decent and acceptable limits. Regulationism, while considerably eclipsed in the late nineteenth century in Western Europe, remained central to colonial regulations of sex and sexuality and informed state polices in various places around the world, as well as continuing within the context of studies of crime in Western European societies (Lombroso and Ferrero 1895; Pivar 1981; Stoler 1991).

While this approach to prostitution remained embedded in many state laws and policies throughout the twentieth century, it again became pronounced through various studies and programs on sexually transmitted disease and HIV/AIDS in the 1980s. De Zalduondo (1991) and Murray and Robinson (1996) note that in the new discourses on HIV/AIDS, women in prostitution are commonly stigmatized as "sexual deviants," "reservoirs of infection," and "vectors of disease." Female prostitutes, particularly in societies where HIV/AIDS is predominantly heterosexually transmitted, are again identified as a primary social problem, and are made the objects of practical intervention programs, state health regulations, and academic research initiatives. Often ignoring broader socioeconomic and political factors in the epidemiology of sexually transmitted infections and disease, as well as specific cultural constructions of sexual desire and gendered power, the close scrutiny and control of prostitutes, predominantly in non-Western and developing countries, tends to obscure the racialized and gendered implications of the approach. It is from prostitute organizations and critical feminist and social theorists that challenges to this nineteenth-century legacy have been produced (Hammonds 1997; NWSP 1998). Indeed, it is likely that through the intensified efforts on a world scale to control HIV/AIDS with the concomitant growing resistance from prostitutes to state regulation, stigmatization, and discrimination, such challenges continue in the twenty-first century.

Abolitionism: Victorian and Radical Feminist Perspectives

Whereas issues of female pathology and public health governed the regulation-ist approach, male power and dominance were the key concerns of a second framework that stressed the abolition of prostitution. This abolitionist frame-work first gained prominence during the latter part of the nineteenth century, and drew from Christianity for its vision of a moral society. Shaped by the politics of anti-slavery abolition movements and empowered by the woman's suffrage movement in both Europe and the United States, it also emerged within the context of the institutionalization of the nuclear, heterosexual family, and notions of sex as a biological duty for reproductive purposes. Colonial discourses of race formed the broader ideological backdrop for considerations of sex (Gilman 1986; McClintock 1995). With the medical profession producing evidence to support conceptions of different sexual needs and urges of men and women, ideas abounded that "special excitements and sexual intercourse too frequently repeated had pathological consequences" for women (Corbin 1990: 196). "Loose" and frequent sexual relations were defined not only as immoral but also as hazardous for women. However, given that some intercourse was considered a necessary function for women for the reproduction of family and nation, Victorian prostitution abolitionists did not advocate the complete disappearance of sex acts from society. Instead, non-marital manifestations were targeted for eradication, and state regulations and policies for the management of prostitution were contested.

Central to the articulation of the early abolitionists' perspective were the activities of an English woman, Josephine Butler, who laid the foundations for campaigns against prostitution and the traffic in women (Walkowitz 1983). It was the passing of the Contagious Disease Acts in the 1880s in England, designed to regulate the spread of venereal disease, that brought coherence and force to her view. Her feminist abolitionist crusade challenged the Acts, exposing and critiquing the male privilege encoded within them, and advocating a particular notion of domesticated, bourgeois womanhood. An integral part of the crusade was to rescue "fallen" women from vicious and degrading male practices and to assist them in taking up their "rightful" position in society as mothers and wives. Middle-class and elite women were viewed as "the moral guardians of the family and community," and prostitutes as victims of male privilege and power. In their insistence on protecting and defending helpless "daughters," an authoritative and custodial position of the middle-class feminist abolitionists was established in relationship to working-class women. Furthermore, analogous to the enslaved condition of Africans, "white slavery" was adopted by the abolitionists to refer to the denial of liberty to women. Underpinning this term was the idea that many white, European women were enticed, captured, enslaved, or forced into sexual servitude by non-Western, Black or Native American men of "immoral," "savage," and "barbaric" cultures (Grittner 1990; Guy 1991). The movement thus supported colonial projects that denounced the lack of Christian morals among non-Western peoples, and which called for civilizing efforts in non-European societies.

The nineteenth-century Victorian abolitionist perspective had a significant influence in international legislation during the first half of the twentieth century, which led to the creation of the 1949 United Nations Convention "For the Suppression of the Traffic in Persons and of the Exploitation of the Prostitution of Others." It also remains profoundly important to feminist conceptualizations of prostitution. In the 1970s, earlier abolitionist feminist definitions of prostitution as expressions of patriarchy and male violence to women were drawn upon and expanded by radical feminists. Kathleen Barry, for example, made popular the term "female sexual slavery" to refer to "all situations where women and girls cannot change the immediate conditions of their existence; where regardless of how they got into those conditions they cannot get out; and where they are subject to sexual violence and exploitation" (1984: 40). Sexual slavery, Barry determined, constituted the very essence of sexual and gender politics, with male dominance comprising the primary cause for this oppression. Struggles for the abolition of prostitution were thus re-emphasized. The notion of sexual slavery has been widely used around the world since then to describe and identify prostitution. In particular, it has been central to the retelling of the history of "Comfort Women," who were drafted from Korea, China, Taiwan, Indonesia, Thailand, the Philippines, and Japan to sexually service Japan's Imperial Army during the 1930s and 1940s. It has informed activities by international human rights agencies and women's non-governmental organizations around the world against forced prostitution and trafficking in women, and continues to be influential in the formulation of early twenty-first-century international conventions and policies on women and transnational crime.

While contemporary feminist abolitionists owe much to their nineteenth-century sisters, a marked difference lies in the shift of focus regarding the "victims" who are to be "saved," rescued, and rehabilitated. Whereas in the nineteenth century the casualties of male violence were defined as white, European, working-class women, in the latter part of the twentieth century, poor, third world, and non-Western women were identified as the primary helpless, passive victims of male domination and violence. Legacies of class inequalities and Western imperialism in this account of prostitution are yet to be fully addressed by advocates of this perspective.

From Classical Anthropology to the Prostitutes' Rights Movement

The saying that prostitution is the "oldest profession in the world" reflects a third approach in the study of prostitution. Claiming historical evidence of non-marital sexual relations in every society, culture, and civilization, this approach initially sought to describe a social practice as a universal human activity. Jamaican anthropologist Fernando Henriques was one of the first twentieth-century scholars to comprehensively document historical, contemporary, Western and non-Western forms of prostitution (1961, 1962, 1965). He defined prostitution as "sexual acts, including those which do not actually involve copulation, habitually performed by individuals with other individuals of their own or opposite sex, for a consideration which is non-sexual," showing that they existed throughout human history in a variety of contexts (1961: 17). His work identified two factors that were critical to the construction of prostitution through history: religion and marriage arrangements. These, he argued, determined social attitudes toward adultery, the domestic role of women, procreation, the transferal of property, and the expression of sexual passion, which shaped and conditioned the social value accorded to prostitution in any given time and place. Within specific contexts, "matriarchy," polygyny, and slavery were identified as additional factors that contributed to the structuring of prostitution. The universal appearance of prostitution identified by Henriques, and an emphasis on the cultural constructions of sexual desire and sexual relations, are echoed in the historical surveys of Bullough and Bullough (1987) and in more recent studies of male and transgender prostitution in various parts of the world (Aggleton 1999; Kulick 1998). The wide range of transactions, arrangements, and identities produced in and through prostitution relations are seen to complicate static or fixed notions of culture, and sexual and gender relations, and the approach insists upon fluid and culturally contextualized understandings of prostitution. This anthropological gaze offers rich descriptions of gender and sexual relations in diverse cultures and historical periods.

The premise of prostitution as a universal feature of human society has also been articulated by women working in the sex trade. Expressed in the politics of the twentieth-century prostitutes' rights movements in the United States and Western Europe, prostitution and other activities in sex industries, such as stripping, exotic dancing, and acting for adult films, are claimed as legitimate and respectable professions for women, parallel to many other occupations (Bell 1987; Delacoste and Alexander 1987; Jenness 1993; Pheterson 1989). Struggles ensuing from this perspective often center on liberal conceptions of individual

259

human and civil rights and freedoms, the right of occupational choice, decriminalization of prostitutes, destigmatization of the profession, and sex worker empowerment. This perspective challenges assumptions and representations of prostitutes as social deviants, victims, and sexual slaves, and locates the voices and experiences of women who work in various sectors of the sex industry as central to theoretical, political, and social projects. It is critical to making prostitution visible by the actors themselves, and for the articulation of a distinct prostitute identity (Bell 1994). Nevertheless, it has been critiqued for its encouragement of moral relativism and a liberal, reformist political agenda as well as its disregard for local and international relations of power and privilege around gender, ethnicity, culture, and the economy. Premised on notions of the objective and infinitely variable sex acts for purposes other than reproduction or love, prostitution is conceptualized as neither inherently socially devalued, nor as intrinsically oppressive to women. As a full- or part-time occupation, prostitution and other forms of sex work continue to be viewed as a consistent part of social life throughout history, and one that will continue.

Sexual Labor and the Emergence of Sex Work Studies

Ideas about prostitution as "sex work" were launched through the prostitutes' rights movement, and, together with feminist critiques of capitalism, patriarchy, and racism, gave rise to the most recent approach. First introduced by social activist Carol Leigh, in the late 1970s (Leigh 1997), and more fully elaborated theoretically by sociologists Than Dam Truong (1990) and Wendy Chapkis (1997), the idea of "sex work" captures not simply a profession or occupation, but also the organization and structuring of sexual and erotic labor through gendered, racial, and economic processes (see also Van de Veen 2001). Prostitution, as Truong argues, is not the only form of sexual labor that rests upon the employment and use of sexualized, eroticized bodies and energies, demonstrating little universal expression or meaning. Rather, it complements activities such as wet-nursing and "breeding" of black slaves in Plantation America, as well as exotic dancing, which also draw upon sexual energies and sexualized labor power in very specific social arrangements at different moments in history, and under specific material, cultural, and economic conditions. A historicized and contextualized account of the organization and meaning of sexual labor is thus crucial to this approach (O'Neill 2001). Also important here is the agency of people who trade sex. From the assumption that it is people who make social history, those who engage in sex work are taken as actors who, as in any other social arena, contribute to the shaping and remaking of social life. Nevertheless, with the understanding that under patriarchal and capitalist conditions female sexual labor is organized into specific commercial acts that commonly confirm hegemonic masculine power and the wider global economy, structural gendered exploitations and inequalities are understood as important parameters within which most prostitution activities and sex worker agency occur (Moon 1997; White 1990). Taking heed of structural inequalities within which the organization of sexual labor takes place, others have brought race and ethnic relations as well as issues of women's agency and multiple positionality more centrally into the analysis (Brock 1998; Kempadoo and Doezema 1998; Nencel 2001; O'Neill 2001; Shrage 1994; Thorbeck and Pattanaik 2002). By complicating the notion of prostitution through analyses of intersections of oppressions, exploitations, subjectivities, and resistances, and with attention to contradictions and ambiguities that arise from this matrix, these studies pose questions to earlier approaches that have explained prostitution as natural or universal, or as unidimensional outcomes of patriarchal power or capitalist economic relations. Taking gender to be mediated by race, class, and international relations, this perspective provides conceptual space and legitimacy for examinations of different positionalities and relations of power in the global sex trade, including those associated with tourism industries. Moreover, due to its focus on the organization of labor, it connects activities, identities, and political struggles of workers in sex industries to those of other women workers in local, national, and global economies, and disrupts discourses that distinguish between "good" and "bad" women on the basis of their economic and labor market activities. It also points to a continued need for feminist analyses to continue to examine colonial, imperial, and neocolonial histories in the construction of "the prostitute" and the global sex trade. Ongoing discussions and exchanges among scholars affiliated to academic institutions and activists in sex worker rights organizations in countries such as India, Thailand, the Dominican Republic, Brazil, South Africa, the USA, Canada, and the Netherlands ensures that this analysis in prostitution studies is lodged in concrete material conditions and lived experiences. Furthermore, much of this new direction supports the development of activities, research strategies, and policies of non-governmental organizations that deal with global and local realities of the sex trade, such as the Network for Sex Work Projects (NWSP), the Foundation Against Trafficking in Women (STV), and the Global Alliance Against Traffic in Women (GAATW). This intertwining of theory and praxis remains central to the new scholarship on prostitution, and provides the impetus not simply to produce new feminist academic studies, but, as importantly, also to contribute to political, gendered, grassroots struggles to challenge social injustices and to transform gendered and sexual relations of power.

Characteristic to this body of work is a high degree of cooperation between researchers and activists. This applies also to the naming of the field. At the International Women's Week conference, "The Business of Bodies: Women and the Global Sex Market" (University of Colorado-Boulder, March 6–8, 2002), we proposed the term "sex work studies" as a way of acknowledging the scope of our work. The idea was endorsed by a number of sex worker rights activists,

261

scholars, and students, who participated in the conference, and was also adopted in the conference resolution. Moreover, although not institutionalized as a specific program or field, the number of studies of the organization of sexual labor in and through sex industries and in various political, cultural, and economic contexts have proliferated since the late 1990s. Sex Work Studies is thus practiced widely today by academic researchers. Increasingly, these studies are linked conceptually to sexuality studies and to studies of gender in the global political economy and form part of various academic curricula and conferences in international relations, geography, economics, and also in labor, migration, women's, ethnic, and LGBT (lesbian, gay, bisexual, and transgender) studies.

Despite the specific conceptual framework that rests on theoretical assumptions of intersectionalities of gender, race, sexual, class, and international labor relations, an attachment to a historical materialist analysis, and the centrality of agency to the theorization of the sex trade, the notion of Sex Work Studies often embraces work that exclusively centers on prostitutes' rights and agency. Furthermore, the academic "politics of silence" on the subjectivity of sex workers of the global South is being gradually broken. The emphasis on labor that initially dominated studies of the global sex trade in the 1990s is complicated by interrogations of expressions of sexual desire and social identities of people who work in the global sex trade, and of relations that are not strictly tied to economic activities and which involve intimate emotional attachments, such as "transactional sex" or "romance tourism." Fueled by research and activism around male and transgender sex work, as well as questions about female heterosexuality, some sex work researchers have thus begun to probe the ways in which sex work activities infuse meanings of sexuality. As Sex Work Studies gains more momentum, it can be expected that sex worker agency and sexual subjectivity will continue to be empirically explored and theoretically elaborated.

Critique that is leveled at researchers who conduct Sex Work Studies is that they produce scholarship that supports women's subordination and lack a comprehensive theoretical account of prostitution. Both points derive from a feminist perspective that is wedded to a notion of a grand, singular theory to explain the oppression of women, and which depends upon an homogenizing, fixed, and ahistorical understanding of male dominance and constructions of sexuality and gender. However, it has also been noted by some of the same critics that the type of substantive research and theorizing reflected in recent Sex Work Studies is central to a critical dialogue within feminism, for it recognizes the need for a "more complex, nuanced, and relational vision of gendered power" and "invites examination of the contradictory and conflictual ways gender, race, and class come into existence in and through relation to each other" (Brace and O'Connell Davidson 2000: 1047). Epistemological differences that have been only marginally addressed in feminist work on the subject of prostitution, such as suggested here, may thus take on greater significance in the future and could clarify the debate further.

From its grounding in sex workers' lived experiences and politics of resistance and in its adherence to a feminist theoretical framework that takes as a starting point the intersection of gender with other categories around which social relations and power are organized, Sex Work Studies holds the potential to simultaneously support struggles against gendered oppressions and further feminist theory. The theoretical and political thrust of this new field of study stands to be more fully articulated and realized as, under the intensification of a neoliberal global political economy, systemic inequalities of wealth and power along gendered, ethnic, racialized, and national axes become more marked, and the sex trade takes on greater or even more varied proportions. As sex work becomes a basis of livelihood for increasingly more women and men under new global arrangements, and struggles against the oppression and discrimination of sex workers become more visible, it is thus also likely that many more transnational, postcolonial, and other critical feminist and anti-racist scholars will continue to find ways to research and theorize intersections between sexuality and economic life.

References

Acton, W. (1968) *Prostitution*, ed. Peter Fryer (New York; originally published in 1858).

Aggleton, P. (ed.) (1999) *Men Who Sell Sex: International Perspectives on Male Prostitution and HIV/AIDS* (Philadelphia: Temple University Press).

Barry, K. (1984) *Female Sexual Slavery* (New York and London: New York University Press).

Bell, L. (ed.) (1987) *Good Girls, Bad Girls: Feminists and Sex Trade Workers Face to Face* (Toronto: Seal Press).

Bell, S. (1994) *Reading Writing and Rewriting the Prostitute Body* (Bloomington: Indiana University Press).

Brace, L. and O'Connell Davidson, J. (2000) "Minding the Gap: General and Substantive Theorizing on Power and Exploitation," *Signs: Journal of Women in Culture and Society* 25/4: 1043–50.

Brock, D. R. (1998) *Making Work, Making Trouble: Prostitution as a Social Problem* (Toronto: University of Toronto Press).

Bullough, V. and Bullough, B. (1987) *Women and Prostitution: A Social History* (New York: Prometheus Press).

Chapkis, W. (1997) *Live Sex Acts: Women Performing Erotic Labor* (New York: Routledge).

Corbin, A. (1990) *Women for Hire: Prostitution and Sexuality in France After 1850* (Cambridge, MA: Harvard University Press).

Delacoste, F. and Alexander, P. (1987) *Sex Work: Writings by Women in the Sex Industry* (Pittsburgh: Cleis Press).

de Zalduondo, B. O. (1991) "Prostitution Viewed Cross-culturally: Toward Recontextualizing Sex Work in AIDS Intervention Research," *Journal of Sex Research* 28: 223–48.

Gilman, S. (1986) "Black Bodies, White Bodies: Toward an Iconography of Female Sexuality in Late Nineteenth Century Art, Medicine and Literature," in Henry Louis Gates Jr. (ed.), *"Race," Writing and Difference* (Chicago: University of Chicago Press).

Grittner, F. K. (1990) *White Slavery: Myth, Ideology and American Law* (New York: Garland).

Guy, D. J. (1991) *Sex and Danger in Buenos Aires: Prostitution, Family, and Nation in Argentina* (Lincoln: University of Nebraska Press).

Hammonds, E. M. (1997) "Toward a Genealogy of Black Female Sexuality: The Problematic of Silence," in M. Jacqui Alexander and Chandra Talpade Mohanty (eds.), *Feminist Genealogies, Colonial Legacies, Democratic Futures* (New York: Routledge).

Henriques, F. (1961) *Stews and Strumpets: A Survey of Prostitution* (London: MacGibbon and Kee).

Henriques, F. (1962) *Prostitution and Society: Primitive, Classical and Oriental* (London: MacGibbon and Kee).

Henriques, F. (1965) *Prostitution in Europe and the Americas* (New York: Citadel Press).

Jenness, V. (1993) *Making it Work: The Prostitutes' Rights Movement in Perspective* (Hawthorne, New York: Aldine de Gruyter).

Kempadoo, K. and Doezema, J. (eds.) (1998) *Global Sex Workers: Rights, Resistance, and Redefinition* (New York: Routledge).

Kulick, D. (1998) *Travesti: Sex, Gender, and Culture and Brazilian Transgendered Prostitutes* (Chicago and London: University of Chicago Press).

Lacroix, P. (1851) *History of Prostitution* (New York: Covici Friede Publishers).

Leigh, C. (1997) "Inventing Sex Work," in Jill Nagle (ed.), *Whores and Other Feminists* (New York: Routledge).

Lombroso, C. and Ferrero, G. (1895) *The Female Offender: The Normal Woman and the Prostitute* (London: Fisher Unwin).

McClintock, A. (1995) *Imperial Leather: Race, Gender and Sexuality in the Colonial Contest* (New York: Routledge).

Moon, K. H. S. (1997) *Sex Among Allies: Military Prostitution in US–Korea Relations* (New York: Columbia University Press).

Murray, A. and Robinson, T. (1996) "Minding your Peers and Queers: female sex workers in the AIDS discourse in Australia and South-east Asia," *Gender, Place and Culture* 3/1: 43–59.

Nencel, L. (2001) *Ethnography and Prostitution in Peru* (London: Pluto Press).

NWSP (1998) *Making Sex Work Safe: A Practical Guide for Programme Managers, Policy-Makers and Field Workers* (London: Network of Sex Work Projects).

O'Neill, M. (2001) *Prostitution and Feminism: Towards a Politics of Feeling* (Cambridge: Polity).

Parent-Duchalet, A. (1836) *Policing Prostitution in Nineteenth Century Paris* (Paris: Bailliere).

Pheterson, G. (ed.) (1989) *A Vindication of the Rights of Whores* (Washington: Seal Press).

Pivar, D. J. (1981) "The Military, Prostitution and Colonial Peoples: India and the Philippines, 1885–1917," *The Journal of Sex Research* 17: 256–67.

Shrage, L. (1994) *Moral Dilemmas of Feminism* (London and New York: Routledge).

Stoler, A. (1991) "Carnal Knowledge and Imperial Power; Gender Race and Morality in Colonial Asia," in Micaela di Leonardo (ed.), *Gender at the Crossroads of Knowledge* (Berkeley: University of California Press).

Thorbeck, S. and Pattanaik, B. (eds.) (2002) *Transnational Prostitution: Changing Global Patterns* (London: Zed Books).

Truong, T. D. (1990) *Sex, Money and Morality: The Political Economy of Prostitution and Tourism in South-East Asia* (London: Zed Books).

Van de Veen, M. (2001) "Rethinking Commodification and Prostitution: An Effort at Peacemaking in the Battles over Prostitution," *Rethinking Marxism* 13: 30–51.

Walkowitz, J. R. (1983) *Prostitution and Victorian Society: Women, Class and the State* (Cambridge: Cambridge University Press).

White, L. (1990) *The Comforts of Home: Prostitution in Colonial Nigeria* (Chicago: University of Chicago Press).

Further reading

Bishop, R. and Robinson, L. S. (1998) *Night Market: Sexual Cultures and the Thai Economic Miracle* (New York: Routledge).

Elias, J. E., Bullough, V., Elias, V., and Brewer, G. (eds.) (1998) *Prostitution: On Whores, Hustlers and Johns* (New York: Prometheus Books).

Feminist Review 67 (Spring 2001): "Sex Work Reassessed."

Lim, L. L. (ed.) (1998) *The Sex Sector: The Economic and Social Bases of Prostitution in Southeast Asia* (Geneva: International Labour Office).

Pheterson, G. (1996) *The Prostitution Prism* (Amsterdam: Amsterdam University Press).

CHAPTER EIGHTEEN

Global Social Movements

Nitza Berkovitch and Sara Helman

Contrary to conventional wisdom, global social movements are not a new phenomenon. They are part of the globalization of contentious politics dating back to the mid-nineteenth century. During the last quarter of the twentieth century these movements became prominent and vivid players in the international, national, and local arena (Boli and Thomas 1999; Della Porta et al. 1999; Guidry et al. 2000; Keck and Sikkink 1998; Smith et al. 1997).

This chapter explores instances of transnational social movements that globalize conflicts and protests on issues of gender and sexuality, notably the international women's and the gay and lesbian movements. The women's movement was already emerging during the last quarter of the nineteenth century, but didn't gain momentum until after the Second World War; it proliferated rapidly during the last three decades of the twentieth century. Among gay organizations too there existed cross-national connections more than a hundred years ago. But the global gay and lesbian movement gained visibility only as recently as the 1980s. In what follows, we will discuss the two movements within the larger context of the globalization of social movements, their political strategies, and organizational character. Our focus lies on the cultural aspects of these movements and on the formation, expansion, and transformation of a transnational collective identity that challenges extant public representations and institutional arrangements on issues of gender and sexuality. We will show how the two movements, while mobilizing hegemonic categories of gender and sexuality, have destabilized and challenged the dominant gender order, while simultaneously widening the scope of actors deemed as legitimate participants in the public sphere (for similar analysis see Helman 1999). Moreover, these movements promote new models of actorhood which become part and parcel of the transnational public sphere and are, in turn, diffused by networks of activists across national boundaries.

By global or transnational social movements, we mean collective action that crosses national boundaries and brings together groups and individuals from various countries for the purpose of bringing about some form of social change, either on a global, national, or local scale (for a different conceptualization, see

Tarrow 2001). These movements and their proliferation have to be considered within the wider framework of economic, cultural, and political globalization. In the last few decades, we have witnessed a growing interconnectedness of the world as a result of the weakening of technological and political barriers. This has brought about a massive flow of people, ideas, information, capital, and commodities among countries in the different parts of the world and, consequently, has led to an increasing integration of the world. An integral part of globalization is the emergence of a world polity – a world cultural and political system – composed of various international actors, operating at the supranational level and whose action cannot be reduced merely to the interests of the states that comprise them (Meyer et al. 1997). This world polity is an important part of a transnational public sphere, "a space in which both residents of distinct places (states and localities) and members of transnational entities (organizations and firms) elaborate discourses and practices whose consumption moves beyond national boundaries" (Guidry et al. 2000: 6). More specifically, the transnational public sphere is composed of a grid of supranational and international institutions that serve as sites towards which different actors address their claims. The formation of interstate organizations, the elaboration of international normative regimes, and the power of international organizations to initiate the formulation of normative rules all provide new arenas of action for social movement actors (Passy 1999: 151). Particularly important in this context are the international normative regimes embodied in the United Nations Declaration of Human Rights, and the different international conferences that serve as sites around which social movement actors press their claims and seek access as legitimate participants in the transnational public sphere.

Issues of gender have occupied central attention in the emerging transnational public sphere. Its carriers – i.e., social movements' actors – formulated gender oppression in terms that resonated with other issues that became part of global discourse and which mobilized transnational collective action. These issues vary from bringing to an end armed conflicts and bringing about peace, to protecting and preserving the environment, guaranteeing the human rights of various groups, transforming political regimes, improving labor conditions, and fighting the AIDS epidemic, to mention only a few (Union of International Associations, various years). Toward the end of the 1990s, corporate-driven economic globalization became a central stimulator for anti-globalization global protest as well (see, e.g., the debate in *Millennium* 29/1 (2000) and Falk 1995) and placed the phenomenon at the center of public attention.

Transnational collective action takes many forms, ranging from loose networks, exchange of information, and ad hoc or continuous joint projects to frequent conferences and sustained international campaigns. Often, the joint activity mounts to founding formal organizational infrastructure in the form of international non-governmental organizations (INGOs), whose members are individuals and/or associations from several countries. In spite of the fact that there is a large variation between movements in the different countries in terms of their strength, agenda, tactics and form of incorporation into the national polity, they have adopted similar repertoires of contention. One can find International Women's Day celebrations, gay parades, gay pride week, gay games, public testimonies/tribunals, peace camps, Take Back the Night marches, and international petitions alongside battles for anti-discrimination legislation in polities that differ along every conceivable dimension.

Gender as a Global Issue

The international women's movement is a dynamic form of cooperation between several hundred women's INGOs, networks, and individual activists, which results in various forms of collective action transcending national boundaries and aimed at changing extant public representations of gender and the institutional arrangements that sustain them. Within this framework one can find single-issue movements (e.g., the International Women's Health Movement) and organizations (e.g., Feminist International Network of Resistance to Reproductive and Genetic Engineering) as well as movements that promote a wider agenda in which they combine the goal of "ending patriarchy" with other struggles (e.g., the International Women's Peace Movement). The different groupings vary according to their structures, strategies, constituencies, and aims. Some are established hierarchical centralized organizations, while others maintain an open, non-hierarchical, non-bureaucratic, network kind of structure. Some employ a "mainstreaming" strategy, which means working for change within an existing institutional order, while others "disengage" – i.e., remain outsiders that provide a critique and formulate alternative visions. Some settle for promoting cooperation among women, while others advocate eliminating patriarchal order in all spheres of life (Prugle and Meyer 1999; Stienstra 1994, 2000).

The gay and lesbian movement is a new recognized actor in the transnational public space. The earliest attempts to formalize cross-national contacts took place in 1921 with the creation of the World League for Sexual Reform, which functioned mainly as an arena for the exchange of information and collaboration for those interested in the reform of sex crimes codes (Hunt 1999). It was only in 1978, with the establishment of the International Lesbian and Gay Association (ILGA), that the first truly transnational gay organization appeared on the global arena. It succeeded earlier short-lived and geographically limited attempts at organizing, and has become the largest and most influential international gay organization. During the 1980s and 1990s, about another 30 international gay and lesbian organizations were founded. They range from focusing on changing public and professional attitudes (e.g., Association of Gay, Lesbian and Bisexual Psychologists) to exchanging information (International Information Service), liberalizing national and international laws (e.g., International Gay and Lesbian Human Rights Commission), organizing cultural and sports events (e.g., Federation of Gay Games), and providing social support for themselves and their families (e.g., Gay and Lesbian Parents Coalition) (Union of International Associations, various years).

The Transformative Impact of Gender-focused Social Movements

In order to have input in the formulation of global and national policy, to have an effect on public attitudes, and to widen their constituency, transnational movements operate on multiple levels. In addition to lobbying the state, they also target individuals and campaign international institutions (Smith 1997). Thus, for example, the ILGA succeeded in 1991, after a prolonged campaign, to bring Amnesty International to broaden its mandate to include, as eligible for recognition as prisoners of conscience, people detained because of their sexual orientation. It also pressured the World Health Organization to remove homosexuality from its tenth edition of the International Classification of Diseases. On the national level, the Association's efforts focus on legal reforms to decriminalize homosexuality and to include sexual orientation in anti-discrimination laws regarding employment, immigration, family benefits, parental rights, etc. (Hollmaat and Pistor 1988; Ramakers 1997). Likewise, the international women's movement managed (with varying degrees of success) to have an impact on global population policy, to broaden the definition of human rights to include women's rights, to introduce gender issues and perspectives into matters of development, and to have an imprint on global environmental agendas (Ashworth 1995; Meyer and Prugle 1999).

At first glance it seems that these movements act, by and large, as interest groups that aim at inserting their concerns into the wider agenda and struggle for rights and resources for their own constituency. However, this kind of conceptualization underestimates and misreads the meanings of changes in the global agenda as specified above, as the struggle is not confined to an adage of "add women (or gays) and stir," but to a transformation of the very structures and ways of thinking so as to accommodate the needs, life experiences, and social position of men and women. In the case of women and human rights, for example, the conventional definition refers to harms done by state agencies to individuals on political grounds. Defining harms done to women in the private sphere as a violation of human rights, and recognizing individuals as perpetrators, transforms the very definition of "human rights" and challenges the validity of the public/private split on which the whole notion of "rights" and "human rights" is based (Cook 1994; Peters and Wolper 1995).

Similarly, the decriminalization and demedicalization of homosexuality, and convincing the international community that the fundamental rights for lesbians and gay men need to be recognized as part of international human rights law, have much wider implications than achievements for gay men and women. Granting ILGA a non-governmental status with the United Nations Economic and Social Council redefines the global agenda to include matters of sexuality and paves the way for incorporation of the interests and concerns of lesbians and gay men. These steps defy long-held beliefs regarding appropriate forms of sexuality and desire. In doing so, they destabilize the hegemonic role and status of the pillar of patriarchy – heterosexuality.

Moreover, the very fact that women organized themselves and demanded that their voices should be heard in international forums challenged the gender paradigm that reserved the political arena, especially the international one, for men alone. This holds true especially for the beginning of the international women's movement, when women played an active role in the emerging transnational public sphere, without themselves being recognized political actors. Women took leading roles – alongside men – in many transnational campaigns aimed at correcting social evils and moral wrongs, but more importantly these campaigns were part and parcel of their own movements and organizations. Informative examples are the suffrage movement, the international women's temperance movement, and the international women's socialist movement (Berkovitch 1999a; Rupp 1997). These movements advocated women's suffrage and access to education and employment not just as a cause in their own right but also as a means for the "betterment of the world." Women's movements mobilized the hegemonic notions of the "separate spheres" and "gender differences," but turned them into a symbolic resource in their struggle for the transformation of society and their own place in it. A dramatic example of the ways in which this discourse was used to challenge the notion of the "domestic women" and "public men" was provided by the women's international peace movement in its formative congress at the Hague in 1915 (Berkovitch 1999b; Foster 1989). (For a general discussion on the effects of social movements, see Giugni 1998.)

Challenging Normative Heterosexuality

During that early period, when women challenged patriarchy and gender hierarchy by organizing and holding international conferences, campaigns, and petitions, gay men and women started to find ways to contest another aspect of patriarchy – the perception of heterosexuality as the only legitimate and appropriate form of sexuality. But this was done in a much lower key. In many European countries, homosexuality was punishable under criminal law and any such public action was likely to bring about a loss of jobs, imprisonment, and harsh social sanctions. Thus, the early stages of the transnational gay movement took the form of informal forums for the exchange of ideas, lectures, and visits of people from different countries; soon after, a more open and assertive movement arose.

It is known that homosexuality, as a form of sexual practice, has existed throughout human history. Moreover, there is evidence that indicates the existence of homosexual networks and a gay male world in various large European cities in the seventeenth and eighteenth centuries (Adam 1995). But since the late nineteenth century, homosexuality, as a result of engagement in collective action, became politicized and mobilized as a base and material for identity building and claims making. The main carriers of the new identity were organizations that combined scientific and political work, such as the Scientific Humanitarian Committee, founded in Berlin in 1897. This was the first homosexual *rights* organization and was soon to be followed by others both in Germany and elsewhere. They lobbied political parties and sent petitions against their subjection to legal penalty and for legal reform. They also campaigned to change the attitudes of the public and the medical profession toward homosexuality. This model of collective action spread across Europe. Members of the organizations toured other countries, gave lectures, and held meetings, inspiring the founding of similar groups in Northern Europe and bringing about an embryonic movement in the United States. Their greatest impact was felt in Britain, where scholarly societies devoted to the scientific study of homosexuals flourished (Adam 1995; Hunt 1999).

Attempts to build a transnational community based on the notion of a commonality of fate continued during the 1920s but came to a halt with the rise of fascist regimes in Europe and with outbreak of the Second World War. The holocaust wiped away most of the early gay culture and its movement through systematic extermination and ideological control (Adam 1995).

After World War II, conservative forces in North America and Western Europe posed new constraints on homosexuals, the harshest pressure being exerted in the United States, where homosexuals were defined as destroyers of society and as "security risks." The few organizations that did emerge adopted a low profile, and an accommodating stand to heterosexuality and society. This position was manifested also in several small-scale international conferences held during the 1950s (Clark 1993). Still, gay and lesbian writing began to flourish, and issues of bisexuality, butch/femme, and pedophilia were discussed in gay magazines and newspapers (Adam 1995; Blasius and Phelan 1997). The members of this emerging community – being mainly white, European, and of middle-class backgrounds – concentrated on the reform of heterosexist legal and medical norms and did not try to formulate a wider agenda in which other forms of oppression were recognized. Like the international women's movement at that time, which cultivated a collective identity that aimed at transcending all differences among women and was based on the notion of shared fate of all women because of their gender alone, so too did the international gay movement emphasize sexuality alone.

Gender Tensions in the Gay Movement

Challenging heterosexuality did not inevitably lead to a critique of patriarchy. The problematic relations between men and women had been apparent in the gay movement since its inception. Men dominated the scene and male sexuality was the prime issue, hence replicating gender hierarchy once again. Only in a few instances, such as in the German Scientific Humanitarian Committee, were women involved from the start, and the concept of homosexual oppression was framed as integrally related to wider issues of sexuality and women's rights in society, and not in isolation from them (Blasius and Phelan 1997). But this was an exception. Even the ILGA, one of the few gender-mixed organizations, has been dominated by men. Its original title was the International Gay Association, and only in 1986, eight years after its foundation, was the word "lesbian" added to its title. This symbolic change was not satisfactory, and, in response, women decided to set up an autonomous international organization – the International Lesbian Information Service (ILIS) (Hollmaat and Pistor 1988). In the 1980s, the cleavage between gay men and women deepened as some members argued that gays and lesbians could not form a community because gender differences are greater than the shared rejection of heterosexuality (Blasius and Phelan 1997).

Lesbian women had to fight for their place within the women's movement as well. Their gradual acceptance can be detected by looking at the events of the United Nations world conferences. At the first International Women's Conference in Mexico in 1975, the issue of lesbian women was raised but put aside. At the 1980 Conference in Copenhagen, no lesbian workshop was organized and the issue was only discussed in unofficial gatherings. Only in 1985, at the UN Conference at Nairobi, was the issue of lesbian women raised and discussed for the first time at an official UN gathering. The presence of lesbians was visible at the unofficial UN forum, where the ILIS held several workshops; a lesbian caucus meeting was convened every day; and a lesbian press conference was held, attracting wide attention. As a result of the Nairobi conference, the ILIS organized the first ever lesbian international conference in 1986 in Geneva, attended by 800 women from five continents, where South American and Asian women laid the foundation for regional lesbian networks (Borren 1988).

Thus, questions regarding the role and place of lesbian women within the women's movement and the gay movement troubled both groups along their history. Lesbians posed a challenge that involved not only power and leadership roles but also the definition of what constitutes "women's interests," the meaning of the category "woman," and, likewise, what constitutes "homosexuality" and what should homosexual people fight for.

The success of the women's and the gay movement in constituting a political subject in the name of which claims were made gave rise to controversies over the identity of this political subject. Tensions developed over the inclusiveness and exclusiveness of the collective identity, as the latter defined women and gays and lesbians across and beyond the different cultural, national, class, and ethnic affiliation. Thus, struggles over the definition of the political subject were entwined with the very process of challenging hegemonic definitions of the gender order. Indeed, controversies over identity, and consequently of political strategy and interests, not only in regard to lesbian women, have been an unresolved issue throughout the history of the two movements.

Identity Politics

The salience and content of the conflicts over these issues were shaped, to a large degree, by the changing opportunity structure, and the composition of the movements and cultural frames. Thus, for example, class conflict within the women's movement surfaced with the creation of the League of Nations and the International Labor Organization (ILO), after the First World War. The formation of these two organizations opened a new arena for transnational mobilization by offering a central world focal point that theretofore had been lacking. This changing opportunity structure led to further mobilization and higher degrees of cooperation for the purpose of lobbying both organizations to include women's rights in their agenda (Miller 1994). But these very intensified lobbying efforts brought up the thorny question of what actually constitutes women's interests. Working-class women lobbied the ILO to adopt international labor standards that would guarantee protective labor legislation, and objected to the Equal Rights Treaty promoted by middle-class women. The latter saw protective legislation as limiting women's opportunity for employment and not as an achievement in improving working conditions (Berkovitch 1999a).

Similar questions of representation of class interests, sexuality, ethnicity, and cultural differences became acute during the 1970s, with the changing political and cultural climate, the upheaval that swept Europe, and the flourishing of the two movements both on the national and the international scale. The salience of these issues increased, especially when the two movements expanded their geographical distribution and diversified their social composition. Issues of global power hierarchies, such as those between the South and the North, were added and interacted with matters of cultural, class, sexual, and ethnic differences.

To put it more generally, social movements articulate a collective identity and new models of actorhood through the subversion of hegemonic discourses. However, as movements grow and come to include wider constituencies and expand across different locations, a different dynamic develops within movements themselves (Steinberg 1998). The political subject that movements claim to represent is conceived as oppressing or silencing interests of new constituencies. Thus, within movements themselves a process of contention over the meaning of actorhood developed, as is the case in the women's movement and its relation to the non-Western world and to gays and lesbians. This process may eventually lead to an expansion of models in order to account for diversity, or to the emergence of new movements (Keck and Sikkink 2000).

Indeed, the expansion of the transnational women's movement, attributed to the United Nations Decade of Women (1976–85) and its three world conferences, led to the inclusion of many women and groups from various parts of the world, mainly from third world countries. With this, new perceptions, new needs, and new agendas were brought in, challenging long-held views regarding what a feminist agenda and struggles consist of. The leading notion of commonality

273

among all women – a "global sisterhood" sharing the same fate and suffering the same oppression because of their gender – came under serious attack for promoting the interests of white, middle-class women from the North (see, e.g., Kaplan 1997; Mohanty 1992).

Paradoxically, the same events – the United Nations world conferences – that stimulated the expansion of the movement became a site to voice and enact these contentions and to question the very possibility of an existence of a truly transnational women's movement. The main controversy concerned the relations between gender oppression and other forms of oppression. Women of color and from the South saw struggles against imperialism, apartheid, racism, and redistribution of wealth as feminist struggles. The oppression that resulted from these different regimes was considered as an integral part of oppressive sexism. First world women denounced this argument as a "politicization" of women's issues and preferred to focus on what they defined as women's issues alone. Moreover, there was a strong criticism of Western-style feminism that portrayed Western feminists as the saviors of third world women, the latter being the passive victims of their circumstances. The last two meetings – in 1985 at Nairobi and in 1995 in Beijing – were characterized by the conspicuous presence of women of color from the North and of women from the South, and were less conflictual and more cooperative in spirit and in action, but not all conflicts were resolved. Indeed, the agenda was broadened to include issues that concerned women from the South alongside more traditional Western feminist issues (see various articles in *Signs* 1 (1986) and 1 (1996)). However, debates over the meaning of feminism and possibilities of cooperation continued, framed in the context of resisting century-old imperialist tendencies of white patronizing feminism (Amos and Parmer 1984).

Multiple Identities and Struggles

New understandings, modes of cooperation, and ways of organizing emerged during the 1980s and 1990s. These new understandings did not assume any notion of universality, nor did they erase old divisions and controversies as is manifested by the new terms of "negotiated solidarity" and "strategic sisterhood." Coalition-building, ad hoc alliances, and network organizations became the new forms that define much of the international women's movement. Instead of hierarchical organizations that dictate policy and action to the local groups, the latter, though aided by international support, gain autonomy and focus on day-to-day work and needs (Mohanty 1992; Johnson-Odim 1991). Similar processes marked the rise of the contemporary gay and lesbian movement in the 1970s and its expansion in the ensuing decades. The trigger for the appearance of the movement was the formation of the Gay Liberation Front and the Stonewall riots (both in 1969) in New York City. From there, it spread throughout the US, Canada, and Western Europe and later to other parts of the world. It was the first time that the movement became truly transnational. During this period, we witness the emergence of homosexual groups in Mexico, Brazil, and Peru. Similar organizations became visible also in South Africa, Australia, and New Zealand as well as in Asia and Africa and Eastern and Central Europe (Tatchell 1990; Clark 1993).

This process of expansion awakened similar controversies as in the women's movement. Paramount among them was the relation between gay liberation and other liberation movements. Note for example the debate within lesbian women's groups. On the one hand, they formed their own organizations after being disappointed by their gay brothers when the latter proved to be no less sexist and patronizing than heterosexual men. On the other, however, lesbian women were criticized for holding a narrow vision of gender and for ignoring black lesbians' need to cooperate with their brothers to confront racism.

Issues of sexuality, sexual practices, and identity added another layer to the internal conflicts, as was manifested in the "sex wars" of the 1970s and 1980s. Lesbian feminists have been critical of gay men's sexual practices. Conflicts over issues such as pornography, S/M, pedophilia, and the age and meaning of consent have divided the groups from the 1970s to the present day. But the sex wars drew a line not only between men and women, but also between lesbian women themselves. "Sex radicals" reclaim a culture for their sexual practices (S/M, butch/femme) as potentially valuable and transformative. In so doing, they reopened alliances with gay men. Other lesbian women claimed that only "woman-identified" love is "true lesbianism" and conceived of S/M and pornography as anti-women and anti-feminists (Blasius and Phelan 1997).

The AIDS epidemic has transformed, to a large degree, the politics, strength, and identity of the gay movement. The creation of ACT UP, the Aids Coalition to Unleash Power, in 1987 marks the beginning of what has since been called AIDS activism, and led to further transnationalization of the movement. It spread quickly and by the early 1990s it had close to 100 chapters around the world. The struggle against AIDS had some paradoxical results. On the one hand, the mobilization to fight the disease through public education, attracting media attention, and exerting political pressure led to a further politicization of the gay movement and gay activity and to the diffusion of similar modes of action around the world. It also led to coalition-building with other groups in society and various community services. On the other hand, AIDS organizations also went through a process of "de-gaying," thus losing the gay edge of their politics, exactly at the time when they were gaining more power and influence. AIDS politics also mitigated much of the conflict between gay men and lesbians when many women joined the AIDS campaign. But this renewed coalition brought to the surface the issue of economic inequality and social class, which meant unequal access to health services (Blasius and Phelan 1997).

In addition, new currents pose fundamental new challenges to established gay politics. Queer politics problematized the binary conception of fixed gender identities as well as of all other identities, thereby challenging an essentialized gay identity, the cornerstone of identity politics and a powerful mobilizing strategy. Queer politics has also destabilized the relationship between sex, gender, and sexuality, thus awakening new questions as to how these relations should be articulated in collective identities and the politics of the individual, and paving the way for coalitions with other minorities.

To conclude: the claims made by the different social movements' actors have implications not only for the political subjects they claim to represent; they also affect others and bring about changes in socio-political relations and in the distribution of power. Thus, transnational social movements such as the women's movement and the gay and lesbian movements, as we have demonstrated in the short historical and analytical accounts above, challenge extant constructions of gender and actorhood. And by so doing, they redefine the criteria of membership in the transnational public sphere as well as the distribution of power within it.

References

Adam, D. B. (1995) *The Rise of a Gay and Lesbian Movement* (New York: Twayne).

Amos, V. and Parmer, P. (1984) "Challenging Imperial Feminism," *Feminist Review* 17: 3–19.

Ashworth, G. (ed.) (1995) *A Diplomacy of the Oppressed: New Directions in International Feminism* (London and New Jersey: Zed Books).

Berkovitch, N. (1999a) "The Emergence and Transformation of the International Women's Movement," in J. Boli and G. Thomas (eds.), *Constructing World Culture: International Nongovernmental Organizations Since 1875* (Stanford: Stanford University Press).

Berkovitch, N. (1999b) *From Motherhood to Citizenship: Women's Rights and International Organizations* (Baltimore, MD: Johns Hopkins University Press).

Blasius, M. and Phelan, S. (1997) *We are Everywhere: a Historical Sourcebook of Gay and Lesbian Politics* (New York: Routledge).

Boli, J. and Thomas, G. M. (eds.) (1999) *Constructing World Culture: International Non-Governmental Organizations since 1875* (Stanford: Stanford University Press).

Borren, S. (1988) "Lesbian Organizations in Latin America," in The Pink Book Editing Team (ed.), *The Second ILGA Book: A Global View of Lesbian and Gay Liberation and Oppression* (Utrecht: International Gay and Lesbian Association).

Clark, J. (1993) "The Global Lesbian and Gay Movement: Mass Movement, Grassroots, or by Invitation Only," in A. Hendriks, R. Thelman, and E. van der Veen (eds.), *The Third Pink Book: A Global View of Lesbian and Gay Liberation and Oppression* (Buffalo, NY: Prometheus Books).

Cook, R. J. (ed.) (1994) *Human Rights of Women* (Philadelphia: University of Pennsylvania Press).

Della Porta, D., Kriesi, H., and Rucht, D. (eds.) (1999) *Social Movements in a Globalizing World* (London: Macmillan).

Falk, R. (1995) *On Humane Governance: Toward a New Global Politics* (Cambridge: Polity).

Foster, C. (1989) *Women for All Seasons: The Story of the Women's International League for Peace and Freedom* (Athens and London: The University of Georgia Press).

Giugni, M. G. (1998) "Was it Worth the Effort: The Outcomes and Consequences of Social Movements," *Annual Review of Sociology* 98: 371–93.

Guidry, J. A., Kennedy, M. D., and Zald, M. N. (2000) "Globalizations and Social Movements," in J. A. Guidry, M. D. Kennedy, and M. N. Zald (eds.), *Globalizations and Social Movements: Culture, Power and the Transnational Public Sphere* (Ann Arbor: The University of Michigan Press).

Helman, S. (1999) "From Soldiering and Motherhood to Citizenship: a Study of Four Israeli Peace Protest Movements," *Social Politics* 6: 292–313.

Hollmaat, H. and Pistor, R. (1988) "Ten Years of International Gay and Lesbian Solidarity: Ten Years of ILGA," in The Pink Book Editing Team (ed.), *The Second ILGA Book: A Global View of Lesbian and Gay Liberation and Oppression* (Utrecht: International Gay and Lesbian Association).

Hunt, R. (1999) *Historical Dictionary of the Gay Liberation Movement: Gay Men and the Quest for Social Justice* (Lanham, MD: Scarecrow).

Johnson-Odim, Cheryl (1991) "Common Themes, Different Contexts: Third World Women and Feminism," in Chandra Talpade Mohanty, Ann Russo, and Lourdes Torres (eds.), *Third World Women and the Politics of Feminism* (Bloomington and Indianapolis: Indiana University Press).

Kaplan, C. (1997) "The Politics of Location as Transnational Feminist Critical Practice," in I. Grewal and C. Kaplan (eds.), *Scattered Hegemonies: Postmodernity and Transnational Feminist Practices* (Minneapolis: University of Minnesota Press).

Keck, M. E. and Sikkink, K. (1998) *Activists Beyond Borders: Advocacy Networks in International Politics* (Ithaca: Cornell University Press).

Keck, M. E. and Sikkink, K. (2000) "Historical Precursors of Modern Transnational Social Movements and Networks," in J. A. Guidry, M. D. Kennedy, and M. N. Zald (eds.), *Globalizations and Social Movements: Culture, Power and the Transnational Public Sphere* (Ann Arbor: University of Michigan Press).

Meyer, J. W., Boli, J., Thomas, G. M., and Ramirez, F. O. (1997) "World Society and the Nation-State," *American Journal of Sociology* 103: 144–81.

Meyer, M. K. and Prugle, E. (eds.) (1999) *Gender Politics in Global Governance* (Lanham, MD: Rowman & Littlefield).

Miller, C. (1994) "'Geneva: The Key to Equality'," *Women's History Review* 3: 219–20.

Mohanty, C. T. (1992) "Feminist Encounters: Locating the Politics of Experience," in B. Michele and A. Phillips (eds.), *Destabilizing Theory: Contemporary Feminist Debates* (Stanford: Stanford University Press).

Passy, F. (1999) "Supranational Political Opportunities as a Channel of Globalization of Political Conflicts: The Case of the Rights of Indigenous People," in D. Della Porta, H. Kriesi, and D. Rucht (eds.), *Social Movements in a Globalizing World* (London: Macmillan).

Peters, J. and Wolper, A. (eds.) (1995) *Women's Rights, Human Rights: International Feminist Perspective* (New York and London: Routledge).

Prugle, E. and Meyer, M. K. (1999) "Gender Politics in Global Governance," in M. K. Meyer and E. Prugle (eds.), *Gender Politics in Global Governance* (Lanham, MD: Rowman & Littlefield).

Ramakers, M. (1997) "The International Lesbian and Gay Association Five Years Later: Towards a Truly Worldwide Movement?" in M. Blasius and S. Phelan (eds.), *We are Everywhere: a Historical Sourcebook of Gay and Lesbian Politics* (New York: Routledge).

Rupp, L. J. (1997) *Worlds of Women: The Making of an International Women's Movement* (Princeton, NJ: Princeton University Press).

Smith, J. (1997) "Characteristics of the Modern Social Movement Sector," in J. Smith, C. Chattfield, and R. Pagnuco (eds.), *Transnational Social Movements and Global Politics* (Syracuse: Syracuse University Press).

Smith, J., Chatfield, C., and Pagnucco, R. (eds.) (1997) *Transnational Social Movements and Global Politics: Solidarity Beyond the State* (Syracuse, NY: Syracuse University Press).

Steinberg, M. W. (1998) "Tilting the Frame: Considerations on Collective Action Farming from a Discursive Turn," *Theory and Society* 27: 845–72.

Stienstra, D. (1994) *Women's Movements and International Organizations* (New York: St. Martin's Press).

Stienstra, D. (2000) "Making Global Connections Among Women, 1979–99," in R. Cohen and M. S. Rai (eds.), *Global Social Movements* (London and New Brunswick: The Athlone Press).

Tatchell, P. (1990) *Out in Europe* (London: Rouge).

Tarrow, S. (2001) "Transnational Politics: Contention and Institutions in International Politics," *Annual Reviews of Political Science* 4: 1–20.

Union of International Associations (various years) *Yearbook of International Organizations* (Munich: K. G. Saur).

Further reading

Adam, D. B., Duyvendak, J. W., and Krouwel, A. (eds.) (1999) *The Global Emergence of Gay and Lesbian Politics: National Imprints of a Worldwide Movement* (Philadelphia: Temple University Press).

Altman, D. (1997) "Global Gaze/Global Gay," *Gay and Lesbian Quarterly* 3: 417–36.

Bulbeck, C. (1988) *One World's Women's Movement* (London: Pluto Press).

Bulbeck, C. (1998) *Re-Orienting Western Feminism: Women's Diversity in a Postcolonial World* (Cambridge: Cambridge University Press).

Cohen, R. and Rai, M. S. (eds.) (2000) *Global Social Movements* (London and New Brunswick: Athlone Press).

Dean, J. (1996) *Solidarity of Strangers: Feminism after Identity Politics* (Berkeley: University of California Press).

Gamson, J. (1995) "Must Identity Movements Self-Destruct? A Queer Dilemma," *Social Problems* 42: 390–406.

Gamson, J. (1997) "Messages of Exclusion: Gender, Movements, and Symbolic Boundaries," *Gender & Society* 11: 178–99.

Grewal, I. and Kaplan, C. (eds.) (1994) *Scattered Hegemonies: Postmodernity and Transnational Feminist Practices* (Minneapolis: University of Minnesota Press).

Hendriks, A., Tielman, R., and van der Veen, E. (eds.) (1993) *The Third Pink Book: A Global View of Lesbian and Gay Liberation and Oppression* (Buffalo, NY: Prometheus Books).

Melucci, A. (1995) "The Process of Collective Identity," in H. Johnston and B. Klandermans (eds.), *Social Movements and Culture* (Minneapolis: University of Minnesota Press).

Polleta, F. and Jasper, J. M. (2001) "Collective Identity and Social Movements," *Annual Review of Sociology* 27: 283–305.

CHAPTER NINETEEN

Arab Women:
Beyond Politics

Ratiba Hadj-Moussa

Introduction

How does one speak about gender relations in the "Muslim World"[1] without falling back upon generalizations? How does one point to what is at stake knowing full well that in this world every society is distinctive, that each society possesses its own unique history and its particular positioning? How can one avoid the pitfalls of the homogenizing discourse of *el Umma* (the communion of believers) and its simplifications and yet recognize that the so-called Muslim societies have been shaped by a common complexification? In this chapter I will not be dealing with the whole world (is it even possible to do so?). I will mainly be considering one of its regions, the Arab one, and within this region, I will be concentrating on a few countries. On occasion, I will refer to the Iranian and the Turkish experiences to emphasize a point.

In order to assess what is at stake in the Arab Muslim region when interpreting gender relations, I will, without a historical overview, examine the various women's movements,[2] their relation to the state and questions of nationalism, and how they have been positioned vis-à-vis Islamic movements. Finally, I will sketch out the underlying dynamic of attempts to re-islamicize the Arab region.

Reform Movements and Women's Movements

The emergence of a women's movement in North Africa and the Middle East coincides with the work that was started towards the end of the nineteenth century by the Muslim reformers who sprung from the mid-nineteenth-century "renaissance," or *el Nahda*. This was most notable in Egypt, which was one of its principal fountainheads, as well as in Syria,[3] followed at a later date by other Arab countries such as Tunisia and Algeria. Fundamentally anti-colonialist and anti-Orientalist, the reform movement attempted, through a rereading of the Koran, to provide answers to the pressures of the modern world. It is important to note that the reform movement arose out of contact with the West and that the movement represents several tendencies, from the most conservative (Algeria) to the most radical (Tunisia's Tahar Haddad: see Marzouki 1993: 27–30). Although all the reformers have placed women at the heart of the Muslim nation, in the role of maintaining its pulse, not all reformers have done so with emancipatory intent. Such is the case of Algeria, where women were to be schooled only to the extent that they would serve as shields against aggressive French colonialism. However, in most cases, for example in Egypt, the work of reformers such as Mohamed Abdu was vital because they faced the woes of the Muslim world by starting from the inside, from the Koran, in order to shed new light, to bring a new reading (of the sacred text), and to the search for new solutions and the retailoring of old ones. Ahmed (1992) points out that Abdu was well versed in the exegesis of the Koran, and contrasts this expertise with a particular embracing of modernization. As much as Abdu wanted profitably to harness Western technological progress, he also resisted Western values and argued that Islam plays the role of forerunner in the liberation of women. Islam was not to blame for the lamentable situation in which women found themselves. Rather, the causes lie with certain interpretations of Islam and the mutations Islam has suffered. This is a crucial line of argumentation, for it will be taken up later not only by some Islamic feminists (e.g. Z. El Ghozali in Egypt), or by feminists adept at reinterpreting the Koran (F. Mernissi), but also by secular views such as those of N. El Saadawi (1986: 19). However, in its Middle Eastern as well as its North African manifestations, the reform movement remains indebted to tradition (the Sunna) and to *salafiyya*.

In the Arab Muslim context, male reformers have played an important role in attempts to open up spaces previously inaccessible to women. Moreover, like the reformers, the women's movements have in effect adopted anti-colonial and anti-imperialist positions. Some of the reformers, such as Tunisia's Tahar Haddad, have paid dearly for their rethinking of tradition. Following the 1930 publication of his book, *Notre femme dans la loi religieuse et la société*, Haddad became a favorite target of learned polemic and el Zaytouna true-thinking defending Islamic orthodoxy. It was inconceivable for these guardians of orthodoxy that "one could claim respect for Islamic orthodoxy while holding, on the question of feminism, anti-conformist views" (Mérad 1967: 324). It should henceforth be impossible to confuse the reform with the "modernist"[4] movement although both have the education of women as a common goal. However, like the modern-ist movement, the reformers have engaged with modernity. Thus the reform movement cannot simply be construed as a canonical voice opposed to modern ideas. One needs to consider the context of its emergence. As Mervat Hatem has noted, the modernists have not even thought about the relevance of Islam to contemporary society. They have mainly concentrated on the education of women in the hopes that the partition of space along gender lines could accommodate new conditions (Hatem 1993: 38). The amelioration of the situation of women in no ways meant that male dominance was challenged. Counting very few exceptions and despite perceptible advances, this modernist discourse reinscribed gender inequality by closely tying women to family.

This positioning of women and family rests upon a major and long-lived presupposition which continues to affect the ways in which relations between the sexes are thought of in the Arab Muslim region. The positioning of women with family presupposed the link between women and culture to be indissoluble, that women and culture belong on the same continuum. In this regard, Ahmed demonstrates the paradoxical similarity between Western discourse on the status of Arab women and the local counter-discourse: "The resemblance between the two positions is not coincidental: They are mirror images of each other. The resistance narrative contested the colonial thesis by inverting it – thereby also, ironically, grounding itself in the premises of the colonial thesis" (Ahmed 1992: 166). In leveraging the fusion between women and culture, colonial France studiously attempts to co-opt women. The nationalist response throughout the Maghreb and across all tendencies has been to protect women from the colonizer either by exhorting them to ignore the latter's enticements or by providing them with the tools (education) to resist. Daoud notes that "the [Moroccan] leaders of Istqlal *now* invoke women as more sacred than the earth or than freedom, as the holy carriers of honor and dignity" (1993: 252; my emphasis). We will come back to the link between women and culture.

The nexus between women and family occupies a prominent place in the discourse surrounding the liberation of women. The first women's groups, whether in Egypt (Badran 1995), Palestine (Rishmawi 1986: 82), Lebanon (Fleischmann 1999: 102) or Tunisia (Marzouki 1993: 42–3), were mutual aid societies and educational centers, which operated in the context of what Badran calls "traditional camouflage" (1993: 30) and of what I call the new domesticity. Here, women were taught to sew as well as trained in the techniques of Western-style hygiene, all in order to create the modern mother. These developments are contemporaneous with the emergence of feminist writing – particularly so in countries such as Egypt, Lebanon, Turkey, and Iran – a vein of writing depth and richness which is only now beginning to be appreciated. The women's movements were also highly interested in schooling for girls, an interest that was buoyed by massive state-sponsored reforms, as was the case, for example, in Egypt under Mohamed Ali (Ahmed 1992: 131ff) and in the other Arab countries. Let us recall that the opening up of educational opportunities was also due in large part to the impact of colonialization. The degree of change varied from context to context: weak in Algeria (few Algerians had access to formal schooling), very high in Egypt and Tunisia. However, the great determining factors remain the extent of urbanization and class structure. Upper-class girls were the first to benefit. The dominant feminist movement, the one that espouses making Western feminist positions "native" and which is exemplified in the person of Huda El Shahraoui, an Egyptian woman, will continue to carry the traces of these class-related factors and will thereafter, despite the widespread recognition of its agenda, garner but a small following. For its part, the other feminism is indigenous and vernacular, and finds its inspiration in Islam (Z. El Ghozali in Egypt and B. Ben Mrad in Tunisia).

It is now important to note that beyond the individual chronology of each particular women's movement, there is an undercurrent that flows through the various discourses and practices of these movements as they related to reformers, modernists, colonists, former colonial powers, or governments. This undercurrent has usually been approached in terms of the paradigm that sets modernity and tradition in opposition to each other. It would be more productive to consider this opposition as the indissoluble parts of a totality. On this score, Shakry's "Schooled Mothers and Structured Play" (1998) is quite remarkable. Shakry's article shows that, despite the Egyptian reformers' attempts to distance themselves from the West and to rely upon native sources, their teachings resonate strongly with Western doctrines. "Hence the 'modernist' focus on hygiene and the cultivation and discipline of the body (tarbiyat al-jasad) was not antithetical to Islamic discourse at the turn of the century but was in fact complementary to it" (ibid.: 155).

There is an annoying tendency exhibited by research on the family in Arab countries to liken the family to tradition. Notwithstanding some significant progress, modern state structures, despite the introduction of formal schooling and the struggle against colonialism, have not enabled families (and perforce women) to escape the repetitive groove of tradition. However, if one stops to consider ever so briefly the turmoil experienced by Arab countries, one quickly sees that for a long time now the "traditional family" has ceased to exist as I have claimed is the case for the Algerian family (Hadj-Moussa 2003). Indeed, how can one take stock of the rural–urban shift throughout the Arab world and the structural upheaval of agrarian society (very extensive in the case of Algeria and still significant in other countries), and fail to recognize that the objective conditions and the subjective circumstances of the traditional family no longer exist? We need to make the effort in our theorization *and* exercise political vigilance.

I would like to illustrate this need for political vigilance vis-à-vis the tradition–modernity opposition with a recent example. The tradition–modernity opposition can be used to further political ends. It is not inaccurate to claim, in reports about the Algerian situation, that the Algerian Islamist movement, when deftly conflated with armed Islamist groups responsible for spreading death and terror, is presented as the enemy of democracy, the foe of modernity, and therefore an adversary of women's liberation. Given considerations of space, I will not examine the validity of this characterization. I will simply state that women, in particular feminists, have been hailed by the governing powers as fervent advocates of democracy and liberty. The Western world has been comforted by this very reassuring image and its contrast with "Islamist barbarity." But if one considers for an instant Algeria's history, one quickly realizes that it is the very same governing powers that proclaimed in 1984 (well before the civil war, which began in 1992) edicts to the effect that family law should be based on the sharia (Islamic law), a legal code against which women were struggling. We can see from these examples that it is important when considering gender relations, especially in non-Western countries, to be aware of the stakes when the well-worn opposition between modernity and tradition is invoked. From the outset, the women's movements have supplied the modernity–tradition opposition with its dynamism in so far as, following Belhassen and Bessis (1992), it is women themselves who are at stake.

From Ideologization to Institutionalization

The Arab reform movement of the second half of the nineteenth century tried to resolve the developmental lag of the Arab countries by accepting the technological advances of the West, all the while replacing an ideology based on the refusal of imitation (*taglid*) with a moralizing ideology whose values were to be implemented principally by women. Thus, women had to act both as nation builders and as an antidote to colonialism. As to the first phase of feminist movements, they essentially tried to align themselves with this opportunity through initially timid and then progressively more and more assertive demands. Nonetheless, they did so all in a framework of subordination to nationalist interests.

It is easy to understand that the emergence of nationalist movements, particularly in the Middle East, posed a challenge for the women's movements in those countries. This was the case in Iran at the beginning of the twentieth century as well as in Egypt and in Palestine (but not in Algeria where to a certain extent an autonomous women's movement did not exist until the end of the Second World War and where the women's movement was incarnated in the form of action groups for women set up by the political parties). In Egypt, El Shahraoui's association was from the outset an endorser of the nationalist positions of the El Wafd party (Badran 1995: 74ff). Women's groups in Tunisia and Palestine also endorsed nationalist positions (Fleischmann 1999: 90). In Morocco, as Daoud (1993) reminds us, the wife of Moroccan nationalist Allal El Fasi (a supporter of feminist positions from at least the beginnings of his engagement in the struggle against the French protectorate) herself delivered correspondence to King Mohamed V when her husband was in exile. As stressed by Fleischmann, the question facing women's groups was "gender or nation, which first?" (1999: 92), a statement alongside which we may place Sandoval's (2000) expression "oppositional consciousness," and which Fleischmann, ever sensitive to the specificity of the Middle Eastern women's movements, glosses as "the ability to read the current situation of power" (1999: 92). These formulations and characterizations help us to understand the historical and political contexts of these women's movements. In other words, these contexts favored nationalist struggles for independence over women's social and political struggles. However, this interpretation should be limited to certain distinct cases, such as those of Egypt or Iran at the beginning of the twentieth century (ibid.: 108). But in the case of other independence movements, for example in Palestine or Algeria, the women question was from the outset inscribed within the framework of a nationalist struggle, often, as in the case of Algeria, without major political support from women (Amrane 1993). Thus the women question, as will be the case with feminist movements, quickly became a highly charged ideological question and is strictly circumscribed to the domain of liberation struggles. No freedom without nationalism! Indeed, in Palestine, "Palestinian women were ideologically defined to suit the official priorities of the PLO and had the burden of being 'mothers of the nation.' As such they were encouraged to concentrate on grass roots activity leaving the main battlefield – military or political – to 'real soldiers'" (Jamal 2001: 258–9).[5] Also, "women's entry into politics in Algeria as everywhere else thus occurs under the sponsorship of organizations whose agendas they support but who do not per se reach out to women. . . . Women will participate in the liberation struggles but always in a subordinate role" (Gadant 1995: 132–3). Peteet, however, provides a more nuanced view: "Women's entry into formal national politics did not necessarily marginalize the women's movement. But the process of formal integration into the national political body diluted their movement's potential commitment to women's issues and autonomy over their policies, positions and development" (2001: 137).

We can point to the instrumentalization of women (Tahon 1993) just as much as we can point to the opposite given the absence of women's political organizations even at the height of the revolution (Haddad 2000: 305). At stake in this debate is not, I believe, the truth of women's co-option, nor is it, as we have seen, the unjustified panic and fear-mongering expressed by certain Arab feminists vis-à-vis the specter of the Algerian experience. Rather, what is at stake is the ideological continuity that brought to the fore a national identity that women were obligated literally to make flesh and to incorporate. Also at stake is the passage from ideological appeals to women to the institutionalization of feminism in almost every country of the Middle East (especially those that experienced "socialism," such as Iraq and Egypt, not to forget the three countries of the Maghreb which soon followed suit).

This type of institutionalization, of course, stems from the centralizing nature of the state, which, in neutralizing political pluralism, acquires satellite organs whose function is to distill the regime's ideology. This phenomenon was evident under Nasser in Egypt, the Baath party in Iraq, and the FLN in Algeria, as well as the paradoxical and perverse regimes of Bourguiba in Tunisia[6] and Kemel Atatürk in Turkey. Where it did exist, as in Egypt, the women's movement held a relative but real autonomy under various nationalisms but progressively lost its autonomy with state independence. The women's movement became an instrument of the ruling apparatus and was thus meaningless. Indeed, the main ideological proposition consisted in recognizing women's participation in the construction of a national state which was, by definition, modern, but at the same time women were regarded as strong pillars of the "Arab Muslim personality." Moreover, in Algeria, where this thinking dominated the discourse, women were not to fight for their freedom, for they had acquired it thanks to the struggle in which they engaged during the war of liberation (regarding Turkey, see Arat-Koc 1999: 182). The new states expressed their identity through the status of women just as nationalist movements did during the struggle against colonialism. According to several commentators, these societies are schizophrenic in that their constitutions are anti-discriminatory on the matter of the relation between the sexes but the Personal Status Law, based on the Sharia, denies women their rights and perpetually treats them as minors. The institutionalization of feminism has sapped the extraordinary work initiated in the early decades of the twentieth century. Furthermore, this institutionalization has contributed to the distancing of women's movements from women of the middle classes (which gained prominence during the period from the 1950s to the 1970s), and, most tragically, isolated the movement from poor and rural women. The groups that have managed to resist the governing power – such as that led by the Islamist feminist Zeineb El Ghozali in Egypt[7] – have been violently repressed. The same fate befell El Saadawi and the Arab Women's Solidarity Association.

Autonomy?

Arising concurrently with the "straw women" of institutionalized feminism are the women's groups that emerged between the end of the 1970s and today. These groups want no more meddling by political parties or by the state and jealously guard their autonomy. They were faced by rising Islamism and the delegitimation of political regimes, which, far from fulfilling their promises, contributed to the impoverishment of the middle classes and the deepening social crisis (expressed in the form of riots, for, like the Maghreb, legitimate political protest was stifled). Nevertheless, these women's groups managed to create for themselves a place of some significance. The regimes have reacted to this activity by pitting one group against the other. It is not a strategy without consequences, as Saddat discovered when, following the path of "denasserization," he allowed Islamist groups to thrive (Sullivan and Abed-Kotob 1998: 73), but they turned against him when he recognized the state of Israel. In Algeria, the legalization of the Islamist and feminist movements in 1989 seemed to have been a change in *modus operandi*. Still, the strength of the Islamist movement is rooted in its proven history of collusion with the ruling party from which it attempts to distance itself by becoming the foremost oppositional force. Lacking similar means, the feminist movement has succeeded in carving out a small bit of space. After the elections of 1991 were halted, when they seemed to be leading to an Islamist victory, the ruling party attempted to bring women to the forefront as a way of demonstrating the legitimacy of its suppression of the Islamists, yet without moving to reform the Personal Status Law. Terrorism, not women, captured the spotlight. Both governments and media[8] in the West were lulled into believing that the moves towards democracy were genuine and the West reconsidered the servicing of the national debt and the extension of foreign aid in order to fight the menace of the possible fusion of Islam and the state. Women in this pitched battle were the chosen figureheads of the so-called progressive movement, given their explanation of the struggle against terrorists and political activists lumped together under the rubric "Islamist extremists." It is not only Western observers or the ruling elites who failed to distinguish between terrorists and activists. Many intellectuals and feminists proceeding from a strong Orientalist bias did likewise. However, it was not only women's groups that were drafted into this particular struggle, nor were they all created with the express purpose of combating terrorism. Such is the case of the Rassemblement algérien des femmes democrates (RAFD, which means "refusal" in Arabic). The women's groups know they are caught between a rock and a hard place. They find themselves in opposition to the ruling power and in opposition to the Islamists (Hadj-Moussa 1995). In Tunisia, before the general repression which befell democratic forces and Islamists alike, women were turning their attention to human rights. In Morocco, despite some progress, women's groups continue to present their grievances before the king, the only worthwhile hearing available. It is a habit that the independent press does not hesitate to criticize.[9]

The Not-so Silent Game

Before concluding, I would like to touch upon, by way of an anthropological perspective, a subject that has been debated by an impressive array of authors and raises perhaps more questions than answers. That subject is the matter of the hijab or the Islamic veil. It is not my intention here to discuss the validity of wearing the veil and whether or not women who adopt the veil can do so freely as an expression of agency or of individuality. Rather, my aim is to ask some simple but hard questions as to why the hijab is so important and what interests it stirs up. Does it tie women to culture? Following the recent historical and anthropological work of Benkheira (1996) and Colonna (1995) on the relations between popular and learned Islam, I would like to propose that the Islamic veil resonates deeply with some fundamental process at play in Arab Muslim societies and perhaps even beyond: that is, the retreat of popular Islam from learned and scriptural forms of Islam and the radical reformulation of social space. What do women have to do with this fundamental process, one may ask? As Benkheira rightly recalls, "women often constitute a source of resistance" (1996: 20), for it is with them that popular Islam and the cult of saints and marabouts find their basis. To conquer this, needless to say, quite strong resistance is to make possible and legitimate a learned Islam that rests upon the written word. Benkheira rightly indicates that the Islamic veil is regulated by a certain discourse while the traditional veil (in all its forms) is not subject to such a discourse. The undermining of popular by learned Islam, which was well in hand during the period of Muslim reformism, is conducted through women, or, to be more precise, through their bodies. Thus, instead of ecstatically prostrating themselves on the tombs of marabouts, women sit soberly listening to a sermon in a mosque. This is the expression of rationalism. Whether it is a modern rationalism remains an open question. It is a rationalism that wished to burn away the heretical dross of popular Islam in its crucible. "In making the mosque the only legitimate place for the expression of religious authority, fundamentalism does not seek to challenge the traditional hierarchy between the sexes but rather to destroy traditional religion" (ibid.: 21).[10] The struggle continues. and one must pay attention to the turn of attacks and counter-attacks by one side and the other.

Yet, whatever the goal may be, it is now true that many women who wear the Islamic veil enjoy access to the sacred texts. Certain feminists see in this a route to salvation. Unlike their mothers who had but little understanding of the Koran, these women are perceived as "revolutionaries" under the veil, to paraphrase the title of Adelkhah's 1991 book. They answer to God alone (Bessis and Belhassen 1992; Daoud 1993; Tahon 1994), not to men who, like themselves, are creatures of this earth and in need of improvement. We see in this phenomenon a kind of protestant revolution, which began, we may recall, within the walls of universities, centers of knowledge. But from the university, through the city streets and into homes, duplicitous governments (past and present), and towards the desire for a secular and democratic society, how much more wandering is there to be done?

Notes

1 The scare quotes are used to signal the complexity and the heterogeneity of this world.

2 Like the authors of *Remaking Women* (Abu-Lughod 1998), I leave the application of the designation open. Although an ambiguous term, "women's movement" allows me to include in its purview groups and organizations that have worked to raise awareness of women's issues without necessarily precluding the participation of men.

3 As Mérad (1987: 29) has demonstrated, *el Nahda* was also influenced by the Indian subcontinent through the important work of Sayyid Ahman Khan (1817–98). Those interested in pursuing the matter might wish to examine the replies to Renan's theories of a decadent and inferior Muslim world (E. Renan, *Oeuvres complètes*, vol. 1 (Paris, Calman Levy, 1947), p. 946) by the critique mounted by the reformers, notably Jamel El Din El Afghani who insisted on the effects of colonialization and its expansionist ethos.

4 As Mérad (1967) explains it, the Algerian reform movement emerged during a time when society was completely fragmented and facing a succession crisis. Furthermore, "although they perceived themselves as moderate Ibn Badis and his peers were all but moderate in matters dealing with women" (Lazrag 1994: 86).

5 I believe it is important to make the distinction between modernist and reform movements because when it is a question of redefining the place of women in society, the Koran and the Sunna, principal sources of authority, are not, except in a few isolated cases, reinterpreted. But just like the reformers, they seek to understand the causes for the lag in the development of their respective countries. But the two movements are subject to different sets of influences. The modernist for the most part looks to Western sources and European models.

6 Bourguiba, the charismatic Tunisian president, promulgated Family Law which is considered as the most liberal of the Arab world. It so happens, with the passage of time, that reform could not be led by women's struggles but always by the "Supreme Chief," who decided what was appropriate for women.

7 This amazing woman, an ardent defender of Islam, and a contemporary more or less of that other mythic figure of Egyptian feminism El Ashoroui, and supporter of the positions of the Muslim brethren, not only refused to allow her association to become a vassal of the Society of Muslim Brothers, but also refused to step down under pressure from Nasser. She was imprisoned and tortured and her association was dissolved (Sullivan and Abed-Kotob 1998).

8 During the first few years of the civil war, women and intellectuals were portrayed as the principal targets of the Islamists, while in reality it was young men who were hardest hit by violence.

9 Naima Bendriss very kindly kept me up to date with developments in Morocco (cf. Berraoui 2001).

10 Considering Algeria alone, the zaouias (confraternities dedicated to the cult of the marabouts) have since the days of independence been subject to governmental attacks (notably because of the role as go-between that some of these organizations played during the colonial period). But since the civil war, the state has been deploying considerable effort in establishing the visibility of the remaining zaouias to block the Islamists. The Moroccan regime certainly has been mindful of their importance and has since always counted upon them as reliable allies.

References

Abdelkhah, F. (1991) *La révolution sous le voile. Femmes islamiques d'Iran* (Revolution under the veil. Muslim women of Iran) (Paris: Karthala).

Abu-Lughod, L. (ed.) (1998) *Remaking Women. Feminism and Modernity in the Middle East* (Princeton: Princeton University Press).

Ahmed, L. (1992) *Women and Gender in Islam. Historical Roots of a Modern Debate* (New Haven & London: Yale University Press).

Amrane, D. (1993) *Femmes au combat* (Women in the battlefield) (Algiers: Rahma).

Arat-Koc, S. (1999) "Coming to Terms with *hijab* in Canada and Turkey: Agonies of a Secular and Anti-Orientalist Emigré Feminist," in A. Heitlinger (ed.), *Émigré Feminism: Transnational Perspectives* (Toronto: University of Toronto Press).

Badran, M. (1993) "Independent Women. More than a Century of Feminism in Egypt," in J.-E. Tucker (ed.), *Arab Women. Old Boundaries, New Frontiers* (Bloomington: Indiana University Press).

Badran, M. (1995) *Feminists, Islam, and Nation. Gender and the Making of Modern Egypt* (Princeton: Princeton University Press).

Benkheira, M. H. (1996) "Le Visage de la femme. Entre la *sharia* et la coutume" (The woman's face. Between the sharia and the custom), *Anthropologie et sociétés* 20/2: 15–36.

Berraoui, J. (2001) "Du courage politique" (Of political courage), *La Gazette du Maroc*, 3 June.

Bessis, S. and Belhassen, S. (1992) *Femmes du Maghreb: L'enjeu* (Women of the Maghreb: the stake) (Paris: JC Lattès).

Colonna, F. (1995) *Les Versets de l'invincibilité. Permanence et changements religieux dans l'Algérie contemporaine* (The verses of invincibility. Continuity and religious changes in contemporary Algeria) (Paris: Presses de Sciences Po).

Daoud, Z. (1993) *Feminisme et politique au Maghreb. Soixante ans de lutte* (Feminism and politics in the Maghreb. Sixty years of struggle) (Paris and Rabat: Editions Eddif & ACCT).

El Saadawi, N. (1986) "The Political Challenges Facing Arab Women at the End of the Twentieth Century," in N. Toubia (ed.), *Women of the Arab World* (London, New Jersey: np).

Fleischmann, E. L. (1999) "The Other 'Awakening': The Emergence of Women's Movements in the Modern Middle East, 1900–1940," in M. L. Meriwether and J. E. Tucker (eds.), *Women and Gender in the Modern Middle East* (New Jersey: Westview Press).

Gadant, M. (1995) *Le Nationalisme algérien et les femmes* (Algerian nationalism and women) (Paris: L'Harmattan).

Haddad, Z. (2000) "Les Femmes, la guerre de libération et la politique en Algérie" (Women, the war of liberation and politics in Algeria), in I. Med (ed), *Les Algériennes, citoyenne en devenir* (Algerian women, becoming citizens) (Oran and Roma: CMM and Istituto per il Mediterraneo).

Hadj-Moussa, R. (1995) *Le Mouvement associatif en Algérie: Quelques perspectives* (Grass-Roots Associations in Algeria: Some Perspectives) (Montreal: Arab Studies Center for Development (CEAD)).

Hadj-Moussa, R. (2003) "New Media, Community and Politics in Algeria," *Media, Culture and Society* 25/4: 451–68.

Hatem, M. (1993) "Toward the Development of Post-Islamist and Post-Nationalist Feminist Discourses in the Middle East," in J.-E. Tucker (ed.), *Arab Women. Old Boundaries, New Frontiers* (Bloomington: Indiana University Press).

Jamal, A. (2001) "Engendering the State-building. The Women's Movements and Gender-Regime in Palestine," *Middle East Journal* 55/2: 56–76.

Lazrag, M. (1994) *The Eloquence of Silence. Algerian Women in Question* (London and New York: Routledge).

Marzouki, I. (1993) *Le Mouvement des Femmes en Tunisie au XXème siècle* (The women's movement in Tunisia in the twentieth century) (Paris: Maisonneuve et Larose).

Mérad, A. (1967) *Le Réformisme musulman en Algérie de 1925 à 1940* (Muslim reformism in Algeria from 1925 to 1940) (Paris and LaHaye: Mouton).

Mérad, A. (1987) *L'Islam contemporain* (Contemporary Islam) (Paris: Presses Universitaires de France).

Peteet, J. (2001) "Women and the Palestinian Movement: No Going Back?" in S. Joseph and S. Slyomovics (eds.), *Women and Power in the Middle East* (Philadelphia: University of Pennsylvania Press).

Rishmawi, M. (1986) "The Legal Status of Palestinian Women in the Occupied Territories," in N. Toubia (ed.), *Women of the Arab World* (London and New Jersey: Zed Books).

Sandoval, Chela (2000) *Methodology of the Oppressed* (Minneapolis: University of Minnesota Press).

Shakry, O. (1998) "Schooled Mothers and Structured Play: Child Rearing in Turn-of-the-Century Egypt," in L. Abu-Lughod (ed.), *Remaking Women. Feminism and Modernity in the Middle East* (Princeton: Princeton University Press).

Sullivan, D.-J. and Abed-Kotob, S. (1998) *Islam in Contemporary Egypt. Civil Society vs. the State* (Boulder and London: Lynne Rienner Publishers).

Tahon, M. B. (1993) "En Algérie: Des Citoyennes 'à part entière'" (In Algeria: female citizens "entirely" apart), in *Genèse de l'état moderne en méditerranée* (Emergence of the modern state in the Mediterranean) (Rome: Ecole Française de Rome).

Tahon, M. B. (1994) "Islamité et féminin pluriel" (Islamity and the plural feminine), *Anthropologie et Sociétés* 18/1: 185–202.

PART FIVE

Mobility

CHAPTER TWENTY

Development under Globalization

Enakshi Dua

Since the mid-1970s, feminist theorists and activists have been engaged with gender development theory, policies, and practices. As the dominant practice among development practitioners has been to ignore the ways in which the processes of development impact on women, feminists have illustrated that development not only positions women very differently from men, but that development itself is a profoundly gendered project. Despite such accomplishments, at this conjuncture, the field of gender and development is at a crossroads. Since the 1990s, we have witnessed what many have called the "demise of the development project" (Sachs 1992). As Sachs has noted: "The idea of development was once a towering monument inspiring international enthusiasm. Today, the structure is falling apart and in danger of total collapse" (ibid.: 5).

While it may be exaggerated to proclaim a demise of development, changes in the international political economy and within the third world have transformed how development is being constituted. As we shall see, for much of the postcolonial period, the "development project" has been constituted as state-led, nationally based strategies for economic growth. However, the current ascendancy of the forces of globalization, with its concomitant regimes of neoliberalism and structural adjustments, have threatened the ability of third world states to undertake such a project. In addition, as new patterns of regional and class, gender and race differentiation have emerged within and among third world countries, many members of these societies have begun to question the efficacy of "development." As a result, the multi-class support that the development project once enjoyed has been eroded. Such changes in global and local political economies have led many theorists to question whether the "development project" is still possible (Booth 1994; Leys 1996).

These changes pose particular challenges for those who work in gender and development. As much of the work in this area has been set on ensuring that development theory, policy, and practice include a gender focus, such forces threaten not only the development project, but also the field of gender and development. Ironically, rather than disappearing, an interest in both development and gender and development remain. Indeed, the 1990s witnessed greater attention to a gender analysis, as several international donor agencies and governments integrated a gender framework into their programs. However, as we shall see, in the past decade, the fields of development and gender and development have undergone radical changes. As the social bases for the development project have been undermined, development policies have been reconstituted. As a result, gender and development policies have increasingly been tied to mitigating the effects of globalization. Missing in this new focus are policies and programs that attempt to undertake meaningful development. As a result, despite the radical visions that have characterized the field since its inception, current policies and programs fail to offer women in the third world meaningful development alternatives.

In this chapter, I explore the meaning of the transformation of the development project for those attempting to gender "development." The chapter is divided into four sections. I begin by defining and outlining the history of the "development project." As we shall see, "development" was a project of economic and social change that emerged in the postcolonial period. The second section documents the ways in which feminists have endeavored to gender "development." Next, I discuss the forces that have led to the erosion of the development project. I conclude by discussing the implications of globalization for gender and development. While each country, region, and community has its own story to tell, my focus is to provide a certain coherence to the common experience with development, and with engendering development.

The Development Project

Between 1945 and 1965 more than 50 colonies located in Africa, Asia, and the Caribbean achieved political sovereignty. These countries joined those in South America that had gained political independence in the pre-war period to create a category of the "third world." What third world countries shared was that political independence was accompanied by a distorted and underdeveloped economic structure. Colonization had left these countries unable to provide the basic necessities of food, shelter, education, and healthcare for their members. Colonial policies had distorted the ability to be self-sufficient in the production of foods and prevented the development of industry. Education facilities and health facilities were virtually non-existent. While political independence had been achieved, many of the leaders of anti-colonial movements felt that it would be meaningless if the economies of these countries remained underdeveloped (see, for example, Castro 1968; Nehru 1946; Nyerere 1974).

It is in this context, that the project of "development" was born. It was a political and intellectual response to the underdevelopment of third world societies at the historical moment of decolonization. While the development project has taken on different forms across time and space, for leaders and development planners of the emerging nations in Latin America, the Caribbean, Asia, and Africa, the pressing task was to transform the economies of underdeveloped societies. Ironically, in part, European powers shared this goal. Leys has pointed out that, as postcolonial nations were of prime importance in postwar global restructuring, leaders of advanced capitalist countries, international capital, and international organizations shared in the concern of increasing the economic productivity of the former colonies (1996: 5). For those countries that followed a capitalist model, two central components were seen as necessary for "development": the creation of a national economy and that this should be a state-led process.

Given that in the colonial period integration in the world economy had led to the underdevelopment of third world societies, it is not surprising that development initiatives would prioritize national economic development. As a result of international integration, the economies of the colonies had become specialized in the production of agricultural or mineral commodities for export, prohibiting the indigenous development of industry and thereby creating a dependence on the import of consumer and industrial products. As the price of agricultural and mineral commodities had historically been set at levels lower than that of consumer and industrial products, the dependence on imports of industrial goods led to a flow of wealth out of the country. Given such terms of trade, many development theorists and planners argued that as long as third world countries remained dependent on imports, they would remain impoverished (see, for example, Furtardo 1970; Prebisch 1971). As a result of such an analysis of underdevelopment, in many countries the focus of development was to facilitate the emergence of self-sufficient nationally based economies. Importantly, self-sufficiency was most often defined as the development of an internal industrial structure.

A second characteristic of the development project was that it was constituted as a state-led process. Assuming that the development of capitalism in the third world would have to replicate the conditions that characterized the emergence of capitalism in Europe, theorists argued that industrialization required a combination of an entrepreneurial "class" with a market for capital, conditions absent in most third world countries (for examples, see Rostow 1971; Warren 1980). In order to overcome these deficiencies, development theorists advocated that state managers be given powers and responsibilities that would allow them to restructure underdeveloped economies (see, for example, Kalecki 1972). These powers ranged from centralized planning of production to the power to enter into the economy directly. A strong state was seen as a key component of the development project. Indeed, many of the countries that have been more successful in implementing the development project have been characterized by strong developmentalist states (Deyo 1987; Evans 1995).

In order to implement such a model of development, leaders of third world countries required both national and international support. Despite claims to implementing a strategy of development that would benefit all members of a nation, in most cases the development project was a classed project. Indigenous elites (landowning classes, comprador capitalist classes, and emerging industrial capitalist classes), which had taken over political and economic power from colonizers, put forward strategies of development that privileged their interests: the prioritization of industrial development and agro-industry. Notably, such strategies led to a massive transfer of wealth from the poor to industrialists and large farmers (for a more detailed analysis, see Chenery 1974). As a result, those that have benefited the most from the development project have been capitalist and landowning classes (see, for example, Cardosso and Faletto 1979; Petnaik 1975, 1979).

Given the class character of the development project, leaders of third world countries needed to establish multi-class political coalitions to insure support for such policies. In Latin America and India, this coalition building included commercial farmers, public employees, urban industrialists, merchants, and labor unions. Support of the rural and urban poor was facilitated by subsidies for basic food commodities, health and education programs (Evans 1979; Petnaik 1979). In Mexico, political support was also facilitated by corporatist political parties such as the PRI (Institutional Revolutionary Party), which integrated popular organizations, workers, and peasants into a formal political structure (Hellman 1983). In the case of South Korea, the development alliance was forged through land reforms, which insured that wealth was more evenly distributed between urban and rural constituencies (Deyo 1987). In other countries, such as Chile and Algeria, authoritarian regimes enforced such policies.

As important as forging internal support for the development project was mobilizing international support, both economic and political. In order to implement ambitious strategies of industrial development, the third world would need first world technological and financial resources. However, Western powers had a different vision of how to constitute the development project. While there was a shared concern over increasing productivity of the former colonies, leaders of Western nations and international organizations did not share the focus on nationally based economic policies. Crucial to reconstituting post-colonial political and economic relationships was the construction of the Bretton Woods system. In 1944, leaders of 44 nations met to reconstruct a postwar economy. This meeting led to the Bretton Woods agreement, which brought into being four major institutions: the IMF (International Monetary Fund), IBRD (International Bank for Reconstruction and Development) – after the World Bank – the UN (United Nations), and GATT (General Agreement on Tariffs and Trade), which were given the powers to regulate the postwar international economy.

Notably, at this conference the representatives of third world countries lobbied to alter the way in which prices were set for primary exports, an essential component for the development project. In contrast, representatives of Western nations, particularly the United States, argued that what was required for development was more of the same: that third world governments needed to expand third world primary imports to earn foreign currency for purchasing first world exports. The representatives of third world countries were unable to gain support for their position (Adams 1993; Rich 1994). Without being able to generate revenue from the exports, third world governments would become dependent on international agencies and Western governments for loans and aid, a dependency that allowed donor agencies to exert influence over development policies.

Despite these limitations, as several writers have recently noted the impact of the Bretton Woods agreement on the development project has been contradictory, as it also allowed for the political and economic space for economic development (Leys 1996). Importantly, the agreement allowed for nationally based state-managed (and funded) economic development. As Leys has pointed out, by insuring that "capital was not allowed to flow across frontiers without national approval, which permitted governments to determine domestic interest rates, fix the exchange rate of the national currency, and tax and spend as they saw fit" the Bretton Woods agreement gave third world state managers the power to manage their economies according to national objectives (ibid.: 6).

Thus, the development project was an ambitious attempt to restructure the economies of third world nations, as well as the international economic order. However, the development project was also characterized by a number of contradictions. First, despite its claim to economic enfranchisement, indigenous elites succeeded in imposing a project of national bourgeois development. Second, despite attempts to reconfigure the political and economic relationships between the West and the third world, the project was dependent on the political and economic support of Western leaders. As we shall see, in the last 20 years these contradictions have become apparent, and are serving to undermine the development project.

Alternative Visions: Gendering the Development Project

It was as such contradictions in the development project were becoming apparent that feminist scholarship and activism around development began to take place. Feminist critiques have been engaged with demonstrating that national economic development was not benefiting all groups, particularly women and the poor. In the 1970s, feminist activists challenged the exclusion of women from the development process. In 1970, Ester Boserup wrote what was to become a seminal work, in which she pointed out that development planners had tended to ignore the significance of women's unpaid labor for national economies, labor that was critical in sustaining local and national economies. Boserup argued that because of such gender biases, the development project was working to undermine rather than improve the status of women in third world economies. Boserup's article, combined with feminist activism, has led to the emergence of a large body of knowledge that is engaged with engendering development theory, policy, and practice.

In the emerging scholarship and activism, feminists would challenge the universalistic discourse surrounding development by illustrating the ways in which development impacted differently on women. In doing so, they would present alternative visions with which the development project could be framed. However, there would be little consensus among feminists on how to reconstitute the development project. For some, this simply involved broadening the current parameters of development to include women. Others suggested that engendering development was not a simple matter of adding women to the development formula, but involved questioning the way in which development was being defined and shaped. It would require challenging the class and gender forces that were shaping development policy. These differences have led to four distinct theoretical and political approaches to gendering development: Women In Development (WID), Women and Development (WAD), Gender and Development (GAD), and postcolonial approaches (for a more detailed review, see Rathgeber 1990; Visvanathan et al. 1997).

Drawing from Boserup's conclusion that women had been excluded from the development process, those working within the WID approach went on to document the ways in which women have been excluded in four key sites: access to education and training, to paid employment, to political rights, and to legal rights. These writers and activists called for the inclusion of women in the total development effort. Moreover, they argued that such inclusion was possible within the framework of the development project – that what was needed was to "mainstream" gender analysis at the national and international levels. While this approach has been important for raising the issues of gender biases, as several writers have pointed out, the WID approach tended to ignore the structural and socio-economic forces within which gender inequalities are embedded, and through which development was constituted (Jackson and Pearson 1998; Pearson et al. 1984; Tiano 1982). This failure has led to a number of alternative approaches to gendering the development project.

In 1987, Sen and Grown questioned the link between development and national and international capitalism. They began by documenting the systemic crises arising from the development project, illustrating that in its short history development had resulted in the deterioration of the environment as well as increasing levels of poverty, especially for women (1987: 41). Notably, Sen and Grown argued that the reason that the development project fell short of its goals was because it incorporated bourgeois liberal assumptions of equality. They illustrated the ways in which the discursive understanding of economic activity that was embedded in the development project encouraged the exploitation of the poor, land and natural resources, open global markets, and militarism. Given such a framework, they questioned whether equality for poor women was possible within the framework of the development project, and called for socialist alternatives to development.

However, the WAD approach was also subject to criticism. Many feminist writers and activists pointed out that the singular preoccupation with class and capital did not allow for an analysis of the ways in which relationships between men and women shaped gender inequality. As Pearson (Jackson and Pearson 1998; Pearson et al. 1984) pointed out, it is the inequality of gender relations that ensured the continuity of the subordination of women. In addition, Kabeer (1994; Kabeer and Subrahmanian 1996) pointed out that a closer examination suggests that the development process was not only constituted through liberal bourgeois notions of the economy, but also through gendered understanding of what constituted the public and the private realms. Maria Mies (1986) argued that what was needed was an approach that emphasized gender relations in both the economy and the reproductive sphere. Drawing on these ideas, several writers have developed what is referred to as the Gender and Development (GAD) approach, which focuses on the way in which gender operates as a pervasive allocational principle, linking production with reproduction, domestic with public domains, and the macro-economy with the local-level institutions (see Kabeer 1991; 1994; Kabeer and Subrahmanian 1996). This body of research suggests that gender is constantly drawn on to construct the terms on which women and men enter and participate in public life and the marketplace (Young 1993).

More recently, feminists have offered another powerful critique of the development project. In 1988, Chandra Mohanty illustrated that development practice was often defined through a "Western gaze," one that reinforces and maintains the discourse of modernity as essential to Northern hegemony and development practices. Several writers have demonstrated that WID, WAD, and GAD models often portrayed third world women as poor and vulnerable, and presented a view of gender inequality that drew on earlier colonizing discourses of pre-modern gender relations (Mohanty 1998; Ong 1998; Parpart 1995; Hirschman 1995). Others have demonstrated that such discourses are also adopted by mainstream developmental programs, with the result that development programs reinforce notions of a North/South divide, with the assumption that the North is more developed and controls the key technology and modernity required by the South (Hirschman 1995; Rathgeber 1990). In addition, these writers have pointed out that the emphasis on poor women has led development theorists and practitioners to homogenize women in the third world. The role of class, sexuality, age, and ability are ignored. The result is that differences among women in the South are erased.

Feminist interventions have had considerable influence on development scholarship as well as on policy and practice. Feminist activism led to the UN International Women's Decade, which, in turn, led to four UN conferences of women (Tinker 1990). It has led to the collection of data on many aspects of women's work and lives, as well as resulted in the wider use of gender-analysis frameworks for agriculture, land use, poverty alleviation, community participation, and environmental policies among governments and NGOs. As Tinker (1997) argues, such initiatives have not only increased the visibility of women within third world economies, but also allowed feminist activists to influence development planning. Moreover, by gendering the development project, feminists have raised important questions regarding the ways in which the project has been constituted through postcolonial, class, and gender inequalities. Feminist scholarship has illustrated the ways in which the development project incorporated bourgeois liberal assumptions of equality. Most feminist writers have argued that resolving such inequities is not possible within the parameters of development, but requires fundamental social transformation of the development project itself. Such a focus of social transformation takes on new meaning as we witness the demise of the development project.

Undermining Development: Increasing Regional and Social Differentiation in an Era of Globalization

By the mid-1980s, the development project would begin to unravel. A new phase of globalization began to reintegrate third world countries into the international economy. Globalization introduced new rules and conditions for economic activity, rules that undermined state managed nationally based approaches to economic development. As third world economies were being reintegrated into the international economy, new patterns of economic differentiation among and within third world countries forced both a theoretical and a political re-evaluation of the development project.

As many writers have illustrated, the mid-1970s brought about a new phase in the organization of the international economy. A crisis in accumulation among advanced capitalist countries, combined with the emergence of new communications technologies, allowed for an internationalization of the processes of production. Globalization introduced new patterns in the international division of labor, as industrial production began to be transferred to third world locations (Harvey 1989). Just as importantly, it introduced new discursive frameworks for economic activity, often referred to as liberalization.

In the third world, the globalization project began with a debt crisis that occurred in many countries in the early 1980s. This paved the way for the integration of the third world into a new phase of globalization, as it allowed international donor agencies to impose structural adjustment programs (South Commission 1990). Debt managers demanded a shrinking state: a reduction of social spending on education, healthcare, and food subsidies, and the privatization of state enterprises. In addition, international donor agencies tied new loans to the condition that the recipient country implement economic policies that shifted manufacturing and agriculture production toward exports rather than for domestic markets, that allowed for a free rein of market forces, and eliminated barriers to international investment.

Structural adjustment policies have had profound effects on the ability of third world governments to pursue the development project. In the economic sphere, it has led to the emergence of a new international division of labor, the integration of financial markets, and the growing power of multinational corporations. In the political sphere, the discourse of markets and free trade has undermined the powers of states. In 1988 the Bretton Woods agreement was replaced with a new GATT regime, which limited the ability of states to regulate national currencies, provide subsidies to key sectors of the economy, and to regulate the flow of capital (Raghavan 1990). These changes eroded the integrity of the national territorial state as the location for a coherent political economy. As Leys (1996) has argued, this new discursive framework reframed the development project so that a state-led national project is no longer possible.

Importantly, the project of globalization has been facilitated by the new patterns of economic and social differentiation within the Third World. Those who have benefited from development – the bourgeoisie and the middle classes (especially those located in the private sector) – have been promoters of policies of neoliberalization and globalization. Indeed, in many countries, structural adjustment programs often garnered support from state managers, the bourgeoisie, and those in the middle classes who were not employed in the public sector (Sklair 1999). On the other hand, those who have been excluded from the development project are also increasingly disenfranchised from the idea of development. At the same time, new patterns of power are emerging in the international political arena, as newly industrializing countries, such as China, South Korea, Taiwan, Singapore, and India, are also exerting geopolitical influence. Ironically, the success of these countries played an important role in the rise of neoliberalism, as international donor agencies and neo–conservative economists attributed their success to integration in the global economy (see, for example, Ballasa 1981).

Structural adjustment programs, the cutbacks to social welfare, and the integration of third world economies into global capitalism has impacted very differently on women than on men. While it is important to note that globalization impacts on women differentially, depending on their regional location, class position, and sexual orientation, women generally have been particularly affected (Afshar and Dennis 1992; Enloe 1990). In some countries, the search for cheap labor has led to a feminization of the labor force (see Elson 1991). The withering away of state programs has been particularly regressive for women, as it has retrenched domestic and reproductive roles, and reinforced the public/private divide in the economy (Weigersma 1994). The largest cutbacks in the public sector have been to health and education, which affect women both as teachers and as health workers. The results have been decreases in real wages and employment for women. State cutbacks have meant that the access that women and girls have to healthcare and education has decreased (Manuh 1997; UN 1989). At the same time rising neo-traditionalist and familialist movements are imposing more "traditional" family and gender roles on many women, subjecting them to renewed surveillance and control. As Agarwal (1988) has noted, a different kind of restriction on women's reproductive rights occurs when fundamental regimes limit access to family planning. Women are reinscribed as markers of community boundaries, signifiers of cultural difference, and as reproducers both physically and culturally (Yuval-Davis 1989).

The rejuvenation of global capitalism has severely constrained the attractiveness and viability of the development project. As importantly, the erosion of state powers has undermined the ability of state managers to implement autonomous policies of social or economic development. As a result of these changes, several writers have questioned whether development is indeed possible in the era of globalization. Some writers, such as Leys (1996), have questioned whether autonomous development strategies are possible in an increasingly interdependent and internationally managed global political economy. Others, such as Amin (1990), suggest that if it were combined with socialist principles, democratic controls, and a commitment to national sovereignty, the opening of the global economy could potentially lead to new political trajectories of development.

Lost Visions: Gender and Development in the Era of Globalization: Mitigating the Social Costs of Adjustment

What has happened to the interrelated projects of development and of gender and development in the era of globalization? As the new rules of the international economy curtail the ability of third world states to pursue policies of economic development, and as international donor agencies have forced these governments to curtail their commitment to social programs, it certainly is reasonable to expect that "development" would wither away. However, as I shall illustrate through a critical read of recent United Nations Development Program (UNDP) documents, rather than disappearing, a discourse of "development" is surprisingly central to globalization. Since the 1990s, governments, international agencies, and development agencies have continued to employ a language of "development." However, it is clear that development is taking on a very different meaning.

One of the notable transformations has been that the "task" of development is increasingly undertaken not by local states, but by advanced capitalists and international donor agencies. As Hewitt (1996) has suggested, as third world states lose their ability to undertake social and economic transformation, the main agents and sources for funding development initiatives have been advanced capitalist countries and international agencies. Not surprisingly, this increase in the influence of international agencies has come with a cost. As Ravenhill has argued: "The North now enjoys a leverage unprecedented since decolonization over the economic strategies pursued in most of Africa, Latin America and South America" (1990).

Reflecting international interests, international donor agencies have targeted development resources towards integrating third world countries into the global economy. Duffield (1996), based on an extensive discourse analysis of international development policies, found that in the 1990s economic globalization had become the new discourse of development. My review of UNDP documents also indicated that international agencies have redefined "development" as participation in the global economy. For example, in a recent statement, UNDP claimed that its new mandate was "to strengthen the capacity of the least developed countries to benefit from the global economy" (UNDP 2001a: 1).

Interestingly, gender and development (and the poor) have taken on a new urgency in development discourse. Since the 1990s, international development and donor agencies have argued that priority needs to be placed on providing assistance for women and the poor. For example, a 2001 UNDP document declared that their priority was in "helping developing countries plan and implement strategies and solutions for reducing poverty. The goal is to get to the multidimensional roots of poverty, including through the creation of economic opportunity; the empowerment of women; participatory approaches to government budgets; and the better delivery of social services" (UNDP 2001a: 1). Chowdhry (1995: 32) found that the vast majority of development funds are being targeted towards providing social assistance for marginalized groups.

Despite the longed-for focus on women and the poor, these changes in development policies are problematic because of the neoliberal globalization framework from which they are generated. First, these development and gender and development policies deploy liberal discourses of poverty and inequality. In this discourse, causes of poverty are located in the "limitations" in the individual's ability to participate in the economy. Overlooked in liberal frameworks of poverty are the structural causes of poverty. Second, not only do the new development and gender and development discourses deploy liberal frameworks; in addition, they work to erase the ways in which globalization has increased levels of poverty in the third world. Increasingly, UN policy statements, as well as those made by other donor organizations, have begun to locate poverty in "national dynamics." As a recent UN document states, it wishes to develop "a renewed development cooperation framework which *prioritizes national ownership* of the country's poverty reduction strategy" (UNDP 2001b: 2). Significantly, by locating the causes of poverty within a national context, these policies are able to erase the multifaceted ways in which the process of globalization has and continues to contribute to poverty. Third, despite the focus on women and the deployment of the language of gender, these policies and programs work to reinscribe gender roles. For example, in UNDP gender and development policies the focus on women is legitimized through positioning women in their roles as mothers and caretakers (Chowdhry 1995).

Finally, the new development and gender and development policies work to further erode the autonomy of third world states. International donor and development agencies have been proposing that, in the future, development funding should be tied to "political conditionality." As claimed in a 2001 UNDP statement: "linking debt relief to poverty reduction should be seen as a key entry point for revamping the entire system and methodology of development assistance" and "the promise and delivery of debt relief is both a carrot and a stick to prompt countries to pursue, or persevere, in creating sound policy environments" as "it provides for strengthening conditionality and a potentially stronger role for the IMF in poverty reduction" (UNDP 2001b: 2). As Hoogvelt has suggested, such conditionality "willfully and openly does meddle in the internal affairs of state" (1997: 178).

As I have argued in this section, in the past decade both development and gender and development policies have been redefined in order to integrate third world economies into the global economy. In this context, international donor agencies have deployed development funds to mitigate the effect of globalization and, in this process, women and the poor have taken on a new importance. Despite this, the new development framework is working to reverse earlier development goals. As these policies deploy liberal and gender assumptions, these policies work to reinscribe both the class and gender forces that create inequalities. Rather than offering meaningful visions for development that could transform women's lives, the new approach offers to further the economic, political, and social forces that are perpetuating inequalities and differences in the third world.

In this context, feminist debates on engendering development become even more relevant. Extending the early work of feminist scholars and activists on the ways in which bourgeois liberal assumptions of equality distort projects of development to the new development agenda becomes a pressing task. Feminists need to continue to challenge the ways in which the development discourse is being reconstituted, demanding that the discourse of globalization is deconstructed and that its capitalistic, class, gender, and racialized biases are exposed. The emphasis on social transformation takes on new meaning as we negotiate development in the era of globalization.

References

Afshar, H. and Dennis, C. (1992) *Women and Adjustment Policies in the Third World* (New York: St. Martin's Press).

Allen, T. and Thomas, A. (eds.) (1996) *Poverty and Development in the 1990s* (Oxford: Oxford University Press).

Adams, N. A. (1993) *Worlds Apart: The North–South Divide and the International System* (London: Zed Books).

Agarwal, B. (ed.) (1988) *Structures of Patriarchy* (New Delhi: Kali for Women; London: Zed Books).

Amin, S. (1990) *Delinking* (London: Zed Books).

Balassa, B. (1981) *The Newly Industrializing Countries in the World Economy* (New York: Pergamon Press).

Booth, D. (1994) "Rethinking Social Development," in D. Booth (ed.), *Rethinking Social Development: Theory, Research and Practice* (Harlow: Longman Scientific & Technical).

Boserup, E. (1970) *Women's Role in Economic Development* (New York: St. Martin's and George Allen & Unwin).

Cardosso, F. and Faletto, E. (1979) *Dependency and Development in Latin America* (Berkeley: University of California Press).

Castro, F. (1968) *Major Speeches* (London: Stage 1).

Chenery, H. et al. (1974) *Redistribution with Growth* (Oxford: Oxford University Press).

Chowdhry, G. (1995) "Engendering Development? Women in Development (WID) in International Development Regimes," in Jane L. Parpart and Marianne H. Marchand (eds.), *Feminism, Postmodernism, Development* (London and New York: Routledge).

Deyo, F. C. (ed.) (1987) *The Political Economy of the New Asian Industrialism* (Ithaca, New York: Cornell University Press).

Duffield, M. (1996) *The Symphony of the Damned: Racial Discourse, Complex Political Emergencies and Humanitarian Aid*, occasional paper 2, March (Birmingham: School of Public Policy, University of Birmingham).

Elson, D. (1991) *Male Bias in the Development Process* (Manchester: Manchester University Press).

Enloe, C. (1990) *Bananas, Beaches and Bases: Making Feminist Sense of International Politics* (Berkeley, CA: University of California Press).

Evans, P. B. (1979) *Dependent Development: The Alliance of Multinational, State, and Local Capital in Brazil* (Princeton: Princeton University Press).

Evans, P. B. (1995) *Embedded Autonomy: States and Industrial Transformation* (Princeton, NJ: Princeton University Press).

Furtardo, C. (1970) "The Concept of External Dependency in the Study of Underdevelopment," in C. H. Wilbur (ed.), *The Political Economy Of Development And Underdevelopment* (New York: Random House).

Harvey, D. (1989) *The Condition of Postmodernity* (Oxford: Basil Blackwell).

Hellman, J. A. (1983) *Mexico in Crisis*, 2nd edn. (New York: Holmes and Meier Publishers).

Hewitt, T. (1996) "Developing Countries: 1945–1990," in Tim Allen and Alan Thomas (eds.), *Poverty and Development in the 1990s* (Oxford: Oxford University Press).

Hirschman, M. (1995) "Women and Development: A Critique," in Jane L. Parpart and Marianne H. Marchand (eds.), *Feminism, Postmodernism, Development* (London and New York: Routledge).

Hoogvelt, A. (1997) *Globalization and the Postcolonial World: The New Political Economy of Development* (Baltimore, MD: Johns Hopkins University Press).

Jackson, C. and Pearson, R. (eds.) (1998) *Feminist Visions of Development: Gender Analysis and Policy* (London and New York: Routledge).

Kabeer, N. (1994) *Reversed Realities: Gender Hierarchies in Development Thought* (London and New York: Verso).

Kabeer, N. (1991) *Gender, Production and Well-Being: Rethinking the Household Economy* (Brighton, UK: Institute of Development Studies, University of Sussex).

Kabeer, N. and Subrahmanian, R. (1996) *Institutions, Relations and Outcomes: Framework and Tools for Gender-Aware Planning* (Brighton, UK: Institute of Development Studies, University of Sussex).

Kalecki, M. (1972) *Selected Essays On Economic Growth Of The Socialist And The Mixed Economy* (Cambridge: Cambridge University Press).

Leys, C. (1996) *The Rise and Fall of Development Theory* (Bloomington: Indiana University Press).

Manuh, T. (1997) "Ghana: Women in the Public and Informal Sectors Under the Economic Recovery Program," in Nalini Visvanathan, Lynn Duggan, Laurie Nisanoff, and Nan Weigersma (eds.), *The Women, Gender and Development Reader* (London: Zed Books).

Mies, M. (1986) *Patriarchy and Accumulation on a World Scale: Women in the International Division of Labour* (London: Zed Books).

Mohanty, C. (1988) "Under Western Eyes: Feminist Scholarship and Colonial Discourses," *Feminist Review* 30: 61–88.

Nehru, J. (1946) *The Discovery of India* (New York: J. Day).

Nyerere, J. K. (1974) *Man and Development* (London: Oxford University Press).

Ong, A. (1988) "Colonialism and Modernity: Feminist Re-presentations of Women in Non-Western Societies," *Inscriptions* 3/4: 79–93.

Parpart, J. L. (1995) "Deconstructing the Development 'Expert': Gender, Development and the 'Vulnerable Groups'," in Jane L. Parpart and Marianne H. Marchand (eds.), *Feminism, Postmodernism, Development* (London and New York: Routledge).

Parpart, J. L. and Marchand, M. H. (eds.) (1995) *Feminism, Postmodernism, Development* (London and New York: Routledge).

Pearson, R., Whitehead, A., and Young, K. (1984) "The Continuing Subordination of Women in the Development Process," in Kate Young, Carol Wolkowitz, and Roslyn McCullagh (eds.), *Of Marriage and the Market: Women's Subordination in International Perspective*, 2nd edn. (London: Routledge).

Petnaik, P. (1979) "Industrial Development in India Since Independence," *Social Scientist* 7/10: 3–20.

Petnaik, P. (1975) *Classes in Contemporary Capitalism* (London: New Left Books).

Prebisch, R. (1971) *Change and Development: Latin America's Task; Report Submitted to the Inter-American Development Bank* (New York: Praeger).

Raghavan, C. (1990) *Recolonization: GATT, the Uruguay Round, and the Third World* (London: Zed Books).

Rathgeber, E. M. (1990) "WID, WAD, GAD: Trends in Research and Practice," *Journal of Developing Areas* 24/4: 489–502.

Ravenhill, J. (1990) "The North–South Balance of Power," *International Affairs* 66/4: 731–48.

Rich, B. (1994) *Mortgaging the Earth: The World Bank, Environmental Impoverishment and the Crisis of Development* (Boston: Beacon Press).

Rostow, W. W. (1971) *Politics and the Stages of Growth* (Cambridge: Cambridge University Press).

Sachs, W. (1992) "Development: A Guide to the Ruins," *The New Internationalist* (June): 5.

Sen, G. and Grown, C. (1987) *Development, Crises and Alternative Visions* (London: Earthscan).

Sklair, L. (1999) *Sociology of the Global System* (New York: Harvester/Wheatsheaf).

South Commission (1990) *The Challenge to the South* (Oxford: Oxford University Press).

Tiano, S. (1982) *The Separation of Women's Remunerated and Household Work: Theoretical Perspectives on "Women in Development"* (East Lansing, MI: Women in International Development, Michigan State University).

Tinker, I. (1990) *Persistent Inequalities: Women and World Development* (New York: Oxford University Press).

Tinker, I. (1997) "The Making of a Field: Advocates, Practitioners and Scholars," in Nalini Visvanathan, Lynn Duggan, Laurie Nisanoff, and Nan Weigersma (eds.), *The Women, Gender and Development Reader* (London: Zed Books).

UN (1989) "Women, Debt and Adjustment," *1989 World Survey on the Role of Women in Development* (New York: United Nations).

UNDP (2001a) *The Global Governance of Trade as if Development Really Mattered* (United Nations Development Program).

UNDP (2001b) *Trade, Gender and Poverty* (United Nations Development Program).

Visvanathan, N., Duggan, L., Nisanoff, L., and Weigersma, N. (eds.) (1997) *The Women, Gender and Development Reader* (London: Zed Books).

Warren, B. (1980) *Imperialism: Pioneer Of Capitalism* (London: New Left Books).

Wiegersma, N. (1994) "State Policy and the Restructuring of Women's Industries in Nicaragua," in Nahid Aslanbeigui, Steven Pressman, and Gail Summerfield (eds.), *Women in the Age of Economic Transformation* (New York and London: Routledge).

Young, K. (1993) *Planning Development with Women: Making a World of Difference* (London and Basingstoke: Macmillan Press).

Yuval-Davis, N. (1989) *Gender and Nation* (London and Thousand Oaks, CA: Sage Publications).

CHAPTER TWENTY-ONE

Migration and Refugees

Cecilia Menjívar

With increasing trends of globalization, the gendered nature of migration has been accentuated. Current world systemic political and economic dislocations generate large population movements, most of these punctuated by gender differences. Women in different areas of the world, mainly in Asia, the Caribbean, and Latin America, migrate internally to seek jobs in the ever-increasing export-processing zones in their own countries. Sassen-Koob (1984) observes that these women, through their work in export processing zones, become familiar with the different lifestyles and consumer practices of the countries where investment capital originates. Thus, when they are laid off from the factories (where the turnover rate is very high), they do not go back to the rural areas from where they originated (where their social and economic reinsertion will be difficult), but instead become part of an increasing pool of women who migrate internationally in search of jobs (as domestics or caring for the increasingly ageing population of richer countries, etc.) in the wealthier countries that house the firms that invest in the export-processing zones. Men also participate in large migratory movements, but given the jobs that are available in today's world economy, it is women's migration that has increased both internally and internationally. Thus, men migrate under organized labor recruitment programs, such as those that exist between the Philippines and Gulf countries or between Mexico and the United States. But relatively more women migrate as workers under these recruitment programs, or as family members, while relatively fewer move on their own or independently from these institutionalized practices.

In countries of the South (and East), military confrontations and political upheaval (aided and supported by powerful states in the North and West) produce large numbers of refugees. There are more than 20 million refugees in the world today and it is believed that approximately 80 percent of them are women and children. However, according to the United Nations, data on refugees are often incomplete. Thus, the assumption that women and children predominate in these flows is based on the notion that these movements are representative of the high fertility rates in the countries where they originate (1994: 78), and on the image of women and children as dependents. In any event, up to 90 percent of these refugees stay in developing countries, so the problems faced by refugee women and men are similar to those confronted by women and men in the developing world, such as poverty, high rates of fertility and child mortality, lack of adequate food and drinking water, and relatively poor health.

Women and men have been migrating from East to West and South to North at similar rates, but in some cases women have surpassed men, as in the cases of migration flows from Central and South America, the Caribbean, and Europe to the United States since World War II. Since the 1930s women have comprised a majority of the migrants to the United States, which receives the largest number of legal immigrants worldwide (Houstoun et al. 1984). In spite of this volume, much immigration scholarship was based on the assumption that international migration flows consist mainly of men, and simply extrapolated the experiences of men to women. Since the 1980s, however, more attention has been given to immigrant women in statistics and as actors in the process, to the point where now there is a substantial block of literature that documents their lives and experiences. An examination of trends worldwide points to some similarities between men and women, but, overwhelmingly, we now know that gender exerts significant influence on the experiences of immigrants, as men's and women's motivations for migrating, conditions of travel, and situations at resettlement are fundamentally different.

Gender ideologies permeate the entire migration process, as men and women migrants' experiences of migration are dissimilar and also are perceived differently by the bodies of law that reconstitute groups in the countries where they arrive. For instance, even when men and women flee political persecution or intolerable structural conditions in their homelands, their experiences in those contexts vary. A Salvadoran refugee explained that there was a belief in his country that guerrillas were likely to be men, or that men were more politically active than women; consequently, it was men who were more targeted by the army as potential subversives. In the same context, women were more likely to withstand gender-related attacks, such as rape and abductions, usually because a family member was politically active (Menjívar 1993), a "weapon of war" not uncommon in other politically conflictive regions of the world. Thus, in these situations, both men and women suffer, but gender ideologies shape the differential effects they experience. In the destination countries, women's and men's claims for asylum are accorded different weight. For instance, since the UN definition of a refugee (which has been adopted by the larger receiving countries) does not include a provision for "gender-related violence," the adjudication of asylum and refugee cases still rests on the assumedly gender-neutral conditions that prompt people to flee political turmoil. But the UN guidelines on gender have been used to develop a category whereby the emigration of women from areas of war and conflict can be expedited. Thus, some receiving countries have set immigration and refugee policy specially directed at women. For instance, Canada now identifies gender-specific forms of persecution as bases to request political asylum, and Australia has a category to accept single women and women with children whose partners have been killed or are missing (Manderson et al. 1998). Nonetheless, women are still underrepresented in refugee admissions for permanent resettlement in developed countries, as the legal criteria for granting refugee status (e.g., the UN Convention) do not include gender persecution as grounds for receiving refugee status or political asylum (DeLaet 1999: 9).

Refugee women and men who resettle in countries of the North and West often face the traumatic consequences of an abrupt flight and harrowing journeys, but they must also cope with disrupted lifestyles, culture shock, adaptation to a new economy, and different labor-force demands. Due to gender ideologies that portray women as keepers of the domestic sphere and as caretakers of the ill and young, and that confer on them primary responsibility for the family's well-being, quite possibly, women also have to deal with the psychological trauma of other family members. Thus, whereas men and women may be exposed to the same traumatic situations, different sociocultural expectations influence these experiences, with direct effects on their eventual adjustment in the receiving countries.

For immigrants who move from countries not undergoing political strife, gender exerts a different kind of effect, as more women than men seem to migrate as accompanying spouses, to reunite with their families, or simply, "on behalf of their children" (as indicated in statistics that show more women entering the United States under the family reunification category). However, one must not assume that because women have predominated in the legal category of family reunification, that this is the main reason why women migrate. As DeLaet (1999: 4) observes, women migrate for different and complex reasons but are admitted under family reunification policies that reflect assumptions about gender roles and women as dependents. For instance, often women face cultural practices in their countries that restrict their freedom, mobility, security, and well-being, which make them prime candidates for migration. In general, however, immigration policies, particularly the family reunification laws that stereotype women as dependents, often have a "gender" effect, as they tend to restrict women's mobility and legalization prospects more than men's. When women are admitted as dependents on their husbands' applications (either for refugee status or for regular immigrant admissions), as is the case under the family reunification category, women are made dependent on their husbands and may even avoid reporting domestic violence situations in fear of their husbands' retaliation, which may include stopping the process for the women to become permanent residents.

Sometimes immigration laws also result in the separation of mothers and fathers and their children, as parents (or a parent) often need to migrate first and, some time later, the children follow. In the absence of adequate and affordable childcare in receiving countries and differences in cultural expectations in schools and of the school system, often parents (particularly those in the United States originating in Latin America and the Caribbean) leave children in their homelands in the care of a relative, usually a grandmother. These separations can be traumatic for everyone, but because of ideologies about motherhood and about the pre-eminent role of children in women's lives, they pose more difficulties when mother and child (or children) are separated (see Hondagneu-Sotelo and Avila 1997; Menjívar 2000). Sometimes, however, children arrive with their parents, but given the high crime rates and ubiquity of drugs in some of the cities where many poor immigrants live, the parents or parent send the children back home to protect them from such dangers. Although the material and financial lot of these children (and their relatives, too) improves when the parents send money and goods from the wealthier countries in the form of remittances, this betterment does not come without a price. It is not uncommon that when children finally reunite with their parents (or parent), they find little to share as a family, because they sometimes cannot even physically recognize each other (Menjívar 2000). Men and women who migrate alone and without their children often establish a new family at their destination, which further complicates family reunifications.

Many immigrants (and refugees who are resettled in third countries) travel directly to their destination (e.g., those who travel with a visa or are processed as refugees and thus are legal entrants), but there are large numbers for whom the journey is hardly a straight line from point (a) to point (b) (e.g., the undocumented, which also include those fleeing political strife who are not recognized as refugees in the destination countries). Thus, significant numbers of men and women make their journey by land or by sea, sometimes crossing several international borders and oceans to reach their destination. Refugees travel in ways similar to those of "regular" immigrants because of refugee policies, particularly in the United States, that are in practice an extension of foreign policy. Thus, the United States has facilitated (and at times encouraged) the resettlement of Cubans and of Southeast Asians because receiving them as refugees has constituted a political statement against the (socialist) governments where these refugees originate. On the other hand, Central American immigrants fleeing persecution and turmoil in the 1980s were not officially recognized as refugees (and thus became deportable) because of the strong backing of the US to the governments of the countries where these de facto refugees originated. Therefore, Central Americans fleeing wars utilized the same channels (e.g., already established social networks of kin and friends) to make their journey that "regular" migrants (seeking to better their lives through higher-paying jobs or to reunite with families) use for their migration.

Men and women who travel by land or who cross oceans to reach their destination are exposed to myriad obstacles during their journeys, including delays due to robberies, often at the hands of the very smugglers that they hire to guide them, and even death. In many situations, men and women suffer even more traumatic experiences on their journeys as they did in their home countries. But here again, gender shapes in important ways how immigrants experience these journeys. Women are more vulnerable to being assaulted and raped, but, at the same time, they are more likely to obtain help along the way, such as shelter and food, due to sociocultural ideologies that portray women as in need of help. A Salvadoran who had gone through these experiences explained: "If women encounter good people, they will be treated better than the men because people pity women – you know [laughs], women are believed to be weak. The problem is when women find bad people, then they suffer more than anyone because the first thing that they suffer is, well, that they are [sexually] abused" (Menjívar 2000: 71).

Labor-Force Participation

Although women tend to have lower educational levels than their male counterparts (with direct consequences for their labor-market potential), immigrant women who migrate to seek employment are admitted under a wide range of occupational categories in the host countries (United Nations 1995). (One must remember that not everyone who enters the labor force in the host country is admitted under an occupational category: those who enter under family reunification or refugee categories also join the labor force and work in different sectors and occupations.) While it is true that many immigrants and refugees in developed countries take low-paid and unskilled jobs, the typical image of poorly educated immigrants with few skills is no longer the norm. Refugees' and immigrants' educational levels range from illiteracy, to primary education, to high school, to college and postgraduate schooling, such as engineers, doctors, nurses, and scientists. In fact, immigration policy in several of the largest receiving countries has been geared toward recruiting highly skilled professionals, as in the case of high-tech companies in the US and Germany, which actively seek to employ Indian engineers, and many men are recruited this way. Destination countries also sponsor programs to bring in unskilled or semi-skilled labor. Guest worker programs in Western Europe come to mind as well as the recruitment of Mexican immigrant men to work in US agriculture, a pattern that has been in place for about a hundred years.

Women also migrate as part of organized recruitment efforts, as in the case of Filipina and Caribbean nurses in the US (or Nigerians in the UK), who have been recruited since the 1970s to work in (mostly public, inner-city) hospitals across the country that find it hard to attract native nurses. Women are also recruited for domestic work, as in the case of Filipinas and Indonesians who work in Hong Kong, Singapore, and the Gulf states. The gender composition of the immigrants who are recruited to work in different occupations shows differential hiring practices in different occupations, as men are recruited more often to work in electronics or in science, whereas women are recruited to work in jobs that require "emotion work," such as nurses or as caretakers for children and the elderly. However, these concentrations may reflect differences in educational/occupational opportunities available to men and women in the origin countries as much as the recruitment practices themselves.

It has been noted that rates of self-employment (in the "ethnic economy") are higher among immigrants than among the native population, and men and women alike participate in this type of employment. Although this tendency has been observed in different countries and contexts, it tends to be more pronounced among Asian immigrants in England and the United States. However, it must be borne in mind that many immigrants resort to self-employment because of a lack of opportunities for paid work, which result from racism and/or the structure of the local labor market.

In some cases refugees' and immigrants' skills are easily transferable, but this outcome varies by region. For instance, whereas immigrant men from select countries (e.g., India, Japan, Iran) in the United States during the 1980s seemed able to convert their education into higher occupational statuses at higher rates than even native-born whites, few of their female counterparts were able to do so (Waldinger and Gilbertson 1994). Sometimes professional immigrant and refugee women, even those who are able to transfer their human capital to commensurate jobs in the host countries, are less likely to be promoted than native-born women and immigrant men (Goyette and Xie 1999). Thus, it is not unusual to find immigrant and refugee women with college degrees laboring in unskilled jobs even for years after immigration, particularly in the case of undocumented women or those who find themselves in a legal limbo. Professional immigrant men also land jobs below their human capital potential, but the jobs women tend to perform are less likely to be avenues for upward mobility than those taken by men.

In industrialized countries, where women's labor-force participation is high, immigrant and refugee women find jobs as domestics in the households of affluent and middle-class employers, but also in the homes of working couples who need childcare. For instance, many Latin American women, sometimes in spite of having high educational skills, have been caring for the elderly and children and cleaning homes in Los Angeles, Madrid, and Rome. In fact, because there is always demand for baby-sitters, even during times of recession, Latin American immigrant women in the US have been able to procure jobs more easily than their male counterparts and, thus, to earn more regular, though not necessarily higher, wages (Menjívar 1999).

However, baby-sitting or household chores are not the only jobs women perform that have contributed to their increased financial contributions to the household, since this has also happened when they work in other occupations, such as subcontract workers in the garment industry, as the case of Cambodian refugee women in California exemplifies (see Ui 1991), or generally in low-paid service occupations, such as the case of Latin Americans in New York. Immigrant and refugee women have found jobs in other unskilled and semi-skilled occupations, such as factory work, especially in apparel manufacturing and microelectronics. Immigrant and refugee women with high educational levels also find work in the higher echelons of the service sector, often in the healthcare professions or as office clerks. So one may easily find Nigerian nurses in Britain, Jamaicans in New York, and Filipinas in the West Coast states. Thus, in many cases, women's financial contributions to their families increase considerably after migration, sometimes even surpassing those of men.

Immigrant and refugee men, who generally have higher educational levels and are also more likely to convert past experience and education into commensurate jobs in their destinations, tend to work in a variety of occupations as well. Thus, there are Latin American men working in construction or as busboys, dishwashers, gardeners, or landscapers throughout California, Texas, Arizona, New York, and Washington DC. They also work in agriculture, as is the case of Mexicans and Caribbeans (and in the past, Asians) in California's harvests, or of Africans working in Spanish agriculture. Those with higher levels of education or those who have professional degrees also work in jobs in different economic sectors of the destination countries, as in the higher echelons of the service sector, engineering, computing, and science.

Often, the financial contributions of immigrant and refugee women are not viewed as work and are not limited to their work for pay. Gendered family reunification laws that see women as being dependent on their husbands (and that admit women as such), may exert an influence here, and contribute to the perpetuation of such myths of dependency. Thus, in many instances, women are not seen as workers in their own right, and their work is perceived as simply an extension of their "domestic" responsibilities. (And official rates of labor-force participation do not register these contributions that women make.) This is particularly true when they look after children while tending a cash register or prepare meals that they then consume with the rest of the family in the place of their business. For instance, immigrant family-owned businesses usually rely on and are successful as a result of family labor, as in the case of Asian Indians in England and in the United States and Koreans and Cubans in the United States, a practice that often hides women's real labor-force participation rates. The husband, often with other male relatives, figures as the owner and controls the most important decisions, financial and otherwise. Thus, in such cases, the work that women perform is not recognized as such. Furthermore, it has been observed (Anthias 1983) that men from ethnic and racialized groups who are active in businesses in "ethnic economies" may use their power in the home to counteract their exclusion from the larger society and, thus, exaggerate sexist behavior in the home. However, Bhachu (1988) observes that Sikh women in Britain have taken a more important role in developing business enterprises as a response to the racist exclusions faced by the whole Sikh community.

For immigrant and refugee women who work for pay – whether outside the home or as family labor – cultural practices that reinforce gender inequalities, as well as a lack of knowledge of their rights in the destination country, put them in vulnerable positions. Whereas immigrant and refugee men also suffer abuse as workers (e.g., they are cheated on their payments, fired when they complain; Valenzuela 2001), so too do women. And these abuses are linked to their different experiences as men and women, as women tend to be more susceptible to sexual abuse and harassment, while both are open to fraudulent payments and dismal working conditions. Such incidents seem quite commonplace in the experiences of immigrants and refugees among different groups in the United States, Europe, the Middle East, and Asia. The cases of inhumane abuses on the part of employers (in different occupations) of Filipina and East Asian housekeepers in the Middle East, migrant workers in Malaysia, Caribbean and Central Americans in the United States, and Eastern European women in Western Europe are but a few examples (Bonacich and Appelbaum 2000; Chang 2000; Constable 1997; Hondagneu-Sotelo 2001; Parreñas 2001). In many cases, however, the women suffer at the hands of their own relatives, as in the case of women who work in a family business, or when the husbands turn to excessive drinking to relieve the pressures of work. Also, more seasoned compatriots sometimes take advantage of the labor of newcomers – men and women alike. But immigrants and refugees, both men and women, have at times responded by unionizing and demanding better working conditions, as in the case of the organizers of the Justice for Janitors campaign, which sought better terms of employment for janitors – all immigrants – in Los Angeles (Hamilton and Chinchilla 2001).

Language is a key factor in immigrant and refugee settlement, for both men and women. For instance, immigrants can avail themselves of the social services and support provided by community agencies in the localities where they arrive, which are usually run by compatriots so all transactions tend to be conducted in the immigrants' own language. However, not being fluent in the local language curtails immigrants' chances in the labor market and it impedes them (particularly women) from learning and accessing services in their communities (Nah 1993; Bui and Morash 1999). Some immigrants arrive already fluent in the language of the destination country (because they are well educated or because the origin and destination languages are the same), but many others do not. Usually, immigrants and refugees with limited or no destination country language skills tend to live in communities with other co-ethnics, where they can find jobs (that tend not to offer much opportunity for mobility), as well as the comfort of speaking in their own language.

Gender Relations and Household Division of Labor

A powerful effect of immigration is in the changes in gender relations and in the household division of labor. Although there is extensive evidence that immigrant women may benefit from migration, there are indications (Kibria 1994; Menjívar 1999) that a unilinear progression from gender inequality to parity as a result of migration may not be universal to all groups, or even for the same group at different points in time and place. Although women's increased earnings and labor-force participation in host societies are believed to lead to gender equality in the home, such observations do not hold consistently, as studies have found that immigrant women do not always improve their status in the workplace, at home, or in the community (Hondagneu-Sotelo 1994, 2001; Kibria 1994; Menjívar 1999; Morokvasic 1984).

As immigrant women acquire more status within their families as a result of their increased economic contributions, sometimes gender relations become more egalitarian; but at other times the result is comparatively more unbalanced gender relations in favor of men because the women do not want to upset delicate arrangements in the home that would threaten the men's position (Kudat 1982; Menjívar 1999). Examples of this situation can be found among Asian and Latin American immigrants and refugees in the United States as well as North Africans in Western Europe.

It is difficult to observe what happens within the household. But it seems that in some cases, among professional immigrants, the household division of labor is more equitable because of the smaller gap between these men's and women's earnings. Professional women can command more leverage at home to pressure their husbands into increasing their participation in household chores because of their demanding jobs and the larger financial contributions these signify. Among groups that originate in societies with relatively more egalitarian gender relations, such as among the indigenous Maya of Guatemala in California, migration does not significantly alter gender relations (Menjívar 1999). Notwithstanding these points, generally speaking, gender relations in the home do change in favor of women, even though paid work alone does not seem to promote such changes. Rather, it may be the fact that they live and work in the different social, economic, political, and cultural environment of the destination society, where information networks and exposure to novel gender relations serve as catalysts for important alterations in gender relations as a result of migration (Menjívar 2000).

Men's status is often reduced with immigration, which can lead to marital conflicts and domestic abuse. This situation is compounded when, in some cases, women learn about new opportunities in education and employment, and, in general, about less restrictive lifestyles for women in the destination country (Menjívar 1999, 2000). When women start to question orthodox gender ideologies, it is not uncommon to find conflict and even family disintegration, as husbands and other men in the women's families do not always welcome such changes. But when immigrant and refugee women are victims of domestic abuse, sometimes they face additional structural and cultural constraints – language barriers, legal obstacles, and the expected tolerance in women to men's abusive behaviors – that prevent them from seeking help from legal and social services (Menjívar and Salcido 2002).

But not all immigrant and refugee women find themselves in the same situation, as many network informally and manage to access information and services on their own, often independent of their male partners or family members (Menjívar 2000). For instance, women can obtain information on domestic violence, shelters, and their rights at local community organizations, though their partners do not welcome such knowledge (Menjívar 1999, 2000). A note of caution

315

is in order here, for speaking the destination country language does not mean that immigrant and refugee women will not be victims of domestic violence. There are other factors that exacerbate its occurrence, such as isolation from the woman's own family, cultural norms and practices that buttress these practices, and, in the case of undocumented women, legal instability (Menjívar and Salcido 2002).

There are important public spaces that give immigrants and refugees a sense of increased status in the destination countries, and compensate for the loss in social status that results from migration. An example of these are religious institutions: some churches provide opportunities for men and women to be acknowledged and respected. For instance, in many immigrant churches women play central roles in reproducing cultural practices, where they also have the opportunity to access positions of authority. These expanded roles are linked to their increased levels of education and employment as a result of migration (Ebaugh and Chafetz 1999). In other immigrant churches, however, it is men who attempt to regain the power lost in the home as a result of immigration, and through positions of authority in their churches, as in the case of men migrating from Kerala, India to the United States (George 2000).

Community organizations offer services that immigrant and refugee women are likely to seek, as they are often in charge of the well-being of their families and are responsible for seeking help. These organizations provide assistance with educational and healthcare information, but are also public arenas that afford women a sense of increased status. Community organizations provide women with opportunities to meet other women in similar circumstances, to exchange information about myriad aspects of their lives (including their rights), and to learn about novel practices that may contribute to lessening gender inequities in the home. Immigrant and refugee women's participation in public domains has significant consequences for the well-being of their own families and for community building, as in the case of Cambodian refugee women in the Central Valley of California (Ui 1991). But the men in their families do not always welcome such participation, since it can ultimately have negative consequences for them, particularly when women learn about their new rights, as Salvadoran men and women commented in San Francisco, California, and in Phoenix, Arizona (Menjívar 2000; Menjívar and Bejarano 2004).

In sum, the lives of immigrants are shaped by the dynamics of the labor market in an era of increased interconnections as well as by country-specific immigration laws. But the immigrants' social positions, shaped by gender, class, and race and ethnicity, mediate the effects that immigration laws will have on their lives. Furthermore, in the case of gender, at least two sets of gender ideologies affect immigrants' lives: that of the immigrant group itself and that of the dominant group, which, together with labor market and racialization processes, produce a particular stratification system within an immigrant group (Anthias 1993). And, importantly, receiving countries devise dissimilar immigration laws for different nationality groups, so that immigration laws affect immigrant groups in diverse ways. Thus, immigrant women's and men's lives are inscribed by a multiplicity of factors, but not everyone is affected in the same manner.

References

Anthias, F. (1983) "Sexual Divisions and Ethnic Adaptation: Greek-Cypriot Women," in A. Phizacklea (ed.), *One Way Ticket: Migration and Female Labor* (London: Routledge & Kegan Paul).

Anthias, F. (1993) "Gendered Ethnicities in the British Labour Market," in H. Rudolph and M. Morokvasic (eds.), *Bridging States and Markets: International Migration in the Early 1990s* (Berlin: Ed Sigma).

Bhachu, P. (1988) Apni Marzi Kardhi. "Home and Work: Sikh Women in Britain," in S. Westwood and P. Bhachu (eds.), *Enterprising Women: Home Work and Minority Status Cultures in Britain* (London: Routledge).

Bonacich, E. and Appelbaum, R. (2000) *Behind the Label: Inequality in the Los Angeles Apparel Industry* (Berkeley: University of California Press).

Bui, H. N. and Morash, M. (1999) "Domestic Violence in the Vietnamese Immigrant Community: An Exploratory Study," *Violence Against Women* 5/7: 769–95.

Chang, G. (2000) *Disposable Domestics: Immigrant Women Workers in the Global Economy* (Cambridge, MA: South End Press).

Constable, N. (1997) *Maid to Order in Hong Kong: Stories of Filipina Workers* (Ithaca, NY: Cornell University Press).

DeLaet, D. L. (1999) "Introduction: The Invisibility of Women in Scholarship on International Migration," in G. A. Kelson and D. L. DeLaet (eds.), *Gender and Immigration* (New York: New York University Press).

Ebaugh, H. R. and Chafetz, J. S. (1999) "Agents for Cultural Reproduction and Structural Change: The Ironic Role of Women in Immigrant Religious Institutions," *Social Forces* 78/2: 585–612.

George, S. (2000) "'Dirty Nurses' and 'Men who Play': Gender and Class in Transnational Migration," in M. Burawoy et al. (eds.), *Global Ethnography: Forces, Connections, and Imaginations in a Postmodern World* (Berkeley: University of California Press).

Goyette, K. and Xie, Y. (1999) "The Intersection of Immigration and Gender: Labor Force Outcomes of Immigrant Women Scientists," *Social Science Quarterly* 80/2: 395–408.

Hamilton, N. and Chinchilla, N. S. (2001) *Seeking Community in a Global City: Guatemalans and Salvadorans in Los Angeles* (Philadelphia: Temple University Press).

Hondagneu-Sotelo, P. (1994) *Gendered Transitions: Mexican Experiences of Immigration* (Berkeley: University of California Press).

Hondagneu-Sotelo, P. (2001) *Doméstica: Immigrant Workers Cleaning and Caring in the Shadows of Affluence* (Berkeley: University of California Press).

Hondagneu-Sotelo, P. and Avila, E. (1997) "I'm here, but I'm there: The Meanings of Latina Transnational Motherhood," *Gender and Society* 11/5: 548–71.

Houstoun, M. F., Kramer, R. G., and Barrett, J. M. (1984) "Female Predominance in Immigration to the United States since 1930: A First Look," *International Migration Review* 18/4: 908–63.

Kibria, N. (1994) "Household Structure and Family Ideologies: The Dynamics of Immigrant Economic Adaptation Among Vietnamese Refugees," *Social Problems* 41/1: 81–6.

Kudat, A. (1982) "Personal, Familial and Societal Impacts of Turkish Women's Migration to Europe," in R. G. Parris (ed.), *Living in Two Cultures: The Socio-cultural Situation of Migrant Workers and their Families* (New York: Gower Publishing Co. and UNESCO Press).

317

Manderson, L., Kelaber, M., Markovic, M., and McManus, K. (1998) "A Woman Without a Man is a Woman at Risk: Women at Risk in Australian Humanitarian Programs," *Journal of Refugee Studies* 11/3: 267–83.

Menjívar, C. (1993) "History, Economy, and Politics: Macro- and Micro-level Factors in Recent Salvadoran Migration to the US," *Journal of Refugee Studies* 6/4: 350–71.

Menjívar, C. (1999) "The Intersection of Work and Gender: Central American Immigrant Women and Employment in California," *American Behavioral Scientist* 42/4: 595–621.

Menjívar, C. (2000) *Fragmented Ties: Salvadoran Immigrant Networks in America* (Berkeley and Los Angeles: University of California Press).

Menjívar, C. and Bejarano, C. (2004) "Latino Immigrants' Perceptions of Crime and of Police Authorities: A Case Study from the Phoenix Metropolitan Area," *Ethnic and Racial Studies* 27/1: 120–48.

Menjívar, C. and Salcido, O. (2002) "Immigrant Women and Domestic Violence: Common Experiences in Different Countries," *Gender and Society* 16/6: 898–920.

Morokvasic, M. (1984) "Birds of Passage are also Women," *International Migration Review* 18/4: 886–907.

Nah, K. H. (1993) "Perceived Problems and Service Delivery for Korean Immigrants," *Social Work* 38/3: 289–96.

Parreñas, R. S. (2001) *Servants of Globalization: Women, Migration, and Domestic Work* (Stanford, CA: Stanford University Press).

Sassen-Koob, S. (1984) "Notes on the Incorporation of Third-World Women into Wage-Labor Through Immigration and Off-Shore Production," *International Migration Review* 18/4: 1144–167.

Ui, S. (1991) "Unlikely Heroes: The Evolution of Female Leadership in a Cambodian Ethnic Enclave," in M. Burawoy et al. (eds.), *Ethnography Unbound: Power and Resistance in the Modern Metropolis* (Berkeley, Los Angeles, and Oxford: University of California Press).

United Nations (1994) *The Migration of Women: Methodological Issues in the Measurement and Analysis of Internal and International Migration* (Santo Domingo, Dominican Republic: International Research and Training Institute for the Advancement of Women).

United Nations (1995) *International Migration Policies and the Status of Female Migrants*. Proceedings of the United Nations Expert Group Meeting on International Migration Policies and the Status of Female Migrants, San Miniato, Italy, March 28–31.

Valenzuela Jr., A. (2001) "Day Laborers as Entrepreneurs?" *Journal of Ethnic and Migration Studies* 27/2: 335–52.

Waldinger, R. and Gilbertson, G. (1994) "Immigrants' Progress: Ethnic and Gender Differences Among US Immigrants in the 1980s," *Sociological Perspectives* 37/3: 431–44.

CHAPTER TWENTY-TWO

Class and Globalization

Abigail B. Bakan

Introduction

In this chapter, I consider the relationship between gender and class. Each of these terms refers both to the lived experiences of individuals and groups in specific historical circumstances and to specific ways of analyzing broad social processes. Many other factors – including race and racism, various levels of national economic development, and political forms of governance – figure into the mix. In the former sense, the lived experiences of women and men are shaped by specific class relationships that vary greatly over time, place, and social circumstances. In the latter sense, gender and class are theoretical categories that focus on different aspects of human interaction.

A Case in Point: The Mallory Children

A case study illustrates how class intersects with gender. This is the story of the Mallory Children (Dwyer 1994: 66–7). Some of the Mallory Children are now in their twenties, but they are still known by this name. They were first noticed by a doctor in the state of Metamoros in Mexico at a school for special education. They suffer from a series of severe disabilities bearing similar characteristics, resulting from birth defects. They have webbed feet, webbed hands, broad noses, and bushy eyebrows. Some are deaf. Some cannot walk. Some learn to walk only at age 12 or 13.

The mothers of the Mallory Children all worked while they were pregnant at Mallory Capacitors, later taken over by Duracell Batteries. Like thousands of other employees in the Mexican maquiladora zone along the US border, they worked for a company that faced no health and safety restrictions. The free-trade zone is one of the most profitable in the world, and its profits are directly related to how little investment the companies spend on wages or working conditions. Handling PCBs (polychlorinated biphenals) is banned in US factories because of their known links to cancer, but those same corporate investors use PCBs liberally on the Mexican side of the border. The class interests of the corporate management at Mallory were motivated first and foremost by the drive for profit.

What about the class interests of the employees? The mothers who work in the maquiladora zone were motivated by the same issues that compel millions of women around the world to work for a living – to support themselves and their families. Over 80 percent of the workforce is female: girls and young women between the ages of 14 and 20. They earn an average hourly wage of $US0.80–$1.25. Management strategy in the maquiladora zone, as in export-processing zones in many areas of the third world, favors the hiring of women, who are considered to be a cheap and flexible section of the labor force.

The mothers of the Mallory Children washed the capacitors – small television parts which store an electrical charge – in a liquid they called "electrolito." Their fingernails turned black, and they were always very tired at the end of their shifts. And when they became pregnant, they hid this from their bosses for fear of being fired. Then they saw their babies born with brain damage and webbed feet.

In Mexico's maquiladora zone, there are almost one million workers who daily face conditions similar to the mothers of the Mallory Children. There are approximately 2,300 foreign branch plants operating in the northern border region of Mexico. The vast majority of these, estimated to be as high as 90 percent, are American-owned. The other 10 percent include Canadian, British, Japanese, and German corporations.

The story of the Mallory Children indicates how the drive for profit, a class relationship of exploitation, has an impact in shaping many other relationships, including poverty and the gendered and racialized oppression of young women of color. This has impacted not only on the women who worked at Mallory, but also their mothers and fathers, their husbands and lovers, and of course the lives and futures of the children themselves.

While the case of the Mallory Children seems an extreme case, the maquiladora region which generates this type of health and safety violation has been taken as a model for global corporate investment internationally.

Globalization and Export-processing Zones

Export-processing zones, where multinational corporations with home offices in the most developed countries invest with virtually no regulations regarding health and safety or labor standards, have expanded throughout the poorest sections of the world system, in the least developed countries. The maquiladora zone is the model for a massive expansion of multinational interests throughout the Latin American region. The North American Free Trade Agreement (NAFTA), which includes the US, Canada, and Mexico, is being used as the model for a corporate-led move to expand an even larger hemispheric free-trade zone: the Free Trade Area of the Americas (FTAA). Also, conditions of membership within the World Trade Organization (WTO), which includes the majority of states in the world, operates to encourage the same pattern of investment and trade among member states.

As corporate concentration intensifies, so does the drive for ever-higher profits. Exploitation of cheap labor is one of the key mechanisms to draw in higher profits per investment dollar. Health and safety, environmental protection, and workers' rights all cut into higher profit margins. Class relations impact directly on gender relations. Corporations like Mallory employ women workers in highly vulnerable conditions in order to ensure a high degree of compliance and obedience, even in the face of hazardous and highly exploitative conditions.

Corporate globalization has an impact on virtually every aspect of modern life, from the ecological threat of global warming to the privatization of healthcare services. Corporate control of the world's wealth is now extensive. Since the mid-1980s, the number of multinational corporations (MNCs) has increased from 7,000 to more than 40,000. By the early 2000s, 50 of the top 100 economies in the world were MNCs and 500 corporations controlled 70 percent of world trade. Fully one-half of the total stock in foreign direct investment is owned by 1 percent of the transnational corporations (TNCs) in the world (Clarke 2000).

One trade group, the Asia Pacific Economic Cooperation (APEC), incorporates more than 20 states, including the US, Canada, Mexico, Australia, Japan, China, and the once mighty "Asian Tigers." The intersection of class and gender is clearly indicated in APEC's stated goals and practices. Based on a clear commitment to economic restructuring in the interests of greater profit maximization for corporate investment, APEC states that "issues directly related to poverty alleviation and social issues have by and large not been directly addressed by APEC" (APEC 1996, cited in Bakan 2002: 239).

The living and working conditions of the men and women of Asia are among the poorest in the world. Faced with high rates of unemployment, there is tremendous pressure for the poor to migrate to wealthier countries in search of stable employment. However, as the most secure and well-paying jobs in the advanced states of the global system have tended to be downsized by neoliberal policies, the prospects for legal migration for men and women migrants have tended to decline. Instead, only some of the most vulnerable areas of employment, including live-in domestic labor and "entertainment" that acts as a legal cover for prostitution, are open to foreign workers. The effect of these combined pressures is that today Asian women make up the fastest growing section of migrant workers in the world. Commonly, these migrant women are responsible for supporting extensive family networks across national borders. They send portions of their meager wages back home to their husbands, children, brothers, and sisters in an effort to offset the impact of increasing unemployment and poverty.

APEC has nothing to say about the lives of poor Asian families, or the gendered impact of global restructuring. However, APEC is not blind to issues of gender in another way. Publications from APEC indicate a concern that professionals associated with the organization's management should not be prevented from traveling freely across borders, including professional women. Again, class and gender intersect in the global system.

Class and gender influence the dynamics and structure of the corporations. The history of imperialism, colonial conquest, and slavery has left its marks on the contemporary conditions of class exploitation. While modern corporations no longer generally admit to maintaining a gender or color bar in their hiring processes, class exploitation is not a neutral process. The top executive positions of the multinational corporations reflect the patterns of racism, sexism, and class exploitation in the economically advanced states where the majority base their home offices. For example, few people of color and fewer women of color would find their way into the top executive management offices of the major multinationals. However, the majority of the employees who labor in the export-processing zones of third world countries are people of color, including those who are the descendents of indigenous peoples and slaves. Globalization has also shaped changing relationships between class and gender (Enloe 1989; Ward 1990).

Gender and Class: Theoretical Parameters

What can we understand more generally about the politics of gender by considering class relations? What are the various schools of thought that have attempted to analyze the connections between gender and class? What can we learn by linking gender and class to better understand the nature of oppression, and how we can challenge it? These questions are briefly considered below.

Understanding class relations allows us to see many aspects of how gender is shaped in our society. There are several distinct schools of thought that emphasize class relations. One of the main approaches was developed by Max Weber (1958). Weber emphasized that classes varied by occupational status and income. The wealthier one was in society, the higher the class position. Modern capitalism was therefore seen to be structured in a pyramidical fashion, with the majority of the population in the lower class, a large section in the middle class – itself divided by lower, middle, and upper strata – and a small minority elite class. A Weberian approach to class is largely descriptive, like a snapshot of socio-economic structure in a given moment of time and space.

Karl Marx and his collaborator Friedrich Engels developed a different approach to class (German 1996; Wright 1985). Marx and Engels (1969) saw the history of all human society as the history of class struggle. Classes in this view are defined according to how groups of society labor, or how humans transform nature and in this process transform themselves and relations among themselves. Each mode of production is marked by specific relations among classes – ancient society saw the division between aristocratic masters and oppressed slaves; feudalism between ruling landlords and serfs; capitalism between the capitalists who own and control the means of production, and a working class, or proletariat, who must sell their ability to labor to the capitalists in exchange for a wage. Originally developed in an earlier period of capitalist society when modern classes were less articulated, the Marxist perspective has proved to be very adaptable to changing conditions. In this approach, history and transformation are the key elements.

Capitalism was seen by Marx and Engels as a particular mode of production because of its combined tendency to expand the wealth of human society and, at the same time, its tendency continually to exploit the working class and subordinate the world's resources to profit. The workers' wage, in a Marxist view of class, is sufficient only to ensure that the worker can reproduce him- or herself and their offspring. But the labor of the working class produces much more than this. The surplus of the worker's labor stays in the hands of the capitalist in the form of profit. This surplus is used to expand their productive capacity and compete against other capitalists.

How do these notions of class apply to gender? Some feminists have transformed traditional class theory by maintaining that men in general operate as a ruling class or an elite, and women as a sex are an exploited class (Firestone 1970). Others maintain the relevance of class as a social category useful in understanding women's oppression, but challenge a form of biological determinism, reducing the socially constructed notions of female and male genders to essentialized, unchanging categories (Armstrong and Armstrong 1990). One view suggested by feminists influenced by postmodernist theory is that class is one in a series of forms of oppression experienced within society, similar to racism, sexism, homophobia, discrimination on the basis of ability, etc. (Razack 1998).

Other theorists have emphasized the centrality of class relations but insist that racism in particular is also key (Davis 1981). For example, Mullings has challenged the feminist notion of "patriarchy" on the grounds that it tends to assume that all men are in a similar relationship of power regardless of class or race. She describes the impact of racism on black families in the United States prior to 1900. Even after the end of slavery, the continued legacy of racial oppression meant that black male employees were denied access to land ownership, and paid wages much lower than white males:

In most U.S. cities, the constraints on the ability of the Afro-American man to earn a "family wage" forced Afro-American married women into the labor market in much greater proportions than Euro-American wives. By 1880 50 percent of Afro-American women were in the workforce as compared to 15 percent of Euro-American women. While the majority of working women of both races were unmarried, significantly higher proportions of Afro-American wives worked. (1986: 53)

Another school of thought, broadly termed socialist feminism, has focused on the material conditions and historical context in which the sexual division of labor has developed. These authors have focused on the specific relationship between the labor performed in the home and the labor performed in the public, waged economy. A common thread among socialist feminist theorists is a tendency to view capitalism as a system dominated by two distinct modes of operation – one a mode of production that dominates the world of work and labor, and a second mode of reproduction that regulates the family, sexual relations, and ideology. The former is seen as a capitalist mode of production; the latter a patriarchal mode of reproduction. There are various views, however, of the relationship between gender and class within this school. Some maintain that the labor of women in the home is isolated and alienated (Eisenstein 1979). Others have seen women's work in the home as something that is the only unalienated locus of labor (Sontag 1973). And still other theorists have argued that there is a common interest between men in the working class and the capitalist system's ruling class, which is also male-dominated, in a cross-class patriarchal alliance (Hartmann 1979).

Marxist theorists of gender and socialist feminists, while sharing many assumptions regarding oppression, differ on their causes. Some Marxist theorists, while firmly opposing gender oppression, have objected to the dualistic structure of two modes – one of production and the other of reproduction – suggested by patriarchy theory (Cliff 1984; German 1989; Vogel 1983). Instead, it has been argued that women's oppression is a central part of capitalism, and intrinsic to it as a system. The view here is that Marxist analysis can explain the relationship between productive labor and all human relations in society. From this perspective, the family is itself seen as a historical form of social relationship, one that varies in different periods of time and among different societies.

The real test of analytical theory, however, is the ability to explain the world as it exists in lived experience. Where class analysis of gender has been particularly valuable is in unpacking the complex realm of women's work.

Linking gender and class can allow us to view women's labor in the home as a necessary feature of capitalist reproduction. In the working class, women's labor serves to reproduce the labor power of the current generation of workers, and the next generation of future workers. Capitalism, like earlier class societies, has benefited from the unpaid labor performed by women in the home. The heterosexual nuclear family is presented as the norm in the media, the education system, and other means of promoting state ideology, as if this is an ideal type, and encouraged materially by the structure of the private household. There are many other family forms, including same-sex partnerships or single-parent households. And there are many factors in life affecting the choices of women and men regarding the bearing, raising, and caring of children, including income, access to birth control and abortion, and access to childcare. Gender and class linkages apply not only to women's work in the home, but also to the complex relationship between women's paid and unpaid work.

Working for a Living

Prior to the women's movement of the 1960s and 1970s, the idea was widespread that paid, waged work was the realm of the male breadwinner, and "women's work" consisted of being at home caring for the "man of the house" and raising children. One example of this traditional sexist view is revealed in the following excerpt from a Canadian textbook used in 1950 in Ontario on the instruction of secondary school girls in the subject of home economics:

> Get your work done: Plan your tasks with an eye on the clock. Finish or interrupt them an hour before he is expected. Your anguished cry, "Are you home already?" is not exactly a warm welcome. Have dinner ready: Plan ahead, even the night before, to have a delicious meal – on time. This is a way of letting him know that you have been thinking about him and are concerned about his needs. (*Toronto Star*, March 9, 1994, F5)

Today, this projected image of the future teenage girls, and more accurately white middle-class teenage girls, is so off base as to be laughable. Over recent decades, there has been a dramatic increase in the number of women who work for a wage or a salary, and they do so for the same reasons that men work: to support themselves and their families. In countries all over the world, more and more women have been drawn into full- or part-time paid labor.

Women's paid jobs in the advanced Western economies of Europe and North America have tended to be concentrated in certain sectors, or women's job ghettoes, such as teaching, hospital service, or secretarial work. As global capitalism has expanded, however, more and more women are also employed in "maquiladora" districts similar to the Mexican border zones, working on factory lines in sweatshop conditions and producing everything from shoes to microchips.

At the same time, a majority of women continue to bear the main responsibility of care in the home. While male participation in household chores and childcare has increased to some extent, the "double burden" of women's work – working one shift outside the home for a wage followed by a second unpaid shift in the home – has increasingly set the standard. Employers have benefited from this double burden in two ways. First, female workers are often offered less job security and lower pay than men. Women are treated as secondary wage earners, and are commonly forced to accept part-time jobs and face severe discrimination on the claim that pregnancy and child-rearing interruptions make them "unreliable" workers. Second, women's unpaid labor in the home is a source of economic and social stability for the employing class, ensuring that the private family continues to run smoothly, both daily and over the generations.

It is a myth, however, to presume that there was ever a time when most women were entirely removed from wage labor. The vast majority of women – including poor women, immigrant women, black and other women of color – have historically worked for wages in the paid labor market as well as in the private home. The two spheres of labor have often been artificially counterpoised, separated by what is referred to as the public/private divide (Pateman 1988).

One feature of the relationship between gender and class is starkly revealed in how different groups of women have struggled to cope with this double burden. Ruling-class or elite women, or women of sufficient wealth and means, have historically and in the present hired other women as domestic workers to care for the duties in the home. The majority of women, however, have been among the pool of domestic workers who have had to work long hours in highly exploited conditions as a means of supporting their own families. The domestic service industry can only be understood if class divisions among women and their families are highlighted analytically.

Domestic service, paid or unpaid, is overwhelmingly women's work. Historically in the advanced West, and today in many parts of the world, many women are unable to find paid work unless they enter domestic service. But women with other options leave paid domestic work at the earliest opportunity. The evolution of paid domestic service is difficult to trace precisely, but there are some general patterns that can be described. In general, as capitalist industrialization has expanded, the mass of agricultural workers became impoverished. Traditionally, it was the children of poor farmers who became the servants in urban homes of the wealthy. Far larger numbers were usually available to work than there were jobs for them to fill. Women workers, often young and unmarried, have been available in large numbers to work as servants, sometimes just for the cost of a roof over their heads. In the US, for example, the Labor Department's category of "household workers" – including housekeepers, cooks, maids, launderers, childcare workers, servants, and cleaners – was the largest single category of all employed working women during the nineteenth century. After 1870, the figure declined from a high of 52 percent in that year, and consistently declined after 1900.

The most dramatic turning point in women's work, including in paid domestic service, occurred in the years during and after the Second World War. During the postwar boom, capitalist industry experienced its most sustained and advanced expansion in history, and with it the structure of women's work in both the "public" and "private" realms changed. Not only have more women entered the paid labor force, in particular married women with young children, but new birth control technologies and new ideas about women's rights also affected the structure of work in the family. Average family size in advanced economies has declined; women who have children out of wedlock tend to raise them rather than put them up for adoption; women tend to wait longer to marry and divorce rates are higher; and those women who have children have fewer of them.

There is also a new demand among working mothers for adequate childcare. Few countries in the world have developed national programs to provide quality, accessible childcare. The shortage in childcare, particularly for pre-school-age children, has produced a new and increased demand for private domestic

workers and nannies. As women with citizenship rights and access to employment opportunities formerly denied have increased, immigrant non-citizen
domestic workers have often filled the demand for in-home childcare. Internationally, there is an increasing divide between women of means and women
who perform labor in the home, the latter usually poor women of color of third
world origin.

Throughout the 1980s and 1990s, immigrant female domestic workers – often
from the poorest countries and regions in the world where there are few employment options – worked in domestic service, often enduring highly abusive and
exploitive conditions, only because there was no other work available (Heyzer et
al. 1994). Immigration policies of receiving states have taken advantage of the
demand for in-home childcare by denying rights to foreign domestic workers
that are normally afforded to other immigrants or permanent residents. These
include being forced to live with one's employer, denial of privacy, lack of labor
rights, lack of social security, and, under fear of deportation, abusive conditions
ranging from non-payment of wages to denial of food, imprisonment, sexual
abuse, and seized passports (Bakan and Stasiulis 1997).

Conclusion: Gender, Class, and Resistance

A focus on gender and class highlights specific effects of multiple forms of
oppression. It also, however, highlights a rich tradition of working-class
women's resistance. March 8, International Women's Day, was originally recognized as a day to commemorate a 1909 strike by women garment workers in New
York City, when they took to the streets to protest against dangerous working
conditions and low pay. In 1917, the Russian Revolution was sparked on International Women's Day by a demonstration of women against the brutalities
of the First World War.

Today, a rising movement against the damaging effects of neoliberal policies
has found support and resonance among women from Mexico City to Prague,
from Quebec City to Nice. Working women continue to be at the forefront of
the international movement for liberation from oppression. Gender and class
issues are linked not only in theory, not only in history, but also in the ongoing
movements to challenge oppressive practices in all their manifestations.

References

APEC Economic Committee (1996) *State of Economic and Technical Cooperation in APEC* (Singa-
    pore: APEC Secretariat).
Armstrong, P. and Armstrong, H. (1990) *Theorizing Women's Work* (Toronto: Garamond Press).
Bakan, A. B. (2002) "Capital, Marxism and World Economy: APEC and the MAI," in Abigail B.
    Bakan and Eleanor MacDonald (eds.), *Critical Political Studies: Debates and Dialogues from the
    Left* (Montreal: McGill-Queen's University Press).

Bakan, A. B. and Stasiulis, D. (eds.) (1997) *Not One of the Family: Foreign Domestic Workers in Canada* (Toronto: University of Toronto Press).

Clarke, T. (2000) "The Emergence of Corporate Power and What to do About it." International Forum on Globalization Publications, <http://www.ifg.org/corprule.html>

Cliff, T. (1984) *Class Struggle and Women's Liberation* (London: Bookmarks).

Davis, A. (1981) *Women, Race and Class* (New York: Random House).

Dwyer, A. (1994) *On the Line: Life on the US–Mexican Border* (London: Latin American Bureau).

Eisenstein, Z. (1979) "Developing a Theory of Capitalist Patriarchy and Socialist Feminism," in S. Eisenstein (ed.), *Capitalist Patriarchy and the Case for Socialist Feminism* (New York: Monthly Review Press).

Enloe, C. (1989) *Bananas, Beaches and Bases: Making Feminist Sense of International Politics* (Berkeley: University of California Press).

Firestone, S. (1970) *The Dialectic of Sex: The Case for Feminist Revolution* (New York: William Morrow and Co.).

German, L. (1989) *Sex, Class and Socialism* (London: Bookmarks).

German, L. (1996) *A Question of Class* (London: Bookmarks).

Hartmann, H. (1979) "The Unhappy Marriage of Marxism and Feminism," *Capital and Class* (London edn.) 8 (summer).

Heyzer, N., Lycklama a Nijeholt, G., and Weerakoon, N. (eds.) (1994) *The Trade in Domestic Workers: Causes, Mechanisms and Consequences of International Migration* (Kuala Lumpur and London: Asian and Pacific Development Centre and Zed Books Ltd).

Marx, K. and Engels, F. (1969) "Manifesto of the Communist Party," in *Selected Works* (Moscow: Progress Publishers).

Mullings, L. (1986) "Uneven Development: Class, Race, and Gender in the United States Before 1900," in Eleanor Leacock, Helen I. Safa, et al., *Women's Work* (Massachusetts: Bergin and Garvey).

Pateman, C. (1988) "The Patriarchal Welfare State," in A. Gutmann (ed.), *Democracy and the Welfare State* (Princeton: Princeton University Press).

Razack, S. (1998) *Looking White People in the Eye: Gender, Race and Culture in Courtrooms and Classrooms* (Toronto: University of Toronto Press).

Sontag, S. (1973) "The Third World of Women," *Partisan Review* 60.

Vogel, L. (1983) *Marxism and the Oppression of Women: Toward a Unitary Theory* (New Brunswick, NJ: Rutgers University Press and Pluto Press).

Weber, M. (1958) *From Max Weber*, trans. and ed. H. H. Gerth and C. Wright Mills (New York: Galaxy).

Ward, K. (ed.) (1990) *Women Workers and Global Restructuring* (Ithaca, NY: Cornell University Press).

Wright, E. O. (1985) *Classes* (London: Verso).

CHAPTER TWENTY-THREE

Unions: Resistance and Mobilization

Linda Briskin

Like all social institutions, unions are organized by gender. In many Western countries, evidence, particularly from the nineteenth century, speaks to men's active exclusion of women workers from unions. Ironically, this position often worked against their own class interests, since employers could then more easily hire women workers as cheap replacements. Unions have also been a vehicle for the construction and validation of particular forms of masculinity, and this has increased men's resistance to the presence and participation of women in unions. Gender practices in unions, then, have most often been about difference, exclusion, and power.

However, in the 1970s, union women began to identify their gender status as meaningful, and to organize to resist and reconfigure the gender order of unions. This organizing has exposed taken-for-granted gendered practices, led to the articulation of a proactive agenda for unions to take account of gender realities, and helped to make visible the significance of other social identities based on race, ethnicity, sexuality, and ability. Undoubtedly, it has had a dramatic impact on the structures, policies, practices, and climate of union movements in many countries.

This chapter begins by examining the gendered barriers women face inside unions from both patriarchal and bureaucratic structures and ideologies. It then explores the strategies women have used to transform the gender order of unions: representation, redefining union issues, expanding the collective bargaining agenda, and separate organizing and constituency building. A thread through all the initiatives of union women is the call for a substantively different form of democracy: for structures of participation and inclusivity rather than simply representation. Women's struggle for gender democracy has provided a foundation for alliances with rank-and-file activists of both sexes who are also seeking to transform union practices.

Finally, this chapter considers the current context. Globalization and restructuring are affecting all union movements, although unevenly, and reshaping the significance of gender, race, and citizenship to organizing strategies. These economic and political changes are certainly heightening the relevance of gender to the task of organizing the unorganized into unions as some innovative initiatives by women workers in India and Canada demonstrate.

Since the 1970s a new gender consciousness has strengthened union movements in many countries. In the current context, gender realities must inform opposition to globalization. For union movements to survive and flourish, this chapter contends, they need to shift gendered consciousness from the margin to the center of union resistance. Alliances and coalitions across unions, with social movements and across borders, offer a key strategy to this end.

Two assumptions inform this presentation. First, although this chapter focuses on gender, it recognizes that the categories "women" and "men" homogenize experience and obscure the differences among women and among men based on ethnicity, class, sexuality, racialization, citizenship, age, and ability. It also challenges the traditional privileging of class in much union ideology, arguing instead that the experience of class is gender- and race-specific, and the experience of gender and race is mediated by class locations. So, for example, working–class women experience their class positions differently than working-class men. In the unions, the privileging of class over gender and race hides these differences and undermines solidarity and resistance.

Second, this chapter rejects the paradigm of women as passive victims in the face of a discriminatory gendered order. Despite acknowledging the barriers women face to full citizenship in unions, it highlights agency – that is, the power of women to act individually and collectively on their own behalf. It also resists the deficit model which links women's problems to some inadequacy in women themselves – an ideological strategy of blaming the victim common to the defense of traditional gender relationships. It argues that, by and large, unions, rather than women, need to change despite the value of programs that improve women's self-esteem, develop their assertiveness, and train them in union procedures.

Barriers to Union Participation

A report from the European Trade Union Confederation (ETUC) (Braithwaite and Byrne 1995) identifies four major barriers to union participation, each of which resonates with gendered ideologies: family responsibilities, job segregation, masculine union cultures that structure unions in ways that limit women's inclusion, and traditional stereotypes. When such stereotypes are internalized by women, their confidence in their capacity to organize and lead is weakened, and when they are externalized by men, they result in overt and covert prejudices against women.

Family responsibilities constitute the barrier most often cited. The ETUC concludes that there is a "skewed age and fertility profile of women union leaders, who tend to be younger women without family commitments or older women whose children have grown up" (Braithwaite and Byrne 1995: 13). In a

1993 study of stewards in the United States, "women said that their main conflict was how to keep union responsibilities from interfering with or subtracting from family time . . . male stewards. . . . usually gave priority to the union responsibility" (Roby and Uttal: 367–70).

Australian research found that it is less the presence of children that inhibits women's activism than "lower incomes, an interrupted career and shorter periods of union membership, which are in turn associated with parenting" (Pocock 1995: 387). Cutbacks in social services, which increase the unpaid caring work of women, make union activism even more difficult for women. It is also the case that patterns of occupational stratification, gender power, and union leadership intersect – that is, "union structures reflect the sex-segregated character of the labor market and create barriers for women's advancement" (Braithwaite and Byrne 1995: 13). Women's segregation in low-paid work with often unrecognized skills and little flexibility means that they may not be encouraged into or chosen as union leaders. In a recent American study of custodians, clerks, and cafeteria workers who were members of the Communications Workers of America or the United Auto Workers, Coventry and Morrissey found the same pattern: "Both gender and status discrimination seem to block unskilled women from positions of power within their union and from participation in union activities" (1998: 291).

In assessing the situation of women in Australian unions, Pocock groups barriers under personal, union, and job-related characteristics. She finds that "unions most commonly take action that addresses the personal deficiencies of women rather than deficiencies in the way unions work" (1995: 383). She concludes: "A genuine transformation of the Australian union movement . . . depends upon a shift in perception and action away from 'fixing deficient women' towards a close examination of union methods, organizing habits, and support structures for activism" (ibid.: 399).

Resisting the Gender Order

Union women in both the North and the South have taken initiatives to challenge the traditional gender order of unions: around representation, redefining union issues, expanding the collective bargaining agenda, and separate organizing and constituency building. As a result, unions in many countries have changed the way they do their work, and moved toward greater inclusivity and more democratic practices.

Representation

Many unions and federations now have affirmative action policies that designate or add seats on leadership bodies for women in an attempt to address their under-representation in top elected positions.

In Canada, this process began in 1983 when the Ontario Federation of Labor (OFL) broke new ground by amending its constitution to create five affirmative action positions on its executive board. The increased awareness of representational issues has had effects in other areas: employment equity for union staff; affirmative action seats on Executive Boards of unions for racial minorities, gays and lesbians, and aboriginal peoples; and equitable representation in education courses.

In the year 2000, the Australian Confederation of Trade Unions (ACTU) made world union history with a new executive of 50 percent women. In 1985, ACTU had only one woman on its executive; with the adoption of this policy, it will now have 32 women. And the International Confederation of Free Trade Unions (the ICFTU has 187 affiliates from around the world representing more than 100 million workers) reported that trade union centrals in Austria, Belgium, Botswana, Burkina Faso, Colombia, the Dominican Republic, Fiji, France, Great Britain, Guyana, Israel, Italy, Korea, Malaysia, New Zealand, and the Philippines all set aside special seats for women on their central leadership body (ICFTU 1991: 46–7).

Undoubtedly, women elected into top positions give visibility to women in leadership, challenge stereotypes, and provide role models. Since some of these women are committed to addressing the specific concerns of women as workers and unionists, the profile of these issues has also increased. Penni Richmond of the Women's Bureau of the Canadian Labor Congress (CLC) reports that the presence of "outsiders" on the CLC Executive has "changed the issues raised, changed who gets to hear what we talk about, and changed rank and file perception of who has power; in fact, it has put the discussion of power itself on the agenda" (quoted in Briskin 1999a: 158). Although the affirmative action strategy remains controversial in some countries, there remain many reasons to support it. Interestingly, Melcher et al. found that 63 percent of men but only 27 percent of women agree that "women's concerns are accurately represented by male union leaders" (1992: 277). The authors conclude: "It seems unlikely that [male] leaders who think they are adequately representing the needs of their female constituents will see a compelling need to encourage women's involvement in more influential leadership positions" (ibid.: 278).

Redefining union issues/expanding the collective bargaining agenda

Since the 1970s, union women's organizing has led to a heightened consciousness about gender, and the development of union policy on equality of opportunity and treatment of women workers. For example, the ICFTU reports that 70 percent of its affiliates who responded to a survey indicated that they had specific statements on women's equality (ICFTU 1994: 2).

Women unionists in the industrialized countries have, with varying degrees of success, pressured unions to take up issues of childcare, reproductive rights, sexual harassment, and violence against women, pay equity, and employment equity among others. Despite these important gains, the gap between policy and implementation continues. However, shifts in the understanding of what constitutes a union issue have had impacts on the collective bargaining agenda. In Canada, for example, half the workers covered by major collective agreements now have the protection of a formal sexual harassment clause (up from 20 percent in 1985) and the majority of the major collective agreements contain a non-discrimination clause. Though less dramatic, even the number of pay equity (equal pay for work of equal value) clauses and affirmative action clauses have increased (Jackson and Schellenberg 1998: 18).

Despite such gains, women's issues are susceptible to marginalization. For example, Creese reports that, in the Office and Technical Employees' Union (OCTEU Local 378) at British Columbia Hydro in Canada, "for the most part women's issues continue to be seen as secondary, as issues affecting half of the membership, while traditional issues are presumed to affect all members in the same way. As currently defined, special women's issues are bound to be sidelined during economic restructuring and concession bargaining" (1995: 163).

In order to protect against the potential peripheralization associated with "women's issues," gendering union issues is now on the agenda. This means a move from an identification of a women's platform of concerns to a recognition of the gender implications in all issues such as restructuring, seniority, health and safety, and telework. Such a shift opens the door to taking account of the gender-specific concerns of male workers.

Issues are also being scrutinized for their impact on diverse groups of women. For example, discussions of family benefits increasingly reject traditional definitions of "family" that exclude gay and lesbian couples. Such scrutiny provides the ground for bridge-building among diverse groups of women unionists, and for alliances with marginalized male workers.

Separate organizing and constituency building

Men's active resistance to women's union membership in the nineteenth and early twentieth centuries and the persistence of gendered barriers to full union participation into the twenty-first century have created a legacy of male-dominated structures. In response to imbalances in gender power – in fact, to the exclusionary and almost separatist practices of men – women unionists have often organized separately.

Separate organizing among women has a long history in trade union movements around the world; for example, German and Austrian unions have had women's divisions since the 1890s and a 1991 report from the ICFTU points out that "women's committees are now almost as widespread in developing countries as in industrialised countries" (1991: 44). Separate organizing (sometimes called self-organizing) takes a variety of forms within the union movement: informal women's networks or caucuses; formal, sometimes elected, regional or national women's committees; women-only educational conferences; women's locals of mixed unions; and women-only unions. Separate organizing is increasingly supported by union resources and facilitated by equal opportunity coordinators, newsletters, and women's bureaus. In examining "separate organizing," it is useful to distinguish between separatism as a *goal* – an end in itself, and separate organizing as a *strategy* – a means to an end, in this case, the integration of women as full citizens in unions (Briskin 1999b).

Separate organizing has produced vocal constituencies among women who increasingly identify their gender status as significant and act, as part of a collectivity, on their own behalf. Through such organizing, women have forced unions to take up women's concerns as union members and workers, have promoted women's leadership and challenged traditional leaderships to be accountable, and encouraged unions to be more democratic and participatory.

Women's committees often model more inclusive, flexible, and responsive structures. So separate organizing by union women challenges not only the male domination of unions, but also the domination of an organizational model based on bureaucratic, hierarchical, overly competitive, and often undemocratic practices. Men's power, privilege, and leadership have combined with traditional organizational forms to exclude and disadvantage women. Since women's separate organizing simultaneously contests the gender relations of power and bureaucratic organizational structures, it is often experienced by men as a serious challenge.

Furthermore, as this recent example demonstrates, unions have often resisted separate organizing, claiming that it divides workers. Such an argument privileges class solidarity over gender discrimination. Sahabat Wanita (which means "friends of women"), the only national organization of women workers in Malaysia, grew out of the students' efforts to organize among the workers in the electronics industry in an export-processing zone (EPZ). Its president, Irene Xavier, comments:

> We organise women workers to enable them to form their own trade unions. We encourage them to lead the trade unions they form and address issues that specifically affect women. But this is really an uphill battle . . . so-called progressive trade unionists fear that by forming a women's union, we are dividing workers. (quoted in Cabrera-Balleza 1999)

In fact, separate organizing acknowledges existing differences, helps unions build equality in practice, and increases the potential for inclusive and activist unions.

Women's separate organizing has provided an important precedent. In Canada, for example, women and men of color, lesbians and gay men, and native peoples are now organizing separately inside the union movement, often through Human Rights and Rainbow Committees, Aboriginal Circles, and Pink Triangle Committees. The British UNISON, Europe's largest public-sector union with about 1.4 million members, 75 percent of whom are women, has built separate organizing

– which it calls "self-organizing groups" (SOGS) – for women, black people, lesbians and gay men, and members with disabilities into the structure of its constitution. Such organizing provides "opportunities and support for members suffering similar disadvantage, under-representation, hostility or exclusion, to come together to express their needs, voice their demands and determine their priorities" (Mann et al. 1997: 202).

Despite the self-evident value of separate organizing, recent work on Sweden is a vivid reminder of how strategies such as separate organizing must always be situated within political and ideological contexts. In Sweden, union women have been reluctant to organize "separately," especially through formal structures, inside or outside the unions. An ideology of common interests between women and men has supported innovative family and labor market policies; yet at the same time such a gender-neutral approach has concealed the practices which privilege men, thereby making it difficult to address power imbalances (Briskin 1999a).

Gendering Democracy

Although notions of democracy in the West tend to be linked to representation, an increase in women's participation in union leadership is not sufficient to gender democracy. For representational strategies to be successful, they must be deeply embedded in larger processes of democratizing union culture and organizational practices.

Gendering democracy, then, speaks not only to making the internal practices of unions more inclusive, but also to making them more accessible by taking account of childcare and domestic responsibilities. It means ensuring that the bargaining agenda reflects the needs of women workers, and promoting organizational structures such as women's committees that encourage participation.

The call to gender democracy is useful in moving away from abstractions about democracy. Since women and men have unequal access to political and economic power, and to union power, practices of democracy are not gender-neutral. At the same time, the language of "gendering democracy" does not reflect the specific visions about, and claims for democracy that emerge from other marginalized groups in the unions: lesbian and gay workers, workers of color, workers with disabilities. So, for example, democratizing unions for workers with disabilities will involve, at minimum, increasing accessibility.

Gendering democracy is, however, linked to rank-and-file empowerment, and therefore may help build alliances between progressive male and female unionists. In many contexts, demands by rank-and-file unionists for more democracy, and by union women struggling for more voice, converge. Gallagher made this link nearly two decades ago: "There is still an unwillingness . . . and a real fear of sharing power with women. In some ways, it is a fear of democracy itself, because women's push within the labor movement has represented a demand for a more democratic union. These people who fear democracy, fear women" (1987: 354).

Gendering democracy is a way of actualizing the principles of equality, solidarity, justice, and fairness which are part of union ideology, if not always its practice. The struggle for new forms of democracy within the union movement is critical: it will be the key to gaining and maintaining women's access to, and voice within, the labor movement; it will empower women to stand firm when confronting their employers; and it will help provide a vision for a new kind of unionism for all workers, especially the most marginalized.

Globalization, Restructuring, and Structural Adjustment Programs

The globalization of capital and the growing permeability of national boundaries as a result of regional integration treaties like the North American Free Trade Agreement (NAFTA) and the European Union (EU) are negatively impacting on workers around the world. Political and economic reorganization has meant deregulation, increasingly hostile neoliberal states, "global" employers, wage competition across national boundaries, and increasing corporate rule. The dismantling and redefinition of the welfare state in the industrialized countries, and the introduction of structural adjustment programs (SAPS) in the developing countries have resulted in the privatization of public services and decreased state funding to health, education, and family benefits, programs on which women depend and where they have often worked (in better paid unionized positions).

In response to the search by transnational corporations for ever-cheaper labor, avoidance of labor standards and "union-free" guarantees, developing countries have set up EPZs that are exempt from legislated labor standards and with explicitly anti-union policies. In the EPZs (now present in 50 countries, but concentrated in Central America, and South and South-East Asia), labor-intensive industries depend on a young female labor force. EPZs are characterized by low wages, difficult and unhealthy working conditions, little or no social or job security, and a climate of repression that involves violations of human rights, including physical and sexual abuse, pregnancy tests, forced labor, denial of the right to take breaks, compulsory overtime, and use of amphetamines to keep workers awake. Outside the EPZs, in Africa, Asia, and Latin America, economic crisis and structural adjustment have reduced the opportunities for full-time, permanent employment in the structured sectors of the economy concomitant with a growth of "invisible" labor by women in the domestic, agricultural, and informal sectors.

Workplace restructuring in the industrialized countries has increased calls for labor flexibility; created more non-standard, part-time, part-year service work, often referred to as contingent, precarious or casual labor; and led to more contracting out, homework, and off-shore production in the EPZs.

336

Although gender is undoubtedly implicated in all these changes, they impact unevenly on particular groups of women, depending on their age, race, ability, citizenship, and class. However, the International Labor Organization (ILO) of the United Nations now talks of "a worldwide feminization of the labor force" coincident with an erosion in the quality of women's employment and an increase in inequality. These changes have politicized women workers and brought them to the forefront of resistance.

The process of restructuring is also transforming the work of men, especially in industrialized countries where a sharp decline in the unionization rate for men can be traced to the shift of employment from the heavily unionized male-dominated manufacturing industries to the less-unionized service industries. Given the decline in available employment in those sectors that have been dominated by male workers, the focus has shifted from women seeking non-traditional jobs to men competing for women's jobs.

These economic and political changes are challenging the very foundations of unions: in industrialized countries they have significantly reduced union membership, and in developing countries they have made unionization more difficult. For example, the rate of unionization in the Canadian garment sector has declined from 80 percent to 20 percent in just 30 years.

Yet, in the current context, workers, especially women, need unions more than ever. Union activity fosters personal empowerment, political awareness, and collective solidarity. Unions provide a vehicle for struggling around funda-mental issues affecting home and work lives – economic independence, the right to secure employment, childcare, harassment- and violence-free environments. Unions also lobby to influence government policy and legislation on equality issues. And unionization offers women concrete benefits. For example, in the United States, unionized women earn 38 percent more than non-unionized women workers. Union membership has also narrowed the wage gap between women and men by more than one-third.

Organizing the Unorganized

In order to maintain union density (the percentage of workers who are union-ized) and the ability of unions to represent workers, unions need to develop innovative organizing strategies. The feminization of work and increase in women workers necessitates taking account of gender in organizing the unorganized. Evidence suggests that women have gender-specific attitudes to joining unions, identify different issues than do men as central, and respond to distinct organiz-ing strategies.

The experience of the Service, Office, and Retail Workers' Union of Canada (SORWUC) provides an excellent and oft-cited example in the Canadian context (Baker 1991; Bank Book Collective 1979; Warskett 1988). SORWUC was an explicitly feminist union which, in the 1970s, took on the enormous task of organizing bank workers in Canada. It focused on the banks as a sector of women's low-wage work that had been virtually ignored by the union movement. SORWUC was able to organize many bank branches where others had failed. Their success was related to their recognition of gender-specific concerns such as the double day, pay equity, childcare, and sexual harassment; their adoption of participatory decision-making; and their acknowledgment of the discrimination of women.

In the developing countries, women's employment is concentrated in the EPZs and in the informal sector, both of which fall outside the scope of most countries' labor laws and protections. Given anti-union repression, organizing in EPZs faces great difficulties. Increasingly, international labor organizations such as the ILO and the ICFTU are calling for a social clause that would govern international trade and the EPZs. Such a clause would protect freedom of association, a right to collective bargaining, prohibit child labor, and fight against discrimination in employment. In the informal sector, however, innovative initiatives by women workers in many developing countries, forced by necessity to organize outside of official structures, have been remarkably successful.

Consider the example of India. The great majority of working women in India – 94 percent – are self employed, eking out a marginal livelihood as small-scale vendors selling food, household goods, and garments; home-based producers such as weavers, milk producers, and handicraft producers; and laborers selling their services or labor including agricultural and construction workers, cooks, and cleaners. For these workers, conventional forms of trade unionism are not possible. The Self-Employed Women's Association (SEWA) began in 1972 as a trade union of self-employed women, drawing on Gandhi's notion that a union should cover all aspects of workers' lives, both in the factory and at home. SEWA endorses trade unionism in order to struggle for their rights; it also organizes cooperatives as a vehicle to develop alternative economic systems through which workers control what they produce. SEWA's membership has grown from 6,000 in 1981 to 46,000 in 1994; and from one cooperative to 40 (Jhabvala 1994). SEWA's inspiring success demonstrates that even the most vulnerable of women workers can organize effectively. It also offers an important lesson to union movements about the necessity to take account of gendered class realities to ensure organizing success.

Coalition Building and Transnational Organizing

The globalization of production, mobility of capital, and competitive wage bargaining are putting transnational solidarity on the agenda of unions. Unions increasingly see the need to move across national boundaries to build alliances with workers in other countries. Many key initiatives have originated with women activists who have emphasized the significance of gender to the "new world order".

The successful struggle to improve conditions in the El Salvador plants that produce clothes for the GAP clothing company is an example of such transnational work. A joint campaign was undertaken in the US and Canada by unions and popular organizations, and in El Salvador by workers who put their jobs and often their lives on the line. The goal was to force the GAP to establish and enforce a code of conduct to improve working conditions, and to extend the right to unionize to workers in the EPZs. It was also about preventing maquiladora working conditions from moving north. The campaign mobilized the power of Western consumers and capitalized on the vulnerability of clothing retailers to public criticism (Jeffcott and Yanz 1997).

In 2000, union movements around the world, at the prompting of women activists in both unions and communities, were actively involved in building the World March of Women, the goals of which were to eliminate poverty and violence in women's lives. This action was endorsed by more than 200 countries and 2,200 organizations.

Coalition work has redefined both the ideology and the practice of union solidarity, and now challenges the competitiveness and individualism at the core of corporate and neoliberal state agendas. Perhaps more than any other single strategy, coalition building, nationally and transnationally, will be critical to the resistance that needs to be mounted against corporatization, workplace restructuring, changing state forms, decommodification, and globalization, each of which affects women in gender-specific ways.

Conclusion

The notion of a generic worker with a homogeneous and self-evident set of interests has, more often than not, informed understandings of union solidarity. Such an approach is now contested by a heightened consciousness about the significance of gender, women's organizing inside and outside the unions, and by the corporate agenda itself. Abstractly calling for unity or seeking a common denominator like class will further weaken union movements. Solidarity now must mean "unity in diversity," that is, addressing discriminatory practices inside unions and workplaces based not only on gender but also on racialization, ethnicity, citizenship, ability, age, and sexuality, and inserting a gendered, raced, and classed consciousness into all strategies for organizing against globalization and restructuring.

In the current context, where increasing competition among workers is at the heart of restructuring, unity in diversity must be central to union responses. Social justice and equity, then, need to shift from the margin to the center of union strategy in order to reinvent solidarity for a global context, challenge the neoliberal invocation of patriarchal and individualistic values for workplaces and households, and build alliances across gender, across diversities, and across national boundaries.

References

Baker, Patricia (1991) "Some Unions are More Equal than Others: A Response to Rosemary Warkett's 'Bank Worker Organization and the Law'," *Studies in Political Economy* 34: 219–33.

Bank Book Collective (1979) *An Account to Settle* (Vancouver: Press Gang).

Braithwaite, M. and Byrne, C. (1995) *Women in Decision-making in Trade Unions* (Brussels: European Trade Union Confederation).

Briskin, L. (1999a) "Unions and Women's Organizing in Canada and Sweden," in L. Briskin and M. Eliasson (eds.), *Women's Organizing and Public Policy in Canada and Sweden* (Montreal: McGill-Queen's University Press).

Briskin, L. (1999b) "Autonomy, Diversity and Integration: Union Women's Separate Organizing in North America and Western Europe in the Context of Restructuring and Globalization," *Women's Studies International Forum* 22: 543–54.

Cabrera-Balleza, M. (1999) "Fighting an Uphill Battle," *Women in Action* 2: 26–9.

Coventry, B. and Morrissey, M. (1998) "Unions' Empowerment of Working-class Women: A Case Study," *Sociological Spectrum* 18: 285–310.

Creese, G. (1995) "Gender Equity or Masculine Privilege? Union Strategies and Economic Restructuring in a White Collar Union," *Canadian Journal of Sociology* 20: 143–66.

Gallagher, D. (1987) "Affirmative Action," in R. Argue, C. Gannage, and D. W. Livingstone (eds.), *Working People and Hard Times* (Toronto: Garamond Press).

International Confederation of Free Trade Unions (1991) *Equality: The Continuing Challenge-strategies for Success* (Brussels).

International Confederation of Free Trade Unions (1994) *Implementation of the Programme of Action for the Integration of Women into Trade Union Organisations* (Brussels).

Jackson, A. and Schellenberg, G. (1998) *Unions, Collective Bargaining and Labor Market Outcomes for Canadian Women: Past Gains and Future Challenges* (Ottawa: Canadian Labor Congress).

Jeffcott, J. and Yanz, L. (1997) "Bridging the GAP: Exposing the Labor Behind the Label," *Our Times*: 24–8.

Jhabvala, R. (1994) "Self-Employed Women's Association: Organising Women by Struggle and Development," in S. Mitter and S. Rowbotham (eds.), *Dignity and Daily Bread: New Forms of Economic Organising Among Poor Women in the Third World and the First* (New York: Routledge).

Mann, M., Ledwith, S., and Colgan, F. (1997) "Women's Self-Organising and Union Democracy in the UK: Proportionality and Fair Representation in UNISON," in B. Pocock (ed.), *Strife: Sex and Politics in Unions* (St. Leonards, Australia: Allen and Unwin).

Melcher, D., Eichstedt, J., Eriksen, S., and Clawson, D. (1992) "Women's Participation in Local Union Leadership: The Massachusetts Experience," *Industrial and Labor Relations Review* 45: 267–80.

Pocock, B. (1995) "Gender and Activism in Australian Unions," *Journal of Industrial Relations* 37: 377–400.

Roby, P. and Uttal, L. (1993) "Putting it all Together: The Dilemmas of Rank and File Union Leaders," in D. Cobble (ed.), *Women and Unions: Forging a Partnership* (Ithaca, NY: ILR Press).

Warskett, R. (1998) "Bank Worker Unionization and the Law," *Studies in Political Economy* 25: 41–73.

Further reading

Briskin, L. and McDermott, P. (eds.) (1993) *Women Challenging Unions: Feminism, Democracy and Militancy* (Toronto: University of Toronto Press).

Colgan, F. and Ledwith, S. (eds.) (2001) *Gender, Diversity and Trade Unions: International Perspectives* (London: Routledge).

Cobble, D. (ed.) (1993) *Women and Unions: Forging a Partnership* (Ithaca, NY: ILR Press).

Cunnison, S. and Stageman, J. (1993) *Feminizing the Unions: Challenging the Culture of Masculinity* (Aldershot: Avebury).

Curtin, J. (1999) *Women and Trade Unions: A Comparative Perspective* (Aldershot: Ashgate).

Hunt, G. (ed.) (1999) *Laboring for Rights: Unions and Sexual Diversity Across Nations* (Philadelphia: Temple University Press).

Lawrence, E. (1994) *Gender and Trade Unions* (London: Taylor and Francis).

Martens, M. and Mitter, S. (eds.) (1994) *Women in Trade Unions: Organizing the Unorganized* (Geneva: International Labor Organization).

CHAPTER TWENTY-FOUR

Corporate Masculinity

Agneta H. Fischer and
Annelies E. M. van Vianen

Women and Management

All over the world, the participation of women in the labor force is increasing (United Nations Development Report 1996). Although the economic and social status of women's work is still lower than that of men in all countries, there is also a worldwide increase in the number of female managers. However, despite these changes, the proportion of female managers still progressively decreases when climbing the organizational hierarchy. Moreover, in senior or top management functions, no visible changes in the proportion of women can be detected. In other words, whereas there is a rapid increase of women in the labor force – and even in management functions – the proportion of women in top management functions has hardly changed over the last few decades. The fact that women's careers are stuck at middle-management levels is well documented and has been referred to as the "glass ceiling" effect (Burke and McKeen 1992; Melamed 1995; Morrison and Von Glinow 1990; Morrison et al. 1987). It should be noticed that the glass ceiling does not only exist for women, but for all other social categories that do not comprise white, middle-aged men (Essed 1991; Ferdman 1999). In this chapter, we focus on the gendered aspects of management and organizational cultures in Western societies. However, many of the mechanisms that we will describe are general in nature and can be applied to other social groups which are excluded from higher management.

The "glass ceiling" effect has attracted considerable attention from social scientists, feminists, and currently also from managers, who all consider this skewed balance in senior positions as an undesirable state of affairs. In the literature on the glass ceiling a variety of explanations have been offered to answer the question why women, or more generally, other social categories than middle-aged white men (Ferdman 1999; Whitehead and Moodley 1999), have such great difficulties in acquiring and maintaining these top positions. These explanations can be broadly categorized into two perspectives. The first is often labeled as a "sex-difference" or "person-centered" approach (Horner 1972;

Morrison and Von Glinow 1990; Riger and Galligan 1980) focusing on the differences in men's and women's skills, abilities, attributes, ambitions, or private circumstances, while hardly considering the organizational context. A second perspective, the structural or situational approach, emphasizes the structural barriers in women's careers (Ferguson 1984; Kanter 1977) by explaining women's subordinate position by the fewer organizational opportunities that are created for women compared to men.

Several authors, however, have argued that women's slow career advancement cannot be explained by either personal or structural variables, but should be seen as the result of an interaction between the two sets of variables (see, for example, Marshall 1995). A third approach therefore has been advanced, emphasizing a contextual explanation of women's roles and behaviors (Deaux and LaFrance 1998; Deaux and Major 1987). In this view, women's under-representation in higher management functions is seen as the result of an interplay between the organizational context and small, but nonetheless existing differences between men and women. We will call this the "gender-in-context" approach (for similar perspectives, see Fagenson 1990, 1993; Marshall 1995; Parker and Fagenson 1994). The basic assumption of this approach is that there are small differences between men and women in the beginning of their careers (due, for example, to different socialization histories), and that these small differences accumulate as a function of a gendered organizational context (see also Valian 1998). For example, it has often been found that women are less self-confident, and that they have a tendency to play down their performance and capacities to a greater extent than do men (Melamed 1996; Tannen 1990; Van Vianen and Keizer 1996). This sex difference is likely to be enlarged in an organization where overt competition is valued, or where all women have lower status and positions than men. The gendered nature of organizations thus refers to those aspects of the organization that reproduce dissimilarities between men and women, in power, status, positions, jobs, salary, or roles. It is also reflected in the beliefs about different characteristics, motives, or abilities that are ascribed to men and women and in the formation of social networks that often follow gender lines. In other words, gender is a distinct and crucial organizational principle in many organizations (Marshall 1993; Sheppard 1989): "advantage and disadvantage, exploitation and control, action and emotion, meaning and identity, are patterned through and in terms of a distinction between male and female, masculine and feminine" (Acker 1991: 167). Indeed, the denial or failure to recognize the genderedness of organizational culture is in itself a gendered observation (Sheppard 1989). In our view then, gender differences in careers do not only exist because men and women may be different in some respects, but rather because organizations tend to reproduce and increase these differences (see also Acker 1991; Connell 1987).

The genderedness of an organization is clearly reflected in its culture. An organizational culture refers to the shared assumptions, beliefs, norms, and social practices within the organization. Because they are shared, they are often, though not necessarily, tacit. People are generally not aware that they form part of a cultural meaning system, except when they leave the organization, or when outsiders enter it. Recent research and theorizing has drawn attention to the masculine nature of organizational culture as a likely explanation for the persistence of the glass ceiling phenomenon (Cassell and Walsh 1997; Gherardi 1994; Maddock 1999; Maier 1999; Marshall 1993; Mills 1992; Sheppard 1989). The basic assumption is twofold. First, the more men in organizations dominate women in terms of numbers, status, and power, the more masculine values and practices will prevail. Of course, there are different types of masculine values, depending on national culture, age, or ethnicity, but we are referring to a specific type of white masculinity that applies especially to the top of large (international) organizations. Second, gender differences in organizations are reproduced because it is mainly men who feel attracted to and are selected into these masculine cultures (Marshall 1984, 1993; Sheppard 1989). In the next sections, we will further explore these two assumptions.

The Masculine Nature of Organizational Cultures

One way to study organizational culture is to focus on the norms and values that are considered important in the organization, for example as reflected in mission statements or management courses. Obviously, masculinity is not a universal concept and is related to other social categories. However, the masculine nature of organizational cultures has some core features that can be found in many organizations all over the world. On the basis of a large number of studies on organizational culture (Furnham and Gunter 1993; Quinn 1988; Williams et al. 1989), two dimensions have been identified. The first reflects a "task orientation," with an emphasis on productivity, efficiency, control, and task motivation, the second a "people orientation," with a concern for employees, relationships, team spirit, individual motivation, and development. Comparable labels that have been used in the literature are "power-oriented" cultures versus "people-oriented" cultures (Williams et al. 1989), "power and achievement" cultures versus "support and role" cultures (Schein 1985), and "rational goal" cultures versus "human relations" cultures (Quinn 1988). Often these organizational and behavioral values have been presented as gender-neutral, or gender-irrelevant, because they are seen as manifestations of the objective nature of the goals and values in the organization.

However, several authors have argued that these values are influenced by gender, not only because they have been produced by men in male-dominated organizations, but also because they are characterized by gendered patterns of power (e.g., Marshall 1984, 1993; Sheppard 1989). In many Western countries values such as competition, achievement orientation, rationality, hierarchy, command and control, task efficiency, and independence are considered to be stereotypically masculine and are highly approved of. Interdependence, cooperation, receptivity, grounding, intuition, commitment, community,

344

diversity, empowerment of others, inclusiveness, gentleness, and caring, on the other hand, are stereotypical feminine values which would be undervalued and suppressed in most Western organizational contexts (Maier 1999). Maier characterizes these masculine ways of being and behaving as "corporate masculinity." Corporate masculinity is reflected not only in organizational goals, or management requirements, but also in views of self, definitions of success, organizational roles and commitments, sources for taking decisions, styles of communication, or approaches to solving conflicts.

More direct evidence for the masculine nature of organizational cultures can be found in research on the characteristics of successful managers. In a large number of studies it has been shown that both male and female managers believe that the characteristics associated with managerial success were more likely to be held by men than by women (Schein 1973, 1975). Recent replications of this study showed the same pattern of results in the US, China, the UK, and Germany (though not in Japan); however, this was only the case for male managers and management students (Brenner et al. 1989; Schein et al. 1989). The male respondents rated women as much less likely to have leadership ability, be competitive, ambitious, skilled in business matters, or to desire responsibility than men (Schein 1994). Female managers and management students on the other hand no longer sex-typed the managerial position, and rated men and women as possessing similar characteristics as do managers.

Another more direct way of investigating the masculine nature of organizational culture is by examining managers' stereotypical or even discriminatory views. According to Maddock and Parkin (1994), corporate managers play a significant role in creating gendered cultures. They vividly illustrate that the extent to which cultures can be labeled as masculine depends largely on male managers' attitudes towards women. They distinguish two different types of gendered culture. The first is the traditional culture, such as the gentleman's club, which is characterized by male managers' beliefs that men and women are fundamentally different in nature and should therefore be assigned different roles and status. The consequence of this ideology is that women are denied any status and excluded from higher positions. More modern cultures on the other hand, such as the "gender blind," or the "smart macho," proclaim that men and women are more or less equal and that they have the same abilities, attributes, and opportunities as do men. However, this does not imply that these cultures are gender-neutral, because women and men are still considered members of distinct social categories and treated accordingly. In the "paying lip service" culture, for example, the new breed of male managers think of themselves as non-sexist, and although they pay lip service to equal opportunity programs, they actually do very little to promote women. Thus, this "similarity" attitude generally has not resulted in an equal distribution of women and men in higher management. In a similar manner, Kvande and Rasmussen (1994) also distinguished different types of gendered culture, by focusing on the way men typically react to encounters with new female colleagues in order to protect their own professional identity. These types of men fit perfectly in the different gendered cultures as identified by Maddock and Parkin (1994), with the "cavaliers" fitting in the traditional cultures, and the "competitors," "comrades," and "comets" forming the new male managers who advocate equality, but constitute a firm masculine order at a deeper level.

The conclusion that is generally drawn from this literature is that in the majority of organizations masculine values, views, and practices prevail. This "corporate masculinity" is reflected not only in male managers' views on women, but also more implicitly in the values that an organization considers important, like independence, autonomy, hierarchical relations, competition, status, and authority. However, Maddock and Parkin's depiction of modern organizational cultures suggests that they may not be as overtly masculine as is often implied. In fact, more modern organizations would adhere to more liberal views toward women and advocate more democratic and human-oriented views on leadership and management. This raises the question what the major determinants are for an organizational culture to be predominantly masculine. Is it the sheer number of men, and their views on women, that are the best predictors of a masculine culture? Or is it, rather, the specific goals or tasks within an organization, such as engineering, or managing, or still other factors that contribute to the masculinity of organizational cultures?

Masked Masculinity

In order to answer the question to what extent today's organizations can still be considered masculine, we conducted a large-scale empirical study. We compared six large organizations in the Netherlands in terms of the organizational values and the management requirements they promote (Fischer and Rodriguez Mosquera 2001). The organizations differed in nature (a financial institution, an IT organization, an industrial company, a hospital, a temp agency, and a governmental organization), and could also be distinguished by the percentage of women in top functions. We first of all administered questionnaires to the top managers of these institutions concerning the organizational values that they themselves considered important in their organization. We found that feminine values, such as positive feedback, loyalty towards colleagues, personal develop-ment, a balance between work and private life, and participation of employees in decision-taking, were rated as far more important than traditional masculine values, like competition, achievement orientation, high efforts, material rewards, and explicit hierarchical relations. This was found for all organizations, inde-pendently of the percentage of women in the top positions or the nature of the organizational tasks. Moreover, women did not differ from the men in these top functions in what they considered as important values. This implies that it is not one's biological sex, but rather one's social role that reinforces the advance-ment of specific values. Once women have a firm position in top management, they apparently tend to act and think globally the same way as their male colleagues.

In order to investigate whether the percentage of women in top functions made any difference to which values were considered most important, we categorized the six institutions into two types: namely the more service-oriented (or feminine) organizations and the more industrial (or masculine) organizations. The first type also had more women in top positions (between 15 and 20 percent), whereas the second type could be characterized by a lower percentage of women at the top (around 5 percent). A comparison of both types showed that there were no differences in the ratings of the feminine values. This supports the idea that current management ideologies proclaim feminine values independently of organizational context or sex of the manager. We did, however, find some differences with respect to the masculine values. Service-oriented organizations considered hierarchy as more important, whereas industrial organizations considered achievement and material rewards as more important. This suggests that there are multiple masculinities at work (Maier 1999) and that the specific dimensions of masculinity may differ with the type of organization (see also Collinson and Hearn 1996).

Yet, the most noticeable finding is that the top managers in these organizations rate feminine values as much more important than masculine values. These results may suggest that organizational cultures have indeed become feminine. This is in line with the characterization of recent cultures by Maddock and Parkin (1994), who argue that there is a growing consensus, at least in Western organizations, that men and women are equals and thus should have equal opportunities. Further, the results reflect modern management ideologies, such as human resource management and empowerment, in which a people-oriented dimension of management is advocated. In other words, there seems to be a shift toward more feminine values in management and more liberal ideologies concerning the roles of men and women.

However, the point is that this shift has not resulted in a shattering of the glass ceiling, for women's position in higher management has not changed dramatically during the last decade. Apparently, more subtle gender dynamics are at work, as is suggested by Maddock and Parkin (1994), and we should delve deeper into the dungeons of organizational culture in order to solve this paradox.

We therefore investigated the more implicit criteria for being a successful manager in these organizations and found that masculine persons are conceived of as the best leaders and a masculine style is perceived as the best and only way of doing the job. Stereotypical masculine attributes like charisma, enterprise, ambition, a strong will, independence, and self-confidence were rated as most important for a manager to be successful, whereas more stereotypically feminine characteristics – like understanding, cooperation, sociability and tact – were considered less important. Moreover, ego-boosting emotions, like pride, anger, and irritation, more typically associated with men (Fischer 2000; Timmers et al. 1998), are allowed to be expressed by managers, whereas emotions that are

347

considered as stereotypically feminine – like shame, doubt, or uncertainty (Fischer 1993) – are seen as undermining one's qualities as a leader. We also considered the actual working hours of these top managers and found that they worked on average more than 10 hours above their contract hours, which sheds another light on the importance they claimed to assign to a balance between private life and work.

All in all, these more implicit measures clearly showed a preference for masculine norms and masculine ways of doing the job. We may interpret these results as reflecting a firm masculine culture that is masked by a "feminine" management ideology. In other words, "corporate masculinity" (Maier 1994, 1999) is still solidly extant, but has become less visible. In large organizations, both in traditional masculine and in feminine domains, and irrespective of the number of women in top functions, masculine styles, norms, and behaviors still prevail, and only the espoused values have changed. However, espoused values, which predict what people say, may often be incongruent with the basic assumptions, which predict what people actually do in situations where these values should be operating (e.g., Schein 1985). This explains why current equality ideologies have not yet resulted in significant changes in women's positions in senior management. The essence of organizational culture – that is, the actual practices and basic assumptions – has not moved in a more feminine direction.

Organizational Culture as Exclusion and Self-exclusion Mechanism

The question that still remains is how masked masculinity blocks women's careers. The basic argument of the gender-in-context approach is that differences between men and women at the start of their careers accumulate over the years, basically as a function of a gendered organizational context. Of course, there are important constraints for women's careers outside the organization, such as their greater responsibility for household tasks and care for children (Hochschild 1989; Lewis 1994), but the way in which the organization deals with these differences makes the crucial difference.

In order to explain the role of organizational cultures in women's career success, we must distinguish two complementary processes. The first focuses on exclusion, the second on self-exclusion. Exclusion refers to all processes that involve managers' negative behavior toward or judgments of female subordinates. There are several ways in which women may consciously or unconsciously be excluded from senior management functions. For example, a study in which male and female executives in a financial organization were compared (Lyness and Thompson 1997) showed that women received less authority and as a consequence fewer stock options than did the male executives. In the same way, other research has shown that organizations create fewer promotion opportunities for women and lend them relatively little support (Ohlott et al.

1994). Moreover, women meet more obstacles in the form of overt discrimination or prejudice on their way to the top than do men (Melamed 1995). However, our characterization of more recent organizational cultures as "masked masculinity" suggests that more subtle forms of prejudice are also operating.

It should be noted that the judgments concerning a person's suitability for a management position are largely based on the impression of their competence and leadership abilities, and less on more "objective" credentials such as education. Abundant psychological research has demonstrated that gender stereotypes and gender schemes play an important role in the assessment of women's and men's performance (Bartol 1999; Eagly et al. 1992; Graves 1999; Valian 1998). Gender schemas or stereotypes are cognitive structures that contain general information about a social group, i.e. men and women, and influence our judgments of individual members of a group, generally without our being aware of it. This is especially the case when the criteria for judging someone are subjective (Powell 1999); the information about the applicant is sparse; and gender is a central feature of an interviewer's ideal applicant prototype (Van Vianen and Willemsen 1992). In these situations, information about gender becomes salient and is used to fill the gap in our knowledge about the individual person and thus may lead to gender bias and discrimination.

In a meta-analysis of 61 studies on the evaluation of male and female leaders, Eagly et al. (1992) showed that there is a small, but significant overall tendency to evaluate female leaders more negatively than male leaders. The evaluation of leaders due to their sex depended on organizational context, however. The preference for male leaders was larger in traditional masculine settings (e.g., basketball coaches, and managers in business or manufacturing contexts) than in other organizational contexts. This implies that male managers in traditional masculine settings seem to have more prejudiced views toward women and may have more masculine views on management tasks, compared to men in organizations where women make up a considerable proportion of the managers. In this way, gender differences are reproduced within organizations. In addition, recent research has shown that other gender-related variables – like clothing, non-verbal behavior, or attractiveness – have an effect on performance evaluations and hiring decisions. Feminine clothing, for example, leads to less positive recommendations than masculine clothing (Forsythe 1990). In addition, undesirable physical features, like obesity or unattractiveness, are more likely to lead to discrimination for women than for men (Graves 1999).

In sum, this research suggests that gender and gender-related traits form important ingredients of the schemas of decision-makers, which increases the likelihood of gender discrimination. We have shown that masculine attributes still form the essence of what is seen as a successful manager, and that a masculine communication style and a masculine way of doing the job is still the most dominant practice. This gives men an advantage from the beginning of their careers onwards. These gender schemas flourish in all organizations, irrespective of the espoused feminine values. The fact that the masculine nature of organizational cultures is masked makes it more difficult to discuss and criticize it, because managers will always refer to the espoused values, and not to the basic assumptions and actual practices.

The second process focuses on women's own motives and intentions to pursue a career into higher management. This does not imply a person-centered focus: on the contrary. Self-selection presumes that contextual and organizational variables are highly relevant. Women may feel less attracted to cultures dominated by masculine norms and values, which may be reflected in weaker motives to be promoted into a senior management function. On the other hand, the masculine nature of organizational culture is not very visible, and therefore the attractiveness of top cultures may be similar for men and women. The question is thus whether men and women differ in what they consider attractive or off-putting in an organizational culture that is characterized by masked masculinity.

In our large field study of six organizations, we asked men and women in middle-level management positions ("potentials") which cultural norms they considered important. The items were the same as the ones administered to top managers, in order to make comparison possible. The results showed that, like top managers, men and women both favored feminine values over masculine ones. However, we also found a sex difference: women rated feminine values as more important than did men, whereas men rated masculine values as more important than did women. Men especially valued material rewards, hierarchical relations, and a competitive atmosphere more highly than did women (Fischer and Rodriguez Mosquera 2001). This suggests that men may feel more at home in a culture that is dominated by those masculine basic assumptions. Moreover, we asked these potentials to report which reasons would be applicable for them to decline an offer of a senior management function. It appeared that both men and women more often mention time-related motives ("I would have less free time," "I would have less time for caring-related tasks"), and that there was only a sex difference with respect to stress-related motives ("It would mean too much stress," "the job is too demanding," "the atmosphere is too competitive"): women more often reported such motives to decline an offer for a higher management function than did men. In other words, it is not so much the expected amount of time that inhibits women more than men, but rather the expected stress that is evoked by the requirements for top managers. The stress is expected because the potentials know that top managers have to meet high demands and that the culture at the top is highly competitive.

Conclusion

This review aimed to offer an explanation for the fact that the glass ceiling is such a persistent phenomenon. Why is it that women still form a small minority of top managers? Current trends in management theory and practice seem to contradict the idea that they have difficulty reaching higher management functions.

The number of female managers has dramatically increased during and since the 1990s; managers make public statements in which they express their concern for the lack of female top managers; current management ideologies reflect values that are stereotypically feminine; and women are proclaimed as the new managers of the twenty-first century. Why is it, then, that these developments have not resulted in any actual changes in the proportion of women in higher management?

We have reviewed research that shows that these trends in Western societies are about espoused values and not about the actual practices and basic assumptions in organizational cultures. The underlying organizational culture, at least in large organizations, is still predominantly masculine, which is reflected in the actual imbalance between the life and work of top managers, in the preferred communication styles, and in the ideal attributes that are expected from successful managers. Those less visible, but more essential aspects of organizational culture show less change in a feminine direction than do more artificial and explicit levels of culture. We may therefore characterize modern organizational cultures as "masked masculinity": masculine values are still dominant but they are masked by a feminine management ideology to which most managers pay lip service. This implies that women are still excluded from top management because of the subtle workings of gender schemas. More important, it shows that it has become more difficult to criticize and lay bare these gendered mechanisms and the gendered aspects of culture, especially because they are hidden and not publicly expressed or acknowledged. Because the visible levels of organizational culture have become more feminine, it seems more obvious to blame women for their absence in higher management and to attribute this phenomenon to a lack of ambition. This is why it is important to show the inconsistency between the visible, espoused values and the hidden, underlying assumptions and practices in organizations.

Future research should further examine to what extent women are more sensitive than men to the hidden aspects of organizational cultures and behaviors. Cultures are very difficult to change. The large body of research on mechanisms of exclusion did not lead to a more equal division of power in organizations. Therefore, researchers should also focus on the potential strengths women have in breaking the glass ceiling.

References

Acker, J. (1991) "Hierarchies, Jobs, Bodies: A Theory of Gendered Organizations," in J. Lorber and S. A. Farrell (eds.), *The Social Construction of Gender* (Newbury Park: Sage).

Bartol, K. M. (1999) "Gender Influences on Performance Evaluations," in G. N. Powell (ed.), *Handbook of Gender and Work* (Thousand Oaks, CA: Sage Publications).

Brenner, O. C., Tomkievicz, J., and Schein, V. E. (1989) "The Relationship Between Sex-Role Stereotypes and Requisite Management Characteristics Revisited," *Academy of Management Journal* 32: 662–9.

Burke, R. J. and McKeen, C. A. (1992) "Women in Management," in C. I. Cooper and I. T. Robertson (eds.), *International Review of Industrial and Organizational Psychology*, vol. 7 (Chichester, UK: John Wiley).

Cassell, C. and Walsh, S. (1997) "Organizational Cultures, Gender Management Strategies, and Women's Experience Of Work," *Feminism and Psychology* 7: 224–30.

Collinson, D. L. and Hearn, J. (eds.) (1996) *Men as Managers, Managers as Men: Critical Perspectives of Men, Masculinities, and Managements* (Thousand Oaks, CA: Sage).

Connell, R. W. (1987) *Gender and Power* (Stanford, CA: Stanford University Press).

Deaux, K. and LaFrance, M. (1998) "Gender," in D. Gilbert, S. T. Fiske, and G. T. Lindzey (eds.), *Handbook of Social Psychology*, 4th edn. (New York: McGraw-Hill).

Deaux, K. and Major, B. (1987) "Putting Gender into Context: An Interactive Model of Gender-related Behavior," *Psychological Review* 94: 369–89.

Eagly, A. H., Makhijani, M. G., and Klonsky, B. G. (1992) "Gender and the Evaluation of Leaders: A Meta-Analysis," *Psychological Bulletin* 111: 3–22.

Essed, Ph. (1991) *Understanding Every Day Racism: An Interdisciplinary Theory* (Newbury Park, CA: Sage).

Fagenson, E. A. (1990) "At the Heart of Women in Management Research," *Journal of Business Ethics* 9: 1–8.

Fagenson, E. A. (1993) "Diversity in Management: Introduction and the Importance of Women in Management," in E. A. Fagenson (ed.), *Women in Management: Trends, Issues and Challenges in Managerial Diversity* (Newbury Park, CA: Sage).

Ferdman, B. M. (1999) "The Color and Culture of Gender in Organizations. Attending to Race and Ethnicity," in G. N. Powell (ed.), *Handbook of Gender and Work* (Thousand Oaks, CA: Sage).

Ferguson, K. E. (1984) *The Feminist Case Against Bureaucracy* (Philadelphia: Temple University Press).

Fischer, A. H. (1993) "Sex Differences in Emotionality: Fact or Stereotype," *Feminism and Psychology* 3: 303–18.

Fischer, A. H. (ed.) (2000) *Gender and Emotion: Social Psychological Perspectives* (Cambridge: Cambridge University Press).

Fischer, A. H. and Rodriguez Mosquera, P. M. (2001) "Masked Masculinity in Management." Paper presented at the EAESP Small Group Meeting on Gender Role Research, Graz, Austria.

Forsythe, S. M. (1990) "Effect of Applicant's Clothing on Interviewers' Decision to Hire," *Journal of Applied Social Psychology* 20: 1579–95.

Furnham, A. and Gunter, B. (1993) "Corporate Culture: Definition, Diagnosis and Change," *International Review of Industrial and Organizational Psychology* 8: 233–61.

Gherardi, S. (1994) "The Gender We Think, The Gender We Do in our Everyday Organizational Lives," *Human Relations* 41: 591–610.

Graves, L. M. (1999) "Gender Bias in Interviewers' Evaluations of Applicants: When and How Does It Occur?" in G. N. Powell (ed.), *Handbook of Gender and Work* (Thousand Oaks, CA: Sage).

Hochschild, A. (1989) *The Second Shift* (London: Piatkus).

Horner, M. (1972) "Toward an Understanding of Achievement Related Conflicts in Women," *Journal of Social Issues* 28: 157–76.

Kanter, R. Moss (1977) *Men and Women of the Corporation* (New York: Basic Books).

Kvande, E. and Rasmussen, B. (1994) "Men in Male-Dominated Organizations and their Encounter with Women Intruders," *Scandinavian Journal of Management* 10: 163–73.

Lewis, S. (1994) "Role Tensions and Dual Career Couples," in M. J. Davidson and R. J. Burke (eds.), *Women in Management* (London: Paul Chapman).

Lyness, K. S. and Thompson, D. E. (1997) "Above the Glass Ceiling? A Comparison of Matched Samples of Female and Male Executives," *Journal of Applied Psychology* 82: 259–75.

Maddock, S. (1999) *Challenging Women* (London: Sage).

Maddock, S. and Parkin, D. (1994) "Gender Cultures: How They Affect Men and Women at Work," in M. J. Davidson and R. J. Burke (eds.), *Women in Management* (London: Paul Chapman).

Maier, M. (1994) "Glass Ceilings, Glass Prisons: Reflections on the Gender Barrier," *The Diversity Factor* 2: 32–7.

Maier, M. (1999) "On the Gendered Substructure of Organization: Dimensions and Dilemmas of Corporate Masculinity," in G. N. Powell (ed.), *Handbook of Gender and Work* (Thousand Oaks, CA: Sage).

Marshall, J. (1984) *Women Managers: Travellers in a Male World* (Chichester: Wiley).

Marshall, J. (1993) "Organizational Cultures and Women Managers: Exploring the Dynamics of Resilience," *Applied Psychology: An International Review* 42: 313–22.

Marshall, J. (1995) "Gender and Management: A Critical Review of Research," *British Journal of Management* 6: 553–62.

Melamed, T. (1995) "Barriers to Women's Career Success: Human Capital, Career Choices, Structural Determinants, or Simply Gender Discrimination," *Applied Psychology: An International Review* 44: 295–314.

Melamed, T. (1996) "Career Success: An Assessment of a Gender-specific Model," *Journal of Occupational and Organizational Psychology* 69: 217–42.

Mills, A. J. (1992) "Organization, Gender, and Culture," in A. J. Mills and P. Tancred (eds.), *Gendering Organizational Analysis* (Newbury Park, CA: Sage).

Morrison, A. M. and Von Glinow, M. A. (1990) "Women and Minorities in Management," *American Psychologist* 45: 200–8.

Morrison, A. M., White, R. P., and Van Velsor, E. (1987) *Breaking the Glass Ceiling* (Reading, MA: Addison-Wesley).

Ohlott, P. J., Ruderman, M. N., and McCauley, C. D. (1994) "Gender Differences in Managers' Developmental Experiences," *Academy of Management Journal* 37: 46–67.

Parker, B. and Fagenson, E. A. (1994) "An Introductory Overview of Women in Corporate Management," in M. J. Davidson and R. J. Burke (eds.), *Women in Management: Current Research Issues* (London: Paul Chapman).

Powell, G. N. (1999) "Reflections on the Glass Ceiling. Recent Trends and Future Prospects," in G. N. Powell (ed.), *Handbook of Gender and Work* (Thousand Oaks, CA: Sage).

Quinn, R. E. (1988) *Beyond Rational Management* (San Francisco, CA: Jossey-Bass Publishers).

Riger, S. and Galligan, P. (1980) "Women in Management; An Exploration of Competing Paradigms," *American Psychologist* 35: 902–10.

Schein, E. H. (1985) *Organizational Culture and Leadership* (San Francisco, CA: Jossey-Bass; 2nd edn. 1992).

Schein, V. E. (1973) "The Relationship Between Gender-Role Stereotypes and Requisite Management Characteristics," *Journal of Applied Psychology* 57: 95–100.

Schein, V. E. (1975) "The Relationship Between Sex-Role Stereotypes and Requisite Management Characteristics Among Female Managers," *Journal of Applied Psychology* 60: 340–4.

Schein, V. E. (1994) "Managerial Sex Typing: A Persistent and Pervasive Barrier to Women's Opportunities," in M. J. Davidson and R. J. Burke (eds.), *Women in Management* (London: Paul Chapman).

Schein, V. E., Müller, R., and Jacobson, C. (1989) "The Relationship Between Sex-Role Stereotypes and Requisite Management Characteristics Among College Students," *Sex Roles* 20: 103–10.

Sheppard, D. L. (1989) "Organizations, Power and Sexuality. The Image and Self-Image of Women Managers," in J. Hearn, D. L. Sheppard, P. Tancred-Sheriff, and G. Burrell (eds.), *The Sexuality of Organizations* (London: Sage).

Tannen, D. (1990) *You Just Don't Understand. Women and Men in Conversation* (New York: Ballantine).

Timmers, M., Fischer, A. H., and Manstead, A. S. R. (1998) "Gender Differences in Motives for Regulating Emotions," *Personality and Social Psychology Bulletin* 24: 974–86.

United Nations Development Report (1996) *Human Development Report 1996* (New York: Oxford University Press).

Valian, V. (1998) *Why So Slow? The Advancement of Women* (Cambridge, MA: MIT Press).

Van Vianen, A. E. M. and Keizer, W. A. J. (1996) "Gender Differences in Managerial Intention," *Gender, Work and Organization* 3: 103–14.

Van Vianen, A. E. M. and Willemsen, T. M. (1992) "The Employment Interview: The Role of Sex Stereotypes in the Evaluation of Male and Female Job Applicants in the Netherlands," *Journal of Applied Social Psychology* 22: 471–91.

Whitehead, S. and Moodley, R. (eds.) (1999) *Transforming Managers. Gendering Change in the Public Sector* (London: UCL Press).

Williams, A., Dobson, P., and Walters, M. (1989) *Changing Culture: New Organizational Approaches* (London: Institute for Personnel Management).

PART SIX

Familiality

CHAPTER TWENTY-FIVE

Family and Culture in Africa

Ifi Amadiume

Feminism and Women's Studies have complicated what used to be a simplistic understanding of gender as corresponding to biological sex. What we do with our sexed bodies is now known to be contextually, socially, and culturally defined. Equally, roles and statuses in society do not readily fit into simple dichotomous categories of male and female gender. Some cultures indicate more flexibility in gender classification by employing mechanisms of a neuter pronoun, gender-crossing, or gender-bending. Cross-cultural comparison and in-depth study of social processes show more evidence of gender cooperation and the subversion of assumed binaries than was previously thought. I will give some examples of roles and statuses in marriage, kinship, and the family in Africa. Obviously, this picture, although representative of some general patterns, is incomplete given the impossibility of covering the huge continent and its many societies, languages, cultures, and countries. I use a feminist perspective to explore the topic of gender, culture, and the family in Africa. In looking at the ways that gender relations have been constituted and reconstituted in Africa, I will draw illustrations from the different regions – West Africa, North Africa, East Africa, Central Africa, and Southern Africa – as I compare traditional societies/cultures and urban cosmopolitan experiences in towns. What are women's realities and choices? How do new realities effect new understandings of kinship, marriage, and the family as a result of the influences of status, class, sexuality, geography, place, and location?

From a structuralist and class analysis there seems to be an interconnection between economic wealth and women's cultural and political expression of power. Up until the early twentieth century, just before the complete colonization of most of Africa, women in West African societies (for example Nupe, Igbo, Yoruba, Asante, Mende, etc.) and many other regions of Africa controlled subsistence production and were heavily involved in farming, marketing, trade, and commerce in rural and urban settings. Wealthy women could convert economic wealth into cultural and political power, because of a general economic gendered division of labor and separate maintenance of finances. Long histories of slavery, colonialism, and capitalism reversed women's economic gains and domination of agriculture and markets, especially in West Africa, and pushed women into urban areas and petty trading during the nineteenth century (White 1999). In the early twentieth century, women became more liable to state interference and control (Amadiume 2000; Mikell 1997a; Parpart and Staudt 1989). New stratification and gender hierarchy emerged, but women's solidarity groups that are involved in social, economic, and cultural production continue into the present. It is the culture of these women's solidarity groups in kinship, marriage, and the family that I focus on, as it provides insights into women's own constructions of cultural systems and women's active involvement in social processes. This certainly demands that new questions be asked of old and existing institutions: what conditions and what institutions make possible women's solidarity? Choice involves moving forward in developing organically what is "good," viable, and empowering in one's heritage.

Gender, Culture, and Family

The topic of gender, culture, and the family in Africa is complex and has been tackled from many perspectives. Feminist approaches have problematized relations of gender in the family, focusing on the dominance and privileges of males, elders, and Islamic clerics who use "custom" and "tradition" to oppress females. Studies on gender that focus on Islamic cultures in North, West, and East Africa have tended to emphasize the struggle for legal reforms that would promote more equal family relations in matters of divorce, polygamy, the veil, the seclusion of women, rights to property and inheritance, early marriage, women's education, female circumcision, etc. At the national level, in relation to the state and family practices, feminist concerns have focused on issues of reproductive sex, abortion, contraception, prostitution, HIV/AIDS, rape, and domestic violence. These issues undoubtedly call for an advocacy approach, which unfortunately tends to lead to single-issue concerns at the expense of a holistic or relational approach to gender and women's total well-being. In an advocacy approach, all that remains are issues and fragmented women without a historical or organizational context. A relational approach through a structuralist and class analysis that also considers the socio-economic basis of gender abuse would provide a critical evaluation of all related factors and interests (Amadiume 2000: 135). Such an approach does not lose sight of issues of abuse and oppression, but goes beyond women's victimhood to also consider their cultural and political expressions of resistance and power. In this approach, African women who have experienced a history of slavery and colonialism can interrogate and historicize problems of unfreedom, sexism and abuse in the family, disease, and poverty. I believe that this perspective, which also considers the contextual social and cultural framework, is necessary for a more egalitarian future of gender.

It is important to understand the complex dynamics of the current period in which we are situating studies of gender relations and the family in Africa. Given what Africa has experienced, many would simply assume that the twenty-first century means the victory of industrial, technological, and global capitalism over non-industrial communities that are unequally tied to globalization, even though they are still more grounded in clan, descent, and kinship systems. Such an assumption would thus see an inquiry into gender and the family more as a concern with family relations or family conditions that allow individual choice, women's leadership, and support for working or professional women. Issues of culture, such as mentoring, collaboration, sharing information and power, and collective action, are essential to successful working conditions and product-ivity. Ironically, the same issues of culture apply to gender and the family in all socio-economic conditions in Africa, whether rural or urban, industrial or non-industrial. African societies have been inventing and reinventing gender, culture, and the family since human and cultural origins in the continent and thus have a rich history of diversity of cultures and family traditions (Diop 1989; Knight 1991; Oppong 1983; Radcliffe-Brown and Forde 1950).

Patriarchal paradigms of gender misrepresented the roles, statuses, and situations of women in kinship and marriage in Africa. Traditional anthropological studies of kinship and the family were patrifocal and male-biased, ignoring or misrepresenting the very important matriarchal roles of women in the household (Amadiume 1997). Rights to property, inheritance, and succession were defined according to a Eurocentric father–son paradigm of rights, especially rights of husband over wife. In this perspective, women are no more than possessed objects of exchange in marriage and invisible members of descent and kinship groups. On the contrary, women in Africa gained social power and political clout from their central role in African economies, from gathering food in hunter-gathering economies, agricultural production and home industry, and doing over 80 percent of the agricultural work (Boserup 1970). Under postcolonial conditions and the development of nuclear families, there are increased gender differences in men's and women's work patterns and use of income. This has resulted in the economic separation of husband and wife, as for example the unpaid labor of women, which is a source of potential conflict within the family (Adepoju 1994: 38–41).

There is a new pattern of oppression and isolation of women as a result of rural–urban migration and women's wage labor, which Obbo (1980) has shown to weaken the family structure, and which has produced the phenomenon of the single woman in urban and rural Uganda. For a group of young Swazi female textile workers, marriage would confer legal status, as well as access to land and credit. But this high cultural valuation of marriage in the Swazi tradition is contradicted by the low percentage of those young women who were actually married, which was 20 percent, while 66 percent were single. Some of the women were married to migrant workers in South Africa, yet 82 percent had children regardless of their marital status (Harris 1997). The young women are making new choices and the growing emphasis on the nuclear family and urban migration has resulted in Swazi women being overburdened with domestic, agricultural, and textile work in a context where they are no longer able to rely on traditional kinship support for childcare or on organized women's cultural systems.

We can generalize about transformations in family structure as a result of colonial and postcolonial land alienation, migration, and wage employment. All of this has led to the emergence of the nuclear family, while the desertion of men has contributed to an increase in female-headed households. According to government statistics, 40 percent of households in Kenya were female-headed in 1979 and among plantation workers this increased to over 45 percent (Adagala 1991). Colonial policies and postcolonial conditions have also introduced tensions between matrilineal kinship and values of the nuclear family, with categories and terms of emphasis shifting from mothers and children to wives and children. Attesting to women's weaker economic situations and new poverty, Manuh (1997) writes that in Ghana 89 percent of workers in trade and sales are women, but the economic gains from market trading for most of these women are small. About one-third are in polygynous marriages, with each mother caring for about six children. Under such circumstances, it is not surprising that the concern of government and advocacy groups, which they obviously consider modern, is for the economic rights of wives and children. Yet, in urban Ghana 33 percent of households are female-headed and the figure in rural Ghana for this type of family is 28–9 percent. Modern thinking also expects men to support their wives and children.

This modernist thinking is behind Ghana's Intestate Succession Law of 1985, which guaranteed legitimate status and the right of wives and children to the inheritance of property. Women's groups (church groups, "benevolent" associations and market groups) and traditional authorities (councils of chiefs and traditional rulers) were involved in petitioning the colonial government to recognize customary marriage and the rights of wives and children in these marriages. Subverting traditional marriage practice, a British colonial Marriage Ordinance of 1884 imposed the laws of England on marriage in Ghana, according new status and roles to women married according to the Ordinance and two-thirds property inheritance to "legitimate" children, leaving one-third of the property governed by customary law (Manuh 1997: 83). Colonialism and the patriarchal state sowed the seeds of discord by privileging monogamous marriage, the nuclear family, and conjugal relations over wider kinship ties and loyalty. The result is a high rate of divorce, economic hardship, and women resorting to suing men for maintenance, something Akan women say that their mothers would never have supported (Mikell 1997b). We can certainly historicize new postcolonial fragmented patterns of gender relations in the family.

We may wonder why mothers of Akan women in Ghana were against the use of law to settle marital disputes by their daughters. The answer is probably due to economic and cultural differences, with the older generation of women less economically dependent on their men, and certainly less culturally fragmented. Present experiences and trends show that state and development policies have based decisions about state legislation and development projects on the assumption that men are husbands, fathers, and heads of households and families, to the marginalization of women.

Gender, Culture, and Kinship

Modern conditions might favor new definitions of the family in Africa that also incorporate a European definition of the family based on monogamy and the male-headed nuclear family. Such modern forms of marriage include marriage as a civil contract and Christian or Muslim marriage as a vow made with God's blessing. To see marriage only in these terms would grossly misrepresent the complex reality, since in Africa the family is traditionally understood as part of kinship and descent. In the Western metropolis, which is so multicultural and diverse, it is possible that people do not view themselves and others in terms of kinship. In Africa, everyone has a kin and is expected to be guided by the rules of kinship morality (Fortes 1949; Goody 1997). Although the terms of relations are shrinking in line with narrow, individualistic, European models, Africans cannot escape their kinship obligations. In spite of charity work by religious organizations and non-governmental organizations (NGOs), kinship, even if weaker, is still the basis of social welfare in Africa (Amadiume 2000; Goody 1997). Kinship as a support system provides better management of potentially fragmenting experiences like divorce, widowhood, and orphanhood.

Common ancestry, blood, marriage, and adoption define kinship groups as biological and non-biological lineage. Kinship and family are thus social and cultural. Gendered kinship values are reflected in cultural and political systems, depending on whether they are centralized or decentralized (no centralized rulers). The language of gender relations is also reflected in the political culture of a people, depending on matriarchal or patriarchal orientation. Anthropological literature has classified the huge diversity of kinship and descent systems in Africa into confusing and not very helpful terms such as patrilineal, matrilineal, double descent, cognatic, etc. These terms render women's systems in kinship and descent invisible (Amadiume 1997). Gendered kinship values define identity, marriage, and citizenship, therefore the roles and statuses of women – but more importantly the possibilities of women's access to resources such as land and property, control of people and solidarity groups.

In so-called matrilineal descent systems such as the Asante and Akan in Ghana, children trace citizenship in their clan through their mothers, who also pass on property such as land. However, anthropologists tell us that political authority in this system resides with the men – that is, mothers' brothers. Matrilineal systems practice "avunculocal" residence, in which there are several residential options but, in keeping with the theory of male authority, only two

361

are frequently cited. These are when a sister's son goes to live with his mother's brother and when a woman moves to her husband's village. The man is taken as the point of reference, which does not correctly describe what really takes place in the social process. Thus we learn that in "uxorilocal" residence a man moves to his wife's village, but the literature does not tell us that the woman remains at home after marriage. In actuality, the matricentric unit is collectivist and gender-inclusive (Amadiume 1997). It is not gender–casted and limited to only females as we can see from this informed description by a Ghanaian scholar of a matricentric household that she defines as a matrilineal family:

> Matrilineal family members are united by the possession of common blood [*mogya*]. In the matrilineal family [the *abusua*] the blood passes exclusively through the female line, and the typical family is made up of woman, her uterine sisters and brothers, her children (both male and female), her sisters' children, her daughters' children, and so on. It is membership in this group that determines what rights, interests, and duties an individual can possess or owe. (Manuh 1997: 79)

Manuh further writes:

> Children in the matrilineal system are by definition members of their mothers' families, but *not* of their fathers' families. Even though children are not considered to possess the same blood as their fathers, there are strong bonds between fathers and their children in all matrilineal communities in Ghana, arising from their possession of a common controlling spirit [the *ntoro* or *kra*]. A man's public recognition of the infant after birth gives the child legitimacy and his/her cult affiliation, and also the attendant supernatural prohibitions. (ibid.: 80)

Even though the matricentric unit is gender inclusive, the consistency of the unity of the matricentric unit shows that the husband was the outsider and home (family) was with the mother. The use of European categories thus completely misrepresents these traditional kinship realities.

While patrilineal Ga practice separate residence for men and women in the lineage ("duolocal" residence), matrilineal Akan, who make up to 40 percent of the population of Ghana, combine avunculocal (supposedly male residence with his matrilineal kin group) and duolocal (separate residence for men and women at marriage) options of residence after marriage. Manuh writes: "Although their roles vary according to their kinship and ethnic groups, women are not defined as members of their husbands' families in either patrilineal or matrilineal systems" (ibid.: 79). On the traditional status of wives and children, Manuh writes: "In both matrilineal and patrilineal descent systems, wives are not members of their husbands' families and have no inheritance rights to husbands' property" (ibid.). I use these quotes to show the shift in focus from the unity of the matricentric unit to a European nuclear family–type model and thinking in which the woman as wife is expected to be the moveable entity and is dislodged from her organic matriarchal kinship base.

What is interesting in these residential options is that there are traditional marriage residential arrangements where there is no dispersal of the matricentric unit of kinship that is centered around mother and children. I have described this kinship paradigm as a basic production unit in economic and cultural production for a matriarchal ideology (Amadiume 1987; 1997: chs. 1 and 3). At the national level, the matricentric unit generated a matriarchal superstructure in early ancient Egyptian kingdoms and in ancient African kingdoms, where queens and their male and female children ruled in a tripartite palace system (Amadiume 1997: ch. 4). These political cultures valued peace and harmony (ibid.: chs. 2 and 5; Diop 1987, 1991). They are certainly distinct from European, patriarchal, centralized states, which embarked on conquest and imperialism, enslaved and colonized Africans, and finally imposed the present problematic systems of nation and state on disparate ethnic nationalities and languages in Africa.

We now have a better understanding of our past and contemporary needs, and knowledge of ourselves calls for major revisions in anthropological understanding of gender, personalities, and cultures of kinship relations. For example, avuncular or complementary affiliations are said to have relations of indulgence that are the opposite of the kinship category that controls property and authority. This category often constitutes relations traced through the mother. An understanding of matriarchal values of love and compassion better describes gender equity practices in kin relations that often necessitate a flexibility of gender such as gender-bending. The Mbuti forest people of Central Africa achieve gender cooperation by sharing motherhood between mothers and fathers who play the role of "male mothers" (Turnbull 1981: 212). We have an example in the practice of the sister's brother and sister's son in southern African societies like the Tsonga of Mozambique and the Nama of Namibia, where, to the child, his mother's brother is the same as his mother and is called "male mother" and he gives his best cattle to his nephew. In patrilineal systems the father's sister shares patriarchal authority and is called "female father" by her nephew (Barnard 1997: 452–3). We have a comparable practice of "male daughters" or "female husbands" in the Igbo society of Nnobi where daughters' children called *Nwadiana* have a relationship of love, indulgence, and compassion with their mother's lineage called *Ndiochie* (Amadiume 1987: 63). In short, in matriarchal values, the mother's relatives to whom she is a daughter have a relationship of love and indulgence with their daughter's child. This points to matriarchal values with regard to the multiple roles and cultures of women as mothers and as mother's daughter and mothers as sisters that anthropological lineage terms do not capture.

Classical anthropological approaches to the study of kinship, marriage, and the family in Africa do not teach us much about daughters. We often learn that sons are preferred to daughters, since they have juridical authority in the clan and family and will confer ancestorhood on fathers, which daughters and women cannot do (Fortes 1987). We also learn that daughters have no property and that the bridewealth paid for them at marriage served as marriage payment for their brother's marriage. In effect, daughters are represented as unwanted and propertyless objects of exchange. Now, if we change the lens to a relational matriarchal model and view daughters in relation to their mothers and other women in the lineage, all the different statuses of women assume an importance in relation to their culture of interdependence, sharing, mentoring, cooperation, and solidarity.

We can assess the controversial issues of bridewealth (often called bride price) and polygamy from a relational, matriarchal model and women's perspective. Bridewealth is usually in the forms of money, essential goods or cattle that are transferred from the groom's kin to the bride's. It is not a one-off complete transaction, since, according to the Igbo, this payment is never completed. The Igbo, for example, and many other societies even take back their daughter's corpse at her death and receive additional ritual payments (Amadiume 1987: 79–81). Bridewealth is therefore a transfer of wealth at marriage that establishes legal rights over sexual access, services, and offspring. The woman also gets legal rights and protection from abuse. When a woman makes these transfers in a woman and woman marriage – which I will discuss presently – she gets the same rights over another woman, even though she herself does not consummate the marriage. Therefore, woman and woman marriage practice in African societies and cultures is different from gay and lesbian same-sex marriage. However, they all share an idea of same-sex marriage, but deal differently with its potentialities, which are dependent on culture, social development, and social change. We can safely say that Africa originated the idea of same-sex marriage in kinship options with utilitarian intentions, not as a romantic equal partnership.

Plural and complex marriage practices, just like same-sex marriage, also challenge European assumptions of monogamy and the nuclear family. Levirate (widow inheritance by the brothers of a woman's deceased husband) can be viewed as a kind of patrilineage polyandry, with women married to more than one man in a group marriage (Amadiume 1987: 83). Polygyny, which is when one man is married to more than one woman, is the most common form of plural marriage and accounts for an average of more than a third of all marriages in African societies, with over 40 percent in West Africa, 30 percent in East Africa, and 20 percent in southern Africa. While, in the past, we could argue that the demand for polygyny resulted in early marriage for girls, in cosmopolitan Africa today, mature and highly educated women are rationally choosing this loose association. The attractions seem to be co-wives and a large number of children, a support system, freedom of movement, and the ability to live separately that polygyny provides. Thus, polygyny is increasing in urban cities.

Polygynous marriage practice, it seems, is creative and is changing to suit the times, including the privileges of wealth and the demands of globalization. A wealthy African man who travels a lot might even have wives of different nationalities, including white and Asian women, in major cities of the world. In the context of survival strategies in the cities, Goody argues that rather than polygyny, it is the high rates of polycoity (multiple sexual partners) that has increased AIDS in Africa, for which he blames rural–urban migration, prostitution and single travelers (1997: 464).

Woman and woman marriage was widely practiced in many African societies (O'Brien 1977), including Igbo (Amadiume 1987), Lovedu (Krige 1974; Krige and Krige 1943), Nandi (Oboler 1980), Gikuyu (Clark 1980; Leakey [1938] 1977), Nuer (Evans-Pritchard 1945; 1951), etc. This flexible gender practice gave us the institution of "female husbands" which subverts dichotomous gender categories and rigid gender roles. The combination of polygyny, woman and woman marriage, and a flexible gender culture helps toward solving problems such as a woman's infertility. They also enhance the social status of an economically successful woman or powerful daughter, give relief to a tired wife, build up and extend the clientage of women chiefs or royal princesses and queens. They are a means of ensuring a vibrant matricentric household; they increase a woman's labor or the number of workers in agriculture or trade and give women an agency by which to secure family property and their own choice of succession and inheritance. There are all these social benefits, but there is also a negative one – namely, that such practices also create class difference between women: one woman pays bridewealth and claims rights over another. Still, they point the way toward gender flexibility and gender equity when roles are genderless, such as the Igbo word for husband: *di*. The role of the husband shows the interconnection of culture and economics, since the role of the husband facilitates economic accumulation and is therefore a means to social and political power.

The African institutions of polygyny, same-sex marriage, and levirate (a brother or son takes the place of a diseased husband and inherits his wife) represent a creative subversion of orthodox European assumptions that the "natural" family is constituted simply by a union between a man and a woman. These untidy African institutions separate heterosexuality or homosexuality and marriage practice. Marriage seems to supersede sexual orientation. In other words, the flexibility in marriage practices accommodates the diversity of sexuality that also includes problems of infertility and impotence. Consequently, marriage practice relates to the values of a gendered, structured community and gendered kinship, not simply the will of elders and Islamic clerics and their control of women, as is often claimed. Obviously, these gendered communities are different from the proto-patriarchal European state that regulates and legitimates sex, marriage, and family, and is today posing great difficulties to norm-conforming gay and lesbian families in their struggle for legal same-sex marriage.

The role of the "female husband" shows a class difference between poorer women and men, but it also indicates women's leadership as a result of a complex classificatory system and a diversity of family and household choices, for children belong to a family compound or a house, a lineage, and a clan. Children are more often called after their mother's name. All children come under a house-name and are not singularly tagged, which is an advantage these days for relocating rape babies and war orphans. In response to Oboler (1980) on whether a "female husband" is a man, to call the children in a same-sex marriage Ifi's children would not make one see Ifi as a father, but more as a Big Mama. We might therefore consider using the term "Mama husband" in place of "male husband" in order to de-link her from the patriarchal culture. Ifi as "Mama husband" is the matriarch of a complex matricentric household. In the term "female husband," genderless roles are disengaged from biological kin, and social motherhood is stressed so that "Mama husband" best describes this role. A similar notion of a larger national role of social motherhood is stressed in the ritual political roles of women chiefs, royal princesses, and constitutional queen mothers in African societies. There are examples from the Asante, Igbo, Benin, Kanuri, Hausa, Kogu, Yoruba, etc. in some West African societies and Rwanda, Burundi, Lozi, Lovedu, Zulu, etc. from East and Southern Africa and many examples in all African regions (Kaplan 1997; Paulme 1963).

The culture of matriarchy is used in national women's organizations for the mobilization of women, as I have pointed out elsewhere, citing the examples of many African first ladies and leaders of umbrella organizations and their national development projects (Amadiume 2000). Similarly, in traditional cultures, social mothering provided women leadership roles as teachers and mentors in girls' transition and initiation rituals into women's societies and organizations whereby girls become adult women and come under the mentorship of designated women in their societies and other adult women in general, as, for example, Sande of the Mende in Sierra Leone and Liberia (MacCormack 1975) and Chisungu of the Bemba in Zambia (Richards [1956] 1992). Women's leadership and social mothering continued into spirit possession groups, especially Bori and Zar in Islamized African societies in Nigeria, Sudan, Somalia, and North Africa (Lewis 1989; Lewis et al. 1991). In other African societies women's leadership and social mothering can be seen in postcolonial religious movements in African Christianity, Holy Spirit, prophetic, and Pentecostal churches (Hackett 1987). Here, a kinship or lineage matriarch becomes "Big Mama Prayer." Women in all these social family situations show leadership and exhibit a culture of solidarity in participation, sharing, mentoring, and healing. Through the social mothering and spiritual leadership that these women provide, they also aspire to spiritual perfection and immortality just like men and their ancestors. This relational, matriarchal model provides a gender perspective that subverts the patrifocal monopoly on religion and political authority that legitimizes male leadership and power to the exclusion of women and subordinate males.

As well as class, race, and gender, migration, unemployment, and poverty are some of the factors splintering kinship, families, and households both in rural and urban Africa. Ironically, these are also some of the factors that pro-duce the urban version of the rural matricentric household in female-headed households in urban towns. Increasing numbers of complex but single-sex and female-headed households in Africa and the African Diaspora communities in Britain, the Caribbean, and the United States exhibit poverty due to androcentric and patrifocal state policies that undermine and undervalue the efforts and achievements of female leadership. But these complex families, which contain different combinations of kin, also need to be celebrated, and their matriarchal leadership praised rather than berated as being maladjusted, social security and welfare dependents. These models of family that reflect specific contemporary situations challenge us to focus on women's choices and strategies of resistance and struggle against odds.

The imposition of the European model of the nuclear family on Africans by colonial rule and legislation of the postcolonial state has greatly transformed relations of gender, culture, family, and kinship. Sadly, monogamous marriage has not proven to be a happy-ever-after affair, and the nuclear family is no haven from the imagined oppressions and hell of polygyny. We can point to a higher rate of divorce, domestic violence, and lack of a support system experienced by women under the constraints of the nuclear family. When we compare simple and fragmented families with complex families, kinship, and lineage on the question of the situating of children, women, and individuals in general, we find that many of the current problems around individual responsibility that arise in cases of adoption and parenting often do not apply in complex families. The African adage that it takes a village to raise a person speaks to the principle of community and shared responsibilities. The Igbo say that to have people is to have wealth. The point here is not to deny the transformations in postcolonial cultures in African societies and cosmopolitan cities, but to raise questions about the conservatism and narrowness of the imported transforming cultures.

In an effort to transform a public male culture that has generated stressful and oppressive individualist and fragmenting conditions of work, some in the West are proposing more conducive, relational working conditions that would be more favorable to women and people in general. By so doing, they are appropriating values from "simple" societies by preaching interdependence and collectivism (Fletcher 1999). Just as we can demand support and mutuality at the point of production, we also need to be concerned with redistribution of profit at the end of production. If not, mutuality will be no more than a club of successful sisters; a club of rich women who are disconnected from the majority of poorer women. It is important to change and transform the institutional culture of power that is based on patriarchy; but it is not just a question of increasing the number of women in leadership positions and creating more powerful "male females," important as it is to correct sexism and balance the gender equation at the top.

By far the most important issues to be reconsidered by feminists involve the choice between the traditional African flexibility in the ameliorating role and compassionate culture of the "Mama husband" that many progressive men adopt these days, and the masculinized, European, patriarchal gender role of the hard father and head of a household. All these issues beg for the recognition and the rethinking of the traditional relational, matriarchal model of kinship, whose support system can easily absorb innovations and choices in marriage, kinship, and the family.

References

Adagala, K. (1991) "Households and Historical changes on Plantations in Kenya," in Eleonora Masini and Susan Stratigos (eds.), *Women, Households and Change* (Tokyo, Japan: The United Nations University Press).

Adepoju, A. (1994) *Gender, Work, and Population in Sub Saharan Africa* (London: James Curry).

Amadiume, I. (1987) *Male Daughters, Female Husbands: Gender and Sex in an African Society* (London and New Jersey: Zed Books).

Amadiume, I. (1997) "Part One Re-writing History," *Reinventing Africa: Matriarchy, Religion and Culture* (London and New York: Zed Books).

Amadiume, I. (2000) *Daughters of the Goddess, Daughters of Imperialism: African Women, Culture, Power and Democracy* (London and New Jersey: Zed Books).

Barnard, A. (1997) "Kinship and Descent," in John Middleton (ed.), *Encyclopedia of Africa South of the Sahara*, vol. 2 (New York: Macmillan Library Reference USA).

Boserup, E. (1970) *Woman's Role in Economic Development* (London: Allen and Unwin).

Clark, C. M. (1980) "Land and Food, Women and Power, in Nineteenth Century Kikuyu," *Africa* 50/4: 357–69.

Diop, C. A. (1987) *Precolonial Black Africa: A Comparative Study of the Political and Social System of Europe and Black Africa, From Antiquity to the Formation of Modern States* (Westport, CT: Lawrence Hill & Co.).

Diop, C. A. (1989) *The Cultural Unity of Black Africa: The Domains of Matriarchy and of Patriarchy in Classical Antiquity* (London: Karnak House).

Diop, C. A. (1991) *Civilization or Barbarism: An Authentic Anthropology*. New York: Lawrence Hill Books.

Evans-Pritchard, E. E. (1945) *Some Aspects of Marriage and the Family Among the Nuer* (Livingstone, Northern Rhodesia: The Rhodes-Livingstone Institute).

Evans-Pritchard, E. E. (1951) *Kinship and Marriage Among the Nuer* (Oxford: Clarendon Press).

Fletcher, J. K. (1999) *Disappearing Acts: Gender, Power and Relational Practice at Work* (Cambridge, MA: MIT Press).

Fortes, M. (1949) *The Web of Kinship Among the Tallensi* (Oxford: Oxford University Press).

Fortes, M. (1987) *Religion, Morality and the Person: Essays on Tallensi Religion* (New York: Cambridge University Press).

Goody, J. (1997) "Kinship and Marriage," in John Middleton (ed.), *Encyclopedia of Africa South of the Sahara*, vol. 2 (New York: Macmillan Library Reference USA).

Hackett, R. (1987) *New Religious Movements in Nigeria* (Lewiston, NY: The Edwin Mellen Press).

Harris, B. J. (1997) "Swazi Women Workers in Cottage Industries and Factories," in Gwendolyn Mikell (ed.), *African Feminism: The Politics of Survival in Sub-Saharan Africa* (Philadelphia: University of Pennsylvania Press).

Kaplan, F. E. (ed.) (1997) *Queens, Queen Mothers, Priestesses and Power: Case Studies in African Gender* (New York: New York Academy of Sciences).

Knight, C. (1991) *Blood Relations: Menstruation and the Origins of Culture* (New Haven and London: Yale University Press).

Krige, E. J. (1974) "Woman–Marriage, with Special Reference to the Lovedu – its Significance for Definition of Marriage," *Africa* 44: 11–37.

Krige, J. D. and Krige, E. J. (1943) *The Realm of a Rain Queen* (Oxford: Oxford University Press).

Leakey, L. S. B. ([1938] 1977) *The Southern Kikuyu Before 1903* (New York: Academic Press).

Lewis, I. M. (1989) *Ecstatic Religion: A Study of Shamanism and Spirit Possession*, 2nd edn. (London and New York: Routledge).

Lewis, I. M., Al-Safi, A., and Hurreiz, S. (eds.) (1991) *Women's Medicine: The Zar-Bori Cult in Africa and Beyond* (Edinburgh: Edinburgh University Press for the International African Institute).

MacCormack, C. P. (1975) "Sande Women and Political Power in Sierra Leone," *West African Journal of Sociology and Political Science* 1: 42–50.

Manuh, T. (1997) "Wives, Children, and Intestate Succession in Ghana," in Gwendolyn Mikell (ed.), *African Feminism: The Politics of Survival in Sub-Saharan Africa* (Philadelphia: University of Pennsylvania Press).

Mikell, G. (ed.) (1997a) *African Feminism: The Politics of Survival in Sub-Saharan Africa* (Philadelphia: University of Pennsylvania Press).

Mikell, G. (1997b) "Pleas for Domestic Relief: Akan Women and Family Courts," in Gwendolyn Mikell (ed.), *African Feminism: The Politics of Survival in Sub-Saharan Africa* (Philadelphia: University of Pennsylvania Press).

Obbo, C. (1980) *African Women: Their Struggle for Economic Independence* (London: Zed Books).

Oboler, R. S. (1980) "Is the Female Husband a Man? Woman/Woman Marriage Among the Nandi of Kenya," *Ethnology* 19: 69–88.

O'Brien, D. (1977) "Female Husbands in Southern Bantu Societies," in Alice Schlegel (ed.), *Sexual Stratification: A Cross-Cultural View* (New York: Columbia University Press).

Oppong, C. (ed.) (1983) *Male and Female in West Africa* (London: Allen and Unwin).

Parpart, J. L. and Staudt, K. A. (eds.) (1989) *Women and the State in Africa* (Boulder, CO: Lynne Reinner Publishers).

Paulme, D. (ed.) (1963) *Women of Tropical Africa* (Berkeley and Los Angeles: University of California Press).

Radcliffe-Brown, A. R. and Forde, D. (eds.) (1950) *African Systems of Kinship and Marriage* (New York: Oxford University Press).

Richards, A. ([1956] 1992) *Chisungu: A Girl's Initiation Ceremony Among the Bemba of Zambia* (London: Routledge).

Turnbull, C. M. (1981) "Mbuti Womanhood," in Frances Dahlberg (ed.), *Woman the Gatherer* (New Haven: Yale University Press).

White, F. E. (1999) "Women in West and West-Central Africa," in Iris Berger and Frances White, *Women in Sub-Saharan Africa: Restoring Women to History* (Bloomington: Indiana University Press).

CHAPTER TWENTY-SIX

The Caribbean Family?

D. Alissa Trotz

Introduction

This brief chapter provides an overview of some of the historical and contemporary debates on the family in the Caribbean. The Caribbean covers a heterogeneous combination of (primarily island) countries, including Belize in Central America, countries on the northeastern shoulder of South America, and the islands below the Bahamas. Some also include in this definition the Caribbean/Atlantic coasts of such Latin American countries as Costa Rica, Nicaragua, Colombia, and Venezuela. The region consists of those countries in the Americas that were among the first to be colonized by Europe, and this history of colonial oppression and creative resistance often constitutes the basis for speaking of the Caribbean as a coherent area. Such definitions mark an incredibly contingent and diverse space, comprising a medley of colonial histories, tongues (French, Dutch, Spanish, English, along with a vast array of indigenous and Creole languages), political systems, and ethnic groups. The Caribbean is the site of one of the first diasporas following European colonization, the consequence of the decimation and displacement of the original peoples of the Americas, and the transplantation of populations from other parts of the world. Given this history, and with current migration levels out of the region, one could say that the Caribbean, in its pasts, presents, and futures, is both situated and everywhere (Girvan 2001).

Consequently, in the section on theoretical debates that follows, it is perhaps wiser to speak of the idea of the Caribbean family without attempting to cleanly delineate boundaries and certainties. Even in doing so, it is important that we recognize the limitations in the scholarly literature (and the geographical limits of this chapter). The bulk of the literature has tended to focus on the English-speaking Caribbean, and on the experiences of Black Caribbeans, the descendents of slaves transplanted from Africa. (To cite one example, Barrow's extensive overview (1996) of the family in the Caribbean is based almost exclusively on research in the Anglophone countries.) There is far less material on, for example, the descendents of indentured laborers from India who have settled in such countries as Trinidad, Guyana, Martinique, Suriname, and Jamaica. Many of the examples here will be drawn from secondary research in relation to these groups, which constitute the largest populations in the region. The lack of research on other underrepresented groups is even more apparent, while the existing literature on family structures in Amerindian populations tends to be disconnected from broader questions of their marginalization in the postcolonial Caribbean.

The second section of this chapter considers some of the challenges facing families in the current neoliberal conjuncture in the Caribbean. It is critical that we see these two sections as mutually implicated, for one could argue that in this area more than any other, theorizing has translated into policies and limits that are placed on the practice of everyday living. This requires that we be open to and less ignorant of our role as intellectuals, and our contribution to stereotypes and misrepresentations that can and do have real material effects.

An Overview of Debates

Conceptual stereotypes

Research and policy have historically been preoccupied with two central issues in the study of Caribbean families. The first related to high levels of female-headed households, especially among the black population. The second concerned the apparently different forms of familial formation and organization along class and ethnic divides. Briefly, working-class and predominantly black households exhibited a wide array of male–female arrangements ranging from the visiting union (where partners did not reside together) to common-law relationships and marriage. As one moved up the social ladder, marriage was far more common. Moreover, for other groups – and particularly among Indian households – research showed marriage rates to be far higher, regardless of class position. Early efforts to identify, classify, and explain these specificities traversed a broad range of questions: the extent to which these differences were derived from the "Old World" (such as Africa and India) or newly constituted Creole forms; whether "different" family types were part of a single stratification system or fit into a plural society model of non-overlapping segments with their own internal evaluative systems; whether we were witnessing simply the adaptation of family forms, especially among the poor, to the exigencies of everyday life.

These positions all shared the notion of the domestic as an essentially unchanging feminine and bounded domain. This premise was especially clear in the respectability-reputation paradigm developed by Peter Wilson, which identified women with respectability and the colonial status quo – as represented, for instance, in the household and the church – and vested Caribbean men with the responsibility for subverting such norms (for a critique of this paradigm, see Besson 1993). The starting point for researchers and policy-makers was that "normal" households necessarily took a nuclear form. The imposition of this external norm refused to acknowledge the patterns of family life and relations in the region as anything other than an aberration if they did not conform to such Eurocentric expectations.

Such notions of normative familiality plagued especially the debates surrounding women-headed households. "Matrifocality," a term originally developed by anthropologist R. T. Smith to denote the centrality of women in the domestic domain in their role as mothers, whether they lived with a man or not, soon became widely used by others interchangeably with female-headedness and female dominance. The Afro-Caribbean female-headed household would become shorthand for "the Caribbean family," a gatekeeping concept marshaled to provide contrasts with, say, the machismo of Latin America or the patriarchies of South Asia. This deployment of the term not only erases the racialized specificity of the concept within the Caribbean, it also evokes a notion of cultural difference across geographic spaces, all falsely homogenized. Moreover, this concern with the female-headed household is a project of restoration. That is to say, if the nuclear family form is the ideal, then the Caribbean family becomes symptomatic of pathology and lack, with female-headed households labeled variously as deviant, disintegrated, denuded, and incomplete, a legacy that remains to this day in the region as well as in the diasporas (in other renderings, the female head becomes emblematic of excess, the strong indefatigable matriarch). Attempts to find explanations, many of which revolved around the incapacity of men to fulfill their breadwinner role, exemplified the underlying ideology of nuclearity that fueled such debates. Such stereotypical frameworks do not attempt to consider women outside of the domestic domain, or to raise questions about the effects of this idea of the family on the modes of organizing people's family lives. Nor is there any effort to interrogate the power dynamics within families, including the nuclear model itself.

Gender, culture, and class: feminist and other critiques

Feminist critiques, especially since the mid-1970s, have countered these portrayals, and their primary responses, broadly summarized, are as follows: demonstrate the centrality of women in the forging of Caribbean culture; point out that families involve networks that extend beyond the physical boundaries of the household, the yard, the city, and even the country – and often include non-kin; underline women's involvement beyond the domestic domain; highlight how the gendered division of labor in the family is not a natural fact, but a social relation that can only be understood by locating it in a historical context; and make the case that studies of the family can shed valuable light on wider political and social relations in the region. Below is a brief outline of some of the current directions of this work.

The challenge to established wisdom about the Caribbean family received a huge impetus from the University of the West Indies' ambitious Women in the

Caribbean Project (WICP), a multidisciplinary study conducted among thousands of women across the Anglophone Caribbean between 1979 and 1982 (Senior 1991). Although based primarily on the lives of a relatively homogeneous sample of linguistically similar, low-income Afro-Caribbean women, and while it did not provide any theoretical framework for analyzing the existence and reproduction of gender inequality, the WICP was extremely valuable for documenting the limitations of previous work that regarded women only within families. Moreover, by identifying some of the obstacles women faced within the domestic domain and beyond, the study also questioned notions that Caribbean women had parity with men or that Caribbean society was matriarchal. A recent text that presents Haitian women's narratives is a critical contribution to our understanding of how Caribbean women experience the family across territory and political systems (Bell 2001). What is striking about this publication is the attention given to the public domain and especially to state violence, concerns that are clearly not as central to the WICP study.

Historical research has offered exciting possibilities for uncovering the hidden dimensions of families and the ways in which these are constituted by, and constitutive of, broader structures of power. Martinez-Alier's early seminal text on colonial Cuba (1974) elucidated connections between the development of marriage laws based on the doctrine of purity of blood, and wider stratification systems based on gender, color, and class. In the Anglophone Caribbean, a somewhat similar analytical lens has been effectively trained on the ideology and practices of elite Jamaican families (Douglass 1992). Smith (1988) has pointed out that "illegitimate" relationships (often seen as part and parcel of female-headedness and matrifocality), far from being a correlate of poverty, permeate all levels of society. In fact, they are a structuring principle of class, gender, and racial subordination, as higher-status men tend to marry social equals but maintain extra-marital relationships with lower-status women. That working-class families – and black families in particular – continue to be decried as exclusively practicing non-legalized relationships speaks to social power and the ability to define normality while rendering invisible the ways in which such practices are common throughout the Caribbean across class lines. On the other hand, challenges to dominant norms have effected policy changes in such countries as Antigua, where understandings and kinship practices among the "common order" eventually found their way into state legislation relating to family law (Lazarus-Black 1994). Lazarus-Black (1995) also takes issue with the notion that "matrifocal" women father children, arguing that kinship events and activities are quite clearly defined along gender lines, so that women in their roles as mothers are not compensating or substituting for men but are rather performing culturally and historically produced responsibilities that are quite distinct from fathers' duties. At any rate, focusing on men in their role as fathers detracts attention from the ways in which men participate in the family as uncles, sons, grandfathers, and other kinship roles. Finally, it seems fair to say that while this more recent work challenges the power dynamics embedded in heterosexual

relations, there is little that explicitly engages with the construction and reproduction of heteronormativity. Exceptions include Jacqui Alexander's seminal
work (1997) on intersections of state formation, citizenship, and sexuality in
Trinidad and the Bahamas, and Gloria Wekker's research (1997) that discusses
entrenched and accepted practices of same sex relations (mati work) in Afro-
Surinamese working class culture.

Labor, colonial legacies, and postcolonial nationalisms

Researchers have also investigated notions of family and domesticity in the
context of men's and women's relationships to the labor force. Rather than
studying women in relation to the family and men in relation to the labor force,
we should pay close attention to how they develop different relations to both
domains. For example, Indian women came to the Caribbean as indentured
laborers for the sugar plantations beginning in the mid-nineteenth century. To
examine dominant understandings and self-conceptions of Indian women as
housewives today, and to dislodge arguments that this domestic role is a timeless
cultural predisposition, we need to trace the ways in which women's labor has
become increasingly relocated from the waged workforce to the "nuclear" or
joint household, differentiated among various groups of women, and distinguished definitionally from men's labor. We must look at the emergence of the
male breadwinner ideology and how it came to be taken up not only by the state
and employers but also by male workers and the trade unions that represented
their interests. In the case of black women, the emphatic link between mothering
and wage work must be placed in the context of the historically continuous
relationship of such women to paid labor, even though it takes place in a highly
stratified market which continues to severely compromise women's ability to be
autonomous vis-à-vis men (Reddock 1994).

We are also beginning to comprehend how the Caribbean experience provides
a different inflection and new insights into the theorizing of familial dynamics.
Whereas the family was initially seen in Euro-American feminist scholarship as
the site of women's oppression, researchers have shown how for slave women
from Africa and indentured women from India and China, the family (and male
prerogatives of control over the disposal of female labor power) was a privilege
reserved for the white planter class. In the transition to a post-slavery and post-
indentureship society, the family became a critical site of struggle for autonomy
and cultural identity, one in which women often invested as heavily as men. This
does not mean that women did not have to face gender subordination within the
homespace, but rather that they may have traded one form of control for another.

Understanding the complex loyalty the family evokes in the postcolonial
era requires moving beyond a narrow focus on gender and considering group
membership of other sorts of constituencies. In particular, the relationship between
the rhetoric of the family/kinship and appeals to collective racialized identities
in the name of culture and tradition, and the implications of this for women as

bearers of future generations, constitute a promising area for future research. Indeed, there is exciting new work that reveals how discourses and practices of morality, respectability, and legitimacy were central both to the shaping of the family and the making of the public domain. Here we see clearly the shadow of domesticity that haunts the constitution of anti-colonial and national identities and selective claims to citizenship (Macpherson 2003). The narratives in Beverly Bell's collection (2001), with their powerful testimonies of state violence perpetrated against women who transgressed the boundaries of acceptable behavior, offer a powerful reminder of the differentiated consequences of defining and confining women in this way.

These recent interventions have enabled us to move beyond the pathologization of Caribbean family life, to make tentative connections between the ways in which familiar, private spaces are related to each other as well as to states and public spaces, and examine how these relationships are informed by the enduring legacy of our colonial pasts.

Contemporary Challenges

The impact of structural adjustment policies

As we have seen in the previous section, familial relations and the inequalities that stem from them are historically and diversely constituted. Yet notwithstanding developments in scholarship, "family" continues to suggest a certain timelessness or a taken-for-granted quality. In the contemporary Caribbean, as elsewhere, hegemonic notions of what "normal" and natural families should look like persist, notwithstanding differences in the ways and spaces in which people live their everyday lives. Such dominant renderings of "the Caribbean family" have a number of consequences, especially where academic work and policy-making converge. One good example is the work of T. S. Simey, a colonial social welfare officer in the Caribbean who in the 1940s authored a study decrying the widespread existence of female-headed households. In the contemporary moment, rewarding male breadwinners because of persistent notions that men head families means that female household heads remain disadvantaged and over-represented among the poor in the region. Forms of homophobic legislation that are underpinned by heterosexist assumptions of family formation further stigmatize large segments of Caribbean populations. In Guyana, for example, recent attempts to pass a parliamentary bill outlawing forms of discrimination based on sexual orientation provoked such an outcry from influential segments of society that it was returned to parliament for further debate.

Any discussion of the contemporary challenges facing the restructuring of familial life in the Caribbean must also address the widespread adoption of neoliberal policies across the region during the past decade. Massive reductions in the provision of basic social infrastructure by the state mean that unpaid

375

reproductive labor now has to bear the costs. At the level of the household, because of the still entrenched notion (among both women and men) that women bear the primary responsibility for the domestic domain, they have had to shoulder a disproportionate share of the displaced burden. This includes caring for the young, the elderly, and the infirm, budgeting, and searching for cheaper goods and services, all of which involve increased outlays of time. Coping mechanisms in the Caribbean tend to consist largely of making individual adjustments at the household level and drawing on close extended networks of family and friends for support.

The restructuring of the labor market is another domain that both affects and is affected by familial arrangements and identities. Women are intensifying their involvement in the paid labor force. This is partly in response to specific demands for female labor in those countries where export-oriented manufacturing and service industries are located, such as Barbados, Cuba, the Dominican Republic, Haiti, Jamaica, and Puerto Rico. For the most part, however, the increase is driven more by economic necessity on the part of households rather than a generalized expansion of demand. This is reflected in drastic cutbacks in the public sector that have resulted in the displacement of large numbers of women (predominantly black women in countries like Trinidad and Tobago and Guyana), the growth of informal sector activities, and continuing stratification of both the formal and informal labor markets in ways that persistently disadvantage women and are based on stereotypes that belie the extent of their contribution to or responsibility for their families. Men's ability to be breadwinners is also being eroded by the increasing uncertainty and insecurity of paid work that is the hallmark of the current conjuncture (referred to by some as "feminization" to denote the degradation of conditions across increasing sectors, such that general conditions now resemble those previously faced only by women). Moreover, the Caribbean has had a long-standing tradition of working women relying on extended confederations of female kin to assist with domestic activities. Such networks are being attenuated as more women, and older women especially, are entering/re-entering the paid workforce.

"Traditional" notions of the family also stigmatize women who are finding niches in the spaces opened up in Caribbean economies. Tourism, for example, plays a critical role in most of the Caribbean, and sex work is one largely informal sector activity that provides some income for working women and men in the region. Official refusal to acknowledge that regional economies depend in part on sexual labor – prostitution is regulated and penalized in various ways across the Caribbean, and Curaçao is the only country that has a state-legalized brothel where women are licensed to work – has meant little if any protection for female sex workers who are labeled as morally loose and irresponsible, although research has shown that support of families is a frequently cited reason for women's entry into sex work (Kempadoo 1999). Efforts to shore up the family are also giving rise to women entering some spheres of non-traditional work (like the private security guard industry), suggesting that in this respect men's gender identities may be far more resilient and resistant to change under crisis, especially in a context in which jobs that are sex-typed as feminine are associated with a devaluation of social prestige and remuneration.

Migration

Large-scale migration, especially to major North American cities, is another phenomenon that is reconfiguring the shape and meaning of familial life for Caribbeans (Chamberlain 1998). If the parameters of Caribbean families have always been fluid, they have now assumed an international dimension that makes the notion of boundaries even more difficult to define. The networks to which such flows have given rise are so entrenched that researchers now speak of transnational families as a way of capturing these rich and dynamic linkages across place. Some initial research also suggests that women are centrally involved in building diasporic communities, and participate in movements aimed at influencing or tracking events back in the Caribbean (Charles 1995).

Intra- and extra-regional movement of peoples in the relative absence of local opportunity is certainly not new (in fact it constitutes the foundations of the modern Caribbean as we know it). What distinguishes the contemporary trend from previous flows is the scale, and the fact that more women than men are now leaving. This gender imbalance results in large part from women's additional efforts to maintain those left behind through the provision of remittances, advice, marriage partners, and possible eventual sponsorship for closest kin, and cannot be divorced from the bond between women's social identities and the future welfare of their families. The tendency in the literature on transnationalism to depict migratory strategies as signifying change overlooks the fact that for many individuals, leaving home is a means of remaining the same, in the sense of keeping families afloat that may not have been able to cope otherwise. These shifts are taking place in a global context in which borders are opening up to international capital while becoming increasingly intransigent in the face of the movement of racialized and gendered bodies and labor from the "South" to the "North." The result for the vast majority of migrants is underpaid work in the undocumented sector, often with little possibility of familial reunion with those who remain "at home."

This brief discussion suggests that households and families are not simply being passively buffeted by, but are also reshaping, wider social forces. It also raises the question of how gender relations within domesticity are being pushed in new directions. There are some indications that in the workplace and at home, women may be negotiating new positionalities, recreating and revaluing themselves and their activities. The performance of similar, gender-typed work under different circumstances may change the meaning and status given to those activities (Freeman 2000; Peake and Trotz 1999). One study of export-processing workers in the Hispanic Caribbean (Puerto Rico, the Dominican Republic, and Cuba) makes the case that women have been more effective in challenging gender subordination in the family than on the production line (Safa 1995). Nonetheless, recognizing the initiatives that women are taking should not lead us back to the depiction of Caribbean females as heroic miracle workers or matriarchs, a stereotype that vastly underestimates the daily struggles all women face and ignores the fact that many are simply not coping. Increasing entry of women into the labor force is not always a guarantee of the emergence of fundamentally more egalitarian familial relationships, especially where men's jobs are threatened. The result may instead be estrangement and greater numbers of female heads in a region in which such households are more or less culturally accepted but where the acknowledgment of female familial responsibility does not translate into financial or other forms of equity. Domestic violence (across gender and generation) is an area where further research is needed to pinpoint some of the relationships between abuse and economic crisis, and there is still precious little work being done on men and masculine identities. At this stage, one can only surmise that the physical and mental regulation of women's bodies is a likely outcome under conditions in which the material basis for the performance of masculinities is being singularly eroded by the onslaught of global capitalism. In the Anglophone Caribbean in particular, the notion of male marginalization (and the accompanying myth that women are taking over), which has some of its roots in (misunderstandings of) the matrifocal thesis, is gaining increasing ground in popular and decision-making circles, and is certain to contribute to further tensions in this area (Barriteau 2000).

Conclusion

Familial experiences vary across a number of social relations that include age, household structure, class, and ethnicity. For instance, while black women's intensified involvement in the labor force is partly a continuation of a historical practice that has generated a perception that the social identities of mother and worker are compatible, paid work has not had the same continuous resonance for Indian women and indicates a different set of challenges in the contemporary context. Female heads with young children will face economic and other practical challenges relating to childcare that women living with extended family members may not feel as sharply. Thus, while practices of social reproduction are becoming increasingly commensurate under conditions of economic immiseration, this should not necessarily lead us to conclude that the meanings attached to those practices will be the same across different constituencies. Moreover, as we have seen in the previous sections, women and men have investments in the family as a site of difference from "other" women and men, so that political allegiances and collective identities cannot be automatically assumed to emerge straightforwardly along gender lines. Women's groups (including those in the diaspora) have been at the forefront of campaigns addressing structural adjustment, state-sponsored and domestic violence, women's reproductive rights, and a host of other issues that explicitly make the connections between the public and the private (Reddock 1998). For these and other organizations that are committed to challenging the hierarchies within families and making explicit the ways in which state practices are invested in harnessing a particular vision of the Caribbean family to neoliberal policies, it is critical that the forging of common political positions acknowledges and works through specific histories, while recognizing that the family consists of complexly interwoven networks that offer both pleasure as well as betrayal for its members, and especially for women.

References

Alexander, J. (1997) "Erotic Autonomy as a Politics of Decolonization: An Anatomy of Feminist and State Practice in the Bahamas Tourist Economy," in Jacqui Alexander and Chandra Talpade Mohanty (eds.), *Feminist Genealogies, Colonial Legacies, Democratic Futures* (London: Routledge).

Barriteau, E. (2000) "Examining the Issues of Men, Male Marginalisation and Masculinity in the Caribbean: Policy Implications." Working Paper No. 4, Center for Gender and Development Studies, University of the West Indies at Cave Hill.

Barrow, C. (1996) *Family in the Caribbean: Themes and Perspectives* (Kingston, Jamaica: Ian Randle Publishers).

Bell, B. (2001) *Walking on Fire: Haitian Women's Stories of Survival and Resistance* (Ithaca, NY: Cornell University Press).

Besson, J. (1993) "Reputation and Respectability Reconsidered: A New Perspective on Afro-Caribbean Peasant Women," in J. H. Momsen (ed.), *Women and Change in the Caribbean: A Pan-Caribbean Perspective* (London: James Currey).

Chamberlain, M. (1998) *Caribbean Migration: Globalised Identities* (London: Routledge).

Charles, C. (1995) "Gender and Politics in Contemporary Haiti: The Duvalierist State, Transnationalism, and the Emergence of a New Feminism (1980–1990)," *Feminist Studies* 21/1: 135–64.

Douglass, L. (1992) *The Power of Sentiment: Love, Hierarchy, and the Jamaican Family Elite* (Boulder, CO: Westview Press).

Freeman, C. (2000) *High Tech and High Heels in the Global Economy: Women, Work, and Pink-Collar Identities in the Caribbean* (Durham: Duke University Press).

Girvan, N. (2001) "Reinterpreting the Caribbean," in Brian Meeks and Folke Lindahl (eds.), *New Caribbean Thought: A Reader* (Kingston, Jamaica: University of the West Indies Press).

Kempadoo, K. (ed.) (1999) *Sun, Sex, and Gold: Tourism and Sex Work in the Caribbean* (Lanham, MD: Rowman & Littlefield Publishers).

Lazarus-Black, M. (1994) *Legitimate Acts and Illegal Encounters: Law and Society in Antigua and Barbuda* (Washington, DC: Smithsonian Institution Press).

Lazarus-Black, M. (1995) "My Mother Never Fathered Me: Rethinking Kinship and the Governing of Families," *Social and Economic Studies* 44/1: 49–71.

Macpherson, A. (2003) "Imagining the Colonial Nation: Race, Gender, and Middle-Class Politics in Belize, 1888–1898," in Nancy Appelbaum, Anne S. Macpherson, and Karin Alejandra Rosemblatt (eds.), *Race and Nation in Modern Latin America* (Chapel Hill: University of North Carolina Press).

Martinez-Alier, V. (1974) *Marriage, Class and Colour in Nineteenth-Century Cuba: A Study of Racial Attitudes and Sexual Values in a Slave Society* (London: Cambridge University Press).

Peake, L. and Trotz, D. A. (1999) *Gender, Ethnicity and Place: Women and Identities in Guyana* (London: Routledge).

D. Alissa Trotz

Reddock, R. (1998) "Women's Organizations and Movements in the Commonwealth Caribbean: The Response to Global Economic Crisis in the 1980s," *Feminist Review* 59: 57–73.

Reddock, R. (1994) *Women, Labour and Politics in Trinidad and Tobago* (London: Zed Books).

Safa, H. (1995) *The Myth of the Male Breadwinner: Women and Industrialization in the Caribbean* (Boulder, CO: Westview Press).

Senior, O. (1991) *Working Miracles: Women's Lives in the English-Speaking Caribbean* (Bloomington: Indiana University Press).

Smith, R. T. (1988) *Kinship and Class in the West Indies: A Genealogical Study of Jamaica and Guyana* (Cambridge: Cambridge University Press).

Wekker, G. (1997) "One Finger Does Not Drink Okra Soup: Afro-Surinamese Women and Critical Agency," in Jacqui Alexander and Chandra Talpade Mohanty (eds.), *Feminist Genealogies, Colonial Legacies, Democratic Futures* (London: Routledge).

Further reading

Brereton, B. (1999) "Family Strategies, Gender and the Shift to Wage Labor in the British Caribbean," in B. Brereton and K. Yelvington (eds.), *The Colonial Caribbean in Transition: Essays on Postemancipation Social and Cultural History* (Kingston: University of the West Indies Press).

Smith, R. T. (1996) *The Matrifocal Family: Power, Pluralism and Politics* (London: Routledge).

Suárez Findlay, E. J. (1999) *Imposing Decency: The Politics of Sexuality and Race in Puerto Rico, 1870–1920* (Durham: Duke University Press).

CHAPTER TWENTY-SEVEN

Family and Household in Latin America

Nina Laurie

Introduction

Studies of the family in Latin America must highlight the wider context of development in an age of globalization. Development ideologies and policy have framed the family within notions of the household. Household acts as the ultimate scale of analysis, the micro level at which development is expected to make material improvements in the quality of people's lives. Although many families do not live as a single unified household and many households are not forged through direct family ties, development policies often imply that the family and the household are the same thing.

Since Oscar Lewis first published his work on the culture of poverty (1975), perceptions of the Latin American household/family as "poor" have dominated social sciences and the development planning industry. The household has become one of the main targets of development and the reference point for analyzing and measuring poverty. In turn, the material realities of oppression (economic and political) have influenced the ways in which academics have conceptualized development, gender, and feminism in the region. The Latin American household and family are seen as home to "everyday" forms of resistance to oppression. Household survival strategies are assumed to carry individuals through fluctuations in the political and economic fortunes of Latin American nation-states.

Despite the poverty-focused generalizations made by development policy, it is not possible to speak about "the Latin American" family/household. Different development trajectories, colonial histories, indigenous cultures, and rural and urban geographies make an anathema of such a homogenizing category. Nevertheless, it is important to discuss the impact of universal political and economic processes on households and families. For example, authoritarian regimes and violent repression were experienced throughout Latin America in the 1980s, affecting families and households in diverse ways, across differences of class, ethnicity, and location. This general situation was compounded by the implementation of uniform neoliberal structural adjustment packages. These reforms increased the burden on families and households by removing subsidies, privatizing services, and decreasing the role played by the state in social provisioning. These measures were intended to compensate for losses accrued by governments during the "lost decade of development" in the 1980s, when increased interest rates created a debt crisis of continental proportions. The ways in which household survival strategies and gender relations responded to these universal conditions became the focus of much work by Latin American and western scholars in the 1980s and 1990s. In recent years, attention has shifted somewhat from this crisis-led conceptualization of the family to focus on wider aspects of identity formation within family and household units. In the first part of this chapter, I examine how a development context has framed the Latin American household and family, with specific attention to the impact of feminist critiques. This will introduce the second part, in which I explain how and why a gender analysis of "family" benefits from highlighting the role played by identity formation in development processes.

Gender, Development, and Households

Research has shown how men and women are differentially engaged in and affected by development processes. With an analysis of women's economic contributions to development, Boserup (1970) set in motion the Women in Development (WID) paradigm that aimed to insure that women were included in development processes. Critiqued by Gender and Development (GAD) analyzes for failing to focus on the power relations between women and men and question modernization interpretations of development, WID approaches became overshadowed by the 1980s (Rathgeber 1990). An important success of both paradigms has been to make visible the ways in which the conceptualizations of change adopted by development planners reflect "male bias," that is the prioritization and institutionalization of masculine activities and values (Elson 1991). WID and GAD have also raised important questions about methods for gathering statistics on development, and have crucially promoted feminist data-collection techniques that focus on the micro level in order to analyze how development affects different individuals within households, rather than the unit as a whole. For example, Ostergaard (1992) contrasts the calorie intake of boys and girls in poor households in Bangladesh. She shows how the collection of household statistics obscures very real patterns of "son preference" in many homes, whereby boys are given more nutritious meals than girls. Therefore, while much local analysis examines the household, feminist critiques of household-based research have emphasized the ways in which unequal power relations within households structure access to resources and development more widely. Such studies gained particular importance in the 1990s as critiques of structural adjustment packages showed how their impacts were clearly gendered. Not only do women generally bear the burden of adjustment, but also analyses show how specific groups of women, such as the elderly and indigenous, are doubly disadvantaged. As formal jobs are cut back with the demand for increased flexibility in labor markets under structural adjustment, pressure on the informal sector increases (Tanski 1994). Competition for jobs rises and the opportunities available to elderly and indigenous women who face stereotyping and discrimination become more limited (Crain 1996; Gill 1994). This situation is compounded by the restricted access of older and indigenous women to urban community survival mechanisms such as community soup kitchens (Clark and Laurie 2000).

Feminist critiques of Latin American adjustment have had a significant impact on state and NGO policy. In particular, two gender-sensitive policy approaches toward the Latin American family and household have become institutionalized as important tools in development planning. These are basic and strategic gender needs and a focus on female-headed households. Drawing on a longitudinal study in Guayaquil, Ecuador, Moser (1993) indicates that poor households are not endlessly elastic in their ability to absorb the impact of adjustment. Analyzing the way in which women in households develop mechanisms to cope with change led Moser to identify practical and strategic gender needs as a model that could be used in targeting development planning. Practical needs address immediate concerns such as the provision of services and access to resources, whereas strategic needs focus on changing unequal relations of power (securing rights for women and promoting women's empowerment in the long term). Moser's approach, which was based on Maxine Molyneux's work on the gender interest in the Nicaraguan revolution (1986), was adopted by key funders such as the World Bank. While there have been many critiques of the instrumentalist approach towards gender inherent within this model (see Arnold and Yapita 1996; Calla and Paulson 2000; Lind 1992; Paulson and Crespo 1997), its impact on NGO and state activities in Latin America cannot be underestimated. This model has become one of the key tools by which gender has been "mainstreamed."

Similarly, authors have been rightly cautious about the exaggeration of estimates of female-headed households globally (Varley 1996). Yet, this work has been important in informing policy-makers that the poorest households in Latin America are often those headed by women (Chant 1997; Delpino 1990; Mujer y Ajuste 1994). Data-collection categories in large-scale surveys, including in some countries the national census, have changed as a result of these sorts of study. Categories now seek to identify different types of household and to disaggregate the responsibilities and decision-making powers of individual household members. In most large data surveys it is no longer assumed that the head of the household is a man. Conceptualizations of female-headed households have also shifted to include a focus on women-maintained households (households financially supported by women but with male partners present) (Laurie 1999a). New policies embrace different understandings of the household types as seen in the "workfare"-style programs that target women in poor households in Argentina and in Chile (Valenzuela et al. 1995; MTSS 1996). In Chile, SERNAM, the Ministry for Women, developed a program specifically for female heads of households as part of the nationwide poverty alleviation program.

Paid Work, Gender, and the Household

Scholars have been centrally concerned with the importance of paid work in the Latin American household since the promotion of postwar Import Substitution Industries (ISI) (Radcliffe 1999). ISI policies were intended to protect and build up national industries such as steel, petroleum, and manufacturing in order to move national economies away from dependence on imports. Some of the earliest feminist scholarship focused on women entering the formal and informal labor markets associated with industrial and service-sector expansion. This work highlighted the double and triple burdens placed on women who, upon obtaining paid work, still shouldered household and community responsibilities. It also analyzed gendered segregation in labor markets, noting that women often occupy the worst jobs (Scott 1995; WGSG 1997). The increased feminization of the labor force (more women entering paid employment) and its informalization (the move away from formal jobs with security and benefits to insecure contract and piece work) have been linked to globalization and restructuring in recent years (Laurie 1999b; Laurie et al. 1999; Radcliffe 1999). Early analyses of the international division of labor suggested that the shift to footloose factory employment (where factories are not tied to a particular area by dependence on skilled labor but instead move in search of cheap manual labor) bypassed Latin America with the exception of the Mexican border region (Pearson 1986). NAFTA gave a high profile to the activities in this border region, and maquiladora industries (small workshops and factories along the US/Mexico border) have come to dominate much of the literature on globalization and gender in Latin America (see Tiano 1990; Tiano and Ladino 1999; Wright 1997). While they have received less attention, outworking and homeworking practices in the rest of Latin America have also increased significantly in recent years. This increase is particularly relevant to this chapter, as these practices, associated with restructuring and globalization, locate work in the heart of the family and household. As a result, women's roles as domestic and household actors have come to the fore as a "household ideology" that is used "to mobilize women in a restricted and relatively powerless domain" (Radcliffe 1999: 202). Women enter the labor force but remain within domestic space. They do not experience the external workspace, where worker solidarities can influence the fight for better working conditions. Recent analyses of household ideologies in industrial outputting chains and micro-enterprise (see Hays-Mitchell 1999; Lawson 1999) have drawn on and rejuvenated longstanding feminist interest in Latin American informal economies, notably in the domestic work and street-hawking sectors (see, for example, Chaney and Bunster 1989; Delpino 1990).

The influences of the new workspaces associated with restructuring and globalization on gender relations, femininities, and masculinities, however, remain unclear and vary from place to place (Laurie et al. 1999; Radcliffe 1999). In some cases, homeworking opportunities in teleworking and data input for women in Latin America mirror those of women in marginalized areas of countries of the North, as technological advances associated with globalization provide new "female" jobs. In poorer Latin American countries, however, where the provision of credit plays a key role in state and NGO poverty alleviation, home-based enterprises are dominated by small-scale, often semi-artisan production. In Bolivia, for example, home-based workshop production in textiles relies heavily on kinship networks linking rural and urban areas to secure credit and labor (Laurie 2000). Young rural workers come from villages to work and live in the city with *padrinos* ("godfathers"). They train in small domestic workshops before raising capital to establish their own businesses. In this way, close familial ties of kinship and ethnicity sustain an export economy producing fake designer goods with globalized logos. The households involved in this economy have strong diasporas as inter- and intra-generational links are maintained across rural–urban space and family members move across national borders to trade. The Bolivian diaspora in the Brazilian and Argentinean export markets also provides support for family and community members to work (often illegally) for a number of years, enabling them to acquire skills and save capital to start a new business in Bolivia. The informal home-based enterprise sector in Bolivia is therefore as dependent on transnational relationships as the better-known maquiladora industries in Mexico.

The remittances that these and other diasporas invest in maintaining rural communities are well established in the anthropological literature. It is not only Andean families that rely on remittances and contact with international diasporas for domestic reproduction. After decades of forced migration resulting from authoritarian regimes, economic crisis and civil war, households in most Latin American countries are characterized by close diasporic ties with North America and Europe as well as within the region.

Social Movements and Development

Latin American social movements have inspired radical politics and academic thought for as long as any social scientist can remember. The most recent debates have focused on the emergence of so-called "new social movements" (Escobar and Alvarez 1992), which are viewed as new partly because of the gender democracy they supposedly reflect (Chinchilla 1992). It is claimed that men and women participate more equally in social movements than they do in conventional party politics. However, what has given gender such a high profile in Latin American social movements is the way in which women, mobilizing as mothers demanding a better deal politically and economically for their families and households, have become emblematic of social movement activity.

The image of the "supermadre" (super mother) has come to dominate literature on economic survival strategies such as soup kitchens and human rights literature on women's protests about their "disappeared" family members. A rich body of literature in Spanish and English now exists on these topics. Despite the fact that these movements have become less active with the return to electoral politics in the southern zone and Central America and the passing of the shock periods of economic adjustment in the Andes, many representations in the west still focus on these events. Supermadre survivalist representations of femininities in Latin America are therefore often reified in academic work. In order to avoid fixed conceptualizations of change, feminists need to engage with the contemporary democratic, post-adjustment scenarios facing Latin American households. Gender-sensitive analyses must examine the diverse range of collective and individual strategies of reproduction and development rather than continue to be vexed by questions about social movements that ask "where have all the women gone?" As has been argued elsewhere (Laurie et al. 1999), women who have been activists in soup kitchens and human rights groups do not simply disappear into households once initial crises pass. Rather, their experience continues to inform personal decisions about individual and family social reproduction as well as the more performative sorts of cultural politics outlined by Alvarez et al. (1998). The cultural politics of gender-based social movements have started to embrace a series of new tactics and issues in recent years. The mothers of the disappeared have been joined by grandmothers, and currently human rights movements and other issue-related Latin American alliances focus as much on transnational networks as on local collective activism involving associations of families/households.

Transnational networks have been particularly important in the new alliances around gay rights in Latin America, with organizations such as Amnesty International monitoring discrimination against gays and activists in countries of the North becoming active in Latin American campaigns. Globalized campaigning tactics such as rights marches and Mardi Gras festivals, together with an emerging body of academic writing, are overtly focusing on discriminatory gender ideologies maintained in many cases by the church and the family (Bossio 1995; MacRae 1992; Pink Paper 2001; Prieur 1996; Ugarteche 1996).

Women, Men, and Ethnicity

The various gender and development paradigms of the 1980s–90s have been criticized in Latin America for their failure to engage with ethnicity and for leaving men out of gender studies and policies (Calla and Paulson 2000). Where gender and ethnicity have been examined together, this has tended to be in the sorts of poverty studies mentioned above, where indigenous women appear as the most poor (those with the least education and worst access to rights and resources). While poverty statistics should not be ignored, the predominance of these representations has tended to exacerbate what Mohanty (1991) identifies as freezing indigenous women as vulnerable victims and sidelining their agency. The freezing of indigenous family identity is expressed in a number of academic approaches. It is apparent in some of the more fundamentalist interpretations of gender relations in indigenous households that emphasize the "natural balance" of the household unit (see for example Apffel-Marglin 1998). In examinations of household and family strategies for upward mobility, it is apparent that fixed notions of indigeneity influence the ways in which men and women are seen. Indigenous men and women are both assumed to be influenced by a fixed hegemonic assumption in mestizo society that "no one wants to be an Indian" (Oliart 2001a: 1). The fixing of indigenous identities also occurs in the often essentialist assumptions that underlie interpretations of women's relationships with the environment that ignore their role in household reproduction (Townsend 1995).

While the increase in studies on social movements has given a new profile to indigenous agency in Latin America (see Brysk 2000), there is evidence that even in this literature indigenous voices can be homogenized (Laurie et al. 2002). With the scaling up of social movements through transnational practices, such as consciousness-raising on the internet, indigeneity can become prioritized over a homogenized gender identity, which sees women only as mothers, and representations of strategic alliances therefore become partial (Laurie 2000). The fact that partial representations of gender and ethnic identities and alliances are common in Latin American analyses of the family, household, and development reflects what Calla and Paulson (2000) have identified as polarized conceptualizations.

Although gender-sensitive and ethnic-sensitive approaches illuminate inter-related facets of Andean life, they are repeatedly polarized in popular and political discourse. Gender theory has been variously associated with modernity: opponents of modern development see gender analysis as an imperialist tool for annihilating unique, complementary, and harmonious identities and relationships, while development partisans see gender analysis as a positive tool for democratizing discriminatory local identities and relationships (Calla and Paulson 2000: 123).

At least in the Andes, these polarizations are attributable in part to the institutionalization of these approaches in the academy and development organizations, as well as the political biographies of those who implement policies (Calla and Paulson 2000). Gender and development was well established by the late 1980s and preceded the more recent focus on ethnic exclusion in development planning and donor funding in Latin America. It is only in the last few years that donors have moved to identify indigenous networks and households as "social capital," thus shifting ideas away from poverty-fixed representations of indigenous people (Radcliffe et al. 2001).

While donor and government rhetoric is moving toward incorporating gender and ethnicity as "transversal themes" at all scales of analysis, academic studies have apparently been slower to bring the approaches together in systematic reconceptualizations, notwithstanding the long tradition of Latin American scholarship focused on the family and household in both fields. However, an emerging literature is beginning to theorize gender and ethnicity. Postcolonial studies identify intersections of race, class and gender (Barrig and Henríquez 1995; Rivera Cusicanqui 1996) and specific studies on employment and education are indicating the ways in which gender and ethnicity are mutually constituted (Calla 2000; Montecino et al. 1994; Oliart 2001a, 2001b). Some of the work on education focuses specifically on masculinities and examines the new ways in which young men are negotiating family aspirations for professional education with new ways of being indigenous (Oliart 2001a). Emerging literature on masculinities addresses a number of issues, including macho identity and notions of family and belonging (see, for example, Gutmann 1996; Montecino and Acuña 1996) and complements studies of masculine gay identities in social movements discussed above. Studies of masculinities are being "mainstreamed" into the curricula in most established academic Gender Studies centers in Latin America (these include the University of Chile, the Catholic University of Lima and San Simón University in Bolivia).

However, there is still a need to link the largely localized ethnographic literature on masculinities to interrogations of dominant configurations of gender relations across a range of scales. Work by international political economy scholars such as Charlotte Hooper (2000) on embodiment and globalization points toward ways of interrogating the gendering of neoliberal practices and their resistances in specific locations and contexts (Laurie and Calla 2001). More work is needed, however, on how these current expressions of masculinist development are embodied in the household and the family in Latin America. If the recent focus on masculinities and reworked understandings of the cross–cutting construction of gender and ethnic identities is to become more than merely another trend in development planning, then there must be a dialogue about scale. If the household and family are to have an impact on development rather than merely be units of analysis that are "impacted upon," then the embodied practices of power that they express must be examined in relation to other scales of analysis and action. The ways in which household and family ideologies of gender articulate with communities, regions, nations, and processes of globalization remain key issues for feminists.

References

Alvarez, S., Dagnino, E., and Escobar, A. (1998) *Cultures of Politics, Politics of Cultures: Re-visioning Latin American Social Movements* (Boulder, CO: Westview Press).

Apffel-Marglin, F. (1998) *The Spirit of Regeneration: Andean Culture Confronting Western Notions of Development* (London: Zed Books).

Arnold, D. and Yapita, J. D. (1996) "Los caminos de género en Qaqachaka: saberes femeninos y discursos textuales alternativos en los Andes," in S. Rivera Cusicanqui (ed.), *Ser mujer indígena, chola o birlocha en la Bolivia postcolonial de los años 90* (La Paz: Ministerio de Desarrollo Humano).

Barrig, M. and Henríquez, N. (eds.) (1995) *Otros pieles, género, historia y cultura* (Lima: Pontificia Universidad Católica del Perú).

Boserup, E. (1970) *Women's Role in Economic Development* (London: George Allen and Unwin).

Bossio, E. (1995) "Interview with a Gay Activist," in O. Starn, C. Ivan de Gregori, and R. Kirk (eds.), *The Peru Reader: History, Culture, Politics* (London: LAB).

Brysk, A. (2000) *From Tribal Village to Global Village: Indian Rights and International Relations in Latin America* (Stanford, CA: Stanford University Press).

Calla, P. and Paulson, S. (2000) "Gender and Ethnicity in Bolivian Politics: Transformation or Paternalism," *Journal of Latin American Anthropology* 5/2: 112–49.

Calla, P. (2000) "Gender, Ethnicity and Intercultural Education." Paper presented at workshop on "Current Challenges to the Bolivian State: Issues of Gender, Ethnicity and Citizenship," Newcastle University, November.

Chaney, E. and Bunster, X. (1989) *Sellers and Servants: Working Women in Lima, Peru* (Massachusetts: Bergin and Garvey Publishers Inc.).

Chant, S. (1997) *Women-headed Households: Diversity and Dynamics in the Developing World* (Basingstoke: Macmillan).

Chinchilla, N. (1992) "Marxism, Feminism, and the Struggle for Democracy in Latin America," in A. Escobar and S. Alvarez (eds.), *The Making of Social Movements in Latin America: Identity, Strategy, and Democracy* (Boulder, CO: Westview Press).

Clark, F. and Laurie, N. (2000) "Gender, Age and Exclusion: A Challenge to Lima's Community Organisations," *Gender and Development* 8/2: 80–8.

Crain, M. (1996) "The Gendering of Ethnicity in the Ecuadorian Andes: Native Women's Self-Fashioning in the Urban Marketplace," in M. Melhuus and K. Stolen (eds.), *Machos, Mistresses, Madonnas: Contesting the Power of Latin American Gender Imagery* (London: Verso).

Delpino, N. (1990) *Saliendo a Flote. La Jefa de la Familia Popular* (Lima: Fundación Friedrich Naumann).

Elson, D. (ed.) (1991) *Male Bias in the Development Process* (Manchester: Manchester University Press).

Escobar, A. and Alvarez, S. (1992) *The Making of Social Movements in Latin America: Identity, Strategy, and Democracy* (Boulder, CO: Westview Press).

Gill, L. (1994) *Precarious Dependencies: Gender, Class, and Domestic Service in Bolivia* (New York: Columbia University Press).

Gutmann, M. (1996) *The Meaning of Macho: Being a Man in Mexico City* (Berkeley: University of California Press).

Hays-Mitchell, M. (1999) "From Survivor to Entrepreneur: Gendered Dimensions of Microenterprise Development in Peru," *Environment and Planning* A 31/2: 251–72.

Hooper, C. (2000) "Disembodiment, Embodiment and the Construction of Hegemonic Masculinity," in G. Youngs (ed.), *Political Economy, Power and the Body* (London: Macmillan Press).

Laurie, N. and Calla, P. (2001) "Who Is This Lady 'La Co-Ordinadora'? Gendering the Cochabamba Water Conflict." Paper presented at the Annual Conference of Canadian Geographers, Montreal, June.

Laurie, N. (1999a) "More than the Blood of Earth Mothers," *Gender, Place and Culture* 6/4: 393–400.

Laurie, N. (1999b) "Negotiating Femininities in the Provinces. Women and Emergency Employment in Peru," *Environment and Planning* A 31/2: 229–50.

Laurie, N. (2000) "Globalising Fakes: The Home-Based Production of Fake Designer Wear in Bolivia, Turkey and India." Paper presented at the international annual conference of feminist economists, Istanbul, August.

Laurie, N., Dwyer, C., Holloway, S., and Smith, F. (1999) *Geographies of "New" Femininities* (London: Longman).

Laurie, N., Radcliffe, S., and Andolina, R. (2002) "The New Excluded 'Indigenous'?: The Implications of Multi-Ethnic Policies for Water Reform in Bolivia," in R. Sneider (ed.), *Pluri-Cultural and Multi-Ethnic Implications for State and Society in Mesoamerica and the Andes* (London: Palgrave).

Lawson, V. (1999) "Tailoring is a Profession, Seamstressing is Work! Resisting Work and Reworking Gender Identities Among Artisanal Workers in Quito," *Environment and Planning* A 31/2: 209–28.

Lewis, O. (1975) *Five Families: Mexican Case Studies in the Culture of Poverty* (New York: Basil Books).

Lind, A. (1992) "Power, Gender, and Development: Popular Women's Organizations and the Politics of Needs in Ecuador," in A. Escobar and S. Alvarez (eds.), *The Making of Social Movements in Latin America: Identity, Strategy, and Democracy* (Boulder, CO: Westview Press).

MacRae, E. (1992) "Homosexual Identities in Transnational Brazilian Politics," in A. Escobar and S. Alvarez (eds.), *The Making of Social Movements in Latin America: Identity, Strategy, and Democracy* (Boulder, CO: Westview Press).

Mohanty, C. (1991) "Cartographies of Struggle: Third World Women and the Politics of Feminism," in C. Mohanty, A. Russo, and L. Torres (eds.), *Third World Women and the Politics of Feminism* (Bloomington: Indiana University Press).

Molyneux, M. (1986) "Mobilization Without Emancipation?: Women's Interests, State and Revolution," in R. Fagen, C. Deer, and J. Coraggio (eds.), *Transitions and Development: Problems of Third World Socialism* (New York: Monthly Review Press).

Montecino, S., Rebolledo, L., and Willson, A. (1994) *Diagnostico Sobre Inserción Laboral de Mujeres Mapuche Rurales y Urbanas* (Santiago: Universidad de Chile y SERNAM).

Montecino, S. and Acuña, M. E. (eds.) (1996) *Diálogos sobre el género masculino en Chile* (Santiago: Bravo y Allende Editores).

Moser, C. (1993) "Adjustment From Below: Low-Income Women, Time and the Triple Role in Guayaquil, Ecuador," in S. Radcliffe and S. Westwood (eds.), *"Viva" Women and Popular Protest in Latin America* (London: Routledge).

MTSS (1996) *Programa de servicios comunitarios*, Resolución 453/96. Buenos Aires, Ministerio de Trabajo y Seguridad Social.

Mujer y Ajuste (1996) *Ajuste Estructural Debate y Propuestas. El Ajuste Estructural en el Perú; una Mirada Desde las Mujeres* (Lima: Ediciones Mujeres y Ajuste).

Oliart, P. (2001a) "University Life and Masculine Identities Among Education Students in Ayacucho." Paper Presented at the Workshop on Education and Ethnicity in the Peru Center for Development Research, Copenhagen, June.

Oliart, P. (2001b) "Vida universitario e identidades masculinas en Ayacucho después de la Guerra," *Informe final para el PRODIR III* (Lima: Fundación Carlos Chagas).

Ostergaard, L. (1992) *Gender and Development: A Practical Guide* (London: Routledge).

Paulson, S. and Crespo, M. (1997) *Teorías y Prácticas de Género: una conversación dialéctica* (La Paz: Embajada Real de los Países Bajos).

Pearson, R. (1986) "Latin American Women and the New International Division of Labor: A Reassessment," *Bulletin of Latin American Research* 5: 67–79.

Pink Paper (2001) Issue 692, June 29.

Prieur, A. (1996) "Domination and Desire: Male Homosexuality and the Construction of Masculinity in Mexico," in M. Melhuus and K. Stolen (eds.), *Machos, Mistresses, Madonnas Contesting the Power of Latin American Gender Imagery* (London: Verso).

Radcliffe, S. (1999) "Latina Labor: New Directions in Gender and Work in Latin America," *Environment and Planning* A, 31/2: 191–5.

Radcliffe, S., Laurie, N., and Andolina, R. (2001) "Indigenous Movement Representation in Transnational Circuits: Tales of Poverty and Social Capital." Paper presented at the Annual Conference of the Association of American Geographers, New York, February.

Rathgeber, E. (1990) "WID, WAD, GAD: Trends in Research and Practice," *The Journal of Developing Area Studies* 24: 489–502.

Rivera Cusicanqui, S. (ed.) (1996) *Ser mujer indígena, chola o birlocha en la Bolivia postcolonial de los años 90* (La Paz: Ministerio de Desarrollo Humano).

Scott, A. (1995) "Informal Sector or Female Sector? Gender Bias in Urban Labor Market Models," in D. Elson (ed.), *Male Bias in the Development Process*, 2nd edn. (Manchester: Manchester University Press).

Tanski, J. (1994) "The Impact of Crisis, Stabilization and Structural Adjustment on Women in Lima, Peru," *World Development* 22/11: 1627–42.

Tiano, S. (1990) "Maquiladora Women: A New Category of Workers," in K. Ward (ed.), *Women Workers and Global Restructuring* (Ithaca, NY: ILR Press).

Tiano, S. and Ladino, C. (1999) "Dating, Mating, and Motherhood: Identity Construction Among Mexican Maquila Workers," *Environment and Planning A* 31/2 (February).

Townsend, J. (1995) *Women's Voices From the Rainforest* (London: Routledge).

Ugarteche, O. (1997) *India bonita, o, Del amor y otras artes: ensayos de cultura gay en el Perú* (Lima, Peru: MHOL).

Valenzuela, M., Venegas, S., and Andrade, C. (eds.) (1995) *De Mujer Sola a Jefa de Hogar: Género, Pobreza y Políticas Públicas* (Santiago: Servicio Nacional de la Mujer (SERNAM)).

Varley, A. (1996) "Women Heading Households: Some More Equal than Others?" *World Development* 24/3: 505–20.

WGSG (1997) *Feminist Geographies: Explorations in Diversity and Difference* (London: Longman; Women in Geography Study Group).

Wright, M. W. (1997) "Crossing the Factory Frontier: Gender, Place, and Power in the Mexican Maquiladora," *Antipode* 29/3: 278–302.

CHAPTER TWENTY-EIGHT

Family in Europe

Joanna Regulska

European Family: Do We Have One?

Families in Europe are increasingly similar, but does that allow one to conclude
that there is one European family? Diverse mediating factors ranging from
cultural influences (e.g. the role of the Church, intergenerational linkages, traditions and customs) through social and economic circumstances (e.g. economic
and housing crises, new career paths for women) and political ideologies (including interventionist policies of the state) have fostered changes in the formation
and breakdown of families. Examination of demographic data could lead one
to believe that the convergence or homogenization of family behavior seems
unquestionable among member states of the European Union (EU) (Begeot and
Fernandez-Cordon 1997; Segalen 1997). The decrease in fertility rates; new
forms of cohabitation and, connected with these, an increase in the number of
children born in new unions; the increase in the number of divorces; the widespread growth in the number of women engaged in professional activities and,
as a result, the increase in dual-income households (altering the economy of
relationships within the family); the increase in intergenerational linkages: these
are only a few of the new developments that make families in European countries
more similar. While these similarities in family development do indeed bring
European countries together, their differences are significant enough for one
to conclude that it is not sufficient to talk about the European family without
acknowledging differences within and between countries. Commaille and de
Singly stated simply: "The French family is as great an illusion (as great a
reality) as the European family" (1997: 5).

Some scholars argue that what distinguishes one country from another is the
rate of change rather than the direction of change (Begeot and Fernandez-
Cordon 1997). They point out that while all the countries of the EU have an
average total fertility rate that is lower than two children per woman, specific
groups of countries have exhibited differences in the timing of the decline in
fertility rates and the actual levels they have ultimately reached (in 1998 the highest

levels were registered in Iceland and Ireland, with 2.0 and 1.8 children per woman respectively, and the lowest were in Spain and Italy, each with 1.2 children: McDevitt 1999). Similarly, the number of children born outside heterosexual marriages has increased dramatically (e.g. in the UK from 10 percent in 1977 to 39 percent in 2000) and has reached over 55 percent in Sweden and 40 percent in Denmark, France, and Finland. This is no doubt a result of new behavioral patterns. The emergence of similar patterns can also be noticed in post-1989 Central and Eastern Europe (CEE), where birth rates have decreased across the region and marriage rates have declined (while divorce has increased), indicating that cohabitation has begun to replace marriage. The younger generation is also more likely to be unmarried at the birth of the first child, and single motherhood is rising. Still, women in CEE tend to marry at a much younger age in comparison with their counterparts in the EU (UNICEF 1999).

While xenophobia and racism have fueled debates over the construction of a "fortress Europe," and despite repeated violence against Turkish minorities in Germany, Albanians in Italy, or Romany groups across Europe, there is not enough awareness of the needs of different ethnic families that are frequently separated from their surrounding neighbors by legal status, culture, and often the color of their skin (Eide 1998). Research on the family in Europe often ignores race and ethnicity and the fact that the construction of ethnicity is relevant to the family formation process and its daily practices (Commaille and de Singly 1997; Hantrais and Letablier 1996; but see Joly 1998). Yet as Bhopal (2000) has shown, the traditional practices of "arranged marriages" and dowries have been undergoing redefinition by women of the South Asian community living in London (especially among British-born South Asian women) and thus the process through which women make decisions about getting married and forming a family is also being altered. Similarly, Moroccan women living in Italy have been re-examining their cultural and religious identity as they struggle with exclusion and yet also become increasingly rooted within Italian society (Salih 2000). Research on Romany women indicates different family practices, as women marry at a comparatively young age and have an above-average number of children. This latter pattern is caused, among other factors, by one of the highest rates of infant mortality in Europe. Romany women are often faced with different but intertwining forms of discrimination as members of a marginalized minority and as women in a patriarchal community, where they are frequently sold to the male head of the household (Mrsevic and Prodanovic 2000). Men are the owners of the assets and the main decision-makers, yet women are the breadwinners. Notwithstanding women's fiscal contributions, their position as the economic provider receives little recognition. These patterns of ignorance, exclusion, and discrimination for ethnically diverse families continue to prevail across Europe.

Given the emergence of new familial behavioral patterns, the question of how to define the family has become more diversified as well. While Bjornberg (1997) contends that the numerous changes and family policy innovations in Sweden have not to any large extent contributed to the break-up of the classical family model relations, one can no longer speak in the name of all families. Patrilineal extended families of the Asian diaspora, where relations between brothers are significant, or extended families in which mothers-in-law have considerable power over their daughters-in-law, are not uncommon. Lesbian, gay, or heterosexual families that consist of single parents, multiple partners of the same and opposite sex, as well as children raised by several parents, grandparents, foster parents or friends, or lesbian mothers and gay fathers are also no longer unique. While legal or blood ties were the common markings that defined the heterosexual family, this cannot be taken for granted by lesbians or gays who create new unions. Griffin rightly pointed out that when lesbians consider creating a family, then "how we define family and determine its members is called into question" (1997: 21). Do we continue to privilege biology and therefore identify only the bio-logical mother as the mother? If so, where does this leave the non-biological partner who has raised the child? Is the two-mother family a family? And what is the place or role of the biological father from a previous heterosexual marriage? Considering cases of self-insemination, how does one talk about parenthood if the donor remains invisible? The frequent non-recognition and non-support of same-sex unions by the state, public discourse, religious organizations, and often families themselves create new spaces of contestation and tensions for the notion of family.

Familial Power Relations

Who has the power and authority within these diversified family forms varies with class, race, religion, ethnicity, sexuality, and culture. The traditional distinctions between private and public are no longer sufficient to explain the dynamics of familial power and processes. How do we explain the fact that in some countries the traditional "nuclear" family, where the father's role is primarily seen as that of a breadwinner, has increasingly become subject to questioning and negotiation as individual family members move through the life cycle? In Finland, Denmark, and Sweden, for example, the meaning of fatherhood shows a much greater complexity than in other locations. Here, questions of care, intimacy, masculinity, and gender equality have been for decades subject to constant (re)negotiation of the gender contract (Crompton 1999; Harvey 2000). New partnerships/unions question the power dynamic within the family. Is it the social parents or the biological mother or father who have power and author-ity? And does the power have to reside with one person only, or can it be shared, or interchanged? The diversity of familial decision-making patterns indicates that specific solutions do not depend only on negotiated contracts within fam-ilies, in which social and biological parents from past heterosexual marriages and present unions, children, grandparents, friends or donors participate. The outside environment (state, teachers, neighbors, children's friends) also needs to be considered. As Griffin and Mulholland (1997) revealed, there exists an obvious paradox between the "freedom" of the internal world of gay and lesbian families, which provides for autonomy and choice to make every possible contract that they wish for, and which will not fall under legal scrutiny, and an outside world of social and legal norms that often does not recognize these families. Only rarely are such contradictions acknowledged through practices such as in Denmark, where social welfare authorities offer unofficial counseling to separating lesbian couples. Lesbian and gay parents increasingly test the government's legal framework as to who (e.g. the non-biological mother and/or the father), and under what circumstances (adoption, fostering, visitation), can be legally seen as parents and have legal rights to act and therefore use power and authority to make decisions.

External social pressures undoubtedly shape, in detrimental ways, how each individual's internal relationships within the space of the home will be negotiated, as in the case of a lesbian mother and gay father who live under one roof in Denmark, or biological parents who live together with their children, although divorced, in Bulgaria and in France, or when lesbian mothers forgo custody rights altogether in the UK. The patriarchal underpinnings and privileging of masculinities as far as family relations are considered are especially visible when a father's custody rights are considered or when mothers are ready to relinquish their custody rights. It is often the case that heterosexual fathers after (in many cases prolonged) court battles will have wide-ranging rights to visitation and shared decision-making privileges regarding their children's future, but in practice they will exercise these rights occasionally and only when there is a danger that they may lose some of the control they have. But when women assign custody rights to the father, such a solution is also questioned, as traditionally it is the mother who should take care of children. The recent reshaping of the notion of the family in Europe thus suggests that while the new forms of unions and partnerships challenge stereotypes, they also raise new conflicts and tensions.

The widespread perception of the family as a safe site, where members are provided with love, security, and safety, is increasingly losing ground and has become discredited. As evidence shows, the family is frequently a site of domestic violence against women and girls. "Violence in the domestic sphere is usually perpetrated by males who are, or who have been, in positions of trust and intimacy and power – husbands, boyfriends, fathers, fathers-in-law, stepfathers, brothers, uncles, sons, or other relatives" (UNICEF 2000: 3). Surveys conducted in various countries point to the different magnitudes with which domestic violence takes place. A Eurobarometer/INRA survey reported that almost 40 percent of respondents in Finland, 35 percent in the UK, over 30 percent in the Netherlands, and 25 percent in Ireland have a close friend or relative who has been subjected to violence by her husband or partner (for 15 EU member states this figure is over 20 percent) (European Commission 1999). In CEE these numbers are higher and over the last few years they have been on the rise. In Poland, a 1993 survey indicated that 60 percent of divorced women have been hit at least once by their ex-husband and 25 percent reported repeated violence (UNICEF 2000: 5). Femicide – the murder of women by their batterers – while low in Western European countries, emerged as noticeable in Russia (ibid.: 6; UNICEF 1999).

Extensive kinship networks have also added complexity to the ways in which power is exercised within the context of family. What is different in contemporary kinship relationships is their social rather than biological (blood ties) base, so long distinguished in Europe as the organizing principle. Segalen (1997) asserts that the "rediscovery" of kinship is an outcome of several forces, among which the reintegration of the economic factor into kinship is of primary importance. The increasing participation of women in the labor force and therefore the impact of women's new wage-earning capacities on family behavioral patterns (e.g. division of labor within the family, family demographics, new intergenerational patterns, decision-making capacities) are among the decisive factors. In some countries, especially in the North, the state, with its extensive social benefits system, has substituted, to a certain degree, for kin support, without diminishing its significance. In countries such as Spain, on the other hand, the extended family and kinship play an important supportive role, since state subsidies for childcare in these countries are among the lowest in Europe, and men's contributions to childcare and housework are almost non-existent (Garcia-Ramon and Ortiz 1998; Le Bras 1997). In Central and Eastern Europe, kinship networks, while traditionally performing significant services, have gained further significance and power as a result of the repositioning of the states in the post-1989 political and economic transformation, and as support and services to families have lessened (UNICEF 1999).

Changing Family Culture

Technological changes, new social norms, and the free flow of people across national borders are altering the ways in which family formation processes take place and how the relationships between family members are maintained. Chief among these changes is the process by which the conception of a child takes place, as procreation and sexuality have become separated. A child can be conceived within the confines of a marital heterosexual relationship, but this can also be achieved through artificial and self-insemination, with the help of a same-sex partner, or a gay friend or family member. Furthermore, potential mothers/fathers/parents have, in many cases, control over the timing, race, or other desired characteristics of the child. While religious faith and economic means, as well as traditional and customary rules, play a definite role in regulating procreation, these new realities result for many families in multi-births and multi-parents. They also shatter our assumptions about the meaning of motherhood/fatherhood/parenthood and responsibilities that have been traditionally embedded in these identities. They question the meaning of "private" and "public" and create new linkages between biology and social relationships. They create new conditions for identity formation in children and will affect their sense of belonging. What is the meaning of fatherhood, when the father has already been dead for many years at the time when his sperm is actually used? Or how should the meaning of motherhood be configured when a mother's womb is used to carry the child of her child?

The changing notion of family is not immune to the current reconfigurations of social, political, and economic spaces of Europe. The opening of borders within the EU and free flow of people implicates family and introduces new residential patterns, especially of the more mobile segments of the population (younger, professional). While there are no specific studies evaluating these changes, they do raise the question of increasing dispersion of family members and potential implications for the availability of family members to provide care, assistance, and support. Two simultaneous processes seem to be at work. On the one hand, the fact that people live longer means that often several generations can act jointly as kin by interacting materially, socially, emotionally, or symbolically (Segalen 1997). Parents often continue to provide support and care for children into late adulthood. Older adults provide more assistance to younger family members. The needs of the disabled, both children and adults, are often satisfied through the informal network of friends and family members. On the other hand, the dispersal of family members means that often these new familial spatial arrangements began to be delineated not by geographic proximity, but rather through technological linkages, and not by biological links but by social relationships. How does the perception of distance alter familial intergenerational linkages? How do class, race, and ethnicity mediate these geographically distant relationships? What kind of care can be offered from a distance? Who becomes the more significant caregiver: the distant biological family member who can be reached easily, but whose physical presence is more restricted, or the nearby neighbor (who de facto is perceived as a family member) and who can be physically present? Not surprisingly, the greater heterogeneity of families, with diverse forms and patterns of partnerships, and the simultaneous crises of welfare states have put new demands on the caregiving role of women (of all ages), who have across the generations provided services to each other, their families, partners, and friends (Fredriksen-Goldsen and Scharlach 2001; Himmelweit 2000; Segalen 1997).

State Policies and Interventions

State responses to the plurality of family forms and arrangements of private life reflect not only present social, economic, and political realities but, equally strongly, they are imbedded in national conventions and traditions. While in France the family is a public/state concern, in the UK it is a private space. Accordingly, family policy in France has regularly been a subject of political and media debates and strong state intervention. French family policy, which is controlled to a large degree by employment policy, represents a mixture of measures which, on one hand, respond to the demands of working mothers (through the "Allowance for Childcare at Home") and, on the other hand, support the male breadwinner scheme (Fagnani 1998). Despite creating a large pool of publicly funded childcare, the French allowance scheme has been criticized for its class-based approach, which caters primarily for middle-class families, and for creating large numbers of low-paying and low-status jobs. Such jobs are filled predominantly by migrant women of color whose prospects of being hired have increased, but who otherwise are stuck in these menial non-unionized jobs. Furthermore, critics have asserted that through the combination of part-time jobs, childrearing benefits, career breaks, and unpaid parental leave, the French state continues to promote the male breadwinner model. In the end, French policy does not foster more gender equality in the division of labor, but in fact reinforces gender discrimination and prejudice against women employees. This, in turn, further erodes women's earning capacities. What the French example illustrates is the power that the state exercises over the formation of family policy and ultimately family practices.

In CEE countries during the communist period, the family was a sanctuary of private space, where its members could gain temporary relief from an oppressive state. Yet, the communist state regulated family behavior by providing housing, setting pro-natalist policies, and at the same time, as in many West European countries, ignoring violence. In the post-1989 conditions, while the constraining uniformity of communist ideology quickly faded, the confrontation between the states' new priorities and the desire for the rediscovery of cultural traditions produced a mixture of diverse measures (UNICEF 1999). In the early 1990s, for example, many CEE states improved their income-support schemes and provided new cash benefits, but by the end of the decade a shift to family allowances was noticed in several countries. With the general erosion of the value of the benefits, many low-income families experienced a drastic reduction in their disposable income. In addition, as family allowances are usually attached to women's wages, any losses in benefits have, in fact, resulted in income losses for women. The impact of the lower value of benefits was further compounded in CEE countries by a rapid decline in low-cost public childcare. Newly gained powers of local governments, combined with prevailing patriarchal family structures, quickly reduced the availability of nurseries, kindergartens, and pre-school services. While maternity and parental leave entitlements in most CEE countries remained available and therefore still provided childcare options for mothers, they are being challenged by the vigorous emergence of the private sector and the simultaneous elimination of public jobs through which women could secure access to these benefits.

Supporting a "family" is also not an easy task for lesbian or gay partners. States try to limit support by restricting payments to lesbian mothers. In Sweden, for example, lack of information regarding the biological father limits eligibility for public assistance. In the UK, lesbian mothers may face a 20 percent reduction in the level of benefits if they cannot provide such information. In Russia, on the other hand, lesbian mothers have an option at the birth of a child to withdraw information regarding the biological father. Not only does the lack of this information not affect payments, but it also shelters mothers from future custody and other parental rights-related claims (Mulholland 1997).

States' wide-ranging responses are also visible when the interrelations between family and work are considered. Women's higher level of labor force participation (39 percent in 1985, 42 percent in 1995, projected to grow to well over 44 percent by 2010) is observable across Europe (European Communities 2001). While West European women have made substantial gains, interestingly these rates continue to be higher for women in CEE countries (47.3 percent in 1995), despite major social and economic transformations and increasing unemployment, and women want to maintain their active labor force participation (UNICEF 1999). At the same time, the rates for men in the EU have been in decline (66.6 percent in 1994). Attempts by states to mediate and reconcile family and work through taxation, childcare and child benefits, and health and welfare provisions have affected women's relation to work. In Spain, Ireland, Italy, and Greece, where the breadwinner/housewife contract is predominant, a gendered division of labor at home privileges women's role as mother and care-giver and the labor market is marked by widespread part-time and flexible employment arrangements for women. But flexible work arrangements, which were seen by many policy-makers as an attempt to facilitate a reconciliation between family and work, often failed. As Spanish research indicated, these policy measures resulted for women in increased job insecurity and employment instability, and their dependence on a male breadwinner or the state (Garcia-Ramon and Ortiz 1998; Perrons 1999).

Where states and EU institutions seem to be failing and show only limited progress is in the lack of measures addressing racism and ethnic discrimination (Phillips 1998). Repeatedly, voices have been raised claiming that EU attitudes toward the family have been racist. Not only do legislation and policy development measures lag behind as far as race relations are concerned, but also equal treatment legislation, while prohibiting discrimination based on nationality, neither includes provisions for ethnic minorities nor prohibits racism. Where policies do exist, such as the family unification policy, they are racially based (Hoskyns and Orsini-Jones 1995; Knocke 1995; Kofman 1999; Kofman et al. 2000). In some cases, such as Romany families, against whom discrimination, prejudice, and violence have reached very high levels (e.g. in Spain and the UK, as well as in Hungary and Slovakia), the need for more forceful and visible actions on the part of the EU as well as the national governments has been called for (Barani Project 2002; British Council 1999; Romani World 2002).

Increasingly, calls are also made for an integrated approach toward eliminating violence against women, which would provide support to women both via formal systems – the state, the judiciary, healthcare services, Parliament – as well as informal networks such as family, friends, neighbors, and local community groups. Yet unless men also re-evaluate their role in the family and examine cultural and social assumptions of masculinity, the gender norms that have been accepted for centuries will prevail. The White Ribbon Campaign – efforts by men working to put an end to violence against women – which originated in Canada and has expanded to other countries, including Western Europe, still represents a rare form of mobilization (UNICEF 2000: 16). Nevertheless, the EU has begun to recognize the extent of the violence against women within the family, and the increased social pressures to address it (90 percent of respondents in a survey felt that the EU should be involved in combating violence against women), and initiated the "Breaking of Silence" campaign through its four-year Daphne program (European Commission 1999).

The existing diversity of patterns and responses precludes the notion of a common European family policy or uniform state intervention. Yet, as the research on flexible arrangements indicated, despite acknowledged differences between countries, low-income families or single mothers do share similar problems, while middle-class and elite families share similar privileges. This reinforces the notion that markings of gender, class, sexuality, and race remain significant. What also becomes evident is that the state is only one of many actors involved in shaping family policies. Public/state, private business, organized social actors such as trade-unions, associations, NGOs, women's groups, and family groups, as well as auto-regulation by families themselves have all shaped circumstances under which interventions are made. What further differentiates these responses is the lens through which these actors choose to intervene, stressing the family, individual, or social context. In the end, these heterogeneous approaches reflect the mix of cultural traditions, institutional arrangements, and political compromises that often exclude those most affected by policy outcomes.

References

Barani Project (2002) "Romany Women and the Spanish Criminal Justice System," *The Barani Project* (<www.web.jet.es/gea21/ing.htm>).

Begeot, F. and Fernandez-Cordon, J. A. (1997) "Demographic Convergence Beyond National Differences," in J. Commaille and F. de Singly (eds.), *The European Family* (Dordrecht, The Netherlands: Kluwer Academic Publisher).

Bhopal, K. (2000) "South Asian Women in East London: The Impact of Education," *European Journal of Women's Studies* 7/1: 35–52.

Bjornberg, U. (1997) "Cultural and Political Limits to the Transformation of Family Roles," in J. Commaille and F. de Singly (eds.), *The European Family* (Dordrecht, The Netherlands: Kluwer Academic Publisher).

British Council (1999) "Unequal Access to Public Services," *Governance* (<www.britishcouncil.org/governance/viv/roma/r3.htm>).

Commaille, J. and de Singly, F. (eds.) (1997) *The European Family* (Dordrecht, The Netherlands: Kluwer Academic Publisher).

Crompton, R. (ed.) (1999) *Restructuring Gender Relations and Employment* (Oxford: Oxford University Press).

Eide, A. (1998) "Racial and Ethnic Discrimination in Europe: Past, Present and Future," in D. Joly (ed.), *Scapegoats and Social Actors: The Exclusion and Integration of Minorities in Western and Eastern Europe* (London: Macmillan Press; New York: St. Martin's Press).

European Commission (1999) *Breaking the Silence* (Luxembourg: Office for Official Publications of the European Communities).

European Communities (2001) "Regional Labour Force in the EU: Recent Patterns and Future Perspectives," *Statistics in Focus: Theme 1–2* (Brussels: Eurostat).

Fagnani, J. (1998) "Recent Changes in Family Policy in France: Political Trade-Offs and Economic Constraints," in E. Drew, E. Ruth, and E. Mahon (eds.), *Women, Work and the Family in Europe* (London and New York: Routledge).

Fredriksen-Goldsen, K. I. and Scharlach, A. E. (2001) *Families and Work: New Directions in the Twenty-first Century* (New York and Oxford: Oxford University Press).

Garcia-Ramon, M.-D. and Ortiz, A. (1998) *Flexible Working and the Reconciliation of Work and Family Life or New Form of Precariousness*, National report from Spain, prepared for DGV Economic and Social Affairs Unit European Commission V/768/98 CE-V/2-98-003-EN-C (Brussels: European Commission).

Griffin, K. (1997) "Family Structures," in K. Griffin and L. A. Mulholland (eds.), *Lesbian Motherhood in Europe* (London and Washington, DC: Cassell).

Griffin, K. and Mulholland, L. A. (eds.) (1997) *Lesbian Motherhood in Europe* (London and Washington, DC: Cassell).

Hantrais, L. and Letablier, M.Th. (1996) *Families and Family Policies in Europe* (London and New York: Longman).

Harvey, C. D. H. (ed.) (2000) *Walking a Tightrope: Meeting the Challenges of Work and Family* (Aldershot, UK: Ashgate).

Himmelweit, S. (2000) *Inside the Household: From Labour to Care* (New York: St. Martin's Press).

Hoskyns, C. and Orsini-Jones, M. (1995) "Immigrant Women in Italy: Perspectives from Brussels and Bologna," *European Journal of Women's Studies* 2/1: 51–76.

Joly, D. (ed.) (1998) *Scapegoats and Social Actors: The Exclusion and Integration of Minorities in Western and Eastern Europe* (London: Macmillan Press; New York: St. Martin's Press).

Knocke, W. (1995) "Migrant and Ethnic Minority Women: The Effects of Gender-neutral Legislation in the European Community," *Social Politics* (summer): 225–38.

Kofman, E. (1999) "Gender, Migrants and Rights in the European Union," in T. Fenster (ed.), *Gender, Planning and Human Rights* (London: Routledge).

Kofman, E., Phizaacklea, A., Raghuram, P., and Sales, R. (2000) *Gender and International Migration in Europe* (London: Routledge).

Le Bras, H. (1997) "Fertility: The Condition of Self-perpetuation. Differing Trends in Europe," in M. Gullestad and M. Segalen (eds.), *Family and Kinship in Europe* (London and Washington, DC: Pinter).

McDevitt, T. M. (1999) *World Population Profile: 1998* (Washington, DC: US Government Printing Office).

Mrsevic, Z. and Prodanovic, A. (2000) "Roma Women Speak Out," *Oxfam GB Gender Newsletter – Links*, November (<www.oxfam.org.uk/policy/gender/oonov/1100roma.htm>).

Mulholland, L. A. (1997) "The World Outside," in K. Griffin and L. A. Mulholland (eds.), *Lesbian Motherhood in Europe* (London and Washington, DC: Cassell).

Perrons, D. (1999) "Flexible Working Patterns and Equal Opportunities in the European Union. Conflict or compatibility?" *European Journal of Women's Studies* 6: 391–418.

Phillips, A. (1998) "Minority Rights: Some New Intergovernmental Approaches in Europe," in D. Joly (ed.), *Scapegoats and Social Actors: The Exclusion and Integration of Minorities in Western and Eastern Europe* (London: Macmillan Press; New York: St. Martin's Press).

Romani World (2002) "Romani Emancipation: The Social and Economic Inclusion of the Roma: Equal Rights? The Challenge Facing Romani Women in Europe," *Romani World Quarterly* (<www.romaniworld.com/publst04.htm>).

Salih, R. (2000) "Between Tradition and Transformation: Shifting Boundaries of Self and Other: Moroccan Migrant Women in Italy," *European Journal of Women's Studies* 7/3: 321–35.

Segalen, M. (1997) "Introduction," in M. Gullestad and M. Segalen (eds.), *Family and Kinship in Europe* (London and Washington, DC: Pinter).

UNICEF (1999) *Women in Transition*, The MONEE Project, Regional Monitoring Report No. 6 (Florence, Italy: United Nations Children's Fund).

UNICEF (2000) *Domestic Violence Against Women and Girls*, Innocenti Digest No. 6 (Florence, Italy: United Nations Children's Fund).

PART SEVEN

Physicality

CHAPTER TWENTY-NINE

Reproduction

Laura Shanner

Because women gestate pregnancies while men do not, one's sex necessarily *matters* in reproductive contexts vastly more than in any other domain. Indeed, biological reproductive roles are the likely origin of most social distinctions involving sex and gender.

Reproduction is not merely a biological process, however, but touches nearly every aspect of human life. Significant physical, sexual, economic, social, psychological, and ethical ramifications follow from producing offspring, and reproductive choices necessarily involve attitudes about sexuality, gender roles, and family structures. The personal meanings of kinship, generations, parenting, and embodied reproductive experiences interact with population trends and environmental sustainability. Rapidly evolving reproductive and genetic technologies make gender-sensitive analysis of procreation particularly urgent.

The portrayal of reproductive biology is often peculiar, silencing, and even contradictory. Medieval theories of the "homunculus" posited that tiny, fully formed babies existed in the heads of sperm, needing only a fertile place in which to grow (Pinto-Correia 1997), and yet women have traditionally been held responsible both for unwanted pregnancies and infertility. Contemporary discussions about abortion, prenatal testing, and prevention of prenatal harm often ignore the fact that fetuses reside in a woman's body (Mahowald 1995), as if women were merely "fetal containers" (Purdy 1996); women literally fall out of view in prenatal imaging techniques (Petchesky 1987; Stabile 1992). We often speak of infertility treatment for "couples," when the most invasive procedures occur in the bodies of women rather than men (Kirejczyk and van der Ploeg 1992). "Labour and delivery" remain excluded from most economic models, in a notable category of women's uncompensated work (Anderson 1990; Schwarzenbach 1987).

Men's reproductive needs and experiences are usually overlooked entirely. Very little attention is paid to protecting or restoring men's reproductive health despite global evidence of falling sperm counts (Colborn et al. 1996), and men have very few contraceptive options to exercise. Men's perspectives on reproductive choices, and especially infertility, are only recently garnering significant attention (Becker 2000; Mason 1993). Sperm banks and cloning make some wonder if men are even needed for reproduction any longer. What, then, is the meaning of fatherhood?

The sexes have unequal needs for collaboration to produce offspring: women need sperm, but men need both an ovum and someone to gestate the pregnancy. Potential fathers thus face poignant limitations regarding whether, when, and how a pregnancy is initiated, maintained, or terminated. All eyes focus on the expectant mother, who is vividly experiencing the pregnancy (or its loss), with the expectant father shuffled to the shadows unable to share most of the phenomenon. Accordingly, many men feel significantly left out of the reproductive experience, or that fatherhood is beyond their control.

Reproduction and Sexism

Societies typically promote "pronatalist" reproductive imperatives to ensure future generations and social continuity (Peck and Senderowitz 1974), while sexual and reproductive controls aim to prevent unsupported children and the risk of genetic anomalies from incest. Pronatalist policies and attitudes usually fail to reflect the burdens of reproducing and parenting, however, and are widely viewed by feminists as an impediment to non-reproductive goals.

Exactly how reproductive roles contribute to sexist theories and social practices is a matter of ongoing debate. One view is that pregnancy is women's greatest weakness, described by de Beauvoir as "a fatiguing task of no individual benefit to the woman but on the contrary demanding heavy sacrifices" (de Beauvoir 1952: 33). More radically, motherhood has been called "the annihilation of women" in which women's bodies are appropriated by men "as a resource to reproduce patriarchy" (Allen 1983: 317). The social importance not just of reproducing, but also of producing healthy or "high quality" offspring, supports increasingly invasive initiation and "management" of pregnancy. In contrast, a "matrist" approach (Bunkle 1988) depicts childbearing as a source of women's inherent power; the drive to subjugate this power explains the development of male social dominance (Corea 1979). Medical and social control of contraception, abortion, infertility treatments, genetics, and childbirth are thus seen as "an attempt by men to sublimate their envy of women's awesome creative force; to imitate it, extract it, and finally to exorcize its power over them" (Bunkle 1988: 96). Broader social restrictions on sexuality, marriage, divorce, and women's participation in professional and political realms would be indirect, but more pervasive mechanisms to control women's reproductive capacities. "Womb envy" has even been invoked to invert Freud's theories of female neurosis rooted in penis envy (Kittay 1983). Firestone (1970) was rare in her optimism that genetic engineering and artificial wombs will free women from their biological constraints in reproducing; the much more common feminist view is that new technologies subject women to *greater* control (Klein 1989; O'Brien 1989; Overall 1993; Purdy 1996; Sherwin 1992; Spallone 1989).

The pronatalist imperative typically applies only to *married* women, however, and the outlook for unwed mothers has generally been grim. Options for handling pregnancy out of wedlock vary widely among cultures and economic classes, and may even reinforce class distinctions: in the US in the mid-twentieth century, for example, pregnant white teens were typically sent to maternity homes and gave their babies up for adoption to middle-class couples, while black teens were more likely to keep their children and become entrenched in poverty (Solinger 1992).

Population rates and birth patterns have been strongly correlated with education and economic opportunities for women (Demographic and Health Surveys 2002; United Nations Population Division 2002). In most of Western Europe and North America, birth rates have dropped steadily to equal or even dip below the population replacement rate as women delay childbearing and reduce family size to focus on paid employment. The United Nations highlighted this correlation as the key to population control in impoverished parts of the world at the 1994 International Conference on Population and Development in Cairo, and emphasized education and economic opportunities for women in the Beijing Declaration at the Fourth World Conference on Women (United Nations 1995).

Wanting Children

Men and women typically share many common interests in having children, which may be acutely painful when infertility arises (Burns and Covington 1999; Zoldbrod 1993). Reaching reproductive maturity, and especially becoming a parent, are almost universally viewed as the hallmarks of adulthood; adults without children are often viewed by others as immature, unreliable, or even selfish, and typically feel left out of family-oriented social activities. Additional motivations include liking children and wanting them to be present in one's life, a woman's desire to experience being pregnant, or relieving angst about our mortality by having our children survive our death.

When women have few options for education, employment, or social status outside of marriage and motherhood, childbearing may be socially and economically necessary for survival. Even in societies that promote women's equality and opportunity, though, "real women" are expected to want children and to experience pregnancy (Lang 1991). Men typically have other avenues of social and economic success outside of parenting, but stereotypes of masculinity still emphasize a man's ability to father a child.

The phrase "reproductive rights" must be defined carefully, as several different types of claim may be at stake (Cook 1993; Robertson 1983; Shanner 1995). A right of refusal or to be left alone – e.g., a right to avoid forced reproduction, sterilization without consent, or perhaps carrying an unwanted fetus – is

407

quite different from asking for assistance to achieve one's goals, or for a right to create a new person. Rights of equality and nondiscrimination are often invoked regarding interests in parenting regardless of infertility, disability, sexual orientation (Hanscombe 1983), marital status, advanced age, or socio-economic status. The key challenge to rights-based approaches to reproduction is that children cannot agree to whatever arrangement brings them into existence.

Avoiding Reproduction

The enormous psychological, social, legal, economic, and (for women) physical implications of having children lead many people to avoid procreating, at least during certain phases of their lives. Many social and religious norms, as well as personal choices, may restrict sexual activity; contraceptives, sterilization, and abortion can prevent unwanted births. It is notable that, except for vasectomy, the available forms of contraception all involve chemicals or objects being introduced into a woman's body.

The availability of safe and effective birth control pills in the 1960s prompted widespread changes in sexual norms and gender roles in many parts of the world. The "sexual revolution" was far from complete, however. Japan and several insurance companies in the US made Viagra (recently introduced for erectile dysfunction) legally available or covered by insurance before they did the same for oral contraceptives that have existed for more than 30 years. In many parts of the world, hormonal contraceptives are prohibitively expensive, simply unavailable, or of variable and unreliable quality. Research into new contraceptive methods tends to be done on the poorest and most marginalized populations both globally and within specific regions; the long controversy over the safety of Depo-Provera is only the most prominent case.

Surgical sterilization for both men and women is gaining popularity in various parts of the world as a form of birth control, especially for mid-life adults who already have children. Vasectomy is less invasive and safer for men than tubal ligation is for women, and offers men the only form of contraception that can be fully under their own control. The social implications of widespread vasectomy in male-dominated communities are unclear, however. Other forms of contraceptives may seem unnecessary, leaving women vulnerable to sexually transmitted diseases and pregnancies as a result of rape, a partner who wants more children over her objections, and non-marital sexuality.

Abortion

The rancorous debate over abortion (Beckman and Harvey 1998; Luker 1984) often emphasizes the moral and legal status of fetuses: is removing a fetus more like murder or merely the removal of tissue from a woman's body? The moral status of the fetus is not a scientific or factual matter, but is most often couched in religious teachings about ensoulment that vary widely (Maguire 2001), ranging from conception (e.g., Catholicism) through various points in mid-pregnancy (Islam, Orthodox Judaism, many sects of Christianity) to live birth (non-Orthodox Judaism). Belief systems that include multiple lifetimes (Buddhism, Hinduism) or souls in all living things offer significantly different approaches. Embryos and fetuses may also be described as related to us genetically, developmentally, and through pregnancy, leading many to give them some intermediate status above that of mere objects but still below the status of persons.

Even if the fetus is considered a person, Thomson (1971) persuasively launched the argument – echoed in more recent analogies between pregnancy and organ donation – that one's right to impose oneself on the body and life of another person is minimal. Attempting to balance the rights of fetuses and pregnant women is a particularly Western concept, however. Pregnancy and abortion are viewed quite differently in different geographic, social, religious, and economic contexts (Kulczycki 1999); abortions may be restricted for reasons having little to do with fetal rights, or may be taken in stride without the distress that dominates many countries.

Reproductive and Genetic Technologies (RGTs)

In the new millennium, initiating pregnancy frequently involves complex technology and multiple collaborators. The least technical options include insemination with donor sperm (Daniels and Haimes 1998), surgical repair of damaged reproductive organs, and hormonal stimulation. In vitro fertilization (IVF) requires a woman to undergo hormonal stimulation and surgical extraction of ova, which are then fertilized in the lab. Resulting embryos may be transferred to the uterus of the same woman or to a "surrogate mother," donated to an infertility patient, used in research, or kept indefinitely in frozen storage. In addition to physical risks of hormones and ovum retrieval, RGTs often pose substantial emotional, social, and financial costs (Shanner and Nisker 2001). Cutting-edge research into cloning and stem cells must therefore be recognized as having differential impact on the sexes due to the need for women to provide ova (Mahowald 2000).

The new technologies allow us to mix and match parents as never before in human history (Shanley 2001; Strathern 1992), and no society appears to have appropriate social and legal mechanisms to deal with these new options. Same-sex partners can procreate with the help of sperm donors or contracted pregnancies, people can procreate after their deaths, and women in their 40s have given birth to their own genetic grandchildren on behalf of their infertile daughters. What does it feel like for a man to watch his mother-in-law give birth to his child, and what role should the birth mother/grandmother play in raising the child? Men's reactions to watching their wives inseminated with another man's sperm can be complex and disturbing (Blizzard 1977; Lauritzen 1990). Offspring of sperm donors in several countries are seeking to open donor records, as they are denied important information about their kinship lines and medical family history in a system that almost universally favors secrecy. Some men who were sperm donors years ago are also expressing a changed desire to know whether they have offspring in the world, and that they are doing well.

Even the most basic concepts require re-examination in the modern age of pro-creation. "Biological fatherhood" refers to genetic parentage; "biological mother-hood" involves both genetics and gestation. In vitro fertilization fragmented biological motherhood and created enormous social and legal complications unimaginable in all of previous human history. If Mary's ovum is transferred to Susan's uterus, who is the biological mother of the child (Rothman 1989)? The mother is usually deemed to be Susan if Mary is an ovum donor and Susan is an infertility patient, but is Mary if she is the infertility patient and Susan is a "gestational carrier" or "surrogate mother." Very few jurisdictions have updated their laws regarding birth certificates. The word "surrogate" is controversial, as it implies that a woman in this role is merely a stand-in; from the newborn's perspective, though, the birth mother is the first and only relationship. How should we understand the importance of genetics, physiological bonds, the relationship of the mother(s) to the father of the child, and the different parent-ing desires of various reproductive collaborators? What are the implications for women if gestation is devalued, and for offspring if their progenitors are haphazardly identified? Our increasing confusion over such basic biological and social relationships is troubling.

Genetic tests can be done on embryos, preventing the need for later prenatal diagnosis and possible abortion. Avoiding a "tentative pregnancy" (Rothman 1986) can be a blessing for those at genetic risk, but may also subject healthy women to invasive, unnecessary infertility interventions in order to avoid the pregnancy. The earlier the test is done, the easier it is to reject a potential child; when are the medical, personal, and social harms of being born with a given trait "serious" enough to balance the harms of going through the bodies of women to test potential offspring? The choice of a baby's sex is particularly contentious, as sex is not a disease or inherent disability, and gender preferences tend to be based on rather stereotypical assumptions. The rapid advancement of genetic science raises the fear that offspring will be increasingly subject to "quality control" measures, and that women will increasingly bear liability for failing to take available tests or failing to prevent the birth of a child with socially undesir-able traits.

The role of expensive reproductive and genetic technologies is significantly larger in rich, Western countries than in many other parts of the world. Indeed, the problems raised by RGTs are sometimes viewed as disguised blessings com-pared to the lack of basic medications, hospitals, and public health protections faced by many developing economies. On the other hand, international "family planning" efforts are often viewed with skepticism or even fear if they emphasize contraception without infertility relief. Being told not to have babies, but not being assisted to have them when wanted and appropriate, can be perceived as a racist agenda. Genetic technologies may well increase the gaps between the world's "haves" and "have-nots," as only the wealthy will be able to afford genetic enhancements for their children.

Being Pregnant

One of the most exciting developments in feminist scholarship is rigorous phenomenological reflection on pregnancy as an embodied experience. Pregnant physiology, fetal development, recognition of the fetus by the mother and by others, and the woman's coming to view herself as a mother all evolve gradually, over time, and through almost imperceptible changes (Bergum 1997; Gatens-Robinson 1992; Mackenzie 1992; Martin 1987; Young 1984). There simply is no such thing as a fetus without a pregnant woman sustaining it; describing pregnancy as a lived phenomenon or as part of the narrative of a woman's life refocuses our attention on this often-neglected fact, and establishes pregnancy as an ethical, purposeful and creative activity rather than merely an instinctive happening. Gilligan (1982) articulated the relationships and responsibilities that women perceive to their fetuses; significantly, abortion, adoption, and keeping a child one cannot support can *all* be viewed as failures to maintain the mothering relationship.

Histories of procreation mythologies (Weigle 1989) and prenatal care (Oakley 1986) show how far our insight into pregnancy has come. On the other hand, the old images of women as empty vessels or baby machines are inadvertently being reinforced by life-sustaining technology such as ventilators: a brain-dead (legally deceased) woman's body can be maintained so that the fetus she carried at the time of her death might survive to birth by caesarean section (Nelson 1994). What does it mean for living pregnant women if dead women can do what they do? What does it mean for a child to be born from a corpse?

Outside the domain of feminist scholarship, literature on pregnancy tends to focus on fetuses: their development, their legal and ethical status, and the interests of various parties in the well-being or fate of the fetus. Western ethics, law, and medicine often approach pregnancy as a conflict of interests between women and fetuses they carry, but pregnant women and fetuses are not entirely separate parties. The moral significance of birth has been given shockingly little serious philosophical attention (Held 1989; Warren 1989) compared to the vastly greater reflection on the meanings of death. The beginning of life, and a woman's role in making it possible, are frequently taken for granted, and much more work is needed to fully articulate the unique relationship that pregnancy entails.

When pregnancy is perceived to be primarily about fetuses rather than pregnant persons, the political, social, and economic implications for all women can

411

be enormous. Women's employment opportunities (Frazier and Hage 1998) and lifestyle choices may be curtailed to prevent prenatal injury, and, in the extreme, women may suffer forced prenatal interventions and even criminal penalties for engaging in otherwise legal activities when pregnant (Mathieu 1996). How best to prevent prenatal injury while protecting women remains a difficult challenge.

The Future of Reproduction

Reproductive roles are anything but static in the twenty-first century. New technologies may one day allow men to carry pregnancies, or ectogenesis (mechanical wombs) may allow babies to be born without anyone being pregnant. Cloning and genetic engineering might allow a person to reproduce him- or herself without corresponding sperm or ovum providers, or to create wholly new individuals related to nobody. These shifting reproductive roles may significantly redefine gender roles on a broader social scale, just as contraception prompted significant advances for women in many cultures. We live in interesting but unsettling times.

In any envisioned future, though, at least some people will continue to reproduce in the old-fashioned, fun way – with sex, without technology or collaborators, and with unpredictable results. The vast majority of future people will continue to be carried and birthed by women. Choices about children will therefore always remain deeply personal, socially important, and profoundly gender-sensitive matters.

Note

I would like to thank the Canadian Institutes of Health Research and the Alberta Heritage Foundation for Medical Research for their research support.

References

Allen, J. (1983) "Motherhood: The Annihilation of Women," in J. Trebilcot (ed.), *Mothering: Essays in Feminist Theory* (Savage, MD: Rowman and Littlefield).

Anderson, E. S. (1990) "Is Women's Labor a Commodity?" *Philosophy and Public Affairs* 19/1: 71–92.

Becker, G. (2000) *The Elusive Embryo: How Men and Women Approach New Reproductive Technologies* (Berkeley: University of California Press).

Beckman, L. J. and Harvey, S. M. (1998) *The New Civil War: The Psychology, Culture, and Politics of Abortion* (Washington, DC: American Psychological Association).

Bergum, V. (1997) *A Child on Her Mind* (Westport, CT: Bergin & Garvey).

Blizzard, J. (1977) *Blizzard and the Holy Ghost* (London: Peter Owen).

Bunkle, P. (1988) *Second Opinion: The Politics of Women's Health in New Zealand* (Auckland, NZ: Oxford University Press).

Burns, L. H. and Covington, S. N. (1999) *Infertility Counseling: A Comprehensive Handbook for Clinicians* (New York: Parthenon Publishing Group).

Colborn, T., Dumanoski, D., and Myers, J. P. (1996) *Our Stolen Future* (New York: Dutton).

Cook, R. J. (1993) "International Human Rights and Women's Reproductive Health," *Studies in Family Planning* 24: 73–86.

Corea, G. (1979) *The Mother Machine* (New York: Harper & Row).

Daniels, K. and Haimes, E. (1998) *Donor Insemination: International Social Science Perspectives* (New York: Cambridge University Press).

De Beauvoir, S. (1952) *The Second Sex* (New York: Vintage).

Demographic and Health Surveys (2002) <http://www.measuredhs.com/> (last accessed August 30, 2002).

Firestone, S. (1970) *The Dialectic of Sex* (New York: William Morrow).

Frazier, L. M. and Hage, M. L. (1998) *Reproductive Hazards of the Workplace* (Scarborough, ON/ New York: Van Nostrand Reinhold/International Thomson).

Gatens-Robinson, E. (1992) "A Defense of Women's Choice: Abortion and the Ethics of Care," *Southern Journal of Philosophy* 30/3: 39–66.

Gilligan, C. (1982) *In A Different Voice* (Cambridge, MA: Harvard University Press).

Hanscombe, G. (1983) "The Right to Lesbian Parenthood," *Journal of Medical Ethics* 9: 133–5.

Held, V. (1989) "Birth and Death," *Ethics* 99 (January): 362–88.

Kirejczyk, M. and van der Ploeg, I. (1992) "Pregnant Couples: Medical Technology and Social Constructions around Fertility and Reproduction," *Issues in Reproductive and Genetic Engineering* 5/2: 113–25.

Kittay, E. F. (1983) "Womb Envy: An Explanatory Concept," in Joyce Trebilcot (ed.), *Mothering: Essays in Feminist Theory* (Savage MD: Rowman & Littlefield).

Klein, R. (1989) *Infertility: Women Speak Out about Their Experiences of Reproductive Medicine* (London: Pandora).

Kulczycki, A. (1999) *The Abortion Debate in the World Arena* (New York: Routledge).

Lang, S. S. (1991) *Women without Children: The Reasons, the Rewards, the Regrets* (Holbrook, MA: Adams Media Corporation).

Lauritzen, P. (1990) "What Price Parenthood?" *Hastings Center Report* 20/2: 38–46.

Luker, K. (1984) *Abortion and the Politics of Motherhood* (Berkeley: University of California Press).

Mackenzie, C. (1992) "Abortion and Embodiment," *Australian Journal of Philosophy* 70/2: 136–55.

Maguire, D. C. (2001) *Sacred Choices: The Right to Contraception and Abortion in Ten World Religions* (Minneapolis: Fortress Press).

Mahowald, M. (1995) "As If There Were Fetuses Without Women: A Remedial Essay," in J. Callahan (ed.), *Reproduction, Ethics, and the Law* (Bloomington: Indiana University Press).

Mahowald, M. (2000) *Genes, Women, Equality* (New York: Oxford University Press).

Martin, E. (1987) *The Woman in the Body: The Cultural Analysis of Reproduction* (Boston: Beacon Press).

Mason, M.-C. (1993) *Male Infertility – Men Talking* (London: Routledge).

Mathieu, D. (1996) *Preventing Prenatal Harm: Should the State Intervene?* 2nd edn. (Washington, DC: Georgetown University Press).

Nelson, H. L. (1994) "The Architect and the Bee: Some Reflections on Postmortem Pregnancy," *Bioethics* 8/3: 247–67.

O'Brien, M. (1989) *Reproducing the World* (Boulder, CO: Westview Press).

Oakley, A. (1986) *The Captured Womb: A History of the Medical Care of Pregnant Women* (New York: Basil Blackwell).

Overall, C. (1993) *Human Reproduction: Principles, Practices, Policies* (Toronto: Oxford University Press).

Peck, E. and Senderowitz, J. (1974) *Pronatalism: The Myth of Mom and Apple Pie* (New York: Crowell).

Petchesky, R. (1987) "Foetal Images: The Power of Visual Culture in the Politics of Reproduction," in M. Stanworth (ed.), *Reproductive Technologies: Gender Motherhood and Medicine* (Minneapolis: University of Minnesota Press).

Pinto-Correia, C. (1997) *The Ovary of Eve: Egg and Sperm and Preformation* (Chicago, IL: University of Chicago Press).

Purdy, L. M. (1996) *Reproducing Persons: Issues in Feminist Bioethics* (Ithaca, NY: Cornell University Press).

Robertson, J. (1983) "Procreative Liberty and the Control of Conception, Pregnancy and Childbirth," *Virginia Law Review* 69: 405–62.

Rothman, B. K. (1986) *The Tentative Pregnancy: The Prenatal Diagnosis and the Future of Motherhood* (New York: Viking).

Rothman, B. K. (1989) *Recreating Motherhood: Ideology and Technology in a Patriarchal Society* (New York: W. W. Norton).

Schwarzenbach, S. (1987) "Rawls and Ownership: The Forgotten Category of Reproductive Labor," *Canadian Journal of Philosophy* 13: 136–66.

Shanley, M. (2001) *Making Babies, Making Families: What Matters Most in an Age of Reproductive Technologies, Surrogacy, Adoption, and Same-Sex and Unwed Parents' Rights* (Boston: Beacon Press).

Shanner, L. (1995) "The Right to Procreate: When Rights Claims Have Gone Wrong," *McGill Law Journal* 40/4: 823–7.

Shanner, L. and Nisker, J. (2001) "Bioethics for Clinicians: 26. Assisted Reproductive Technologies," *Canadian Medical Association Journal* 164/11: 1589–94.

Sherwin, S. (1992) *No Longer Patient: Feminist Ethics and Health Care* (Philadelphia: Temple University Press).

Solinger, R. (1992) *Wake Up Little Susie: Single Pregnancy and Race Before Roe v. Wade* (New York and London: Routledge).

Spallone, P. (1989) *Beyond Conception: The New Politics of Reproduction* (Granby, MA: Bergin & Garvey).

Stabile, C. (1992) "Shooting the Mother: Fetal Photography and the Politics of Disappearance," *Camera Obscura* 28: 179–205.

Strathern, M. (1992) *Reproducing the Future* (New York: Routledge).

Thomson, J. J. (1971) "A Defense of Abortion," *Philosophy and Public Affairs* 1/1: 47–66.

United Nations (1995) Report of the Fourth World Conference on Women: Beijing Declaration and Platform for Action <http://www.un.org/womenwatch/confer/beijing/reports/plateng.htm> (last accessed August 30, 2002).

United Nations Population Division (2002) <http://www.un.org/esa/population/unpop.htm> (last accessed August 30, 2002).

Warren, M. A. (1989) "The Moral Significance of Birth," *Hypatia* 4/3: 46–65.

Weigle, M. (1989) *Creation and Procreation: Feminist Reflections on Mythologies of Cosmogony and Parturition* (Philadelphia: University of Pennsylvania Press).

Young, I. M. (1984) "Pregnant Embodiment: Subjectivity and Alienation," *Journal of Medicine & Philosophy* 9: 45–62.

Zolbrod, A. (1993) *Men, Women and Infertility: Intervention and Treatment Strategies* (New York: Lexington Books).

CHAPTER THIRTY

Disability

Anita Silvers

Body and Role

For at least a century and a half, appeals to biological destiny have functioned as the ascendant rationale for defending assignments of groups of people to undesirable social roles. Social history is replete with examples of people unfairly excluded from leading the lives they desire and deserve because their biological characteristics are surmised to suit them for some other kind of life. Often reputed to have biological flaws, people of color, women, and people with disabilities traditionally have been cast as subordinates or dependents.

Gender Studies explores a subset of these examples, namely those that involve constructions that link the characteristics of biological sex to gendered social roles. Gender Studies has much to offer to scholars concerned about outsider populations, even those groups that are neither classified with reference to sex nor associated with standard gendered roles. The irrepressible, fertile, insightful scholarship of Gender Studies has greatly advanced our understanding of how biological and social factors interact in the construction of personal and group identity.

Gender Studies has developed a variety of models of the linkage of sex and gender. These are a rich resource for analyzing the material and the social aspects of outsiders whose bodies are atypical and who thereby either become invisible or are assigned oppositional identities. For example, Crenshaw (1991) has shown how the dislocation of black women from conventional roles has weakened their legal protection against both sexual harassment and racial discrimination. Her work has stimulated analogous examinations of the feebleness of discrimination protection for women with disabilities. Concomitantly, broadening the inquiry to include more than just the sexual elements of human biology, and more than the gendered aspects of social roles, can deepen our grasp of the ways in which outsider populations are exposed to disadvantage by their corporeal differences.

Gender and disability may be thought of as conceptual frames that give meaning to the body. In this chapter, I will suggest how some theoretical approaches pioneered in Gender Studies can be adapted to the analytic categories of disability and impairment, the concepts that frame current research in disability studies. Concomitantly, I will indicate where attending to the subtle realities of disabled people's lives can press gender-specific approaches to theorizing beyond their present boundaries. In doing so, I will often refer to how self and social experience act on, and become attuned to, each other in distinctive ways when our daily activities are mediated by corporeal, material, or biological limitations.

I count so-called cognitive, emotional, and psychiatric limitations as biological for three reasons. First, the vast majority are now correlated with genetic, congenital, chemical, or nervous system anomalies. Even conditions that are traceable to external events, such as post-traumatic stress syndrome, appear to involve chronic disruptions of bodily processes. Second, living these conditions is experienced as being of a piece with, rather than as constituted by, separate physical and mental events. For example, individuals with bipolar conditions experience periods of unbounded physical energy characterized by such manifestations as wanting little sleep, interleaved with periods of deadening, horizonless lethargy when it is impossible to move their bodies to get out of bed. Third, historically, social responses to people with physical and mental disabilities have had much in common. For example, people with mental retardation, cerebral palsy, and deafness have had their children removed or have been sterilized by the state, denied access to public education on the ground that their presence harms other children, and been institutionalized to remove them from social contact with citizens who function in species-typical ways. (As have native people, women, gays, and lesbians.)

This last example reminds us of the ways in which social exclusion amplifies and exacerbates disadvantage for people with cognitive, emotional, and psychiatric anomalies. Further, the degree to which a particular kind of biological anomaly courts disadvantage shifts from culture to culture. For example, in contemporary European and North American culture, extremely heavy people are judged defective and are shunned, while to appear to be virtually emaciated is to be sought after and admired. Some of the indigenous cultures of Polynesia, to the contrary, require tremendous corpulence in those who ascend to the most prominent social roles. There is no consistency across cultures regarding the social opportunities available to individuals with a particular biological limitation, although all cultures appear to impose some exclusions on some such people.

Biological Difference and Social Segregation

Enforced segregation of biologically anomalous population groups is an egregious but by no means isolated example of the influence of presumptions about biological fitness. In this vein, courts have endorsed the separation of people identified as being of different races by advancing the rationale that segregating social schemes merely acknowledge "natural" affinities among people of the same race and "natural" antipathies among people of different races (Silvers and Stein 2002a). Indeed, confidence in the benefits of biological separatism was so entrenched in earlier thinking that even liberationists like the early feminist writer Charlotte Perkins Gilman subscribed to it. The women's utopia Perkins describes in her novel *Herland* (1979 [1915]) is a single-sex society, and its citizens flourish because they can congregate with their own kind.

The supposed benefits of biological separatism have often been evoked to deny women employment that would place them in the company of men. For example, a state law denying women the opportunity to be employed as bartenders was adjudged to be in compliance with the US Constitution's guarantee of equal protection. The US Supreme Court held that there is no requirement that different kinds of people be treated the same. The Court declared that women's presence "naturally" incites males to lust and violence, and that women typically do not have the physical ability to impose orderly behavior on the rowdy patrons of a bar (Silvers and Stein 2002a, 2002b).

Similar accounts of women's nature as physically, intellectually, and emotionally frail have been used to strip them of control of their property, and of custody of their children. These practices have been defended with the rationale that "nature" has made women physically, intellectually, and emotionally frail (Miles 1988: 187). Gay and lesbian people have been denied the legal protections of marriage on the basis of claims about the "unnaturalness" of partnering with someone of the same sex. Similarly, people with disabilities have been characterized as being too biologically inferior to execute the responsibilities and thereby enjoy the privileges of citizenship to work and play with non-disabled people, and to be permitted reproductive freedom.

Deep in Our Cells, or Only Skin-deep?

The initial line of resistance to such unfavorable and unfair treatment of a group usually has been to deny that their biological differences reduce their capabilities. To illustrate: a typical first step in opposing racism is to declare that persons with different pigmentations are the same under the skin. Notice, however, that this kind of reassurance does not preclude privileging individuals who conform to the common standard over people who fall away from perceived biological optimality. For example, believing that the characteristic pigmentations of all the primary population groups (Caucasian, African, Asian) should be considered typical of the species and refusing to associate these differences in pigmentation with greater or lesser biological optimality do not entail rejecting all considerations of color in assigning social status. Even people convinced of the fundamental similarity of humans with the diverse pigmentations associated with different races usually do not extend their tolerance to individuals with albinism. Such individuals are not accepted as being the same as everyone else "under the skin."

Albinism is associated with disability rather than with race, and so the tolerance of "color-blindness" is not extended to these extraordinarily white people (Silvers 1998).

Of course, the embodied nature of human experience argues against theories that obscure or disregard bodily differences. Women's bodies undeniably are different from men's, and women's fleshly awareness also is different. Liberal feminism has been criticized for obscuring these differences. Liberal feminism seeks to increase women's access to the most advantageous areas of existing social practice without regard for the question of whether adopting male roles obscures or subordinates women's differences. Cultural feminists propose instead to elevate women's distinctive roles and reform social practice by enhancing the influence of women's distinctive ways and values. Cultural feminists therefore are proponents of conventions that reflect biological difference without privileging favored differences or rejecting disfavored ones.

Cultural feminism has been criticized, however, for the essentialism of equating women with their traditional social roles, and for identifying the difference between men and women with the difference in their gendered roles. Further, not all women are admitted to women's roles. Barron, who has engaged in extensive studies of the lives of young women with disabilities in European culture, observes that we place great value on the womanly art of caring for dependents, but the traditional dependent position of young women with disabilities prevents them from perfecting this art (Barron 1997: 234). We should be clear that what precludes young women like those Barron studied from being homemakers and mothers is not their lack of potential for executing these roles but, instead, their having been assigned to an alternative social position, one defined in terms of such dependence that their capacity to nurture others becomes virtually inconceivable.

Where being acknowledged as a socially worthwhile person requires being perceived as competent to fulfill gendered roles, we find important differences in the social and economic well-being of men and women with disabilities. Census data show that women with disabilities have a much lower socio-cultural participation rate than their non-disabled and male counterparts. More than half of non-disabled men and women, and disabled men, are employed, but less than half of women with disabilities have employment. They are the group most likely to remain unmarried. Among persons who have married and are not widowed, 12 percent of male non-disabled, 15 percent of female non-disabled, 11 percent of male disabled, but 25 percent of female disabled are divorced or separated (Bureau of the Census 1984). These data show the socio-cultural participation rate of women with disabilities descending below the combined straight-line projections of the participation rates of non-disabled women and men with disabilities, thereby suggesting that, combined, the two stigmas have a more than additive negative effect (Deegan and Brooks 1985; Hanna and Rogovsky 1991).

Regardless of how women may resent the added burdens placed on them by a spouse who develops a disability, they typically remain in the relationship, while men in heterosexual relationships do not as commonly do so (Cohen 1996). Presumably, fewer men than women identify with care-giving as a self-affirming role. Further, men and women with the same disability have different reactions to their being denied the opportunity to engage in certain performances. When gender and disability intersect, disabled women often lose all gendered identity. On the other hand, when disability and gendered behavior intersect, disabled men often feel that they are being feminized. For example, this chapter's author, a wheelchair-using female old enough to have been socialized in an era when men opened doors for women, was startled to learn that some of her wheelchair-using male friends felt themselves demeaned when an able-bodied man opens doors for them.

Regardless of whether they are biologically capable of executing ordinary roles, disabled individuals' differences thus are reified into reasons for denying them access to the normal opportunity ranges of gendered roles. To illustrate, because individuals with albinism are stigmatized as witches in Zimbabwe, they are considered too dangerous to bring into a family through marriage (Silvers 1998). Although the expression of the genetic anomalies associated with albinism often is no more than skin-deep, individuals with albinism may face profound limitations in their access to gendered roles. In the same vein, in European culture, families discourage their members from partnering with individuals with disabilities because of imagined burdens they fear having to assume.

Is Dependency the Difference?

Gender Studies has produced an extensive literature about the power relationships that influence the privileging of certain gendered roles over others. Nevertheless, Gender Studies has paid scant attention to the consequences for disabled individuals, who are pressed into gendered roles they do not embrace, or who are perceived as unqualified for the gendered roles usually adopted by individuals of their sex. Disability Studies addresses analogous problems about the valorization of current social roles, but from the perspectives of disabled people. Disability Studies documents how exclusion from the usual range of social roles, even from the least esteemed of these, marginalizes biologically anomalous individuals.

Early versions of the social model of disability were aimed at eliminating the many artificial barriers that exclude people with disabilities from social participation. Proponents urged the disentanglement of disability from illness, pointing out that many individuals with disabilities are as strong and capable of productivity as non-disabled people, and therefore should not be consigned to the limitations of the "sick" role (Silvers et al. 1998). Other writers, such as Wendell (1996), object to this approach. They say that illness is itself disabling, and that chronically ill individuals constitute a prominent part of the population considered to be disabled. Many such people experience pain, fatigue, feebleness, and disorientation to a degree that forestalls productivity, saps self-sufficiency, and even may alienate them from their own bodies or minds. To make the healthy rather than the ill disabled paradigmatic of the disability category obscures the disabled's differences. Worse, doing so perpetuates our culture's devaluing of dependency and inflating of the importance of autonomy and self-sufficiency.

More and more voices are being raised in celebration of dependence. The philosopher Alasdair MacIntyre (1999) has pointed out that it is only human to be dependent and that good societies cultivate virtues of dependence. Feminist philosopher and legal studies scholar Martha Nussbaum suggests that "instead of picturing one another as rough equals making a bargain, we may be better off thinking of one another as people with varying degrees of capacity and disability, in a variety of different relationships of interdependency with one another" (2001: B9). Nussbaum echoes an observation made by other feminist writers when she criticizes traditional justice theory for casting citizens in the role of bargainers who develop reciprocal relations with other people primarily for their own benefit rather than to benefit the other. To think of this role as the pre-eminent one for citizens "effaces the more asymmetrical forms of dependency that human life contains: the need for care in infancy, extreme age, and periods of severe illness or a lifetime of severe disability" (ibid.).

Nussbaum comments that we must preserve the self-respect of dependents without exploiting care-givers, since women, who do a very large proportion of care-giving, have their equality compromised unless the role of carer is adequately acknowledged and compensated. If the primary social assignment for disabled people is to be in extended dependency, however, the system that provides for their care may be the self-same system that impugns their self-respect. First, as Tronto (1993) finds, the power imbalance between care-givers and care-receivers carries with it a potential for oppression. Helping relationships are voluntary, but asymmetrically so. Help-givers choose how they will help, but recipients of help cannot choose how they will be helped, for if one's connection to others is as the recipient of help, rejecting others' choice of proffered help leaves one in a solitary position (Silvers 1995).

In systems where individuals viewed as incompetent to care for themselves are coerced into compliance "for their own good," people with disabilities are too easily typecast as subordinate. It is well documented that where non-disabled people relate to disabled people primarily by caring for them, it becomes socially incumbent upon the former to profess incompetence even where they are more competent than the latter (Scott 1969). It was not too long ago, recall, when all women were expected to dissemble this way to make men more secure in their masculine role.

Second, it is a mistake to think that children and aged people do not relate reciprocally just because they are consumers of care. The latter have contributed to the support of others, and the former will do so when they grow up. We care for children to facilitate their growth into caring adults, and devotion to our elders is a tribute to their earlier contributions. That the very young and very old are dependent does not thereby identify them as being non-reciprocating. The same cannot be said, of course, for anyone whose lifetime role is to be a dependent. In other words, a social system structured so that disabled people are required to assume roles of dependency may inherently curtail others' respect for them and in so doing corrode their self-respect.

Consequently, we should ask why disabled people are identified with extended dependency. Do disabled people's biological properties destine them for this role? Trying to imagine how people who do not see, hear, walk, or think in species-typical ways execute the activities of daily life may invite an affirmative response. People who can function species-typically rarely master the skills of navigating without seeing, mobilizing without walking, communicating without hearing, or operating in a cognitively overwhelming environment. They therefore presume that remaining independent presents enormous difficulties for individuals who lose these abilities. People who have been temporarily disabled often complain about the difficulties of performing their daily activities under this condition. While temporarily disabled people are more likely to notice the hostility of the everyday environment than non-disabled people, they are no more expert judges of the real limitations of a disability than a student who complains, after completing a semester's study of French, that she can't say anything in French because the language is so severely limited. Nevertheless, disabled people often find that medical and social service experts are employed to be their spokespeople, as a hallmark of contemporary dependency systems is to disregard or dismiss the judgment of individuals who are assumed to need such systems.

Privileging Species-typicality

Like queer theory, Disability Studies investigates how the authority of people who fall away from species-typicality is undermined. For example, in a departure from the usual epistemic standard, we privilege non-disabled people's characterizations of the difficulties of disabled people's lives over disabled people's own assessments. Ordinarily, we defer to first-person reports of subjective states, and we take the testimony of people with great and varied experience of a subject over those with less experience.

As Milligan points out, many blind people have experienced both sightedness and blindness, while very few sighted people have done so. Applying the usual standard, we should acknowledge that blind people possess the most expertise about the importance of seeing (Magee and Milligan 1995). In actual practice, however, we expect blind people to defer to sighted people, who have no direct knowledge basis for comparing the difficulties of living blind and living sighted, rather than to blind people, who are much more knowledgeable. This is evidently a political rather than an epistemological decision. Species-typical individuals are in the majority, of course. As Canguilhem (1998) has observed, we take the biological characteristics of the most populous or otherwise dominant group to be normal for the species. Because biologically anomalous people are, by definition, minorities, their epistemic expertise is discounted even where doing so violates standard evidentiary practice.

Given the ubiquity of discursive practices that disregard disabled people's epistemic authority, we should not be surprised that non-disabled people ignore compelling evidence of the competence of disabled people. For example, I recently listened to a non-disabled colleague in a working group insist that blind people's quality of life must be lower than that of sighted people. The speaker, a famous bioethicist, cited the great difficulty he was sure blind people must suffer in finding their way around. He advanced this proposition despite having observed (although apparently not having registered) that the blind members of the working group invariably found their way without complaint to unfamiliar restaurants, while some sighted members arrived late or failed to arrive because they could not find the restaurant.

Similarly discounting disabled people's authority in regard to their own lives, Daniels (2002) acknowledges that "people with longstanding disabilities will often rank their welfare higher than would other people who are merely imagining life with such disabilities." He speculates that "perhaps people with disabilities accommodate by adjusting their goals and expectations" (ibid.). Even if they are subjectively happy with their lives, Daniels maintains, objectively they have limited access to the normal opportunity range. Not only should society implement preventative healthcare programs so that citizens can avoid the limitations of disability, but he argues as well that therapeutic healthcare to restore biologically anomalous people must be allocated to them.

Daniels assumes that there are straightforward connections between people's biological and social performances. We cannot generalize, however, about the degree to which a physical or cognitive anomaly will limit a person. People whose biological conditions appear to be identical achieve very different levels and ranges of social functioning. People with biologically similar hearing losses differ in their abilities to use and understand speech. People with biologically similar vision losses differ in their ability to navigate in the same city. Some are masters of public transportation, while others depend on special paratransit services. Some people with Down syndrome and Williams syndrome have college degrees, while others are not able to execute basic cognitive activities of daily life.

Moreover, sometimes vast differences in functioning are occasioned by relatively small differences in impairment, while at other times relatively severe impairments are only minimally dysfunctional. There is no fixed proportional relation between having any specific impairment and being dysfunctional. Wendell (1996) makes this fact about becoming impaired very clear in her narrative of her own disabling illness. How to handle such functional differences occasions much debate in Disability Studies.

Differences About Disability

The first wave of Disability Studies scholars often took these functional differences as reflections of the degree to which various social environments are accommodating or hostile to the disabled. Analyzing disability as a category of oppression was initiated during the 1970s by crossovers from radical philosophy to the disability movement in Britain. Subsequently, American disability activists adopted the model because it both illuminated how they experienced limitations and gave direction to social reform (Silvers et al. 1998).

Their thematic principle has been that disability is the remediable product of flawed public policy, not the irremediable outcome of personal failings of body or mind. On this view, impairments are material facts, but disabilities are social facts. An impairment is a given, but given a particular impairment, an individual will function more or less independently depending on how accommodatingly her living conditions are arranged. Contra Daniels, on this view it is wrong to pursue therapeutic interventions to make biologically anomalous individuals more normal. Doing so is risky. They sometimes lose more function than they gain. To illustrate, children born with phocomelia as a result of their mothers' ingestion of thalidomide during pregnancy had their shortened limbs amputated so they could be fitted with more normal appearing artificial arms or legs. These proved so heavy and awkward as to be dysfunctional, and when the children were old enough to reject the role of compliant dependent, they discarded their prosthetics (Satz and Silvers 1999).

The medical history of disabled people is replete with such examples, which parallel oppressions imposed to alter other minority groups. For example, medicine has treated women like disabled people, intervening in their bodies to eliminate or discipline (to use Foucault's term) those parts that mark their identification with a purportedly inferior group. To give another example, in North America native children and deaf children were removed from their homes to residential schools and punished for using the language most natural to them. In view of this history, early Disability Studies theorists proposed to treat impaired embodiments as givens, and to reject all practices directed at altering them as being coercive instruments for further subordinating disabled people by inducing feelings of inadequacy and self-hate.

Embodiments

Gender Studies scholars may be reminded of a similar debate in their own field. Biological sex and the division of humans into two sexes, male and female, initially were taken as givens. On this account, the properties of bodies were supposed to be presocial: biology adapts the sexes to different social roles, but society unfairly devalues the roles for which women's biology destines them.

423

On reflection, however, facts about sex and gender muddy this picture. First, there are intersexed people, born with the biological markers of both female and male. Our allegiance to sexual dualism demands they be submitted to medical intervention that (usually through amputation) presses their bodies into one or the other sexual mold. Second, having a woman's body does not necessarily suit a person for feminine roles, nor do all those with men's bodies find themselves fitting comfortably into masculine roles. There are individuals who adapt with facility to gendered roles that are not traditional for their sex. Others, however, find their sexual characteristics too restricting for the roles they adopt and consequently seek to change these elements of their bodies through surgical and chemical intervention. The materiality of sexual characteristics does not make them unbreachable constants. Further, the body's limitations cannot always be discounted. While some people do not think their corporeal alteration is required to comfortably fit into opposite gendered roles, others seek medical intervention to facilitate their transgendering. Thus, the experiences of transgendered people suggest that there are circumstances in which altering one's body to better execute preferred social roles can be an affirming, rather than a degrading, choice.

Transferring this insight to disabled people helps us to see the over-simplification in condemning medical transformations of the body as being expressions of self-hatred. No firewall segregates our awareness of our biological properties from our interpersonal experiences. Our bodies' responses and responsiveness mark the social as well as the solitary aspects of our experiences. How our own bodies feel to us is shaped by social discourse. Nor is social practice isolated from, or prior to, materiality. An individual's impairments are no more neutral than her sexual characteristics are, for they mediate much of the content of her consciousness of the world with which she interacts. Performing major life functions such as mobilizing, hearing, seeing, interpreting, and infer- ring are such intimate elements of the fabric of our experience that what we view as within our reach in the world around us – and thereby what we take as the objects of our ambition – arises out of the scope and facility of our biological functioning.

Like Gender Studies, Disability Studies foregrounds transgressive actions as a way of stretching our imaginations. People with disabilities often are stigmatized because their adaptive functioning strikes others as disruptive. From a Disability Studies perspective, however, adaptive functioning offers a rich and largely unexplored resource for developing more adequate concepts of the materiality of human experience and of our personhood. People who talk or read with their fingers, walk with their hands, recoil from other people's touches, or float through the day on waves of pain, often develop innovative approaches to fleshly func- tion. Disabled people often are the first to incorporate adaptive technology into their lives. From typewriters (typewriters were invented to permit blind people to write) to computerized talking devices (computerized speech output was invented to permit blind people to read), disabled people have piloted the use of mechanical devices that now are integral to so many lives. Machines combine with fleshly effort to secure their basic capabilities: they hear with amplifiers, breathe with respirators, mobilize in wheelchairs they guard with more concern than the care they give their bodies.

Considering these examples should indicate the impoverishment of our typical thoughts about executing basic functions. Often, however, disabled people's use of prosthetics becomes yet another reason to stigmatize them. When disabled athlete Casey Martin sought to use a golf cart to play in Professional Golf Association (PGA) tournaments for which he had qualified, PGA officials rejected the request by evoking a Frankensteinian slippery slope: if Martin could mobilize with a golf cart while normal golfers walked, what would prevent a future contender, an upper limb amputee, from strapping on a bionic arm that could drive a golf ball more than two miles (Silvers and Wasserman 1998)?

Such cyborgian competitors are not far off. Lower-leg amputees have been banned from competitive running because their prostheses made them run too slowly. Now, however, new materials and designs have created special springy sportsfeet that permit their wearers, when very skilled and talented, to run faster than can be done with fleshly feet. Dory Selinger now bicycles with a cleated peg replacing his amputated foot. Because it does not flex, the peg is more efficient at pedaling than a fleshly foot. Selinger's best time is only four seconds off the longstanding world record for "normal" racers (Squatrighlia 2001). Arguably, it is unfair to exclude racers when prosthetics render them uncompetitive, and also to exclude them when better prosthetics make them very competitive. Given the fight the PGA put up to exclude Casey Martin's golf cart, however, it is unlikely the Olympic Committee will welcome being infiltrated by individuals whose impairments require machined parts more intimately connected to them than the golf cart is to Martin.

Identities

We continue to impose segregation on biologically anomalous population groups when they are identified with disability. An important reason is that, like male and female, normality and disability often are considered to be binary properties that mark oppositional identities. Davis writes that "the 'normal' body always is in a dialectical play with the disabled body. . . . [O]ur representations of the body are really investigations of and defenses against the notion that the body is anything but a seamless, whole, complete, unfragmented entity" (1997: 68). In a similar vein, Mitchell and Snyder characterize the record of representing disability in the visual and literary media as a history of "metaphorical opportunism" (1997: 17). They think our culture colonizes and exploits people with various kinds of impairments, or at least their images, in order to nourish non-disabled people's fictions about their own perfections (ibid.: 12). Embodied normalcy thus is both understood and embraced by means of the identical process wherein disability is denied or distanced.

According to Thomson, "the disabled figure operates as a code for insufficiency, contingency, and abjection – for deviant particularity – thus establishing the contours of a canonical body that garners the prerogatives and privileges of a supposedly stable, universalized normalcy" (1997: 136). Referring to disability as a lack and to impairment as an absence establishes normalcy as complete, present, and thereby as regulative. If we understand disability as an oppositional identity in this way, the segregation of biologically anomalous and species-typical populations is inescapable. The alternative is to reform the discourses of pathology and charity that heretofore have confined them.

Doing so requires us to invent ways of experiencing our materiality that are not organized around the construction of norms. Neither sexuality nor other major life activities should be structured in terms of oppositions around which power is contested and secured. Neither Disability Studies nor Gender Studies has fully rid itself of a dualistic framework that is torn between privileging the material or the social elements of experience. In this regard, Gender Studies and Disability Studies have to meet very similar conceptual challenges. To learn how to eliminate biological determinism without erasing biological difference, scholars should maintain currency with the issues and approaches of both fields.

References

Barron, K. (1997) "The Bumpy Road To Womanhood," *Disability & Society* 12/2: 223–9.

Bureau of the Census (1984) *Survey of Income and Program Participants*, SIPP84-R3 (Washington, DC: Bureau of Commerce).

Canguilhem, G. (1989) *The Normal and the Pathological* (New York: Zone Books).

Cohen, Marion Deutsche (1996) *Dirty Details: The Days and Nights of a Well Spouse* (Philadelphia: Temple University Press).

Crenshaw, K. (1991) "Mapping the Margins: Intersectionality, Identity Politics, and Violence Against Women of Color," *Stanford Law Review* 43.

Daniels, N. (2002) "Justice, Health, and Healthcare," in R. Rhodes, M. Battin, and A. Silvers (eds.), *Medicine and Social Justice* (Oxford: Oxford University Press).

Davis, L. (1997) "Nude Venuses, Medusa's Body, and Phantom Limbs: Disability and Visuality," in D. Mitchell and S. Snyder (eds.), *Discourses of Disability* (Ann Arbor: University of Michigan Press).

Deegan, M. J. and Brooks, N. (1985) *Women and Disability: The Double Handicap* (New Jersey: Transaction Press).

Gilman, C. P. (1979) *Herland* (New York: Pantheon).

Hanna, W. J. and Rogovsky, E. (1991) "Women with Disabilities: Two Handicaps Plus," *Disability, Handicap & Society* 6/1.

MacIntyre, A. (1999) *Rational Dependent Animals* (Chicago: Open Court).

Magee, B. and Milligan, M. (1985) *On Blindness* (Oxford: Oxford University Press).

Miles, R. (1988) *A Women's History of the World* (London: Michael Joseph).

Mitchell, D. and Snyder, S. (eds.) (1997) *The Body and Physical Difference: Discourses of Disability* (Ann Arbor: University of Michigan Press).

Nussbaum, M. (2001) "The Enduring Significance of John Rawls," *The Chronicle of Higher Education*, sect. 2 (July): B7–B9.

Satz, A. and Silvers, A. (2000) "Disability and Biotechnology," in M. Mehlman and T. Murray (eds.), *The Encyclopedia of Biotechnology: Ethical, Legal, and Policy Issues* (New York: John Wiley and Sons).

Scott, Robert (1969) *The Making of Blind Men: A Study Of Adult Socialization* (New York: The Russell Sage Foundation).

Shakespeare, T., Gillespie-Sells, K., and Davies, D. (1996) *The Sexual Politics of Disability* (London: Cassell).

Silvers, A. (1995) "Reconciling Equality To Difference: Caring (F)or Justice For People With Disabilities," *Hypatia* 10/1: 30–55.

Silvers, A. (1998) "A Fatal Attraction To Normalizing: Treating Disabilities As Deviations From 'Species-Typical' Functioning," in E. Parens (ed.), *Enhancing Human Capacities: Conceptual Complexities and Ethical Implications* (Washington DC: Georgetown University Press).

Silvers, A. and Stein, M. A. (2002a) "From Plessy (1896) and Goesart (1948) to Cleburne (1986) and Garrett (2001): A Chill Wind From the Past Blows Equal Protection Away," in L. Krieger (ed.), *Backlash Against the ADA: Interdisciplinary Perspectives* (Ann Arbor: University of Michigan Press).

Silvers, A. and Stein, M. A. (2002b) "Disability, Equal Protection, and the Supreme Court: Standing at the Crossroads of Progressive and Retrogressive Logic in Constitutional Classification," *The Michigan Journal of Law Reform*.

Silvers, A. and Wasserman, D. (1998) "The Double Edge of Convention: Disability Rights in Sports and Education," *Philosophy and Public Policy Newsletter* 16/4.

Silvers, A., Wasserman, D., and Mahowald, M. (1998) *Disability, Difference, Discrimination: Perspectives on Justice in Bioethics and Public Policy* (Lanham, MD: Rowman and Littlefield).

Squatrighlia, D. (2001) "Triumph Out of Tragedy," *San Francisco Chronicle* (July 1): A19, A22.

Thomson, R. G. (1997) *Extraordinary Bodies: Physical Disability in American Culture and Literature* (New York: Columbia University Press).

Tronto, J. (1993) *Moral Boundaries* (London: Routledge).

Wendell, S. (1996) *The Rejected Body* (London: Routledge).

CHAPTER THIRTY-ONE

Health

Lesley Doyal

Introduction

Since the 1980s, we have seen a significant expansion of work on the links between gender and well-being. Much of this has been done by women, with the practical aim of improving their own health and healthcare. More recently, men have begun to explore the impact of masculinity from a similar perspective. This chapter will review the main conclusions from this literature and will examine its broader significance for Gender Studies.

A quick examination of global patterns of health and illness reveals marked differences between women and men in the same social groups. Women usually have a longer average life expectancy, yet they also tend to report more sickness and distress than their male relatives and partners. There are also marked variations in the rates of specific diseases between men and women. Men are more likely than women in the same communities to die prematurely from heart disease, for example, while women are more likely than men to suffer from auto-immune diseases or musculo-skeletal disorders and also from anxiety and depression. Patterns of use of health services also vary between women and men living in similar socio-economic circumstances.

The discussion presented here will explore the reasons for these differences. It will begin with an examination of male and female biology which takes on much greater significance in discussions relating to health than in other areas of gender analysis. Women's capacity to become pregnant and give birth is potentially the single most important determinant of their well-being. In many of the most impoverished parts of the world, the lack of reproductive healthcare means that women's lives continue to be either damaged or foreshortened in very profound ways. Hence these biological differences need to be taken seriously as determinants of health.

However, biological characteristics are not the only determinants of health in either women or men. Male and female patterns of health and illness are also shaped by gender influences. As we shall see, the daily lives of men and women in the same communities are often very different and this affects their exposure to health risks, as well as their access to resources to promote their own health. Hence the work of social scientists is now being laid alongside that of biomedical researchers in an attempt to clarify the links between sex, gender, and health.

Both biological and social differences are therefore important in shaping male and female patterns of health and illness. But of course their effects are inextricably interlinked with a range of other influences including race, class, and geopolitical status. The potential risks of childbearing, for example, will be multiplied in settings where poverty is most acute. Similarly, the health impact of gender inequalities in resource allocation will be greatest in those societies where patriarchal values are strongest. In order to reflect these complex interrelationships, we will begin by exploring biological and gender influences on health and will then move on to place these debates in a broader context of economic, social, and cultural diversity.

The Biology of Risk

In biomedical theory and practice, the analysis of maleness and femaleness starts (and usually ends) with sex differences in reproductive systems. Because of their reproductive biology, women face sex-specific risks that will affect their lives in fundamental ways. Without access to the resources necessary to control their fertility and to ensure healthy pregnancy and childbirth, they may be unable to maintain either mental or physical well-being (Sen and Snow 1994). They therefore have "special needs," which must be met if they are to achieve their potential for health (UNFPA 2000). Both men and women may also be at risk from sex specific diseases such as cancers of the prostate and cervix.

Alongside these widely recognized biological differences, there are also more subtle genetic, hormonal, metabolic, and other variations between women and men. More research is needed into these, but it is clear that they are involved in shaping sex differences in the causes, the incidence, and the prognosis of a number of health problems (Wizemann and Pardue 2001). These include HIV/AIDS, tropical infectious diseases, tuberculosis, and coronary heart disease (Garenne and Lafon 1998; Hudelson 1996; Sen et al. 2002; Vlassoff and Bonilla 1994). Men are more susceptible than women to developing heart disease early in life, for example, and this is an important factor in explaining their lower life expectancy.

Complex biological variations in patterns of risk and susceptibility therefore play an important part in any explanation of sex differences in mortality and morbidity. But these biological influences can tell only part of the story. Socially constructed inequalities or gender differences between males and females are also important in determining whether individuals are able to realize their potential for a long and a healthy life. And it is generally males who have a significant advantage over females of the same social group as themselves in access to health-related resources.

The Hazards of Female Gender

In many societies, there is a sharp divide along a male/female axis. This means that those falling on opposite sides of the divide are seen as fundamentally different types of creature with different duties and responsibilities as well as different entitlements. Of course, in most societies there are not just differences but also inequalities inherent in the social definitions of femaleness and maleness. Those things defined as male are usually valued more highly than those things defined as female, and men and women are rewarded accordingly (Charles 1993; Papanek 1990). The precise detail of what comes to be defined as feminine or masculine will differ between communities, but gender remains a basic divide. Not surprisingly, the associated inequalities have significant effects on the health of both men and women, though so far it is only their impact on women that has been explored in any detail.

In recent years women and their advocates have built up a large body of work demonstrating the intimate interrelationship between gender inequalities and both mental and physical health (Annandale and Hunt 2000; Doyal 1995; Stein 1997; WHO 1998). These studies have looked not just at life expectancy but also at more qualitative dimensions of well-being. They have shown that many of the health problems faced by women are reflections of the discrimination and disadvantage so many continue to experience as they carry out the gendered activities that make up their daily lives (Sen et al. 2002). Anxiety and depression, for instance, are more common among females than among males in most parts of the world (Desjarlais et al. 1995). Yet there is no evidence that women are constitutionally more susceptible to these problems than men (Busfield 1996).

Gender inequalities in income and wealth make women especially vulnerable to poverty. Though levels of discrimination vary significantly between societies, millions do not have sufficient means to acquire the basic necessities for a healthy life (UNDP 1995). Poverty can affect both males and females, but women and girls often suffer additional disadvantage as a result of discrimination (Jackson 1998). Lack of adequate nourishment and unequal access to healthcare mean that sometimes their most basic needs are not met (Tinker et al. 1994). The gender division of work means that women are often denied the opportunity to meet other basic needs such as time for rest and recuperation.

Within the household, women often have little support and too many end up being abused by others (Doyal 1995: ch. 2; Heise et al. 1995; WHO 1999). As a result, their need for physical and psychological security may also be denied. The process of "growing up female" influences the type of identity girls are able to develop. Being raised as members of the gender that society has identified as less valuable can make it difficult for women to develop the positive sense of themselves that is usually associated with good mental health (Papanek 1990). In many societies this means that female identities are shaped in ways that encourage them to put the well-being of others before their own (Kandiyoti 1998).

As well as affecting their health, gender inequalities may also limit women's access to healthcare. Around the world, many millions of women continue to be denied access to basic healthcare as a result of poverty and discrimination (Alan Guttmacher Institute 1999; UNFPA 2000). Even when these financial obstacles are alleviated, there is still evidence that women are treated by some doctors as less valuable than men. This can lead to demeaning attitudes as well as the unequal allocation of clinical resources (Sen et al. 2002). This gender bias is especially evident in the context of medical research, where studies have shown that women have traditionally been excluded from many studies for what are now seen as inappropriate reasons (Mastroianni et al. 1994).

We can see that gender inequalities in access to a wide range of resources have a significant impact on the health of women. Though they have a longer average life expectancy than men, women do not necessarily lead healthier lives. And most importantly, a considerable amount of the illness they experience can be traced back in one way or another to the gendered nature of their daily lives and should therefore be preventable through public policy.

Male Gender: A Mixed Blessing?

Thus far, relatively little attention has been paid to the impact of gender on the lives of men. This has now begun to change with the development of the sociology of masculinities, Men's Studies and associated men's movements (Connell 1995; Mac an Ghaill 1996). A major focus of many of those working in these new paradigms has been the exploration of male (homo)sexualities and their implications for health promotion in the context of the HIV/AIDS epidemic (Kimmel and Levine 1993). Other aspects of men's health have received less attention, but important links are now beginning to emerge between gender, heterosexuality, and well-being (Huggins and Lamb 1998; Sabo and Gordon 1993).

It is evident that in some societies the stereotyped role of provider increases the risk of men dying prematurely from occupational accidents. Just as women face hazards in carrying out their domestic tasks, so many men may also be at risk from doing the duties that are socially expected of them (Waldron 1985). However, the other risks associated with maleness are of a rather different order from those linked to femaleness. Gender inequalities themselves rarely deprive men of the resources to meet their needs. If anything, they operate in the other direction. However, it does appear that constructing and maintaining a hetero-sexual male identity often requires the taking of risks that can be seriously hazardous to health.

431

Many men feel compelled to engage in risky behavior in order to "prove" their masculinity and to "do" gender in the socially approved way (Kimmel and Messner 1993). Their behavior has been shaped by what Connell calls the "hegemonic" version of masculinity, and as a result men are more likely than women to be murdered, to die in a car accident or in dangerous sporting activities (Canaan 1996; Connell 1995; Schofield et al. 2000). In most societies they are also more likely than women to drink to excess and to smoke, which in turn increases their biological predisposition to early heart disease and other health problems (Waldron 1995). They also seem to be more likely than women to desire unsafe sex (Zeidenstein and Moore 1996).

The significance of a male identity in the arena of mental health has also received attention, especially from participants in the new men's movements. It has been argued that growing up as male renders many men unable to realize what might be their emotional potential. The desire to be seen as a "hard" man, for instance, may prevent them from exploring the "caring" side of their nature. The dilemmas inherent in developing a masculine identity have also been blamed for the increased rates of suicide among young males in many parts of the world (Charlton et al. 1993).

The implications of male gender for health have been highlighted by debates about mortality and morbidity in Central and Eastern Europe (Chenet 2000). In many countries, the health of both men and women has been deteriorating since the 1960s and this trend has accelerated over the past decade. However, the impact has been much greater on men and there is now a 14-year gap in life expectancy between the two groups (ibid.). Some of this difference can be explained by gender differences in accidents and in smoking and alcohol consumption (Leon et al. 1997; Peto et al. 1992). However, more qualitative variations in the lives of men and women have also been implicated (Bobak et al. 1998; Chenet 2000; Watson 1995, 1998).

Both men and women have been affected by the disruption of civil society, which can result in feelings of hopelessness and lack of control (Bobak et al. 1998). The collapse of state socialism highlighted the importance of the family as a locus for "getting by." In this context, women's social support networks and their capacity to generate survival strategies have come to the fore. This has meant that unmarried men may be materially and socially disadvantaged by lack of a family and this is reflected in their higher mortality rates. At the same time, economic decline has led to higher rates of unemployment, especially among men. This has generated feelings of helplessness and frustration, which have been linked both directly and indirectly to the greater decline in male health (ibid.; Watson 1995).

Men too, experience gender-related problems in using healthcare. Given the fact that men earn on average more than women, the practical and financial obstacles that limit many women's access to services are less likely to affect men in similar socio-economic circumstances. However, a reluctance to admit weakness may prevent them taking health-promotion messages seriously and from consulting a doctor when problems arise (Scofield et al. 2000). Indeed, illness itself may be especially feared because of its capacity to reduce men to what one study has called "marginalized masculinity" (Cameron and Bernardes 1998). Thus many men have to grapple not with external obstacles, but with gendered internal constraints in order to get the health services they need.

Sex, Gender, and Diversity in Health

We have now explored the biological and the social commonalities that identify men and women as separate groups. But of course this does not imply homogeneity within each group. Socio-economic, cultural, and age differences among women and among men also need careful exploration in order to assess their interaction with sex and gender in the shaping of human health (Krieger 2003).

Despite the fact that they share the same biology, it is clear that women's reproductive health status is profoundly affected by who they are and where they live. The technical means to ensure safe contraception, abortion, and childbearing do exist, but they are not equally available to all. Half a million women still die each year as a result of pregnancy, and virtually all of these avoidable deaths occur in poor countries where there is insufficient access to trained health workers (UNFPA 2000; WHO 1995). It is therefore impossible to understand the impact of sex on health without also taking factors such as class, race, and geopolitical status into account.

Shifting to the gender differences between men and women, again we have to take seriously the issue of diversity. The reality of "maleness" and "femaleness" varies significantly between cultures and communities. Hence the impact of gender on well-being will vary too. The implications on health for a woman will be very different depending on whether the "femaleness" in question is mediated through poverty or wealth, through an urban cosmopolitan existence or life in a traditional village. To be a single female lawyer in an affluent London suburb may well be considerably healthier than being a working–class mother of two in a run-down tower block in the same city. However, both will face many fewer social and economic constraints on their health than a landless woman with seven children in a village in Bangladesh.

Age too is crucial. It is increasingly clear that the health needs of men and women and the resources available to meet these needs vary significantly across the life cycle. But again, these differences are complex. On the one hand, the special needs of women for reproductive care are at their most acute during the childbearing years, when they are most dependent on men. In mid–life, levels of need may be reduced, only to rise again in old age. Yet in many societies older women lose what little status they had with the disappearance of childbearing potential and the sexual allure of youth (Owen 1996). This mix of social and biological influences has profound effects on the nature of gender relations at different ages, and these need to be included in any model for understanding the health status of males and females.

433

Conclusion

It is clear from this analysis that the relationships between sex, gender, and health raise important issues for a wider debate in the arena of Gender Studies. One of the most important lessons to be learned is that we ignore biological issues at our peril. Recent developments in sociological theory have been extremely valuable in drawing attention to the social construction of much that had previously been taken as "natural." However, there is a danger that our understanding of the material dimension of human life will be undermined by the spread of radically deconstructionist approaches. Detailed analysis of the differences in the health of women and men illustrate very clearly the need to retain the biological dimension in any explanatory framework.

The analysis has also shown the importance of a social model for explaining patterns of morbidity and mortality. The health of individuals will be shaped not only by their biological constitution, but also by the circumstances of their daily lives. These in turn are shaped by a range of social and economic factors that include not only gender but also other variables such as race and class. The patterns of causality are complex and not easy to disentangle, but greater clarity is essential if these insights are to be transferred into the policy arena in pursuit of greater equity in health and healthcare (Doyal 2000).

One of the main challenges is to bring the perspectives from different disciplines together. Cross-boundary work of this kind is never easy, but important insights are emerging into how it can best be done. In the context of HIV/AIDS, for instance, many biomedical scientists have come to recognize the importance of social and cultural factors in explaining the epidemic. At the same time, an increasing number of social scientists have begun to explore the nature of "material embodiment" and its differential implications for the health of women and men (Davis 1997; Scott and Morgan 1993; Shilling 1993). Further work of this kind can provide the knowledge base for promoting the health of both sexes, while also making an important contribution to the further development of Gender Studies.

References

Alan Guttmacher Institute (1999) *Sharing Responsibility: Women, Society and Abortion Worldwide* (New York: The Alan Guttmacher Institute).

Annandale, E. and Hunt, K. (2000) *Gender Inequalities in Health* (Buckingham: Open University Press).

Boback, M., Pikhart, H., Hertzman, C., Rose, R., and Marmot, M. (1998) "Socio-Economic Factors, Perceived Control and Self-Reported Health in Russia. A Cross Sectional Survey," *Social Science and Medicine* 47/2: 269–79.

Busfield, J. (1996) *Men, Women and Madness: Understanding Gender and Mental Disorder* (London: Macmillan).

Cameron, C. and Bernardes, D. (1998) "Gender and Disadvantage in Health: Men's Health for a Change," *Sociology of Health and Illness* 18/3: 673–93.

Canaan, J. (1996) "One Thing Leads to Another: Drinking, Fighting and Working Class Masculinities," in M. Mac an Ghaill (ed.), *Understanding Masculinities* (Buckingham: Open University Press).

Charles, N. (1993) *Gender Divisions and Social Change* (Hemel Hempstead: Harvester Wheatsheaf).

Charlton, J. et al. (1993) "Suicide Trends in England and Wales: Trends in Factors Associated With Suicide Deaths," *Population Trends* 71 (spring).

Chenet, L. (2000) "Gender and Socio-Economic Inequalities in Health," in E. Annandale and K. Hunt (eds.), *Gender Inequalities in Health* (Buckingham: Open University Press).

Connell, R. (1995) *Masculinities* (Cambridge: Polity).

Davis, K. (1997) *Embodied Practices* (London: Sage).

Desjarlais, R., Eisenberg, L., Good, B., and Kleinman, A. (1995) *World Mental Health: Problems and Priorities in Low Income Countries* (Oxford: Oxford University Press).

Doyal, L. (1995) *What Makes Women Sick, Gender and the Political Economy of Health* (London: Macmillan).

Doyal, L. (2000) "Gender Equity in Health: Debates and Dilemmas," *Social Science and Medicine* 51: 931–9.

Garenne, M. and Lafon, M. (1998) "Sexist Diseases," *Perspectives in Biology and Medicine* 42/2: 773–87.

Heise, L., Moore, K., and Toubia, N. (1995) *Sexual Coercion and Reproductive Health: A Focus on Research* (New York: Population Control Council).

Hudelson, P. (1996) "Gender Differentials in Tuberculosis: The Role of Socioeconomic Factors," *Tubercle and Lung Disease* 77: 391–400.

Huggins, A. and Lamb, B. (1998) *Social Perspectives on Men's Health in Australia* (Melbourne: Maclennan and Petty).

Jackson, C. (1998) "Rescuing Gender from the Poverty Trap," in C. Jackson and R. Pearson, *Feminist Visions of Development* (London: Routledge).

Kandiyoti, D. (1998) "Bargaining with patriarchy," *Gender and Society* 2/3: 274–90.

Kimmel, M. and Levine, M. (1993) "Men and AIDS," in M. Kimmel and M. Messner (eds.), *Men's Lives* (New York: Macmillan).

Kimmel, M. and Messner, M. (eds.) (1993) *Men's Lives* (New York: Macmillan).

Krieger, N. (2003) "Genders, Sexes and Health: What Are the Connections – and Why Does It Matter?" *International Journal of Epidemiology* 32: 652–7.

Leon, D., Chenet, L., Shkolnikov, V., Zakharov, S., Shapiro, S., Rakhmanova, G., Vassin, S., and McKee, M. (1997) "Huge Variations in Russian Mortality Rates 1984–94: Artifact, Alcohol or What?" *Lancet* 350: 383–8.

Mac an Ghaill, M. (ed.) (1996) *Understanding Masculinities* (Buckingham: Open University Press).

Mastroianni, A., Faden, R., and Federman, D. (eds.) (1994) *Women and Health Research: Ethical and Legal Issues of Including Women in Clinical Studies*, vols. 1 and 2 (Washington, DC: National Academic Press).

Owen, M. (1996) *A World of Widows* (London: Zed Books).

Papanek, H. (1990) "To Each Less Than She Needs, From Each More Than She Can Do: Allocations, Entitlements and Value," in I. Tinker (ed.), *Persistent Inequalities: Women and World Development* (Oxford: Oxford University Press).

Peto, R., Lopez, A., Boreham, J., Thun, M., and Heath, C. (1992) "Mortality From Tobacco in Developed Countries: Indirect Estimation for National Vital Statistics," *Lancet* 339: 1268–78.

Sabo, D. and Gordon, G. (1993) *Men's Health and Illness: Gender, Power and the Body* (London: Sage Publications).

Schofield, T., Connell, R., Walker, L., Wood, J., and Butland, D. (2000) "Understanding Men's Health and Illness: A Gender Relations Approach to Policy, Research and Practice," *Journal of American College Health* 48 (May): 247–58.

Scott, S. and Morgan, D. (eds.) (1993) *Body Matters. Essays on the Sociology of the Body* (London: Falmer Press).

Sen, G. and Snow, R. (1994) *Power and Decision: The Social Control of Reproduction* (Boston: Harvard University Press).

Sen, G., George, A., and Ostlin, P. (2002) *Engendering International Health: The Challenge of Equity* (Cambridge, MA: Harvard University Press).

Shilling, C. (1993) *The Body and Social Theory* (London: Sage).

Stein, J. (1997) *Empowerment and Women's Health: Theory, Methods and Practice* (London: Zed Books).

Tinker, A., Daly, P., Green, C., Saxeman, H., Lakshminarayan, R., and Gill, K. (1994) *Women's Health and Nutrition: Making a Difference* (Washington, DC: World Bank).

UNDP (1995) *Human Development Report 1995* (New York: United Nations Development Programme).

UNFPA (2000) *The State of the World Population 2000: Lives Together, World Apart* (United Nations Population Fund).

Vlassoff, C. and Bonilla, E. (1994) "Gender Related Differences in the Impact of Tropical Diseases on Women: What Do We Know?" *Journal of Biosocial Science* 26: 37–53.

Waldron, I. (1995) "Contributions of Changing Gender Differentials in Behaviour to Changing Gender Differences in Mortality," in D. Sabo and G. Gordon (eds.), *Men's Health and Illness: Gender, Power and the Body* (London: Sage Publications).

Watson, P. (1995) "Explaining Rising Mortality Among Men in Eastern Europe," *Social Science and Medicine* 41/7: 923–4.

Watson, P. (1997) "Health Differences in Eastern Europe: Preliminary Findings from the Nowa Huta Study," *Social Science and Medicine* 46/4–5: 549–58.

WHO (1995) "Global Estimates of Maternal Mortality for 1995; Results of an In-Depth Review, Analysis and Estimation Strategy" (Geneva: World Health Organization).

WHO (1998) *Gender and Health: A Technical Document* (Geneva: World Health Organization).

WHO (1999) *Annotated Bibliography on Violence Against Women: A Health and Human Rights Concern* (Geneva: World Health Organization).

Wizemann, S. and Pardue, M.-L. (2001) *Exploring the Biological Contribution to Human Health: Does Sex Matter?* (Washington DC: National Academy Press).

Zeidenstein, S. and Moore, K. (1996) *Learning About Sexuality: A Practical Beginning* (Washington, DC: World Bank).

CHAPTER THIRTY-TWO

Sport

Martha Saavedra

An introductory course on gender so often begins with this distinction: sex is about the physical differences between female and male, while gender is about the social constructions involved in being female and male. Of course, this distinction has been challenged, stretched, and examined in a myriad of ways (e.g. Hoodwilliams 1995; Oyewumi 1997). Whether the distinction holds, it does suggest an underlying question: what is the relationship of the corporeal body to social practice? In the practice of sport, the body is central. The physical manipulation of one's body to achieve an end is, of course, mapped with multiple political, economic, social, cultural, psychological, and spiritual forces. Yet the body remains pivotal to the practice. Hence, within sport, the varied social practices that rest on beliefs and assumptions about physical possibilities, including those of sexual difference, are magnified. One historically specific expression of this naturalizes sport as masculine and a code for heterosexual male superiority and domination over the feminine, which in turn is distinctly unathletic. Under such an ideology, female athletes, gay or straight, put their "femininity" at risk, threaten the social order, and invite disapproval and hostility because they "act" male. In spite of this, many feminists view (and female athletes have certainly experienced) sport as an embodied practice which can liberate girls and women from a constraining hegemonic feminine ideal. Gay male athletes also disrupt this social order that equates "masculine" physicality with heterosexuality. In a milieu where sport occupies an important social role and the normative for sport is heterosexual and male, an athlete who deviates poses a critical challenge.

Since the 1980s, scholars have mined this nexus of ideas, constructs, and phenomena to examine how gender and sex operate in sport. Closely linked with this scholarly interest has been the increased participation of and activism around women and girls in organized sport, with gay and lesbian athletes and pro-feminist men also asserting their space. In this chapter, I will identify major trends, questions, and new directions in the literature on gender and sport. To narrow the focus, some major approaches, such as media studies and psychological studies, will not be addressed here. Two particular interests inform my review: exploring how the physicality of sport conjoins with Western constructions of masculinity, femininity, and sexuality, and broadening the scope of inquiry to non-Western and postcolonial settings. The latter will highlight variations in practice that will help to tease out the complexities of the former, challenge the construct of "sport-as-masculine hegemony," and reveal global and transnational forces that interact with sporting practice throughout the world.

Overview of the Field

With contributions from many scholarly disciplines, the study of gender and sport has been marked by a progression of methods and theories. Early efforts documented previously disregarded histories and analyzed exclusion and inequity from a liberal feminist perspective. The field of psychology contributed assessments of attitudes, personality traits and motivations, and studies of sex role socialization and role conflict studies. Marxism and its variations weighed in with analyses of structure and material circumstances. Finally, postmodern cultural studies, with influence from cultural Marxism and hegemony theory, have conceptualized the interplay between sport and gender as diffuse and complex, dependent on unequal power relations marked by domination, compliance, subversion, and resistance (Cole 1994; Hargreaves 1994; Rail and Harvey 1995; Theberge and Birrell 1994; Wigmore 1996). The initial impetus, to study and claim a space for "women and sport," opened the way for re-evaluations of broader cultural meanings of sport, including its "relevance as a site for the critical analysis of masculinity" (Andrews and Cole 1999: 322). Sport emerges as a primary site for the reproduction of gender relations and hegemonic sexualities as well as a contended space of contradictions and struggles contained in multiple experiences and representations of embodied experiences that are marked by sexuality, class, race, ethnicity, (dis)ability, age, nationality, and postcolonial position.

For the larger field of Gender Studies, a focus on sport pushes the issue of the body, physicality, and embodied power to the front, where the meaning of physical sexual difference, in biological "fact," in cultural belief, or in social practice, can be scrutinized. As will be explored later, the study of gender and sport through analysis of the public and physical performance of sexuality makes an important contribution to understanding the construction, maintenance, and subversions of hegemonic sexualities and their contradictions. It examines the social production and public consumption of the ways in which individuals occupy and manipulate space and how that translates into a particular gendered system.

In Cultural Studies, an emerging area is the study of popular culture in which sports are central and have deep local, cultural meanings, yet are still vitally intertwined with state-building, nationalism, globalization, and transnational movements. For instance, analyses of the spread of Western sports, especially football, have shown how sport has been a complex and often contradictory nexus for local popular expression, government control, and international influence (Alegi 2000; Arbena 1996; Archetti 1996; Darby 2001; Finn and Giulianotti 2000). When these studies address gender questions, they do so mostly by exploring masculinity (Mangan 1996, 2000; Nauright 1997). The very nature of this approach depends on a comparative perspective and, as will be explored later, more work needs to be done to investigate the interaction of sport and gender around the world.

Popular culture, itself, is rapidly adding to the discourse. A growing number of popularly targeted fictional and personal accounts, biographies, magazines, newsletters, movies, documentaries, CD-ROMS, and glossy coffee-table pictorials specifically deal with women and sport. Indeed, despite "conflicting attitudes toward physical power and feminine aesthetics" (anon. 1998a), the corporate publishing world has discovered women and sport as a market (anon. 1998b; anon. 1999). Not blind to the issues at stake, publishers have explicitly cashed in on the public struggle over gender and sexuality, as Davis reveals in her study of *Sports Illustrated*'s annual swimsuit issue (Davis 1997; Young 1998). And, as Davis's book also shows, this corporate fascination with women's sport becomes fodder for Cultural Studies scholars.

Claiming Sport for Girls and Women: Recovering History, Confronting Hegemony

The ancient and pre-modern Western world

One of the first impulses in the study of gender and sport was to document women's involvement in sport and to recover forgotten and obscured pasts. Earlier work tended to come from a liberal feminist perspective in which history was presented as the "gradual, progressive unfolding of increased opportunities for participation" (Parratt 1994: 11). Historical analyses have now moved to a more critical stance, raising conceptual and methodological issues such as the inappropriateness of standard periodization (e.g., sport history begins with the Greeks) and certain concepts (e.g., sport is by definition competitive) (ibid.: 6–7). They also embrace the importance of theory, especially feminist theory, to understand "how sport has been implicated in the social construction and maintenance of gender relations" (ibid.: 11). Descriptive work, however, was and remains important in documenting women's and girls' involvement in and struggles around sport, providing the data to challenge the hegemonic mid-twentieth-century Western view of sport as a male preserve. Two examples of these trends are the historical analyses of the ancient Mediterranean world and physical education in twentieth-century North America.

Modern sport has been defined as a non-utilitarian physical contest where there is competition against nature, self, or others (Guttmann 1978). Many of the elements that make sport "modern" are exactly those with which feminist scholars have grappled: secularization, role specialization, rationality (rules), bureaucratization (hierarchy), and quantification. Tracing the development of modern organized sport has been a major occupation of historians. Scholars (and promoters) have spent much energy looking for historical precedents of particular games and sporting ideologies in the ancient Western civilization. For instance, while the modern Olympic games emerged squarely from late nineteenth-century social and political conditions, they were inspired by understandings of ancient Greek competitions that lauded male power and agency and obscured the involvement of women. Hence, feminist sport historians have re-examined data for evidence of women's participation.

Interestingly enough, for early Western civilizations (e.g., Egypt, Greece – with Sparta standing out as unique – Crete, and Rome) the verdict on female participation is unclear. Yes, evidence can be found which indicates that some women did engage in leisure and religious activities that were physical and even competitive in nature, including running, swimming, and boating. Furthermore, they were likely more active than previous sport historians have acknowledged. Greek culture, according to the bulk of evidence, discouraged female athleticism; Euripides derided as "abominable" the racing and wrestling of Spartan girls. Still, quadrennial competitive athletic festivals honoring the goddess Hera attracted girls and young women from throughout the Greek world to run in foot races. The games were held at Olympia a month before the men's games, from which women were excluded even as spectators (Guttmann 1991: 20–7; Kennard and Carter 1994: 20–2). Written descriptions of the Heraia games, bronzes of Spartan girls running, and Cretan frescoes of girls bull-leaping inspire advocates of sporting women. But how widely, how often, and under what conditions girls and women participated remains largely a matter of speculation. Conclusions are often arrived at by analogy to anthropological data from the non-Western world, a methodology that is open to much criticism (Guttmann 1991).

Historians have followed gender and the development of and struggles over sport from the medieval period through the industrialization and colonial era, although most work concerns the late nineteenth and twentieth centuries (Cahn 1994; Eisen 1991; Guttmann 1991; Hall 1999; Hargreaves 1993, 1994; McCrone 1988, 1991; Mangan and Park 1987; Riordan 1991; Struna 1991). Yet, as Guttmann points out in his 1991 bibliographical note: "the history of women's sports is a badly underdeveloped field" (1991: 317). There is work, though, that does not directly examine women's sport, but does address gender issues.

Explorations of sport in relation to the state and nation, on one hand, and to Christianity, on the other, are two interesting lines of inquiry in sport history in Europe and North America that have gender implications. In the first case, the question revolves around how and with what consequence states have used sport and physical education in nation-building and domination. States that saw value in sport and physical culture developed educational and political strategies that sought "to discipline and correct individual behaviour; and to mobilize, bring together and shape . . . the masses" (Faure 1996: 77). At the beginning of the nineteenth century in Prussia, for instance, Frederick Ludwig Jahn developed *Turnkunst*, a form of gymnastics that employed paramilitary methods and nationalistic rhetoric, connecting physical fitness with national welfare. Eventually this became an important part of the education in nineteenth-century German states, and in the twentieth century it was absorbed into the Nazi system, albeit in a different form (Guttmann 1991: 183–4; Vertinsky 1994: 68). The French, in turn, adopted gymnastics to prepare the masses to be soldiers for a nation seeking revenge (Faure 1996: 78–9). As will be addressed later, recruiting methods of the British state encouraged the use of competitive games in British public schools to develop public servants, particularly for the Empire. Most often, the explicit target of these various strategies were men, with particular visions of masculinity endorsed (Holt 1991; Krüger 1991; Mangan 1996, 1999, 2000).

The work on Christianity and sport also addresses gender mainly by exploring masculinity. Several recent works explore the muscular Christianity movement of the nineteenth and early twentieth centuries that represented a distancing from an ascetic, anti-physical, spiritual (or even "feminine") norm to one which embraced physicality, robustness, and "manliness" as a sign of devotion (Hall 1994; Ladd and Mathisen 1999; Putney 2001). A current evangelical men's movement (e.g. the Promise Keepers in the United States) also draws on the image and practice of sport for proselytizing and promoting an idealized patriarchal gender order where men are clearly at the head of their households (Claussen 1999, 2000; Mathisen 1990; Mazer 1994; Williams 2001). Undoubtedly part of the backlash against feminism, this movement's lasting impact remains to be seen.

Physical education and gender in twentieth-century North America

A major issue in Western twentieth-century women's sport has been asserting the right and capacity of women to even engage in sport – i.e., claiming space for girls and women and, in turn, challenging the assumption that sport is a masculine (and heterosexual) endeavor. Much of the history of women's sport in the West has concerned the struggle to gain access to resources, facilities, organizational support, and acceptance. One of the strategic challenges has been whether to seek access to inherently masculinist extent structures, to establish separate feminine/feminist spaces, or to seek and demand the transformation of the dominant mode of sport experienced by all. This dilemma is not at all specific to women and sport, but is shared by other movements such as the civil rights movements and the larger feminist struggle. When those engaging in sport do not fit or philosophically reject the hegemonic ideal (in this case, masculine), is it better, and even natural, to develop a separate space allowing for difference and practices free from the demands of the dominant practice? Does the segregated space constitute resistance? Or does it avoid direct challenge, and thereby rein-force hegemonic practice? Can it get far enough away from the dominant culture norms to establish a real alternative? The struggle over female physical education and athletic competition in the twentieth-century United States exemplifies this core conundrum in the practice of sport.

Early in the twentieth century in the US, women physical education profes-sionals in mostly white middle-class and elite institutions developed a philosophy and program for women's sport that sought a separate sphere and asserted values distinct from those in the male sporting world. They balanced Victorian notions of the body (sturdiness of body contributes to strength of character), fem-ininity (the cult of domesticity), and emerging medical views (limited exercise improved women's health and reproductive capacity; excessive exercise damaged it). Their program would "balance the rigors of intellectual life with healthful and *appropriate* sporting activities" (Hult 1994: 85). In this, they deemed it vital to avoid the commercialism, corruption, aggression, competitiveness, and elitism of male sport. Furthermore, they asserted that their non-elitist, minimally competitive, sports-for-all approach was more inclusive and democratic. Creat-ing their own form of appropriate feminine physicality also became a way to distinguish what they promoted from "mannish," or later "lesbian," athleticism. The philosophy, its application, and the organizations promoting it evolved considerably over the next 70 years, e.g. allowing for more sports, more exer-tion, and more competition. These early physical educators and their feminist inheritors in organizations such as the National Association for Girls' and Women's Sports (NAGWS) and the Association for Intercollegiate Athletics for Women (AIAW) continued to organize, advocate, and struggle for an alternative vision to the male sporting world. Their legacy was very much behind the drive to pass Title IX in 1972, federal legislation which prohibited sex discrimination in educational programs or activities (Cahn 1994; Festle 1996; Griffin 1998; Guttmann 1991; Hult 1994).

The approach of the physical educators was grounded squarely in a white, upper-middle-class milieu. Alternative venues for women's sport reveal some of its shortcomings, and how race and class intersect with gender. For instance, industrial and commercial leagues embraced high-level competition, and many working-class women, who generally did not have access to higher education, took part. While some elite African American schools and colleges adopted the physical educators' philosophy that maintained an appropriate "feminine" decorum and avoided the lesbian label through asserting a separate space and alternative values (e.g., anti-competitive, non-elitist, sports-for-all), most did not. Schools, colleges, churches, and others organized competitive sporting opportunities for black women, particularly in basketball and athletics (track and field). In both of these venues, other femininities – more exuberant, physical, and erotic, albeit still very heterosexual – were expressed.

While the working-class and African American institutions did not engage in debate or struggle with the white women physical educators, male-dominated organizations such as the Amateur Athletic Union, and later the National Collegiate Athletic Administration, did, especially in the realm of intercollegiate and elite sports. By the time the effects of Title IX gained momentum, the AIAW had lost the battle, folding in 1982. Other women's sport organizations remain, but now operate in the realm of advocacy, not in the organization of sport for women. The vast majority of college, elite, and professional sports for women occur within frameworks organized and controlled by the same entities that control men's sports. Title IX did see the numbers of athletic opportunities and scholarships for girls and women increase. But the number of female coaches and athletic administrators declined as women's athletic programs were folded into men's programs and coaching females actually became lucrative. Simultaneous with increased access and opportunity for female athletes in the US has been the loss of control by women's athletic organizations and women coaches and administrators (Cahn 1994; Festle 1996; Himes Gissendanner 1994).

The female physical educators may have been visionaries in their attempt to provide an alternative to the crassness and corruption of male sport. Yet theirs could also be understood as a white, middle-class project that excluded working-class, minority, and rural poor women. Alternatively, it could have been a strategy to claim turf from competing organizations or an ill-conceived tactic to "protect" women which, in fact, only set them back. Another interpretation is that it was a heterosexist and homophobic effort to make female athletes conform to prevailing hegemonic notions of femininity. Examining the specific and subtle ways the physicality of sport conjoins with constructions of sexuality will help in appreciating the dilemmas confronted.

Analyzing the Hegemonic Gender Order: Sex, Sexuality, and Physicality

Of all the gender issues raised when addressing the topic of women in sport, none gets so quickly to the heart of the matter as does that of lesbians and sport. Likewise, discussing gay male athletes leads directly to a core issue of sport – hegemonic masculinity. As Pronger states, gays and lesbians live "on the paradoxical edge of orthodox culture" (1990: 216). Homosexuality undermines the myth of gender, and the Western hegemonic practice of modern sport has much invested in the myth of gender. Yet, the very practice of sport, whether by men and, especially, by women, constantly pulls apart this myth.

Modern sport in the West has developed as a key site for the reproduction of a particular, albeit shifting, gender order. As emphasized earlier, the basic hegemonic ideology is that athletic endeavors are defined as male. Over time, exceptions have been allowed, but only if they do not threaten the underlying gender order in which men are considered superior and in control where women play a subordinate and supporting role. Key in this ideology is compulsory heterosexuality. Those with power rely on this particular conjunction of roles, but, as with other hegemonic social orders, this one is "leaky" (Cole 1994). Deviance, resistance, and subversion abound. Without reifying it too much, the hegemonic order "responds" in ways to try to control, disempower, and contain these "leaks." Thus, the relationship between sport and homosexuality is one of intimacy, struggle, and paradox. To understand this one must understand how sport in the West serves to support and reproduce a hegemonic heterosexual masculinity that intersects with other very powerful interests in society.

In the emerging twentieth-century Western gender order, sport took on several functions: teaching masculinity skills to boys, providing a safe environment for male bonding and intimacy, reinforcing male privilege and female inferiority, establishing status among other males, and reinforcing heterosexuality (Griffin 1998; Lenskyj 1990; McKay et al. 2000; Messner 1992; Messner and Sabo 1990, 1994; Nelson 1994). Sport, particularly team sports, provides a socializing system for males into the public world of power, whether that be political, economic, or social. Sport prepares "boys" to be "men" in a corporate capitalist world. Sport itself became constituted in the corporate, capitalist, Western-centric system as:

> a discursive construct that organizes multiple practices (science, medicine, technology, governing institutions, and the media) that intersect with and produce multiple bodies (raced, sexed, classed, heterosexualized, reproductive, prosthetic, cyborg, etc.) embedded in normalizing technologies (classification, hierarchization, identity production) and consumer culture. (Cole 1994: 6)

The masculinity produced by sport serves to uphold this construct.

A twist remains, however: "At the centre of a world that is supposed to symbolize and celebrate masculinity, and which in fact is supposed to endow men with a powerful sense of heterosexual masculinity, is a fascinating homosexual paradox" (Pronger 1999: 182). As Pronger argues, sport is an expression of macho heterosexual identity with an important, yet denied, homoerotic dimension. The allure of masculinity keeps men hooked, yet fear and hostility emerge when the desire for masculinity becomes explicit. The homoerotic theme is powerful and at least intuitively shared widely, but it is denied because it is immensely threatening and subversive. Hence, to conceal and disempower this homoerotic element, a hyper-heterosexual masculinity emerges in men's sport affecting athletes, spectators, and promoters. At its extreme, this masculinity is marked by violence, particularly against women and queers. A discourse of race and class may be invoked to distance the core from phenomena such as football hooliganism and violent male athletes. Yet at a minimum, there remains a hostile environment for anyone transgressing the "safe" boundaries; a stingy toleration may only be forthcoming if an athlete's skills, such as the rebounding of Dennis Rodman, are lucrative enough for the corporate interests.

Women's involvement in sport questions this version of masculinity and the power that emanates from it. Hence, as a control mechanism, female athletes' femininity is questioned. As the "order" has moved over the last 100 years to accept strong women, ambivalence remains. Embracing "celebrity feminism" (Cole 2000: 5; Cole and Hribar 1995), Nike may name its largest building after Mia Hamm – the power forward on the 1999 world champion US women's national soccer team, and considered by many to be the best all-round player in the world – but physically powerful and competent women are still suspect. Starting in the 1960s, the International Olympic Committee and many international sporting federations required official "sex-testing" of women athletes, lest a man be tempted to pose as a female athlete in order to win. The IOC only dropped this after much protest and discrediting from the scientific community in 1999. Yet, it still reserves the right to "investigate" as needed.

If a strong woman is not a man, then she might be a lesbian. In this hegemonic ideology, lesbians represent a conscious rejection of the superiority and privilege of men, and thus constitute a threat. As recounted earlier, avoiding the lesbian label and providing heterosexual credentials was central to the experience of the early US female physical educators. The lesbian label has served as a powerful means of social control to keep women athletes within the boundaries. Stigmatizing lesbian identity is a measure to control women, divide them, mute their power, and limit "access to the benefits of sport participation in the physical and psychological empowerment available in sport" (Griffin 1998: 20). The threat of the label affects all women, lesbian or not.

For female athletes, this has resulted in a push for a hyper-femininity matched with a new sporting persona. If one is going to be an athlete, then one must go to extra lengths to prove one's femininity and heterosexuality. The pressure is also to render lesbians invisible in women's sport, as speedy official denials of lesbianism on "our team" or in "our sport" indicate. For lesbian athletes, silence and fear are the outcome. Assessing the personal risk of being out, many choose to remain in the closet. Consequences of being out(ed) include ostracism, verbal and physical attacks, and loss of scholarships, jobs, recruits, and endorsements. The "chilly climate" remains despite the attraction that many lesbians and straight women have toward sport exactly because female participation transgresses rigid gender boundaries (Blinde and Taub 1992; Blum 1994; Griffin 1998; Palzkill 1990; Phillips 1996; Rogers 1994; Sykes 1996).

Yet, do the correlations of "sport-as-male" and "female-athlete-as-transgressor" always hold? Perhaps these "hegemonic" assumptions are very Western, even Anglo-Saxon. Fastings and Scraton (1997) found that the stereo-type connecting playing certain sports (e.g. physical team sports like soccer, rugby, and softball) with a (butch) lesbian identity was a concern among English female football players, but apparently *not* among Norwegian players (cited by Caudwell 1999: 395). Lopez (1997) also found that other European countries and federations were much more open to women's football than the English Football Association. As alluded to earlier, the mid-twentieth-century African American community received female athleticism much more positively than did the white middle-class community. If intra-Western comparisons begin to challenge the sport-as-male construct, a comparison with non-Western sport goes even further. In the next section, I will explore non-Western experiences, with examples from China and Senegal, and their contribution to understandings of the interrelations between gender and sport.

Gender Hegemony: Globalized or Challenged Beyond the West

The emergence of modern sport in the West coincided with European colonialism and imperialism. Western sporting practice and the concomitant ideologies on gender and bodies were not simply carried with European expansion as a side product (e.g., through the leisure practices of individuals), but were often central to the method of domination, particularly in the case of British imperialism. For example, because of its "character-building qualities," public school athletic achievement was an important factor in the recruitment of British colonial officers (Kirk-Greene 1987). In promoting organized sport in schools and communities, colonial officers and missionaries extended a vision of "muscular Christianity," which would help to civilize natives by building the moral character, work discipline, and sense of duty that they "so lacked" (Fair 1997; Mangan and Park 1987). It was also an attempt to shape and control local expressions of identity (Ranger 1987), including masculinity and femininity. For instance, from the 1920s to the 1950s in Zanzibar, colonial administrators and local elite promoted men's soccer as an alternative to *ngoma* dances, which they considered "vulgar and obscene," because in these dances men dressed like women (Fair 1997: 236–7).

While Western forms of sport were adopted, adapted, modified, ignored, and rejected by colonial subjects, an international mode of sport dominated by the West emerged. Even where local forms of sport have thrived, they may reflect Western influence, such as in Senegalese wrestling in which two top contenders in the late 1990s were known as Mike Tyson I and Mike Tyson II. The wrestlers not only adopted the name of the storied heavyweight American boxer; they also make explicit references to American culture, such as when Mike Tyson I, Mohamed Ndoa, wrapped himself in the American flag and chose to fight a big match on July 4 (Muhammad 1999; Reuters 1998; Saavedra 1999).

Discourse, practice, and policy affecting gender in these globalized sporting regimes also travel. Mandates by international sporting bodies, such as the IOC and FIFA, to regional and national federations to increase the number of women and girls represented in sport do have some effect, especially when they are backed by resources to accomplish this. Global corporate entities from leagues to sporting apparel companies to beverage conglomerates also make their presence known in supporting the development of athletes and facilities, and in the marketing and production of their products. Global commodity chains for sports apparel and equipment, in fact, explicitly and exploitatively link "third world" women with the "hegemonic sporting model" in the West (Lafrance

1998: 130–5). Still, the Western "model" is not simply replicated as received. Local responses to the external forces as well as indigenous practices that affect and change the "global" sporting practice create a local sporting experience that must be understood on its own terms, including the ways in which gender is constructed and performed.

Women's sporting experience in China provides a clear challenge to the way sport and gender are understood in the West, particularly in the United States. By the 1990s Chinese women were formidable contenders on the international sporting scene, winning championships and setting records in many sports. In fact, their presence was much more palpable than that of Chinese men. The doping scandals that seemed to explain much of their success, especially in Western discourse (Plymire 1999), obscure local and historical factors that propelled Chinese women to the top of the sporting world. As with many non-Western, postcolonial countries, sport serves as a way to achieve global recognition, status, and honor for the athlete's country, particularly when the value of a political system is opposed or at least posited as an alternative to Western, liberal capitalist democracies. In turn, successful athletes can become national heroes regardless of their sex (e.g., Fatouma Roba of Ethiopia, gold medallist in the 1996 Olympic women's marathon). In China, several factors merged to make it more likely that women as opposed to men would succeed internationally, such that official priority was given to elite women's sports. Hence, "training the body for China" (Brownell 1995) supersedes gender considerations.

Still other factors – including historical attitudes toward sport and women's physicality and the socio-economic status of sport, the influence of Confucian and socialist ideology about women – propelled Chinese female athletes forward. A long history of women's involvement in combative and other sports meant that sport was not understood to be a male preserve as in the West. With the development of the Imperial bureaucracy, elite education emphasized the mind over the body, and sport became an endeavor more suited to the lower classes and to women. Significant numbers of the current elite female athletes come from lower socio-economic and educational backgrounds. Furthermore, in Confucian ideology, being obedient, humble, compliant, and respectful are particularly important for women – thereby making women athletes much more malleable, or able to "eat bitterness," than men in the hands of strict coaches with arduous training regimens. Finally, socialist ideology under Mao extolled the hardworking peasant and women. Though uneven, advancement and oppor-tunities for both groups did grow. In the post-Cultural Revolution era, then, the stage was set for women to excel in internationally competitive sports (Brownell 1995; Dong and Mangan 1998; Plymire 1999; Riordan and Dong 1996).

Comparing the Chinese to the Western experience shows how particular social, cultural, political, and historical factors condition the relationship between gender and sport. Examining these factors also shows that gaining international success and official priority are not necessarily the marks of progress for women, for, in the case of China, it is exactly women's lower status that marked them for success in sport. Yet the situation remains dynamic, with international sporting contacts and individual rewards gained by women athletes becoming resources for them to negotiate their position in society.

The Senegalese case reflects the dynamic mix of local and external cultural, political, and economic influences on the participation of men and women in sport. These influences include a French colonial past, a structurally adjusted, globally linked postcolonial present, an active diaspora, ethnic diversity with Wolof domination at the center, competing Islamic discourses, powerful indigenous Islamic brotherhoods, an increasingly urban and youthful population, and a longstanding official support for the "emancipation" of women. The resulting overall cultural and institutional structures for sport still favor the participation of boys and men, yet the climate in Senegal does not forbid – and sometimes even encourages – athletic women. In Senegal, women's basketball is the third most popular spectator sport behind men's football and wrestling. While women pursuing teaching, refereeing, and administrative careers in sport have had to overcome negative attitudes and neglect, their way has not been officially blocked and is in fact legally upheld. Hence, qualified women can and have refereed men's football and wrestling matches, opportunities that are only beginning to open up for women in North America and Europe.

Concerns about sport masculinizing women and girls are common in Senegal, but they do not fully parallel the Western experience. A 1994 study in four Dakar schools found that secondary-school students ranked handball as the most feminine sport, followed by basketball, volleyball, and gymnastics. Interestingly enough in that study, judo, a combative sport, was ranked sixth, while wrestling, only traditionally practiced by Dioula women in the southern province of Casamance, ranked last at tenth. Football (soccer) ranked ninth (Manga 1994). Although there are several women's soccer teams and a concerted effort by some to promote women's football, many expressed in interviews that women's football suffered from an image of being "too physical and brutal," whereas basketball is considered "graceful" and "feminine." However, observers of women's basketball matches can attest to the hard physicality of the game and the players (Saavedra 1999).

In an environment where unemployment is high, opportunities are limited, and women have not been traditionally excluded from productive activities, sports that offer financial and social reward and potential overseas opportunities to women, such as basketball, have come to be defined as "feminine." A consideration of muscles, femininity, and sexuality in Senegal is not (yet) an issue about lesbianism, but, as in China, about economic and social status. Competing femininities reflect this: the rural, muscled, toiling, agrarian woman versus the more privileged, urban woman who did not need to labor physically. In the urban milieu exist two idealized femininities that are decidedly non-muscular: the *disquette* (young, slim, Western-oriented) and the *drianke* (large, soft, round, and economically established) (Biaya 2000; Saavedra 1999). With female basketball players serving as popular icons, athletically inspired girls and women have other models to draw on, but still they must navigate these other powerful images.

Conclusion

The promise of comparative work is great, but considerably more research and analysis must be done. I posit three points here that should be taken into account. First, the researcher, whether Western or not, must not assume a teleological paradigm in which the Western experience (as varied as it is) with its various indicators of participation, cultural representations, and institutional forms is the "end point." This applies whether one might view the "end point" as a desirable achievement or an inevitable state of being. It is true that global and transnational forces such as the IOC, international sporting federations, powerful leagues, and the generalized, hegemonic power of Western economic, political, and cultural forms are formidable. Yet, we already know that "local" histories and forces powerfully shape the "local" experience of sporting practice and the gendered aspects of that. The global forces themselves are not monolithic or unchanging and are influenced and acted on by the "local." My view is that homogenization is not to be expected. Furthermore, the variations and different trajectories found in other parts of the world will lead to a deeper, nuanced understanding of processes in the West.

Second, it is important to move the field of gender and sport beyond the Western world by recognizing the work of third world scholars and proceeding collaboratively. Already, significant local research has been and is being done. The library at the Institut National Supérieur de l'Education Populaire et du Sport (INSEPS) in Dakar is full of research on sport in Senegal and West Africa. The research covers a vast number of topics, methods, and perspectives and is produced by those taking various degrees in physical education. While gender analysis in the study of sport is not universal at INSEPS (and the study of women is not to be confused with the study of gender), I identified at least 11 studies done between 1984 and 1998 which specifically explored some aspects of women and sport. These range from general studies of women and sport in Guinea, Senegal, Togo (Béte née de Souza 1988; Faye 1986; Ka Diaw 1984; Tonguino née Sissoko 1996–8) to historical, motivational and physiology studies of women in particular sports, such as football, handball, judo, and wrestling (Manga 1994; Menqué 1998; Sarr 1990; Thiam 1996; Touré 1986) to an analysis of Islamic law and culture in reference to women in sport (Sissoko 1990). Many more such studies are likely on the shelves of sport and physical education training institutes around the world. Western scholars should seek out those that produced these studies, and work with these institutes to broaden understandings of gender and sport transnationally.

Finally, as the Chinese case shows, to caution that Western gendered notions in sport are not universal does not mean that non-Western sporting experiences

449

are to be idealized. Nor are advocates for, say, women's sport in the developing world to be embraced uncritically (Hargreaves 1999). Rather, the point is to expand the possibilities in practice and theory. Several questions can be posed in the comparative study of gender and sport. For instance, historically how has sport been valued in a particular society? How does gender affect access to and opportunities in sport? What have been the articulations of historically and contemporary visions of sport and gender with external and global manifestations? Who controls legal and administrative access? How does sport relate to other networks of power (political, economic, social, and cultural)? Does participation in sport provide access to these other networks? Does sport have autonomy? Is it dependent or co-opted, and in what ways? Notions of sexuality, economic opportunity, political power, symbolic representation, and resource availability all come into play. The power of sport as found in its organizations, facilities, and popularity must be explored. The role of the state in promoting sport for social, political, and developmental purposes must also be examined. The relationship between the state, organizing bodies, athletes, spectators, and supporters all must be taken into consideration. Truly, this will be an ongoing process of research, reflection, and practice, with considerable contributions to understandings of gender, sexuality, and physicality.

References

Alegi, P. (2000) "Keep Your Eye On The Ball: A Social History of Soccer in South Africa, 1910–1976." PhD, Boston University.

Andrews, D. L. and Cole, C. L. (1999) "Review of A. Baker and T. Boyd (eds.), *Out Of Bounds: Sports, Media and the Politics of Identity*, and T. Boyd, *Am I Black Enough For You? Popular Culture From the Hood And Beyond*," *Men and Masculinities* 1/3: 319–24.

anon. (1998) "Women Account for 73% of All Sports Apparel Spending," *About Women & Marketing* 11/11 (November 19).

anon. (1998) "Women's Sports Magazines Seeking Identity, Advertisers," *Media Report to Women* 26/1 (winter), p. 1.

anon. (1999) "The 68% solution: Women's sports publishing," *Publishers Weekly* (March 22), p. 56.

Arbena, J. (1996) "Nationalism and Sport in Latin America, 1850–1990: The Paradox of Promoting and Performing 'European' Sports," in J. A. Mangan (ed.), *Tribal Identities: Nationalism, Europe, Sport* (London; Portland, OR: Frank Cass).

Archetti, E. P. (1996) "In Search of National Identity: Argentinian Football and Europe," in J. A. Mangan (ed.), *Tribal Identities: Nationalism, Europe, Sport* (London; Portland, OR: Frank Cass).

Béte née de Souza, A. A. (1988) *Le Sport féminin au Togo*. Mémoire en vue de Certificat d'Aptitude aux Fonctions d'Inspecteur de la Jeunesse et des Sports à Titre Estrager Session 1986–1988, Institut National de la Jeunesse, Marly-le-Roi (France).

Biaya, T. K. (2000) "'Crushing the pistachio': Eroticism in Senegal and the Art of Ousmane Dago," *Public Culture* 12/3.

Blinde, E. M. and Taub, D. E. (1992) "Homophobia and Women's Sport – The Disempowerment of Athletes," *Sociological Focus* 25/2: 151–66.

Blum, D. E. (1994) "'Colleges Sports' L-word," *Chronicle of Higher Education* 40/27 (March 9): A35.

Brownell, S. (1995) *Training the Body for China: Sports in the Moral Order of the People's Republic* (Chicago: University of Chicago Press).

Cahn, S. K. (1994) *Coming on Strong: Gender and Sexuality in Twentieth-century Women's Sport* (New York: Free Press).

Caudwell, J. (1999) "Women's Football in the United Kingdom: Theorizing Gender and Unpacking the Butch Lesbian Image," *Journal of Sport and Social Issues* 23/4: 390–402.

Claussen, D. S. (1999) *Standing on the Promises: The Promise Keepers and the Revival of Manhood* (Cleveland, OH: Pilgrim Press).

Claussen, D. S. (2000) *The Promise Keepers: Essays on Masculinity and Christianity* (Jefferson, NC: McFarland).

Cole, C. L. (1994) "Resisting the Canon: Feminist Cultural Studies, Sport, and Technologies of the Body," in S. Birrell and C. L. Cole (eds.), *Women, Sport, and Culture* (Champaign, IL: Human Kinetics).

Cole, C. L. (2000) "The Year that Girls Ruled," *Journal of Sports and Social Issues* 24/1: 3–7.

Cole, C. L. and Hribar, A. (1995) "Celebrity Feminism – Nike Style Post-Fordism, Transcendence, and Consumer Power," *Sociology of Sport Journal* 12/4: 347–69.

Darby, P. (2001) *Africa, Football and FIFA: Politics, Colonialism and Resistance* (London: Frank Cass).

Davis, L. R. (1997) *The Swimsuit Issue and Sport: Hegemonic Masculinity in Sports Illustrated* (Albany: State University of New York Press).

Dong, J. and Mangan, J. A. (1998) "Gender Relations in Chinese Sports: Continuity and Change in Traditional Gender Culture," International Sociological Association (ISA).

Eisen, G. (1991) "Sport, Recreation and Gender: Jewish Immigrant Women in Turn-of-the-century America (1880–1920)," *Journal of Sport History* 18/1: 103–20.

Fair, L. (1997) "'Kickin' It: Leisure, Politics and Football in Colonial Zanzibar, 1900s–1950s," *Africa* 67/2: 224–51.

Fastings, K. and Scraton, S. (1997) "The Myth of the Masculinisation of the Female Athlete: The Experiences of European Sporting Women." Paper presented at the North American Society for the Sociology of Sport Conference, Toronto, Canada.

Faure, J.-M. (1996) "Forging a French Fighting Spirit: The Nation, Sport, Violence and War," in J. A. Mangan (ed.), *Tribal Identities: Nationalism, Europe, Sport* (London and Portland, OR: Frank Cass).

Faye, C. (1986) *Contribution de sport à l'évolution de la condition de la femme au Sénégal.* Mémoire de Maîtrise de Science et Technique de l'Activité Physique et du Sport (STAPS), Institut National Supérieur de l'Education Populaire et du Sport.

Festle, M. J. (1996) *Playing Nice: Politics and Apologies in Women's Sports* (New York: Columbia University Press).

Finn, G. P. T. and Giulianotti, R. (2000) *Football Culture: Local Contests, Global Visions* (London and Portland, OR: Frank Cass).

Griffin, P. (1998) *Strong Women, Deep Closets: Lesbians and Homophobia in Sport* (Champaign, IL: Human Kinetics).

Guttmann, A. (1978) *From Ritual to Record: The Nature of Modern Sports* (New York: Columbia University Press).

Guttmann, A. (1991) *Women's Sports: A History* (New York: Columbia University Press).

Hall, D. E. (1994) *Muscular Christianity: Embodying the Victorian Age* (Cambridge and New York: Cambridge University Press).

Hall, M. A. (1999) "Creators of the Lost and Perfect Game? Gender, History and Canadian Sport," in P. White and K. Young (eds.), *Sport and Gender in Canada* (Ontario: Oxford University Press).

Hargreaves, J. (1993) "The Victorian Cult of the Family and the Early Years of Female Sports," in E. G. Dunning, J. A. Maguire, and R. E. Pearton (eds.), *The Sports Process: A Comparative and Developmental Approach* (Champaign, IL: Human Kinetics).

Hargreaves, J. (1994) *Sporting Females: Critical Issues in the History and Sociology of Women's Sports* (London and New York: Routledge).

Hargreaves, J. (1999) "The 'Women's International Sports Movement': Local–Global Strategies and Empowerment," *Women's Studies International Forum* 22/5: 461–71.

Himes Gissendanner, C. (1994) "African-American Women and Competitive Sport, 1920–1960," in S. Birrell and C. L. Cole (eds.), *Women, Sport, and Culture* (Champaign, IL: Human Kinetics).

Holt, R. (1991) "Women, Men and Sport in France, c.1870–1914: An Introductory Survey," *Journal of Sport History* 18/1: 121–34.

Hoodwilliams, J. (1995) "Sexing the Athletes," *Sociology of Sport Journal* 12/3: 290–305.

Hult, J. S. (1994) "The Story of Women's Athletics: Manipulating a Dream 1890–1985," in D. M. Costa and S. R. Guthrie (eds.), *Women and Sport: Interdisciplinary Perspectives* (Champaign, IL: Human Kinetics).

Ka Diaw, M. (1984) *Activités physiques et sportives et femme sénégalaise*. Mémoire pour l'Obtention du Certificat d'Aptitude aux Fonctions d'Inspecteur Adjoint de l'Education Populaire de la Jeunesse et des Sports. Promotion 1982–1984, Centre National d'Education Populaire et Sportive (Theis).

Kennard, J. and Carter, J. M. (1994) "In the Beginning: The Ancient and Medieval Worlds," in D. M. Costa and S. R. Guthrie (eds.), *Women and Sport: Interdisciplinary Perspectives* (Champaign IL: Human Kinetics).

Kirk-Greene, A. (1987) "Imperial Administration and the Athletic Imperative: The Case of the District Officer in Africa," in W. J. Baker and J. A. Mangan (eds.), *Sport in Africa: Essays in Social History* (New York and London: Africana Publishing Company).

Krüger, A. (1991) "There Goes This Art of Manliness: Naturism and Racial Hygiene in Germany," *Journal of Sport History* 18/1: 135–58.

Ladd, T. and Mathisen, J. A. (1999) *Muscular Christianity: Evangelical Protestants and the Development of American Sport* (Grand Rapids, MI: Baker Books).

Lafrance, M. R. (1998) "Colonizing The Feminine: Nike's Intersections of Postfeminism and Hyperconsumption," in G. Rail (ed.), *Sport and Postmodern Times* (Albany: State University of New York Press).

Lenskyj, H. (1990) "Power and Play: Gender and Sexuality Issues in Sport and Physical Activity," *International Review for the Sociology of Sport* 25/3: 235–46.

Lopez, S. (1997) *Women on the Ball: A Guide to Women's Football* (London: Scarlet Press).

McCrone, K. E. (1988) *Playing the Game: Sport and Physical Education of English Women, 1870–1914* (Lexington: The University Press of Kentucky).

McCrone, K. E. (1991) "Class, Gender and English Women's Sport, c.1890–1914," *Journal of Sport History* 18/1: 159–82.

McKay, J., Messner, M. A., and Sabo, D. F. (2000) *Masculinities, Gender Relations, and Sport* (Thousand Oaks, CA: Sage Publications).

Manga, J.-J. (1994) *La Pratique féminine des sports de combat vue par les élèves de quartre lycées de Dakar: L'exemple du judo et de la lutte*. Mémoire de Maîtrise de Science et Technique de l'Activité Physique et du Sport (STAPS), Institut National Supérieur de l'Education Populaire et du Sport.

Mangan, J. A. (1996) "Duty Unto Death: English Masculinity and Militarism in the Age of the New Imperialism," in J. A. Mangan (ed.), *Tribal Identities: Nationalism, Europe, Sport* (London and Portland, OR: Frank Cass).

Mangan, J. A. (1999) *Sport in Europe: Politics, Class, Gender* (London: Frank Cass).

Mangan, J. A. (2000) *Making European Masculinities: Sport, Europe, Gender* (London and Portland, OR: Frank Cass).

Mangan, J. A. and Park, R. J. (eds.) (1987) *From "Fair Sex" to Feminism: Sport and the Socialization of Women in the Industrial and Post-Industrial Eras* (London: Frank Cass).

Mathisen, J. A. (1990) "Reviving 'Muscular Christianity': Gil Dodds and the Institutionalization of Sport Evangelism," *Sociological Focus* 23/3: 233–49.

Mazer, S. (1994) "The Power Team: Muscular Christianity and the Spectacle of Conversion," *TDR* (Cambridge, MA) 38/4 (winter), p. 162.

Menqué, N. (1998) *Les Motivations liées à la participation des femmes sénégalaises au sport*. Mémoire de Maîtrise de Science et Technique de l'Activité Physique et du Sport (STAPS), Institut National Supérieur de l'Education Populaire et du Sport.

Messner, M. A. (1992) *Power at Play: Sports and the Problem of Masculinity* (Boston: Beacon Press).

Messner, M. A. and Sabo, D. F. (eds.) (1990) *Sport, Men, and the Gender Order: Critical Feminist Perspectives* (Champaign, IL: Human Kinetics).

Messner, M. A. and Sabo, D. F. (1994) *Sex, Violence and Power in Sports: Rethinking Masculinity* (Freedom, CA: Crossing Press).

Muhammad, R. D. (1999) "Culture Clash – How American Culture is Seducing African Youth," *Final Call* (June 8), accessed via New California Media ONLINE (<http://www.ncmonline.com/in-depth/1999-06-11/clash.html>).

Nauright, J. (1997) "Masculinity, Muscular Islam and Popular Culture: 'Coloured' Rugby's Cultural Symbolism in Working-class Cape Town c.1930–70," *The International Journal of the History of Sport* 14/1: 184–90.

Nelson, M. B. (1994) *The Stronger Women Get, the More Men Love Football: Sexism and the American Culture of Sports* (New York: Harcourt Brace).

Oyewumi, O. (1997) *The Invention of Women: Making an African Sense of Western Gender Discourses* (Minneapolis: University of Minnesota Press).

Palzkill, B. (1990) "Between Gymshoes and High-Heels: The Development of a Lesbian Identity and Existence in Top-class Sport," *International Review for the Sociology of Sport* 25/3: 221–34.

Parratt, C. (1994) "From the History of Women in Sport to Women's Sport History: A Research Agenda," in D. M. Costa and S. R. Guthrie (eds.), *Women and Sport: Interdisciplinary Perspectives* (Champaign, IL: Human Kinetics).

Phillips, J. (1996) "Intolerable: Does the Ben Wright Saga Signal an End to the Fight Against Homophobia in Women's Sports, Or Just the Beginning?" *Women's Sports and Fitness* 18/5 (May–June), p. 23.

Plymire, D. C. (1999) "Too Much, Too Fast, Too Soon: Chinese Women Runners, Accusations of Steroid Use, and the Politics of American Track and Field," *Sociology of Sport Journal* 16/2: 155–73.

Pronger, B. (1990) *The Arena of Masculinity: Sports, Homosexuality and the Meaning of Sex* (New York: St. Martin's Press).

Pronger, B. (1999) "Fear and Trembling: Homophobia in Men's Sport," in P. White and K. Young (eds.), *Sport and Gender in Canada* (Ontario: Oxford University Press).

Putney, C. (2001) *Muscular Christianity: Manhood and Sports in Protestant America, 1880–1920* (Cambridge, MA: Harvard University Press).

Rail, G. and Harvey, J. (1995) "Body at Work – Michel Foucault and the Sociology of Sport," *Sociology of Sport Journal* 12/2: 164–79.

Ranger, T. (1987) "Pugilism and Pathology: African Boxing and the Black Urban Experience in Southern Rhodesia," in W. J. Baker and J. A. Mangan (eds.), *Sport in Africa: Essays in Social History* (New York and London: Africana Publishing Company).

Reuters (1998) "Wrestling: Tyson Namesake Wins Senegal's Fight of Century," *Nando Sports Server: The Sports Page* (April 12) (<http://archive.sportserver.com/newsroom/sports/oth/1998/oth/mor/feat/archive/041298/mor19847.html>).

Riordan, J. (1991) "The Rise, Fall and Rebirth of Sporting Women in Russia and the USSR," *Journal of Sport History* 18/1: 183–99.

Riordan, J. and Dong, J. X. (1996) "Chinese Women and Sport: Success, Sexuality and Suspicion," *China Quarterly* 145: 130–52.

Rogers, S. F. (1994) *Sportsdykes: Stories from on and off the Field* (New York: St. Martin's Press).

Saavedra, M. (1999) *Muscular Femininity: Women, Sports and Development in Dakar, Senegal* (Columbus, OH: African Studies Association Annual Meeting).

Sarr, I. L. (1990) *Importance de la cohésion sur la performance des équipes féminines de handball dans le championnat d'élite 1989–1990 au Senegal*. Mémoire de Maîtrise de Science et Technique de l'Activité Physique et du Sport (STAPS), Institut National Supérieur de l'Education Populaire et du Sport.

Sissoko, C. S. D. (1990) *La femme, les activités physiques et sportives et l'Islam*. Mémoire de Maîtrise de Science et Technique de l'Activité Physique et du Sport (STAPS), Institut National Supérieur de l'Education Populaire et du Sport.

Struna, N. (1991) "Gender and Sporting Practice in Early America, 1750–1810," *Journal of Sport History* 18/1: 10–30.

Sykes, H. (1996) "Constr(i)(u)cting Lesbian Identities in Physical Education: Feminist and Post-structural Approaches to Research Sexuality," *Quest* 43: 459–69.

Theberge, N. and Birrell, S. (1994) "The Sociological Study of Women and Sport," in D. M. Costa and S. R. Guthrie (eds.), *Women and Sport: Interdisciplinary Perspectives*. (Champaign, IL: Human Kinetics).

Thiam, A. B. (1996) *Evaluation de certaines qualités physiques chez les footballeuses sénégalaises*. Mémoire de Maîtrise de Science et Technique de l'Activité Physique et du Sport (STAPS), Institut National Supérieur de l'Education Populaire et du Sport.

Tonguino née Sissoko, F. (1996–98) *La Femme et le sport en République de Guinée (cas de la ville de Conakry)*. Monograph de Fin de Formation d'Inspecteur de l'Education Populaire de la Jeunesse et des Sports, Institut National Supérieur de l'Education Populaire et du Sport.

Touré, N. D. (1986) *Le Judo féminin au Senegal: Blocages et perspectives de développement*. Mémoire de Maîtrise de Science et Technique de l'Activité Physique et du Sport (STAPS), Institut National Supérieur de l'Education Populaire et du Sport.

Vertinsky, P. (1994) "Women, Sport, and Exercise in the 19th century," in D. M. Costa and S. R. Guthrie (eds.), *Women and Sport: Interdisciplinary Perspectives* (Champaign, IL: Human Kinetics).

Wigmore, S. (1996) "Gender and Sport: The Last 5 Years," *Sport Science Review* 5/2: 53–71.

Williams, R. H. (2001) *Promise Keepers and the New Masculinity: Private Lives and Public Morality* (Lanham, MD: Lexington Books; co-published with the Association for the Sociology of Religion).

Young, K. (1998) "The Swimsuit Issue and Sport: Hegemonic Masculinity in Sports Illustrated," *Gender & Society* 12/4 (August), p. 479.

PART EIGHT

Spatiality

CHAPTER THIRTY-THREE

Environment and Sustainable Development

Irene Dankelman

A Short History

Environment has become a major socio-political issue only during the past 40 years. Societal concern for the environment has developed not because people started to value it per se, but because of environmental problems, which were becoming increasingly visible. Until the 1960s the environment was the exclusive research subject of the natural sciences, while the social, political, and historical sciences primarily studied human relations. The environmental and social spheres of life seemed to be completely separated. Only a few attempted to bridge these spheres, for example, in studies on people's interaction with the physical environment by some anthropologists and production scientists (such as forestry and agricultural scientists).

Rachel Carson, a biologist from the US, had studied and published widely on ocean life. Her book *The Sea Around Us*, initially published in 1950, was an immense success. In 1958, prompted by a letter from a friend who told of her own bitter experience of a world made lifeless, Carson realized that she had to write her next book, *Silent Spring* (1962). It became the most controversial and instrumental publication in raising environmental awareness. Carson showed in appealing prose how pollution by pesticides and other toxins would endanger many non-target species, and finally (higher in the food chain) people themselves. Carson would shake and awaken the world, as Hynes (1989) mentioned in her biography of the scientist. Carson's work resulted in extensive environmental legislation and the establishment of environmental agencies in many countries, as well as bans on dangerous pesticides like DDT. She wrote as a woman inside the scientific field, and captured a fundamental struggle of women in science. She was underlining the need for an analysis of science and its technologies. She challenged the directions, priorities, and values of the science–industry–government complex: "Man's attitude toward nature is today critically important,

457

simply because of his new found power to destroy it. . . . We now wage war on other organisms, turning against them all the terrible armaments of modern chemistry, and we assume a right to push whole species on the brink of extinction" (1962).

A decade later, the English political scientist Barbara Ward warned that the two worlds of man – the biosphere of his inheritance and the technosphere of his creation – are out of balance and in deep conflict. But humankind inhabits only one earth (Ward and Dubos 1972). This work laid the foundation for the first United Nations Conference on the Human Environment, held at Stockholm in June 1972.

In that same year Donella Meadows was the principal author of the controversial book *The Limits to Growth*, or what was later called the report of the Club of Rome. With Dennis Meadows, Jørgen Randers, and Willem H. Behrens she formed a young team of scientists at the Massachusetts Institute of Technology (MIT). They spent two years programming a computer to act as a model of the entire world: "World 3." In scenario after scenario, World 3 collapsed at a certain point, due to accelerating population growth, resource use, and pollution (Meadows et al. 1972). Atkisson (1999) likened her prophetic work to that of Cassandra, the youngest daughter of the last King of Troy. Apollo gave her the gift of prophecy, but in such a way that nobody would believe her prophecies. Cassandra could see the dangers threatening others, but was unable to prevent them.

Although nature conservation organizations such as the IUCN (International Union for the Conservation of Nature) and WWF (World Wildlife Fund) had been in existence since 1948, environmental organizations working at local and national levels emerged largely in the 1970s, as concerns about the interconnections between the human environment, or sociosphere, and the natural world, the biosphere, became more central. The World Conservation Strategy underlined in 1980 that natural resources conservation was essential for the sustainable development of humankind (IUCN, UNEP, WWF 1980). The World Commission on Environment and Development – or Brundtland Commission, named after its chairperson Mrs. Gro Harlem Brundtland from Norway – elaborated the concept of sustainable development in its report, *Our Common Future*. It defined sustainable development as "development that meets the needs of present generations without compromising the possibilities of future generations to meet their needs" (WCED 1987). This paved the road for the United Nations Conference on Environment and Development (UNCED), held in Rio de Janeiro in 1992.

Gender-neutral?

At first sight, the relationship between society and the physical environment appears gender-neutral, affecting both men and women in a similar way. But a closer look reveals that it is not neutral at all: the socio-cultural construction of relationships between men and women means that the linkages between people and the environment work differently for them. The development of UNCED and its outcome, Agenda 21, illustrated this very clearly. Women from around the world were convinced that men should not set the agenda exclusively in this UN process that addressed the future of humankind, and that women's voices and concerns should also be included. Women entered the UNCED process with their own comprehensive and integrated vision, which emerged from the First Women's World Congress for a Healthy Planet, organized by the Women's Environment and Development Organization (WEDO) and attended by 1,500 women from 83 countries in 1991 (in Miami). That congress adopted its own platform – "Women's Action Agenda 21" – which presented a gender-conscious perspective on major global issues such as governance, economy, poverty, food security, environment, health, energy, and technology (WEDO 1991). In the women's tent, the "Planeta Femina" at the NGO Forum in 1992 in Rio de Janeiro, women from all corners of the world shared their views on these global development issues. The result at UNCED was an engendered Agenda 21, which included a separate chapter (24) entitled: "Global Action for Women towards Sustainable and Equitable Development." It acknowledged the need to integrate women and gender at all governmental levels and in all UN-related activities on sustainable development.

How did an engendered vision of environment and sustainable development come about? And why was it a logical step?

In 1980 the historian of science Carolyn Merchant published her germinal book *The Death of Nature: Women, Ecology and the Scientific Revolution*. The book reassesses the scientific revolution of the sixteenth and seventeenth centuries, during which Western culture took its present technologically oriented, growth-minded form. Merchant also explores the historical connections between women's issues and ecology. When the scientific revolution, with founders of modern science such as Francis Bacon, William Harvey, and René Descartes, took hold, the cosmos ceased to be viewed as an organism and instead became a machine that could be regulated and manipulated. This crucial shift toward the mechanistic world-view – or "the death of nature" – accelerated the exploitation of human and natural resources in the name of progress. As nature was reduced to a resource for economic production to be controlled and dissected through experiment, women were reduced to psychic and reproductive resources. The Scottish Protestant reformer John Knox, for example, advocated in his book *First Blast of the Trumpet* (1558) that women should be kept in their place in the natural order, which was passive, physically weaker, and that of an obedient servant. With Knox, many others espoused men's command over women (Merchant 1980).

Women and the Environment

Some organizations that focused on the day-to-day lives of women and men adopted a different premise, arguing that women had been rendered invisible in environmental concerns and debates. The Center for Science and Environment (CSE), based in New Delhi, argued:

> Probably no other group is more affected by environmental destruction than poor village women. Every dawn brings with it a long march in search of fuel, fodder and water. It does not matter if the women are old, young or pregnant: crucial household needs have to be met day after weary day. As ecological conditions worsen, the long march becomes even longer and more tiresome. Caught between poverty and environmental destruction, poor rural women in India could well be reaching the limits of physical endurance. (CSE 1985: 172)

In 1985, the second UN Decade for Women Conference was held in Nairobi. At the NGO Forum '85, the international organization Environment Liaison Center (now ELCI) organized a series of workshops on "women, environment, and development," which aimed at a better understanding of the relationships between women and the environment. In the workshops, more than 25 women leaders from all parts of the world – with a much larger audience of women and men – presented their local and regional case studies on women and the global environmental crisis, addressing and engendering subjects such as forests, energy, agriculture, and water management. Women bear the highest costs of the environmental crisis because of their role in providing water, food, and energy for their families. On the other hand, women also have the potential to contribute significantly to environmental crisis solutions precisely because of their management of those primary resources. The growth of women's power and the sustainability of development are ecologically tied. It is therefore imperative that women are enabled to participate at all levels of development planning throughout the industrialized and developing worlds, according to the ELC statement to the UN conference (ELC 1985).

One of the recommendations of these workshops was to make more visible the practical relationships between women and the environment. An information-gathering project launched on the basis of this recommendation resulted in *Women and Environment in the Third World: Alliance for the Future*, by Irene Dankelman and Joan Davidson (1988). The authors argue that recent developments had worsened the position of women worldwide: Western colonization, increasing dependency of Southern countries on the Western monetary economy, technological changes, including agricultural modernization, and the sharpening global division of labour: "The accelerating degradation of the living environment is the latest and, in many ways, the most dangerous of the threats they face" (ibid.: 6). Based upon a wide range of case studies, the book describes the different roles of women in managing land, water, and forests – as fuel, food, production sites, fodder, energy, and human settlements. Food gathering was primarily a female responsibility. Feminist writers such as Boserup (1989) argue that it was actually "woman-the-gatherer" (and not "man-the-hunter") who was a source of a sustainable food supply. Women, who dealt daily with vegetable foods and wild seeds and experimented with planting, have played a major role in the revolutionary transition from gathering to agricultural food production. Environmental changes crucially affect women's lives, adding to their work load and worsening their health and social position.

Dankelman and Davidson also describe women's roles in environmental conservation and sustainable development, which include conservation work, training in family planning, and organizing at local, national, and international levels. This is not a new phenomenon – in the eighteenth century some women under the leadership of Amrita Sen waged an environmental struggle for survival in Gujarat (India). In Cape Verde, which was struck by severe droughts in the late 1970s, women started growing half a million seedlings per year. And the women's organization Açao Democrática Feminina Gaúcha, which originally focused on social and educational issues, has prioritized environmental issues on its agenda since 1974, so much so that it renamed itself Friends of the Earth Brazil (ibid.).

In her article on ecological transitions and the changing context of women's work in tribal India, Geeta Menon (1991) describes work as the active, labor-based interaction of human beings with the material world. Historically, this interaction has been intricately based upon the natural environment in which human populations survived. Menon distinguishes major areas of human work: food procurement, the protection of life, property, and territory, and childbearing and rearing, including maintenance of basic health standards. Many traditional economies were based on a division of labor along gender lines. This means that in women's work lies the direct connection to the environment.

Gender and Environment

Since the late 1980s we have witnessed the publication of a myriad of studies describing women's roles in specific environmental sectors and in particular regional contexts, along with studies featuring a more global perspective. The first publications focused on women as a singular social group and their relationship with the environment. However, several writers have critiqued this notion of women as a monolithic group, arguing that there are vast economic, cultural, and social differences among women. Distinguishing factors include class and caste, race, kinship, age, and national origin. Even within the same village, women of different classes and castes may have very different positions and roles. The same is true for women living in a rural or an urban setting. The position of a tribal woman can be completely different from that of her female neighbors from a settler's family. These differences are as crucial as those between women and men (Kelkar and Nathan 1991).

The insight grew that it is not enough to look at the position of women and the environment in isolation. Power relations between and among both sexes are determining factors, so a shift towards "gender" took place, which considered the interdependent nature of women's and men's positions in society (Barrig and Wehkamp 1994). The current gender and development approach is not only concerned with women, but also with the social constitution of gender and the assignment of specific roles, responsibilities, and expectations to women and men.

Access to and effective control over natural resources, such as land, water, and forests, are important indicators of gender positions. The use and management of these resources is also gender differentiated. Other critical factors include access to income and credit, appropriate technology, training and education, housing, and freedom of organization. These factors have diverse implications among genders, and play a role at micro-, meso-, and macro-levels of society.

Clearly, the quality or quantity of environmental resources directly affect the work and energy of the resource managers (often women), thereby limiting their other development options. Improving women's positions thus requires not only a redistribution of roles, tasks, and control over resources, but also a healthier and more productive environment.

Ecofeminism

The term "ecofeminism" was probably first used in 1974 by the French feminist Françoise d'Eaubonne. Ecofeminists like Carolyn Merchant argue that women are closer to nature than men, while men are closer to the dominant culture. They see a connection between the domination of nature and the domination of women. Indian physicist Vandana Shiva argues (1988) that paternalistic, colonial, and neocolonial forces and values have marginalized women and their scientific knowledge. Based on experiences in Northern India, she claims that women's knowledge and experiences are superior in promoting egalitarian societies in harmony with nature, and notes that women often lead popular movements. Shiva contends that male-dominated "mal-development" has caused major social and environmental problems. Seager (1993) argues that a feminist analysis of environmental problems must be rooted in an analysis of the social, cultural, and political institutions that are responsible for environmental distress. She underlines that the institutional culture that is responsible for most of the environmental calamities in the last century is a masculinist culture: "Environmental problems are quintessentially social problems, whose roots lie deep in a long-standing matrix of cultural proclivities" (ibid.). In *Eco-feminism*, co-authored with Shiva, German sociologist Maria Mies emphasized that ideas about a different science and society should be based on different ethical and methodological principles, in which subject-subject reciprocity is central: "We should never lose sight of the fact that we ourselves are part of Nature, that we have a body, that we are dependent on Mother Earth, that we are born by women, and that we die" (1993: 52). Mies and Shiva stress that science and technology, economy, trade, and politicians must finally prove themselves responsible to society at large.

Beyond Ecofeminism

Critics of ecofeminism, such as Agarwal (1998) and Braidotti et al. (1994), underscore that ecofeminists have focused on ideological arguments and failed to address power and economic differences as important sources of dominance. Ecofeminists, the critique holds, did not differentiate women by class, ethnicity, and caste, or recognize that concepts of nature, culture, and gender vary across cultures. They have not really addressed the material relationship that women may have with nature, and present a utopian notion of harmonious, ecological, traditional societies.

Agarwal (1998) suggested the alternative concept of "feminist environmentalism." This concept insists that the link between women and the environment should be seen as "structured by a given gender and class/caste/race organization of production, reproduction and distribution." She speaks of class-gender effects of environmental change, and underlines the need to transform the actual division of work and access to resources. The class-gender effects of environmental change are manifested as pressures on women's time, their income, their nutrition and health, their social support networks, and their knowledge. Agarwal's approach is similar to what Rocheleau (1995) has called "feminist political ecology," and both emphasize material relations and their structuring by gender relationships. These are particularly expressed in dynamic and cumulative gendered knowledge of environment, sciences, and technologies. Moreover several studies underline the need for a rights-based approach in gender, environment, and sustainable development (NEDA 1997).

In Practice

Organizations working on environment and development have produced materials and guidelines for dealing with the gendered aspects of their work. For example, the Dutch Ministry for Development Cooperation published two working papers in 1997: "Gender and Environment; a delicate balance between profit and loss" and "Rights of Women to the Natural Resources Land and Water." Based upon policy and project practice, both offer an analysis of the issues at stake and some practical guidelines. One of the conclusions notes: "The definition of gender relationships and anticipation of the opportunities and problems relating to them are prerequisites of the more sustainable use and management of natural resources and of improvements in the position of women."

Other organizations, such as the United Nations Center for Human Settlements and the United Nations Environment Program (2000), have developed practical guidelines on integrating gender responsiveness in environmental planning and management, advocating for the balanced allocation, management, and utilization of available resources, promoting women's access to equal opportunities, and reorganization of the gendered division of labor and decision-making processes. Thais Corral developed a set of practical guidelines for integrating gender in Local Agenda 21 processes (WEDO 2001).

Neefjes (2000) distinguished several critical issues with implications for praxis: the gendered division of labor and responsibility; gendered property rights; gendered positioning in households, communities, and other institutions; the influence on gender relationships and gender–environment relations of the wider political economy; and ecological characteristics that determine the processes of gender and environmental change. Education and training on these issues is crucial as well, and in this regard Martin (1994) developed a teaching program on environmental literacy and gender, in which she explores the metaphor of interdependence. Guijt's (1996) training video and manual on gender and class-specific participatory processes for rural appraisal also centers gender in practical projects. Lorena Aguilar and colleagues have developed a whole series of publications that enable the integration of gender aspects in environmental conservation activities (see <www.generoambiente.org>).

Forward Looking

In this chapter I have shown that recognition of the link between gender and environment has developed only recently, and has different roots: the environmental and the feminist movements. Three major perspectives can be distinguished: first, the study of women and gender relations with the environment being observed as sociological subject of study; second, the expression of women's and feminist visions of the contexts in which they live, including feminist critiques of dominant development, science, and technology; and, third, a combination of both, in which particularly local women are encouraged to express their own vision of development. While it has various roots, the theme of gender, environment, and development (GED) is an important basis for coalitions, as it can build bridges between different movements and schools and develop into the focal point of a major countervailing force (see also Braidotti et al. 1994).

Although securing the rights of women of all classes to a sustainable livelihood is an important step, articulating critiques of development and creating alternative visions, theories and methods are principal concerns for women and all those engaged in GED. These are primary prerequisites for building a more sustainable and just society.

Women do not want to be mainstreamed into the polluted stream. They want to clean the stream and transform it into a fresh and flowing body: "one that moves in a new direction – a world at peace, that respects rights for all, renders economic justice and provides a sound and healthy environment" (Bella Abzug, former US congress woman and founder of WEDO).

References

Agarwal, B. (1998) "The Gender and Environment Debate," in Roger Keil (ed.), *Political Ecology: Global and Local* (London and New York: Routledge).

Atkisson, A. (1999) *Believing Cassandra: An Optimist Looks at a Pessimist's World* (White River Junction: Chelsea Green Publishing Company).

Barrig, M. and Wehkamp, A. (eds.) (1994) *Engendering Development: Experiences in Gender and Development Planning* (The Hague: Novib).

Boserup, E. (1989) *Women's Role in Economic Development* (London: Earthscan).

Braidotti, R., Charkiewics, E., Haüsler, S., and Wieringa, S. (1994) *Women, the Environment and Sustainable Development: Towards a Theoretical Synthesis* (London: Zed Books).

Carson, R. (1950) *The Sea Around Us* (Geneva: Western Publishing/Hachette International).

Carson, R. (1960) *Silent Spring* (Greenwich, CT: Fawcett Publications).

CSE (1985) *The State of India's Environment 1984–1985: The Second Citizens' Report* (New Delhi: Center for Science and Environment).

Dankelman, I. and Davidson, J. (1988) *Women and Environment in the Third World: Alliance for the Future* (London: Earthscan).

ELC (1985) *Women and the Environmental Crisis: A Report of the Proceedings of the Workshops on Women, Environment and Development*, July 10 to 20 (Nairobi, Kenya: Environment Liaison Center).

Guijt, I. (1996) *Questions of Difference: PRA, Gender and Environment* (training video; London: IIED).

Hynes, H. P. (1989) *The Recurring Silent Spring* (New York: Pergamon Press).

IUCN, UNEP, WWF (1980) *World Conservation Strategy. Living Resources Conservation for Sustainable Development* (Washington, DC: IUCN).

Kelkar, K. and Nathan, D. (1991) *Gender and Tribe: Women, Land and Forests in Jharkhand* (New Delhi: Kali for Women).

Martin, J. (1994) "Interbeing and the 'I' Habit: An Experiment in Environmental Literacy," in Wendy Harcourt (ed.), *Feminist Perspectives on Sustainable Development* (London: Zed Books).

Meadows, D. et al. (1972) *The Limits to Growth: A Report for the Club of Rome Project on the Predicament of Mankind* (New York: Universe Books).

Menon, G. (1991) "Ecological Transitions and the Changing Context of Women's Work in Tribal India," *Purusartham*: 291–314.

Merchant, C. (1980) *The Death of Nature: Women, Ecology and the Scientific Revolution* (London: Wildwood House).

Mies, M. and Shiva, V. (1993) *Ecofeminism* (London: Zed Books).

NEDA (1997) *Gender and Environment: A Delicate Balance Between Profit and Loss*. Working Paper Women and Development no. 1 (The Hague: Ministry of Foreign Affairs).

Neefjes, K. (2000) *Environments and Livelihoods: Strategies for Sustainability* (Oxford: Oxfam).

Rocheleau, D. (1995) "Gender and Biodiversity: A Feminist Political Ecology Perspective," in Susan Joekes et al. (eds.), *Gender Relations and Environmental Change*, IDS Bulletin 26/1 (Brighton: Institute for Development Studies).

Seager, J. (1993) *Earth Follies: Feminism, Politics and the Environment* (London: Earthscan Publications).

Shiva, V. (1988) *Staying Alive: Women, Ecology and Development* (London: Zed Books).

Ward, B. and Dubos, R. (1972) *Only One Earth: The Care and Maintenance of a Small Planet* (Harmondsworth: Penguin Books).

WCED (1987) *Our Common Future*. World Commission on Environment and Development (Oxford: Oxford University Press).

WEDO (1991) *Women's Action Agenda 21* (New York: Women's Environment and Development Organization).

WEDO (2001) *Engendering Local Agenda 21: Primer* (New York: Women's Environment and Development Organization).

Further reading

Hombergh, H. van den (1993) *Gender, Environment and Development: A Guide to the Literature* (Utrecht: International Books).

NEDA (1997) *Rights of Women to the Natural Resources Land and Water*. Working Paper Women and Development no. 2 (The Hague: Ministry of Foreign Affairs).

UNCHS/UNEP (2000) *Integrating Gender Responsiveness in Environmental Planning and Management*. The EPM Source Book Series (Nairobi: UNCHS/UNEP).

UNIFEM (1992) *Agenda 21: An Easy Reference to the Specific Recommendations on Women* (New York: UNIFEM).

CHAPTER THIRTY-FOUR

Space and Cultural Meanings

Tovi Fenster

One afternoon, my kids were bored and being naughty, as there is no playground in the neighborhood; so I thought why not take them to the park that we have at the entrance to the town. You know, it is so beautiful, full of grass and flowers . . . very pleasant. After all, why do we need this if we can't use it? So I went for the first time with my kids and after maybe ten or fifteen minutes my husband came hurrying to take me back to the neighborhood. He was angry, and told me "Don't you know it is forbidden?" Apparently his brother drove along the road and saw me, and went straight to my husband to tell him. (April 21, 1995)

This is the story of Azziza Ibrahim,[1] a Bedouin woman living in Rahat, a Bedouin town located in Southern Israel. Azziza is married with four children; she is university-educated and works in a white-collar profession. But in the culturally constructed gendered role division, she is the one in charge of the productive and domestic roles in the household. Her husband is in charge of her dignity, among his other duties. Her story is the story of millions of women and men around the world who are caught up in cultural norms and values that construct space in terms of symbolic values so that the notions of forbidden and permitted spaces are established.

There are several ways to interpret Azziza's story. One way is by critically emphasizing how gender and culturally "neutral-blinded" assumptions made by the planners of the town about the use of this park result in having a park that is not used, mainly because its location near the main entrance to the town increases the risk of unwanted encounters between Bedouin women and men. This is just one side of a whole situation of the "shrinking of women's permitted spaces" in Bedouin modernized towns, which ends their spatial mobility in their own neighborhood. It is the result of modernist urban planning, which assumes space to be "absolute" and "neutral" and thus plans Bedouin towns accordingly (creating central service locations such as parks and shopping centers).

Another way of analyzing this narrative is by exploring and highlighting Azziza's resistance to the spatial restrictions she faces. By taking her children to the park, a well-known forbidden place, she protests against intertwined discrimination, both as a member of Bedouin society and as a woman. As a member of Bedouin society and a citizen of Israel, she objects to the ethnic discrimination implied in the lack of appropriate services in her neighborhood, which is part of what the Bedouin citizens of Israel are exposed to. As a woman in a Bedouin community she also defies the patriarchal appropriation of public space and its articulation as forbidden by women and men in her community.

Azziza's story helps us to highlight several themes in relation to gender and space. First, space is not a neutral entity; rather, it is culturally constructed, creating symbolic meanings with regard to gender relations, roles, and values. Secondly, gender relations and their expressions in space are linked to notions of power relations and citizen identity both between communities and the state and between men and women in specific communities. Thirdly, the notions of gender and space are highly connected to human rights issues. The rationale behind this connection is that space is more than relevant in understanding individual human rights violations, especially those that contain gender dimensions. Some of the most brutal cases of human rights abuse are connected to the lack of freedom of movement in space caused by imprisonment at home or imposed rules which are the result of cultural meanings of space as forbidden and permitted. These violations are individual, but they derive from cultural norms and restrictions that are constructed by cultural communities ruled by patriarchal ways of thinking.

Let us elaborate on these three themes.

Gender, Space, and its Symbolism

Massey argues: "We need to conceptualize space as constructed out of inter-relations as the simultaneous coexistence of social interrelations and interactions at all spatial scales, from the most local level to the most global" (1994: 264). The ways spaces are culturally and symbolically constructed reflect the legitimacy and power taken to exclude men and women from access to resources. Such aspects of symbolism of space are usually formulated by the patriarchy. The most common are the private/public devices, which for many women in different cultural contexts mean permitted/forbidden spaces. Sometimes this means that women in the cities are unable to wander around the streets and parks on their own (ibid.) and, in some cultures, are unable to wander around at all. For Bedouin and Ethiopian women in Israel, the cultural codes and sense of ethnicity influence perceptions and meanings of space in ways that prohibit or accept their use of public space. There are also some spaces in Israeli cities, such as the Mea Shearim ultra-orthodox neighborhood in Jerusalem, that are restricted only to women who are modestly dressed.

In the case of Bedouin women, it means that all spaces outside their home are forbidden. Symbolic spaces are mostly relevant to women, as they play a major role in the construction and defense of cultural and ethnic collectivities. They often symbolize a particular national collectivity, its roots and spirit (Yuval Davis 1995). Therefore, their spatial mobility is very much dictated, if not controlled, by these cultural symbolic meanings of space. In this way, cultural and ethnic norms create "spaces of modesty and immodesty" which then become forbidden and permitted spaces for Bedouin women in Israel or "spaces of purity and impurity" for Ethiopian women (Fenster 1998). "The cultural guards" of society – i.e., men – usually dictate the boundaries of these spaces (Fenster 1999a). Thus, the "home" is usually considered as "private" – the women's space, the space of stability, reliability, and authenticity – the nostalgia for something lost which is female. "Home is where the heart is and where the woman (mother, lover) is also" (Massey 1994). Outside home is considered as "public" – sometimes forbidden or restricted for women. The boundaries between the two are connected in certain cultures to notions of the body and clothing.

The roles of body modesty and clothing are a major element in articulating "forbidden" and "permitted" space. One example is the description of modest clothing which appears in big street signs at the entrances to the ultra-orthodox neighborhoods in Jerusalem. These signs mention very specifically what kinds of clothes are considered modest or immodest (for example, long-sleeved shirt, long skirts, head cover, etc.). Women are asked not to cross and use the public streets in these neighborhoods if they are not dressed accordingly. Another striking story that emphasizes the role of the body and clothing in marking the boundaries between the forbidden and the permitted relates to Arab women married to Bedouin men in the Negev. Those women are now living in a traditional context and wear traditional Bedouin clothes.[2] Before marriage, they lived in modern Arab cities and were dressed in modern Western style. On monthly visits to their parents (who still live in Arab cities) they wear traditional Bedouin clothing when leaving the Bedouin town but, as they leave the "forbidden" spaces, they ask their husband to stop the car so that they can change from traditional to modern dress. They note that the boundaries between the forbidden and the permitted are usually a bit further away from the town, where they can reappear as "modern" women. Interestingly enough, Muslim Bedouin women's experiences in the Negev are quite similar to the experience of young Muslim women living in London, who "are defined as caught between two cultures of home and school, torn by a culture clash between the secular/modern world of the school and the 'traditional/fundamentalist' world of the home" (Knott and Khokher 1993, cited in Dwyer 1998). The latter represents the same dilemma with a much stronger cultural clash regarding the expressions of their bodies as "contested sites of cultural representation," which results in a process of negotiation around different styles of dress in different spaces.

As already emphasized, the cases of bodily norms and clothing are not exclusive to women in Muslim cultures: the notion of clothing as a mechanism of control is known also to young people in other "controlled" areas, such as shopping malls. Young people in the Wood Green Mall in London, UK have expressed anxieties about being chased by the security people just because of the clothes they wear (Jackson 1998). Thus, clothing is a mechanism by which personal and social identities are expressed, but it is also contested by cultural norms mostly related to specific spaces. Let us now discuss norms of the body and clothing in their theoretical context.

Gender, Citizen, Ethnic Identities, and their Spatial Expressions

Gender, ethnic, and citizen identities are highly important in understanding how the tension between equal rights (citizen identity) and respect for difference (ethnic identity) is playing out in the lives of both men and women in different cultural contexts. It is necessary at the outset to clarify the meanings of the concepts "gendered ethnic identity" and "gendered citizen identity" and their spatial relevance.

Much has been written about ethnicity and ethnic identities.[3] In the context of this chapter, ethnic identity is about the distinctive values and norms that distinguish a community from other communities. Ethnicity is often recognized in distinctive components such as language, religion, customs, festivals, ceremonies, clothes, food, and so on, formed and preserved by a particular group of people. What is important in this context is to highlight the gendered dimension of ethnicity. Ethnic identities are intrinsically gendered, and are often highly differentiated between women and men. In many cultural contexts women play distinctive and major roles in the construction and defense of ethnic collective identities. For example, the spirit and the roots of an ethnic group are frequently symbolized in feminine terms (Yuval Davis 1995, 1997). These include women's and men's clothing which are made by women, ethnic food which is usually the domain of women, ethnic and national symbols which are connected to the "mother land," "mother tongue," etc. Ethnically specific constructions and understandings of spaces are also often differentiated in gendered terms. One effect of this is that women's mobility may be circumscribed by cultural constructions of space. Consequently, they are, in a sense, sometimes imprisoned by the symbolism that defines their ethnicity, as seen in Azziza's case.

Whereas ethnicity emphasizes differences between groups, the concept of citizenship draws attention to principles of sameness, such as equal rights and equal treatment for all.[4] What characterizes women's as opposed to men's citizenship in many societies is that women are still dependent in certain areas on traditional/religious rules, such as those of marriage and divorce, which have a more negative effect on women than on men. Thus women more than men face a situation where, in the first instance, they are included in the general body of citizenship legislation and in the laws and policies of the state which defend individuals' rights, but at the same time they are still subject to a special body of religious legislation. This is sometimes framed in protective terms but it generally expresses and contributes to women's subordinate position, especially with regard to principles of marriage and divorce. This is commonly the case in Israel for Jewish, Muslim, or Christian women, and will remain so for as long as there is a separation between civil and religious legislation in the country.

The geographical and environmental context of this complicated situation is perhaps expressed in the notion of "spaces of citizenship" (Painter and Philo 1995) and the distinctions usually made in the literature between the "public" and the "private" sphere. The latter plays an integral part in framing the limits of state intervention in the lives of individuals. Thus, the home is becoming a different space of citizenship from the public space. This distinction is deeply gendered so that, according to Lister (1995), we cannot understand gendered patterns of entry into the public sphere, where the formal rights of citizenship are exercised, without taking into account sexual divisions within the private sphere. But the distinction is also culturally variable, and is therefore a key point of intersection between gender, ethnicity, and citizenship (Yuval-Davis 1991). In a multicultural concept of citizenship, a right to equality is combined with respect for ethnic difference (Fenster 1996, 1998), including issues of gendered inequality in access to natural resources such as land, water, and minerals, and access to public facilities such as welfare services, education, and employment.

Gender, Space, and Human Rights Discourse

So far, we have discussed the gendered dimensions of citizenship rights, which are usually constructed within the formal frameworks of state apparatus. Another body of "rights" concerns the basic human rights of individuals, and encompasses a much larger frame of reference – i.e., not only citizens of particular countries, but also people in general, including refugees, displaced people, political assailants, etc.

Human rights are tragically gendered. Women and their dependent children make up most of the world's refugees and displaced people (Amnesty International 1995). Human rights are also gendered because women represent a large majority of the poor in every country. To acknowledge economic well-being as a human rights issue would certainly help to eradicate poverty. The exclusion of women from positions of public power, especially at the national scale, is another aspect of gendered human rights. This exclusion prevents women from being involved in decision-making in terms of shaping laws and institutions that affect women's and men's lives.

The geographies and spatiality of human rights challenge the traditional treatments of human rights that are cast exclusively in legal frameworks (Fenster 1999b). Space, it is argued, is more than relevant for understanding human rights violations. One of the major concerns of the human rights discourse is the practice of locking up men and women, or forbidding them from moving freely in their environments either because of political reasons or because of internal cultural norms that seek to ensure women's faithfulness and modesty. The right to work and the right to political participation are also abused because of a lack of freedom of movement (Nussbaum 1995). Fear of violence makes men and women avoid certain spaces. If women go to the bar for a drink, as do men, the response in certain parts of the world may be sexual terrorism. Or if men in different ethnic contexts go to public spaces that are sometimes appropriated by people of "the majority," the response may be ethnic or racial terrorism. In certain cases, men's or a minority's control over public spaces such as urban parks in the evening makes women and men fear violence, deterring most of them from being independent, even those who live otherwise successful professional lives. Thus, women's and sometimes men's inhibited use and occupation of public space is seen as a spatial expression of patriarchy (Bunch 1995; Valentine 1989) and as a violation of human rights. Here, patriarchy is taken in its wider meaning to express power relations between men and women, but also between the state and men and women. These examples show that space is never neutral; instead, it affects and is affected by social and power relations in society.

The spatiality of the human rights discourse is usually expressed in the legal distinction drawn between "private" and "public" spheres, as mentioned earlier. The large number of definitions of and perspectives on the two dimensions indicates how easily they can be confused (Cook 1995). This distinction is not only a gendered matter, but also one of race and class (Sullivan 1995). In many cases the notion of public interest has been replaced by the notion of "the wealthier upper class public interest" (Eisenstein 1996), thus making this distinction not so much women-oriented as men- and women-oriented. Thus, public spaces are renegotiated for the interests of only some members of the "public," and power relations define the boundaries between private and public and in many cases between what and where it is forbidden and what and where it is permitted. A clear example of such contradictions is the reduced investment by governments in public services such as playgrounds or parks in poor neighborhoods, as shown in the Bedouin case, while tax breaks and other public mechanisms facilitate gentrification and up-market developments for the affluent "public" living in gated suburbs.

Thus, boundaries between private and public or forbidden and permitted are not only gendered, but are also matters of class, culture, and politics. Their lines of demarcation and meanings may change among different classes, races, and geographical regions within a country, between urban and rural environments (Sullivan 1995) and between densely populated or dispersed areas. Perhaps the most explicit evidence of the "elasticity" and contradiction between these definitions is the fact that new practices and new scales of organization within global capitalism are currently redefining the public/private divide in both first and third world countries. Mega-corporations are replacing the power of governments, and economies are being built on global scales. In this context, private/public divides are no longer clear-cut (Eisenstein 1996), because services, spaces, and activities such as health, childcare, and care of the elderly, which used to be public in industrialized welfare states, are now privatized. In developing countries, the opposite is occurring: what was the duty of the family is now in the hands of the state (child and care of the elderly in third world countries), while global corporations have taken over employment that was formerly locally organized. The process of transitional economic intrusion into third world countries means, in many cases, further exploitation of both men and women as poverty-waged workers, and in particular women as factory workers.

Conclusion: Is Space Gendered?

The aim of this chapter is to show how space is, indeed, gendered, especially if we look at its symbolic construction through the "rights" lens, whether we are talking about human or citizen rights. The case studies presented here represent women's and men's everyday life experiences in Israel, but in fact they reflect a general trend in which cultural, social, and ethnic norms become the spatial abuse of women's rights. In order to substantiate this argument, three themes have been discussed. First, I have considered the extent to which cultural symbolism creates gendered forbidden and permitted spaces, which affect men and women's freedom to move in space. Secondly, I discussed the mechanisms by which expressions of power relations and identities both between communities and the state and between men and women dictate the conceptualization of gendered ethnic and citizen identities and rights, a definition that is culturally constructed. Thirdly, I discussed the extent to which the connection between gender and space is very much inherent in the discussion on human rights.

I hope that this analysis emphasizes the strong connection between cultural and social articulation of space and gender relations. There cannot be any in-depth discussion on notions of identities, citizenship, ethnicity, or human rights without looking at the intersection between gender relations, power, and their expressions in space.

Notes

1 A pseudonym.
2 The use of the labels "traditional" and "modern" is sometimes problematic, but it seems appropriate to use them in this context precisely because they reflect the static situation faced by these women.
3 To mention only a few: Erikson (1993); Horowitz (1985); Smith (1991); Van den Berge (1983); Yuval Davis (1995, 1997).
4 For elaboration on citizenship and gender and citizenship, see Fenster (1996); Kofman (1995); Lister (1995); Marshall (1975, 1981); Yuval Davis (1995, 1997).

References

Amnesty International (1995) *Human Rights and Women's Rights* (Amnesty International).

Bunch, C. (1995) "Transforming Human Rights from a Feminist Perspective," in J. Peters and A. Wolper (eds.), *Women's Rights Human Rights* (New York: Routledge).

Cook, R. (1995) "Women's International Human Rights Law: The Way Forward," in R. Cook (ed.), *Human Rights of Women* (Philadelphia, PA: University of Pennsylvania Press).

Dwyer, C. (1998) "Contested Identities: Challenging Dominant Representations of Young British Muslim Women," in T. Skelton and G. Valentine (eds.), *Cool Places* (London: Routledge).

Eisenstein, Z. (1996) "Women's Publics and the Search for New Democracies." Paper presented at the Conference "Women, Citizenship and Difference," London.

Erikson, T. H. (1993) *Ethnicity and Nationalism* (London: Pluto Press).

Fenster, T. (1996) "Ethnicity and Citizen Identity in Planning and Development for Minority Groups," *Political Geography* 15/5: 405–18.

Fenster, T. (1998) "Ethnicity, Citizenship, Planning and Gender: The Case of Ethiopian Immigrant Women in Israel," *Gender, Place and Culture* 5/2: 177–89.

Fenster, T. (1999a) "Space for Gender: Cultural Roles of the Forbidden and the Permitted," *Society and Space* 17: 227–46.

Fenster, T. (1999b) "Gender and Human Rights: Implications for Planning and Development," in T. Fenster (ed.) *Gender, Planning and Human Rights* (London: Routledge).

Horowitz, D. L. (1985) *Ethnic Groups in Conflict* (Berkeley, CA: University of California Press).

Jackson, P. (1998) "Domesticating the Street: The Contested Spaces of the High Street and the Mall," in N. Fyfe (ed.), *The Images of the Street* (London: Routledge).

Knott, K. and Khokher, S. (1993) "Religious and Ethnic Identity Among Young Muslim Women in Bradford," *New Community* 19/4: 593–610.

Kofman, E. (1995) "Citizenship for Some but Not for Others: Spaces of Citizenship in Contemporary Europe," *Political Geography* 14/2: 121–37.

Lister, R. (1995) "Dilemmas in Engendering Citizenship," *Economy and Society* 24/1: 2–40.

Marshall, T. H. (1975) *Social Policy in the Twentieth Century* (London: Hutchinson).

Marshall, T. H. (1981) *The Right to Welfare and Other Essays* (London: Heinemann Educational).

Massey, D. (1994) *Space, Place and Gender* (Cambridge: Polity).

Nussbaum, M. (1995) "Human Capabilities, Female Human Beings," in M. Nussbaum and J. Glover (eds.), *Women, Culture and Development* (Oxford, Clarendon Press).

Painter, C. and Philo, C. (1995) "Spaces of Citizenship: An Introduction," *Political Geography* 14/2: 107–20.

Smith, A. (1991) *National Identity* (London: Penguin).

Sullivan, D. (1995) "The Public/Private Distinction in International Human Rights Law," in J. Peters and A. Wolper (eds.), *Women's Rights Human Rights* (New York: Routledge).

Valentine, G. (1989) "The Geography of Women's Fear," *Area* 21/4: 385–90.

Van den Berge, P. L. (1983) "Class, Race and Ethnicity in Africa," *Ethnic and Racial Studies* 6: 221–36.

Yuval Davis, N. (1991) "The Citizenship Debate: Women Ethnic Process and the State," *Feminist Review* 39: 56–68.

Yuval Davis, N. (1995) "Ethnicity, Gender Relations and Multiculturalism." Paper presented at the Euro Conference on "Migration and Multiculturalism," London.

Yuval Davis, N. (1997) *Gender and Nation* (London: Sage).

CHAPTER THIRTY-FIVE

Architecture and Planning

Mona Domosh

That architecture is gendered must come as a surprise to many people. The buildings in which we live, work, and play are often considered neutral backdrops to our activities. Following this line of thinking, architecture provides, at its best, aesthetically pleasing solutions to functional problems (like keeping us warm and dry), and neither of these goals has much to do with women or gender or feminism. Yet consider the most mundane and commonplace example of architecture: the home and the house. The very idea of home already resonates with gender – in most cultures and throughout much of human history, home has been associated with women and with feminine identities. In many cultures, the physical form of the house is gendered. The traditional house form of the Navajos living in the American southwest, the *hogan*, is divided literally and symbolically into a feminine and masculine half. The homes of wealthy Muslims are often divided into private feminine spaces and public masculine spaces. In Euro-American culture, the kitchens, living-rooms and bedrooms are generally considered feminine spaces, while the man of the house is identified with the outside yard, the basement, and the garage. And certain types of house reflect and shape masculine and feminine identities: the suburban, postwar houses in the United States and Canada are often seen as the embodiment of the happy housewife ideal of 1950s domesticity, while the penthouse – urban "bachelor pads" – expressed and reinforced the new "free" sexuality of a 1960s masculinity.

As art and artifact, then, architecture is deeply gendered; as a creation of society, it reflects, expresses, reinforces – and at times challenges – gender roles, behaviors, and identities. Women and men tend to create and inhabit buildings and spaces differently from each other, and masculine and feminine identities are performed through and reflected in particular built environments. So too architecture is related to sexuality – the 1960s bachelor pad reflected and reinforced norms of hetero-masculinity, while many scholars argue that gentrified inner-city neighborhoods are heavily associated with gay and lesbian populations. To explore the complex relationships between architecture and gender, therefore, I have divided this chapter into three (assuredly overlapping) sections: architecture/women, architecture/gender and architecture/sexualities.

Architecture/Women

From its origins in the late nineteenth century as a professional discipline to its contemporary practices, architecture is decidedly a masculine and masculinist occupation. To separate themselves from, and elevate their position above, "mere" builders, a group of elite, male architects secured their position by forming in 1857 a professional association: the American Institute of Architects (AIA). This association created and enforced educational and licensing requirements that greatly limited entry into the profession. Eligibility "requirements" and social norms have kept the group predominantly white, and almost exclusively male, ever since. In 1995, only 9.1 percent of the membership of the AIA consisted of women (Coleman 1996: xiii).

Even without taking an essentialist position (that is, without assuming that women and men are essentially different from each other), it is not difficult to understand in what ways the overwhelming maleness of the profession matters in everyday life. The priorities and perspectives of the architectural profession have been shaped by this male-only social world. As Boys (1984) has pointed out, it only takes one attempt to navigate through city streets as a single woman with children in tow and in trolley to appreciate how the built environments of most cities have been created with little regard to the reproductive sphere of life – that most often assigned to women. Most modern cities and towns have been planned and/or have evolved around the notion of individual mobility, with large distances between home and paid employment, and with highways constructed at the expense of public transport. As Boys points out, "that this is a male, white, middle-class 'norm' (look at almost any cross-section of car drivers during rush hour) is ignored by the makers of our physical surroundings" (1984: 41).

Yet women have ventured into this masculine profession, although many of their accomplishments have been tarnished by critics and historians. Sophia Hayden, the first woman graduate of MIT with a degree in architecture, designed the Woman's Building at the 1893 World's Columbian Exposition in Chicago. Though a popular building in terms of crowd appeal (with its tea-room, model kitchen and roof garden, visitors thronged the building), it was deemed by contemporary critics to be an architectural failure. The *American Architect and Building News* commented: "It is simply weak and commonplace. . . . The roof garden is a hen-coop for petticoated hens, old and young" (1892: 86). Disheartened by her critics and prospects, Hayden found it difficult to continue as an architect.

Colomina (1996) has documented a very particular (but telling) case of how the accomplishments of women architects have been erased from history. A summer house designed by the architect Eileen Gray on the coast in southern

France in the mid-1920s became infamous when Le Corbusier occupied the house in the late 1930s and painted, against the wishes of Gray who still owned the house, a series of murals on the walls depicting nude women. According to Colomina, this act of defacement "went hand in hand with the effacement of Gray as an architect" (1996: 173). In the books and articles that documented and depicted the murals, the authorship of the house by Gray was never mentioned, and most historians assumed that it had been designed by Le Corbusier. The erasure continues. As Colomina argues: "Gray's name does not figure, even as a footnote, in most histories of modern architecture, including the most recent and ostensibly critical ones" (ibid.).

Strengthening this historical erasure is the relative absence of writings by women architects. As Favro points out, "architecture is as much about words as about actual buildings" (1996: 295). Since the mid-nineteenth century, architects have produced written texts that explain, expound upon, and document their theories and their lives. These writings have appeared in professional journals and in monographs, and, according to Favro, the undercurrent of much of this writing is a legitimization and celebration of the role of the architect as artist/ genius. Not surprisingly, given the dearth of women in the profession, most of these words have been produced by men. And the architects who are women have rarely written about themselves or their works. For example, Julia Morgan, who designed more than 500 projects in the early to mid-twentieth century, "scrupulously avoided being what she disparagingly labeled 'a talking architect'" (ibid.: 297), preferring to let her work be evaluated on its own terms.

This is not to say that the words of women have had little impact on the architectural arena; only that those words have not become part of the architectural "canon." As Favro shows, although throughout much of the nineteenth and twentieth centuries women were denied entry into the professional circles of architecture, they were encouraged to participate in the world of letters. Since part of the proper, middle-class woman's role was to serve as the moral and cultural center of family and society, they were encouraged to write about, for example, the correct furnishings of a home or the proper physical environment for raising children. And many of these writings gained a wide audience. The women's magazine, *Godey's Lady's Book*, had 70,000 subscribers in 1851 (ibid.: 302). The male-dominated profession did its best to distance itself from such matters, "proclaiming the autonomy of architecture as art and demonstrating an open hostility to mass culture" (ibid.: 303), resulting in a split between two views of architecture: architecture as art, divorced from the concerns of society and conceived of as masculine, and architecture as built environment, linked to notions of social reform and conceived of as feminine. One could argue that this problematic separation continues today, with grand architectural statements (both as buildings and texts) valued much more highly than, for example, the design of environmentally sensitive offices or affordable housing. Such concerns, as Weisman contends, have been grievously ignored in the education of architects, leading to a discipline that she believes could become "anachronistic and irrelevant" (1996:

273). Weisman's call for architectural training that teaches students how to evaluate buildings, not only aesthetically but also in terms of their environmental sustainability and whether they reinforce socially just norms, might well go a long way toward making what many have considered the "feminine" concerns of architecture center-stage within the profession.

Architecture/Gender

Even though the masculine profession of architecture might try to divorce itself from explicitly social concerns, architecture itself is inherently social. Built environments, whether designed by a lone architect as "artist" or created from the plans of clients or built in response to purely functional considerations, reflect and reinforce the norms and ideologies of society. For example, as many scholars have pointed out, the postwar suburbs that encircle most Western cities embodied a very particular societal view of renewed domesticity and patri-archal family structure. In the United States, the pent-up demand for housing after World War II was large, given that few homes had been built during the Great Depression or the war years, yet this demand could have been at least partially fulfilled by building and renovating apartments and homes within the existing urban borders. Instead, government programs encouraged the con-struction of single-family homes in the new suburban fringes, connected to the city by new roadways. This suburban lifestyle fulfilled several ideological goals at the same time: women who had earlier, during the war, worked in factories and other jobs were removed physically and psychologically from the productive site of the city to the reproductive site of the home; soldiers "returned" to their jobs in the city and their role as patriarch in the home; new home construction and decoration increased consumption, boosting the economy; and single-family home-ownership maintained a good workforce (monthly mortgage payments were thought to ensure reliable workers) and fought communism (individual ownership of property was thought to be the corner-stone of capitalism).

Coincident with this suburban explosion, American cities witnessed the con-struction of modern office buildings to house the many white-collar (and almost exclusively male) workers of the new corporate economy. The rationalized and hierarchical world of corporate capitalism was both reflected and reinforced in these sleek, well-ordered buildings. As Ockman argues, the International Style, as it was called, "explicitly embodied the values of technocracy – the ethos of rationalism, bureaucracy, and technoscientific progress on which both big busi-ness and government were predicated" (1996: 191). Most of the women who worked in these symbols of bureaucratic, masculine control were secretaries, relegated, as Spain (1992) points out, either to the "office pool," where they had no individual control over space, or to open-door "front" offices, without privacy – either way, as spaces always open to surveillance, they reflected and reinforced the subservient position of secretaries and women within the corporation, and within patriarchal society.

In addition to reflecting and shaping gendered ideologies, buildings and spaces also provide frameworks in which particular forms of feminine and masculine identities are performed. For example, the single-family suburban home embodied, as we have seen, the postwar gendered norms of renewed domesticity; at the same time, it was in and through the spaces of these homes that particular forms of femininity and masculinity were performed. The Sunday afternoon ritual of mowing the lawn became an important identity marker of a domesticated masculinity – men were removed from the rough-and-tumble bachelor world of the city, yet maintained their masculinity through the association with the outdoors, and with technology. The suburban housewife, on the other hand, acted out her role as caregiver, consumer, and community-builder by attending PTA meetings, arranging neighborhood social activities, cooking healthy meals as dictated by women's magazines, and purchasing tasteful household commodities on Saturdays, when her husband relinquished the family's automobile. A suburban woman seen working in the city was out of place, and risked losing her respectable, feminine identity.

Similarly, the masculinity of a man found shopping in a department store on a midday afternoon was certainly suspect, because spaces of consumption have been culturally constructed as feminine. Exactly how and why this has happened is particularly interesting, given the proliferation of consumer spaces in contemporary cities. Many scholars trace the association of the feminine sphere with consumption and the masculine sphere with production to the early modern city (sixteenth–eighteenth centuries), and the articulation of the ideology of separate spheres: women and the feminine were assigned to the domestic realm of the home, while men and the masculine were in charge of the public world of work. This separation of spheres was accelerated and strengthened in the nineteenth century, when the industrial economy led to the proliferation of consumer goods. A successful industrial economy required a societal commitment to two different value systems: the values of hard work, diligence, and self-denial were necessary to keep men working hard in the factories, while the values of self-indulgence, leisure, and playfulness were required to create open-ended demand for consumer goods. Yet these two value systems contradicted each other, leading to societal anxieties: how can you encourage self-indulgence at the same time as hard work? One effective way of dealing with these anxieties was to ally the values of production with men, and those of consumption with women. Men would work hard to support the indulgences of women. And since gender ideology spoke of women as naturally moral beings, they could consume wisely, without ruining their family's economic situation. So women became the class of shoppers, and a particular vision of femininity was aligned with the spaces of consumption. In fact, many entrepreneurs, eager to encourage women shoppers, made sure their stores fitted into nineteenth-century gendered notions of femininity. The large department stores that lined the streets of many American cities, for example, were purposely designed to resemble public cultural buildings more than commercial ones: they were extremely decorative, well-arranged, and commodious, bringing the domestic into the city, functioning almost as parlor spaces for middle-class women. A woman seen shopping in one of these ornate buildings was performing the rites of nineteenth-century femininity. A man performing the same role was a societal threat: he should be occupying the spaces of production.

Architectural space, therefore, reinforces particular gendered identities. As such, it can also pose a threat to certain identities. As Wagner (1996) shows, the 1960s ideal of the urban bachelor pad was in many respects a reaction to a loss of masculine control over space. The 1950s emphasis on reproduction and its manifestation in the suburban lifestyle threatened the masculine image of the urban man-about-town, in control of his fate – an ideal already under threat in the hierarchical corporate world, where most white-collar workers were far removed from any real economic control. In contrast to the relatively insignific-ant position most men occupied in the work world, the ideal bachelor pad was perched above the city in a penthouse, affording its occupant a surveilling gaze of its delights. The occupant was a lone, single man, in complete control of the design of the space. And the design, with its emphasis on furnishings and high-tech gadgets geared to seduction, functioned as a "space of imagined lib-eration, in which technology serves as an extension of sexual desire" (Wagner 1996: 199). The bachelor pad, then, represented a masculinity freed from domestic and feminine control, where the rough-and-tumble predatory world of the single man would reign supreme. A reinvigorated masculinity was performed and imagined in and through these new urban scenes.

Architecture/Sexualities

As we can see from the example of the bachelor pad, not only do architectural spaces reflect gendered identities and norms, they also reflect sexual identities – the bachelor pad housed a single and, most decidedly, a heterosexual man. Indeed, given the extreme regulation of sexuality in most societies, and the normalization of heterosexual behavior, one could argue that almost all architectural spaces incorporate and reinforce those norms. Most residences, commercial buildings, and public spaces are and were designed to embody and reinforce heteronormative behavior. For example, most middle-class homes are built to accommodate the patriarchal, heterosexual family: a "master" bedroom for the heterosexual couple, smaller bedrooms for children, a family room for leisure time with the children, the kitchen as feminine domestic space, and the living- and dining-rooms for the public display of the norms of "family" life. In fact, often the furniture itself tells us about those norms. In Victorian times, it was common for parlors to be equipped with a matching suite of furnishings: a "father's" chair, a less grand side chair for the mother, and the couch for visitors and children.

Similarly, the strictly enforced social norms that govern the uses of public and commercial buildings ensure that these are heterosexual spaces. Even spaces that are defined by activities seemingly removed from any sexual behavior are implicated in reinforcing heterosexuality. In her study of the everyday working lives of men and women employed in the banking industry in London, McDowell found that professional jobs, "once seen as the epitome of disembodied, rational workers," are in fact "characterized by sexual performances" (1995: 76). For example, she found that to be a successful stock trader, it was necessary to perform as an aggressive heterosexual male, including participating in sexual banter about "conquests" and "the possession of 'iron balls'" (ibid.: 85). This acting out of particular sexualized identities defines these workspaces; once thought of as neutral backdrops to economic, disembodied activity, we are now understanding that many workplaces are sites that reinforce heteronormative behaviors.

Yet the presence of gay men and lesbian women is not entirely erased in these heteronormative spaces. Space itself, as Chauncey reminds us, has "no natural character, no inherent meaning" (1996: 224). It is not itself heterosexual; rather, it is put to heterosexual use and regulated under a heterosexual gaze. As such, under particular circumstances, space can become homosexual, it can be "used by queers or put to queer use" (ibid.: 224). Chauncey documents such a circumstance in 1920s and '30s New York City, when gay men devised a series of tactics to express their identities in the public spaces of the city, spaces dominated by heterosexual norms. Certain unspoken rules of how to "cruise" the city's parks and beaches afforded gay men introductions to others, and an intricate social geography of street patterns and interactions associated certain areas and street corners as gay. This "gay geography" of the city was available only to those who knew the intimate tactics, allowing gay men to use spaces governed by the dominant culture in ways that were decidedly queer – for homosocial events, sexual encounters, chance meetings.

Such queer uses of heteronormative spaces certainly continue in today's cities, and some of the tactics have become more visible to the dominant culture. For example, scholars have documented the multilayered association of gentrification with gay life. Gentrification – a process whereby urban residential and commercial neighborhoods, abandoned by the middle classes in the 1960s and 1970s in favor of the suburbs, are "rediscovered" – was from its inception a development promoted by gay men. It is not difficult to understand why. The heteronormative structure of postwar suburban life as outlined above was clearly not an environment comfortable for most gay men; while urban neighborhoods undergoing gentrification were ideal for white, middle-class gay men seeking economic, cultural, and political power. Urban governments and elites were happy to have white, tax-paying professionals in the city, and therefore tolerated some "deviant" behavior. Gay men were often directly involved in gentrification as real-estate agents, architects, developers, and designers. As a result, many cities have experienced a "homosexualization of gentrified areas" (Knopp 1995: 152) – that is, neighborhoods dominated by openly gay businesses, activities, and

481

lifestyles. Lesbians too have often found gentrified urban neighborhoods comfortable places for expressing their identities. Park Slope in Brooklyn, for example, is a gentrified neighborhood which, in the early 1990s, was home to the largest concentration of lesbians in the New York metropolitan area. Although less spatially visible than gay-identified neighborhoods, in the sense that lesbian activities are more often performed in private, not public spaces, Park Slope is "associated with the creation of [a lesbian] identity, and the collectivity of identities transforms the place" (Rothenberg 1995: 179). We could, then, begin to think of some gentrified neighborhoods, such as Park Slope, the Castro in San Francisco, and "the Village" in Manchester, UK, as "queer spaces" – that is, as places that are visible reflections and symbols of homosocial and homosexual identities; places that are partially removed from the regulations of the heterosexual gaze.

Although I started this chapter by reflecting on the overwhelming heteromasculinism of the architecture profession, it is important to recognize the challenges to its norms. Particular built environments, as we have seen here, can be transformed into alternate spaces. The nineteenth-century brownstones of Park Slope, originally built to house middle-class, heterosexual, nuclear families, are now arenas for the expression of lesbian identities. Many postwar suburban homes became sites for women's social activities, activities that in some cases led to feminist and environmental political caucuses and actions. And feminist architects and planners are mapping out new ways to organize, design, and use space in order to promote more socially just and environmentally sustainable homes, neighborhoods, and cities. As architect Leslie Kanes Weisman argues, even though architecture is the "expression of an established social order" and therefore "is not easily changed until the society that produced it is changed," this does not mean that it cannot participate in a progressive, feminist politics (1992: 179). I borrow my conclusion from hers: "The nature of the built environment is such that it can suggest the world transformed as well as the means for its transformation. If we are to design a society in which all people matter, more architects and planners need to become feminists and more feminists need to concern themselves with the design of our physical surroundings" (ibid.).

References

American Architect and Building News 38/86 (1892).

Boys, J. (1984) "Women and Public Space," in Matrix (ed.), *Making Space: Women and the Man-Made Environment* (London: Pluto Press).

Chauncey, G. (1996) "Privacy could only be had in Public: Gay uses of the Streets," in J. Sanders (ed.), *Stud: Architectures of Masculinity* (New York: Princeton Architectural Press).

Coleman, D. (1996) "Introduction," in D. Coleman, E. Danze, and C. Henderson (eds.), *Architecture and Feminism* (New York: Princeton Architectural Press).

Colomina, B. (1996) "Battle Lines: E.1027," in D. Agrest, P. Conway, and L. K. Weisman (eds.), *The Sex of Architecture* (New York: Harry N. Abrams, Inc.).

Favro, D. (1996) "The Pen is Mightier than the Building: Writing on Architecture 1850–1940," in D. Agrest, P. Conway, and L. K. Weisman (eds.), *The Sex of Architecture* (New York: Harry N. Abrams, Inc.).

Knopp, L. (1995) "Sexuality and Urban Space: A Framework for Analysis," in D. Bell and G. Valentine (eds.), *Mapping Desire: Geographies of Sexualities* (New York: Routledge).

McDowell, L. (1995) "Body Work: Heterosexual Gender Performances in City Workplaces," in D. Bell and G. Valentine (eds.), *Mapping Desire: Geographies of Sexualities* (New York: Routledge).

Ockman, J. (1996) "Mirror Images: Technology, Consumption, and the Representation of Gender in American Architecture since World War II," in D. Agrest, P. Conway, and L. K. Weisman (eds.), *The Sex of Architecture* (New York: Harry N. Abrams, Inc.).

Rothenberg, T. (1995) "'And She Told Two Friends': Lesbians Creating Urban Social Spaces," in D. Bell and G. Valentine (eds.), *Mapping Desire: Geographies of Sexualities* (New York: Routledge).

Spain, D. (1992) *Gendered Spaces* (Chapel Hill: University of North Carolina Press).

Wagner, G. (1996) "The Lair of the Bachelor," in D. Coleman, E. Danze, and C. Henderson (eds.), *Architecture and Feminism* (New York: Princeton Architectural Press).

Weisman, L. K. (1992) *Discrimination by Design: A Feminist Critique of the Man-Made Environment* (Urbana: University of Illinois Press).

Weisman, L. K. (1996) "Diversity by Design: Feminist Reflections on the Future of Architectural Education and Practice," in D. Agrest, P. Conway, and L. K. Weisman (eds.), *The Sex of Architecture* (New York: Harry N. Abrams, Inc.).

Further reading

Boyer, M. C. (1983) *Dreaming the Rational City: The Myth of American City Planning* (Cambridge, MA: MIT Press).

Colomina, B. (ed.) (1992) *Sexuality and Space* (New York: Princeton Architectural Press).

Duncan, N. (ed.) (1996) *Body Space: Destabilizing Geographies of Gender and Sexuality* (New York: Routledge).

Ingram, G. B., Bouthillette, A. M., and Retter, Y. (eds.) (1997) *Queers in Space: Communities, Public Places, Sites of Resistance* (San Francisco: Bay Press).

Jones, J. P., Nast, H. J., and Roberts, S. M. (eds.) (1997) *Thresholds in Feminist Geography: Difference, Methodology, Representation* (Lanham, MD: Rowman and Littlefield Publishers).

Silverstone, R. (ed.) (1997) *Visions of Suburbia* (New York: Routledge).

CHAPTER THIRTY-SIX

Museums

Ellen Fernandez-Sacco

Gender is about relations.[1] In the context of the museum, gender shapes the power relations between people, objects, and their social interactions. In this chapter, I offer a series of brief meditations on aspects of those relationships that point to the complexity of gender relations to the museum, interlaced with my own observations from a recent museum visit. In the five sections that follow, I move from consumption, to architectural spaces and heroic architecture, then to a consideration of the changed expectations brought by war, a consideration of gender as an object of museum studies, and finally, a brief conclusion. The locations discussed are specific, as I will deal with established museums in New York City, San Francisco, and Bilbao, Spain.

It is not my aim to offer an overview of museum history, but, rather, to point to particular intersections which involve relations of power expressed through gender, or relations dependent on a traditional binary formulation of "male" and "female." If I maintain a focus on understanding the museum solely as a manifestation of national identity, I simply miss the boat. The meanings and interconnections of the museum as an institution to the larger world shift continuously. Worldwide, the number of museums continues to grow, and a new pattern of relations has developed that disengages national identity from the museum. This new pattern of relations emerges from a larger global political framework outlined by sociologists Anibal Quijano and Ramon Grosfoguel as the "coloniality of power" (Grosfoguel and Georas 1998; Quijano 1998). Colonialism, as both scholars explain, extended from 1492 to 1945; after 1945, the structures of colonial administration were lost, but colonialism's structuring of social relations survive, thereby preserving older patterns of gender relations. Museums remain among the institutions that represent and interpret various forms of social relations, material culture, and identity. In turn, these social processes have the capacity to shape their institutional structures.

The museum emerged in the late eighteenth century to lend materiality to the processes of colonialism (Prösler 1996). Instead of a developmental sequence for the museum, my perspective connects gender ideologies to racial and societal hierarchies. This connection unites the seeming disparities in my approach to the museum. Rather than separate gender out from other dimensions, I retain its shifting ambiguities, contradictions, and complexities for the reader.

Consuming Displays, Consuming Architecture

Does gender permeate the space of the museum, or is it marked on its exterior? Is it present in the interiors of rooms, vitrines, and display cases? Do objects – paintings, installations, video, sculpture, photographs, virtual objects – become feminized by virtue of the visitor's gaze?

Gauging the effects of gender dominance in the Western museum is much more complex than in previous decades, because of shifts in demographics and hiring practices and the end of segregation. From the early to mid-twentieth century, white males dominated architectural firms, ran civic institutions, and participated in expeditions which supplied museums with major collections drawn from indigenous cultures in North and South America, Greece, Egypt, and Africa. The activities of colonial administrators sent expeditions to discover, record, and collect antiquities and ethnographic data. Colonial countries were frequently represented in feminized terms or as children in need of care. From 1890 to 1930, women who "entered the art museum profession entered on unequal terms with their male colleagues" (Downs 1996). More often, women worked in museums in many different capacities – as curators, educators, secretarial staff, docents, or as custodial staff. The exceptions were the few white women who participated in expeditions, ran their own architectural firms, and, if affluent enough, participated in civic projects that involved founding institutions.

> I pass through massive entrance doors, purchase my admission ticket in the main atrium, and pause to look at the staff. I see mostly young women and men who issue tickets, offer membership information, or work in the museum store. The museum's curatorial staff are mostly invisible, save for the lists in exhibition catalogs and event schedules. Among the works displayed it seems women are more visible . . . particularly when an institution shows contemporary works. A museum's audience changes gradually, but for the most part remain middle or upper class. My ticket taken, I walk upstairs to spend time among a selected group of artifacts in the galleries.

The change in museum staff arrived through legal initiatives, and the development of programs for different constituencies in the wake of Civil Rights movements.[2] The older, embodied ideals of national identity changed in several sites as museums gradually began to serve a visibly different demographic. Relevance to the community that surrounds a museum, attention to outreach, and diversity are characteristic of the concerns of many contemporary arts institutions.[3]

485

Museum visitors vary; they have different needs and different constituencies – yet they are so overwhelmingly white. Why? Almost all of the museum guards are people of color. As for the audience, it is not representative of the local area's demographics. Most of the guards on the West Coast are Filipino, older women, and men who watch the visitors. In New York, I knew museum guards from Puerto Rico, West Africa, and other places. We watch from the margins. Fred Wilson's installation, "Guarded View" (1991), makes visible those seemingly anonymous brown mannequins in the uniform worn by guards at several museums. He asked a group to meet him in the gallery, where he waited, wearing a guard's uniform, near his work. They all walked right past him, never noticing him in his outfit.[4] I don't know if he would have had the same experience outside of the United States.

Technological improvements since the First World War enabled artists to travel more extensively, their ability to reach distant locales enhanced by the technologies of print and transportation. In the early 1900s members of the DaDa movement could travel from Cologne to Paris in a matter of hours, effectively bridging distance and culture. References to a specific nationality fragment as people emigrate, or spend long periods of time exiled in different countries because of the disruptions of wartime. In the US, during the Cold War years of the 1950s, it was (white) male artists, rather than female artists, who signified the nation-state. Images of these men also served dual functions as sign and index of culture, civilization, and innovation. This view of the ideal artist harks back to the expositions and world fairs of the nineteenth and twentieth centuries. Artists continue to travel across continents in an accelerated fashion since the appearance of jet planes collapsed the distance between towns, cities, and countries; for instance, artists, exhibitions, performances, and installations move from city to city or across countries. Some artists work to disseminate political resistance, while others are considered national representatives, and some readily declared their allegiance to or alienation from the nation. Museums were part of the conduit along which these representations of masculinity were disseminated to the public.

What has vanished from representations and discussion of the museum's halls of cases and rooms filled with art objects is the physical labor needed to run these sites. The labor of hands that clean, order, and maintain the museum recedes further from view, and this disappearance obscures the gendered and frequently racialized relations of capital wrought by tourism and its service economy.[5] Such an economy produces limited access for segments of society, which remain excluded from the network society.[6]

Consumption – and with this term I invoke its fullest definition of activities in which visitors expect to participate – includes seeing, reading, eating, traveling, walking, and shopping, all of which require care taken by members of a service economy. The museum is another axis of power along which the relations of consumption involve ideas of value, hierarchy, and the marking of time. Today, we witness a progressive disengagement of the museum from its former identity as a world in miniature that illustrated the nation-state and kept the material culture of former colonies within the display case. There is no going back.

Consuming Online: Divides Between Real and Virtual Space

In North America and Europe, the close of the twentieth century was marked by a rush to build new and different structures to house museum collections. Accompanying the materiality of buildings were simulations of representative sites and works that occupied digital space. Internationally, an array of buildings continue to be erected, from spectacular exteriors of commissioned architectural works to thought-provoking meditations on the complexity of relationships between architecture, space, identity, digitization, and globalization. Frequently, these new museum structures physically dominate the cultural landscape they are located in, and are often accompanied by a strong virtual presence. The improvement of technologies that support simulations and communication networks, as with the museum's spaces, also veil the relations of labor that enable the availability and progressively lower the costs of such virtual presence. Despite the appearance of virtual media as a presence independent of the body, its possibility is dependent on workers meshed into a transnational, global economy who manufacture, assemble, and test electronic equipment before it reaches its final destination. In this manufacturing realm, there is a preference for female labor to perform tasks from the preparation of silicon, to soldering connections on circuit boards, to assembling plastic housings.[7]

Through a series of links, artist Preema Murthy's *Mythic Hybrid* (2002) utilizes two Quicktime film clips separated by a quote from Asian women microelectronics workers. On the left are clips of women working in factories in Southeast Asia, and on the right narrated clips from Siemens promotional videos for its microelectronics division, which produces "hybrid microcircuts for telecommunications." The noise of the factory accompanied by glimpses of women working competes with a man's English accented voice speaking of the design and benefit of production for the high-tech market. This transnational network of labor, usually invisible to the consumer, comprises a dependency on the development strategies of transnational corporations in the third world. Murthy's work is itself a museum, offering displays of a gendered division of labor, a visual record of contemporary advertising practice, and links to regional women's worker organizations.[8]

On the web, some museums can offer glimpses of its external architecture, 360-degree views of interiors via webcam, images of current and recent exhibitions, permanent collections, and virtual works commissioned for online viewing. Catalogues also appear on CD-ROM, condensing the space of a book onto the flat, ribbed surfaces of each small disk. In this format, our experience of the book is further deferred by the momentary wait for the hard drive to spin and

487

load the media. We look, see, and even listen, but cannot touch the book, or get close to the objects displayed on a website.

How do these shifts in sensory capacity register in the newfound virtual space of the museum? The web does not yet offer the visceral sensation of a site to the body. Audiences are not simply corporeal, nor are museums simply aggregates of material culture. Museums still offer a secular space in which to engage a particular subject, moment, or object in time, an experience not yet approximated online. This is similar to the problem that occurs when one teaches with projected representations of artworks – which contrast intensely with the expectation of students engaging the materiality of objects and forms that are not necessarily web-based. One still needs to visit to see and experience it for oneself. For the museum visitor in virtual space, gender relations can take ambiguous forms that escape particular categorizations.

Thus, the "content" of the Western art museum progressively moves away from its external form. A visitor's reception of a representation of the collection, and a museum's holdings – its actual array of objects – are two distinctly different things. These experiences can be conflated when a museum's space or its forms are perceived on the bitmap screen of a computer monitor. From inside a museum, access to far more online content is possible than from an internet connection at home. The ability to connect to these sites raises questions concerning access (by whom and when) to information. Using data on access to the museum via technology is part of a larger map of unequal power relations. These relations in turn are frequently couched in language descriptive of gender inequity, sexual subordination, and domination.

Branding: Gender and Architecture

> About five years ago, two friends from Germany, my husband, and I sat in the expansive plaza of the Getty Museum in Los Angeles, soon after its opening. Both artists, the friends were excited at the opportunity to walk around the hilltop, through its buildings and its spectacular views. "We don't care to look inside," they told us. "We came to see the outside!"

Outside, museum architecture remains, for the most part, the province of white male architects who accumulate cultural capital in the construction of massive, contemporary exteriors. Each structure is branded by the architect rather than by the collection, or a collector. In other words, the aim is to build spaces that fuse art and architecture. Architectural firms involved in museum redesign include Yoshio Taniguchi and Associates, who worked on MOMA, New York; the Marugame Genichiro-Inokuma Museum of Contemporary Art; the Toyota Municipal Museum of Art in Toyota City; and the Higashiyama Kaii Gallery in Nagano City, Japan. The projects of Jacques Herzog and Pierre de Meuron include the Walker Art Center, Minneapolis, and the De Young Museum in

San Francisco. Arata Osozako designed the Guggenheim Museum in Soho. Frank Gehry's firm has produced the Guggenheim Museum in Bilbao, Spain, the Experience Music Project in Seattle, the Fredrick R. Weisman Art Museum in Minnesota, and the Los Angeles Concert Hall. Santiago Calatrava designed the Quadracci Pavilion, a 58,000-foot addition that considerably expands the Milwaukee Art Museum. Also prominent are Richard Meier, who designed the travertine-surfaced Getty Museum and the Museum of Television and Video in Los Angeles, and Rem Koolhaas, responsible for the exterior of the Guggenheim-Hermitage Museum in Las Vegas, whose interior was designed by Frank Gehry. Each of these commissions demonstrates how central high-profile architectural projects are in enhancing the perception of the city as an important tourist destination.

Although these firms include women as partners or employees, a firm's public profile is frequently embodied as a male venture, as seen in the partial listing above. Few professional female architects have had such large commissioned projects offered to them by an institution. To date, there is only one commission for the architect Zahad Hadid to design the Cincinnati Contemporary Arts Center in Ohio.[9] Although the gendered identity of the professional or "star" architect does not detract from a building's stunning views, the spatial reconfigurations of its interiors, and the creative use of materials to shape institutional space inside and out, museum buildings remain informed by notions of value inflected with masculine ideals (Anderson 1999). Could the equivalence of monumental scale together with the perception of an ebullient masculinity signal a return to nationalist concepts of traditional sex/gender roles? Does this make the building a masculine domain? Architect Leslie Naa Norle Lokko (2000) points to such "overworked" terms as race, gender, and class to ask how they remain relevant to the reality of architectural practice. Does it matter that five of the seven architects mentioned at the outset are white males?

Can we ask whether professionalization is a process by which the specificity of the architect, the director, the curator, is rendered a merely neutral issue? This "neutrality," then, is something outside and transitional, yet the museum, envisioned as a "neutral space," is one that works to create social order. The neutral, according to Kevin Hetherington (1996), "stands apart, it constitutes sites of difference within a process, a neutralization, and from this emerges a new social ordering; a new form of sameness. The process of utopics is what lies behind the museum." Many of these contradictions are embodied by the events surrounding the initiation and building of the Guggenheim-Bilbao Museum.

War: Gender, Tourism, the Everyday

The Guggenheim-Bilbao Museum brought a new strategy of expansion beyond that of travel, and a shift in the way cultural organizations operate. Aside from the flexible titanium exterior of Gehry's spectacular building, there is a morphing of form that involves the museum's transformation into a branded product franchised to the right city with the right budget. It is, of course, more complex than that, yet the planned expansion of the Guggenheim Museum in global cities closely resembled the strategies of a transnational corporation. The museum and riverfront complex was proposed as a solution for a deindustrialized region with high unemployment, an area racked by the violent acts of the Basque nationalist-regionalist group ETA (*Euskadi 'ta Azakatazuna*, Basque Land and Freedom).[10] Their tactics, which include planned car bombs, assassinations, kidnappings, and extortion, have given rise to the formation of a Basque professional class accompanied by bodyguards. More than 800 people have died from ETA acts over the last 30 years. Although ETA declared a cease-fire in 1998, it is still possible that a resurgence of violence may occur (Zulaika 1997).[11] By locating a major cultural institution on the banks of the Nervion River, city planners and international developers sought to reinforce a sense of control. Perhaps the museum was a symbol of "civilization," a visual deterrent to the idea of the potential of terrorist attacks.

Bilbao's history, like that of Glasgow, the other city with which Bilbao is associated, has its roots in empire. Sociologist María V. Gómez points to a series of similarities shared by Bilbao and Glasgow – their peripheral location in relation to the continent, and the fact that both were once crucial industrial centers. In terms of the landscape, both cities "are built over old mines, illustrating how minerals played a key role in their regional prosperity" (2000: 113) and have a navigable river upon which its former economy depended. Most importantly, as post-industrial cities of the twenty-first century, the administrations of Bilbao and Glasgow are committed participants in reconstructing the city's image, key to a new service economy that replaces the old. Each region has undergone tremendous social change in the wake of deindustrialization, which resulted in the "huge loss of full time male employment in manufacturing" (ibid.). Rather than its former economy based on materials and their processing, the city governments of Glasgow and Bilbao are now relying on something less tangible, which is "image." This entails a transformation from each city's former "image problem" as an industrial city, into its new role as a cultural center. This new image is equivalent to a new economic base, which uses a fashionable landscape on the banks of the Nervion River as a first step toward attracting international capital (ibid.).

Image for Bilbao marks its arrival in the stream of global tourist traffic (ibid.: esp. 114–15).[12] Instead of shipbuilding and iron-smelting, a new service economy based on tourism would catapult the region into the company of other global actors. Geographer Donald McNeill sees this change as a symbolic reterritorialization, a counter-move by a distinctive cultural region that plays against the imagined landscapes of Europe's capital cities (McNeill 2000: 490–2). This move toward a tourist economy is the solution to unemployment in a post-industrial age, a structure that bears within it shifts in the patterns of gender relations. In Bilbao, unemployment for male laborers reached 25 percent or more, with the loss of 40,000 industrial jobs. Despite the claims made for the new economy, unemployment remains steady, with 60 percent of young Bilbainos remaining without work (Zulaika 1997). However, rehabilitating the perception of Metropolitan Bilbao meant enhancement by the shaping of the built environment by marketers, architects, and planners. It was a process aimed at saturating the media with the city's new image, a process that may parallel the aggressive marketing of Viagra. As a result, the museum was credited with sparking an economic boom, for within a year of being opened, 1.3 million visitors had passed through its doors (Wilson Lloyd 2001).

To explain how he achieved his goal of franchising the museum to the Basque city, Thomas Krens, then director of the New York Guggenheim Museum, who brokered the deal, described his job as "Seduction – that's the business I am in. I am a professional *seducteur*. I don't earn the money, but I raise it. I seduce people into giving $20 million gifts. I am, in a way, the greatest prostitute in the world."[13] By using language that wields transnational monetary potential, Krens tips his analogy away from feminization. "Prostitute," "*seducteur*": these are ironic terms, given that the exchange of sexual services for money has long been a feature of tourist economies.

A service economy, like those of North America and cities on every continent, is an economy based on tourism. Cynthia Enloe wrote that tourism "symbolized a country's entrance into the world community." She explains:

> Tourism doesn't fit neatly into public preoccupations with military conflict and high finance. Although it is infused with masculine ideals about adventure, pleasure and the exotic, those are deemed "private" and thus kept off the stage in debates about international politics. Yet since World War II, planners, investors and workers in the tourist industry, and tourists themselves, have been weaving unequal patterns that are restructuring international politics. And they depend on women for their success. (1990: 31–5)

Enloe points out that the jobs in this economy tend to be part time and seasonal, and offer little opportunity for advancement; they are therefore more likely to be filled by women. Underpinning this system are concepts of masculinity and femininity and their enforcement in both the societies of departure and destination. Without them, as Enloe notes, "it would be impossible to sustain the tourism industry and its political agenda in their current form" (ibid.: 40–1).[14] In Bilbao, this new economy offers women employment, shifting the structure of gender relations across society.

This new economy exemplifies the consolidation of a "network society," which collapses national boundaries, extends itself transnationally, and ultimately erodes the perception of "nation." The result is that the museum is no longer a site from which to imagine the nation-state; rather, museums increasingly establish cities as sites for micro-national imagining. Networks define this micro-national identification with a city, rather than the nation-state overall (McNeill 2000: 491).

The museum plays an increasingly central role in this redefinition of the city and the perception of its public space through the commission of spectacular architectural works.

Rippling Effects in Global Economies

In part, the recent burst of exuberant museum-building in the latter 1990s was fueled by economic euphoria produced by investments in internet businesses and related technology. This has rapidly decelerated since 2001. With the collapse of the tech market, unemployment rose, traffic is lighter, rents have dropped, and the economy is slowly recovering.

In many cities, smaller art spaces disappeared, and, unable to maintain a steady stream of cash, those sites that partook of more experimental and critical approaches faced closure. Similarly, economic change registered in gallery opening notices, visible in a cautious return to the stability of "blue-chip" artists – largely (but not exclusively) male artists with high-value works shown by more established galleries. Overall in the US, the economic downturn shrank the venues available for new artists, and political critique lapsed as the war went on and sections of the economy staggered.

New York area museums anticipate cuts in city cultural budgets along with a decline in tourism and charitable donations, the worst financial forecast for non-profit cultural institutions there in 30 years. In 2002, the Guggenheim Museum in Manhattan, not uncharacteristic of the state of museums more generally, announced a 20 percent cut in staffing (which equated to 80 positions), no doubt disproportionately affecting women employees.

At the museum's periphery is a growing awareness that the nation-state no longer holds sway in the imaginary of US populations. The US is no different, no less vulnerable than anywhere else worldwide. Is a site – of reflection, exhibition, memorialization – feminized under violent processes, such as the assault on the World Trade Center in September 2001? Does its meaning change? Efforts to stem violence may be part of an ideological attempt to restore the masculine power of the nation-state through the increasing militarization of police and the rapid military response to terrorism. Regardless of the gender of the actors involved in such efforts, the threat posed to memorializing sites, museums, and, by extension, the nation find perpetual expression through the binary of masculine and feminine.

Notes

Thanks to Francesca Barrientos, Blanca Gordo, Lynne Horiuchi, and Jeff Ow for their comments on an earlier draft of this chapter, and to the Beatrice M. Bain Research Group on Gender at the University of California, Berkeley.

1   I find Carol Cohn's definition of gender useful (1993). By gender, I am referencing a constellation of meanings assigned to biological sex differences, and a symbolic system that is one of the central organizing discourses of culture. I add race to Cohn's definition, because it is another and important organizing discourse in American popular culture, and cannot be separated out from gender.

2   Exactly how to gauge these demographic shifts in museum personnel overall is a difficult proposition. Statistics from the US Census Bureau's Statistics of US Businesses (1998) records that just over 66,000 individuals worked in 3,714 museums and historic sites. Museums are defined as: "Establishments primarily engaged in the commercial or noncommercial operation of museums and art galleries. Historical, cultural and educational societies whose functions are primarily providing attractions for the public are included here. Art galleries or art dealers primarily selling to the general public are classified in Retail Trade, Industry 5999" (<http://www.census.gov/epcd/susb/1998/US71211.HTM#table1>).

The actual breakdown according to gender and ethnic background are unavailable on a national level; state agencies may have this information, but there is no one site from which to access this data.

3   "The initiative begins with the premise that each museum – in the extraordinary varieties of communities across the country that have created and cherished them – has a deeply rooted community connection that is uniquely its own. Building on these distinctive connections will give communities greater cultural vitality and museums renewed relevance" ("American Association of Museums Launches Groundbreaking Museums and Community Initiative," AAM Press Release. Washington, DC, May 3, 2000; <http://www.aam-us.org/pressreleases/may3.htm>)

4   Personal communication, Fred Wilson, 2000.

5   On one artist's work whose performance elevates the everyday acts of labor and reveals the ideological underpinnings of the museum space, see "Mierle Laderman Ukeles, *Maintenance Art Activity* (1973)," Miwon Kwon, "In Appreciation of Invisible Work," Helen Molesworth, "Work Stoppages: Mierle Laderman Ukeles' Theory of Labor Value." And "Democracy is Empty." Discussion by Doug Ashford and Mierle Laderman Ukeles *Documents* 10, Fall 1997, 5–30. I wish to thank Mario Ontiveros for this reference.

6   The term "network society" was coined by Manuel Castells. "Digital destitution" – the resulting economic, political, and social ramifications of exclusion – is theorized by urban planner Blanca Gordo (2000).

7   The issues of gender, workers, and global networks of labor have long been a focus of workers' organizations and Feminist Studies. For an overview of issues involved in globalization, see Evelyne Hong, "Women as Consumers and Producers in the World Market," one of the links in Murthy's *Mythic Hybrid*.

8   Preema Murthy, *Mythic Hybrid*, with funds from the Greenwall Foundation. One worker's quote (a circuit assembly worker) illuminates the difficulties: "The boss tells me not to bring our 'women's problems' with us to work if we want to be treated equal. I am only one person – and I bring my whole self to work with me. So what does he mean, don't bring my 'women's problems' here?" Another details the working conditions and hazards faced by women working in Southeast Asia (http://turbulence.org/Works/mythichybrid/webpages/search_array.html>).

9   "Contemporary Arts Center Landmark in Cincinatti," *Art Museum Network News*, Tuesday, May 28, 2002 (<http://news.amn.org/press.jsp?id=497>).

10 For background on ETA terrorism and its effects on the educational and political institutions in the Basque country see Carmelo Garitaonandia, "The Basque Country: A Country of Bodyguards," Press Freedom, World Association of Newspapers, 2001 (<http://www.wan-press.org/pt/europe/basque.report/paper.html>); Press Release, Bilbao, Spain, September 14, 2001, "Media Condemn Spanish, US Terrorism"; World Association of Newspapers, "Terrorism Against the Media: An International Conference on Violence Against the Media in the Basque Region of Spain," September 14, 2001, Palacio Euskalduna, Bilbao

(<http://www.wan-press.org/pt/europe/basque.report/terrorism.html>). Juan Miguel Linian Macias, Ministry of Defense of Spain, "Counterterrorism: An Example of Co-operation," *NATO Seminar: The Role of the EAPC in Combating Terrorism*, Warsaw, Poland, February 22, 2002, NATO/OTAN online library (<http://www.nato.int/docu/speech/2002/s020222i.htm>)

11 Zulaika asks: "Wooed by the Guggenheim Museum, the Basque people gained an architectural masterpiece, but at what price?"

12 Gomez's conclusions are less than reassuring for the future of Bilbao: "The picture, then, leads to the conclusion that the new economic role pursued for Glasgow has not had a real impact on its employment structure."

13 Quoted from a 1997 interview between Joseba Zulaika and Thomas Krens, arranged by Frank Gehry. Zulaika, "The Seduction of Bilbao."

14 As Enloe sums up: "international tourism needs patriarchy to survive" (1990: 40–1).

References

Anderson, C. (1999) "Masculinity and English Architectural Classicism," in Gill Perry (ed.), *Gender and Art* (New Haven, CT: Yale University Press).

Cohn, C. (1993) "War, Wimps, and Women: Talking Gender and Thinking War," in Miriam Cooke and Angela Woollacott (eds.), *Gendering War Talk* (Princeton: Princeton University Press).

Downs, L. (1996) "A Recent History of Women Educators in Art Museums," in Jane R. Glazer and Artemis A. Zenetou (eds.), *Gender Perspectives: Essays on Women in Museums* (Washington, DC: Smithsonian Institute Press).

Enloe, C. (1990) *Bananas, Beaches and Bases: Making Feminist Sense of International Politics* (Berkeley: University of California Press).

Gomez, M. V. (2000) "Reflective Images: The Case of Urban Regeneration in Glasgow and Bilbao," *Journal of Urban and Regional Research* 22/1: 106–21.

Gordo, B. (2000) "The Digital Divide and the Persistence of Urban Poverty," in *Planners Network Publications*, newsletter, May/June (<http://www.plannersnetwork.org/htm/pub/archives/141/gordo.html>).

Grosfoguel, R. and Georas, C. S. (1998) "'Coloniality of Power' and 'Racial Dynamics': Notes Toward a Reinterpretation of Latino Caribbeans in New York City," *Identities*, 7/1: 85–125.

Heatherington, K. (1996) "The Utopics of Social Ordering," in Sharon Macdonald and Gordon Fyfe (eds.), *Theorizing Museums* (Oxford: Blackwell Publishers).

Lokko, L. N. N. (ed.) (2000) "Introduction," in *White Paper, Black Marks: Architecture, Race, Culture* (New York: Routledge).

McNeill, D. (2000) "McGuggenisation? National identity and globalisation in the Basque Country," *Political Geography* 19: 473–94.

Prösler, M. (1996) "Museums and Globalization," in Sharon Macdonald and Gordon Fyfe (eds.), *Theorizing Museums* (Oxford: Blackwell Publishers).

Quijano, A. (1998) "La colonialidad de poder y la experiencia cultural latinoamericana," in Roberto Briseno-Leon and Heinz R. Sonntag (eds.), *Pueblo, época y desarrollo: la sociología de América Latina* (Caracas: Nueva Sociedad).

Wilson Lloyd, A. (2001) "Architecture for Art's Sake – Exciting New Buildings can Burnish Art Museums' Reputation, and Museums are Commissioning Lots of Them," *The Atlantic Monthly* 287 (June): 6, 85.

Zulaika, J. (1997) "The Seduction of Bilbao" (Guggenheim Museum, Bilbao, Spain), *Architecture* 86/12: 60–4.

PART NINE

Reflectivity

CHAPTER THIRTY-SEVEN

Ethics

Vikki Bell

The question of ethics has never been as centrally debated within feminist theory as it is at present; nor has it been so fraught. Insofar as feminism's express concern is to mobilize against injustice and to see instituted a universal value of equality, it is, like ethics, concerned with the quality of the spaces between people, and with the key ethical questions of responsiveness and responsibility. Indeed, as Cornell has argued, the history of feminism has been a series of challenges to reimagine the values by which human beings live, especially in terms of seeking to have harms that were not regarded as harmful (discrimination against women, sexual violences) seen differently: feminism presents an "endless challenge to the ethical imagination" (1995: 79). However, there has been of late an increasing amount of work that renders the intimacy between feminism and ethics problematic. Some feminists are now highly skeptical of the possibility of "an ethical (way of) being" and thus the pursuit of "feminist ethics" or "ethical feminism" has been placed under question. This is not to say, however, that the question of ethics could be simply rendered obsolete; feminism cannot abandon the question of ethics because feminism's political hope rests upon being able to be confidently responsive and responsible. It would not be hyperbolic to suggest that, currently, it is on the ground of ethics that the possible architecture of that hope is being most hotly debated. In this chapter I want to give some sense of the development of these debates, and the current complexities and directions to which I have alluded.

For a long time, feminists working within philosophy have criticized the discipline's subdivision "ethics," attacking in particular its historical failure to include women within its image of the ethical subject or to reflect upon the *situated* and contextually *contingent* nature of values. The development of mainstream ethical theory through the twentieth century has meant that the notion as proposed at the beginning of the century – that to study ethics is to pursue a "systematic and precise general knowledge of what is right and what makes judgements valid" (Sidgwick, quoted in Walker 1998) – has now been left behind. So, too, the distinction between the study of ethics and the study of a realm of "practical ethics" in which that systematic knowledge is "applied" as if it were a set of formulae, has collapsed. It would be an overstatement to say that feminist critiques brought about these developments, not just because "male-stream philosophers," as Alison Jaggar (2000) has noted, have tended to ignore feminist interventions in ethics, but because others – Walker lists "Aristotelians, Humeans, communitarians, contemporary casuists, pragmatists, historicists, Wittgensteinians, and others" (1998: 53) – have also pursued lines of argument that have forced ethicists to consider the profound consequences of foregrounding the situated nature of the ethical subject and, indeed, the ethical theorist. Universal ethical theory, with its attendant universal ethical subject, unencumbered by any aspect of his context, is now regarded suspiciously not just by feminists, but by most contributors to debates on ethics.

If feminism didn't cause this volte-face, feminists certainly contributed to the groundswell, with the boldest and most celebrated feminist contribution to this decline in faith in the code-following ethical subject – Carol Gilligan's *In A Different Voice* (1982) – asserting that the notion of an abstract moral code was biased toward masculine modes of thinking. Gilligan's work criticized those who understood the highest stages of moral reasoning, as implicit in much ethics philosophy and as defined in the developmental theory of Kohlberg, as those in which people follow abstract rules rather than "merely" respond to the specifics of the situation in which they find themselves. Gilligan argued that many women in her study were reasoning about ethical decisions at what Kohlberg would understand as a "lower" stage, where the preservation of relationships within the situation was considered paramount. Refusing to conclude that women were reasoning at a less developed level, Gilligan forced a reconsideration of whether it is possible to think about a unitary ungendered ethical subject, and whether it was a masculinist bias to understand ethics as involving, at its most developed, abstract rules and codes.

Although Gilligan has emphasized that the notion of a different voice should be understood as characterized by the mode of reasoning and not by the gender of the speaker, it is associated by her, and by others, with women, whose socially defined roles overdetermine them as those who will value the connections between people over "the (moral) law." Unsurprisingly therefore, Gilligan's work has been heavily criticized, not least for its tendencies toward essentialist modes of thought (as if being female was all that was needed to produce caring behavior), as well as for its naivety in thinking these themes are spontaneously produced (were the responses an effect of the interviewees in Gilligan's study responding as women "should"?). It has also been seen as dangerously close to a sort of "slave morality" where care is extended to all, including one's abuser (Card 1990) and as unable to satisfactorily distinguish between appropriate and inappropriate forms of care (Jaggar 1995). Furthermore, some feminists have balked at the image of women as all-caring. Some time ago Elizabeth Spelman argued that feminists must not be too quick to "feel virtuous about attending to the virtues of feeling, the marvel of care" (1991: 229), and that the history of women's capacities to be inhumane to other women cannot be simply removed from the discussion of ethics.

Nevertheless, the notion of care has been enormously influential, connecting with developments elsewhere within feminist thought and with a wider main-stream search within ethics for an alternative to the impartial and universalist eth-ical subject of the Kantian and utilitarian frameworks which had dominated ethical philosophy (and as evidenced in the revival of interest in Aristotelian ethics with its emphasis on virtue and community) (Friedman 2000: 207). Many feminists were intrigued to explore the potential to be wrought by placing care and connection at the center of their analyses. The term provides an umbrella term for wide-ranging considerations of women's everyday inter-actions as gendered ethical practices, from styles of conversation, to mothering practices, to embodied negotiations of space. Moreover, placing "care" centrally, several feminists have suggested, would provide for an improved focus for feminist political demands, and if these demands are met, an improved world where care and connection counter the tendencies of the masculinist world to individualist approaches to life (this has taken many forms: e.g. Jaggar 1995; Noddings 1984; Ruddick 1989; Toronto 1993; for a more recent example in the context of women in British politics, see MacKay 2001).

Importantly, the work of "care" theorists has underscored the argument that in terms of how people live their daily lives ethical theory is "entirely dispensable as a guide to right action" (Jaggar 2000: 370). Attending to the *situated* nature of ethical reasoning respects the space between people with much more nuance and detail than an emptied-out version of abstract universal moral codes ever could. The ideal observer is revealed as ideal only for those who wish for the (im)possibility of being able to abstract oneself away from socially embedded existence so as to compare situations as if they were alike, a compar-ison by substitution that many feminist writers have questioned (e.g. Arnault 1990: 195). Indeed, Benhabib argued that the abstraction of the other that occurs whenever the concrete other magically dissolves into the generalized other of an abstract moral code effectively denies difference *tout court* (1987: 89), as in the process of being likened to an instance to which a general code applies, the specificities of this concrete other and her situation are rendered irrelevant. That a form of ethical reasoning could have the effect of eliminating difference is a devastating charge, since by definition ethics is meant to guide the negotiation of difference.

Feminist ethics could be said, by the end of the 1980s, to have been com-mitted to two principles, which have remained important in feminist work: first, an engagement with ethics as embodied and situated that arose counter to the history of thinking the ethical subject as an abstract rational code-following ideal being; and secondly, an engagement with an appreciation of difference, that arose out of the concern that abstraction had effectively eliminated the central point of ethics, that is, the responsiveness to the (concrete) other. The critique of abstraction forced an engagement with intersubjectivity as an embodied, visceral encounter, with an emphasis on the encounter as a moment in which there should be respect for all differences, not solely gendered difference.

These points continue to inform feminist work. Margaret Walker begins her *Moral Understandings: A Feminist Study in Ethics* from the premise that moral philosophy should abandon the juridico-theoretical model that seeks "unsituated purely moral knowledge" that would provide an "internal guidance system" (1998: 8). We should talk instead about "how human beings actually live and judge" (ibid.: x). Her perspective is to develop what she terms an "expressive-collaborative" account, where moral life is regarded as "a continuing negotiation among people, a practice of mutually allotting, assuming, or deflecting responsibilities of important kinds, and understanding the implications of doing so" (ibid.: 60). She suggests that this model works both descriptively, aiming to reveal what morality "is" – what kinds of interaction are regarded as moral in any given community – and normatively, since it suggests what morality is "for" – that is, what in human life depends upon these practices and how can they work well or less well (ibid.: 60). Interestingly, she also argues that it is imperative to give attention to the existing "geographies of responsibilities" (ibid.: 99) within which ethical practices occur. Drawing on the work of Marion Smiley (1992), Walker suggests that the assessment of responsibility involved in moral judgments turns in large part upon assessments of who can be blamed as well as what it makes sense to hold human beings responsible for. The assessments are therefore tied up with changes in the world (such as global interdependencies or new political balances of power) or in perspectives on understanding the world (what are wealthy nations' responsibilities to less developed countries). How these are understood affects how responsibilities are allocated and therefore how ethical decision processes are approached (1998: 98).

With her attention to the situated interpersonal and social features of morality, and with the choices of themes by which to explore the implications of her perspective, Walker's work dovetails with other feminist arguments. For example, the importance of regarding ethics as embodied negotiation might be seen to echo the engagement with embodied intersubjectivity that has been at the forefront of critiques of Habermasian theories of communication, especially deliberative democracy, indeed, wherever it is assumed that democratic debates are disembodied rational encounters in which strength of reasoning is all that is relevant to the sway of collective judgment. Iris Marion Young (1995) has been most vocal in insisting that democratic debates entail persuasive, rhetorical, and embodied tactics. Democratic participation, therefore, cannot be plural and diverse without recognizing that the space between people is not about formal "recognition" nor about simply being permitted to speak, but also about the quality of the interaction, which modes of speech are valued and accorded persuasive status. Similarly, Walker's work echoes Cockburn's *The Space Between Us* (1998), which could be regarded as a study of the situated and negotiated quality of feminist ethics in practice. Cockburn focused on the work of "peace-building" taking place in three women's projects in three countries where there were wars involving different ethno-nationalist groups: Northern Ireland, Israel/ Palestine, and Bosnia. She draws attention to how women of different ethnic backgrounds or national belonging came together to create within the project a space in which the "difficult reality of unavoidable, un-ending, careful, respectful struggle" (what Cockburn terms, drawing on William Connolly (1991), "agonistic democracy") could be addressed and enacted (1998: 216). The hope that Cockburn found in these projects was not a form of transcendence of differences but an affirmation of them, although, importantly, with "non-closure," that is, without assumptions being made on the basis of a woman's stated identity. The projects were ethical spaces that reduced polarization by emphasizing other differences beyond those that nationalist discourse would allow, that acknowledged injustices and asymmetries (Walker's maps of responsibilities) between ethno-national groups without allowing them to flood "the space between" the women. Cockburn's work is exemplary in its insistence that peace cannot be won through a gestural jettisoning of identity; but at the same time the first task for women in resisting nationalist renderings of the nation is "impropriety" – unsettling notions of "proper" peoples, names, and lands. These projects, she suggests, were examples of women withstanding the allure of tidy closures and conclusions that support imaginary dreams and, ultimately, war.

The exploration of ethical intersubjectivity, therefore, has come a long way from any sense that women can simply be understood to have a more care-orientated, less rule-orientated ethical capacity than men. Characterizing the quality of the "space between us" has become a complicated endeavor. For example, Oliver (2001) has argued that it is time to move beyond the inherited focus on the term "recognition" with its attendant philosophico-political history and its privileging of visibility, as the way to think the ethics of the intersubjective encounter. Drawing on the work of Merleau-Ponty as well as Irigaray and Levinas, as many other feminist writers on ethical encounters have done (e.g. Chanter 1994), Oliver argues, along with Cathryn Vasseleu (1998), that the intersubjective encounter is not only about seeing and recognizing, which privilege light and the eyes, but it also involves a more visceral, sensual receptivity to what she broadly terms "energies." These are psychic and affective energies that are also social energies. It is our ethical obligation, Oliver argues, to attend to these energies that constitute the space between us and the kinds of reception possible between us, not only because subjectivities are founded upon one's responsiveness to these energies, but because they connect each of us to other people and to the world (2001: 196).

However, and as these authors recognize, there are several reasons why the intersubjective and the level of the visceral is limited as the sole focus of feminist explorations. Let three reasons suffice here. First, because intersubjectivity is not merely about two people meeting; it is about a whole complex of power/knowledge relations that constitute differences historically, discursively, and materially. Secondly, because ethics is also about non-intersubjective and non-embodied encounters, between people who have and never will meet, and necessarily involves the powerful mediation of language (let alone the relationship to non-human actors or technologies) and thus the endlessly fraught questions of representation. The question of ethics is not simply "How should I act in relation to the other?" but also one of dimensions, that is, "How far – across how much space and time, encompassing how many people – should I care?" And thirdly, the intersubjective is inadequate as a focus because pursuing the attention to the other implicitly raises the issue of other others who are left unattended: the paradox of the unethical at the heart of the ethical. I will address these three points in turn in order to give some sense of the feminist explorations that take their cue from them.

Feminists have long argued that intersubjectivity is an encounter that is criss-crossed by the lines of power and knowledge that constitute the participants' differences in particular historically and culturally specific ways. Those feminists who have been influenced by the work of Michel Foucault have formulated this thought in his terms – i.e., an ethical encounter is never purely a question of intersubjectivity because it takes place within regimes of power/knowledge. Thus, although there is merit in attending to the intersubjective as a response to the abstraction of moral philosophy as code, the focus will always become wider again as one attends to the historical and contingent conditions of possibility by which the forms of comprehension present within it have arisen. There is, from this perspective, no room for a "spontaneous" ethics. The one to whom we are responsive and to whom we feel accountable is not encountered in a vacuum: our historically and culturally trained modes of comprehension construct him/her and instruct us in our modes of engagement. Not only this, but we know that the very construction of issues *as* ethical and modes of response *as* "ethical" are historically constituted, so that our attentions are never free or innocent even in our most intensely "ethical moments" (see, for example, Valverde 1998, who draws on Foucault in her work on the history of the production of the ethical subject). Within contemporary American popular culture certain versions of what it means to be ethical circulate; Berlant (2000) has warned feminists not to get drawn into the forms of sentimentality that abound in popular American culture, that collapse the ethical into the sensual, that regard feeling bad as a sign of injustice and feeling good as a sign of justice, to the extent that the pursuit of the ethical becomes the expression of forms of (often psychological) pain that are relieved when they are recognized, especially by law. Political work, she argues, requires attention to those levels of the everyday that cannot be articulated merely as forms of private pain.

These conditions of possibility cannot be removed from the encounter by fiat, nor are they readily intelligible, so that ethics becomes a continual assessment not between the right and the wrong way to behave, but between the risky and the more risky (as Foucault said, "we must decide what is the greatest danger"). This would be the approach informing the stance adopted by feminists such as Judith Butler, who would posit the subject as radically contingent cultural production, who continually risks the repetition of discursive formations that further enmesh one in dominant lines of power/knowledge. Because no one can simply step out of these lines, the ethical is understood by Butler as attention to modes of "citation" by which we produce ourselves and others. In her discussion of hate speech in *Excitable Speech*, for example, she suggests that we are doomed to repeat, since to do otherwise would be to risk our status as subjects, so the question is *how* do we repeat? The agency of the subject is an effect of power, Butler writes, but it is not fully "determined in advance" (1997: 139). Thus it is possible to think about moments of rupture where one finds moments of decontextualization, where the authorization of the (speech) act might be sought from sources other than those that have gained (hegemonic) authority.

Secondly, the focus on the intersubjective has to expand in order to consider the ethics of relationships that extend beyond the present moment and place. Some of the most challenging work is relevant at this juncture. Feminists working on trauma and, relatedly, on questions of testimony have produced some extraordinarily provocative work that challenges us to think about the ethical relationship that exists between those in the present and those in the past. How are we to *remember* ethically? On the one hand, there is a question of historical collective remembering: that is, how is it possible to bring aspects of people's lives in the past into our present concerns without denying their singularity, without merely using them for one's own purposes, and without making displays or spectacles of their lives, especially when they can no longer raise objections or make contradictions? On the other hand, there is an ethical question with a more psychoanalytic inflection, which is about how others enter the individual psyche and how that form of "carrying" the trace of the other is or is not able to be "ethical." I do not have space to discuss these lines of thought fully, but they pervade feminist explorations of memory and memorials, especially in relation to catastrophes and past violences, and the related question of "testimony." One concept that has been put to interesting use in this area is that of heteroempathic identification, a concept employed in the work of Silverman (1996). In contrast to a tradition of thinking about women's ethical modus operandi as empathy, and feminism's engine as the sort of sameness found in consciousness raising, this concept attempts to describe an ethical responsivity that does not replace the other with oneself – "that happened to me also" or "I'm just like you" – nor does it simply maintain separation – "I wasn't there" or "we're different." Instead, heteroempathic identification offers a response to the other that maintains identity and difference: "it could have been me" or "it was me also and at the same time it was not me" (see, for example, Radstone 2001).

Many feminists are currently grappling with the possibility of ethical sensibilities that respect differences across geographic distance. Within an unequal global economy, with its colonial legacies and its continuing uneven forms of development, it is clear that feminism has to pay attention to how international relations affect women worldwide. For example, feminists working in development ethics have observed how "development" policies often discriminate against women by denying them land ownership and credit; and some have also noted how women are disproportionately affected by the structural adjustments mandated by international lending institutions which have drastically reduced the welfare functions of states in the developing world (Jaggar 2000: 364, summarizing Moser 1993). Similarly, women working within environmental ethics have suggested that environmental degradation has specific consequences for women, especially poor women and mothers (Warren 1990). But it is in the attempt to grapple with the notion of ethical relationships that are globally extensive and comprehensive that much feminist work has raised ethical concerns. Mohanty (1993) raised the question directly some years ago when she argued that the notion of "third world women" was being used within Western feminism in a way that produced many millions of women as a homogeneous category that could be incorporated into the forms of universalism that Western feminism inherited from legacies of colonial dominance. Her argument was that feminists need to speak and hear each other with attention to their respective cultural formations so that, for example, different modes of comprehension, criticism, and resistance could be appreciated without the imposition of a single ethical standard and vision. A similar form of argument surrounds the more recent debate on the "relationship" of feminism to multiculturalism in the United States; Volpp (2001), responding to Susan Moller Okin, has argued that to set up a debate under the title "Is multiculturalism bad for feminism?" carries with it a legacy of assumptions in which white women are depicted as free of culture and as the owners of "feminism," with non-white women depicted as laboring under archaic forms of "cultural problems." How debates are structured affects their course and conclusions, so that the question of the ethical is not outside the moments of representation that take place within feminist discourse itself.

Gayatri Spivak has been most vociferous in her exploration of the problems and the possibilities of ethical representation in relation to feminism's desire to talk of "women" in the face of the complexities of women's differences within countries and across the globe. Influenced, inter alia, by critical theory and by Derrida's deconstructionism, Spivak's arguments have always attended to the question of representation where the textual and the political are entwined. The influence of her article "Can the Subaltern Speak?" (1988) continues to be felt in feminist work on ethics, as elsewhere. In it, she opposed the idea that a subaltern group could be merely represented without a form of violence being done both to the heterogeneity of the group (and their interests) supposedly so named, or without a certain disingenuousness in the forgetting of the role of colonialism played in producing the subaltern. Elsewhere she has explained:

> [I]t is not a solution, the idea of the disenfranchised speaking for themselves, or the radical critics speaking for them, [because] this question of representation, self-representation, representing others, is a problem. On the other hand, we cannot put it under the carpet with demands for authentic voices; we have to remind ourselves that as we do this we might be compounding the problem even as we are trying to solve it. (1990: 63)

What possibility is there, Spivak asks, of generating a radical feminist politics that is responsive to others without encouraging "the metropolitan feminist" to ask "all women to become like herself" in a world where economic development is mistaken for health and all relevant debates are approached as if they are (to be) structured just as they are in the "Western world" (1998: 342)? This leads to a reduction of the other to the same, so that, for example, Western feminists consider their model of themselves as rights-bearing citizens as the future for women elsewhere.

Spivak's negotiations of the (im)possibility of maintaining an ethical relation with the singularity of the other have led her to consider a notion of ethical *translation* as a means of engagement which, as Sara Ahmed has noted, "moves between distance and proximity" so that the necessity and dangers of the decisions made in the "reading" are admitted and foregrounded (1998: 63). Ahmed herself (2000) has explored this aspect of Spivak's work in relation to her own consideration of the ethical possibilities of an unfetishized approach to "the other." Spivak has also made the *pedagogic* a central concern, and the role of teaching has become a privileged site of ethical relations in her work. She has spoken, for example, about the possibilities of feminist teachers teaching (themselves and) their students not to hide behind the pretence of self effacing gestures that remove their right to speak about and criticize things outside their immediate identity or experience. Educating oneself about the historical construction of one's own positionality and that of other people can earn one the right to speak and be heard respectfully, Spivak argues, and saying "I can't speak about that" because of what one is (such as white, male, or privileged) is another way of salving one's conscience in the name of political correctness (1990: 62).

As one can sense from the direction of much of this work, there is a certain inevitability that the feminist critique of ethical theory would place the feminist pursuit of ethics itself under question. For a start, this is because feminists have long been circling around the argument that feelings of virtue are not always entirely innocently come by, not even in feminism, and "being a good feminist" probably involves sentiments that are less than ethically defensible. Some have suggested that the logic of feminist political argument could be understood as based on *resentiment*, arguments that imagine a (male) figure who has that of which women are deprived, whose place women seek to occupy or usurp (Brown 1995). If envy and anger are bases for feminist political movement, and it is power (Flax 1993) rather than an ethical world that women want, why bother dallying with questions of ethics? Furthermore, from a different line of attack, the question of ethics has come under pressure from the combined force of the philosophies of Levinas and Derrida, who, for different reasons, make ethics highly problematic. Derrida has argued in *The Gift of Death* (1995), for example, that being responsive to the other involves simultaneous irresponsiveness to all others (while I engage with you, I cannot engage with her), and that ethical response doesn't proclaim its reasoning because the response to the other in his or her singularity demands also a secrecy, a non-accountability to a third.

Feminism is unlikely to be able to characterize its actions as ethical on these terms, and by the act of giving account, it cancels its own claims to ethical responsibility. Elsewhere, I have suggested that given the impossibility of achieving Levinas's depiction of ethical non-(in)difference within a *politics* (because the move from ethics to politics in Levinas's thought involves a hiatus rather than a flow), feminist politics can only be understood as the negotiation of the necessarily unethical business of political rallying and representation (choosing this and not that topic, for example, or even the making symmetrical of the asymmetry of the relationship between myself and the other through my knowledge and representation of her, count as "unethical") (see, for example, Levinas 1985, 1987). "The ethical" is not what is *expressed* within feminist politics, even as the impulses that initiate and provide the check on feminist endeavors are "ethical" (Bell 2001).

Yet still it seems that feminist work wants to circle this question of ethics formulating preferred routes away from the necessary difficulties therein. Feminists remain energetic in the search for a figure for ethical reflections, and for new terms to describe ethical relations. A number of feminists – including Chanter (1994), Oliver (2001), hooks (2000), even Spivak (1998: 340) – are returning, somewhat surprisingly, to the term "love" as the site of ethical explorations. Concepts such as forgiveness and empathy also seem to be (re)circulating in feminist discourses (Toronto 2000) as a way of thinking about empathetic ethical attitudes toward enemies past and present. While these elevations of sentiment seem optimistic and even hopelessly romantic, this same impulse to sentiment is arguably as it must be, since it is the manifestation of a sort of ethical impulse. One recent collection describes this persistent excavation of "the good" as itself a bold endeavor – *Daring to be Good* (Bar On 1998) – in the face of philosophical skepticism. But the collection's contents reflect the varied stances it is possible to take when the notion of ethics has become so broadly defined. Perhaps it is because the ethical impulse cannot be removed, since a confident sense of open responsiveness is necessary in a politics that draws upon that sense to question sedimented norms, to speak of justice, and to make judgments about modes of living. However, nor can the ethical question be "solved" once and for all: it must remain fraught. In relation to its ethical sensibilities, feminism cannot have a heroic narrative that is fixed on its path of resistance once and for all. For all the reasons discussed above, feminist ethics must be interrupted and questioned. Indeed, one could give the name "ethics" both to what prompts feminism and to what interrupts and questions its formulations, decisions, and imaginations.

References

Ahmed, S. (1998) *Differences that Matter: Feminist Theory and Postmodernism* (Cambridge: Cambridge University Press).

Ahmed, S. (2000) *Strange Encounters: Embodied Others in Post-Coloniality* (London: Routledge).

Arnault, L. (1990) "The Radical Future of Classical Moral Theory," in A. Jaggar and S. Bordo (eds.), *Gender/Body/Knowledge: Feminist Reconstructions of Being and Knowing* (New Brunswick, NJ: Rutgers University Press).

Bar On, B.-A. and Ferguson, A. (eds.) (1998) *Daring to Be Good: Essays in Feminist Ethico-Politics* (New York: Routledge).

Bell, V. (2001) "On Ethics and Feminism: Reflecting on Levinas: Ethics of Non-(in)difference," *Feminist Theory* 2/2.

Benhabib, S. (1987) "The Generalised and the Concrete Other: The Kohlberg–Gilligan Controversy and Feminist Theory," in S. Benhabib and D. Cornell (eds.), *Feminism as Critique* (Cambridge: Polity).

Berlant, L. (2000) "The Subject of True Feeling: Pain, Privacy and Politics," in S. Ahmed, J. Kilby, C. Lury, M. McNeil, and B. Skeggs, *Transformations: Thinking Through Feminism* (London: Routledge).

Brown, W. (1995) *States of Injury: Power and Freedom in Late Modernity* (Princeton: Princeton University Press).

Butler, J. (1997) *Excitable Speech: A Politics of the Performative* (New York: Routledge).

Card, C. (1990) "Gender and Moral Luck," in Owen Flanagan and Amélie Oksenberg Rorty, *Identity, Character and Morality* (Cambridge, MA: MIT Press).

Chanter, T. (1994) *Ethics of Eros: Irigaray's Rewriting of the Philosophers* (London: Routledge).

Cockburn, C. (1998) *The Space between Us: Negotiating Gender and National Identities in Conflict* (London: Zed Books).

Connolly, W. (1991) *Identity/Difference: Democratic Negotiations of Political Paradox* (Ithaca, NY: Cornell University Press).

Cornell, D. (1995) "What is an Ethical Feminism?" in S. Benhabib, J. Butler, D. Cornell, and N. Fraser, *Feminist Contentions: A Philosophical Exchange* (New York: Routledge).

Derrida, J. (1995) *The Gift of Death*, trans. David Wills (Chicago: University of Chicago Press).

Flax, J. (1992) "The End of Innocence," in J. Butler and J. Scott, *Feminists Theorize the Political* (London: Routledge).

Friedman, M. (2000) "Feminism in Ethics: Conceptions of Autonomy," in M. Fricker and J. Hornsby, *The Cambridge Companion to Feminism in Philosophy* (Cambridge: Cambridge University Press).

Gilligan, C. (1982) *In a Different Voice: Psychological Theory and Women's Development* (Cambridge, MA: Harvard University Press).

hooks, b. (2000) *All About Love* (London: Women's Press).

Jaggar, A. (1995) "Caring as a Feminist Practice of Moral Reason," in Virginia Held (ed.), *Justice and Care: Essential Readings in Feminist Ethics* (Boulder, CO: Westview).

Jaggar, A. (2000) "Feminist Ethics," in Hugh LaFollette (ed.), *The Blackwell Guide to Ethical Theory* (Oxford: Blackwell).

Levinas, E. (1985) *Ethics and Infinity: Conversations with Philippe Nemo*, trans. R. Cohen (Pittsburgh, PA: Duquesne University Press).

Levinas, E. (1987) *Time and the Other*, trans. R. Cohen (Pittsburgh, PA: Duquesne University Press).

MacKay, F. (2001) *Love and Politics: Women Politicians and the Ethics of Care* (London: Continuum).

Mohanty, C. (1993) "Under Western Eyes: Feminist Scholarship and Colonial Discourses," in P. Williams and L. Chrisman (eds.), *Colonial Discourse and Post-Colonial Theory* (Hemel Hempstead: Harvester Wheatsheaf).

Moser, C. (1993) *Gender, Planning and Development* (London: Routledge).

Noddings, N. (1984) *Caring* (Berkeley and Los Angeles: University of California Press).

Oliver, K. (2001) *Witnessing: Beyond Recognition* (Minneapolis: University of Minnesota Press).

Radstone, S. (2001) "Social Bonds and Psychical Order: Testimonies," *Cultural Values* 5/1.

Ruddick, S. (1989) *Maternal Thinking* (New York: Ballatine Books).

Silverman, K. (1996) *Threshold of the Visible World* (New York: Routledge).

Smiley, M. (1992) *Moral Responsibility and the Boundaries of Community* (Chicago: University of Chicago Press).

Spelman, E. V. (1991) "Feeling Virtuous and the Virtue of Feeling," in C. Card (ed.), *Feminist Ethics* (Lawrence, KA: University Press of Kansas).

Spivak, G. (1988) "Can the Subaltern Speak?" in C. Nelson and L. Grossberg (eds.), *Marxism and the Interpretation of Culture* (Urbana: University of Illinois Press).

Spivak, G. (1990) *The Postcolonial Critic* (New York: Routledge).

Spivak, G. (1998) "Cultural Talks in the Hot Peace: Revisiting the 'Global Village'," in P. Cheah and B. Robbins (eds.), *Cosmopolitics: Thinking and Feeling Beyond the Nation* (Minneapolis: University of Minnesota Press).

Toronto, J. (2000) "Time's Place," Unpublished conference paper, "Gendering Ethics Conference," University of Leeds, UK.

Valverde, M. (1998) *Diseases of the Will* (Cambridge: Cambridge University Press).

Vasseleu, C. (1998) *Textures of Light: Vision and Touch in Irigaray, Lévinas and Merleau-Ponty* (London: Routledge).

Volpp, L. (2001) "Feminism Versus Multiculturalism," *Columbia Law Review* 101/5.

Walker, M. U. (1998) *Moral Understandings: A Feminist Study in Ethics* (New York: Routledge).

Warren, K. J. (1990) "The Power and Promise of Ecological Feminism," *Environmental Ethics* 12/2.

Young, I. M. (1995) "Communication and the Other: Beyond Deliberative Democracy," in S. Benhabib (ed.), *Democracy and Difference: Contesting the Boundaries of the Political* (Princeton: Princeton University Press).

CHAPTER THIRTY-EIGHT

Religion

Pamela Dickey Young

It is not self-evident how religion ought to be defined. Even the scholarly notion of specific religious traditions is a particularly Westernized notion that grows out of a Christian-informed imperialistic view that often classifies religions in categories that best fit Christianity and only more tenuously fit other traditions. That said, however, there is much usefulness in examining religious traditions giving attention to questions of gender.

King writes: "Religion is the organization of life around the depth dimensions of experience – varied in form, completeness and clarity in accordance with the environing culture" ([1987] 1995: 285). It is the notion of "depth dimension" that is useful here to focus attention toward something in the way religious people conceive of and organize the totality of their world such that these conceptions and organizations provide structure for understanding the universe and for acting in response to it. Thus, religions tend to deal especially with the most puzzling of human questions and predicaments and provide means to deal with these issues: such as evil or death, for example. Religions provide symbol systems, that is, particular ways to understand and portray what is thought to be ultimate. Frequently, there is a central symbol or symbols: god(s), nirvana, the Tao, for example. Religion often employs myths, poetry, or metaphor rather than direct description, to evoke the ultimate quality of what it is trying to embody. Sometimes these symbols, myths, and metaphors are embodied in sacred texts, sometimes passed on through oral traditions. Religion regularly uses rituals as a means to bring the participant into contact with whatever is conceived as ultimate and to hold at bay the chaotic forces of the universe. There might be sacred places or objects. Historically, religion has been communal, but in the modern Western world, at least, people tend more and more to individualized belief and practice to deal with this "depth dimension."

In North America today, the word "spirituality" has become popular as many people view "religion" or being religious negatively, equating it with dominant forms of organized religious traditions, Christianity in particular. "Spirituality" has become a way to name a picking and choosing of particular elements in what

I would call a personal religiosity. In this chapter I will use "religion" and "religiosity" to cover the gamut of both communal and individual belief and practice.

King also draws attention to the notion of the "environing culture." It is important at the outset to understand the vast diversity of forms taken by even a single religious tradition over time, in various geographical settings and even in specific individual and/or communal contexts. "Religion" is not a monolith; nor is any religious tradition. It is helpful here also if we make a distinction between the "official" way in which any religious tradition presents itself and the host of "unofficial" forms such a tradition might take. While the "official" form often dominantly or exclusively presents males in positions of action and authority, there may well be other faces or presentations of that same tradition that understand women as important actors or authority figures. Thus, for example the "official" face of Roman Catholic Christianity is almost exclusively male in form, represented by the Pope, the Cardinals, and exclusively male language and imagery for God. But there are many feminist Roman Catholics who actively live out their faith in relatively autonomous religious terms (nuns) or as parish lay leaders, who fully recognize the patriarchal nature of official Roman Catholicism and yet who remain within the church. Their interpretation of the symbol system is feminist rather than traditional. They refuse to see the Pope as the only legitimate face of Roman Catholicism or patriarchy as its only form.

Religious traditions have often been seen as tools of patriarchy – or what Fiorenza calls "kyriarchy," rule of the "lords" over everything that is under them (1994: 14) – and indeed they can be and have been. But people who might be considered powerless within a patriarchal or kyriarchal tradition continue to be religious in a whole host of ways in part because their particular way of being religious does not reduce it to its patriarchal or kyriarchal manifestations. Such people have often found a liberating message or practice in their religious tradition despite its seemingly overt kyriarchy.

Gender

"Gender" is a term and a category of analysis that, depending on how it is used, can sometimes illuminate and sometimes mask what is going on in any given cultural pursuit. It can mask what is happening when we pass over the very real differentials of power and position between women and men to some assumed "gender neutrality." As Juschka says:

> The movement into gender analysis in the study of religion could be lauded for its apparent trend toward a more objective appreciation of gender as a facet of socio-historical change, particularly that related to religion (rather than using it apologetically or politically) were it not for the suspicious juxtaposition of this objectivizing tendency with the replacement of women and feminism by gender. (1999: 93)

510

The use of the lens of gender can illuminate when it takes feminist critique and consciousness seriously. It can also illuminate when it seeks to understand the construction of maleness as well as femaleness.

In many, perhaps most, religious traditions, sex and gender have been seen as basically synonymous. One is ascribed certain gender roles on the basis of an essentialized view of one's biological sex. Thus, one's biological sex becomes the marker for assigning particular gendered religious and moral roles and expectations. Even though there are certain religious exceptions to this – for example, the *berdache* in native North American traditions, who represents both male and female power (Hultkranz 1967: 3), or in androgynous portrayals of Siva within Hinduism – these exceptions are clearly seen to be exceptions from the norm of relatively rigidly codified sex/gender roles. Although within many religious traditions in the contemporary world there has been some movement on the front of the reconstruction of gender roles – for example, the ordination of women in most Protestant Christian Churches and in liberal Judaism – there has been virtually no recognition of how most religious traditions use the supposed "bedrock" of biological sex to provide categories and concepts on which much is based and from which much flows. Thus, the whole notion of "sex" remains highly bifurcated, as male and female, and treated as a "given" whether from God or the universe. And in addition to bifurcation and ossification of the roles, rights, and privileges of men and women, this essentialized stance also influences how religious symbols are seen and interpreted: the "maleness" of the God of Western monotheistic traditions, for example, or the interactions of the gods and goddesses of Hinduism. This leaves unexamined how "sex" itself is socially constructed to have meaning and cultural import.

Following Ruether's (1972) astute analysis of "dualisms" within Christianity, feminist critiques of religion noticed from a very early stage that the way in which male over female was a dualism informed the dualism of mind/soul over body/nature in Christianity. Thus, feminist analysis of gender within religious traditions began as an analysis of the dualisms that connected men to God (or the ultimate) as well as to mind and spirit, and women to body and nature. In looking at religious traditions from a feminist perspective, one often sees that men are closer to whatever is considered most important, and women to that which is of lesser value, sometimes even problematic.

Symbols and Social Structure

Mary Daly argues: "If God is male, then the male is God" (1973: 19). What she means is that in monotheistic religious traditions such as Christianity or Judaism, the portrayal of God as male gives license to men to wield social power because they are more godlike than women.

Religious symbols are socially constructed and they reflect the cultural values of the times and places in which they are constructed. The monotheism of

Judaism, Christianity, and Islam, for example, arose in the Ancient Near East in a religious environment of polytheism, where there were both male and female gods. Thus, when only one god becomes ascendant over (and ultimately is said to conquer) all the other gods and goddesses, it is no surprise that this god is portrayed as male rather than as female, especially when "he" is often portrayed in stereotypically male fashion as warrior, ruler, and so on.

The "maleness" of God in monotheisms is not absolute, however. Most practitioners of Western monotheisms, will, if confronted with the maleness of language for God, argue that God "himself" is not "biologically" male, but that, for a variety of reasons, male language is the most appropriate way to speak of God. Judaism and Islam have prohibitions against imaging God in pictorial terms. And there are both female and non-personal ways to refer to God within the scriptures of Judaism and Christianity. Thus, within these traditions are the roots of their own critique.

The relation between the gender of central symbols and the structure of society is not an absolute. Daly's assumptions that the maleness of God ensures male power is not a strict causal relationship. As Bynum (1986) points out, the relationship between the gender of symbols and the structure of power is complex. In Hinduism, for instance, there are a variety of gods and goddesses. If Daly is correct, one would expect that societies where Hinduism predominates would be more egalitarian than those where male monotheisms predominate. But that does not seem to be the case. Thus, the gendered nature of god-language is only one issue in the complex structuring of societal power relationships. Still, there is much that Western feminists can learn from the symbols system of Hinduism about the complex and multifaceted nature of both goddesses and gods.

Language is not an insignificant issue, however. I understand the relationship between language and social structure to be somewhat circular. Language both reflects and creates realities. One reinforces the other, but neither by itself is totally explanatory of power relationships. If one always uses male language to describe or address the God who is considered ultimate, then one might begin to think that maleness is more like divinity than femaleness is, especially if people react in horror or distress when female language is used. Conversely, the reaction of horror or distress might well be because human male power is seen as that which is most important and valuable, and thus that any description of God would have to make use of the most important and most valuable language available.

Some forms of neo-paganism in the West have sought to balance gods and goddesses in their mythic and ritual structures. Some draw only on goddess traditions and images. The latter often rest on the assumption that people, mostly women, need the goddess to counteract traditional patriarchal religious views. Interestingly enough, Western neo-paganism in most of its forms is itself a reinscription of the bifurcation of male and female and of the unalterable connection between sex and gender, for goddesses are often portrayed as stereotypically female (giving birth, akin to nature) and gods as stereotypically male (warriors) (Berger 1999).

Feminist attention to the gender of ultimate symbols has to address, then, not only whether the symbols are male, female, or neutral, but how these symbols are joined to concepts of human power and whether they are fixed or fluid. Symbols that simply reinscribe gender roles will not be able to foster social change. But the same symbols may be used both as tools of oppression and as tools of liberation. What sort of god or goddess is being described? What is his or her power? How are humans able to act in the face of the god, goddess, or other power structures of the universe? Religious traditions often contain within themselves a variety of answers to these questions, even though traditional (and often patriarchal) answers might predominate.

Who is Normatively Human? Who Acts?

Historically, in most religious traditions the "official" actors have been men. Men have mostly been the official interpreters of sacred texts and the official ritual celebrants. Men have been in the most powerful decision-making roles in religious traditions. Men have been normative religious actors, and women, when they have been "official" actors at all, have been interpreted from the point of view of history looking back as extraordinary actors. One thinks of Aisha, wife of Muhammad, who is said to have been his teacher in many things or Maitreyí, the wife of Upanisadic philosopher Yajñavalkya.

The way religious traditions tell their own official gender histories, however, sometimes belies the fact that the sex of the main actors might have been more fluid at certain historical times (often at the beginnings of a religious movement or in times of transition). Certain interpretations of history become normative even when historians have discovered that there may be room for doubt about the official interpretation. For example, the Vatican insists that there have never been women priests. Yet, textual, inscriptional, and pictorial evidence from the early centuries of Christianity has shown that women were in roles of liturgical and ecclesial leadership. What seems to have happened is that as Christianity made the move across four centuries from charismatic movement to official religion of the Roman empire, women became less and less "appropriate" actors. Then, official readings of the history fail to note women's more-than-extraordinary presence at the beginnings of the movement.

There have also been religious roles specifically for women, and there have been rituals specifically for women to perform, especially ritual roles in the home that are women's alone to perform (see Falk and Gross 2001). Early Buddhism had orders of nuns as well as of monks, a tradition that is just being rediscovered and reasserted today with interesting discussions about whether monks are or are not to be absolutely obeyed by nuns. Nuns within Buddhism and Catholic Christianity were able to attain a measure of independence from male control simply by living and working most of their lives apart from men. Likewise, because in Orthodox Judaism or in some cultural forms of Islam women are often separate from men for large portions of their lives, there are many ways of asserting a certain amount of religious independence.

Recently in liberal Judaism and Protestant Christianity and in some forms of Hinduism and Western Buddhism, women have been recognized as official public teachers and ritual actors. The arguments that paved the way for their ordination in liberal Judaism and in Protestant Christianity were based on the view that there is only one human nature and that everyone, male or female, is equal in the eyes of god. There was certainly no idea that women would change the clerical role, only that they would adopt the male-defined clerical role as their own. Clericalism was never gender neutral. And it has taken decades for ordained women to come to be seen as normative actors in their own right rather than as aberrations of the male clerical norm. Nonetheless, this is happening and has happened in many places. And, indeed, the clerical norm begins to change in response to it.

Fundamentalisms

In many of the world's religious traditions there have been resurgences of funda-mentalism. Fundamentalism is hard to define. The notion of fundamentalism grew out of the American Christian context of the early twentieth century when a series of pamphlets called "The Fundamentals" was published. But more recently, fundamentalism has been used to describe particular movements within many world religions, which, among other things, are opposed to Enlightenment values of critical and rational inquiry and depend on a highly structured and authoritarian view of the particular religious tradition. The major leadership roles in most religious fundamentalisms are taken by males, with a charismatic male leader (Lawrence 1989). The male charismatic leader then becomes the final arbiter of truth and morals for those who follow him.

Fundamentalisms reinscribe traditional gender roles based on the view that men and women, if considered equal at all, are "separate but equal," and that women should act and are free within their own (usually highly circumscribed) spheres. If women seek to act outside these spheres, they are flouting not just social custom but also the laws of the universe that have dictated men's and women's status and roles from eternity.

Often when traditional religious institutions are seeking to put forward or defend positions that are against advances in the status and roles of women, they use female spokespersons to assure listeners that there are women who do not want these gains: ordination, access to both religious and secular education, access to safe, legal abortions, more social funding for women raising children alone, and so on. This strategy is supposed to make one think that only "radicals" or outsiders want such changes. It is meant to pit women against one another. It is also deceptive in

514

that it shifts the focus from the question of whether something provides justice for the marginalized to the question of whether "all women" want this.

Sexuality

Most world religions have traditionally had highly prescriptive views of sexuality based on the assumed bifurcation and separation of male and female. In many traditions women have been seen as temptresses to sexual misconduct (Eve). And in most traditions, where having children is important religiously as well as socially, women have historically been blamed for failure to conceive. Male sexuality and female sexuality have often been seen differently. When men's sexuality is restricted, it is because of their need to perform certain religious roles. Women's sexuality is restricted because they are the possessions of men, serving male religious need. In Orthodox Judaism, for instance, although female sexuality needs to be regulated to keep it from being unruly, male sexuality is also highly regulated because of the importance of sperm. Thus, arguments about birth control revolve around whether sperm is being wasted or misused. In Hinduism, renunciation of sexuality for a period of time is important to male performance of expected religious roles.

Because most religious traditions depend on essentialist views of male and female nature and regulate sexuality accordingly, homosexuality has been a huge theoretical as well as practical challenge, often seen as a violation of "nature." Religious traditions are just beginning to grapple with this challenge, especially in North America, where some Christian and Jewish groups have begun to rethink traditional negative positions on homosexuality. Where they have met this challenge to date, it usually involves an argument that actually reinscribes essentialism still further by arguing that gays and lesbians are created as they are by God and that one cannot argue with or change how God creates. Churches and synagogues have yet to begin to grapple in any meaningful way with the notion that sexuality may be at least in part socially constructed.

Curiously, although female sexuality is seen as more dangerous than male sexuality, lesbianism is often seen as more benign than being gay. For example, male homosexuality in Orthodox Judaism is treated with far greater seriousness than lesbianism, because sperm is at issue. But lesbianism is a problem, nonetheless, because it takes women out of the sphere of male control.

Trends

Feminist and gender critiques of religious traditions developed initially in North America and Northern Europe from Christian and Jewish feminists, some of whom quickly became post-Christian and post-Jewish as the critiques became more developed. The use of gender as a category of analysis still falls almost entirely to female scholars and religious practitioners. The origins of a feminist critique of religion was also largely white and middle class as well as geographically bound.

Issues of race and class have been raised by womanist (African-American), *mujerista* (Hispanic, both within and beyond North America), and other feminist Christian liberation theologians. For womanists, for example, the black church has often been a place in which to stand to engage in critique of racism as well as a community where women can find solidarity with one another. *Mujerista* theologians know that the conjunction of women and poverty in Latin America means that any interpretation of religion is insufficient if it does not address political solutions to the very real questions of class and power as well as questions of more abstract meaning. The contemporary North American goddess movements have had to grapple with the recognition that they are for the most part composed of white, educated, middle-class women.

There is a basic agreement among feminist adherents of religion that difference needs to be recognized and privileged. There is no agreement about how to do this. The struggle to make a variety of voices heard and to take these voices seriously is one in which most religious feminists are engaged. But, as with most other feminist pursuits, it is difficult to know how to do this without losing the ties that bind women together in solidarity. And, in this discussion, in addition to race and class, the very real factor of Western, Christian imperialism has been a huge issue. Christianity has been dominant on the Western landscape, asserting its presumed superiority over other religious traditions for centuries. Initially, feminist critiques arose from within and were influenced by Christianity. Understandably, those outside Christianity do not want a Christian feminist imperialism any more than they want a Christian patriarchal imperialism. Thus, feminist categories need to be continually re-examined for their Western, Christian hegemonic assumptions.

One of the issues with which feminist critiques of religious traditions struggle is the question of tradition. When is one still part of the tradition one criticizes and when has one moved beyond it? This issue also raises the question of reforming communities from within. Although many religious women have heard and understood Audre Lorde's view (1984) that the master's tools cannot dismantle the master's house, many also want to remain part of something that has, at least to some extent, given them something that they themselves need or appreciate. Thus, rather than simply walking away, they often employ strategies of resistance from within. For example, women have insisted on becoming educated interpreters of the texts and traditions even when "official" roles have not been open to them. Women have developed their own worshipping communities and rituals within traditions parallel to the official communities. They have often used the venue of the academy or the parallel ritual communities for presenting ideas and alternatives until the official religious community starts to take them seriously.

Another issue is who gets to criticize a tradition on feminist or gender lines and whose feminism or gender critique counts. Feminist critiques of Christianity and Judaism arose first from the pens of Christian and Jewish feminists. But feminist critiques of Islam, Hinduism, and Buddhism, for example, came first from the viewpoints of "outsiders." The critique has been taken up by insiders, to be sure, but there need to be more critiques arising from within these traditions that take specific locales of race, class, and culture into view.

Although it cannot yet be said to be a trend within religious institutions, some feminist academics, many of whom are also adherents of religious traditions, are beginning to push religious traditions to rethink their stable and essentialized views of sex and gender. Because so much religious tradition often rests on these views, this is a difficult task and one that is hardly begun yet. Another task that is needed but hardly begun is to begin theorizing maleness and masculinity in religious systems. Still, the task of "gender" analysis is left to women within religious traditions, because they stand to gain much more than they lose in this analysis. Much work remains to be done.

References

Berger, H. A. (1999) *A Community of Witches: Contemporary Neo-Paganism and Witchcraft in the United States* (Columbia: University of South Carolina Press).

Bynum, C. W. (1986) "Introduction: The Complexity of Symbols," in Caroline Walker Bynum, Stevan Harrell, and Paula Richman (eds.), *Gender and Religion: On the Complexity of Symbols* (Boston: Beacon).

Daly, M. (1973) *Beyond God the Father: Toward a Philosophy of Women's Liberation* (Boston: Beacon Press).

Falk, N. A. and Gross, R. M. (eds.) (2001) *Unspoken Worlds: Women's Religious Lives*, 3rd edn. (Belmont, CA: Wadsworth).

Fiorenza, E. S. (1994) *Jesus; Miriam's Child, Sophia's Prophet: Critical Issues in Feminist Christology* (New York: Continuum).

Hultkranz, Å. (1967) *The Religions of the American Indians* (Berkeley: University of California Press).

Juschka, D. (1999) "The Category of Gender in the Study of Religion," *Method and Theory in the Study of Religion* 22: 77–105.

King, W. L. ([1987] 1995) "Religion," in *Encyclopedia of Religion*, vol. 12 (New York: Macmillan).

Lawrence, B. (1989) *Defenders of God: The Fundamentalist Revolt Against the Modern Age* (San Francisco: Harper and Row).

Lorde, A. (1984) "The Master's Tools Will Never Dismantle the Master's House," in *Sister Outsider: Essays and Speeches* (Trumansburg, NY: Crossing Press).

Ruether, R. R. (1972) *Liberation Theology: Human Hope Confronts Christian History and American Power* (New York: Paulist).

Further reading

Anderson, L. and Young, P. D. (eds.) (2004) *Women and Religious Traditions* (Toronto: Oxford University Press).

Gross, R., et al. (2000) "Roundtable Discussion; Feminist Theology and Religious Diversity," *Journal of Feminist Studies in Religion* 16: 73–131.

Isasi-Díaz, A. M. (1996) *Mujerista Theology* (Maryknoll, NY: Orbis).

Joy, M. and Neumaier-Dargyay, E. (eds.) (1995) *Gender, Genre and Religion: Feminist Reflections* (Waterloo, ON: Wilfrid Laurier University Press).

Juschka, D. (ed.) (2001) *Feminism in the Study of Religion* (London: Continuum).

King, U. (ed.) (1995) *Religion and Gender* (Oxford: Blackwell).

Sharma, A. and Young, K. K. (eds.) (1999) *Feminism and World Religions* (Albany: State University of New York Press).

Williams, D. S. (1994) *Sisters in the Wilderness: The Challenge of Womanist God-talk* (Maryknoll, NY: Orbis).

CHAPTER .THIRTY-NINE

Discourse

Ruth Wodak

Introduction: Gender Identities and Discourse

How is talking to and about each other conditioned? How do people perceive and judge each other? How do they mutually construct their relationships? It seems to be the case for each person and of utmost importance that they are noticed and paid attention to by others and that self/other identity is ratified. We become irritated when we are incorrectly addressed by persons we know personally. We cannot tolerate it when doctors at the hospital speak about us as if they are merely discussing a medical case (Buchholtz et al. 1999; Hetherington 1998; Peyer and Groth 1996; Schoenthal 1992; Wodak 1996, 2001, 2003; Woodward 1997).

Women often find themselves in situations in which their identity as a "human being" is not ratified, for the simple reason that they are not perceived or discursively constructed as members of the human species or other groups that they actually belong to (Kotthoff and Wodak 1997; Wodak 1997; Wodak and Benke 1997). There is a passage in the "Ode to Joy" that says "All people will become brothers." The ninth of the Ten Commandments, which pertains to all people, proclaims: "Thou shall not covet thy neighbour's wife." And something heftier from a newspaper article: "No healthy person can be without a woman for three or six weeks." In spite of these and other examples, it seems generally implied that women should, may, must, in these cases, feel that they are also being addressed. This also pertains to so-called neutral terms that generally apply to men such as "every," "one," "the doctor," or "the politician."

That which language does not define – where no expressions exist, where no words are available – has no function in society and no societal worth; it simply does not exist. Women have, for thousands of years, been excluded from public life. The consequence of this for the lexicon is, taking German as an example, that specific descriptions are simply absent for women. Moreover, this absence was as systematic as the traditional exclusion of women in the public sphere (Kargl et al. 1997; Lalouschek and Wodak 1997).

Equal rights between men and women and their equal treatment at work and in public life was striven for, even before the turn of the twentieth century, by distinguished women and women's organizations (Saurer 2004). Equal rights and equal opportunities have in the meantime been anchored in the legislations of many Western countries. Attitudes, values, and role models are nonetheless still heavily influenced by patriarchal traditions. Unequal treatment at work and in public life still commonly occurs. This unequal treatment of men and women in our society – for example, less pay for the same work and the often-cited increased workload – is realized in language and in language use. Language gets constructed by people with respect to "reality." That is, language is influenced by the social situations in which people interact. In this way, language structure is reflected in social structure and, at the same time, influences people through world-views and ideologies, and thus legitimizes this economic imbalance (Billig 1992; Essed 1997; Raethzel 1997; Van Dijk 1998). Social power is exercised. The powerful are everywhere and they are, for the most part, comprised of white men. Because of this, the same behavior is assessed differently for women from how it is for men; we speak of "career-driven women" and, in contrast, of "dynamic men."

Many stereotypes also become reinforced in Women's Studies. Take the so-called "deficiency hypothesis" (Lakoff 1975) as an example. Here it is argued that women lack certain qualities that men possess; in those areas where men can assert themselves, women appear uncertain and hesitant. Dichotomizations dominated and still in part dominate the discussion (Cameron 1997; Tannen 1998): men are evil and dominant and tend toward competitiveness, while women are good, subordinate, and cooperative (see, however, Sheldon 1997). They even stem from different cultures (Cameron 1997). I suggest that there is mixing of levels here that, as the examples below will show, stand in a mutually consti-tutive relationship to one another: the level of stereotypes, the level of power and hierarchy, and, finally, the level of observed and authentic behavior.

Language and Power

What relationships exist between language (discourse) as a social phenomenon and language (discourse) as social power (Fairclough and Wodak 1997)? How are power and power relationships realized in interaction? How is power exercised through language? With which discursive tools is power (parents, lawyers, doctors, teachers, the "state") realized? There have been in recent years a number of studies that have addressed these issues (Chouliaraki and Fairclough 1999; Mumby 1993; Reisigl and Wodak 2001; Wetschanow 2003; Wodak et al. 1989).

In interaction, social power means discursive control. Who has access to varying types of discourse? Who can and cannot in which situations speak how to whom about what? Who determines the topic of discussion, who interrupts whom, who is listened to? The more powerful people are, the greater are their capabilities of expressing themselves in discourse. They may, for instance, use low address terms (in German, "*Du*") to address their interlocutors, while the latter use high address terms (in German, "*Sie*"). The powerful party in the interaction determines the direction the discussion takes, the theme, and how people are supposed to speak to each other. This also means, however, that no "socially sterile" situations exist in which all speakers possess the same discursive resources (Wodak 1996; Kendall and Tannen 1997).

These inequities are strongly present in parent–child relationships. Unfortunately, the parents' power often gets transformed into physical violence and even into child abuse. However, there also exist more subtle forms. In the sciences and in the media, men are listened to. Their authority is indisputable. Women, on the other hand, are often only looked at and are also judged on the basis of their appearance and not on their capabilities. Women must put much more time and energy into constructing themselves discursively as authoritative. Women must therefore still do twice the amount of work to achieve the same goals. Women's statements and knowledge are often attributed to men; in discussions, men are mostly referred to and sometimes not the women who have made the statement in question. Even powerful women, such as politicians, are interviewed differently by journalists as compared to their male colleagues: women are interrupted more frequently, questioned more intensely, and interviewed in a more aggressive tone. It is especially appalling when numerous poorly valued roles appear simultaneously; such as when a single mother from the lower classes must appear before the social security office or the courts. The unfolding of talk is of a significantly different quality: it is condescending, cynical, and accusatory (Leodolter 1975). To come to the point: we argue that women must still always justify their existence in the public sphere and must always fight against conservative stereotypes, while men are absolved of this kind of pressure to justify their roles and actions (Martin Rojo and Esteban 2003). Men are simply accepted. At this point, though, it must be emphasized that the two categories "women" and "men" are much too undifferentiated. Hierarchy, ethnicity, profession, race, and political affiliation play a big role in evaluating persons and human beings. Thus, women from certain political parties in power who possess dominant roles, as politicians, chancellors, top managers, etc., certainly are more respected than powerless men who belong to a stigmatized minority. Context is therefore the most important variable to be considered while analyzing specific cases and settings (Kotthoff and Wodak 1997).

Today, complex approaches to the communication of gender are advocated, starting from an interrelationship of diverse factors which exert influence on conversation: as asymmetrical societal power relationships between the subcultural interaction strategies which develop in its course, ideal images of femininity and masculinity are transmitted by the mass media, traditional gender ideologies, and a self communicatively positioning her- or himself in this context, continuously interacting with the environment (Bilden 1991; Kotthoff 1996). Furthermore, assertive, self-confident communicative behavior on the part of women is no

521

guarantee that they will thereby obtain the same opportunities as men (Wodak 2003). In fact, the production of symmetry/asymmetry occurs on various levels, which do not necessarily always coincide.

There is, for example, an extensive literature showing that boys and girls learn different verbal and non-verbal behavior forms in their mainly same-sex children's and youth groups and at school (summarized, among others, in Enders-Dragässer and Fuchs 1989; Goodwin 1990; Günthner and Kotthoff 1991; Kotthoff 1994; Swann 1992; Thorne 1993; Wodak and Schultz 1986; Sheldon 1997). It is still hard to say where conversational differences originate. Psychoanalytic, linguistic, and sociological approaches must be combined to produce explanations. Communicative style differences also play a role for adults in many situations (Maltz and Borker 1982; Tannen 1994, 1996). But there is evidence that both sexes generally know a large variety of styles which they can use to create specific contexts and relationships.

Let us have a look at one example of speech activities (directives). Goodwin writes:

> Both boys and girls make use of directives to coordinate behavior in task activities. However, they construct these actions in quite different ways. By selecting alternative ways of formatting directive moves and responding to them, and by distributing rights to perform directives differently, the two groups build alternative forms of social organizations. Boys' directives are formatted as imperatives from super-ordinates to subordinates, or as requests, generally upward in rank. . . . Among the girls, however, all participants use the same actions reciprocally with each other. The party issuing the directive includes herself as one of the agents in the action to be performed, and avoids using strategies which would differentiate herself from others. . . . I [therefore] want to emphasize that the girls have full competence with bold or aggravated forms of action and also systematically use them in appropriate circumstances. Indeed, in some circumstances, such as playing house, they create hierarchies similar to those of the boys. (1990: 116 ff.)

Later, at school, different discourse roles are assigned to boys and girls. Boys are allowed to dominate and control the interaction, while girls are expected to be silent, cooperative and help the teacher. The institution helps to train boys for future leadership roles.

In the past few years, it has been shown that so-called female behavior is held in high esteem; organizational sociology trainers are increasingly finding that cooperative, consumer-friendly behavior can improve efficiency and satisfaction at the workplace. A mixture of womanly and motherly stereotypes is taking place here: powerful women are being squeezed into a mother role and are confronted with these kinds of positive as well as negative implications. The "Mama" is indisputably powerful but, at the same time, protective and understanding. Because of this, employees often behave like "children" in all of these available registers of conduct (Tannen 1998; Wodak 1997; Wodak and Schultz 1986).

This probably sounds all too familiar or even trivial. I claim, however, that these quasi-banalities cannot be often enough repeated, since they are still often not present in our general consciousness. Most importantly, vital changes such as easier or similar career developments for women and men and equal opportunities and treatment in the public sphere are barely visible (Diem-Wille 1996; Martin Rojo 2000). I would like to emphasize, however, that gender is not to be separated from other identities. Identities and roles always appear in combinations and so it is important to examine behavior and interaction holistically rather than trying to isolate one gender variable. It is for this reason that it should be important to focus on "multiple identities" of women and men in many settings and cultures. In broader terms, the concept of "fragmented and multiple identities" should be addressed (Wodak et al. 1999).

The Analysis of Conversation and Discourse

Discourse analysis in gender research – which examines the use of language – concerns itself with gender differences in conversation and discourse (oral as well as written). Differences are investigated in the following fields of language use: voice, pronunciation, intonation, choice of words, argumentation, lexicon, syntax, interactional and conversational behavior, as well as visual features and modes and non-verbal communication. The gender-induced differences in the use of language were and are not treated simply as divergent variants standing side by side. Due to a patriarchally organized society, the interpretation of the differences ascertained is of major social and political significance.

The interpretation of the diverse linguistic indicators (like turn-taking, indirectness, interruptions, and overlaps) varies according to the specific gender theory and ideology which underlie the studies.[1] Probably the two best-known theories about the gender-induced use of language are those of "difference" and "dominance" (Cameron 1997; Kendall and Tannen 1997).

Whereas investigations following the "deficit model" have interpreted the use of such indicators as manifestations of "powerless language of women," research in the paradigm of the "difference model" views the linguistic behavior of men and women as originating in opposed modes of socialization and equal in their meaning and impact. Hedging, tag questions, or indirectness can be viewed "negatively" or "positively," either as signs of female insecurity or as supporting conversational work, depending on the context of the discourse and the theoretical approach adopted. This controversy leads to many polemical debates which in the end show the invalidity of such dichotomous distinctions. Thus, nowadays, other research questions have become more important viewing gender as constructed due to context.

Tannen returns to the early work of Erving Goffman to suggest a new theoretical framework for conceptualizing the relationship between language and gender:

> In this framework, ways of speaking are seen as sex-class linked – that is, linked with the class of women or the class of men rather than necessarily with individual members of that class. As Goffman put it in another, related essay, the relationship between language and gender is a matter of "display" rather than "identity." (1996: 195)

In other words, the behavior is not a reflection of the individual's nature (identity) but rather of some performance that the individual is accomplishing (display) (ibid.: 198). Tannen shows that understanding the relationship between language and gender is best approached through the concept of "framing," by which gendered patterns of behavior are seen as sex-class linked rather than sex-linked.

Incidentally, there are studies on the communicative development of children that show that between the ages of 2 and 3, the child begins to understand itself as a boy or a girl and this is based on the outward appearance of the body (display) – for example, hair and clothing – not on the body as such. Associating gender, which arises interactively, with anatomy is for the child itself the last step in the construction of its social gender identity (Cahill 1986). The child develops a sense for her/his sex-class.

Recent theoretical approaches in the feminist study of discourse

The construction of the "sexes" In Judith Butler's arguments (1990) against the tenability of the categories of "woman" and "sex," she refers to postmodernist theories. In the manner of Foucault she ascribes normative power to the idea of gender identity and the attempt to describe it. By the mere act of defining a gender identity many bodies, practices, and discourses are excluded or devalued, whereas the constructed and hence upright character of this gender identity is simultaneously concealed. Thus, in such feminist theories, the idea of two sexes is criticized as being a construction, a prediscursive factor taking the place of reality. Following this interpretation, "sex" cannot be separated into a biologically inherent aspect and a socially acquired one. The category of "sex" itself, in Butler's view, is a purely cultural product of discourse. Such an opinion, of course, relates well to Foucauldian theories of discourse; "sex," therefore, cannot be viewed as a "universal, suprahistorical and extrasocial entity"; it is understood to be a "integral component of every form of life"; such a view relates well to our assumptions of context sensitivity discussed above. On the other hand, "sex," of course, possesses a material basis: in many relevant contexts in our societies, women and men are still evaluated, judged, promoted, or paid due to their biological sex alone. These facts are not accounted for in Butler's approach. More recently, some authors have differentiated Butler's dogmatic position: it is a question of revealing "the reproduction mechanisms, networks and institutional compulsions that ensure that constructions become persistent and resistant and appear timeless, immovable and identical with themselves" (Hirschauer 1992: 333). It is a matter of exposing the arbitrary construction of this binary opposition and hence also its mutability, and not of criticizing the binarily organized perception as unreal.

Doing gender   Unlike a research approach that accepts sexual differences as an aggregation of qualities and deals with the qualitative behavioral tendencies of women and men, ethno-methodologically oriented studies produced a new focus of research: "doing gender." Such an approach complements traditional theories which viewed gender as an aggregation of static attributes and which are concerned with investigating and displaying the peculiarities of women and interpreting them as "gender-specific or gender-typical attributes" so as to reveal the asymmetry of the difference between the sexes, to criticize it, and to make it politically visible. The use of a bundle of characteristics and attributes to define gender complicates or renders impossible an interactional approach, since attributes are "entities" and not processes. This concept entails that definitions of gender cannot change or transform, and are not influenced by spontaneous interactions. A further problem raised by the concept of gender as a concept of attributes is the possibility of individualization; that is, the individual who has been seen to possess or not to possess certain attributes becomes the center of focus, and the level of the social system is neglected. Unlike this non-interactive approach, "doing gender" regards membership of a sex not as a pool of attributes "possessed" by a person, but as something a person "does." In this sense, membership of a gender constitutes a performative act and not a fact. Gender is continually realized in interactional form. Gender is created not only in the everyday activities which characterize "doing gender," but also in the asymmetry of the relationship between the sexes, the dominance of the "male" and its normativeness. Patriarchal inequality is produced and reproduced in every interaction. This concept of "doing gender" stresses the creative potential and the embedding of gender-typical behavior in a social context.

Examples

Female Members of the European Parliament (MEPs), for example, have created very different ways of positioning themselves in interactions with male colleagues in the European Commission or in the European Parliament itself. These sequences manifest the multiple identities which women (and men) constantly adapt and construct in interactions. Interviews with female MEPs (Wodak 2002, 2003) illustrate that they are very conscious of their gender roles and that they tend to construct very different ways of self-presentation in interactions: in particular, one MEP stated the following, in talking about her first experience as a rapporteur.

when I – entered the parliament –	*Orientation (lines 1–3)*
on my first report it was about Leonardo[2]	
I don't know if you know:	
(*laughing*) well – I said "I'm going to speak to the commissioner"	
and – I – / I knew – he only speaks very bad French	
and my ah my French was very bad as well.	
so I said "I want to have interpretation"	
So – I went to the commissioner	*Complicating Actions (lines 4–14)*
with a very good int / int / interpreter	
and I / I / I / I talked more than an hour with him.	
because we talked the same about it	
and at the end he said –	
"well: I have here the advice of my: civil servants but I – agree with you:	
and this and this and this all goes through – "	
so you have to be: – äh: –	
I don't know h / how do we call it in English in / I	
in the Netherlands we say (bruta:l)	
so you have to: (*laughing*) be polite	*Evaluation (lines 16–20)*
but you have to – you: / you mustn't be /	
you mustn't *sit* behind your – / your *desk* –	
because that doesn't help. (*laughing*)	
but then you have the worse system	
that I tried several times	*Coda (22–31)*
then you have the Council. –	

In this example, which has been marked for basic narrative structure according to Labov and Waletzky's (1967) model, we see that the MEP's story is objectively about having a successful meeting with a commissioner while acting as rapporteur on a report about the Leonardo program. In lines 4–6, the complicating actions, she shows how she went to the commissioner with an interpreter, and because she and the commissioner had the same understanding of the issues involved, he was willing to support her, despite contrary advice by his "civil servants" on the matters involved. The main point of the story, or evaluation, from the MEP's perspective, is to show that, as an MEP, to get things done, you must be active and assertive, "not sit behind your desk." Thus, in this narrative, the MEP positions herself as an MEP who is proactive and who will do what it takes, including arguing directly with commissioners, to see that her voice is heard. She also orients to being a rapporteur (line 2), which carries some responsibility in a committee, and to being from the Netherlands (line 17), although this last identity is evoked only to characterize her style of work ("brutal" in Dutch, or "assertive"). (For further details of the analysis, see Wodak 2002, 2001, 2003). This narrative also manifests the complexity of the European Parliament, the interweaving of languages, cultures, positions, political affiliations, and gender roles, as well as professional experiences.

Another of our interviewees, also an MEP, is oriented to a particularly wide range of identities (left, woman, Swedish, mother, political outsider, etc.) during her interview. Most striking is the way in which she repeatedly positions herself as being an "atypical MEP." Here we see one such occasion.

I figure here the most common – äh civil – job. – for an MEP
is äh to be a lawyer.
me myself *I'm far from that*
the job I had doesn't even *exist* outside *Scandinavia.*
so: – it's a sort of a social teacher – so
so I'm / I'm very in / an: / a very special bird in this a:
IF mhm mhm so now you don't feel like you – fit into sort of a *typical* MEP äh
ME *no. no: no: I'm not. I'm left I'm a woman I'm Swedish* and I'm also
   everything-/everything's wrong. (*laughs*)

In this example, the MEP contrasts herself with what she considers to be a typical profile for an MEP (lawyer by profession), emphasizing the degree to which she feels different ("I'm far from that . . . I'm a very special bird . . . everything's wrong"). She also points out many of the identities that she associates with and that she perceives as marking her as different (social teacher, left, female, Swedish). This MEP is very much concerned with her self-presentation as being different, different from other female MEPs and also from male MEPs. Moreover, she explains her success as a female MEP by being exotic and narrates different strategies, which she applies in "doing politics and gender."

Even such short examples illustrate the diversity and complexity of gender roles and make clear why an interdisciplinary, qualitative, and context-sensitive approach is necessary to access the whole domain of "gender and language." To be able to make more general observations, however, much more cross-cultural comparable research is urgently needed.

Notes

1 Due to the fact that there are no comparable studies (standardized) across cultures and social classes as well as contexts and ethnicities, no generalizations about any universal gender or sex-based differences in conversational styles are possible.
2 One of three EU youth and education related programs – Socrates, Leonardo, and Youth for Europe – established in 1995. Leonardo provides financial support for professional development and job training.

References

Bilden, H. (1991) "Geschlechtsspezifische Sozialisation," in K. Hurrelmann and D. Ulrich (eds.), *Neues Handbuch der Sozialisationsforschung* (Weinheim: Beltz).

Billig, M. (1992) *Ideology and Opinions* (London: Sage).

Buchholtz, M., Liang, A. C., and Sutton, L. A. (eds.) (1999) *Reinventing Identities: The Gendered Self in Discourse* (Oxford: Oxford University Press).

Butler, J. (1990) *Gender Trouble* (New York: Routledge).

Cahill, S. (1986) "Childhood Socialization as a Recruitment Process," *Sociological Studies of Child Development* 1: 163–86.

Cameron, D. (1997) "Theoretical Debates in Feminist Linguistics: Questions of Sex and Gender," in Ruth Wodak (ed.), *Gender and Discourse* (London: Sage).

Chouliaraki, L. and Fairclough, N. (1999) *Discourse in Late Modernity: Rethinking Critical Discourse Analysis* (Edinburgh: Edinburgh University Press).

Diem-Wille, G. (1996) *Karrierefrauen und Karrieremänner* (Opladen: Westdeutscher Verlag).

Enders-Dragässer, U. and Fuchs, C. (1989) *Interaktionen der Geschlechter. Sexismusstrukturen in der Schule* (Weinheim, München: Juventa).

Essed, P. (1997) "Race, Gender and Academic Leadership," in Helga Kotthoff and Ruth Wodak (eds.), *Communicating Gender in Context* (Amsterdam: Benjamins).

Fairclough, N. and Wodak, R. (1997) "Critical Discourse Analysis," in T. A. van Dijk (ed.), *Discourse as Social Interaction* (London: Sage).

Goffman, E. (1996) *Interaktionsrituale* (Frankfurt am Main: Suhrkamp).

Goodwin, M. H. (1990) *He-Said-She-Said. Talk as Social Organization Among Black Children* (Bloomington: Indiana University Press).

Günthner, S. and Kotthoff, H. (1991) "Von fremden Stimmen: Weibliches und männliches Sprechen im Kulturvergleich," in Susanne Günthner and Helga Kotthoff (eds.), *Von fremden Stimmen. Weibliches und männliches Sprechen im Kulturvergleich* (Frankfurt am Main: Suhrkamp).

Hetherington, K. (1998) *Expressions of Identity* (London: Sage).

Hirschauer, S. (ed.) (1992) *Die soziale Konstruktion der Transsexualität* (Frankfurt am Main: Suhrkamp).

Kargl, M., Wetschanow, K., Wodak, R., and Perle, N. (1997) "Kreatives Formulieren. Anleitungen zum geschlechtergerechten Sprachgebrauch," *Schriftenreihe der Frauenministerin* 13.

Kendall, S. and Tannen, D. (1997) "Gender and Language in the Workplace," in Ruth Wodak (ed.), *Gender and Discourse* (London: Sage).

Kotthoff, H. (1994) "Geschlechtertypisierung in der kindlichen Kommunikationsentwicklung," in Ulla Bracht et al. (eds.), *Jahrbuch für Pädagogik* (Frankfurt, Berne, New York: Peter Lang).

Kotthoff, H. (1996) "Die Geschlechter in der Gesprächsforschung. Hierarchien, Theorien, Ideologie," *Der Deutschunterricht* 1: 9–15.

Kotthoff, H. and Wodak, R. (eds.) (1997) *Communicating Gender in Context* (Amsterdam: Benjamins).

Labov, W. and Waletzky, J. (1967) "Narrative Analysis. Oral Versions of Personal Experience," in J. Helm (ed.), *Essays on the Verbal and Visual Art* (Seattle: University of Washington Press).

Lakoff, R. (1975) *Language and Women's Place* (New York: Harper & Row).

Lalouschek, J. and Wodak, R. (1997) "Ärztliche Sprachlosigkeit in der Arzt-Patienten-Kommunikation," in *Wiener Klinische Wochenschrift* (Wien: Springer Verlag).

Leodolter, R. (1975) [née Wodak] *Das Sprachverhalten von Angeklagten bei Gericht* (Kronberg/Ts: Scriptor).

Maltz, D. and Borker, R. (1982) "A Cultural Approach to Male-Female Miscommunication," in John Gumperz (ed.), *Language and Social Identity* (Cambridge: Cambridge University Press).

Martin Rojo, L. (2000) "Narratives at Work: When Women Take on the Role of Managers." Workshop on "Theory and Interdisciplinarity in CDA," July 6 and 7, Department of Linguistics, University of Vienna.

Martin Rojo, L. and Esteban, C. G. (2003) "Discourse at Work: When Women Take On the Role of Manager," in Gilbert Weiss and Ruth Wodak (eds.), *Critical Discourse Analysis* (London: Palgrave Macmillan).

Mumby, D. (ed.) (1993) *Narrative and Social Control: Critical Perspectives* (Newbury Park, CA and London: Sage).

Peyer, A. and Groth, R. (eds.) (1996) *Sprache und Geschlecht. Studienbibliographien Sprachwissenschaft* (Heidelberg: Julius Groos).

Reisigl, M. and Wodak, R. (2001) *Discourse and Discrimination: Rhetorics of Racism and Antisemitism* (London and New York: Routledge).

Raethzel, N. (1997) *Gegenbilder* (Opladen: Lesek und Budrich).

Saurer, E. (2004) *Liebe und Arbeit: Geschlechterbeziehungen in Europa* (forthcoming).

Schoenthal, G. (1992) "Sprache, Geschlecht und Macht. Zum Diskussionsstand feministischer Thesen in der Linguistik," *Mitteilungen des deutschen Germanistenverbandes* 3: 5–12.

Sheldon, A. (1997) "Talking Power: Girls, Gender Enculturation and Discourse," in R. Wodak (ed.), *Gender and Discourse* (London: Sage).

Swann, J. (1992) *Girls, Boys and Language* (Oxford: Blackwell).

Tannen, D. (1994) *Gender and Discourse* (New York and Oxford: Oxford University Press).

Tannen, D. (1996) "The Sex-Class Linked Framing of Talk at Work," in *Gender and Discourse* (New York and Oxford: Oxford University Press).

Tannen, D. (1998) *The Argument Culture* (New York: Random House).

Thorne, B. (1993) *Gender Play: Girls and Boys in School* (Rutgers, NJ: Rutgers University Press).

Van Dijk, T. A. (1998) *Ideology. A Multidisciplinary Study* (London: Sage).

Weiss, G. and Wodak, R. (eds.) (2003) *Critical Discourse Analysis* (London: Palgrave Macmillan).

Wetschanow, K. (2003) "Von sexueller Gewalt über gewalttätigen Sex zu 'gewaltigem Sex' – Die Repräsentation von Vergewaltigung in österreichischen *Printmedien*." (University of Vienna: unpublished dissertation).

Wodak, R. (1996) *Disorders of Discourse* (London and New York: Longman).

Wodak, R. (ed.) (1997) *Gender and Discourse* (London: Sage).

Wodak, R. (2001) "'I'm a Very Special Bird': Ideological Gender Conflicts and Identity Dilemmas with EU Parliamentarians," in K. Nordenstam and K. Noren (eds.), *Sprak, Kon och Kultur* (Goeteborg: Goeteborgs University).

Wodak, R. (2002) "Multinational Organizations: Europe in the Search of New Identities," in Christopher N. Candlin (ed.), *Research and Practice in Professional Discourse* (Hong Kong: City University of Hong Kong Press).

Wodak, R. (2003) "Multiple Identities: The Role of Female Parliamentarians in the EU Parliament," in J. Holmes and M. Meyerhoff (eds.), *Handbook of Language and Gender* (London: Blackwell).

Wodak, R. and Benke, G. (1997) "Gender as a Sociolinguistic Variable," in Florian Coulmas (ed.), *The Handbook of Sociolinguistics* (Oxford: Blackwell).

Wodak, R. and Schultz, M. (1986) *The Language of Love and Guilt* (Amsterdam: Benjamins).

Wodak, R., Menz, F., and Lalouschek, J. (1989) *Sprachbarrieren. Die Verständigungskrise in der Gesellschaft* (Wien: Edition Atelier).

Wodak, R., de Cillia, R., Reisigl, M., and Liebhart, K. (1999) *The Discursive Construction of National Identity* (Edinburgh: Edinburgh University Press).

Woodward, K. (ed.) (1997) *Identity and Difference* (London: Sage).

CHAPTER FORTY

The Violence of Gender

Mieke Bal

What is a man, what is a woman, and what else can one be? Since the advent of the second feminist wave, gender has been detached from, then reattached to, biological sex. The process demonstrates a certain futility of definition. Everyone knows there are people with bodies that are, or are considered, sex-specific, and that this is likely to have some relation to the person's behavior and social position. I shun debates on definition as a distraction from the blatant social problem of gender, which I see as follows.

Social structures are *inherently* – but not essentially – inflected by inequalities of power. Since these inequalities have no real basis, no justification, no ethical or moral grounding, anything will do to sustain and rationalize them. Of course, such rationalizations are false. This means that attempts to participate in debates on definitions cannot but be in collusion with, and further advance, what we should instead undermine by ignoring. That, I contend – the distraction that covers up what ought to be addressed and redressed – is the social problem of gender.

The point of gender, then, is not what it is but what it does. This is not simply to reiterate the well-known position most eloquently advocated by Judith Butler – that gender and sex are performative – although I do endorse that view. Rather than defending Butler's position, I wish to suggest that the relevance of gender as an object of study lies other than in splitting hairs over definition and maintaining dichotomies like "man" and "woman" under equally binary headings such as "ontology" versus "performance," or "being" versus "doing." Instead, its relevance lies in tracing not *if* or *that*, but *how* "being" a woman – being assigned that label, rightly or wrongly – is being made an actor in a social game of representation of which the roles are already distributed (Butler 1990, 1993).

The word "roles" points to a performative view that deserves spelling out, however briefly, as an instance of the productivity of interdisciplinary analysis for the study of culture, including the way gender "works" in cultures. In an extremely illuminating article, Jonathan Culler (2000) follows the concept of the performative from philosophy in the 1950s, through literature in the 1980s, to gender studies in the 1990s and back to philosophy in the first decade of the twenty-first century. During the journey, performativity – of a rather special category of words that allows special utterances, but that *do* rather than *state* things – became, first, generalized, to stand for an aspect of any utterance: the aspect of an utterance as *act*. Generalizing further on the basis of iterability, on which all language-use depends, not performativity but its "standard" other – constativity – became a special case of generalized performativity.

But generalization, a useful way of unfixing rigid categories by stretching their boundaries, calls for new orderings. The next step – already in J. L. Austin's founding text (1975 [1962]) – was to analyze the always potentially performative utterances into aspects. This move, from categorization to analysis of each item, is representative of the move from a scientist to an analytic approach to culture. In the case of performativity, the analytical use of the concept facilitated the shift in focus – from the illocutionary act of performing speaking to the perlocutionary act of achieving the speech act, of securing its effect. This shift makes it possible to extend the domain of the performative from language, a category of cultural phenomena, to all sorts of events that happen, because someone does them, in the cultural domain.

The decisive move in this double shift (from category to analytical concept and from agency to effect) has been Derrida's insistence on the citationality that enables and surrounds each speech act. Austin explicitly excluded literature from the analysis because literary speech acts are not "serious." Derrida (1988), on the other hand, by shifting the focus from the speaker's intention to the social conventions that guarantee the very possibility of performing speech acts, made the iterability or citationality of any language-use the standard, thereby subordinating individual intention to social convention. From an originating, founding act performed by a willing, intentional subject, performativity becomes the instance of an endless process of repetition; a repetition involving similarity and difference, and therefore both relativizing and enabling social change and subjects' interventions – in other words, agency. This makes gender and sexual behavior things that are neither individually intended nor biologically determined, but culturally embedded; pressured, but not inescapably fixed.

That roles, including gender roles, have already been assigned is a simple, easily recognizable fact, one that is, however, pregnant with consequences. It has been remarked early and often: before birth, a child is already treated as gendered, even if the extent and manner may differ. This view is notoriously attributed to Lacan; for the purposes of this chapter, it is best explained by Silverman (1996). The baby has no choice; "it" is – is treated as – a boy or a girl; and its name, the gifts given, the wishes uttered by godmothers, the clothes put on it, and the colors surrounding it already tell tales of what and who this child is and will become qua girl or boy. Something that is imposed without being inevitable – without being "natural" – is subject to violence. Gender, in other words, is inherently violent. I am not referring to actual, recognizable violence: the violence of sexual abuse, rape, and simple "small" violence against women, gays, and children is just a specific, in fact, allegorical acting out of the inherent violence that is disciplining (Foucault) and rehearsing, to the point that the performer believes her behavior is "natural."

In the face of this inherent violence, claiming that gender is "just" a performance is a rightful, useful, and socially constructive act. For it gives us some small margin of choice – of behavior, if nothing else. This is why debates on Judith Butler's 1987 statement to the effect that gender is performative are defensive and misguided. Butler has effectively answered objections and corrected misreadings, particularly clearly in the introduction to *Bodies that Matter* (1993). For me, it is more important to explore the consequences of the claim to performance. One such consequence resides in the "gentle" violence. If gender is performed and imposed by reiteration – "citationality" – the imposition is violent, precisely because no "natural" reality or truth supports it. As hard as this is for some people to accept, I deem it extremely important to explore the consequences of this view. For insight into those consequences is empowering, whereas belief in the natural basis of gender is disempowering.

One of the ways to make this claim meaningful is to confront it with "race." In accordance with critical usage, I put "race" in quotation marks. If I refrain from doing this with gender, there are three reasons. First, I wish to mark the paradigmatic position of "race" in the range of socially constructed inequalities. Second, the word "gender" is already privileged to indicate social constructedness, in distinction from "sex." Third, I object to the excessive use of such graphisms, which in fact give away ordinary, readable language and get stuck in the marginality of "difficult." In other words, if one can just accept that "race" only works, socially, as a construction, no matter what the biological "truth" of it may be, enough has been said, and we need only worry about where the problem, the relevance, and the consequences of such distinctions lie.

A few years ago a British photographer whom I did not know at the time, asked me to write an essay to accompany a series of photographs she was publishing on the Dutch tradition of *Zwarte Piet*. I was taken aback because I thought that shameful, deeply racist tradition lay behind me. But the artist, Anna Fox, insisted that I might find her work of interest, so I agreed to take a look at it. When I received the photos, I was both repelled and fascinated. I went to consult two American friends, militant anti-racists like myself, but – lucky them – with no childhood memories of *Zwarte Piet*. Together, we pored over the photographs to see if I could write about them, associating my name with them, without compromising my position (see Fox 1999 for the essay I ended up writing, and Bal 2002 for an extended version).

It is the act of "poring over" that I wish to foreground here. In that act lies the inherent violence of gender and "race" – inherent, and inevitable, because socially constructed. I grew up with this kind of image of racial otherness. It was literally reiterated: every year they came back. *Zwarte Piet* is the generic name for black-faced clowns. They dance, jump about, play the fool. Colorful, festive, full of surprises, they turn boring, grey, early winter days into a period of partying. They knock on windows, while inside, near the hearth, children sing seasonal songs. Sometimes, without anyone leaving the room, the door opens a notch and a handful of candies are thrown inside. They used to threaten and shake their roe, a birch rod of twigs for flogging, but these days they mainly reassure by giving kids candy only. Reassurance? This alone deserves attention.

Fascination and reassurance – hence, a play with anxiety – underlie the Dutch *Sinterklaas* and *Zwarte Piet* tradition. Over a number of years, Anna Fox came to the Netherlands to make portraits of these figures playing the black-faced fools. Portraiture is the genre of individualism, of the bourgeoisie, and of the authentic self. It is the genre that – literally – constructs the subject. Here, this most individualistic genre of "high art" is deployed to undermine, fight, or, if you wish, deconstruct "race" and gender, the one through the other, and through the address to subjectivity as built up – performed – through memory.

I wrote that essay because I felt implicated, in ways that are relevant for my discussion of gender in the present essay. *Zwarte Piet* triggers my oldest memory of fear. While during the rest of the year, the house I grew up in was a safe haven into which, at the onset of darkness, I quickly fled, to escape the growing shadows of strangers on the street, in late November and early December that haven was visited by spooks that I never saw but who left their traces: candy, a warning note, a slightly misplaced shoe. I knew who they were, and that they were benign. Their presence was thrilling, a promise of mystery candy presents. But somehow, they scared me, and that spoiled the fun, the security, the confidence. I was afraid to pass the basement door on my way to the kitchen, afraid to go upstairs during the day. It took half a lifetime for me to stop looking under my bed before daring to lie on it.

That the *Zwarte Piet* tradition is the product of invention seems obvious. Perhaps not only because – as Hobsbawm and Ranger (1983) point out and condemn – governmental and other powers use tradition to manipulate people's memories. It turns out not to be so easy to recover the interests underlying the invention or its agents. But children live it, they don't question it, and thus the tradition shapes their minds.

The images are portraits indeed. What can that mean? Portraiture in itself is a deeply ambivalent tradition. Like racist typology, as a visual discourse it produces and reflects a longstanding interest in the articulation of human variety. Portraiture foregrounds individuality. But it also provides tools with which to speak simultaneously of the sameness in difference and the difference in sameness. This ambivalence of portraiture is what makes it so suitable to offer a "counter-point *within*," to the racism of the *Zwarte Piet* tradition (see van Alphen 1996).

Fox deployed the tradition of portraiture to critically engage the tradition of black-faced fools, from within a position of productive complicity. This is why, in line with Spivak (1999), I use Fox's artwork to state my position (see figs. 1–4). The generic character, *Zwarte Piet*, is decomposed in as many individual

Fig. 1 Anna Fox, *Zwarte Piet* (# 1), color photograph made in The Netherlands between 1993 and 1998

Fig. 2 Anna Fox, *Zwarte Piet* (# 3), color photograph made in The Netherlands between 1993 and 1998

Fig. 3 Anna Fox, *Zwarte Piet* (# 2), color photograph made in The Netherlands between 1993 and 1998

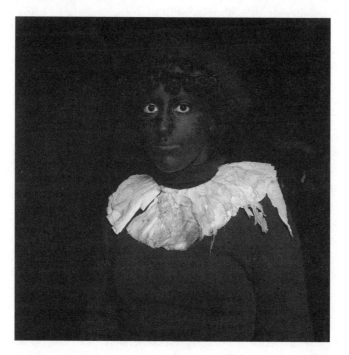

Fig. 4 Anna Fox, *Zwarte Piet* (# 14), color photograph made in The Netherlands between 1993 and 1998

faces, each begging to be named, looked at in detail, understood in terms of what its subject is doing dressing up like this. In the face of a tradition that lumped fantasmatic black men under one generic name as if slavery were still alive, individualizing them according to a class-bound tradition that dates back to the "Golden Age" of which the Dutch culture is so proud is already an act of display that does not simply reiterate. As van Alphen argues, the history of the portrait as a traditional genre is closely linked with specific social historical developments; hence, portraits carry the meanings that context has accrued to the genre.

In these four photographs (figs. 1–4), the specific features of the portrait that stand out are the posing and the dark background. In conjunction with *Zwarte Piet*'s traditional white collar, these features strongly recall traditional Dutch portraiture of the seventeenth century, the period of the joint successes of colonialism, slavery, and capitalism. It is the dark background of the same wealth that enabled the bourgeoisie, rooted in an individualism still with us today and underlying the genre's greatness, to rise to power. A power, incidentally, maintained even in our time, under the name "Golden Age," a term still used, without self-consciousness. A power that, clearly, derived not from biology but from performance.

These photographs, as portraits, thus refer to – without reiterating – a tradition in art that was always already problematic. In addition to engaging with portraiture, Fox's photographs, like tourists traveling to a neighboring country, engage with another significant practice of performance: theater. For, despite the fact that her figures masquerade as powerful, they are not. The casual, less-than-fancy backgrounds that shimmer through the artistic darkness – the radiator, the edge of a formica table – are indexes of the class background within and for which the *Zwarte Piet* play is staged.

A well-known portrait of a black man by Henri Regnault, from 1870, titled *Head of a Moor*, offers an interesting parallel example of the intersection of portraiture and theater. The comparison demonstrates the subtleties of such generic allegiances, and the impossibility of using concepts as labels. In Regnault's work, the perspective from below makes the figure look heroic. Both his gaze – directed outside the image, to the wings so to speak, whereas traditional portraits tend to have the sitter looking at the viewer – and his red mantle, clearly chosen for its coloristic effect, strongly suggest theatricality. But, as a portrait, this work is emphatically *not* performing an appeal to identification. The way color is used emphasizes blackness, in such a way that it can only be seen as "othering," the opposite of identification. It is achieved not only by the facial color – which is black in a way black people rarely are, setting off the whites of the eyes, in turn emphasized by the sideward look – but also by the bright yellow on the left and the deep crimson garment, elements that make this a color picture in more senses than one. Theatrical performance does not come, here, with critical performativity. In this sense, Regnault's work stands in contrast with Velázquez's individualizing portrait of his slave, later painter, Juan de Pareja (Bal 2002).

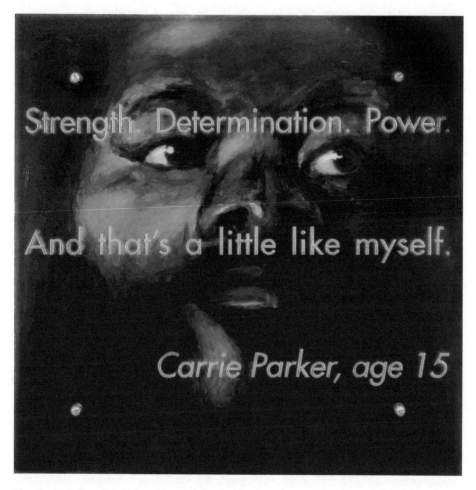

Fig. 5 Ken Aptekar, *Strength, Determination, Power*, 1997, oil on wood, bolts, sandblasted glass, 24 x 24 in. Collection of Dr Lucy C. Daniels, Raleigh, North Carolina. Reproduced by permission.

American artist Ken Aptekar revised Regnault's painting *preposterously* – a term I have developed elsewhere to indicate the historical engagement of the past from a committed position in the present (1999). In a show critically reworking a number of pieces in the collection of the Corcoran Gallery of Art in Washington, DC – as an instance of precisely the double-edged engagement with tradition I am exploring in this essay – Aptekar used Regnault's painting twice, as if to compensate for the absence of black subjects in the collection; at first sight, as a gesture of identity politics. I will only discuss one of these two works (for more on this project, see Aptekar 1997). This is a portrait, and as a minimal intervention in the tradition for which it stands, it has been reversed (see fig. 5). The artist has kept only the most essential part of the face, cropping the portrait and

537

eliminating bright colors. Most importantly, by way of interdiscursive polemic, the painting has become monochromatic, to avoid the picturesque coloring of the source. By being painted in one color, the face regains its nuances, and the visibility taken away by the excessive contrast – which recalls the cultural politics of "invisibility blues" of which Michele Wallace (1991) wrote so powerfully – is reinstated. Visibility itself, Aptekar's work "argues," is a social construction, and "race" is inherently inflected by it.

In addition to making other slight changes to the source paintings, Aptekar mounted glass plates over his paintings of them, on which he wrote short texts. Sometimes these were autobiographical mini-narratives, other times they were quotes, for example of comments made by museum visitors. These words drove the point home that visual images are always overwritten by cultural discourse. The text written over this particular painting was not long, not narrative; it was a snippet from the audience response:

> Strength. Determination. Power.
> And that's a little like myself.
> Carrie Parker, age 15

This text endows the features of the face with the positive feedback that their former invisibility could hardly have been given. It is important to realize that the quoted teenager made these remarks in response to Regnault's, not to Aptekar's, painting. Clearly, my description of Regnault's painting failed to anticipate its possible effects. An image never stands alone; its meanings are never imposed. Heroism, in Regnault's painting, served a purpose the artist could not have foreseen – but not a purpose qua portrait. The visitor responded to the pose and the perspective, the *mise-en-scène*. Moreover, her statement connects the audience to the figure through the explicit identification, based not on skin color but on the features the figure as a person emanates. The figure in the painting is retrospectively given the "Strength. Determination. Power" that he always had, yet could not be given in the portrait as such by Regnault, because the use of color there made his facial features invisible. Carrie Parker, young, female, contemporary, gives the figure these positive features as much as she takes them from him for her own benefit. "And that's a little like myself." Her comment demonstrates the importance of the loving gaze that affirms the subject of the interaction that language most basically is. Parker's response demonstrates the way external images "key" the self to the values presented, to the skin as the shape of the self.

By integrating audience response, Aptekar's painting makes explicit what art can do, what even 15-year-olds can do to *it*, when they respond to art's performativity by offering their counter-performance. This, perhaps, makes empowerment the central theme of Aptekar's project, an empowerment that is also the goal of a cultural analysis of the kind I have been trying to put forward through my engagement with his and Fox's art. But for art to empower, it must be performative. By using theatricality, not to deceive or to impose sentimental identification by means of these reworkings of Regnault's portrait and the tradition it deploys, Aptekar enlists Carrie Parker as an actor, performing – in the two senses of the word: role playing on the basis of a prior score – the Regnault painting – and acting, as in performing a speech act. Combining these two meanings of performing, Parker is performing on the stage (the museum) her speech act of self-empowerment.

This insight helps us to work through Fox's photographic portraits of the Netherlands' most embarrassing tradition. The two conventions of theater and portraiture that have accrued here to my concept of image are reactivated in Fox's work, coming together in their working through of this painful moralistically informed tradition. My hypothetical explanation of the Dutch attachment to this tradition is based on the notion that moralism – even progressive, anti-racist moralism – is less a critique of the tradition than an integral part of it. This collusion is inevitable. Aptekar's works acknowledge it, and have this aspect in common with Fox's photographs.

By virtue of their emphatic interdiscursive relationship with portraiture, Anna Fox's photographs command an individualizing attention that sees the masquerade as part of the subject's individuality. As part of it, along with other parts; but sometimes, also, as synecdoche, as the part standing for the whole, making the rest of the individuality invisible through figurativity. Masquerade, then, comes to stand for a new, disabused form of individuality, in the way that the theatricality of much contemporary art comes to embody a new form of authenticity, one not rooted in a mythical past but in the realization of the possibility of agency that is the reward of a Butlerian view of gender and "race."

Fox's portraits thus become a critique of portraiture from within, a critique of its ruthlessly power-based individualism. But they replace that individualism with one that does not obscure the individual's allegiances and collusions. These updated portraits ask us to look through the disguise, the similarity, the assumption of generic identity that the collective name *Zwarte Piet*, the costume, and the black-facing offer us – at first sight. Gender is not only a key issue here; it is also one of Fox's tools. The subjects are women, but in the photographs, nothing in their traditional gear makes us aware of their gender. No breasts, no feminine clothing, no ornaments, no poses. We are just looking at faces, painted for disguise. Yet, in most of the photographs, we see women.

We see they are white, for many have blue eyes. Still, in some cases I hesitate: is the woman with the blue bonnet, red hood, and white lace collar, who looks me straight in the eye, white or black (fig. 1)? To me, and to the friends to whom I showed the photographs, she "looks black." This demands a closer look. I scrutinize the image with an incurable, acquired, ideological magnifying glass. From my stock of prejudices, I glean all the features I have learned to associate with black people, and here I am detailing the racist taxonomy learned so long ago in geography books at the age when I was also still a little scared of *Zwarte Piet*. This is how the photographs implicate their viewers. The past, they say, is not out there; it is here, today. And, to some extent – which I can neither master nor eradicate – it is inside me. I am alluding to my position of having been raised, schooled, in this tradition. Schools are productive fields for critical fieldwork. See, for example, Mok's detailed analysis (1999) of the racism underlying geography textbooks in the Netherlands. Her study provides extremely useful insights into geography's mapping of racial differences and into the drill through which an entirely white-invented race-consciousness is instilled in Dutch children.

As I am scrutinizing the image for a racial identification, knowing I am doing it, I also see the whiter edges around the subject's eyes, indexes of racial uncertainty, the hand that refuses to assert racial truth. Then I notice the smudge of black paint on the woman's upper lip. This smudge works like a wink, as if she is pulling my leg. "I am not who you think I am," the figure seems to say. Is this a black woman playing a white woman playing a black man? What she is, here, is not the point; *that* is the point. The game she plays involves me, who I am, as much as it involves the she that she does not want to reveal herself to be. This is how Fox, by crossing portraiture with *Zwarte Piet* and soliciting theatricality, denaturalizes tradition. The theatrical space opened up here is the space where the culture of "race" and gender doesn't simply exist but happens.

What this image does to my awareness of the race-consciousness within me, it also does with gender. We see women, all different. Or do we? Is the proud-posing person in the purple mantle, whose wig or bonnet has slipped backwards to reveal, intentionally or by accident, a white hairline, a woman or a man (fig. 2)? The defiance in her gaze and on her lips makes the figure's gender so emphatically ambiguous that I wonder if this is a man posing as a woman posing as a man. And so, again, I realize that sometimes you do not know – and sometimes it does not matter. Sometimes, in other words, it is possible to reject compulsory identification *as*, and to replace it with identification *with*, another. The posing itself, the choice of and the mastery over the way each person is represented in this series, determines whether he or she is of a particular sex or gender, or whether he or she is playing the in-between. Here, gender, like race, is emphatically an event, an effect, not a cause or an origin of social positions. Hence it is bound to the subject choosing to act it, and not an excuse to naturalize social positions and the inequities that come with them.

Each woman in this series is different from every other. But this individuality does not entail distance. Despite resembling the paintings in Dutch museums in some way, they are also very close, very personal. They look me straight in the eye, and invite me to share the pride, boredom, fun, fatigue, resignation, fear, insecurity, comfort, or discomfort that their role-playing entails, despite also resisting the precise reading necessary for such identification. The *Zwarte Piet* in the Italian Renaissance pose – dressed in bright red and blue and a pristine white, with a *Zwarte Piet* clad in yellow in the background – looks the way I dreamed I would look when I knew I would not be chosen to be *Zwarte Piet*, because of my inability to muster that confident prettiness (fig. 3).

This woman, who looks so utterly confident in her Renaissance role and who raises the issue of naturalizing role-playing in general, emanates the success which, for me, defines the class identity of those whose station was just a notch above mine. Having been raised with the ambivalent class-consciousness characteristic of upward-striving, lower middle-class families (the target audience of *Zwarte Piet* in an era of the commercialization of tradition), as a child I would not have been aware that the woman emanated for me the successful impersonation of a superior class position. But I would have sensed it. It would have been part of the drill: the learning of categories and power positions that came with them, which is the main task of children. Even the well-starched, well-ironed collar and the gold bands decorating the costume demonstrated the perfection I knew I would never achieve. The blue eyes are the most secure symptom of the travesty. But the pose of perfection – the head inclined just enough so that it remains a flattering facial representation, yet held proudly and easily at the same time – and the self-confidence of the facial expression are emphatic enough to reveal the artificiality of the pose caught in the act of its success. The acting itself, its visible performance, suggests this is not a wealthy girl, but a lower-middle-class woman posing as an upper-middle-class woman posing as a lower-class man.

While the undermining of racial and gender identities through cross-dressing that creates a space of uncertainty deploys an emphatically artificial conception of theatricality to achieve its effect, this portrait (fig. 3) also probes the limits of realistic theater, or of that form of theater that encourages the audience to forget its own nature and naturalize the spectacle instead. This seems to me to be a highly effective cultural intervention on the part of the artist-cum-model. Subtly approaching class by questioning naturalizing realistic representation, this photograph definitively implicates all viewers – willingly critical or not – in the tensions and ambiguities that representation brings with it, thus undermining its drilling educational effect from within.

My favorite *Zwarte Piet* though – the most effective one as an image that performs a cultural critique of both "race" and gender – looks the way I would have looked given the chance, and seeing her, I know my case was hopeless, even if hers is not. Her hat is as brown as her stained face and eyes. The brown, set off against the shiny, black nylon curls of the wig and the dark background and black costume, here recalls that black isn't black, but just a symptom of a dichotomy that barely covers a physical reality (fig. 4). The brown has been less than well applied; the result is as artificial as the color of the lipstick. Nor is the white white, if the stained collar is any indication. The girl's costume is a bit shabby, her make-up sloppy. This most monochromatic of the portraits is also the most emphatic in its denaturalizing of color on the level of representation. Caught up in a whirlwind of maintained and decomposed traditions, I wonder why this portrait captivates me in particular, and which share of its effect is the woman's, which the artist's, which the character's, and which my own.

The deep ambiguity here, which holds in its sway all the other ambiguities, is a psychological one. The figure's body, clad in black, barely visible, the shoulder with its fraying collar, tells a hundred stories. Straighten your back, her mother must have told her when, growing too tall too quickly and sprouting breasts before her classmates did, she/I tended to hunch her/my shoulders. Hold your head proud instead of looking down, she would have heard when she didn't know she was soliciting her own status as wallflower that she so dreaded. She looks brave, lips slightly parted, as if about to overcome her shyness and actually speak. Her entire face and body are held back just a fraction, perhaps stiff, expressing both the act of posing for the merciless eyes of the camera and the public, and the pain it inflicts on her. Her face speaks to me of fear and bravery, of insecurity and the desire to overcome it. Fear, not of *Zwarte Piet*, but of playing the part in public. This is what I would have liked to be at one time in my life: a tomboy posing as a good feminine girl posing as an exuberant black man. The middle term – a good feminine girl – is the price to pay for the empowerment of the first and the last elements of this theatrical, triple identity.

Trans-gender, trans-racial, and trans-personality travesty merge inextricably in this portrait to perform the kind of intersubjective process that constitutes cultural life and *makes* gender. This, then, the least successful *Zwarte Piet*, is the closest you get to a self-portrait of me as viewer. My own performance as viewer, subjective and unpredictable as it is, thus also belongs to the performance of this work. Tomboy, transvestite, black-faced clown: playing the part of what you are not fulfils a deep desire. Like getting yourself dirty, or doing dirty deeds. Like mastering fear rather than mastering others. Like coping with the entanglements of this tradition rather than simply rejecting it, as if you owned it.

This last case affects my own history; not only my history as a museum-goer and art-lover in training, but my history as a gendered subject of a racially specific and hence racist culture. I grew up with sympathy for Jews and fear of blacks, a theatrical interest in Indians and an earnestness about being a girl. Through the latter training, I learned about the need not to be meek. This is what I like about art. It isn't meek. It entices you to look into the mirror and realize that what you see there is you as product; as theatrical, as enacting scripts and as sometimes forgetting your lines.

You want to know what gender is? Don't even try. The last thing we need is a renewed naturalization of gender. My argument is an impassioned plea for a denaturalization of all such categories. Not that there is nothing "biological" about "race" or gender. Biology, itself a social reality, like medicine, is important. But it can only be effective as a help to sustain and improve life if its social aspects are recognized and worked through. Whether I am a woman or a man, straight or gay, black or white is only important or relevant within the fabric of the social reality, in which the Dutch, for one, insist on maintaining a racist habit, simply because it is traditional. Is tradition natural?

References

Aptekar, K. (1997) *Ken Aptekar: Talking to Pictures*, exhibition catalogue (Washington, DC: Corcoran Gallery of Art).

Austin, J. L. (1975 [1962]) *How to Do Things With Words* (Cambridge, MA: Harvard University Press).

Bal, M. (1999) *Quoting Caravaggio: Contemporary Art, Preposterous History* (Chicago: University of Chicago Press).

Bal, M. (2002) *Travelling Concepts in the Humanities: a Rough Guide* (Toronto: University of Toronto Press).

Butler, J. (1990) *Gender Trouble: Feminism and the Subversion of Identity* (New York: Routledge).

Butler, J. (1993) *Bodies that Matter: On the Discursive Limits of "Sex"* (New York: Routledge).

Culler, J. (2000) "Philosophy and Literature: the Fortunes of the Performative," *Poetics Today* 21/3: 48–67.

Derrida, J. (1988) "Signature, Event, Context," in *Limited Inc.*, trans. Samuel Weber (Evanston, IL: Northwestern University Press).

Fox, A. (1999) *Zwarte Piet* (London: Black Dog Publishing).

Hobsbawm, E., and Ranger, T. (eds.) (1983) *The Invention of Tradition* (Cambridge: Cambridge University Press).

Mok, I. (1999) *In de ban van het ras. Aardrijkskunde tussen wetenschap en samenleving, 1876–1992 (Under the Spell of Race: Geography Between Science and Society, 1876–1992)* PhD dissertation (Amsterdam: ASCA Press).

Silverman, K. (1996) *The Threshold of the Visible World* (New York: Routledge).

Spivak, G. C. (1999) *A Critique of Postcolonial Reason: Toward a History of the Vanishing Present* (Cambridge, MA: Harvard University Press).

van Alphen, E. (1996) "The Portrait's Dispersal: Concepts of Representation and Subjectivity in Contemporary Portraiture," in Joanna Woodall (ed.), *Portraiture: Facing the Subject* (Manchester: Manchester University Press).

Wallace, M. (1991) *Invisibility Blues: From Pop to Theory* (London and New York: Verso).

Index

Numbers in **bold** indicate significant discussions of the topic; numbers in *italics* refer to illustrations

Index

Index